COLLOQUIAL AND

What is colloquial Latin? What can we learn about it from Roman literature, and how does an understanding of colloquial Latin enhance our appreciation of literature? This book sets out to answer such questions, beginning with examinations of how the term 'colloquial' has been used by linguists and by classicists (and how its Latin equivalents were used by the Romans) and continuing with exciting new research on colloquial language in a wide range of Latin authors. Each chapter is written by a leading expert in the relevant area, and the material presented includes new editions of several texts. The introductory section presents the first account in English of developments in the study of colloquial Latin over the last century, and throughout the book findings are presented in clear, lucid and jargon-free language, making a major scholarly debate accessible to a broad range of students and non-specialists.

ELEANOR DICKEY is Associate Professor of Classics at the University of Exeter. She is the author of numerous books and articles on the Greek and Latin languages and linguistics, including *Ancient Greek Scholarship: A Guide to Finding, Reading, and Understanding Scholia, Commentaries, Lexica, and Grammatical Treatises, from their Beginnings to the Byzantine Period* (2007); *Latin Forms of Address: From Plautus to Apuleius* (2002); and *Greek Forms of Address: From Herodotus to Lucian* (1996).

ANNA CHAHOUD is Professor of Latin at Trinity College Dublin. She is the author of *C. Lucilii Reliquiarum Concordantiae* (1998), and of articles on Republican Latin and the grammatical tradition. She has contributed to the *New Oxford Dictionary of National Biography* and is a member of the editorial board of *The Bryn Mawr Classical Review*.

COLLOQUIAL AND LITERARY LATIN

EDITED BY

ELEANOR DICKEY

AND

ANNA CHAHOUD

CAMBRIDGE
UNIVERSITY PRESS

CAMBRIDGE
UNIVERSITY PRESS

University Printing House, Cambridge CB2 8BS, United Kingdom

Cambridge University Press is part of the University of Cambridge.

It furthers the University's mission by disseminating knowledge in the pursuit of education, learning and research at the highest international levels of excellence.

www.cambridge.org
Information on this title: www.cambridge.org/9781107684416

© Cambridge University Press 2010

First published 2010
First paperback edition 2016

A catalogue record for this publication is available from the British Library

Library of Congress Cataloguing in Publication data
Colloquial and literary Latin / edited by Eleanor Dickey, Anna Chahoud.
p. cm.
Includes bibliographical references and index.
ISBN 978-0-521-51395-1
1. Latin language – Style.   2. Latin language, Colloquial.   3. Latin literature – History and criticism.
4. Speech in literature.   I. Dickey, Eleanor.   II. Chahoud, Anna.   III. Title.
PA2311.C65   2010
477 – dc22   2009054015

ISBN 978-0-521-51395-1 Hardback
ISBN 978-1-107-68441-6 Paperback

In honour of

J. N. Adams

Contents

Contributors

PROFESSOR BRIGITTE L. M. BAUER, University of Texas at Austin

DR JOHN BRISCOE, University of Manchester

PROFESSOR ANNA CHAHOUD, Trinity College Dublin

DR JAMES CLACKSON, Jesus College, Cambridge

PROFESSOR KATHLEEN M. COLEMAN, Harvard University

DR WOLFGANG DAVID CIRILO DE MELO, Universiteit van Gent

PROFESSOR ELEANOR DICKEY, University of Exeter

PROFESSOR ROLANDO FERRI, Università di Pisa

DR JAN FELIX GAERTNER, Universität Leipzig

PROFESSOR GIOVANBATTISTA GALDI, University of Cyprus

DR HILLA HALLA-AHO, University of Helsinki

PROFESSOR STEPHEN J. HARRISON, Corpus Christi College, Oxford

DR LEOFRANC HOLFORD-STREVENS, Oxford University Press

DR NIGEL M. KAY, independent scholar

DR PETER KRUSCHWITZ, University of Reading

PROFESSOR DAVID LANGSLOW, University of Manchester

PROFESSOR MICHAEL LAPIDGE, Clare College, Cambridge

DR MARTTI LEIWO, University of Helsinki

PROFESSOR HARM PINKSTER, University of Amsterdam

PROFESSOR PAOLO POCCETTI, Università di Roma 2 'Tor Vergata'

PROFESSOR JONATHAN POWELL, Royal Holloway, University of London

DR PHILOMEN PROBERT, Wolfson College, Oxford

PROFESSOR TOBIAS REINHARDT, Corpus Christi College, Oxford

PROFESSOR DANUTA SHANZER, The University of Illinois at Urbana-Champaign

PROFESSOR RICHARD F. THOMAS, Harvard University

PROFESSOR ANDREAS WILLI, Worcester College, Oxford

PROFESSOR MICHAEL WINTERBOTTOM, Corpus Christi College, Oxford

Acknowledgements

Thanks are due above all to Jim, from all of us, for being the wonderful scholar and mentor that he is. Many of us, unused as we are to working on such topics without consulting him, obtained his assistance in disguise, so he will no doubt find in these pages the results of many queries he responded to with his characteristic generosity. As usual, thank you Jim! And huge thanks, obviously, are due from the editors to all the contributors, not only for their chapters but also for their enthusiasm, support and promptness, not only with initial submission but also with responses to queries. The editors would also like to thank each other! We would also like to thank the numerous friends of Jim's who supported this project and would have liked to contribute to it but were prevented from doing so either by the distance between this volume's topic and their own research or by the strict time frame involved. These include Gualtiero Calboli, Trevor Evans, Mark Janse, John Lee, Robert Maltby, Roland Mayer, Stephen Oakley, John Penney, Olga Spevak and Tony Woodman. Lastly, our warmest thanks go to Iveta Adams, whose expertise and care went far beyond a copy-editor's duties. Her contribution to this volume has been an invaluable and a very special one.

Foreword

David Langslow

The present volume is to honour a man for outstanding contributions to scholarship, and to thank a friend for support and inspiration. Jim Adams is one of the very best and most important students of the Latin language who have ever lived. I attempt to sketch some of his achievements below, but first let me say this: I know that I can speak for the editors and many others besides (not only the contributors to the present volume, but generations of linguists, historians and classicists – not only Latinists – from many different countries), when I say that we are grateful to Jim not only for being the pre-eminent scholar that he is, for opening up and showing the way on numerous new or neglected aspects of Latin, and for publishing his findings so quickly, with such clarity and in such abundance, but also for inspiring us, pointing us in the right direction, and helping us to be better scholars. In my experience – and again I know that I speak for many – Jim has for decades been generous and unfailing in his readiness to share his learning, experience and approach, in answering questions, and in reading and discussing, and commenting and advising on, plans in germ and work in manuscript. For a linguist with work in draft, there are few things so beneficial as having it read by Jim, because he sees straight through the problems and tells you what the solutions are, and where to look to find the evidence to prove it. And he is nearly always right – even when you are actually working on a language other than Latin. Jim is a willing and selfless academic mentor to anyone he thinks may be able to profit from his help, and it has been well said that he is too loyal a friend for his own good. It is hard, if not impossible, truly to deserve what Jim has done for us and our subjects, let alone to reciprocate, given the range and depth of knowledge and understanding necessary to give him equivalent help. At least this volume is a tangible token of how keenly appreciated his help has been in so many of our endeavours over so many years.

Jim was born in Sydney in 1943. He was educated at North Sydney Boys' High School, and graduated from the University of Sydney with the University Medal for Latin (a special award, made by no means every year). A clearly influential teacher, of whom he has often spoken, was G. P. Shipp. After two years as a teaching fellow at his home university, he came to the UK in 1967, and has stayed ever since. He completed his Oxford doctorate, a philological commentary on Tacitus, *Annals* 14.1–54, in under three years (as a Commonwealth Scholar, at Brasenose College), he held the Rouse Research Fellowship in Classics at Christ's College, Cambridge for two years, and was appointed to a lecturership in Greek and Latin at the University of Manchester in 1972, at the age of twenty-nine.

Jim spent twenty-two years in Manchester, being promoted to Senior Lecturer in 1978, to Reader in 1982, and appointed to a personal chair in 1993, the year after his election to a Fellowship of the British Academy. In Manchester, he was Chairman of the Departmental Board from 1983, and Head of Department from 1989. He took leave away from Manchester in 1994–5 in order to take up a one-year Senior Research Fellowship at St John's College, Oxford. Soon after, he moved more permanently, to a professorship at the University of Reading in 1995, and finally, in 1998, to a Senior Research Fellowship at All Souls College, Oxford. Since 1995, he has chaired to enormously good effect the supervisory committee of the *Dictionary of Medieval Latin from British Sources*; it is thanks in no small part to him that this great project is now as far as possible assured of being completed.

Jim's subject has always been the Latin language, in the broadest sense – Latin in all its forms and varieties, from the beginning of our record to the emergence of the Romance languages. This is always the backdrop, no matter how precise his focus at any given moment. This focus is normally very precise indeed, but a signal strength of his work lies in an unusually deft combination of the exhaustive analysis and presentation of details with investigations and conclusions of enormous scope and scale. There are few texts or documents of any sort produced in Latin of any sort, by speakers or would-be speakers of Latin of any period, place, register, ethnic origin or social class that he does not Know (I am happy to be able at last to reflect in print the correct observation made to me by a fellow PhD-examiner in the late 1990s that 'Jim Adams knows Latin with a capital K'!).

He has published steadily, at a high rate since the first year of his Cambridge research fellowship (his first article, on a type of hyperbaton in Latin prose, is from 1971), prolifically since the early 1990s, when the articles came even thicker and faster, and the big books started to appear: *Pelagonius*, *Bilingualism*, and *Regional Diversification* are each longer than

Vulgar Latin Chronicle, Claudius Terentianus, and *Latin Sexual Vocabulary*
put together – and not a syllable less terse. Since 1990 his research has
included (in addition to two jointly authored articles) participation in
four large collaborative projects: on the publication and interpretation of
the texts from Vindolanda (with their editors Alan Bowman and David
Thomas), and, between 1994 and 2005, on jointly organising and editing
the proceedings of three major conferences, respectively on the language
of Latin poetry (with Roland Mayer), bilingualism in ancient society (with
Mark Janse and Simon Swain), and the language of Latin prose (to honour
Michael Winterbottom – with Tobias Reinhardt and Michael Lapidge).

Jim's published work is characterised by the greatest acuity, rigour, efficiency, and good judgement. There is also often a breathtaking boldness
about both the questions that he takes on and the comprehensiveness of
his answers to them. The questions either have never occurred to people
to address before because the necessary connections have not been made,
or they have seemed intractable given the (supposed) state of the evidence,
or they have been much discussed, and the contradictory half-answers are
well known, or they are (surely!) simply too large and difficult for anyone to tackle single-handed. As one reads Jim's findings and discussion of
them, one has the sense of problems and earlier, inadequate solutions being
transformed or swept aside, and a feeling of finality in his conclusions. His
style is refreshingly unselfregarding, his writing is lucid, terse, urgent. The
urgency of his oral delivery (often against a handout containing – for a
one-hour paper – well over a hundred examples), which is transformed into
efficiency and finality on the printed page, is also notable: the lecture that
became the 1999 article on nominative personal pronouns was memorably
compared in discussion both to 'scoring a century before lunch' and to
'driving through the Ardennes'.

Theory is scarce, though not absent; terminology is traditional, at least
from the point of view of linguistics. Jim has always treated more theoretically laden work and new terminology (of the 'old wine in new bottles' type)
with a healthy scepticism, and has regarded with equal respect and purely
on grounds of merit and utility the fashionable and the little-known. An
important consequence of the theoretical neutrality and straightforward
empiricism of his approach is that his early works may still be read with
undiminished profit side by side with his most recent.

His publications address explicitly texts and authors; grammatical and
lexical topics; and, especially more recently in a head-on fashion, some
of the big questions facing the student of Latin and Romance linguistics,
Latin literature, and Roman history. His studies of named literary texts

and authors are concerned with prose much more often than verse – early on, Tacitus, the *Historia Augusta*, Livy, Cicero, Lactantius; most recently, the pseudo-Caesarian *Bellum Africum*, Petronius, Mustio (the subject of Adams 2005a) – but Ausonius, Martial, and Latin epic (especially Virgil) are the subjects of three early articles, Catullus and the Augustan poets are a main focus of the 1999 article mentioned above, Plautus has always been a central point of reference (and is still so in *Bilingualism* and *Regional Diversification*) – and, on the documentary side, let us not forget the remarkable poets of Bu Njem!

The grammatical domains for which Jim is best known are word order and vocabulary. His lexical studies sometimes serve to establish the existence, the form and the meaning of unnoticed or misunderstood words (a good number of veterinary terms, but also such ordinary words as the Latin for 'to canter', are thus saved from lexicographical oblivion or misrepresentation). Other articles or chapters on vocabulary (as in the cases of words for 'put' and 'throw', or of some of the anatomical terms transferred from animals to humans, or of some of the new words attested at Vindolanda) illustrate changes under way in Latin foreshadowing Romance usage. Most, however, provide object lessons in how to use the distribution of synonymous or complementary words as evidence for their register, their social or connotational meaning, so (e.g.) the articles on words for 'woman', 'wife', 'prostitute', 'kill', and the seven chapters of the *Latin Sexual Vocabulary*, the publication of which prompted an article in the *Sunday Times*.

Jim's interest in word order dates from the 1970s. It is the subject of his very first article, on hyperbaton (mentioned above), and 1976 saw the publication of the still-important article on 'a typological approach to Latin word order'. It has yielded along the way the 1991 article on the construction infinitive + *habeo* in late Latin and the origin of the Romance future (Fr. *je chanterai*, Ital. *canterò*, etc.), in which a detail of variable word order is made in masterly fashion to throw light on an important problem of historical morphology and semantics. In many respects, his work on word order supersedes that of the great French Latinist Jules Marouzeau (*L'ordre des mots*), and here more than anywhere embraces recent developments in linguistic theory, notably in pragmatics. Jim's crowning achievement in the study of Latin word order is to have modified (in a pair of long papers both published in 1994) Eduard Fraenkel's modification of Wackernagel's Law by redefining the 'second position' as following not the first word of the clause (so Wackernagel) nor of the 'colon' (so Fraenkel) but rather a 'preferential host', one of a set of accented but not necessarily emphatic words to which unstressed elements (including pronouns and weak forms of the verb 'to be') are attracted. In a brilliant coda to the 'unstressed pronouns' paper, a most appealing and suggestive historical connection is made between the enclisis on the newly observed 'host' in Latin and the proclisis on the verb characteristic of Romance. This is, by any standards and for any language-family, an unusually illuminating and satisfying account of the history of a syntactic pattern, from the prehistoric parent language to the modern vernacular languages.

In truth, however, although lexicography and word order are clearly more prominent in Jim's bibliography, there are few areas of the grammar (from spelling and phonology to sentence structure) that he has not covered in his studies of (e.g.) the *Anonymus Valesianus II*, Claudius Terentianus, C. Novius Eunus, the Bath curse tablets, the ostraca from Bu Njem, the Vindolanda letters, all of which amount to comprehensive, if selective, contrastive grammars of these texts. (I say 'selective' because that is how Jim presents them: in fact, nothing much worth saying is left to say at the end.)

The big questions about Latin that have clearly interested Jim, and continue to interest him, include: (a) What are the limits of variation that we can document within Latin, and against what sort of parameters – chronological, geographical, sociolinguistic, stylistic in the broadest sense – may we describe each variable? (b) What sorts of contact did Latin enjoy with other languages, and what are the grammatical effects, on Latin and on the other language, in each contact situation? (c) How did one language, Latin, evolve into the several Romance languages?

All three questions are addressed already in early publications. The evolution of Latin into Romance is illustrated in 1977 in the foreshadowing of French words in the *Annales regni Francorum*, and numerous aspects of the wider problem are discussed in a 1989 review article of Roger Wright's important book *Late Latin and Early Romance* (1982). Features of bilingualism and consequent linguistic interference are written up in the 1970s first for the influence of Greek on Egyptian Latin. Regional variation is investigated to begin with in the Latin of Egypt and Britain; sociolinguistic variation is documented in features of the Latin of military documents, and in characteristics of female speech in Latin comedy; stylistic variation, and what may be inferred from it about authorship and chronological development, prompts some of Jim's earliest articles, on Tacitus, the writers of the *Historia Augusta*, and Livy.

In pursuing these questions, Jim has for nearly forty years consistently both opened up important new areas to philological study and shed fresh light on familar authors and texts. Many of the writers and documents that he has studied were largely unknown to students of antiquity, and, but for his work, would probably have remained so. Jim has shown that the most unpromising material, examined in the right way, can yield important insights of quite general relevance. His treatment of the high literary, the highly technical, and the most 'hopeless gibberish' alike renders his work essential reading for all Latinists and Roman historians. In many cases, it is evident from the titles or tables of contents of his works that a vast array of literary and documentary evidence will be surveyed and appraised, but the same is true also of, for example, *Pelagonius*, which treats an important but neglected chapter of Roman social history, offers an extraordinary number of instructive insights into the Latin language in various periods and registers, and has much to say on Latin literary topics (cf. my review in *BMCR* 97.04.01). In discussions of international collaborative work on technical Latin, Jim has argued repeatedly and forcefully against restricting oneself to the technical writers, since so much important evidence is to be found in non-technical literary Latin and in inscriptions of all kinds: conversely, to characterise the language of, say, Cicero, Virgil or Ovid with reference just to other literary authors risks no less yielding a partial, impoverished and misleading view.

If, more generally, we may readily agree that we ignore at our peril the contribution that the fullest possible understanding of a language can make to the historical or literary interpretation of texts and their contexts, it remains true that such an understanding of Latin is more easily aspired to than achieved. It is also true that few have approached such an understanding so closely or made its implications so widely available as Jim. A former colleague of mine rightly remarked that 'Jim Adams is as close as we can get to a native speaker of Latin.' The wise philologist, or literary critic or historian, knows to interrogate native speakers. Certainly, the extent to which 'Adams, J. N.' features in a bibliography is a good indicator of the degree to which the author regards the Latin language as of relevance to the theme.

W. M. Lindsay ended his appreciation of the life and work of Franz Skutsch (*CR* 26 [1912] 238) with the words, 'What shall we do now that our protagonist is gone?' Thank Goodness, ours is still with us, and showing no sign of slowing down. May Jim's forthcoming anthology and discussion of non-standard Latin texts and features be very far from his last words on the Latin language!

PART I

Theoretical framework

CHAPTER I

Introduction

Eleanor Dickey

What is colloquial Latin? What is literary Latin? 'Literary' is a famously contested term, and 'colloquial' is no less fraught with difficulties. Not only is its precise meaning unclear, but it is laden with value judgements: some consider it a pejorative term and others a positive one. The word has become involved in the social struggle over the relative value of different varieties of language and as such has been given a wide range of different implications and connotations over the centuries, some complementary and others contradictory. In order to use this word in scholarly discourse, one first needs not only to determine what it means, but also to explain how one's usage resembles and differs from that of others who have used the same term.

The *Concise Oxford Dictionary* (Fowler and Fowler 1995) defines 'colloquial' as 'belonging to or proper to ordinary or familiar conversation, not formal or literary' while defining 'literary' as 'of, constituting, or occupied with books or literature or written composition, esp. of the kind valued for quality of form . . . (of a word or idiom) used chiefly in literary works or other formal writing'. Such definitions tell us a number of different things about the way these terms are normally used:

- 'colloquial' and 'literary' refer to registers[1], with literary being a higher, more formal, register than colloquial;
- they are defined in part by opposition to each other, as is often the case with registers;
- they are genre-dependent, each being proper to particular genres of communication;[2]
- the distinction between them is connected to the distinction between spoken and written language.

---

[1] For the concept of register see p. 10.

[2] In the linguistic, rather than the literary, sense of 'genre': a genre of communication is a type of circumstance in which one might use language, such as a conversation, a formal lecture, a poem, a newspaper article, etc.

The difficulties with such definitions are numerous. First, they give the impression that all linguistic features can be divided between these two categories (i.e., whatever is not literary is colloquial), and yet they cannot.[3] Many words and usages are register-neutral, usable in any variety of language: it would be as silly to ask whether English 'and' is an element of literary or of colloquial language as it would be to ask to which register the English present tense belongs. Moreover literary and colloquial are not the only registers that exist; some words and usages, such as technical terminology, belong to registers distinct from them both.

The connection between register and genre is likewise not as straightforward as it seems. Ordinary familiar conversation is a genre that can span a wide variety of registers, in part because there is a connection between register and social status: the ordinary conversational language of people of high status tends to have more high-register characteristics than the ordinary conversational language of people of low status (indeed the language is considered high-register by speakers precisely because it is characteristic of high-status speakers). The differences between these two extremes of conversational language can be pronounced, to the extent that they may share little that is not common to other registers of the language, and therefore it can be difficult to say anything meaningful about conversational language as a whole.

Recognition of this problem has led to restricted uses of 'colloquial', referring either to the conversational language of low-status people or that of high-status people. When used in the first sense, 'colloquial' can be equivalent to 'ungrammatical' or otherwise 'wrong'.[4] When used in the second sense, however, it can become a kind of Holy Grail of language usage, both for native speakers[5] and for modern students of languages like Latin or ancient Greek (since considerable social prestige has in some recent periods been attached to a full command of those languages).

Restrictions of this type are useful, but they also cause some problems. Often authors use the term in one or the other restricted sense without indicating which one is meant, and this can cause considerable ambiguity. In addition, from any restriction of the term to a particular sort of conversational usage it follows that a substantial segment of the population either

---

[3] Whether all *language* can be divided up among registers is a different question; probably it can. A passage of reasonable length will normally contain enough differentiatable linguistic features to make it possible to classify it as literary, colloquial, or something else, and therefore it is not easy to see how it could be wholly register-neutral.

[4] See Samuel Johnson, quoted in Simpson and Weiner 1989: s.v. 'colloquial' 2: '. . . to refine our language to grammatical purity, and to clear it from colloquial barbarisms'.

[5] See Chapter 2.

lacks a colloquial register entirely or commands it only with difficulty as a partially learned register.[6] This result clashes with the normal meaning of the term 'colloquial' enough to cause a sense of internal contradiction for readers.

On the other side of the register/genre question, most literary genres are capable of accommodating a range of registers. Indeed the interplay of registers is often part of what gives literature its richness. One cannot fully appreciate the language of any literary genre unless one is able to consider the possibility that it may involve register variation, and in many cases one must recognise that literary works include some language belonging to low registers.

The equation of register/genre distinctions with those between speech and writing causes additional difficulties. Literary language (whether this means high-register language or the language of literary genres) is not simply the same as written language, nor is colloquial language (whether this means low-register language or the language of some conversational genre(s)) the same as spoken language. The language of the Homeric poems is generally agreed to be a literary one – that is, elevated, remote from ordinary conversation, and used only for poetry – but also generally agreed to have evolved in a society that had no knowledge of writing. Even in societies where the production of high-register works in literary genres is likely to be aided by writing, their delivery is often oral. In our culture, plays, lectures and speeches are delivered orally, often after being composed in writing – but not always, as many successful speakers do not use a written text and some plays are improvised or incorporate changes to the original script made during rehearsal and not written down. The fact that a member of the audience often cannot tell from the language used whether the giver of a speech or lecture is following a written text, or whether a comedy sketch was written or improvised, shows that there is no clear and simple connection between linguistic register and spoken versus written language production.

In fact, any register can be produced orally: doctors, lawyers and other specialists use technical language as readily as politicians produce their own special genre, and some academics have a habit of delivering in conversation

---

[6] Not all conversation is conducted in the idiom that its speakers find easiest and most natural, because there are often advantages to using a type of language with which one is less familiar. In this context one normally thinks of people of low-status origin who as adults attempt to acquire a higher-status conversational register, e.g. the situation in Shaw's *Pygmalion* or Molière's *Bourgeois gentilhomme*. But the reverse also occurs: people who find themselves surrounded by speakers of a lower conversational register may also try to acquire elements of that register, particularly if use of higher-register features generates hostility in their conversational partners.

sentences so grammatically complex that listeners wish they had been written down. At first glance, however, it seems that the same cannot be said for writing: the language of published books and periodicals, while reasonably diverse, does not have the same range as that of orally delivered speech. But published language is only a subset of written language, and if one turns to non-print media such as the Internet, much greater diversity in written genres becomes apparent. The development of e-mail and text messaging has led to the blossoming of very informal written genres and to the evolution of new linguistic features attached to those genres. Are these genres and their distinctive linguistic features literary because they are found exclusively in written contexts, or are they colloquial because they belong to an informal register? Is the distinction between spoken and written language that seemed so striking in nineteenth- and twentieth-century Western society merely a temporary phenomenon that was born with the rise of publishers and editors and is now becoming obsolete as they lose control over the distribution of written language? These are only a few of the problems with the spoken/written divide; in fact even before the rise of electronic communication linguists were discarding a classification of language based on spoken versus written format and replacing it with classifications based on genre.[7] It is therefore highly problematic to use the written/spoken distinction to help understand the literary/colloquial distinction.

The common usage of the term 'colloquial' is thus of little use to a scholar, but at the same time it is not possible to investigate colloquial Latin without understanding what it is or may be; a clear understanding of the question is essential for answering it. Let us therefore turn to three sources that might be more help: the science of linguistics, the terminology used by the Romans themselves to talk about variation in their language, and the ways scholars have traditionally used the term 'colloquial' in discussing Latin and Greek.

---

[7] See Biber (1988: esp. 52–3) and Chafe and Tannen (1987).

CHAPTER 2

Colloquial language in linguistic studies

James Clackson

The term *colloquial* has had a varied fortune in the history of linguistics. In works written in the nineteenth and the first half of the twentieth centuries it is possible to find references to the colloquial form of language, sometimes contrasted on the one hand with 'formal' or 'literary' language, and on the other hand with 'vulgar' or 'illiterate'. Thus in 1920 the English scholar Henry Wyld could write a book entitled *A History of Modern Colloquial English*, and argue for a separation between the spoken and literary forms. It was clear that Wyld also separated out the colloquial from the vulgar in his later tract on 'the best English' (Wyld 1934: 605), which notoriously maintained that the language spoken by the 'members of the great Public Schools and by those classes in society which normally frequent them' was intrinsically superior to every other type of English speech. Other works on English written in the same period, often aimed at teachers of English or a wider non-specialist public, are more explicit in their classification of the language into three levels (see Kenyon 1948 for citation and discussion of these). Yet it is clear that the simple segregation of language into bands of formal, colloquial and vulgar was never a widely or deeply held view; Wyld himself acknowledges the fact that different varieties may interlock in speech and change takes place through mixture of different codes. Indeed, most scholars writing about the English language were influenced by Murray's diagram of different varieties of English included in the preface to the Oxford English Dictionary (earlier the New English Dictionary, Murray 1888: xvii). Murray's diagram, repeated below, showed 'colloquial' and 'literary' ranged around 'common', with offshoots of scientific, foreign, technical, slang and dialectal. Murray emphasised the fuzzy boundaries between the different varieties, and the movement of lexical items from one category to another over time. The idea of a separate colloquial level of language was firmly put to rest in Kenyon's 1948 paper, which argued that it was important to separate out different functional varieties, such as formal or familiar, from cultural levels such as standard and sub-standard.

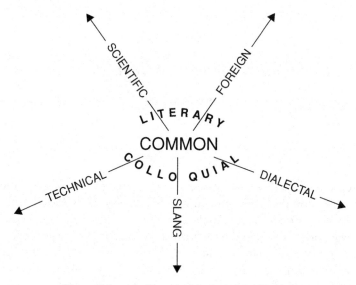

Fig. 2.1 Murray's diagram of the varieties of English

Since Kenyon's paper, the last thoroughgoing attempt by a mainstream linguist to set out a scientific definition of 'colloquial' that has proved to have any influence is that made by Martin Joos in his book *The Five Clocks* (1962, 1967). It is perhaps significant that this work has had more influence on teachers of English, both as a foreign language and in secondary education, and has had less impact on the community of sociolinguists. Joos builds up a categorisation of English into five styles: frozen, formal, consultative, casual and intimate. The colloquial in Joos's definition comprises both the consultative and the casual style (Joos 1967: 29). The consultative style is 'our norm for coming to terms with strangers – people who speak our language but whose personal stock of information may be different' (Joos 1967: 23), and its defining features are that the speaker supplies background information, and the addressee participates continuously. The casual style is used for friends and acquaintances, and is marked by frequent ellipsis and slang. Joos maintains that he is using the term slang in its 'strict' sense, referring to the Webster's definition: 'Language comprising certain widely current but usually ephemeral terms (especially coined or clipped words, or words used in special senses, or phrases, usually metaphors or similes) having a forced, fantastic or grotesque meaning, or exhibiting eccentric or extravagant humor or fancy' (Joos 1967: 24, citing Neilson and Knott 1934). The style which borders the bottom end of the two colloquial styles in Joos's categorisation is the intimate, the language which is used between very tight-knit groups of people, and which relies on shared specialised jargon and a common understanding of familiar sentence patterns to enable speakers to extract a single word or expression from a longer utterance to convey the whole meaning. The style above the colloquial styles is the formal, a style 'strictly determined by the absence of participation' (Joos 1967: 36). Formal text is planned, cohesive and structured, and the speaker does not interact with the addressee. Joos stresses that it is possible within a single conversation, text or even sentence to alternate between different stylistic levels, and his own book is itself an artfully constructed exemplification of this principle: 'your reporter is writing good standard mature formal style, with many borrowings from the consultative and casual styles, plus shreds and patches of frozen style placed with honest care' (1967: 20).

Although Joos's work is still cited in some works on stylistics, linguists writing since him have barely used the term colloquial, except in specific senses related to certain languages: thus, for example, it is possible to talk of 'Colloquial Arabic' to refer to spoken varieties as opposed to the written standard form, Modern Standard Arabic. According to a recent book on bilingualism 'linguists generally don't use the term "colloquial" in any scientific sense. However, "colloquial" is in general use . . . as a term for whatever variety is used in informal situations. This is usually a variety which is not written down' (Myers-Scotton 2006: 84); the non-technical use of the term colloquial is endorsed in the most recent authoritative dictionary of linguistics, Matthews 2007, which has no entry for the word.

Why has the term colloquial fallen out of use amongst linguists? Its demise is no doubt partly due to the fact that it covers too wide a range of different linguistic phenomena to remain a classificatory term. Linguists, generally working on spoken forms of language, have shown that the same speaker may show greater variation than can be caught under a simple split between 'literary' and 'colloquial'. Following the pioneering work of the sociolinguist William Labov in the north-eastern United States in the 1960s, and especially his famous survey of phonological variables, such as the presence or absence of post-vocalic *r*, in New York City (Labov 1966), it became clear that a speaker may frequently vary between two different pronunciations of the same word. Speech variation came to be understood not just in terms of the presence or absence of a feature, but of the frequency of the feature in different circumstances. In one experiment, Labov recorded the frequency of variables over four different styles: in the first, the subject read out a list of minimal pairs (such as *god* and *guard*, potential homophones if the speaker did not pronounce the *r* in *guard*);

in the second, the subject read a passage from a printed text; in the third, he or she was interviewed and recorded in a formal setting; and finally subjects were recorded without their knowledge, using what Labov termed *casual speech*. The speakers in Labov's study showed a progressively higher deviation from the standard forms in the four different styles. As Labov and other sociolinguists have shown, linguistic variation depends on a host of different factors other than the stylistic: age, sex, ethnicity, class and speakers' self-perceptions can all interact with the variation between careful, formal and casual speech. Speakers across different social groups may share a similar pronunciation of a variable in their most careful formal speech, such as reading a word-list of minimal pairs, but in other styles there may be a much greater discrepancy between those of one social group and another.

Labov's work clearly demonstrated that language may vary not only along a stylistic axis, from formal to informal, but also along other axes, relating to speakers' status and group membership. The term colloquial, which had been used both as description of a particular speech style, and as a label of the language of certain social groups, was avoided as it risked confusing two different things: first, variation in the speech of a single speaker, and second, variation between different social groups in a linguistic community. For the first type of variation, linguists since the 1960s have increasingly spoken of linguistic *registers* rather than styles. The term register is used to describe linguistic varieties that are determined by the context of use rather than the user. For example, a doctor might use a technical medical register when discussing a case with colleagues, a familiar register when chatting up a student nurse, and a more formal register when appearing in front of a court on a misconduct charge. Lexical choice is often the most immediate signal of register, but phonological, morphological and syntactic features may also be present. Different speech patterns among different social groups are now more generally described using the term *social dialect* or *sociolect*, which demarcates a range of linguistic varieties used by speakers of the same social class or connected by some shared group membership. Speakers of the same sociolect will deviate from the standard in a similar way and to a similar degree when they are not using a formal register. To return to the example of our fictional doctor given above, he will most likely share a sociolect with other doctors, with his next-door neighbours and with other members of the same golf club, but not with the hospital cleaners.

It has been seen that it is impossible to discuss colloquial language without reference to formal language; colloquialisms are by definition features normally excluded from the formal written register. It is consequently worth briefly considering how this formality in language is constructed. Formal language to a large extent overlaps with what is referred to as standard language, a concept which is unfortunately itself far from clear-cut. Standard languages are typically the languages employed by sovereign powers as the medium of administration, religion, law, science, education and prestige discourse and display. Standard languages show little or no variation, and their status in a society means that speakers usually associate the standard with the 'correct' form of the language. The standard is the variety taught in schools and codified in grammars, and consequently other varieties, including regional and social dialects, are seen as deviations from the standard. Furthermore, lack of proficiency in the standard may be a bar to an individual participating in various official capacities. However, although most states exhibit something which can be called a standard language, the details of its use and its relation to other linguistic varieties may differ from case to case. In some societies, for example, the language of religion may differ from the normal medium of administration – as is the case in countries such as Egypt and Saudi Arabia, which use Koranic Arabic for religion but Modern Standard Arabic for administration; in other states different varieties may be used for literary works; in bilingual societies there may be more than one standard. Linguists (following Haugen 1966) generally agree that all standard languages have passed through four stages: *selection* of a particular variety, such as the language of one particular area or social group, as the model for the standard; *codification* of that variety in written form; *elaboration* of the functional uses of the standard variety, so that, for example, it acquires a vocabulary suitable for the discussion of legal, administrative, technical etc. subjects; and finally its *acceptance* as the correct form by all members of the society. The nature of what is constituted as formal language is therefore dependent on what has been selected and accepted by members of the speech community, especially those members with personal power or prestige. What is acknowledged by the elite as formal language constitutes formal language. Where there are deviations from this language they may be classed as an intrusion from a different stylistic register, and this is more likely to be the case if the speaker or writer who deviates is also able to control the formal register, but decides not to use it. Alternatively, deviations may indicate social variation or dialect, as is more likely if the originator of them has imperfect or limited control over the formal register.

CHAPTER 3

Roman authors on colloquial language

Rolando Ferri and Philomen Probert

I INTRODUCTION

Linguistic register has been characterised as the result of a speaker's choice in a given situation (see Müller 2001: 282–3).[1] It is, nevertheless, impossible to draw a hard-and-fast dividing line between linguistic variables always used by certain speakers and those about which a speaker might choose (so Müller 2001: 283; cf. Coseriu 1980: 111–12). Moreover, speakers and writers do not choose between a finite number of discrete linguistic varieties but modify their language in a continuous way according to the situation. The question what register is, and how it is divided from sociolect, is discussed in Chapter 2. Here we address a simpler question: how did Roman authors conceive of Latin as including options between which speakers and writers had to choose? This question encompasses several more specific ones. What awareness do authors show of a gap between formal and less formal varieties of their language – for example written and oral or official and familiar? What, if any, legitimacy or correctness did they assign to the different varieties, especially the informal ones? What do we learn from the metalanguage of scholars describing linguistic varieties?

We thus leave aside in the first instance passages in which Romans divide Latin into different varieties used by different groups of speakers, since such distinctions reveal concepts of geographical or social variation rather than of register. We will, however, see that register and sociolect are perceived as difficult to separate – and rightly so, in view of what has been said in Chapter 2.

In what follows heavy use will be made of Müller's study of terms for varieties of Latin (Müller 2001). However, rather than discussing individual terms, which tend to be used in more than one way and to shift in meaning

---

[1] We are extremely grateful to Gregory Hutchinson for painstaking and knowledgeable comments, as a result of which we found it essential to rewrite much. Gregory is, of course, not to blame for the results.

over time, cannot be discussed adequately in the space available, and have been exhaustively discussed by Müller, we focus on the types of context in which distinctions suggestive of register appear. We do, however, summarise the main uses of particularly relevant terms in the Appendix.

We concentrate on two kinds of sources: rhetorical theorists (especially the author of the *Ad Herennium*, Cicero and Quintilian) on the one hand, and grammarians and commentators on the other. These two kinds of sources provide us with rather different discussions, and we treat them separately.

2 COLLOQUIAL LANGUAGE IN RHETORICAL THEORY

2.1 Genera dicendi

The notion that speakers can shift between varieties of Latin arises most clearly in discussions of rhetorical *genera dicendi*. Roman rhetoricians inherited from their Greek predecessors the notion that there were three stylistic levels in rhetoric – a grand, medium and simple style.[2] The author of the *Rhetorica ad Herennium* (*c.* 86–82 BC), Cicero and Quintilian regarded it as important for the orator to use all three stylistic levels, switching between them according to the demands of the moment (*Rhet. Her.* 4.16; Cicero, e.g. *Orat.* 99–111; Quint. *Inst.* 12.10.69–72). If linguistic register is taken to be the result of a speaker's choice in a given situation, at least in the hands of these authors the doctrine of the three styles incorporates a notion of linguistic register. The doctrine cannot have reflected actual practice in all respects. Cicero allows that the orator who can use all three styles perfectly is a Platonic ideal rather than a real person (*Orat.* 100–1).[3] Moreover, not everybody agreed with the doctrine even in theory: Cicero battled with Atticists who cultivated a more consistent *exilitas* (Cicero *Brut.* 284; cf. *Orat.* 23, 28). Quintilian looks back to such battles of Cicero's day and suggests that similar ones raged in his own (*Inst.* 12.10.12–15), while also pointing out that in reality there is an almost infinite variety of stylistic levels, not only three (12.10.66–8). However, discussions of the *genera dicendi*, and especially of the lowest *genus*, allow us to glimpse underlying assumptions about ordinary, non-rhetorical Latin whose validity does not depend on the reality of the three styles themselves.

[2] See Kroll 1913: 4–5; Russell 1964: xxxiv–xxxvii. For a contrast between everyday and literary language see Aristotle, *Rhetoric* 1404a9, 1404b2–5, 1406a3.
[3] On the other hand, he saw himself as coming close to the ideal in Latin, and Demosthenes in Greek (*Orat.* 102–11).

In the *Ad Herennium*, the simple style is called *(figura) extenuata* 'diminished' or *attenuata* 'plain' and is described as *demissa . . . usque ad usitatissimam puri consuetudinem sermonis* 'brought down to the most common practice of correct language' (4.11) and *quod ad infimum et cottidianum sermonem demissum est* 'that which is brought down to the lowest, everyday language' (4.14).

Here a variety of Latin describable as *usitatissima puri consuetudo sermonis* 'the most common practice of correct language' or *infimus et cottidianus sermo* 'the lowest, everyday language' is hinted at; the lowest rhetorical style comes close to this variety or makes use of elements of it. As Müller (2001: 94) notes, there is some ambivalence as to the evaluation of this variety. The term *infimus . . . sermo* 'lowest language' suggests a negative evaluation, while *purus . . . sermo* 'correct language' suggests a positive one. The characterisation of the simple style (as opposed to its perversion, the *genus exile*) as having *puris et electis verbis conpositam orationem* 'language composed of correct and select words' (4.16) also suggests a positive evaluation.

A hint at the reason for this ambivalence lies in the author's use of the term *purus* in relation to the language with which the simple style has affinities, and in relation to the simple style itself. In general the word *purus* denotes freedom from something, but not always freedom from the same thing.[4] In rhetorical theory *purus* often means 'restrained, free from ornament' (see Geigenmüller 1908: 19–20; *OLD* s.v. *purus* 10), but the author of the *Ad Herennium* defines *Latinitas* as *quae sermonem purum conservat ab omni vitio remotum* 'what keeps language correct, free from every fault' (4.17; cf. Geigenmüller 1908: 19; Müller 2001: 309). The relevant 'faults' are further specified as solecism and barbarism, so that *purus* would appear here to denote freedom from solecism and barbarism. In describing the kind of Latin with which the simple style has affinities as *usitatissima puri consuetudo sermonis*, and the simple style itself as having *puris et electis verbis conpositam orationem*, the author thus takes care to distinguish a conversational but 'correct' variety from one marred by solecism and barbarism.[5]

---

[4] So the Greek term καθαρός, which can mean free from errors, free from poeticisms, free from digressions, or generally restrained, free from trappings (see Geigenmüller 1908: 17–20). In Hermogenes' discussion of καθαρότης (Περὶ ἰδεῶν λόγου 227–34 Rabe), καθαρότης is the opposite of περιβολή 'abundance, amplification' (227.25–228.1 Rabe; for the translation 'abundance' see Wooten 1987: 9) and characterises a clear, straightforward style free from features of content or language that contribute to περιβολή. One might compare the use of the expression 'free from' by the British supermarket Sainsbury's, which has a product range called 'freefrom'; individual products in this range turn out to be free from gluten, wheat, dairy products, or a combination of these.

[5] A similar distinction is perhaps intended at 4.11, where all *oratio non vitiosa* 'language without faults' is said to belong to one of the three (good) styles. However, at 4.15 the perversions of the three styles are described as *finituma et propinqua vitia* 'neighbouring and nearby faults'; in this context *vitia* refers not to solecism and barbarism but to the rhetorical shortcomings of all three bad styles.

This is, perhaps, the closest ancient discussions come to an explicit distinction between conversational register and low sociolect. At the same time, the very need for warnings against the adoption of non-standard features hints that conversational register and low sociolect will overlap if one is not careful – that the two are dangerously close.[6]

Among Cicero's terms for the simple style are *genus humile* and *oratio humilis* (see Müller 2001: 95, with references). But in other contexts Cicero uses *humilis* of a negatively evaluated, 'too low', style, the equivalent of Greek ταπεινός (Müller 2001: 97–9), and this is the sense in which Quintilian and most subsequent authors use the term (Müller 2001: 99–104).[7] Even in this sense the term appears to refer to language whose affinities are with ordinary conversation – to register rather than sociolect. Thus of pupils whose teacher is too strict Quintilian remarks: *fiunt humiles statim et velut terram spectantes, qui nihil supra cotidianum sermonem attollere audeant* 'they immediately become abject and as it were looking to the ground, and do not dare to raise anything up above everyday language' (*Inst.* 2.4.9); *cotidianus sermo* here appears to refer to the language used by these pupils in everyday contexts, not e.g. to language used by a negatively evaluated social group. The simple style may approach colloquial Latin, but the use of actual, unmediated colloquial Latin is inappropriate in oratory (cf. section 2.4 below). Again the existence of such a thing as *cotidianus sermo* 'everyday language' is taken for granted.

2.2 mollitudo vocis

The *Ad Herennium* (3.23) draws a distinction between three qualities coming under the general heading of 'flexibility of the voice' (*mollitudo vocis*): *sermo*, *contentio* and *amplificatio*. As in the case of the *genera dicendi*, the orator is expected to choose between different possibilities according to the occasion. The first quality, *sermo*, is said to be closest to 'everyday speaking': *sermo est oratio remissa et finitima cottidianae locutioni* '*sermo* is language that is relaxed and closest to everyday speaking' (*Rhet. Her.* 3.23).

---

[6] A warning against the adoption of non-standard features appears also at Cic. *Orat.* 79, where the language of the orator practising the simple style is said to be *purus . . . et Latinus* – though here it is primarily the term *Latinus* that indicates freedom from non-standard features, while *purus* refers primarily to freedom from embellishment (cf. Geigenmüller 1908: 19; *OLD* s.v. *purus* 10; differently Müller 2001: 309 with n. 15).

[7] The term *humilis* is also used in a relative sense, to describe performance that does not meet the demands of the specific content or occasion. Similarly, *tumidus* can describe a style that exceeds the demands of the occasion – one that is 'over the top': *quod alibi magnificum tumidum alibi, et quae humilia circa res magnas apta circa minores videntur* 'what is grand in one place is bloated in another, and what seems mean in connection with great things seems appropriate in connection with smaller things' (Quint. *Inst.* 8.3.18; see Müller 2001: 102–3).

Sermo is itself divided into four categories – *dignitas, demonstratio, narratio* and *iocatio* – appropriate to solemn, expository, narrative and witty speech respectively (3.23).

2.3   Rhetorical and non-rhetorical language

We saw above that the simple rhetorical style is considered to have affinities with a form of language called *usitatissima puri consuetudo sermonis* or *infimus et cottidianus sermo* in the *Ad Herennium* (see above). This form of language is essentially non-rhetorical, i.e. 'ordinary'. Ordinary language will inevitably have been subject to variation in phonology, morphology, syntax and vocabulary. Some of this variation is hinted at when the orator practising the simple style is warned e.g. to use correct and select words (*Rhet. Her.* 4.16); yet no very clear distinction between different sorts of ordinary language is made in contexts where the simple style is said to come close to something non-rhetorical.

A similarly broad distinction between rhetorical and non-rhetorical language is made in contexts where distinctions between different rhetorical styles are not at issue but rhetorical language as a whole is being contrasted with non-rhetorical (i.e. ordinary) language. Thus, in the conclusion to the *Rhetorica ad Herennium*, Herennius is told that if he practises the principles set out in the work he will speak like an orator rather than barely and without embellishments in *vulgaris sermo* (*Rhet. Her.* 4.69; cf. Müller 2001: 119). In a similar vein, Quintilian (*Inst.* 9.3.3) suggests that figures of speech relieve the tedium of speech that is 'everyday and always formed in the same way', and defend us from a common (*vulgare*) manner of speaking.

Cicero in *De officiis* (1.132) draws a contrast between *contentio* (here 'debate') and *sermo* (here 'conversation'). *Sermo* is said to be appropriate *in circulis, disputationibus, congressionibus familiarium* 'in gatherings of people, discussions, and meetings of friends' and in *convivia* 'banquets', contexts that suggest a conversational register. Cicero goes on to remark that there are no teachers or students of *sermo* (*Off.* 1.132) and to claim that the *Socratici* excel at *sermo* (*Off.* 1.134), again suggesting that a register for conversational exchange is intended. However, it is also a register that is appropriate in some rhetorical contexts, as in a *dissimulatio* (*De orat.* 3.203).

In some contexts where rhetorical language is distinguished from ordinary language, poetic language is mentioned as a third variety distinct from both. Thus Cicero in *De oratore* has Crassus mention the occurrence in poetry of rare forms that have passed out of use in 'everyday speech';

orators have less right to these rare forms than poets, but on occasion a 'poetic word' lends grandeur to oratory.[8] The examples Cicero gives are compatible with the dialogue's setting in 91 BC, but also with Cicero's own time (Innes 1988: 309–11; Wisse, Winterbottom and Fantham 2008: 195):

> inusitata sunt prisca fere ac vetuste ab usu cotidiani sermonis iam diu intermissa, quae sunt poetarum licentiae liberiora quam nostrae; sed tamen raro habet etiam in oratione poeticum aliquod verbum dignitatem. neque enim illud fugerim dicere, ut Coelius[9] 'qua tempestate Poenus in Italiam venit', nec 'prolem' aut 'subolem' aut 'effari' aut 'nuncupare' aut, ut tu soles, Catule, 'non rebar' aut 'opinabar';[10] aut alia multa, quibus loco positis grandior atque antiquior oratio saepe videri solet. (Cicero *De orat.* 3.153; cf. also Varro *L.* 9.5, 9.114–15)

Unfamiliar words are virtually ancient ones that have long ago passed out of the usage of everyday conversation through their antiquity; they are more freely available to the licence of the poets than to ours, but occasionally even in oratory some poetic word lends grandeur. For I would not shrink from saying, like Coelius, 'what time the Carthaginian came into Italy', nor 'offspring' or 'scion' or 'utter' or 'declare' or, as you are accustomed to do, Catulus, 'I deemed not' or 'I judged'; or many others through which, when they are used in the proper place, speech often seems grander and more ancient.

Oratory here appears to fall somewhere between everyday speech and poetry in its use of expressions which have passed out of use in everyday speech. A similar notion appears in a passage in which Quintilian discusses an opinion that oratory should be as similar as possible to *cotidianus sermo*:

> adhuc quidam nullam esse naturalem putant eloquentiam nisi quae sit cotidiano sermoni simillima, quo cum amicis coniugibus liberis servis loquamur, contento promere animi voluntatem nihilique arcessiti et elaborati requirente: quidquid huc sit adiectum, id esse adfectationis et ambitiosae in loquendo iactatiae, remotum a veritate fictumque ipsorum gratia verborum, quibus solum natura sit officium attributum servire sensibus. (Quint. *Inst.* 12.10.40)

Besides, some think that no eloquence is natural except one that is as similar as possible to everyday conversation, with which we speak with our friends, wives, children and slaves, which is content to express the mind's intention and does not

---

[8] For the Greek background to this notion of poetic licence, and the orators' licence to participate in moderation, cf. Jonge 2008: 353. For the differences between prose and poetry according to the Greek rhetorical tradition see more generally Jonge 2008: 347–55. For artistic prose as falling somewhere between everyday language on the one hand and poetry on the other see Jonge 2008: 349–50.

[9] We print *Coelius*, not *Caelius*, although we otherwise follow Wilkins' text (OCT 1902); on the text here see Wisse, Winterbottom and Fantham 2008: 195.

[10] On these examples see Lebek 1970: 26–32; Innes 1988: 309–11; Wisse, Winterbottom and Fantham 2008: 195–7. The least obviously archaic is *opinabar*, but the only frequent form of this verb in Cicero is *opinor*, while Cicero avoids the imperfect altogether (Innes 1988: 310; Wisse, Winterbottom and Fantham 2008: 197; cf. Lebek 1970: 31–2).

need anything recherché or perfected: whatever is added to this they think belongs to affectation and ambitious ostentation in speaking, something removed from the truth and fashioned for the sake of the words themselves, whose sole function given by nature they think is to serve the thoughts.

Those who hold this opinion take the speech of the earliest orators to be closest (but, it seems, already not identical) to 'nature' (*natura*) and later orators to be more like poets and, like poets but to a lesser degree, to regard new coinages and transferred usages as positive qualities (Quint. *Inst.* 12.10.42). Those whose opinion Quintilian discusses here do not approve of these more 'poetic' aspects of oratory, whereas Quintilian himself goes on to defend them as long as they are not taken to excess. Those on both sides of this debate appear to agree, however, that in practice oratory falls somewhere between ordinary language and poetry in its use of neologisms and transferred usages.

2.4 Characteristics of conversational language in rhetorical theory

The point for us of identifying various contexts in which conversational language, or something having affinities with conversational language (such as the simple rhetorical style), is discussed by rhetorical theorists is to see if we can learn something from these contexts about features or at least perceived features of conversational language. Indeed, some of the discussions already mentioned quote examples, or mention examples that are available to us, or make relevant comments about the registers in question.

The clearest quoted example of something approaching conversational language is the example of the simple style provided in the *Ad Herennium*:

nam ut forte hic in balneas[11] venit, coepit, postquam perfusus est, defricari; deinde, ubi visum est ut in alveum descenderet, ecce tibi iste de traverso: 'heus', inquit 'adolescens, pueri tui modo me pulsarunt; satis facias oportet'. hic qui id aetatis ab ignoto praeter consuetudinem appellatus esset erubuit. iste clarius eadem et alia dicere coepit. hic vix: 'tamen', inquit, 'sine me considerare'. tum vero iste clamare voce ista quae vel facile cuivis rubores eicere posset: 'ita petulans es atque acer ut ne ad solarium quidem, ut mihi videtur, sed pone scaenam et in eiusmodi locis exercitatus sis'.[12] conturbatus est adolescens; nec mirum, cui etiam nunc pedagogi lites ad oriculas versarentur inperito huiusmodi conviciorum. ubi

---

[11] So all the manuscripts except cod. Paris. lat. 7696 (called 'P' by Marx 1923), which has *balineas* (see Achard's apparatus ad loc., and on the manuscript see Achard 1989: lxii), and cod. Bern. 469 (Achard's β: see Achard 1989: lxix, lxxi–lxxii), which has *balnea* before correction.

[12] The text is full of difficulties here; see Achard's (1989) apparatus and note ad loc.

enim iste vidisset scurram exhausto rubore, qui se putaret nihil habere quod de
existimatione perderet, ut omnia sine famae detrimento facere posset? (*Rhet. Her.*
4.14)

For when he by chance came into the baths, after he had washed he got rubbed
down. Then, when he thought he would go down into the tub, up comes this man
from an unexpected quarter: 'Hey!', he says, 'Young man, your boys just beat me;
you ought to make amends.' This man, seeing as he had unusually been addressed
by a stranger at that age, blushed. The other man started to say the same things and
others in a louder voice. This youth says with difficulty, 'But – let me think about
it.' Then the other man really cried out in that voice that could get blushes out
of anyone, even easily: 'You're so aggressive and violent that you must have spent
time not just at the sundial, it seems to me, but behind the stage and in places
of that sort.' The young man was ruffled – not surprisingly, since a pedagogue's
strictures were still ringing in his ears and he was not used to brawls of this sort.
For where would he have seen a ne'er-do-well with no shame left, who thought he
had no reputation to lose, so that he could do everything without any damage to
his name?

The features of this passage that might particularly exemplify the simple
style have been discussed elsewhere and will not be rediscussed in detail
here.[13] It is, however, of interest that some scholars have seen various
features here as 'vulgarisms', apparently in the sense of lower-class features
(so Marouzeau 1921: 156–7, 1954: 195; Caplan 1954: 262–3 n. *b*), while
others have maintained that the passage displays 'everyday language without
vulgarity, the conversational language of the upper-class' (Leeman 1963:
1.31). Are these views incompatible, or did the 'conversational language of
the upper-class' in fact include some features that also characterise lower-
class Latin?[14]

---

[13] Marouzeau 1921: 156–7, 1954: 195; Caplan 1954: 262–3 n. *b*; Leeman 1963: i.31; Hofmann–Ricottilli
145, 252, 293, 364, 381, 391; Achard 1989: 143 n. 55; Calboli 1993: 293–4, 532–3.

[14] The term *scurra* might put the man so described in a class of rather well-to-do city layabouts,
from whom one would not necessarily expect lower-class language. However, in the first century
BC recipients of the insult *scurra* were not always wealthy. For a brief history of the term, with
bibliography, see Damon 1997: 109–12. Damon (1997: 110) states categorically: 'It is not possible
to pinpoint the financial status of the *scurra* who appears in a sample speech quoted in a treatise
written while Cicero was still a young man, the *Rhetorica ad Herennium*'. The text is often read so
that the *scurra*'s *vox* is said to have been practised *pone scaenam et in eiusmodi locis*. Taking the text
this way, Damon (1997: 110) notes that the language of the *scurra* in our passage was 'associated
with some scruffy parts of Rome'. Even if the text does contain such a metalinguistic comment,
however, it need not refer to anything beyond the *scurra*'s delivery (his *vox* in a fairly narrow sense).
We follow here the text of Achard (1989), who (with some of the manuscripts) reads *pone scaenam
et in eiusmodi locis* as part of an insult addressed from the *scurra* to the youth. If so, the comment is
not a metalinguistic one at all.

Without discussing all relevant expressions, we may note that some features quite clearly fall into categories condemned as substandard by the prescriptive tradition: the monophthongs *e* and *o* in *pedagogi* and *oriculas* (if these have not been introduced in transmission)[15], and the use of the diminutive *oriculas* in the sense of the non-diminutive *aures* (cf. Väänänen 1981: 80).

The use of *e* for *ae* begins as a non-urban feature and is branded as such as early as Lucilius' jibe against a certain Caecilius: *Cecilius pretor ne rusticus fiat* 'let's hope Cecilius doesn't become Pretor Rusticus' (Lucil. 1130 M. = 232 W. = 1146 K. = H85 C.). More explicitly, Varro points out that *haedus* and many other words are pronounced with *ae* in the city and with *e* in the country: *in Latio rure 'hedus', qui in urbe ut in multis A addito 'haedus'*, 'In the Latin countryside that is *hedus* which is *haedus* in the city, with the addition of *a* as in many words' (Varro *L.* 5.97; cf. 7.96). In post-classical times, prescriptive texts warn against confusion between *ae* and *e* (e.g. Diomedes, *GL* 1.452.17–19), which is indeed common in texts with non-standard features.[16] *o* for *au* likewise originated, in all probability, as a non-urban regionalism, and likewise comes to be condemned as a widespread substandard feature. Already in the first century BC, it appears to be characteristic of sub-elite Latin in the city of Rome (see Väänänen 1981: 38–9; Müller 2001: 35–7; Clackson and Horrocks 2007: 241–2). The diminutive *oricla* (a form with widespread Romance reflexes) for *auris* is expressly condemned in the *Appendix Probi* (83 Powell).

---

[15] All the manuscripts have *pedagogi*, although *-e-* for *-ae-* (where variation between grammatically or lexically different words or forms is not at issue) is relatively rare in all manuscripts of *Rhet. Her.* except in proper names. A trawl through Book 4, with Achard's full apparatus criticus, revealed two further examples that are not proper names and are shared by all manuscripts: *teterrima* for *taeterrima* at 4.51; *trop(h)eis for tropaeis* at 4.66. Both are lively examples illustrating figures of thought. At at 4.61 *celestes* appears in all manuscripts that have this word, but the ninth-century manuscripts ('Mutili') have instead *cetes/cetis/ocetes*. No further examples appear in Book 4 in the 'Mutili', though there are some inverse spellings (at 4.23 *quicquae* for *quicque* in P; at 4.50 C has *aegestatis* for *egestatis* at the first occurrence of the word, and H at the second occurrence; at 4.65 the first hand in P has *exampelaexare* for *examplexare*). All four 'Mutili' have *oriculas*, which is emended to *auriculas* by the correctors of P and B. The later 'Integri' and 'Expleti' (which have been extensively normalised: see Achard 1989: lxiii) have *auriculas*: see Achard's apparatus ad loc. None of the manuscripts otherwise shows a tendency towards *-o-* for *-au-*. We counted no further examples in Book 4, in any manuscript. Given these tendencies, the agreement of all four *Mutili* on two monophthongised spellings in this passage is likely to be significant. If so, the spellings either derive from the author of the treatise or (less likely) are due to 'downgrading' of the language of this particular passage at a fairly early stage of transmission. Cf. also Marx's (1894: 165) judgement that our *oriculas* and *pedagogi*, along with *tropeis* at 4. 66, are due to the author of the treatise.

[16] On *e* for *ae* see further Müller 2001: 32–3; Adams 2007: 78–88.

If these features already belong in the first century BC to negatively evaluated linguistic varieties (whether regional or social), their appearance in the example of the simple style would seem inconsistent with the requirement that the simple style should have *puris et electis verbis conpositam orationem* 'language composed of correct and select words' (*Rhet. Her.* 4.16). However, we have seen that there is a certain ambivalence in the evaluation of the 'ordinary' language with which the simple style has affinities. The apparently substandard features in the example of the simple style may be due to a genuine overlap between conversational register (and its close relative the simple style) on the one hand and negatively evaluated sociolect on the other. It is not very clear, though, whether -*e*- for -*ae*- (differently from -*o*- for -*au*-) already belongs to a low sociolect in the first century BC. The evidence from inscriptions and literary testimonia suggests that this feature is primarily a regionalism at this period (see Adams 2007: 87–8), only later a sociolectal feature. In the light of later developments, however, it seems useless to speculate further: we may simply be lacking the evidence for the early stages of development to a substandard urban feature.

The classification of styles in the *Ad Herennium* is a double tripartite one, in which each of the three styles that is appropriate in its place also has a debased form that should be avoided. The *Ad Herennium* therefore provides us also with an example of the debased version of the simple style (the *genus exile*): *nam istic in balineis*[17] *accessit ad hunc; postea dicit: 'hic tuus servus me pulsavit'. postea dicit hic illi: 'considerabo'. post ille convicium fecit et magis magisque praesente multis clamavit*, 'For that man came up to this man in the baths. Afterwards he said, "This slave of yours beat me." Afterwards this man said to that one: "I'll think about it." Afterwards that man started a brawl and shouted out more and more in front of lots of people.' (*Rhet. Her.* 4.16)

If the manuscript evidence can be trusted here, the form *balneas* in the example of the 'good' simple style has here been replaced by *balineis*, as if the author felt that there was a status difference between the two forms. The form with -*i*- has been taken to be substandard (Marouzeau 1921: 157; 1954: 195), and is indeed condemned as such by Caper (*GL* VII.108.7), but the distribution of the two forms does not make for a straightforward assessment of their sociolinguistic status (see *TLL* s.v. *balneum*; Calboli 1993: 297). Other forms that have been taken to be substandard include *istic* for *iste* (on the persistence of forms of the demonstrative with the deictic -*ce* in

---

[17] Of the four ninth-century manuscripts, P and C have *balineis*, H has *bali in eis*, and B has *balneis*. The later 'Integri' have *balneis*, and the 'Expleti' have *balneas*. See Achard's (1989) apparatus ad loc.

Republican and Imperial Latin outside the literary evidence, presumably as a genuine feature of spoken Latin, cf. Adams 1995b: 101); adverbial *post* for *postea* (not in a standard phrase such as *paulo post* or *multis post annis*); and fossilised *praesente* functioning as a preposition.[18] However, all these features would have been at home in an early phase of the language, for example in Terence, a school author (cf. *Eu.* 649 *absente nobis*), without suggesting ungrammaticality. There may also be a question of imitating comic language (Adams 2007: 379–80). Furthermore, both characters perhaps become inappropriately uncouth in their language. The *scurra*, hardly a sympathetic character in either passage, is now made to blurt out *pueri tui modo me pulsarunt* without any conversation-opener (*heus*) or vocative (*adolescens*). The youth now uses the more direct *considerabo* 'I'll think about it' instead of *tamen sine me considerare* 'but – let me think about it'. The second passage may thus fail to achieve *sermocinatio* (*Rhet. Her.* 4.65), direct speech that conforms to the characters of the participants.[19] The most striking artistic difference between the two passages, however, seems to consist in the latter passage's lack of periodic sentences (in fact complete lack of subordinate clauses), and in the monotonous use of connections, especially *postea . . . postea . . . post* (so Calboli 1993: 297; cf. Caplan 1954: 267 n. *d*).[20]

One of the difficulties we experience in dealing with this crucial passage has to do with our ignorance about the level of inclusiveness or tolerance educated Romans were prepared to adopt in speaking. What the author has in mind here is not so much a criticism of conversational language as such, but of the inept importation of conversational forms into a disguised artistic or formal variety. It is one thing to adopt features imitating *sermo*, another to import those forms without any degree of artistic mediation. Quintilian makes this distinction clear in complaining that many speakers think anybody can state facts in *sermo cotidianus*, whereas the most difficult task for an orator is in fact to say something that everybody will afterwards think he would have said (*Inst.* 4.2.37–8).[21]

---

[18] See again Marouzeau (1921: 157, 1954: 195); cf. Leeman 1963: 1.31. On this passage see also Caplan 1954: 266–7 n. *d*; Achard (1989: 145 n. 64); Calboli 1993: 297–8.

[19] We are indebted to Gregory Hutchinson for comments suggesting this line of thought, and for drawing our attention to the relevance of *Rhet. Her.* 4.65.

[20] Cf. the example of false *brevitas* at Cic. *Inv.* 1.28. We are again indebted to Gregory Hutchinson for this comparison.

[21] Cf. also Quintilian's reference to Cicero's 'concealed art' at *Inst.* 4.2.58, quoted below, and Dionysius of Halicarnassus, *Lysias* 3 (ὁμοίως δὲ τοῖς ἰδιώταις διαλέγεσθαι δοκῶν πλεῖστον ὅσον ἰδιώτου διαφέρει 'and yet although he seems to converse like ordinary people, he could not be more different from an ordinary person').

Comparison between the example of the simple style and that of its perversion may thus suggest, on the one hand, variation within conversational language, with the 'good' simple style being comparatively free from forms that may belong to the wrong *sort* of conversation. On the other hand, however, the comparison suggests a difference between genuine conversational language and its appropriate artistic imitation. In the light of this second point, the distinction between these styles, and the author's comment that the 'good' simple style is made *puris et electis verbis*, should not be taken to hint strongly at different sociolects within conversational language. Once again, even the 'good' simple style has some affinities with negatively evaluated sociolects.[22]

Elsewhere, discussions of the *genera dicendi* suggest works or parts of works in which we might look for the simple style. According to Cicero (*Orat.* III), Demosthenes' *Against Leptines* is an example of a speech in the simple style throughout. The fact that this is a Greek work is, of course, symptomatic of the Roman use of Greek models both for rhetorical theory and for rhetorical practice. Perhaps more helpfully, Cicero (*Orat.* 68) tells us that the simple style is required for proof, the middle style to please the audience, and the grand style to win them over; further on he says that something close to *cotidianus sermo* is appropriate for *narrationes*: *narrationes credibiles nec historico sed prope cotidiano sermone explicatae dilucide*, 'Narrationes (should be) credible and laid out clearly not in the language of history but almost in everyday language' (*Orat.* 124; cf. Quint. *Inst.* 4.2.36).

Quintilian, elaborating on Cicero, says that archaisms, transferred usages and neologisms (all features eschewed by the simple style: see below) should be avoided in prologue, narrative and argument, as should elaborate syntax in a *divisio*, while the *humile atque cotidianum sermonis genus* should be avoided in perorations:

ita nec vetera aut tralata aut ficta verba in incipiendo, narrando, argumentando continuabimus, neque decurrentis contexto nitore circumitus ubi dividenda erit causa et in partis suas digerenda, neque humile atque cotidianum sermonis genus et compositione ipsa dissolutum epilogis dabimus... (*Inst.* II.I.6)

---

[22] Tacitus (*Dial.* 32.3) complains that contemporary orators neglect the thorough learning necessary for oratory to such an extent *ut in actionis eorum <hu>ius quoque cotidiani sermonis foeda ac pudenda vitia deprehendantur*. This is normally taken to mean 'that in their pleadings the filthy and shameful vices of our *cotidianus sermo* are detected', and to imply an unusually negative evaluation of *cotidianus sermo*. However, the phrase should probably be taken to mean rather that the orators fell into barbarisms and solecisms even in their use of *cotidianus sermo*: see Mayer 2001: 189, with references. If so, no special explanation for the appearance of such a negative evaluation in Tacitus is needed. Differently Müller 2001: 172.

Thus we shall not keep on using archaic or transferred or newly coined words in prologue, narrative and argument, nor free-running periods with unbroken splendour when a cause is to be divided and arranged into its parts, nor shall we give the humble and everyday style of speech, loose even in its arrangement, to perorations...

In principle the passages just mentioned give us some hints as to the portions of speeches where we might find the simple style (especially prologues, narratives and arguments) and where we might find its opposite (especially perorations). One might expect at least some extant speeches to conform to these expectations (even allowing that Roman rhetorical theory is derived largely from Greek models); clear examples are not necessarily easy to identify, but Quintilian provides an example of Cicero's *callidissima simplicitatis imitatio*, making use of *verba... vulgaria et cotidiana*, in the *narratio* to the *Pro Milone* (28):

... plurimum tamen facit illa callidissima simplicitatis imitatio: 'Milo autem, cum in senatu fuisset eo die quoad senatus est dimissus, domum venit, calceos et vestimenta mutavit, paulisper, dum se uxor, ut fit, comparat, commoratus est.' quam nihil festinato, nihil praeparato fecisse videtur Milo! quod non solum rebus ipsis vir eloquentissimus, quibus moras et lentum profectionis ordinem ducit, sed verbis etiam vulgaribus et cotidianis et arte occulta consecutus est. (*Inst.* 4.2.57–8)

... and that (well-known) very clever imitation of simplicity is the most effective: 'Milo, on the other hand, since he had been in the Senate on that day until the Senate was adjourned, came home, changed his shoes and clothes, and waited a bit while his wife, in the usual way, got ready.' How Milo seems to have done nothing in a hurry, nothing with planning! The great orator achieved this not only through the things themselves, through which he set out the delays and the slow order of proceeding, but also through popular and everyday words and concealed art.[23]

In a different vein, Cicero tells us that to some the language of Plato and of Democritus seems more worthy of being considered poetic, on account of its rhythmical qualities and stylistic ornamentation, than that of the (Greek) comic poets, which, apart from being in verse, is nothing other than *cotidianus sermo*:

quicquid est enim quod sub aurium mensuram aliquam cadit, etiam si abest a versu – nam id quidem orationis est vitium – numerus vocatur, qui Graece ῥυθμὸς dicitur. itaque video visum esse non nullis Platonis et Democriti locutionem, etsi absit a versu, tamen quod incitatius feratur et clarissimis verborum

---

[23] For the *narratio* and the peroration of the *Pro Roscio Amerino* as following Cicero's own later precepts see Landgraf 1914: 40, 263–5.

luminibus utatur, potius poema putandum quam comicorum poetarum; apud quos, nisi quod versiculi sunt, nihil est aliud cotidiani dissimile sermonis. (*Orat.* 67; cf. Jonge 2008: 364–5)

For whatever falls into some measurement by the ears, even if it falls short of being verse – for that indeed is a fault in oratory – is called measure, in Greek ῥυθμός. Therefore I know some have thought that the language of Plato and Democritus, even if it is removed from verse, is nevertheless, because it is delivered more rapidly and with superb verbal flashes, to be considered poetry more than that of the comic poets; their language, apart from the fact that it consists of verses, does not differ at all from everyday conversation.

Here the notion that formal prose falls between verse and everyday language is given something of a twist, since some formal prose turns out to be more poetic than the verse of comedy. We should, however, be wary of seeing everything in serious (Greek or Latin) poetry as belonging to a non-conversational register, in view of Cicero's contention that Homer, Ennius, the other poets and especially the tragedians need not always use the same *contentio* (here 'rhetorical style') but may make frequent changes and *non numquam etiam ad cotidianum genus sermonis accederent* 'sometimes they may even approach everyday conversation' (*Orat.* 109, cf. p. 132 below).

In addition to the provision or suggestion of some actual examples of conversational language or the simple rhetorical style, various authors note qualities of conversational language or of the style of oratory that comes close to it.

We have mentioned (section 2.2 above) the four varieties into which the *Rhetorica ad Herennium* divides the voice quality *sermo*: *dignitas*, *demonstratio*, *narratio* and *iocatio*. These differ from one another in pace and in the use of pauses as well as in other respects that we would consider to belong to 'tone of voice' (*Rhet. Her.* 3.24–5). *Narratio* is itself characterised by variety of pace and tone (3.24). Although *sermo* and its various subdivisions are not intended as descriptions of everyday speaking, the closeness of *sermo* to everyday speaking suggests that variation in the use of the voice, and in pace and the use of pauses, characterised everyday speaking too. It would, of course, be very surprising if Romans ordinarily spoke in a monotone.

As regards more narrowly linguistic or rhetorical features, frequent points are that conversational language and the associated simple style are unadorned (e.g. *Rhet. Her.* 4.69, mentioned above), or more specifically that they lack figures of speech (e.g. Quint. *Inst.* 9.3.3, mentioned above), archaisms (Cicero *De orat.* 3.153, quoted above), neologisms, periphrases and transferred usages (for the last three see Quint. *Inst.* 12.10.41–2). The notion that conversational language and the simple style are, more vaguely, restrained or 'thin' is present in many of the labels given to the simple style (e.g. *(figura) extenuata* and *attenuata* of the *Ad Herennium*; *(oratio) tenuis* and *subtilis* in Cicero). The same notion appears in Quintilian's association between what is *pressum* and *tenue* – and approved of by Atticists – and what is as little removed as possible from *usus cotidianus*: *ipsorum etiam qui rectum dicendi genus sequi volunt alii pressa demum et tenuia et quae minimum ab usu cotidiano recedant sana et vere Attica putant* 'even among those who want to pursue a correct style of speaking, some think that only what is subdued and thin and as little removed as possible from everyday usage is wholesome and truly Attic' (*Inst.* 10.1.44).

The notion that conversational language lacks figures of speech has to be modified, however, as Quintilian perhaps recognises in pointing out that some figures of speech have become so well used (in everyday language?) that they hardly count as figures any more: *quamquam sunt quaedam figurae ita receptae ut paene iam hoc ipsum nomen effugerint: quae etiam si fuerint crebriores, consuetas aures minus ferient*, 'Although some figures are so widespread that they have now almost escaped this very name. Even if these become more frequent, they will impress the accustomed ears less' (*Inst.* 9.3.4).

He also notes a parallelism between figures that produce innovations and mere mistakes, the difference being that figures of speech are created deliberately while mistakes are accidental: *prius fit isdem generibus quibus vitia: esset enim omne eiusmodi schema vitium si non peteretur sed accideret*, 'The first kind (of figure) occurs in the same varieties as faults: indeed, every figure of that kind would be a fault if it happened instead of being sought' (Quint. *Inst.* 9.3.2).

Although conversational language is generally characterised by the absence of stylistic ornaments, the author of the *Ad Herennium* and Quintilian comment with reference to some specific ornaments that examples occur even in *cottidianus sermo*:

harum omnium denominationum magis in praecipiendo divisio quam in quaerendo difficilis inventio est, ideo quod plena consuetudo est non modo poetarum et oratorum, sed etiam cottidiani sermonis huiusmodi denominationum. (*Rhet. Her.* 4.43)

All these metonymies are harder to classify when teaching than to hit on when searching, because the usage not only of poets and orators, but even of everyday conversation is full of metonymies of this kind.

maxime autem in orando valebit numerorum illa libertas. nam et Livius saepe sic dicit: 'Romanus proelio victor', cum Romanos vicisse significat, et contra Cicero ad Brutum 'populo' inquit 'imposuimus et oratores visi sumus', cum de se tantum loqueretur. quod genus non orationis modo ornatus sed etiam cotidiani sermonis usus recipit. (Quint. *Inst.* 8.6.20–1)

In prose, freedom to vary number will be of most value. For Livy often speaks as follows: 'The Roman was victorious in the battle', when he means that the Romans won, and on the other hand Cicero said to Brutus, 'We have imposed on the people and are considered orators', when he was talking about himself alone. This sort is not only an ornament of oratory but is even accepted by the usage of everyday conversation.

sunt et illae breves: 'vagi per silvas ritu ferarum', et illud Ciceronis in Clodium: 'quo ex iudicio velut ex incendio nudus effugit.' quibus similia possunt cuicumque etiam ex cotidiano sermone succurrere. (Quint. *Inst.* 8.3.81, on brief similes)

There are also brief ones [i.e. similes]: 'Roaming through the woods like wild beasts', and that expression of Cicero's against Clodius: 'from which trial he escaped bare as from a fire'. Ones similar to these can occur to anybody even from everyday conversation.

ceterum allegoria parvis quoque ingeniis et cotidiano sermoni frequentissime servit. (Quint. *Inst.* 8.6.51)

But allegory also very often serves meagre intellects and everyday conversation.

Similarly, Cicero gives examples of metaphors that appear in the speech 'not only of city folk but even of *rustici*':

ergo ille tenuis orator . . . erit . . . *ea* translatione fortasse crebrior, qua frequentissime sermo omnis utitur non modo urbanorum, sed etiam rusticorum: si quidem est eorum gemmare vitis, sitire agros, laetas esse segetes, luxuriosa frumenta. (*Orat.* 81)

Therefore let the orator practising the simple style . . . be . . . perhaps rather liberal with those metaphors that all conversation not only of *urbani* but even of *rustici* uses very frequently, considering that they say that vines 'gem', that fields 'are thirsty', that fields are 'happy' [cf. Verg. *G.* 1.1], and that grain is 'luxuriant'.

Finally, although conversational language is seen as characterised by the lack of archaisms and neologisms, much Latin vocabulary was not bound to a particular register but belonged to a common stock, available to all genres (cf. Dickey, this volume p. 4). This point is underlined by Cicero's contention, in connection with the importance of rhythm, that *sermo* and *contentio* (here conversation and debate) do not use distinct words, nor do *usus cotidianus* and the language of stage and festival:

ex hac versus, ex hac eadem dispares numeri conficiuntur; ex hac haec etiam
soluta variis modis multorumque generum oratio; non enim sunt alia sermonis,
alia contentionis verba, neque ex alio genere ad usum cotidianum, alio ad scaenam pompamque sumuntur; sed ea nos cum iacentia sustulimus e medio, sicut
mollissimam ceram ad nostrum arbitrium formamus et fingimus. (*De orat.* 3.177)

Out of this [i.e. speech] verses are composed, out of this irregular rhythms, out of
this prose too in various manners and of many varieties; for there is not one set
of words for conversation, another for debate, nor are words taken from one sort
for everyday use and from another for stage and festival, but when we have taken
these as they lie in front of us, we form and fashion them to our will like the softest
wax.[24]

3 GRAMMARIANS AND COMMENTATORS

We have thus seen that rhetorical theory assigns some place to 'ordinary
language' as a basis for at least the simple style, and helps to identify some
of the perceived characteristics of 'ordinary language'. Rhetorical theory is
however clear that even the simple style is an artistic approximation, artistic
language disguised as spoken language.

Less satisfactory evidence is available on how prepared Roman scholars
were to recognise the existence of different registers in the spoken language
itself, and to deal with the more informal registers of linguistic communication in Latin. Many usages were classified as substandard, without regard
for the level of education of the speakers involved, but evidence for a more
nuanced approach to informal communication is difficult to assemble.[25]

Yet some discussion always went on among the learned; some advocated
a simple, unaffected use of the language at least for simple, everyday
written communication, and perhaps pleaded for such use even in polite
conversation.

Quintilian, for example, reflects some debate about the acceptability
of evolved forms, such as *caldus* for *calidus* (Augustus described the latter as 'hideous': see below),[26] and seems inclined to accept the current

---

[24] Gregory Hutchinson draws our attention also to the Elder Seneca's remark (*Con.* 7.5.9) *Brutus
Bruttedius cotidiano verbo significanter usus est* 'Brutus Bruttedius pointedly used an everyday word'.
The use of *significanter* here suggests that the use of a *cotidianum verbum* did not automatically have
special significance.

[25] This is obviously different from the implicit information about Roman writers' sensitivity to register
which we can glean from the actual written texts themselves, for example a corpus of letters by the
same person, addressing different people, as most notably in the case of Cicero, or the snatches of
dialogue included in Cicero's orations, or in his letters, on which see Hutchinson 1998: 112–38.

[26] *Apud* Quint. *Inst.* 1.6.19 = Augustus, *Epistulae* fr. xxiii Malcovati: *sed Augustus quoque in epistulis ad
C. Caesarem scriptis emendat quod is 'calidum' dicere quam 'caldum' malit, non quia id non sit Latinum,*

pronunciation of others, such as *have* with a non-etymological initial aspiration and without punctilious delivery of the long final *e* (*Inst.* 1.6.19–21).[27] Quintilian's preoccupation seems to be with colloquial forms which have not obtained recognition in written language, but are commonplace at all levels of the spoken language, so much so that the use of the obsolete or etymologically correct form may be regarded as an excessive affectation. This preoccupation emerges also elsewhere: *quaeso* is old enough as it is, why pronounce it *quaiso*? And *reor*, common in the literary evidence, is considered barely 'tolerable', presumably because *puto* seems to Quintilian less pretentious and conspicuous (*Inst.* 8.3.23; cf. Cicero, *De orat.* 3.153, quoted above, and Wisse, Winterbottom and Fantham 2008: 196–7, with bibliography).

An anecdotal piece of information concerns the emperor Augustus, who scolded Tiberius for eschewing the common word *obiter* 'in passing' (he wrote *perviam* instead; discussion in Adams 2003b: 568–9; Adams *et al.* 2005: 7). The same source relates that another emperor with intellectual pretensions, Hadrian, in his turn queried the Latinity (which in this context clearly means 'correctness, acceptability') of the word, and at the same time slighted Augustus' judgement and authority in language matters: *sed divus Hadrianus 'tametsi' inquit 'Augustus non pereruditus homo fuerit, ut id adverbium ex usu potius quam lectione protulerit'*, 'But divine Hadrian said, "Nonetheless Augustus was not a highly learned man, so that he produced that adverb from use rather than reading"' (Charisius 271 Barwick).

Augustus' support for plain language, though not elaborated in contexts in which metalinguistic reflection was explicit, is proof of some awareness of register variation, particularly since his public pronouncements seem to have all been in irreproachable high-style oratory.[28] In one of the fragments from his letters, for example, he complains that he has eaten only 'two mouthfuls', using lexical items which are certainly colloquial: *hodie duas buccas manducavi* (Suet. *Aug.* 76.2). His censure of linguistic 'affectation' is also reported in reference to some relatives' Latin usage. Terms Augustus

---

sed quia sit odiosum et, ut ipse Graeco verbo significavit, περίεργον. *atqui hanc quidam* ὀρθοέπειαν *solam putant, quam ego minime excludo*, 'But even Augustus, in his letters to Gaius Caesar, scolds him for using by preference *calidus* rather than *caldus*, not so much because the former is not "Latin", but because it is hideous and, as he put it using a Greek expression, "overdone". And yet some take *calidus* to be the only correct pronunciation, and I don't absolutely disagree with it.'

[27] This is incidentally one of the few passages where attention to prosodic and phonetic features of lower register and informal Latin emerges.

[28] *Testimonia* in Malcovati 1967: 71–2 (Suet. *Aug.* 86 called his oratorical style *elegans et temperatum*). The most significant fragment is Augustus' *laudatio* in P. Köln vi.249 (in Greek: *princeps* in Koenen 1970).

uses to denote affected use of the language are *moleste* ('tiresomely': Suet. *Aug.* 86.3 *opus est... dare te operam, ne moleste scribas et loquaris*) and *odiosum* or περίεργον ('hideous', 'overdone': *apud* Quint. *Inst.* 1.6.19 – see n. 26).[29]

Roman authors of extant *Artes grammaticae* pay little attention to the spoken language as such. The purpose of grammar was the description of the parts of speech and their properties, as a preliminary step to the correct study and interpretation of poetry. Comments on linguistic correctness and incorrectness occur in the sections devoted to *vitia orationis* (or 'linguistic errors') (Dammer 2001: 15–16), but their approach is prescriptive and classificatory, and not subtle enough to contemplate the possibility of register variation and speaker's choice. Comments on idioms and phrases which we may believe to have had some currency even among the educated, even at an early date (for example the adoption of prepositional combinations, such as *de susum, de post, de mane, de intus*, or the use of the present for the future or the active periphrastics with reference to future events), do not form a special category between acceptable and non-acceptable usage.[30] A passage in Pompeius (active fifth century AD) comes closest to recognising that Latin speakers had a choice without explicit censure: *quotiens ita volueris facere* [i.e. using an infinitive as a noun], *Graece loqueris aperte, 'da mihi bibere'*, δός μοι πιεῖν, 'Whenever you want to use this construction, you'll be patently using a Greek construction: *da mihi bibere*, δός μοι πιεῖν' (Pompeius, *GL* v.213.13). Here the grammarian must have been at a loss as to how to evaluate an established usage which had some currency in poetry, from Plautus and Terence to Virgil,[31] as well as in the spoken language, but

---

[29] *Bucca* in this sense famously occurs at Petr. 44.2 (*buccam panis*); *manduco* is found very early for 'to munch', and Augustus is the first author to use it simply for 'eating', though of course an expressive 'munch' is not out of place in the context.

[30] E.g. Quint. *Inst.* 1.5.38; Pompeius *GL* v.248.17 *multi enim quasi causa communis elocutionis ita locuntur, 'de intus venio', et dicunt, ideo debet de iungi, ut significet de loco* 'for many as if for the sake of common diction speak as follows: *de intus venio*, and they say that *de* needs to be added to indicate motion from'; Pompeius *GL* v.273.26 *item qui male loquuntur modo ita dicunt, 'depost illum ambulat'* 'likewise those who speak badly sometimes speak as follows: *depost illum ambulat'*; Servius *GL* iv.416.17 *nemo enim dicit 'de sero', 'de modo'; unde nec 'de mane' dicere debemus, quod plerique in usu habent*, 'For nobody says *de sero, de modo*; whence we ought not to say *de mane* either, which many people are accustomed to use'; Pompeius *GL* v.235.29–30 *ergo siqui dicat 'festino, quia hodie dico', non bene loquitur, ea ratione quoniam non videtur hoc agere, sed acturus esse. ergo melius dicit 'dicturus sum'*, 'Therefore if anybody says *festino, quia hodie dico* he does not speak well, since he does not seem to be doing this, but to be going to do this. So he does better to say *dicturus sum*.' On the Roman grammarians' comments concerning current language see Biville 1999.

[31] Cf. Pl. *Per.* 821 *bibere da usque plenis cantharis* 'give us to drink up to the brim'; Ter. *An.* 484–5 *quod iussi dari bibere et quantum imperavi date* 'give what I ordered to be given to her to drink and as much as I ordered'. The construction is commonplace in the school handbooks *De sermone cotidiano*, composed in the third or fourth century AD, where one finds *da nobis bibere, date nobis cenare* (Ferri 2008: 131).

it is interesting to note the expression *volueris*, this time not followed by censure.[32]

Another interesting passage, from the grammarian Diomedes (*c.* 380 AD), deals with what we may suspect to have been a widespread construction in informal speech, the use of the indicative in indirect questions:

hanc speciem [i.e. *relativa*, for 'modal attraction', or simply 'subordination'] in consuetudine parum multi observant inperitia lapsi, cum dicunt nescio quid facis, nescio quid fecisti. eruditius enim dicetur nescio quid facias, nescio quid feceris. quo more et Cicero loquitur pro Sexto Roscio [1], 'credo ego vos, iudices, mirari quid sit quod, cum tot summi oratores hominesque nobilissimi sedeant, ego potissimum surrexerim'; non dixit credo vos mirari quid sit quod surrexi, quod est idiotismos. (*GL* 1.395.15)

Many people adopt this construction [i.e. the use of the subjunctive in the *relativa species*] little or not at all in current usage, for lack of knowledge, so that they say *nescio quid facis, nescio quid fecisti*. A more educated way to say this will be *nescio quid facias, nescio quid feceris*. So Cicero speaks in *Pro Sexto Roscio*: *credo ego vos, iudices, mirari quid sit quod, cum tot summi oratores hominesque nobilissimi sedeant, ego potissimum surrexerim*; he did not say *credo vos mirari quid sit quod surrexi*, which is an idiotism.

Interestingly, Diomedes does not condemn the use of the indicative for the subjunctive as *non Latinum*, but recommends the other construction as *eruditius*.[33] In fact we shall see that the use of the significant label ἰδιωτισμός reveals a degree of acceptance of this as a 'current construction'.

More attention to register variation may have been a feature of the school commentary tradition, especially when it dealt with comedy, where it was impossible not to acknowledge variation, both socially determined and situational or contextual. A particularly apt case is the series of Donatus' references to ἰδιωτισμός in the Terence commentary (fourth century AD). The term occurs in rhetorical writers, in contexts where there can be no question of a substandard, incorrect usage, but the reference is clearly to

[32] Donatus describes this usage as current, with mild censure: *consuetudine quam ratione dixit pro: date ei potionem . . . nam duo verba iniuncta nullum habent significatum sine nomine aut pronomine, ut si dicas dic facere*, 'He said this through usage rather than according to logic, for *date ei potionem . . .* for two juxtaposed verbs have no meaning without a noun or pronoun, just as if you were to say *dic facere*' (on Ter. *An.* 484). Penney (1999: 256–7) considers this the mingling of a Greek, learned construction and an inherited one attested as early as Plautus and Cato (*Agr.* 89 *meridie bibere dato* 'at midday he should give them to drink').

[33] The indicative is a mark of uneducated speech in Petronius (44.1), but it occurs occasionally in several texts, such as *Ad Herennium*, Varro's *De lingua Latina*, and Cicero's letters: cf. H–S 538. For its use in inscriptions see Konjetzny 1907: 340; in the *Vetus Latina* Rönsch 1875: 428–9.

a colloquial, familiar expression.[34] The earliest example is in the Elder Seneca:

Hispo Romanius bello idiotismo usus est: 'dixerunt, inquit, amici: eamus ad raptae patrem, hoc curemus; illud domi est.' (Sen. *Con.* 2.3.21)

Hispo Romanius employed a nice colloquial expression. 'My friends said: "Let's go to the girl's father, let us see to that, the other is in the bag."' (trans. Winterbottom, with modifications)

The declaimer is here impersonating a young ravisher, who reports, in direct speech, his friends' advice to go and obtain pardon from the girl's father first, since forgiveness from the young man's own father must be taken for granted. Here *idiotismus* is used for a non-transparent idiomatic phrase, and the presence of direct rather than reported speech in the extract seems significant.

Importantly, the term also occurs in Quintilian:

vim rebus aliquando verborum ipsa humilitas adfert. an cum dicit in Pisonem Cicero 'cum tibi tota cognatio serraco advehatur', incidisse videtur in sordidum nomen, non eo contemptum hominis quem destructum volebat auxisse? . . . unde interim gratus idiotismi decor, qualis est ille apud M. Tullium: 'pusio qui cum maiore sorore cubitabat' et 'Flavius qui cornicum oculos confixit', et pro Milone illud 'heus tu Rufio', et 'Erucius Antoniaster'. id tamen in declamatoribus est notabilius, laudarique me puero solebat 'da patri panem', et in eodem 'etiam canem pascis'. (*Inst.* 8.3.21–2)

Meanness of vocabulary may itself on occasion lend vigour. When Cicero says, in *In Pisonem*, 'when all your kith and kin are carried on a cart', do we think that he has lighted accidentally on the low word, and not deliberately enhanced the contempt felt for the man he was trying to ruin? . . . Hence a colloquial phrase sometimes gives welcome elegance, as in Cicero's 'The little lad who went to bed with his big sister', and 'Flavius, who scratched out the crows' eyes', or (in *Pro Milone*) 'Hi there, Redhead!' and 'Erucius the Antoniast'. This device is obtrusive in the declaimers: when I was a boy, there was praise for 'Give your father bread' and (in the same case) 'You feed even your dog.' (trans. D. A. Russell)

---

[34] We have no means of learning whether comments on *idiotismus* were an innovation by Donatus, or whether there was a tradition of commentaries on comic texts in which attention was paid to this feature. Jakobi (1996: 125–6) discusses ἰδιωτισμός in Donatus but seems to emphasise only the meaning 'characterisation', which is compatible with some of the examples but cuts out some of the implications, and is clearly not what is meant by *idiotismus* in other sources, such as the Elder Seneca, Quintilian, and Diomedes. In fact, the distinction, as it were, between 'convincing characterization' and 'everyday expression' may have been unclear to Donatus too, but it is symptomatic that Donatus never uses *idiotismus* tags when describing lofty, pompous language, conceivably also used for characterisation purposes.

The successful idiotisms exemplified by Quintilian are low-register lexical items such as *pusio*, colloquial neologisms such as the popular suffix *-aster*, and the use of proverbial sentences with a particular metaphorical meaning felt to be colloquial,[35] and an abrupt address form. In the example from *Pro Milone*, Cicero is polemically conjuring up the cross-questioning of one of Clodius' servants, unfit to give evidence because he is not free to speak, and the rough address form, as well as the switch from analysis to dialogue (*heus tu Rufio . . . cave sis mentiare*), is part of the desired effect.[36]

In the Greek tradition, ἰδιωτισμός had an ambivalent status, denoting in different authors 'vulgar' or 'everyday, current'.[37] In Latin, too, this ambivalence must have persisted, but Seneca is explicit enough when he ranges *idiotismus* among the more slippery of the *virtutes orationis* (*Con.* 7 pr. 5).

Donatus too discusses *idiotismus*.[38] His use of the term is rather wide, and ranges from low-register lexical items or phrases, often metaphorical, to phatic and pragmatic elements, for example the use of proper names in order to soften a statement or a request, and even general striking features, such as speaking to oneself aloud. It thus includes several different elements of what Donatus must have perceived as characteristic of Terence's representation of the *sermo cotidianus*.

One interesting example is Ter. *Hec.* 522 *se duxit foras* 'she took herself out', which is labelled as 'an idiotism for *abiit*'. The speaker is a *senex*, Phidippus, not in principle a lower-class character. Interestingly, *se ducere* for simply 'to go' is found elsewhere in informal genres, such as Pollio's letter to Cicero characterised by direct, unadorned style (Cic. *Fam.* 10.32), and is

---

[35] On scratching out crows' eyes cf. Hutchinson 2006: 142.

[36] Interestingly, *heus* occurs only here in Cicero's speeches, in a characterisation of brusque address, as in the passage from *Rhetorica ad Herennium* 4.14 (see above).

[37] The sense 'common, everyday' for ἰδιωτισμός, ἰδιώτης with reference to a metaphorical expression is found in 'Longinus', *On the Sublime* 31 (with reference to a metaphorical expression); Dionysius of Halicarnassus has ἰδιώτης λόγος for 'common language', cf. *Demosthenes* 2 ἡ δὲ ἑτέρα λέξις ἡ λιτὴ καὶ ἀφελὴς καὶ δοκοῦσα κατασκευήν τε καὶ ἰσχὺν τὴν πρὸς ἰδιώτην ἔχειν λόγον καὶ ὁμοιότητα πολλοὺς μὲν ἔσχε καὶ ἀγαθοὺς ἄνδρας προστάτας . . . , 'The other diction, the one that is simple and straightforward and seems to derive its strength and elaboration from its relation to common language, was adopted by several important authors' (trans. after Grube 1952: 263; see also n. 21 above). The tone is reminiscent of the description of the *figura extenuata* in the *Ad Herennium*, and stresses the similarity of the thin diction and 'common, private' language.

[38] In what follows we ascribe to 'Donatus' all comments included in Wessner's Teubner edition. Wessner thought that the extant commentary as he printed it went back to a sixth-century compilation from two different, though genuine, sources, but Wessner's scepticism (1902–8: I.xliv–xlvii) concerns the possibility of restoring the exact form of the Donatus commentary, not the content of the notes. Comments based on highly specific rhetorical terms little known in the Middle Ages, such as 'idiotism', are unlikely to be later interpolations. A highly questionable attempt to separate genuine from interpolated Donatus was made by Karsten 1912–13.

used in the bilingual school conversational books *De sermone cotidiano* (see p. 30, n. 31), where *duc te* is the Latin for colloquial Greek ὕπαγε. Clearly the usage is not substandard in any meaningful way: it is an expressive form, which the commentator saw fit to remark upon for its linguistic colour. The old man is speaking in slightly rough terms of his wife, with whom he is displeased because he is under the misapprehension that she is to blame for causing the young bride to leave the house.

Another field of application of ἰδιωτισμός is in connection with certain metaphorical expressions which are evidently associated with the common language. *Certe captus est, | habet* 'He's certainly captive, he's got it' (Ter. *An.* 82–3), said by the old man in despair at the thought of his son's passion for a courtesan, is quoted by Donatus ad loc. as another instance of ἰδιωτισμός, with another interesting piece of information about *habet*, which is said to be used of gladiators when they are 'done in' in a fight (*proprie de gladiatoribus dicitur 'habet', quia prius alii vident, quam ipsi sentiant se esse percussos*, '"He's got it" is properly said of gladiators, because others see that they have been finished off before they feel it themselves').

At *Andria* 118 the old man Simo describes to his freedman the first appearance of the girl Glycerium, with whom his son is in love, with the words *unam aspicio adulescentulam*, which Donatus comments upon with the following:

ex consuetudine dixit unam ut dicimus 'unus est adulescens'. tolle 'unam' et ita fiet ut sensui nihil desit, sed consuetudo admirantis non erit expressa. 'unam' ergo τῷ ἰδιωτισμῷ dixit.

He said *unam* as in common usage, as we say 'there is one boy'. Take *unam* away and nothing will be lacking from the sense, but the manner of speaking of someone impressed will not be expressed. He said *unam*, then, using an idiotism.

Donatus' acceptance of this apparently non-standard use of *unus* in a way which is close to that of an indefinite article (H–S 193) is remarkable, as is the equivalence of *ex/in/de consuetudine* and τῷ ἰδιωτισμῷ.[39] This is not *consuetudo* as 'the established usage', called upon to support a rule (as at Quint. *Inst.* 1.6.45 *consuetudinem sermonis vocabo consensum eruditorum* 'I shall call "usage" what is agreed on by the learned'), but the current, common language.

A variant of the same term is ἰδιωτικῶς, which can indicate poor lexical usage, for example, in two cases, in reference to all-purpose *facio* with

---

[39] Interestingly, Donatus might be misreading Terence in the light of later evolved Latin usage. Cf. the discussion on the use of *unus* here and in other classical Latin texts and their (possible) significance in the evolution leading up to the Romance indefinite article in Meisterfeld (2000: 320–1).

weakened semantic content: '*Syre cessas ire ac facere*': ἰδιωτικῶς *dicitur* "'Syrus, are you delaying to go and do it?" is said ἰδιωτικῶς' (On Ter. *Ad.* 916; cf. on Ter. *Eu.* 1001).[40] Some instances of this adverb seem employed to mark more decidedly substandard usage, though Donatus is not explicit on this point, as he is predictably reluctant to identify incorrect Latin in a school author such as Terence: '*ut cum matre esset plus una*': ἰδιωτικῶς *dixit, id est: diu ac maiorem partem*, "'That she could spend more time with her mother": he said ἰδιωτικῶς for "long" and "a greater part (of her time)"' (on Ter. *Hec.* 236). Sometimes, however, the label is attached to simply more colourful, emotional language, for example in a curse: ἰδιωτικῶς '*te cum tua monstratione*' '*te cum tua monstratione* [is said] ἰδιωτικῶς' (on Ter. *Ad.* 713).[41]

Donatus clearly has a notion that slaves and free men use or ought to use different vocabulary and phraseology, and that badly educated people make mistakes,[42] but comments about idiotisms apply indifferently to all classes of characters involved: all notion of sociolect is lost. Also remarkable is the pairing of *idioma* or ἰδιωτισμός with an explanatory phrase in which the sentiment conveyed is explained: *consuetudo admirantis* 'an idiom said by one who is taken aback' (on Ter. *An.* 118); *pro contumelia irascentis* 'an idiom

---

[40] See Jakobi 1996: 125–6; Ferri 2008: 137–8. In theory, it is also possible that Donatus is commenting on the construction of *ire* co-ordinated with an infinitive (*ire ac facere* rather than *ire ut facias*), but the construction has high-register parallels: cf. Acc. *trag.* 518 (W.) *cesso hinc ire et capere lucti vestem in leto coniugis?*, 'Why delay going in and dressing in mourning on the death of my spouse?'

[41] Cf. Pl. *Mer.* 793 *At te, vicine, di deaeque perduint* | *Cum tua amica cumque amationibus*, 'But as for you, neighbour, may the gods and goddesses destroy you together with your girlfriend and love affairs.'

[42] E.g. on slaves' language: on Ter. *An.* 496 '*num veritus*': *veretur liber, metuit servus* '*num veritus*: a free man *veretur*, a slave *metuit*'; on Ter. *Eu.* 312 (only slaves make obscene comments) '*ubi tu nervos intendas tuos*': *utrum obscene hoc, ut servus, an* μεταφορικῶς *ubi laborare ac periclitari debeas?* '*ubi tu nervos intendas tuos*: is this obscene, as befits a slave, or metaphorical for "where you ought to work and take a risk"?'; on Ter. *Eu.* 500 (on appropriate responses to orders) '*fiat*': '*faciam*' *vel* '*fiet*' *diceret servus, liber vero tamquam et ipse iubet sibi* '*fiat*': a slave would say "I'll do it" or "it will be done", but a free man as it were also gives an order to himself'; on Ter. *Hec.* 309.2 *adiciendo* '*causa*' *obscuravit elocutionem suam, sed convenit servo haec humilitas orationis* 'by adding *causa* he has obscured his speech, but this lowness of speech befits a slave'; on Ter. *Hec.* 311 <*sed*> ἀνακολουθία *ista convenit servo* '<but> this ἀνακολουθία is appropriate to a slave'; on Ter. *Ph.* 36 '*erat ei de ratiuncula*': *opportuna diminutio in re servili*: '*ratiuncula*' *et* '*pauxillulum*' '*erat ei de ratiuncula*: an appropriate use of diminutives for a matter concerning a slave: *ratiuncula* and *pauxillulum*'; on Ter. *Ph.* 384 '*eho tu sobrinum t(uom)*': *populari quadam vulgarique fatigatione utpote scurra respondit* '*eho tu sobrinum t(uom)*: he responds with a certain popular and common tediousness, as one would expect from a parasite'. On lack of education: on Ter. *Eu.* 405 (of the soldier's lack of linguistic articulation) *proprie hoc morale est stolidis inerudite loquentibus* 'this is properly in character for stupid people who speak uneducatedly'; on Ter. *Eu.* 1063 '*vobis fretus*': *deinde* ἀνακόλουθος *et vitiosa responsio est: nisi enim addideris* '*sum*', *erit soloecismus conveniens loquenti, impolito homini et militi* '*vobis fretus*: the answer is then anacolouthic and faulty; for unless you add *sum*, it will be a solecism appropriate to the speaker, an unpolished man and a soldier'; cf. on Ter. *Eu.* 432.

of one who is reacting against some offence' (on Ter. *Eu.* 796); ἰδιωτισμός *asseverantis* 'ἰδιωτισμός of one who is making an emphatic assertion' (on Ter. *Hec.* 502); *irascentis* 'an idiom of someone who is angry' (on Ter. *Ad.* 329). Furthermore, Donatus often pairs these tags with such explanatory remarks as *sic solemus dicere, sic dicimus,* thus removing the suspicion of a variant determined entirely by social factors.

Besides the ἰδιωτισμός/ἰδιωτικῶς notes, Donatus employs *familiaris, familiariter* with much the same meaning, for example with reference to an ellipsis which is partly filled by the speaker's significant tone (the young Ctesipho, running away into hiding at the news of his father's approach, and saying 'you've not seen me anywhere'): *'nusquam tu me': familiaris* ἔλλειψις *et apta properanti, quare haec omnia et pressa voce cum celeritate pronuntianda sunt, 'nusquam tu me*: a common ellipsis, appropriate for someone in a hurry, so that these words are to be delivered in a low voice and quickly' (on Ter. *Ad.* 539).

Other terms that are clearly used with reference to colloquial language and with some acknowledgement of register variation are:

simpliciter . . . ex usu

'ab Andria est ancilla haec': simpliciter dixit 'ab Andria est' pro 'Andriae est', nam ex usu sic dicere solemus. (on Ter. *An.* 461)

ab Andria est ancilla haec: [The poet] simply said *ab Andria est* for *Andriae est*: for this idiom is common in current usage.

secundum morem cotidianum

'quid senem quoad exspectatis vestrum': animadverte τὸ 'quid' secundum morem cotidianum tum dici, cum fit transitus a mentione alterius rei ad alteram. (on Ter. *Ph.* 147)

quid senem quoad exspectatis vestrum: note that *quid?* is used in common language when someone moves on to a different subject.

(ex/de/in) consuetudine, or simply *sic et nos dicimus*:

'egomet continuo': deest <'me> duco':[43] consuetudine dictum est et ἐλλειπτικῶς (on Ter. *An.* 361)

egomet continuo: me duco is missing, as in normal usage and elliptically

Among Donatus' definitions for colloquial language that are not rhetorical or linguistic in origin are *morale, moraliter* 'characteristic, in character', and

---

[43] The MS reading *duco* requires some supplement.

proverbium, proverbiale, both of which cover some of the same ground as the ἰδιωτισμός series. Finally, a series of words for rhetorical figures are often used as explanatory labels for apparently colloquial usages, such as *elleipsis, anakolouthon, parelkon* (= pleonasm), *hellenismos, attikismos.*

Donatus' awareness of register variation is also evident in comment on formal and non-literal uses of the language, motivated by pragmatic considerations (for example questions intended to convey gentle hints, or straightforward requests). Politeness features and deferential language are occasionally remarked upon in the language of *senes*: '*ego in hac re nihil reperio*': *haec scaena plena est sententiarum senilium ad officia demonstranda*, '*ego in hac re nihil reperio*: this scene is full of phrases suited to old people and intending to show deference' (on Ter. *Ad.* 592).

Donatus' notes on the entire scene of the dialogue between Micio and Hegio are ready to pick up the respectful tone of the two old men, who are careful not to offend one another by touching a delicate point: '*hoc tibi mancipium*': ταπείνωσις τῷ ἀστεισμῷ: '*mancipium' dicit puellam aut virginem*, '*hoc tibi mancipium*: a self-depreciation for good manners. He calls a young girl or young woman *mancipium*' (on Ter. *Eu.* 274).

An interesting term marking the use of formal or perhaps especially tactful language, by free men and slaves, is *honesta locutio/figura*. Donatus comments on a young man's peroration on behalf of his cousin: '*si est, patrue, culpam ut Antipho in se admiserit*': *honesta locutio 'si est ut admiserit' pro 'si admisit'*, '*si est, patrue, culpam ut Antipho in se admiserit: si est ut admiserit* for *si admisit* is an elegant idiom' (on Ter. *Ph.* 270).

The perceived characteristics of the more colloquial passages of comedy discussed by Donatus are (a) the use of certain metaphorical expressions, which are felt to be jargon or to have vulgar content (cf. Augustine's remark in *Locutiones in Heptateuchum* 1.143 on the currency in everyday Latin of the Biblical phrase *misit oculos suos in* for 'took a fancy to',[44] but also Cicero's remarks in *Orator* 81 (see p. 27 above)); (b) pseudo-dialogic moves, exclamatory or interjectional, and parenthetical remarks such as *illud vide* 'look at that', *em tibi* 'there you are!' (on Ter. *Ad.* 228); (c) pleonastic expressions, especially ethical dative constructions (e.g. on Ter. *Ad.* 496, 790); (d) transitional formulae such as *quid*, to change from one subject to another, a well-known idiom, for example from colloquial extracts in Cicero's orations and letters; *quid tum postea* 'and so what?' (on

---

[44] '*et misit uxor domini eius oculos suos in Ioseph*': *solet et apud nos vulgo esse usitata locutio pro eo, quod est 'amavit eum'* '"and his master's wife cast her eyes upon Joseph": this phrase is a common idiom for us too, and is equivalent to "and she fell in love with him"'.

Ter. *Hec.* 561); (d) diminutives, for example *capitulum lepidissumum* (on Ter. *Eu.* 531); (e) elliptic expressions.

The ἰδιωτισμός, ἰδιωτικός series comes closest to recognising explicitly the adoption of familiar, colloquial idioms by Latin speakers at different levels of social and educational background.[45] Donatus is aware of the sophisticated, artistic purpose to which such conversational turns are deployed in Terence, and comments plentifully on this aspect of Terence's art.

APPENDIX

The following is a list of the most important Latin expressions occurring in descriptions of linguistic register/sociolect. The list is intended for quick reference, and a tentative translation has been provided. However, one must be aware that the adoption of sociolinguistic register labels by Roman rhetorical and grammatical writers is by no means consistent, and that, typically, the purpose of a writer using one of these labels is to set up an opposition between 'oral, casual' and 'written up, literary', rather than to explore the existence of different registers.

communis (*sermo*) 'common usage' (Cic. *Fat.* 24; Sen. *Suas.* 2.13; Suet. *De poetis* 2.43.6). Equated with *cotidianus* in Gel. 1.10.1 *in cotidianis communibusque sermonibus* 'in the language of everyday'.

consuetudo 'current language', 'current usage', sometimes with the implication that the 'spoken language' is being referred to. The term translates the Greek technical term συνήθεια. Starting with Varro, for whom *consuetudo* helps to resolve conflicts between analogy and anomaly (see Müller 2001: 190–1), *consuetudo* is also advocated to establish a linguistic norm, although *consuetudo mala* or *depravata* can be considered no foundation for correct usage. In Imperial writers, *consuetudo* is sometimes qualified with *vulgaris* to indicate 'spoken language', sometimes with pejorative connotations and in opposition to *Latinitas*, 'correct usage' (Gel. 9.1.8; less explicitly negative in Nonius Marcellus 330 L. (223.24 M.); Charisius 239 Barwick). *Consuetudine*, with or without a preposition (*in, ex, de*), for 'in the current language', is also sometimes opposed to *ratione*, the term used for 'the expected regular or logical construction', but not necessarily when a source wishes to condemn the current usage on the basis of analogy.

---

[45] Some caution is in order for the occurrences from *Adelphoe*, where the Greek words have fallen out in the MSS, and Wessner prints Stephanus's conjectures.

cot(t)idianus (commonly *sermo c.* 'everyday conversation', but also *locutio c.* 'common idiom' and even 'everyday conversation', *verbum c.* 'common phrase', *usus c.* 'everyday usage'): for 'everyday', often in opposition to 'literary, ornate' speech. It is also adduced as a confirmation for linguistic correctness.

familiariter, familiaris (*sermo, verbum*): Cicero mentions jointly *familiaris* and *cotidianus sermo* at *Caec.* 52, without elaboration, but apparently meaning 'everyday, habitual words'; *familiari... sermone* for 'relaxed conversation' also at *Fam.* 9.24.3. The adverb *familiariter* appears to be used with a straightforward linguistic meaning only in Donatus on Ter. *An.* 539, for our 'familiar, informal'; *consuetudine familiariore* for 'in a common, informal phrase' occurs in Augustine (*Locutiones in Heptateuchum*, lib. 2 (Exodus), locutio 53).

humilis sermo, humiliter: used in reference to words not belonging to poetic or elevated diction, mainly when a critic comments on word choice in a rhetorically elaborated passage, or in a poem (e.g. Cic. *Orat.* 196; Hor. *Ars* 229). From Cicero onwards, the term is also used in a positive sense to characterise the lowest of the three rhetorical styles. In other contexts Cicero uses the term in a negative sense; Quintilian gets around this contradiction by avoiding *humilis* and *humiliter* in connection with the three rhetorical styles (Müller 2001: 93–103). In Servius' commentary on Virgil *humilis* and *humiliter dictum* are used for mentions of everyday objects or other words felt to be out of place in high poetry, but compensated for by rhetorical ornament (e.g. use of adjectives); but like Cicero, Servius also uses *humilis* of the lowest of the three rhetorical styles (Müller 2001: 106–7). In Christian writers, with a different attitude to *humilitas*, *sermo humilis* becomes the 'simple language' of the Bible.

idiotismus 'informal, colloquial usage' (see above, pp. 31–8). Although *idiota, idioticus* can mean 'illiterate', *idiotismus* does not imply incorrectness, and is found in comments by rhetorical writers (Seneca, Quintilian) on the adoption of lower register terms and idioms, for effect, by canonical writers such as Cicero and Terence.

plebeius: in Cicero *Fam.* 9.21.1 *plebeius sermo* is commonly translated as 'plebeian, vulgar vocabulary' ('colloquial style' Shackleton Bailey, cf. below, p. 255); but later in the same text Cicero defines letter-writing as composed with *cotidiana uerba*, thus suggesting a less derogatory interpretation for the idiom. Müller (2001: 85–7) suggests that Cicero is not entirely serious at *Fam.* 9.21.1 but is jokingly rebutting exaggerated praise. Elsewhere the term probably does mean 'lower-class', as

at Gellius 19.10.9, where an unnamed *grammaticus* uses *plebeium* with
reference to the word *praeterpropter* (Gellius himself calls it *usitatum
pervulgatumque verbum*). From Gellius onwards, there are fewer clear
examples of the use of *plebeius* to characterise a form of language or
to connect it with a lower level of society (the *plebs*); Müller (2001:
91–2) suggests that one of the reasons is that *plebs* probably acquires
a Christian sense of 'lay people' (like Greek λαός); Christian authors
use the term *plebeius sermo* in a positive sense, for a stylistic level.

rusticus*, *subrusticum*, *rusticanus: the term (often qualifying *sermo*)
originally referred to language characteristic of rural areas rather than
the city of Rome, but by the classical period it has taken on the
meaning 'incorrect, uneducated'; as such, it refers to a sociolect more
than a register, but it is often difficult to determine how much of
the earlier reference to regional variation is still present. Under the
Empire the term comes to refer to a register, that of everyday Latin as
opposed to the classical standard. (See Müller 2001: 29–78).

usus*, *usitatus* (*sermo*, *verbum*), *usitate: the prepositional phrase *ex/in
usu* is sometimes used for 'from, in current usage, in the spoken
language' (e.g. Charisius 271 Barwick). *usitate* 'in common usage' is
opposed to *recte* in Cic. *Orat.* 157 (where *noveras* is said to be the
'right' form, *noras* that which is 'commonly used').

vulgo, and all *vulgus* derivatives, are used with a wide and often inconsistent range of meanings (Müller 2001: 117–75). The most common
phrases are *vulgo dicitur, ut vulgus dicit, pervulgate, consuetudo/sermo
vulgaris* (*-ius*). (1) 'vulgarism', in opposition to *Latinum, Latine* (at
all levels of the language, from pronunciation to morphosyntax and
lexical choice, as at Servius on Verg. *Aen.* 3.466 *zemas enim vulgare
est non Latinum* 'indeed the word *zema* is the popular term, not
the proper Latin one [i.e. *olla*]'). The implication of a substandard
level of the language becomes increasingly frequent in late antique
sources. (2) 'common, current usage' with no pejorative implications
(Varro *L.* 8.66 *sine reprehensione vulgo alii dicunt in singulari hac
ovi... alii hac ove* 'some say *hac ovi* in the singular, others *hac ove*,
neither form appearing to be wrong'; cf. also Quint. *Inst.* 4.2.58 *verbis... vulgaribus et cotidianis*, of a *narratio* in Cicero, quoted p. 24).
The oppositional system in which *vulgus* derivatives are used is also
crucial, as sometimes *vulg-* definitions are contrasted with archaic,
far-fetched, recherché choice of vocabulary (e.g. Gel. 9.1.8, where
Quadrigarius' use of *defendo* 'keep away from' rather than 'defend'
(*hist.* 85) is said to be *non ex vulgari consuetudine sed admodum proprie*

et Latine, 'not the meaning usual in general usage, but one which is eminently appropriate and correct Latin'). *pervulgate* in Gellius indicates even usages that are technically incorrect but are adopted by a speaker who, although aware and capable of using the precise technical term, prefers to conform to current usage (18.10.6; similarly at 17.10.18). Another context in which *vulgo* and related idioms may occur is that in which a more precise, technical meaning is offered, or a new meaning acquired by a word in a specific context, for example Biblical exegesis.[46]

---

[46] Jerome, *Commentarii in Isaiam* (beginning of the fifth century), lib. 14, cap. 50 par. 10 (ed. M. Adriaen, 1963, Corpus Christianorum, Brepols).

CHAPTER 4

Idiom(s) and literariness in classical literary criticism

Anna Chahoud

I 'COLLOQUIALISM'

Our records trace the English adjective 'colloquial' back to Samuel Johnson (1751)[1] and the noun 'colloquialism' to nineteenth-century poets, who used it to describe characteristics of common speech as distinct from more elevated forms of language – 'the frequent mixture in some translation of mere colloquialisms' (R. Polwhele, writing in 1810) – or the overall quality of a style – 'their language is . . . an actual transcript of the colloquialism of the day' (Samuel Coleridge, writing in 1818).[2] In these modern uses, as in many ancient notes on style, one detects a sense of unease, or curiosity, about the possibility that characteristics of ordinary conversation might creep into the timeless dimension of 'literature'.

The questions addressed in this volume rise from a desire to investigate this process: to what extent, and with what intent, do authors manipulate (generally) spoken language in the construction of their (specific) literary work? Or, in our subject-specific critical terms, what is the relation of 'literary language' (*Kunstsprache*) to 'colloquial language' (*Umgangssprache*) in individual authors, and what trends can be identified in the building of Latin literary language as a whole?

No fruitful approach to this inquiry is possible until a satisfactory definition of the colloquial is reached. Adams has rightly drawn attention to the unhelpful nature of the generalising (and dogmatic) categorisation implied in the usage of the term 'colloquialism', which in fact 'embraces a multitude of phenomena with different distribution and different degrees of acceptability' (Adams 2005b: 86). More often than not scholars and commentators on classical texts thus label features of the language of Latin

---

[1] See Dickey, this volume p. 4 n. 4. To Eleanor Dickey also my warmest thanks for invaluable comments on this contribution.

[2] Cited in Simpson and Weiner 1989 s.v. 'colloquialism'. Note also 'to use a colloquial phrase, such sentiments . . . do one's heart good' (Coleridge), cited ibid. s.v. 'colloquial'.

prose and poetry without explaining why that should be the case, or what is meant exactly by 'colloquialism', or what function the feature plays in the text. The haziness of the notion brings about striking cases of disagreement over the tone of a particular passage:

> sed tamen iste deus qui sit, da, Tityre, nobis.
> (Virgil, *Eclogues* 1.18)

But even so, Tityrus, tell us: who is the god that you mention?

da for *dic* is colloquial (cf. *sed da mihi nunc: satisne probas?* Cic. *Ac.* 1.10), in keeping with the tone of the whole line. The rhythm of *da, Tityre, nobis* pathetically echoes *uix, Tityre, duco* [1.13] . . . (R. Coleman 1977: 77)

da: instead of *dic*, introducing an appropriate note of gravity; cf. Hor. *Serm.* 2.8.4–5 (mock-solemn) *da, si graue non est | quae prima iratum uentrem placauerit esca* . . . Val. Flacc. 5.217–18 *incipe nunc cantus alios, dea, uisaque uobis | Thessalici da bella ducis.* (Clausen 1994: 42)

The difference in interpretation of the feature, and in the selection of support material for the evaluation of its stylistic effect,[3] makes the reader wonder whether Virgil is having Meliboeus speaking like a 'real' shepherd or like an epic poet, and what Virgil was up to when characterising Meliboeus' address to Tityrus one way or the other.

Commentaries on texts that are usually described as 'conversational' (e.g. satire) contain assertions on 'colloquialness' which, rather than explaining the reasons why a certain feature is colloquial, call it colloquial for no apparent reason other than that the word/phrase is found *there*. I give one example:

> qui fit, Maecenas, ut nemo, quam sibi sortem
> seu ratio dederit seu fors obiecerit, illa
> contentus vivat . . . ?   (Hor. *Sat.* 1.1.1–3)

How is it, Maecenas, that no-one lives content with the lot that either choice has granted him or circumstances have thrown his way?

[Hor. *Sat.* 1.1.1 is] surely intended to establish much of the tone of the book, and must serve as a guide to our reading of the rest of the poems. The speaker begins colloquially: *qui fit* and *nemo* are not poetic words.[4]

---

[3] One could have noted, for example, the examples of *do* in this sense in Terence (*Hau.* 10) and Lucilius (758 M. [= 833 W. = 775 K. = 26.16 C.], 1036 M. [= 1066W. = 1072 K. = 30.34 C.], 1249 M. [= 1209 W. = 1266 K. = H117 C.]): cf. Mariotti 1960: 113.

[4] Zetzel 1980: 69 with n. 51, a view reiterated in Freudenburg 1993: 11 ('*qui fit* and *nemo* do not belong to the language of poetry but to prose and everyday speech'), both on the basis of Axelson 1945: 76 and Plessis and Lejay 1911: 10 (ad loc.).

This statement is no doubt a sensitive analysis of Horace's satirical programme in Book 1, of the diatribic persona speaking in this particular
poem, and of Horace's choice of *sermo* as a form of expression on the
whole; the interpretation, though, rests on a straightforward identification
of colloquial with 'unpoetic', which is debatable; moreover, one of the two
pieces of supporting evidence (*qui fit*) does not exactly fit the bill. 'How
come' is an informal phrase in English (Freudenburg 1993: 11); Latin *qui
fit* need not be.[5]

The present study discusses existing scholarly practices in detecting and
evaluating colloquialisms in Latin literary texts, with a view to reach-
ing an acceptable – i.e. as little subjective as possible – set of criteria to
assess the presence of truly conversational features, as opposed to apparent,
or otherwise explainable, departures from the series of expectations that
a particular author, writing within the constraints of a particular genre,
creates. The difficulties presented by this subject are many. One example is the explanation of 'low words in high places', which explores the
relation between 'vulgar language' and 'higher literature', and calls for
a satisfactory definition of 'vulgar language' to begin with (Bain 2007:
45). A related issue is how one goes about distinguishing between 'vulgar'
and 'colloquial', and between either (or both) and 'archaic' usages:[6] while
Latin prose tends to reject archaisms, Latin poetry tends to favour them
(R. Coleman 1999a: 92), and it does make a difference whether an author is
drawing from an early literary model, or from popular language preserving
a usage rejected by the literary canon. The matter is of course not simply
one of lexical choice, but also of prosody, morphology, syntax and word
order. How many of the *seemingly conversational* features of literary texts
repeat *genuinely conversational* usages? Ultimately, these questions concern
the recovery of conversational Latin through literary representations of it,
and address two distinct sets of problems – the correct formulation of the
term against which colloquialism should be defined (formal? poetic? grammatical?), and the validity of the criteria resulting from such formulations.

2 DICHOTOMIES

I give below an overview of how literary studies have approached a
definition of colloquial Latin. As we shall see, the notion of 'colloquial'

---

[5] This phrase and similar questions introduced by adverbial *qui* (e.g. *qui potest/potis est?*) are found in
early high-register poetry (e.g. Acc. *trag.* 418), in Lucretius (1.168) and in formal prose (e.g. Cic. *Fat.*
38; Sal. *Cat.* 51.24). Plessis and Lejay 1911 on Hor. *Sat.* 1.1.1 simply say that *qui fit* is an 'argumentation
formula', just like e.g. *quo fit* in Hor. *Sat.* 2.1.32. No discussion of this phrase as markedly unpoetic
or low-register is found in Axelson 1945, Hofmann 1951, or H–S.
[6] See e.g. Marouzeau 1954: 181–9; Clackson and Horrocks 2007: 91.

(feature, register or language) has emerged from the opposition with such qualities as 'intellectual', 'stylised', 'poetic', 'vulgar' or 'archaic' (feature, register or language).

2.1 Colloquial versus intellectual: emotiveness

The classic texts on literary representations of colloquial Latin carry the name of Johann Baptist Hofmann (1884–1954), who combined modern linguistic theory with the knowledge of the Latin language of one who worked at the *Thesaurus Linguae Latinae* in Munich for nearly fifty years (1909–51). In the wake of Charles Bally's *Traité de stylistique française* (1909) and other works which viewed linguistic phenomena through the dichotomy between 'emotive' (colloquial) and 'intellectual' (stylised) language,[7] Hofmann developed a system for the identification of features of colloquial Latin, publishing his results in *Lateinische Umgangssprache* (first edn 1926, 3rd edn 1951). In the same years Hofmann applied himself to the rewriting of F. Stolz and J. H. Schmalz's *Lateinische Grammatik* (5th edn 1926–8), which resulted in the monumental *Lateinische Syntax und Stilistik* edited, after Hofmann's death, by his collaborator at the *TLL* Anton Szantyr (1965). The section on *Stilistik* contains countless remarks on various registers of colloquial Latin, in which the same criteria are adopted for the stylistic evaluation of features as those used by Hofmann for the description and classification of them in his earlier work. I now give a brief account of Hofmann's method before moving to the discussion of his criteria.

2.1.1 Methodology

Drawing on a brief study of O. Rebing (1873), which first described some syntactical characteristics of 'conversational Latin' (e.g. elliptical and emphatic expressions),[8] Hofmann turned it into a system by applying a methodology recently developed for the study of modern languages – German (Wunderlich), French (Bally) and Italian (Spitzer). Hofmann's reasons are revealed in his praise for Bally's work in particular, as the one that goes to the core of colloquial language by analysing its 'subjectivity, concreteness and emotiveness' (Hofmann 1951: xv). It is this set of traits

---

[7] Hofmann acknowledges his debt to these works in the 'Literaturangaben' prefixed to his work (1951: xv): H. Wunderlich, *Unsere Umgangssprache in der Eigenart ihrer Satzfügung dargestellt* (Weimar and Berlin 1894); L. Spitzer, *Italienische Umgangssprache* (Bonn and Leipzig 1922); H. Sperber, *Über den Affekt als Ursache der Sprachveränderung* (Halle 1914) and *Einführung in die Bedeutungslehre* (Bonn and Leipzig 1923). See discussion in Ricottilli 2003: 25–35 and Traina *et al.* 2002: iv–v.

[8] O. Rebing, *Versuch einer Characteristik der römischen Umgangssprache auf syntaktischem und lexicalischem Gebiete* (Progr. Kiel 1873), discussed in Hofmann 1951: xv = Hofmann–Ricottilli 87; see discussion in Ricottilli 2003: 17–20.

that qualify colloquial style, because they qualify spoken language: 'when written language displays emotive and subjective features, one unfailingly demonstrates that such characteristics come from spoken language'.[9]

Hofmann identified precisely these three main principles governing colloquial language: (a) subjectivity and emotiveness (*Affekt*); (b) vividness ('sensorial', *sinnlich-anschauliche*, and 'concrete', *konkrete*, expressions), and (c) simplification and 'economy' (*Sparsamkeit*).[10] Prevalence of these characteristics distinguishes the 'subjective-emotive phrase' (*Affektsatz*) from sentences showing evident signs of logical elaboration (*Intellektualsatz*).[11] On this basis Hofmann defines colloquial language (*Umgangssprache*) as any form of exchange with a minimum degree of intellectual – i.e. logically elaborated – elements. At the opposite end of the spectrum are forms of stylised speech, which he called *Intellektual-sprache*.

Hofmann's understanding of *Umgangssprache* is 'lively and oral conversation among educated people',[12] as opposed to popular language (*Volkssprache*) or 'vulgar Latin' (*Vulgärlatein*). It is important to note, however, that in practice Hofmann explicitly discarded as insignificant this traditional set of register differentiations ('everyday', 'popular', 'vulgar'),[13] on the grounds that all forms of affective language display analogous features regardless of the social status or level of education of the speakers: any given *homogeneous* group of speakers shares *current* linguistic practices which are produced *without elaboration or effort* and characterised by subjectivity and emotiveness.[14]

[9] Hofmann 1951: 2–3 = Hofmann–Ricottilli 92.
[10] Hofmann 1951: 1 ('Affekt'); 8 ('Der konkrete und sparsame Zug der Umgangssprache') = Hofmann–Ricottilli 92–3, 100–1.
[11] Hofmann 1951: 5 = Hofmann–Ricottilli 97.
[12] 'Umg. als der lebendigen und mündlichen Rede der Gebildeten' (Hofmann 1951: v = Hofmann–Ricottilli 80).
[13] This choice perplexed some of Hofmann's contemporaries, cf. e.g. Anderson 1927: 90; Whatmough 1938: 321; see now Collard 2005: 357.
[14] Hofmann 1951: 1: 'die Umgangssprache in allen ihren Spielarten, dem sermo familiaris der gebildeten Konversation, dem sermo uulgaris des gemeinen Mannes und dem sermo plebeius der Gasse, die in den kleinen und kleinsten Verkehrskreisen Kurswert hat, besitzt ein Höchstmaß affektischer, subjektiver, individuell-anschaulicher, ein Mindestmaß logisch durchdacter, kunstvoll aufgebauter, weite Gedankengebiete klar überschauender und ordnender Elemente' (= Hofmann–Ricottilli 91–2 'La lingua d'uso, che "ha corso" in cerchie ristrette e ristrettissime, in tutte le sue varietà (il *sermo familiaris* della conversazione tra gente colta, il *sermo vulgaris* dell'uomo comune, e il *sermo plebeius* del vicolo), possiede un grado massimo di elementi affettivi, soggettivi, individualmente evidenti, ed un grado minimo di elementi frutto di meditazione logica, di organizzazione artistica, e che abbracciano e ordinano, con chiarezza, ampi domini di pensiero'). Cf. also Hofmann 1951: viii–ix = Hofmann–Ricottilli 84.

2.1.2 Distribution

Hofmann also indicated the literary forms that are most likely to contain representations (or, as he called them, 'refractions')[15] of the colloquial: the dialogues of early Latin comedy (Plautus and Terence); informal letters between equals (Cicero's letters to Atticus; the correspondence between Fronto and Marcus Aurelius); the language of satirists (Lucilius, Horace, Persius and Juvenal) and the freedmen's speeches in Petronius; among the non-satirical poets, Catullus, Phaedrus and Martial; among the prose-writers, Seneca the Elder, with his account of declamation practices, and instances of wit in Cicero's literary works; and finally inscriptions of all kinds (Hofmann 1951: 2–5 = Hofmann–Ricottilli 92–7). Hofmann believed that all these texts exhibit various degrees of approximation to spoken language that differentiate them from stylised forms; genre determines the presence or absence of colloquial idioms in literary texts. Once again he was drawing on theoretical studies of modern languages that pointed to dialogic texts (e.g. comedy) as the clearest evidence of representation of conversational features: when introducing his preference for Plautus as a source for colloquial language, Hofmann stated his debt to Wunderlich's method of using German drama (Hofmann 1951: v–vi = Hofmann–Ricottilli 80).

2.1.3 Criteria and concepts

Hofmann classified and described *umgangssprachliche* characteristics according to his tripartite definition of the colloquial as emotive, vivid and economical. Here below I give an outline of his criteria and features, preserving Hofmann's subdivisions (or lack thereof) and translating his terminology as closely as possible.

(1) Subjectivity and emotiveness[16]
    (A) Emotive phrases containing little or no intellectual element (Hofmann 1951: 9–46 = Hofmann–Ricottilli 103–60):
        (1) Interjections: verbalisations of laughter, pain, surprise, etc. (e.g. *hahae*; *eho*; *ehem*); oaths and equivalent formulae (e.g. *ita vivam*); imprecations (e.g. *malum*); fossilised pronouns (e.g. *cedo*); fossilised imperatives (e.g. *em*);

---

[15] Hofmann 1951: 2 'literarischen Brechungen der lat. Umgangssprache'. Ricottilli explains Hofmann's notion as influenced by Bally's view that literary language is 'une "réfraction" des procédés affectifs du langage de tous' (Bally, cited in Hofmann–Ricottilli 92 n. 1). On the conceptual difference between (straightforward) 'reflection' and (somewhat distorting) 'refraction' see also Ricottilli 2003: 47–8.
[16] 'Die subjective-affektische Seite der Umgangssprache', Hofmann 1951: 9 = Hofmann–Ricottilli 103.

(2) Words for yes/no or equivalent in meaning (e.g. *verum*);
(3) Interrogative particles (e.g. *nunc*);
(4) Stereotyped questions (e.g. *scin tu*).

(B) Emotive brachylogy (Hofmann 1951: 46–58 = Hofmann–
Ricottilli 160–78): ellipsis; exclamation accusatives; exclamation
infinitives; historical infinitives; aposiopesis; interruptions.

(C) Emotive elements in intellectual sentences (Hofmann 1951:
58–102 = Hofmann–Ricottilli 178–242):

(1) Repetition and anaphora (occasionally epiphora);
(2) Emotive exclamations (including cases of 1.2) and rhetorical
questions;
(3) Exaggeration and redundancy: pleonastic adverbs for emphasis (e.g. *belle, probe, valde*); innovative use of negative particles (e.g. *nequaquam*), of expressions of time (e.g. *e vestigio*),
of imprecation and abuse; comic comparatives and superla-
tives; synonymic pairs and series; grouping of corradical or
synonymic terms; epanalepsis; parallelism; redundant use of
magis with comparatives and of personal pronouns, *ille* and
unus.

(D) Emotive sentence structure (Hofmann 1951: 102–9 = Hofmann–
Ricottilli 243–68):

(1) Disjointed syntax: sense unit dismembered into short phrases;
emphatic nominative; [anacoluthon];[17]
(2) Parataxis; hyperbaton; proleptic accusative; parenthesis.

(E) Emotive collocation (Hofmann 1951: 119–24 = Hofmann–
Ricottilli 269–76): anaphora; hysteron proteron; limited use of
chiasmus.

(II) Engagement with the interlocutor[18]

(A) Persuasion formulae (e.g. *inquam, amabo*, parenthetic *rogo, sodes*).
(B) Expressions of *captatio benevolentiae*: pluralis modestiae; ethic
dative; emotive use of possessive (e.g. *homo meus*); loss of
diminutive force due to overwhelming emotive tone; extension

[17] Cases of anacoluthon are given in this section, but the phenomenon as such is not discussed in
Hofmann 1951. Ricottilli (Hofmann–Ricottilli 247 n. 2) tentatively suggests that the reason for the
omission is that the usage is 'vulgar' as opposed to 'colloquial'; but, as noted above, Hofmann
himself did not treat the two registers separately in the *Lateinische Umgangssprache*, a work which he
referred to as a 'Vorarbeit' on 'Umgangs- *und* Volkssprache' (preface to his *Lateinische Grammatik*
1926–8 at p. vii, cited in Traina *et al.* 2002: v; my emphasis).
[18] 'Die Rolle des Partners in der Äußerung des persönlichen Gedanken': Hofmann 1951: 125–52 =
Hofmann–Ricottilli 277–314.

of terms of endearment to non-erotic contexts; polite attenuation of statements (e.g. *fortasse*; weakened *utique*).

(c) Euphemism: substitution of taboo terms, suggestive periphrases, negative expressions (e.g. *minus = non*); litotes and irony.

(III) Vividness and concreteness[19]

(A) Concrete words and phrases: substitution of sensory imagery for intellectual terms (e.g. *mordere* instead of *sollicitare*).

(B) Metaphorical identifications (e.g. Petr. 42.4 *utres inflati ambulamus*).

(c) Colloquial use of adjectives; extended use of possessive adjectives (e.g. *erilis, puerilis*).

(D) Substantival infinitives instead of abstract nouns.

(E) Innovative use of conjunctions and prepositions (e.g. substitution of *quomodo* for 'overworked' and phonetically weak *ut*).

(F) Conflation of phrases (e.g. Pl. *Poen.* 659 *tu...agere tuam rem occasiost*).

(IV) Simplification and economy[20]

Colloquial language exhibits a tendency to use generic words for specific things – e.g. extended use of *esse, facere, dare* instead of more precise terms; *esse* modified by adverbs (e.g. *temere est quod*) or prepositions (e.g. *ad me fuit*) – and to produce various forms of ellipsis (of nouns and verbs).

Hofmann's concept of colloquial Latin, as far as one can extrapolate it from comments repeated throughout his description of features, may be summarised as follows:

(i) Colloquial language is not controlled by intellectual processes of elaboration: emotiveness disrupts the logical order of the sentence, disjointing all its members and bringing subjectively climactic element(s) to initial or otherwise emphatic position.[21]

(ii) Colloquial language is controlled by the need to interact with an interlocutor.

(iii) Colloquial language displays various degrees of speakers' inadequacy to rise to a level of complete abstraction.[22]

[19] 'Der sinnlich-anschauliche Zug der Umgangssprache: Hofmann 1951: 153–64 = Hofmann–Ricottilli 315–33.
[20] 'Der triviale und sparsame Zug der Umgangssprache': Hofmann 1951: 165–72 = Hofmann–Ricottilli 335–47.
[21] See in particular Hofmann 1951: 102–3 = Hofmann–Ricottilli 243–5; Hofmann 1951: 109 = Hofmann–Ricottilli 269.
[22] Cf. Hofmann 1951: 157 = Hofmann–Ricottilli 322.

(iv) Colloquial language works on minimum resource expenditure –
a notion which Hofmann expresses in terms of 'mental idleness'
(*Denkträgheit*).[23]

It is clear that Hofmann's identification of lexical and syntactical features moves entirely from psychological criteria: his principles (i) and
(ii) fall into the category of emotive-subjective expression (*Affektsatz*);
(iii) and (iv) describe, qualifying them as limits, cognitive processes. The
emotive-subjective criterion (*Affekt*) is by far the most significant one, as
the clearest indicator of *Umgangssprache*.[24] The system has some validity.
Attention to the effects of subjectivity led Hofmann to single out factors
operating at a colloquial level such as derive from the interaction of a
speaker with another, whether present (e.g. in comic dialogue) or absent
(e.g. in private letters): verbalisation of contact, immediacy of reaction,
prevalence of implication over fully elaborated expression. If we remove
the psychologising backdrop from Hofmann's theory (as now Ricottilli
2003: 53–61), we are not too far from the opposition 'formal/informal' that
we find in other classifications. As a method for the recovery of conversational language, however, Hofmann's system is not unfailing. While 'vivid'
expressions of 'feelings and engagement' are characteristics of conversational language,[25] it does not necessarily follow from this that they are consequences only of conversational language. Hence one should not assume
that every expression of this kind, by any speaker and in any context, is
conversational.

2.2 Colloquial versus stylised: naturalness

Indicators of conversational style as can be extrapolated from the illustration in Hofmann's *Lateinische Umgangssprache* largely match the categories singled out by studies of Greek colloquial language (Stevens 1976;
Landfester 1997; and Collard 2005). In English-language Greek scholarship the definition of colloquialism is associated with the works of P. T.
Stevens on colloquial expressions in Athenian dramatists, especially
Euripides. Stevens defined colloquialisms as 'such words and phrases as
might naturally be used in everyday conversation, but are avoided in

---

[23] Cf. Hofmann 1951: 165 = Hofmann–Ricottilli 335.
[24] Hofmann 1951: 9 (my emphasis): 'Die Umgangssprache als *die in erster Linie vom Affekt beherrschte Sprache*' (= Hofmann–Ricottilli 103; see Ricottilli's discussion at 103–4 n. 1 on §8).
[25] Courtney 2001: 95 on Petronius' freedmen: 'When J.B. Hofmann was writing his classic book on conversational Latin, he began by seeking a criterion which could define conversational language in general, and found this in "Affekt": this is exactly the quality which we see in these speeches.'

distinctively poetic writing and dignified prose' (Stevens 1937: 182; cf. Collard 1978: 224–5, 2005: 352), subsequently refining the notion through the differentiation of levels of language (poetic, prosaic, neutral and colloquial) and of emotional and intellectual aspects (Stevens 1976: 1–4, in Collard 2005: 352). Drawing on large quantities of material from Euripides and other texts that he identified as 'evidence for colloquial pedigree' (Collard 2005: 352) (comedy, mime, Platonic dialogue and instances of dialogue in Herodotus and Xenophon; Ptolemaic papyri, and ethopoietic representations of plain style in the Attic orators), Stevens produced a set of criteria that cover for Greek much the same ground as Hofmann had covered for Latin (discussed in Collard 2005: 352):

A. Exaggeration [cf. Hofmann 1951: 1.3.c]
B. Pleonasm [cf. Hofmann 1951: 1.3.c]
C. Understatement [cf. Hofmann 1951: II.3]
D. Brevity [cf. Hofmann 1951: 1.2 and IV]
E. Interjections [cf. Hofmann 1951: I.I.a]
F. Particles [cf. Hofmann 1951: I.I.c; 1.3.c; II.2; III.5]
G. Metaphors [cf. Hofmann 1951: III.I, III.2]
H. Miscellaneous idioms [cf. Hofmann 1951: I.I.d; II.I]
I. Forms and syntax [cf. Hofmann 1951: 1.3.a; 1.4; 1.5]

In his supplement to Stevens, Collard also notes the correspondences between Stevens's classification and the indicators of the colloquial as suggested in M. Landfester's comparative study of Greek and Latin style: (1) expressive modes (interjections, exclamations, curses, exaggerations); (2) free syntax, esp. anacoluthon; (3) ellipses; (4) forms of address; (5) plainest words; (6) parataxis; (7) redundancy for emphasis; (8) varieties of crasis; (9) strongly idiomatic expressions (Collard 2005: 357).

2.3 *Colloquial versus poetic: vocabulary selection*

As noted at the beginning, the term 'colloquial' is sometimes used in a restricted sense with reference to lexical items (words or phrases) that depart from the vocabulary normally associated with elevated poetry. This way of thinking tends to identify the 'literary' with the 'poetic', and, by extension, the 'colloquial' with the 'unpoetic'. Both notions are problematic. The first one neglects the fact that, for all its generic constraints, poetry enjoys more freedom than high-register prose: poetic language is a system evolving through mutual exchange between accepted tradition and individual innovations, which in turn set new standards. The second notion establishes a relation between 'colloquial' and 'unpoetic' that does not work both ways: while we may accept that colloquial usages are 'unpoetic', i.e. excluded from the selective world of high-register poetry, the reverse is certainly not the case, i.e. not all usages which are excluded from high-register poetry are necessarily conversational. Confusion over these matters, however, has an ancient scholarly tradition.

2.3.1 Communia verba

In a study of the passage in Suetonius–Donatus' *Life of Virgil* in which one Vipranius objected to Virgil's use of *communia verba* resulting in obscurity,[26] H. D. Jocelyn examined the series of oppositions used in critical language from antiquity to determine the acceptability of words in literary texts. The first of such oppositions is between plain words (*communia verba*) and poetic words (*poetica verba*). This distinction was quite separate in the ancient sources from the one which set 'distinguished' words (*honesta*) against lowly ones (*humilia*): 'Greek teachers warned against ὀνόματα ταπεινά, ἀγοραῖα, αἰσχρά, δημοτικά, δημώδη, εὐτελῆ, ἰδιωτικά, καπηλικά, πτωχικά. Latin teachers similarly denounced *verba humilia, illiberalia, incompta, obscena, plebeia, sordida, trita, turpia, vilia, vulgaria.*'[27] No word of this kind is obviously found in the works of Virgil, which were the most authoritative source for good Latin in the book of all ancient grammarians. Virgil's *communia verba* must be explained otherwise, and Jocelyn, working on the opposition 'common'/'special to a particular art or craft' (i.e. technical), tentatively proposed to read the *detractor*'s charge as a specific reference to Virgil's avoidance of prosaic agricultural terms in the *Georgics*, thus making the didactic poem useless to anyone seeking precise factual information about farming (Jocelyn 1979: 115–18).

Jocelyn observed that the ancient scholarly definitions of *verbum commune* (κοινὸν ὄνομα) 'referred to lexical items which could be expected to occur either in an informal context of speech among men of the social class to which pupils of the grammarians and rhetoricians belonged or in a formal literary work; they carried in themselves no pejorative connotation'.[28] These were words equally distant from Ennianesque poetic diction and markedly low-register usage.

---

[26] Suetonius, *De poetis* 2.43.6 M. *Vipranius a Maecenate eum suppositum appellabat novae cacozeliae repertorem, non tumidae ne exilis, sed ex communibus uerbis atque ideo latentis*, 'Marcus Vipranius used to call him bastard of Maecenas and discoverer of an affected style, not overblown or understated, but coming from everyday words and therefore hidden' (trans. Thomas 2000: 406).

[27] Jocelyn 1979: 114, with lists of sources at 138 f. (nn. 244–8).

[28] Jocelyn 1979: 111, with list of sources at 137 f. (n. 216).

2.3.2 Unpoetische Wörter

Bertil Axelson (1906–84) published his study on the selectivity of poetic Latin diction in 1945. The importance of the book lies in the view – which soon became widely established (see Watson 1985: 430) – that the factor determining the choice of words in Latin poetry is the generic hierarchy of poetic forms (genres). Certain words are regularly avoided in high-register poetry due to their 'archaic', 'vulgar' or 'prosaic' flavour[29]: epic and tragedy use e.g. *fessus* instead of the 'vulgar' form *lassus* (Axelson 1945: 29–30), *fero* instead of *porto* (1945: 30–1); *coniunx* and *famulus* (*-a*)/*minister* (*-tra*) replace the prosaic terms *uxor* (1945: 57–8) and *servus/ancilla* (1945: 58). The distribution of these sets of synonyms (or rather, quasi- and pseudo-synonyms)[30] in lower genres such as lyric and elegy confirms Axelson's idea that genre governs the inclusion or exclusion of word-usage in Latin poetry: the more elevated the genre, the more 'poetic' the style.

One important adjustment was made to Axelson's theory in more recent years. While paying a tribute to the general validity of Axelson's method, Patricia Watson (1985), drawing on Gordon Williams (1968), demonstrated that factors other than genre might enter into the process of 'poetic vocabulary selection', such as subjectivity and context.[31] Nevertheless, Axelson's analysis, statistics and index of 'unpoetic words' remain to this day the main authority called upon by commentators for labelling a Latin word as 'colloquial', whereas it may simply be prosaic. Such is the case with *nemo* in Hor. *Sat.* 1.1.1 (above, p. 43): *nemo* is indeed 'not a poetic word' (Axelson 1945: 76–7), but it is not a colloquial one either.[32]

2.4 *Colloquial versus vulgar: social class and/or chronology*

A dichotomy that draws on some of the (far from consistent) ancient comments on *sermo cotidianus*[33] defines colloquial language as the 'everyday' (or 'familiar') language of the educated élite, as opposed to the 'vulgar' (or

---

[29] Axelson 1945: 'Archaismen und Vulgarismen' (Chapter 2, pp. 25–45), 'Prosaismen' (Chapter 3, pp. 46–97); on these categories, and on the value of Axelson's classification as a whole, see Ernout 1957: 66–86.

[30] Watson 1985: 431, 433–4 (*puella/virgo*), 439 (*pulcher/formosus*).

[31] Watson 1985: 447, at the same time refuting the validity of Williams's claim that it was 'realism' of subject matter (as opposed to genre) that controlled the diction of Latin poets, who used 'everyday' words for everyday contexts and 'poetic' words for distant mythological settings (G. Williams 1968: 743–50).

[32] Cf. its occurrences in formal rhetoric, e.g. Cic. *De orat.* 3.135.

[33] See Ferri and Probert, this volume pp. 14, 39.

'plebeian') practices of the lower classes. Applications of this criterion also tend to introduce a chronological division between Republican and Imperial usages: scholars do not speak of the 'vulgar' Latin of Plautus; nor do they speak of the 'colloquial' Latin of the letters of soldiers from distant Roman provinces.[34] It would appear that in this usage our terminology finds a permanent reference point in the Augustan age: non-literary language of Republican and Augustan Rome is colloquial and (with an implied judgement of value) good; non-literary language of later periods is vulgar and bad.

But sometimes 'colloquial' and 'vulgar' seem to be synonyms. For example, features of the language of imperial satire and epigram are described indifferently as both colloquial and vulgar (apparently because of the conversational nature, or intrinsic openness, of the genres themselves: the (implied) argument is a circular one). A valuable recent commentary on Martial discusses, under the entry 'Everyday language', such disparate forms as prosaic ('unpoetic') words employed by Cicero in his speeches, words and formation 'from the everyday sphere' or 'common in everyday speech', and 'vulgar spellings'[35]: such mixture of criteria and lack of differentiation are hardly helpful.

2.5 Colloquial versus archaic: currency

J. N. Adams defines 'colloquialism' as 'a current, and possibly "popular" usage usually excluded from other higher literary genres except to achieve a special effect' (Adams *et al.* 2005: 7 n. 8). The criterion of currency implies that colloquialism is not an absolute or inalienable feature of a word or usage, as in the other definitions seen so far; rather it is something that a word or usage can gain or lose over time. Since living languages (a category nearly synonymous with languages that are frequently used in casual conversation) are constantly evolving, it is clear that their conversational registers must change over time. Native speakers are aware of this: many words and expressions that were common in conversation of the Elizabethan age, the early twentieth century, or even a few decades ago, are no longer in use and now have an outdated or archaic ring to them. The use, in a literary work of the twenty-first century, of a feature that had been

---

[34] Cf. e.g. 'the loose colloquial idiom of comic diction' (F. Merrill 1972: xxxiv) versus 'the Vulgar Latin of Claudius Terentianus' (Adams 1977a: title and passim).

[35] Watson and Watson 2003: 23, with comments such as follows (my emphasis): 'In **56** [on 3.82] *familiar* language is used to match by its *vulgar* flavour both Zoilus' boorish manner and his sexual tastes; it may also suggest the lowliness of the social class from which he originated. The piece contains an abundance of words with a *colloquial* or *everyday* colouring, many of which make their entry into literature with M[artial].'

common in conversation in the nineteenth century would not have the same effect as the use of a feature that was common in conversation of the writer's own time.

In Latin, however, we do not have native-speaker awareness of language change to guide us, and thus application of the criterion of currency jeopardises the confidence that the other definitions give us of our ability to recover colloquial language. Even supposing Hofmann's criteria to be entirely accurate in their identification of language that was at some point colloquial, they cannot tell us whether the term was still colloquial at the time it was used in any given text where we meet it. Recognising the difficulty thus raised, Adams gives his own suggestions for identifying colloquialisms:

The identification of a colloquialism ... depends largely on its distribution in extant Latin: a usage with a typical 'colloquial' distribution in Republican Latin might occur in Plautus, Terence, possibly farce and/or mime, and Cicero's letters and/or earliest speeches. If it then remains rare in literature but turns up in the Romance languages, it might seem to fit the bill nicely ... There are, however, many factors that can determine the restricted distribution of a usage apart from any colloquial quality that it might have. (Adams *et al.* 2005: 7 n. 8)

This prescription, however, is in some ways a reversion to the timelessness of colloquialisms supposed by other scholars. It seems to imply that in order to be colloquial at any point in the history of Latin a word or usage would have to remain colloquial throughout nearly a thousand years of that history. This restriction seems unnecessary, but on another level Adams's point is important: if one wants to know whether a usage was colloquial in (say) the Augustan age, establishing its colloquial status in early Latin is not enough. One also needs to show that the usage had not in the meantime gone out of fashion and thereby developed an archaic flavour.

3 EVIDENCE

I now move to a discussion of the types of source that have supplied scholars with stylistic indicators for the colloquialness of a text (or features of it), and of the extent to which such criteria may or may not be usefully applied to the evaluation of register.

3.1 *Types of source*

There are three sources one can use to obtain information on colloquial Latin: the Latin of non-literary texts such as private letters, curse tablets,

etc.; extra-literary evidence such as Romance developments; and usage in
literature.

3.1.1 Non-literary evidence

Recent work on non-literary Latin has been invaluable in adjusting whatever monolithic picture of the language one might have derived from
élite literature and grammarians' pronouncements on standards of correctness. The evidence suggests a much greater diversification of usages,
which one would be tempted to call conversational. Nevertheless, the survival of non-literary written records from the Latin-speaking world in antiquity is mostly accidental, and as such results in a limited corpus: private
communications, epitaphs, curses, advertisements and documents written
on papyrus, ostraka, tablets, walls or stones are often isolated expressions
of an individual or a community locally and/or chronologically situated,
such as, for example, the correspondence of Claudius Terentianus from
early second-century AD Egypt,[36] the soldiers' letters from Vindolanda, or
curse tablets from Bath and other parts of Roman Britain from the same
period.[37] Evidence from the Republican period is scanty, and the existence
of ancient comments identifying 'vulgar' and archaic usages can make this
early evidence even more difficult to evaluate, as with Gellius' comment on
the alleged correctness of the verb *sermonari* 'to have a conversation', which
he read in compound form in Quadrigarius, but also survives in an *impre-
catio* from first-century BC Rome.[38] Inscriptions and graffiti are formulaic,
or short, or both, rarely allowing for substantial enough evidence about
particular usages (cf. Adams 1977a: 1). Finally, most of these texts exhibit
a medium to low degree of literacy and a number of interferences. These
varieties – described as substandard or sub-élite Latin (see Clackson and
Horrocks 2007: 229–62) – cast little light on the conversational practices
of the upper classes of the classical period, and therefore on the colloquial
nature of the texts that supposedly represent them.

The very relation between literary and spoken language is defined in
different ways. Clackson and Horrocks speak of 'homogeneity of spoken
Latin', on the grounds that most sub-élite documentary records appear
to be 'striving to be as close to the standards of Virgil and Cicero as
possible' (2007: 235), whereas Herman views substandard ('vulgar') Latin
as a continuum defined by its opposition with a practically non-influential

---

[36] Adams 1977a, 2003a: 593–7; Clackson and Horrocks 2007: 249–51.
[37] See, most recently, Adams 2007: 579–623.
[38] Gel. 17.2.17; cf. *CIL* I². 818.3, 6. On Quadrigarius as a main source for Gellius' 'Republicanisms' see
    Holford-Strevens 2003: 50–1 with n. 24, and index s.v.

literary language (2000: 7). The nature of Latin-speaking practices in any given (chronological, geographical, social) context is difficult to assess; the evaluation of representations of speaking practices in literary texts is an even more complicated matter.

3.1.2 Extra-literary evidence

Romance outcomes give a clear indication of the currency of a usage in a specific area, and of a long-term process. Survival in Romance is no guarantee that the usage was colloquial to the ear of an author from the classical period. I give one example, recently discussed by Adams in the context of regional diversification of Latin (2007: 378–81). Robert Coleman labels Virgil's use of the possessive adj. *cuius, -a, -um* in *Ecl.* 3.1 (*quoium pecus*) as a 'morphological colloquialism' (1977: 301, index s.v.). The evidence produced in support of this view is the frequency of the word in comedy and in a legal formula in Cicero, and its survival in 'popular Latin' (Spanish *cujo, -a*). Virgil's insertion is motivated as a case of 'subliterary character [of the word] deliberately employed for rustic colour' (Coleman ibid.). Other motivations in fact exist and have been put forward by commentators since late antiquity: Servius takes it as an archaism (*antique*) chosen to avoid the homoioteleuton *cuius pecus*; Donatus (or rather the speaker in the *Antibucolica* at Don. *Vita Verg.* 43) labels it as rustic speech (*sic rure loquuntur*); similarly Courtney (1993: 284) speaks of an obvious rustic archaism; Clausen (1994: ad loc.) takes it as a deliberate imitation of Plautus, consistent with the slave-match scene acted by Virgil's shepherds. Distribution points to an archaic, rather than colloquial, quality of the word: outside early comedy and satire, it is found in the formulaic language of prayers and laws.[39] If *cuius* had any currency, it was neither in Virgil's times nor in his area. Virgil's usage is more likely to have been a deliberate imitation of comedy than repetition of an unattested peasant usage in Italy (Adams 2007: 381).

3.1.3 Literary evidence

Scholars generally agree that features of colloquial Latin can be found in literature, but that they must be sought primarily in such literary texts as provide the closest approximation to dialogic interaction and are furthest removed from the elaborate artificiality of elevated prose and poetry – i.e. letters, comedy and satire. Revisions of our classic studies, however, keep

---

[39] Lucilius 1069 M. (= 1021 W. = 1034 K. = 30.56 C.) and conjectural at 965 M. (= 990 W. = 970 K. = SP19 C.); Cato *Agr.* 139; Cic. *Ver.* 2.127, 3.16, 3.68.

emphasising the need to examine each occurrence of an expression in its own context (see Collard 2005: 353–60). Hofmann and Axelson shared the principle that genre predetermines the presence or absence of colloquial features. This is a valid enough method in as far as it is applied sensibly, i.e. does not make assumptions about the conversational quality of a word simply because it is found in a supposedly conversational genre.[40] Literary texts are not written records of actual conversations, but artistic representations of conversational modes. The implication of this is that even the most 'naturalistic' style is still, well, a style. It is certainly true that Plautus' 'colourful and splendid images . . . have been created for their comic power, not their naturalism' (Fantham 1972: 4); but naturalism is a problematic notion. Terence's 'familiar style' imitates models and conforms to standards of élite speech (cf. Traina 1999: 102–3); one may even argue that the supposed naturalism of his diction is no less a construct than the élite whose speech he is supposedly representing,[41] and no less elaborate than Plautus' flamboyant rewriting of Greek comedy, or Lucilius' multi-register *sermones ac ludi*. Mimesis of everyday language in low-register works may result in the humorous invention of word-types associated with everyday language.[42] These are unlikely to have enjoyed any real currency. Hofmann's notion of 'literary refraction' is still a useful one, especially in Ricottilli's reformulation of it in terms of 'dynamic mimesis' whereby the literary text appropriates and, in different ways, integrates features of the colloquial (Ricottilli 2003: 43–8).

3.2 Stylistic indicators and their difficulties

I give below my formulation of such stylistic criteria of colloquialism as emerge from systematic studies of the colloquial and as might facilitate the discussion of the validity of individual features. I also give some examples of the difficulty of applying such criteria.

3.2.1 Expressions of contact (exclamations, curses, fossilised imperatives, stereotyped questions, forms of address, etc.)

The inclusion of specific items in the long list of idioms of this type involves the evaluation of expressions in their context and in relation to

---

[40] A point raised already by Pasquali (1927: 249–50).
[41] Bain (1976: 367): 'One remains doubtful . . . whether trying to reconstruct the speech of that over-rated and semi-fictitious group, the Scipionic circle, is a particularly useful exercise.'
[42] Watson and Watson 2003: 23–4 (e.g. *cenaturire* 'to want a dinner' at Mart. 11.77.3).

distribution. For example, Virgil *Aen.* 5.635 *quin agite* is described as 'a lively and colloquial use which Virgil introduced into poetic language, esp. in this formula' (R. D. Williams 1960 ad loc.). The commentator also refers the reader to a similar use of *quin* + imperative in *Aen.* 4.99 (*quin... exercemus*). Austin's note there reads: 'this use is from conversational speech and marks impatience and annoyance' (Austin 1960 ad loc.). Austin gives numerous Plautine examples for *quin* with imperative or indicative; Hofmann remarks on this kind of question expressing annoyance, amazement and the like (1951: 68–9 = Hofmann–Ricottilli 192–3, with Ricottilli's notes on §§66–7). Other examples in Virgil are likewise interpreted as 'indicat[ing] a challenge' (Thomas 1988 on *G.* 4.329) or '"Why not, while you are about it", as a resentful person says in modern English' (Mynors 1990 on *G.* 4.329), or 'challenging tone' (Clausen 1994 on *Ecl.* 3.52). The colloquial character of *quin age* is inferred from the Plautine use of the *quid* construction, from the combination with a possibly colloquial idiom in *Ecl.* 3.52 *quin age, si quid habes*,[43] and from considerations about the tone of the expression. These arguments, which vary in their worth, tend to obscure the evidence in the other direction: the specific phrase *quin age/agite* is completely unattested in any text normally used as a source for conversational language, but widely used in poetry as a metrically convenient formula.[44]

3.2.2 *Loose syntax (parataxis; parenthesis; anacoluthon; simplified constructions; emotive collocation of words)*

Hofmann described parataxis as the equivalent, at complex-sentence level, of the process of fragmentation of individual phrases and sentences. Elements of the complex sentence appear without grammatical expression of their mutual relation (Hofmann 1951: 105–6 = Hofmann–Ricottilli 249), verbalisation being unnecessary when intonation and context supply the information (Hofmann 1951: 110 = Hofmann–Ricottilli 257). This concept explains comments such as 'colloquial and choppily paratactic style' (Eden 1984: 85 on Sen. *Apoc.* 5.4); 'displacement suggest[ing] incoherence of colloquial speech (R. Coleman 1977 on Verg. *Ecl.* 3.93 ff.); 'disrupted

---

[43] Cf. Pl. *Epid.* 196 *age si quid agis*. Clausen 1994 ad loc. compares Theocritus 5.78 and Herodas 7.47.
[44] It is indeed a formula: *quin agite* opens one hexameter of Lucan (9.282) and two of Valerius Flaccus (2.55, 7.93); as for the singular *quin age* (*Ecl.* 3.52), not a single other example is recorded outside post-Virgilian poetry, where all seven instances occur in the first foot of the hexameter, three of which (Ov. *Ep.* 14.57, V. Fl. 4.469, Stat. *Ach.* 1.949) exhibit a metrical pattern that grammarians illustrate precisely with *Ecl.* 3.52 (cf. Sacerdos *GL* VI.506.24).

style' (Harvey 1981 on Pers. 1.8–12). The question remains as to whether parataxis is mostly an expression of incoherence, and more importantly, whether parataxis should be regarded as colloquial for this reason. As to parenthesis, Augustan poets use it extensively for the sake of pathos (cf. H–S 728–9 = Traina *et al.* 2002: 72–4); on anacoluthon, Adams has rightly drawn attention to the need to distinguish between stylistically motivated choices and isolated instances of imperfect performance (2005b: 89–90).

3.2.3 Brevity (brachylogy, interruptions, aposiopesis; ellipsis; euphemism; pregnant use of words)

Examples of interruptions are frequent in Plautus, Terence and Cicero's letters – a distribution that seems to point to colloquialism. On the other hand only one, uncertain, example is found in Petronius (62.11 *lupus enim villam intravit et omnia pecora*); if valid,[45] this instance would be a case of self-interruption marking the suppression of an offensive word (e.g. Ter. *Eu.* 479 *ego illum eunuchum*; Verg. *Ecl.* 3.8 *novimus et qui te*). This type of euphemism is well documented in literary and non-literary Latin (see Adams 1981a); specific cases, however, may be motivated as imitations of literary models,[46] rather than related to supposedly colloquial features such as reluctance to express cultural taboos[47] or tendency to elliptical expressions.[48]

On the pregnant use of words, I note the disputed quality of *aliquis* 'someone (worth something)'. This usage is found in idioms at Cic. *Att.* 3.15.8, Sen. *Dial.* 5.37.3, Pers. 1.129 and Juv. 1.74. Persius commentators note that this is 'an expression common in Greek and Latin'.[49] Hofmann compares it to Gk εἶναί τι, and treats it as a case of colloquial ellipsis on the analogy of German *einer* (1951: 203 = Hofmann–Ricottilli 385–6). Shackleton Bailey sees nothing colloquial in Cicero saying to Atticus 'wish me to be somebody', implying that 'an exile without civil rights... has no real existence'.[50]

---

[45] Some editors indicate a lacuna (e.g. M. Smith 1975 ad loc.), others supply a verb (e.g. *perculit* Buecheler).
[46] Clausen 1994: 94–5 on Verg. *Ecl.* 3.8, quoting Theocritus 1.105. Cf. Adams (1981a: 128) 'there is a suspicion that the writer has a Greek usage in mind'.
[47] Hofmann 1951: 144–5 = Hofmann–Ricottilli 304–6. Already Servius ad loc.: *subaudis 'corruperint', quod suppressit verecunde.*
[48] As in R. Coleman 1977 ad loc. 'the ellipse of the verb is an instance not of *verecundia* but of colloquialism, like the parenthetic *sed... risere* in the next line'.
[49] Conington and Nettleship 1893 ad loc, with Theocritus 11.79 and Acts 5:36.
[50] Shackleton Bailey 1965: 153 (on Cic. *Att.* 3.15.8), comparing also Mart. 10.27.4 *nemo... natum te... putat* (a phrase incorporated in a joke by Sen. *Apoc.* 3.2: 'proverbial expression'? So Eden 1984: 73, with Petr. 58.10, Mart. 4.83.4).

3.2.4 Redundancy (word repetition including anaphora; pleonasm; periphrasis; exaggeration)

Hofmann's explanation for redundancy in colloquial language is emotive emphasis. Ricottilli remarks on the opportunity to view brevity and redundancy as interdependent features, often coexisting in one and the same context, where pleonastic elements facilitate the 'decoding' of ellipses (Hofmann–Ricottilli 349, Appendix 1).

One problematic evaluation of 'colloquial' emphasis is at Verg. *Ecl.* 3.49 *numquam hodie (effugies)* 'never in your life'. The phrase is taken to be 'probably colloquial at this period' (R. Coleman 1977 ad loc.), 'emphatically colloquial' (Clausen 1994 ad loc., with ref. to *TLL* v/2.2851.14); supporting evidence is usage in early comedy.[51] It is also noted, however, that the entire hemistich repeats the beginning of an iambic senarius in Naevius (*trag.* 14 R. *numquam hodie effugies quin mea moriaris manu*) – not an isolated case of passage from one metre to the other (Clausen 1994 ad loc.) – which almost certainly provided the model for the one other example in high-register poetry, Verg. *Aen.* 2.670 *numquam omnes hodie moriemur inulti.*[52] Donatus brought this very passage into his discussion of Terence *Ad.* 570. No comment on lower register is given in any of the scholia on the *Aeneid* passage (the scholiast to Virgil in fact states that the usage is the same (*sic*) as *Ecl.* 3.49), nor do examples exist outside Virgil and early Latin drama. If the phrase was colloquial in early Latin, it may no longer have been colloquial in Virgil's time. The strong emotive connotation explains its usage in tragic and comic threats; Virgil used it as a parody of dramatic style to characterise Menalcas' address to his opponent in the singing-match of *Ecl.* 3.

3.2.5 Irony (understatement; litotes)

Hofmann interpreted both irony and litotes as acceptable substitutes for blunt expressions, as a reflection of social norms at work among educated speakers, but also at lower levels (1951: 144–52 = Hofmann–Ricottilli 304–14). On the other hand, commentators sometimes take rudeness (as opposed to the avoidance of it) to be an indication of colloquialness. A case like Verg. *Ecl.* 3.23 *si nescis* ('colloquial and rather rude, "I'd have you know"': Clausen 1994 ad loc.) may be supported with parallels from Martial and

---

[51] Cf. Pl. *Mil.* 214; *Rud.* 611; Ter. *Ad.* 570; with second person future the phrase occurs in Pl. *As.* 493 and Ter. *An.* 409.
[52] A case of *furtum Vergilii*, according to Macr. *Sat.* 6.1.38.

Juvenal, and with the ironic use of politeness formulae in comedy.[53] The commentator's perception of rudeness per se does not qualify colloquialism – as seems to be the case with Roncali's inclusion of Sen. *Apoc.* 1.1 *si noluero non respondebo* in her illustration of Seneca's representation of vulgar style.[54]

3.2.6 Imagery (metaphor; ambiguity; concretisation of abstracts)
I mention the use of substantival infinitive, which Hofmann explains as an expression of vividness (1951: 161 = Hofmann–Ricottilli 328). The feature is a favourite one in informal writing (Cicero's letters) and low-register texts (Plautus, Petronius, Persius, Martial). Modern commentators note the distribution and remark on the colloquialness of the usage,[55] whereas ancient ones would note only its Greek origin.[56] It has been noted that 'the poetic and the vulgar registers after all share a concern for concise and vivid expression which will end up in the same place, whether it is a preference for metaphor or for infinitival constructions' (R. Coleman 1999a: 92). Emotiveness brings poetry and conversation together, making the identification of true colloquialisms in poetry more difficult than in plain prose.[57]

3.2.7 Diminutives
The grammatical category of diminutives embraces forms with various degrees of diminutive force and of expressive (e.g. deflationary) connotations. Scholars who, like Hofmann, emphasise the emotive quality of diminutives describe them as a feature of colloquial language:[58] Hofmann and Szantyr count 70 different forms, for a total of 288 instances, in Cicero's letters only; they also note the presence of diminutives in 'those forensic speeches which are closer to a conversational tone'.[59] Others, including Axelson, label diminutives as characteristic of popular language

---

[53] Hofmann included this idiom in his additional illustration of ironic *captatio benevolentiae* (§125 n. 4): see Hofmann–Ricottilli 380.
[54] Roncali 1989: 74. The other example given is the completely different *in buccam venerit* (*Apoc.* 1.2).
[55] Cf. Conington and Nettleship 1893 on Pers. 1.9 (with a long note summarising Wölfflin 1886): 'the infinitive is used as a neuter substantive with a pronoun or an adjective in the colloquial Latin of the classical period'; Harvey (1981: 17): 'its [i.e. the infinitive's] distribution strongly suggests a colloquialism, though the perfect infinitive occurs at Sen. *Oed.* 992'. See also H–S 343–4.
[56] E.g. *Pithou glossae veteres in Persium* 1.9 (*figura Graeca*), in Zetzel 2005: 166.
[57] An argument of Stevens: cf. Collard 2005: 352.
[58] See Hofmann 1951: 139–41 (= Hofmann–Ricottilli 297–9, with Ricottilli's corrections and bibliographical survey at nn. 1–4); E. Löfstedt 1956: II.336–8; Cèbe 1972–99: I.139.40.
[59] H–S 772 = Traina *et al.* 2002: 143.

(*Volkssprache*).[60] Our most complete study of the language of early satire counts some thirty diminutives in the fragments of Lucilius, distinguishing between expressive usages and weakened forms with neither diminutive nor emotive colour (Mariotti 1960: 113–25). A special case of the latter use is the specialisation of diminutives as technical terms (cf. e.g. Reinhardt *et al.* 2005: 160 n. 25).

Commentators who remark on the 'colloquial flavour' of diminutives often rely on Axelson's authority for the avoidance of these forms in poetry, and/or on Hofmann's association of these forms with emotive speech. But how common were diminutives in actual conversation? Hofmann himself drew attention to the fact that a large number of diminutives are ad hoc formations resulting in *hapax legomena* (a well-known case is the double diminutive *subturpicula* in Cic. *Att.* 4.5.1).[61] Hofmann intended to describe not a productive conversational feature, but a tendency of informal language towards expressive innovation: thus for example Plautus and Petronius come up with the most extravagant diminutive formations – the more extravagant, the less likely to have had any currency. Axelson, on the other hand, intended to describe the differentiation of vocabulary selection in prose and poetry. Neither view may safely be adopted as a universal rule for the identification of forms as belonging to the language of actual conversation. Even diminutive forms that have no diminutive force in vulgar Latin or in their Romance outcomes – in other words those most likely to have been conversational – cannot be proven to be colloquial in Latin literary contexts, where the use of such forms may have a different explanation. For example, the diminutive adjective *vetulus*,[62] which eventually replaced *vetus* in Romance, is used in such a variety of functions (term of endearment, deflationary qualification, technical sense) as to make the label 'colloquial' meaningless, whether in contrast, or synonymous with, 'vulgar';[63] and even in conversational texts of the early period, commentators who call the form colloquial disagree as to the precise reason why it should be so.[64]

[60] Axelson 1945: 38–45 (with Ernout's discussion, 1957: 82–6); cf. Gow 1932: 154; on neoteric poetry: Ross 1969: 22–5.

[61] Hofmann 1951: 140 = Hofmann–Ricottilli 298–9; H–S 772 = Traina *et al.* 2002: 142.

[62] For the formation and development of *vetulus* see Hakamies 1951: 26 and 55–7; Ernout 1954: 192; W–H ii.776–8; E–M 730; Leumann 1977: 308.

[63] E.g. Plessis and Lejay (1911 ad loc.) describe the *cornix vetula* of Hor. *Carm.* 4.13.22 as a feature of familiar language (cf. E–M s.v. 'diminutif de la langue familière'); the use is more probably contemptuous; see also Hor. *Carm.* 3.5.11, with Nisbet and Rudd (2004 ad loc.): *vetula* Chloris is a 'stereotype of comedy and epigrams'.

[64] The reference to Hannibal as *lupus vetulus* in Lucil. 826 M. (= 952 W. = 899 K. = 29.58 C.) is explained as an instance of 'military language' (*sermo castrensis*) by Marx (1904–5: ii.287), but his

4 CONCLUSIONS

The value of the existing systematic studies of 'colloquial' Latin lies in the discussion of subjective/informal expressions within two systems of acceptability – the social norms controlling forms of oral communication and the stylistic norms governing literary registers. Features that grammarians and modern scholars perceive as departing from the norms of elevated prose or poetry need not be colloquial; nor do pronouncements on colloquialness always help explain why an author chose that particular feature. Looseness or lack of stylisation is acceptable in informal prose (e.g. Cicero's letters) and widely represented in characterisations of plain language in dialogue (e.g. Plautus, Petronius); but even low-register works are 'literature'. Imitation of everyday language may result in the invention of word-types associated with everyday language, but belonging to the literariness of the particular text, not to spoken idiom.

supporting parallel concerns *lupus* alone (Hor. *Epist.* 2.2.28). Mariotti (1960: 119–20) takes *vetulus* as equivalent to *vetus*, unmarked except for metonymic sense ('incallito nella ferocia', ibid. n. 2; cf. Hanssen 1951: 130 'old and cunning'). On *vetulus* as technical in reference to animals see Hanssen 1951: 110; Adams 1992b: 85–90.

CHAPTER 5

Preliminary conclusions

Eleanor Dickey

What do these investigations tell us about what colloquial Latin is and how to find it? Clackson tells us that there is no point looking to linguistics for an immediate solution to our problem: linguists avoid the term 'colloquial' because of its ambiguities and associated value judgements. Ferri and Probert tell us that the Roman rhetoricians and grammarians do not provide a full answer either: the way the Romans divided up language into registers is not fully understood and was fluid not only diachronically but also synchronically. Chahoud makes it clear that modern research on colloquial Latin is not much more help. For the past century most work on colloquial Latin has relied on stylistic criteria that are supposed to be characteristic of actual conversational usage but have never been clearly demonstrated to have a close connection with it, and there is widespread disagreement among commentators over whether individual passages are colloquial or not. Such disagreement cannot be resolved by any appeal to a generally accepted set of principles about colloquial Latin, for there are no such principles, nor any agreement about what it is.

On the basis of these investigations we can, however, state the range of things that colloquial language and colloquial Latin in particular has been said to be and therefore could be. Colloquial Latin could be the words and usages that Latin speakers (or just those Latin speakers who lived before or during the Augustan age) employed freely in conversation but avoided in their formal literary productions. Or it could be only those conversational features used by a particular segment of Roman society (the upper classes, the lower classes, or some other group), or those that were not seen as offensive by a particular segment of society (or, indeed, those that were seen as offensive). In any of these cases the meaning of 'colloquialism' could be restricted to current usage or could encompass elements that had once fitted the required description but since gone out of common use. Alternatively, colloquial Latin could be words or usages that had certain stylistic characteristics, whether or not these words or usages ever occurred in the ordinary conversational speech of any group or period. Chahoud has made it fairly clear that some such 'colloquialisms' were in fact literary creations that did not occur in conversation, but it is far from clear that authors such as Hofmann would have agreed that they were therefore not colloquial, as Hofmann's basic definition of colloquialism had to do with internal characteristics of language rather than how or where it was actually used.

This last viewpoint on the colloquial is one that we might be tempted to rule out at once on the basis of Clackson's chapter, but there are two reasons for caution in this direction. This type of colloquial language is in essence what the vast majority of previous scholarship has been looking for in Latin, and while it is often convenient to dismiss the majority of previous scholarship on any given question, doing so is usually unwise. Additionally, knowing that some words and usages fit syntactic criteria of colloquialism but were apparently used only in literary works does not tell us how Romans perceived those words and usages. Just as it is possible to invent, for one-time use in a literary work, an insult that sounds low-register (cf. Dickey 2002: 16, 172), it is possible for the writer of a literary work to invent a word or usage that sounds conversational. Some syntactic colloquialisms might fall into this category. If Roman authors deliberately invented words or usages that were supposed to resemble actual conversational language, such 'literary colloquialisms' are an interesting phenomenon in their own right. We would not want to confuse them with features of actual conversational language, but it is not impossible that we could learn something by studying them in the context of that language.

Colloquial Latin, then, could be any of a very wide range of things. There is no basis for deciding between them, as no evidence can be brought to bear where there is no common ground for argument; any decision as to which of these things 'colloquial Latin' is must be arbitrary. And as there is no advantage to supporting a particular definition of the term if the choice of definition is purely arbitrary, we cannot define colloquial Latin.

But it is essential to remove the imprecision and contradiction that have so far plagued the search for colloquial Latin. That can be done without arbitrariness by stating that any *one* characteristic may be postulated as the basis for defining colloquial Latin, but that no further characteristics should be tied to it without convincing proof of a real and necessary connection between them. In other words, it is legitimate to look for colloquial Latin starting from the premise that colloquial Latin is the Latin used conversationally by the upper (or lower) classes during the Republic, or that colloquial Latin is Latin with certain syntactic characteristics, or to adhere to any other single premise, provided the premise is clearly stated. It is not, however, legitimate to mix premises by assuming that language with one characteristic normally associated with the term 'colloquial' must also have any other characteristic: that language with colloquial syntactic characteristics necessarily occurred in someone's conversation (let alone in the conversation of a particular group of Romans), that language that one group found offensive was necessarily used by another group, etc. The wide range of meanings of the term 'colloquial' must not be allowed to colour our analysis of the facts of Latin: we must describe the facts as they are, find explanations that fit them, and build larger theories on those explanations, rather than starting with theories and trying to get the facts to fit them.

Under these circumstances, how would one go about finding colloquial Latin? To the extent that colloquial Latin is the opposite of literary Latin, it would seem that the best place to find it would be in non-literary texts: curse tablets, ostraca, papyrus letters, etc. The publication of so many such texts over the past half century has led to an enormous increase in our understanding of non-literary Latin, such as would never have been possible from literary sources alone, but nevertheless this material has some severe limitations. It is relatively scarce: the sum total of all the non-literary evidence we have comes to far fewer words than Plautus' plays or Cicero's letters. It is chronologically restricted: most non-literary evidence comes from the Imperial period and so can shed little light on the conversational usage of Cicero's day, let alone that of Plautus' day. (Thus, by some definitions, it is vulgar rather than colloquial Latin.) It is restricted in format and topic: most curse tablets and ostraca deal with a narrow range of topics and situations, and many are heavily formulaic, so many words and usages that we would like to know about have no opportunity to occur. It comes preponderantly from the middle and lower classes of society; if one defines colloquial language as belonging to the upper classes, there is little non-literary evidence that could be relevant.

It is time, therefore, to look again at literature, which remains not only our largest body of evidence for colloquial Latin, but also our most diverse and by far our earliest. Until the mid twentieth century this evidence formed almost the sole basis for the study of colloquial Latin; then the discovery of original documentary texts such as papyrus letters, ostraca, curse tablets and the Vindolanda tablets gave scholarship on this topic a fresh, non-literary perspective. The insights offered by documentary material are invaluable, but the concentration on them has led to neglect of the important evidence available in literature. It is now time to re-examine these literary texts, using the understanding gained from documentary sources to take a fresh look at the interplay of colloquial and literary language in Latin literature.

This look will be based on the following questions: What are the characteristics of colloquial and of literary Latin, and what justifies the selection of these characteristics? To what extent are the two types of language antithetical? Are they mutually exclusive, or were there literary colloquialisms in Latin? How does one identify colloquial language in a literary work? How did authors use colloquial language in literary works, and what was its effect for contemporary readers? To what extent was there synchronic variation in colloquial Latin, for example variation associated with class, region or gender, and if there was such variation, to what extent can we recover it? What was the status, in classical Latin, of forms that were recognised to have been colloquialisms in early Latin but that were synchronically seen as archaic (and therefore potentially literary)? Was all classical Latin literary in the post-classical period? Was all Latin literary in the medieval period, or was the concept of 'colloquial Latin' still meaningful – and if the latter, what did it mean?

We do not claim to be able to answer these questions fully; a complete exploration of this subject across all the centuries through which Latin was used would take more than one book. We do, however, think that by raising them and exploring the way they could be addressed and answered we can increase the understanding of colloquial Latin.

PART II

Early Latin

CHAPTER 6

Possessive pronouns in Plautus

Wolfgang David Cirilo de Melo

I INTRODUCTION

Possessive pronouns such as *meus* 'my' or *tuus* 'your' indicate that there is a connection between two entities.[1] This connection may be possessive, as in *my book*, or it may be of a different nature, as in *my friend*. Lexical items often belong to different stylistic registers, for instance the poetic *ensis* 'sword' and its prose equivalent *gladius*.[2] Grammatical items, on the other hand, tend to be stylistically neutral. Nevertheless, possessive pronouns have found a place in several stylistic studies. There are four reasons for this:

(i) Possessive pronouns can be emphatic; in English we can use *his own* rather than simply *his* in this case. Latin has different means of emphasis. One of them is hyperbaton. Adams (1971: 1–16) has demonstrated that verbal hyperbaton (type *magnam habeo gratiam* 'I am very grateful') is still rare in early prose, but becomes more frequent in the classical period, especially when the register is elevated. In Plautus, possessive pronouns are frequently separated from their head nouns and one may wonder what their register is. Does Plautus use hyperbaton for emphasis and stylistic reasons, or is he simply forced to do so by the metre?

(ii) Possessive pronouns can also be emphasised by reinforcing them with dative pronouns:[3]

(1)   suo sibi gladio hunc iugulo.   (Ter. *Ad.* 958)

        I'm killing him with his own sword.

---

[1] I am grateful to Eleanor Dickey for giving me very helpful comments on a draft of this contribution.
[2] Quintilian explicitly states that there is no difference in meaning (*significatio*) between these two words (*Inst.* 10.1.11).
[3] The reinforcement of emphatic possessive pronouns with -*pte* and -*met* is very rare in Plautus; -*pte* is attached to the ablative singular of *meus*, *tuus* and *suus* seven times, but only once to an accusative singular (*Mil.* 391), and -*met* only occurs in the ablative singular *meamet* (*Poen.* 446).

71

This usage is normally considered colloquial (see Landgraf 1893: 43–4, K–S 1.606, or Hofmann–Ricottilli 294 (§127)). Note that example (1) is spoken by Demea, whose speech is characterised by imagery which is 'often low or vulgar in tone' (Maltby 2007: 157). Not only the register, but also the origins of the type *suus sibi* deserve a closer look. *Suus sibi* is sometimes regarded as typically Plautine, which is one of the reasons why I shall concentrate on this author in my article.

(iii) In classical Latin *suus* is mainly used reflexively, that is, if there is a connection between the entity modified by *suus* and a third-person subject. If the connection is between a *possessum* and a third-person constituent other than the subject, the possessive pronoun is typically *eius*. In Plautus there are instances where *suus* encroaches on the territory of *eius*. Since this foreshadows Late Latin and Romance developments, the Plautine usage has been classified as colloquial. The register of this usage obviously needs to be examined, but another question that arises is how frequent it actually is in Plautus.

(iv) Latin is said to use possessive pronouns more sparingly than most modern European languages. There are indeed many cases where English requires possessives, whereas Latin can do without:

(2)   ad fratrem, quo ire dixeram, mox ivero.   (Pl. *Capt.* 194)

        I'll soon go to my brother, where I said I was going.

Here it is clear that *fratrem* refers to the speaker's brother. Plautus does not employ a possessive, while the English translation would sound odd without one. But on the whole Plautus seems to use possessives more often than classical prose, and in many cases the connections between entities would be clear without them. According to Hofmann and Szantyr (H–S 178) this usage is colloquial. But is this really true? I cannot answer this last question here because that would require a large-scale study involving several Latin authors. But I shall examine the other three questions in some detail, beginning with hyperbaton, which needs to be put in the context of more general word order problems.

2 WORD ORDER PROBLEMS

Latin word order is determined by the interplay of four factors: syntactic rules, emphasis, meaning and metre. Some syntactic rules are without exceptions. For instance, two nouns can be co-ordinated in the form *A et*

B or *A B-que*; neither *et* nor *-que* can assume different positions. Other syntactic rules can be overridden by various factors. For example, Adams (1999a) has demonstrated that *ego* and *tu* are typically Wackernagel clitics placed after an emphatic host; however, if these nominative pronouns are emphatic themselves, they are not clitics and often occupy the first position in the clause. We must ask ourselves to what extent emphasis and stylistic factors influence the position of possessive pronouns. Meaning can also be more important than syntactic categories. Adjectives are a case in point. They constitute a syntactic category, but their position with regard to their head nouns is not fixed syntactically. Here semantic categories matter more. De Sutter (1986: 164–9) has shown that at least in Cato adjectives for colour terms and physical properties regularly follow their head nouns, while evaluative adjectives either follow or precede their heads and numerals typically precede them. Finally, it is obvious that in poetry metre has some influence on word order, though the extent of that influence is open to debate. Absolute syntactic rules like the above ones concerning co-ordination cannot be overridden for the sake of metre, but other syntactic rules are mere tendencies a poet may perhaps occasionally ignore. Here the question arises which factors have the upper hand in Plautus. To what extent can metre create artificial word order patterns by overriding for example pragmatic factors like focus?

The study of possessive pronouns offers several advantages over that of other elements modifying nouns, for instance adjectives or nouns in the genitive. First, the meaning of possessive pronouns is simple. They create a connection between two entities; the exact nature of this connection depends on the context, not the pronouns themselves, and need not concern us here. What matters for our purposes is that among possessive pronouns we need not establish semantic subcategories that may or may not influence word order patterns; for adjectives such a procedure is necessary, as De Sutter (1986) has shown. Second, pragmatic functions are much clearer. Adjectives can be focal or non-focal for a variety of reasons: they can introduce new information, contrast with other adjectives, and so on. Since possessive pronouns merely indicate a connection between two elements, they are focal if contrastive and non-focal otherwise. In the phrase *my book*, the word *my* can only be stressed if there is an explicit or implicit contrast (*MY book, not YOURS*). The third reason why it is worthwhile to study possessive pronouns is that whereas their meaning and pragmatic functions are straightforward, they do not all scan in the same way, which enables us to check to what extent word order in Plautus is influenced by metre.

The only context in which the semantics of possessive pronouns may be regarded as more complex consists of vocative phrases. For obvious reasons, only *meus* and *noster* are used here, not *tuus* or other possessive pronouns. The connection which the possessive establishes between speaker and addressee is one of affection, especially in the case of *mi* and *mea* (for the lower emotional intensity of *noster* see Dickey 2002: 224). Naturally, no contrast is involved.[4] Because vocative phrases are typically short, hyperbaton occurs only once, in *mea me ancilla* 'me, my maid' (*Cas.* 646–7). Vocatives of *meus* precede their head nouns 184 times and follow them 80 times.[5] The vocative *noster* is rare; it precedes once and follows once. In what follows, vocative phrases will be ignored entirely.

Possessive pronouns can occupy four positions with respect to their head nouns. What I call position 1 is exemplified by the following two sentences:

(3)   nunc tibi hanc pateram, quae dono mi illi ob virtutem data est,
         Pterela rex qui potitavit, quem ego mea occidi manu,
         Alcumena, tibi condono.   (Pl. *Am.* 534–6)

         Now, Alcumena, I am presenting you with this bowl, which was given
         to me there as a gift because of my valour, and from which King Pterelas
         used to drink, whom I slew with my own hand.

(4)   ... techinam de auro advorsum meum fecit patrem.   (Pl. *Bac.* 392)

         He played a trick concerning the gold on my father.

In these two sentences the possessive pronouns *mea* and *meum* precede their head nouns but are separated from them (in both cases by verb forms). My position 1 corresponds to what others call pre-modifier hyperbaton.[6] Note that in example (3) *mea* is emphatic: the speaker wants to stress that he killed the enemy's commander himself. In example (4) the possessive is unemphatic; there is no contrast between the speaker's father and other fathers.[7]

In what I call position 2, the possessive precedes its head noun, but is not separated from it:

(5)   Saurea, oro | mea caussa ut mittas.   (Pl. *As.* 431–2)

         Saurea, I ask you to let him off the hook for my sake.

---

[4] The only exception is *Poen.* 392–4 *voluptas huius atque odium meum* ... 'his joy and my nuisance ...'.

[5] In addition, *mea* on its own is used as a vocative in *Mil.* 1263 and *Mos.* 346.

[6] For the term see Devine and Stephens 2006: 524. In what follows, I shall not adopt their approach to word order for reasons outlined in de Melo 2007a.

[7] I do not include cases like *vostrumque ingenium* 'and your character' (*St.* 126) under position 1; here it is only the clitic *-que* which mechanically separates possessive and head.

(6)   ME. quid tu solus tecum loquere? EU. meam pauperiem conqueror.

(Pl. *Aul.* 190)

ME. What are you talking about to yourself? EU. I'm complaining about my poverty.

Again there can be emphasis on the possessive, as in example (5), but there need not be any, as example (6) demonstrates, where the speaker is not contrasting his own poverty with that of others.[8]

The possessive pronoun can also follow its head noun without hyperbaton. I refer to this as position 3:

(7)   ... incommodi
si quid tibi evenit, id non est culpa mea.   (Pl. *Mer.* 773–4)

If you had some unpleasant experience, it isn't through my fault.

(8)   manufesto teneo in noxia inimicos meos.   (Pl. *Cas.* 507)

I have caught my enemies red-handed in their crime.

Once again the possessive can be emphatic in this position, but it need not be so. In example (7) the speaker wants to establish a contrast: he is saying that it is not his fault, but the addressee's. In example (8), on the other hand, there is no contrast between the speaker's enemies and other people's.

Finally, the possessive can follow its head noun, but be separated from it (post-modifier hyperbaton). In my terminology this is type 4:

(9)   ... sexaginta milia hominum uno die
volaticorum manibus occidi meis.   (Pl. *Poen.* 472–3)

I killed sixty thousand flying men with my own hands in a single day.

(10)   nunc hinc parasitum in Cariam misi meum.   (Pl. *Cur.* 67)

Now I have sent my hanger-on off to Caria.

Example (9) is quite similar to example (3). In both cases the speaker wants to emphasize that he killed the enemy himself, and in both cases the possessives are separated from their head nouns. But in example (3) the possessive precedes and in example (9) it follows. Example (10) contains unemphatic *meum* in post-modifier hyperbaton.

---

[8] Under position 2 I also subsume cases like *vostras furtificas manus* 'your thieving hands' (*Ps.* 887), where the possessive is not immediately next to its head, but only separated from it by another modifier.

The four positions are not all equally frequent. Table 6.1 presents the absolute and relative frequencies of the four positions for each type of possessive pronoun.

Table 6.1 *The order of possessive pronouns in relation to their heads*[9]

	Position 1	Position 2	Position 3	Position 4	Total
meus	195 (15.97%)	469 (38.41%)	404 (33.09%)	153 (12.53%)	1221
tuus	155 (18.17%)	297 (34.82%)	279 (32.71%)	122 (14.30%)	853
suus (sg./pl.)	56 (13.37%)	133 (31.74%)	141 (33.65%)	89 (21.24%)	419
noster	42 (19.53%)	93 (43.26%)	60 (27.91%)	20 (9.30%)	215
voster	19 (19.79%)	46 (47.92%)	22 (22.92%)	9 (9.38%)	96
Total	467 (16.65%)	1038 (37.02%)	906 (32.31%)	393 (14.02%)	2804

This table ought to be read as follows: in total, there are 1221 tokens of *meus* (and other forms of the first-person possessive); of these 1221 tokens, 195 occur in position 1 (pre-modifier hyperbaton). These 195 tokens constitute 15.97 per cent of the total of 1221.

Several interesting facts emerge from Table 6.1. Regardless of differences in scansion, all possessive pronouns behave in similar ways. In general, the most frequent position possessive pronouns occupy is before their head nouns, but without hyperbaton. On average, this occurs in 37 per cent of the cases. However, the second-most frequent position, that of possessives following their head nouns without hyperbaton, is not much rarer: this position constitutes 32 per cent of the total. What is perhaps most remarkable is the overall frequency of hyperbaton. In Plautus, the two types of hyperbaton make up almost 31 per cent of the total, with pre-modifier hyperbaton slightly more frequent than post-modifier hyperbaton. In early prose hyperbaton, especially with an intervening verb, is still rare and a feature of elevated register (Adams 1971: 1–16). Yet the sheer frequency of hyperbaton in Plautus makes it clear that within the context of early drama discontinuous noun phrases cannot be considered stylistically marked. They may well be an artificial feature of Plautine *Kunstsprache*, but their great frequency should make us careful not to try to look for a rationale for each and every instance, just as a Homeric word needs an explanation in an Attic prose writer, but not in a tragedy.

Two further observations seem to be in order. First, even though all possessive pronouns behave in roughly the same way, the pronouns *meus*,

---

[9] In this and the following table I have counted the type *suus sibi* + immediately following noun under position 2. I have excluded all possessives in vocative phrases and naturally all instances where possessives do not modify nouns (nominalised or predicative possessives). I have also excluded all possessives that are textually problematic.

tuus and *suus* have a slight preference for positions 3 and 4 compared with *noster* and *voster*; that is, *meus, tuus* and *suus* have a slight preference for following the head nouns rather than preceding them, even though only in the case of *suus* is this preference so marked that positions 3 and 4 taken together make up marginally more than half the tokens. This brings me to my second observation. In the case of *suus* position 4 (post-modifier hyperbaton) is even more frequent than in the case of *meus* or *tuus*.

These divergences seem to have metrical reasons. All adjectival forms of *noster* and *voster* are disyllabic,[10] although the second syllable need not count metrically if there is elision in a form like *nostra*, and they all have heavy first syllables. Forms like *meus, tuus* and *suus* can count as disyllabic with a light first syllable or, if there is synizesis, as monosyllabic. In addition, forms like *mea* can elide the final syllable or undergo complete elision of both vowels. Forms of *meus, tuus* and *suus*, with the exception of the very rare genitive plural forms,[11] are thus metrically much more versatile than forms of *noster* and *voster*.

With regard to my first observation above, one question comes to mind immediately. *Meus, tuus* and *suus* prefer positions 3 and 4 when compared with *noster* and *voster*; is this the result of displacing *meus, tuus* and *suus* from their natural positions, or of displacing *noster* and *voster*? I tend towards the first interpretation because there are certain phrases, most notably with *causa* 'for *x*'s sake', where possessives normally precede in prose, but where they can follow in Plautus for metrical reasons. In Plautus *causa* is only attested with possessive pronouns in the singular. He uses the type *mea causa* twelve times[12] and the type *mea . . . causa* with hyperbaton ten times. Both types are common in prose as well. However, Plautus also has the type *causa mea* thirteen times. This type is only used for metrical convenience, as it is practically restricted to iambic line endings; the only exception is *Cur.* 150, where *causa mea* occurs in the middle of a cretic tetrameter, a metre which does not allow for much freedom in word order. In addition, the unnatural order *causa currendo tua* 'for your sake by running' occurs in *Mer.* 151 in a trochaic septenarius; the natural order *tua causa* is metrically impossible at line end and the most common alternative order *causa tua* is impossible because in that case *currendo* would immediately precede and thereby break Meyer's law.[13] The use of an unnatural word order at line

---

[10] In Plautus *nostrorum* and *vostrorum* are attested, but not as adjectives; the forms are genitives of the personal pronouns *nos* and *vos*.

[11] There are eighteen adjectival tokens, all of them with synizesis before *-rum* (including the one in *Cist.* 28 if this is an iambic septenarius (thus the scansion in Questa 1995: 181) and not a trochaic octonarius, as Lindsay would have it in his edition).

[12] I include *tuan causa* in *Capt.* 845, where only *-ne* intervenes.

[13] For Meyer's law and its *raison d'être* see Questa 2007: 393–413.

end should not surprise us. It is no stranger than the use of archaic forms at line end, for instance *duint* instead of *dent* 'may they give', *siem* instead of *sim* 'may I be' and *vortier* instead of *vorti* 'to turn'. These archaic forms were no longer in regular use in Plautus' day and are more or less restricted to line end, a place where there is less metrical freedom than elsewhere and where consequently metrical convenience often overrides regular usage.

As I noted above, not only position 3, but also post-modifier hyperbaton is more common with *meus*, *tuus* and *suus* than with *noster* and *voster*, and my second observation was that among the first three, it is more common with *suus* than with *meus* and *tuus*. If *meus*, *tuus* and *suus* are particularly frequent at line end, we are probably dealing with displacement of these forms rather than with displacement of *noster* and *voster* to positions 1 and 2, because there are often good metrical reasons for post-modifier hyperbaton involving forms like *meus*, *tuus* and *suus* at line end:

(11)   huc mihi venisti sponsam praereptum meam.   (Pl. *Cas.* 102)

You've come here to snatch away my fiancée from me.

(12)   perge, Nox, ut occepisti; gere patri morem meo.   (Pl. *Am.* 277)

Continue, Night, as you began; humour my father.

In example (11), an iambic senarius, the ending *praereptum sponsam meam* would violate Meyer's law. In example (12), a trochaic septenarius, the ending *morem patri meo* would violate the law of Bentley and Luchs.[14] Let us now look at the data: *meus*, *tuus* and *suus* together have 364 tokens in post-modifier hyperbaton; of these 265, that is 72.80 per cent, occur at line end. This high frequency of tokens at line end makes it clear that the higher frequency with which *meus*, *tuus* and *suus* can be found in post-modifier hyperbaton compared with *noster* and *voster* is due to metrical factors.

However, there is no inherent metrical reason why *suus* should be displaced more often than *meus* and *tuus*, as its forms scan just like those of *meus* and *tuus*. But it should be noted that the displacement is not random: while many forms of *meus* and *tuus* in post-modifier hyperbaton are found at line end, this tendency is even more pronounced with *suus*. 69.4 per cent of forms of *meus* and *tuus* in post-modifier hyperbaton are at line end (191 out of 275), but for *suus* the figure is 83.15 per cent (74 out of 89). Thus, we must be dealing with a metrical licence. Why Plautus should make greater use of it in the case of *suus* than in the case of *meus* and *tuus* has to remain unclear, but at least it is clear that we are dealing with a metrical licence, not with displacement for more linguistic reasons.

---

[14] For this law and a rationale for its existence see Questa 2007: 371–8.

I hope that I have managed to show two things in the preceding discussion. First, pre-modifier and post-modifier hyperbaton may be rare in early prose, but in Plautus they are quite common; so common, in fact, that they are unlikely to be stylistically marked within the context of early dramatic *Kunstsprache*. And second, I hope to have demonstrated that metre has a clear influence on word order patterns, but that at least in Plautus this influence is not so pronounced as to distort the word order patterns of natural speech entirely; otherwise there would not be such broad agreement between the patterns of *meus*, *tuus* and *suus* on the one hand and *noster* and *voster* on the other. Plautus should therefore not be disregarded in studies on word order.

But if metre is not enough to explain word order patterns in Plautus, what determines where Plautus places possessive pronouns? It has long been known that emphatic, antithetic modifiers typically precede their head nouns (Adams 1976b: 89; specifically on possessive pronouns Marouzeau 1922: 133). However, with my example sentences above I have demonstrated that a possessive pronoun can be focused whatever position it occurs in. But that does not mean that focus is equally likely in every position. In Table 6.2 I show how many possessives are focused in each position.[15]

Table 6.2 *Focal possessive pronouns*

	Position 1	Position 2	Position 3	Position 4	Total
meus	95 (48.72%)	155 (33.05%)	74 (18.32%)	15 (9.80%)	339 (27.76%)
tuus	66 (42.58%)	93 (31.31%)	44 (15.77%)	12 (9.84%)	215 (25.21%)
suus (sg./pl.)	25 (44.64%)	44 (33.08%)	19 (13.48%)	14 (15.73%)	102 (24.34%)
noster	11 (26.19%)	21 (22.58%)	7 (11.67%)	1 (5%)	40 (18.60%)
voster	10 (52.63%)	5 (10.87%)	3 (13.64%)	1 (11.11%)	18 (18.75%)
Total	207 (44.33%)	317 (30.54%)	147 (16.24%)	43 (10.94%)	714 (25.47%)

The table should be read as follows: *meus* has ninety-five emphatic tokens in pre-modifier hyperbaton; these constitute 48.72 per cent of all instances of *meus* in pre-modifier hyperbaton. It should be clear from these data that in general Plautus is most likely to put focus on possessive pronouns if they are in pre-modifier hyperbaton, and that he is least likely to do so if they are in post-modifier hyperbaton. Almost half the tokens in pre-modifier

---

[15] Classifications of nouns and verbs as focal or non-focal are often highly subjective. For possessive pronouns we are in a better position because they are grammatical rather than purely lexical items. Possessives are focal if they are contrastive and non-focal otherwise. However, despite the simpler semantics of possessive pronouns, it is not always clear whether a given instance is focal or non-focal; Table 6.2 cannot claim absolute accuracy.

hyperbaton are emphatic, but only one tenth of those in post-modifier hyperbaton are. Actually, there seems to be a kind of focus gradation: possessives in position 1 are most likely to be emphatic, followed by those in position 2, then by those in position 3, and the ones in position 4 are typically unemphatic. While this does not enable us to predict where Plautus would place a possessive in any given instance, it does tell us what his preferences are.

The misfits in Table 6.2 are *noster* in position 1, *voster* in position 2 and *suus* in position 4. There are fewer emphatic tokens than expected of *noster* in position 1 and of *voster* in position 2. In both cases the unexpected distribution can be explained by the fact that the absolute number of tokens is low. *Suus* in position 4 has a higher absolute number of tokens, so here the slightly higher number of emphatic ones is less likely to be fortuitous. Above I argued that the relatively high frequency of *suus* in position 4 is the result of displacement for metrical reasons; it now seems that this metrical displacement can to some extent distort the pragmatic tendency to indicate focus through word order. However, the extent to which this can happen is minor, as the general tendencies remain clear in Plautus. In Plautus, metre can make pragmatic factors in placing words less obvious, but it does not override them entirely.

3 THE TYPE *SUUS SIBI*

I am now turning to the type *suus sibi*, in which the possessive is always emphatic. It does not merely assert the existence of a connection between two entities, but indicates its exclusivity (*MY book* = 'my own book; a book that belongs exclusively to me, not to you'):

(13)   quasi, quom caletur, cocleae in occulto latent,
        suo sibi suco vivunt, ros si non cadit,
        item parasiti rebus prolatis latent
        in occulto miseri, victitant suco suo,
        dum ruri rurant homines quos ligurriant.   (Pl. *Capt.* 80–4)

> Just as snails hide in a secret place when it's warm and live on their own juice if no dew falls, hangers-on hide in a secret place during vacation, poor devils, and live on their own juice while the people they sponge on live a country life in the countryside.

This statement by the hanger-on Ergasilus contains two different phrases meaning 'their own juice'. First he uses *suo sibi suco* to indicate that snails live on their own juice, not someone else's; the possessive pronoun precedes its head noun and is strengthened by *sibi*, a pleonastic reflexive pronoun whose presence is certainly not called for by the valency of the verb *vivere* 'live'. But two lines later he says *suco suo* in the same meaning; this time the possessive pronoun, although equally emphatic, follows its head noun and is not strengthened by any dative pronoun.

As far as the origin of the type *suus sibi* is concerned, scholars are agreed that, in certain collocations in which the dative had a proper syntactic function, it was reanalysed as a particle strengthening an accompanying possessive (see for example Lindsay 1907: 41 or Norberg 1944: 65–6).[16] The starting point could have been cases like the following:[17]

(14)   neque puduit eum id aetatis sycophantias
         struere et beneficiis me emere gnatum suum sibi.   (Pl. *As.* 71–2)

         And he was not ashamed to play tricks at his age and to buy for himself
         the affection of me, his son, with these acts of kindness.

Here *suum* and *sibi* stand next to each other, but do not belong together; *suum* modifies *gnatum*, while *sibi* goes with *emere*. However, with the verb *emere* one does not need to specify the recipient, at least not if that recipient is identical with the subject. In cases like this, the string *suum sibi* could be reanalysed as possessive plus strengthener. But this example also differs from the ones with *suum sibi* in the meaning 'his own' in one crucial respect: *suum* is not contrastive.[18]

Actually, it is quite difficult to come up with attested sentences containing verb-governed *sibi* following a form of *suus*. This is why grammars also mention sentences like the following ones as starting points of the reanalysis (both quoted in Lindsay 1907: 41):

(15)   meas mihi ancillas invito me eripis.   (Pl. *Rud.* 712)

         You're dragging my slave-girls away from me against my will.

(16)   iustumst <ut> tuus tibi servus tuo arbitratu serviat.   (Pl. *Bac.* 994)

         It is only fair that your slave should serve you according to your wishes.

---

[16] Hofmann–Ricottilli (1985: 294) speak of a proliferation of the 'ethic' dative, which is rather vague. What is more, there is only one instance of *meus mihi* (see below), whereas all other instances involve third-person *suus sibi*; however, an ethic dative of the third person is unheard of.

[17] Wölfflin (1892a: 476) is far too specific when he states that the starting point was the standard divorce formula (e.g. Pl. *Am.* 928 *tibi habeas res tuas, reddas meas* 'have your own things for yourself and return mine').

[18] The phrase *gnatum suum* as a whole could be emphatic ('his very own son'), but no contrast between *suus* and other potential possessors is involved.

Here we can see *mihi* next to *meas* and *tibi* next to *tuus*, and in each case the dative depends on the verb. However, it is misleading to regard such sentences as the starting point of a new collocation in which the dative merely has emphasising function. The reason is that while *suus sibi* 'his own' is well attested, it has no real parallels in other persons, either in Plautus or in other authors, that is, parallels like *meus mihi* 'my own' or *tuus tibi* 'your own'. In fact, there is only one single instance of this type of possessive with first-person pronouns:[19]

(17)   . . . in tabernam ducor devorsoriam,
              ubi male accipiar mea mihi pecunia.   (Pl. *Truc.* 697–8)

   I'm being led into a tavern where I'll get a bad reception with my own
   money.

If we confront this one instance of *mea mihi pecunia* with eleven tokens of the type *suus sibi* in Plautus, the question immediately arises whether *meus mihi* and *tuus tibi* were ever common and dropped out of use, or whether example (17) is deliberately unusual. Personally, I tend towards the second alternative. There is no particular reason why *suus sibi* should have been maintained while *meus mihi* and *tuus tibi* were lost. What is more, the speaker of example (17) is Truculentus, the eponymic hero of the play, who is well known for his malapropisms. In his first encounter with Astaphium she greeted him by saying *salve* 'be well', which he countered with the words *non salveo* 'I'm diswell' (259); Sacerdos (*GL* VI.433.7–8) comments that Plautus employs this unidiomatic phrase to make fun of the rustic Truculentus. In our passage Truculentus uses the nonce-word *osculentia* (675), probably a blend of *osculum* 'kiss' and *opsequentia* 'obedience'; this is followed by the equally grotesque words *caullator* (683, for *cauillator* 'jester') and *rabo* (688, for *arrabo* 'deposit'), both commented on by Astaphium. In the light of this, *mea mihi pecunia* could be strange Latin as well; the fact that Astaphium does not comment does not mean anything, as Truculentus' statement is an aside.

But if *suus* followed by *sibi* dependent on a verb could be reanalysed as a single phrase *suus sibi* 'his own', why did this not happen to strings like *meus mihi* or *tuus tibi*? What is so special about the third person? Ultimately the answer must have to do with the fact that a third person is more difficult to pin down, and this fact will lead me to a different derivation of the type *suus sibi*. The first person is the speaker, the second person is the addressee,

---

[19] Kühner and Stegmann (K–S I.606) speak of occasional attestations of *meus mihi* and *tuus tibi*, but only quote the one passage I discuss here. The alleged instance of *tuum tibi* in Porphyrio's commentary on Horace (cf. Landgraf 1893: 44) is non-existent.

but the third person can be anyone else. In Latin there are several ways of reducing this vagueness:

(18)   iam aderit tempus quom sese etiam ipse oderit.   (Pl. *Bac.* 417)

Soon the time will come when he will even hate himself.

(19)   sed ipsus eam amat.   (Pl. *Cas.* 195a)

But he himself loves her.

Example (18) contains a reflexive object pronoun to indicate that the object is identical with the grammatical subject; example (19) contains the non-reflexive *eam* to indicate that subject and object are not identical. Latin has essentially the same distinction among possessive pronouns: *suus* is reflexive and *eius* is non-reflexive (but there is a grammatical difference in that *suus* is adjectival, while *eius* is the genitive of *is*). However, things are more complicated here because *suus* can also be used non-reflexively, with reference to the direct or indirect object, if it has the emphatic meaning 'one's own' (H–S 175). This usage is by no means restricted to lower registers. It also occurs in formal Ciceronian prose:

(20)   hunc [*sc.* Hannibalem] sui cives e civitate eiecerunt.   (Cic. *Sest.* 142)

His own fellow citizens threw him [*sc.* Hannibal] out of their state.

Since oblique forms of *is* are used to indicate that subject and object refer to different entities, and since *suus* can also be used non-reflexively if it is emphatic, it should in theory be possible to place a dative *ei* right next to an emphatic *suus*.[20] But prototypically *suus* is reflexive and speakers must have been loath to combine *suus* with *ei* if both refer to the same person. This, then, is why emphatic, non-reflexive *suus*, if combined with a non-reflexive third-person pronoun, need not be combined with *ei*, but can have *sibi* next to it; we could speak of a kind of attraction. The type is attested in Plautus:

(21)   nunc si ille huc salvus revenit, reddam suum sibi.   (Pl. *Trin.* 156)

Now if he returns here safe and sound, I'll return to him what is his.

(22)   suam sibi rem salvam sistam, si illo advenerit.   (Pl. *Poen.* 1083)

I'll give him his possessions back safe and sound, if he arrives there.

---

[20] This is not actually attested for Plautus or Terence. However, in Cicero we find *cum . . . collegam ei suum commendarem* 'when I was commending his own colleague to him' (*De orat.* 2.196).

Example (21) shows nominalised *suum*, example 22 shows *suam* modifying *rem*. In each case the form is non-reflexive, the subject being the first person. And in each case we find *sibi* instead of *ei*, again in non-reflexive function. Since non-reflexive *sibi* does not normally occur elsewhere, it is an oddity in the system, and that is why it was reanalysed as a particle strengthening *suus*. This derivation differs from the traditional ones in that it has non-reflexive, emphatic *suus* and reflexivity-attracted *sibi* as its basis. This approach has two advantages: first, it starts with strings in which the possessive is emphatic, as it is in the reanalysed sequence *suus sibi*. Not all the strings proposed in earlier derivations necessarily contain emphatic possessives; for instance, there is no reason why *meas* in example (15) should be contrastive. Second, if my explanation is correct, it gives us a rationale for the absence of *meus mihi* 'my own' and *tuus tibi* 'your own': *meam mihi rem salvam sistet* 'he'll give me my possessions back safe and sound' contains nothing unusual, nothing that is against the system, nothing that lends itself to reanalysis.

If examples like the ones I have just given are the diachronic basis for the type *suus sibi*, example (23) reflects a type that is older than example (24):

(23)   ut quisque acciderat, eum necabam ilico
          per cerebrum pinna sua sibi quasi turturem.   (Pl. *Poen.* 486–7)

          Whenever one of them had fallen down, I killed him on the spot with his own feather through his brain, like a turtledove.

(24)   earum hic adulescens alteram ecflictim perit,
          suam sibi cognatam, imprudens, neque scit quae siet.   (Pl. *Poen.* 96–7)

          This young man is madly in love with one of the two, his own relative, without having a clue, and he doesn't know who she is.

Example (23) represents the older type because *sua sibi* does not refer back to the subject, whereas *suam sibi* in example (24) does. Note that the reanalysis of *sibi* as a strengthening particle is complete since in example (23) it comes a few words after the non-reflexive *eum*.

The register of the type *suus sibi* is generally said to be colloquial (Lindsay 1907: 9; Norberg 1944: 65). But is it really? When we examine the register of lexemes or constructions, we typically check their distribution patterns over the various literary genres. For early Latin *suus sibi* this is difficult. In the whole of Plautus there are only twelve tokens. Outside Plautus, there is one occurrence in Terence, and there are two more attestations of the collocation *suus sibi* in early drama:[21]

(25)   <est> haec caterva plane gladiatoria,
cum suum sibi alius socius socium sauciat.   (Caecil. *com.* 38–9)

This crowd clearly consists of gladiators, since each comrade is wounding his own comrade.

(26)   vulnere taetro deformatum,
suo sibi lautum sanguine tepido   (Acc. *trag.* 606–7)

disfigured by a horrible wound, washed with his own warm blood.

Example (25) comes from comedy and thus could be argued to fit the bill for colloquial register. However, example (26) comes from tragedy, where colloquialisms are much rarer. For this reason it is worth taking a closer look at the attestations in Plautus. If we ignore the odd *mea mihi pecunia* in *Truc.* 698, we have eleven tokens. Three of these are found in the mouths of slaves (*Mil.* 632, *Per.* 81; *Am.* 269 is spoken by Mercury, who acts as a slave); three more attestations are used by a hanger-on (*Capt.* 81), a soldier (*Poen.* 487), and a free-born young man (*As.* 825). The language in these passages is neutral, or perhaps somewhat colloquial. What is surprising, however, is that five of the eleven tokens occur in prologues, where higher register is quite common (*Capt.* 5, 46, 50, *Poen.* 57, 97). Such a pattern of distribution speaks for neutral register rather than colloquial overtones.

This brings me back to example (1) from Terence and a related passage in Cicero. In example (1) the rustic Demea said *suo sibi gladio hunc iugulo* (Ter. *Ad.* 958), 'I'm killing him with his own sword.' The fact that this is the only attestation of the type *suus sibi* in Terence does not mean much. Terence does avoid vulgarisms, but since Plautus has only twelve tokens, even though his corpus is three times as large, the rarity of the type in Terence probably has nothing to do with the register of the collocation. It is more important here that Demea's statement seems to have been proverbial. Plautus has a similar phrase:

(27)   itaque me malum esse oportet, callidum, astutum admodum,
atque hunc telo suo sibi, malitia, a foribus pellere.   (Pl. *Am.* 268–9)

So I should be very malicious, sly and tricky, and I should drive him away from the door with his own weapon, malice.

---

[21] *Pace* Landgraf (1893: 44), Turp. *com.* 38 does not contain the phrase *suus sibi* in reverse order; *sibi* depends on *indulgentem*, so *sibi suum amicum esse indulgentem et diutinum* means 'that her friend is kind to her and lasting'.

Plautus' *telo suo sibi* corresponds nicely to Terence's *suo sibi gladio*. Cicero, like Terence, speaks of a sword rather than a weapon in the following passage:

(28)   aut tuo, quemadmodum dicitur, gladio aut nostro defensio tua confi-
         ciatur necesse est.   (Cic. *Caec.* 82)

         It is unavoidable that your defence will be destroyed either by your own
         sword, as one says, or by ours.

Dahlén (1964: 178) believes that the type *suus sibi* was not necessarily colloquial in early Latin, as it occurs in Accius as well, but that it survived in colloquial registers. He rightly argues that the phrase *quemadmodum dicitur* points to a proverb, but he also remarks that Cicero avoided the reinforcing dative pronoun because of its register. If Terence provides us with the original form of the proverb, Cicero has clearly modified it by replacing the rather graphic *iugulare* with the more neutral *conficere*. But if my argumentation above is correct, the reason for the absence of a dative pronoun is different: only *sibi* was reanalysed as a reinforcing particle, not *tibi*.

That said, it is remarkable that Cicero does not use *suus sibi* 'his own' at all.[22] Is this absence due to chance? Here it is important to do the synonym test. Hine (2005: 229) points out that even though Seneca uses the word *regina* 'queen' in his tragedies, but not in his prose, we cannot conclude that it is a poetic word; we could only do so if there were a synonym for it in his prose, which is not the case. What synonyms does *suus sibi* have? How else can one express 'one's own'? The most frequent solution is to use the possessive pronoun on its own, as in example (13) above, where the emphasis on *suo* was probably evident from the prosody. Purely lexical alternatives to *suus sibi* exist as well. Under certain circumstances, the adjective *proprius* can stand for 'one's own':

(29)   ego autem hoc miserior sum quam tu, quae es miserrima, quod ipsa
         calamitas communis est utriusque nostrum, sed culpa mea propria est.
                                                              (Cic. *Fam.* 14.3.1)

         But in this respect I am more miserable than you, who are most miserable:
         the misfortune itself is common to us both, but the guilt is mine alone.

---

[22] Landgraf (1893: 44) mentions the phrases *suas sibi segetes* in *Ver.* 3.69 and *suum sibi* in *Phil.* 2.96. In the first passage, however, *sibi* depends on the following *liceret*, and in the second on *venderes*. Hofmann and Szantyr (H–S 94) add *Att.* 7.11.1, but here *sibi* precedes *suam*, is further separated from it by *habeat*, and clearly depends on this verb.

However, this usage of *proprius* is restricted to cases like example (29), where it stands in opposition to *communis* or *alienus* (Menge *et al.* 2000: 101); only in later Latin can *proprius* replace *meus* or *suus* without such an opposition (Krebs and Schmalz 1905–7: 11.408). More common is the reinforcement of possessive pronouns with the genitive *ipsius*:

(30)   ac si restituor, etiam minus videbimur deliquisse, abs teque certe, quo-
         niam nullo nostro, tuo ipsius beneficio diligemur.   (Cic. *Att.* 3.15.4)

         If I am restored, we will seem to have erred less gravely, and at any rate
         we will be loved by you, for the sake of the good you yourself have done
         for us, since we haven't done any for you.

Since possessive pronouns, though agreeing in case with their head nouns, could be regarded as shorthand for the genitive of a noun, it makes sense to reinforce them with the genitive *ipsius*. Naturally, *ipsius* can also modify possessives of the third person, as in *eius ipsius domum* 'into his own house' (Cic. *Pis.* 83). This usage is alien to Plautus and Terence. Perhaps even more commonly Cicero uses *ipsius* on its own when he wants to say 'his own'; this usage occurs in formal prose as well as in the letters, as in *ex ipsius epistula* 'from his own letter' (Cic. *Att.* 9.6.6). Plautus has the genitive *ipsius* only once (*Capt.* 287), and there it is not contrastive, but simply means 'his'. Terence has two tokens of contrastive *ipsius* foreshadowing the Ciceronian usage (*An.* 818, *Ph.* 725).

The existence, and the frequency, of such alternative constructions indicate that Cicero deliberately avoided the type *suus sibi*. If I am correct in saying that this type was not vulgar, the question arises why he did so. Perhaps the answer has to do with linguistic purism. I have discussed a similar case elsewhere (de Melo 2007b: 119–29): Plautus uses the types *cave ne facias*, *cave facias* and *cave feceris* more or less indiscriminately, all meaning 'don't do'. In the second of these, *ne* is left out by analogy with *fac ut venias/fac venias* 'see to it that you come', and the absence of a subordinator enabled speakers to reanalyse *cave* as a prohibition marker similar to *ne*. This is why *cave* (without *ne*) can also be combined with the prohibitive perfect subjunctive. Cicero uses *cave* with perfect subjunctive only once, in a letter (*Q. fr.* 3.7(9).4). The construction was probably not colloquial in Plautus' time. Cicero may have avoided it because for him *cave* was a verb form and the perfect subjunctive would violate the sequence rules. Similarly, it is conceivable that Cicero avoided *suus sibi* because for him *sibi* was a dative, not a particle for emphasis, and a dative not governed by a verb had no place in a Ciceronian possessive construction.

While a purist like Cicero was bound to avoid *suus sibi*, the collocation continued in writers who are neither colloquial nor vulgar, but whose style could be described as more inclusive.[23] Cicero's contemporary Vitruvius once uses the phrase *in suo sibi* 'in its own' (8.6.3). In the first century AD, Columella still says *suus sibi*. Interestingly, three of the four tokens are in what already seems to be a fixed phrase, *suo sibi iure* 'in its own juice' (12.7.2, 12.42.2, 12.56.2).[24] This phrase must have lived on in everyday language; the fourth-century collection of recipes that goes under the name of Apicius has the phrase *suo sibi iure* once, and *ius de suo sibi* 'juice from itself' seventeen times.[25]

The frequency with which the collocation *suus sibi* recurs in the second-century archaists Gellius and especially Apuleius has in all probability nothing to do with its survival in everyday language. Rather, they imitate archaic usages and in particular Plautine ones. Gellius uses the collocation four times.[26] Apuleius has it fifteen times, that is, more often than Plautus himself. Two examples deserve special mention:

(31)   alios vero suis sibi gladiis obtruncatos reliquere.   (Apul. *Met.* 7.13)

They decapitated others with their own swords and left them there.

(32)   cunctisque narratis deprecatur periclitanti sibi ferret auxilium, seque cum
        suo sibi asino tantisper occultaret.   (Apul. *Met.* 9.40)

When all was told, he asked him to help him, since he was in danger, and to hide him together with his ass in the meantime.

The first of these examples is interesting because *suis sibi* refers to the object, not the grammatical subject. Apuleius, like the early Latin writers, uses *suus sibi* regardless of whether Cicero would have used a reflexive or a non-reflexive form. The Apuleius passage also invokes example (1) from Terence, although here the meaning is literal, not metaphorical. The second example shows that in Apuleius *suus sibi* is not necessarily emphatic. No contrast is involved. The meaning is 'his' rather than 'his own'. Apuleius

---

[23] For the term 'inclusive' see Adams *et al.* 2005: 5. However, Petronius' freedmen speak colloquial Latin, and here we also once find the phrase *panem autopyrum de suo sibi* 'whole-meal bread on its own' (Petr. 66.2).

[24] The fourth token is *suo sibi pampino* 'with its own shoot' (Col. *Arb.* 11).

[25] Apart from these instances, *suus sibi* occurs only once in Apicius (4.3.4 *cum sua sibi tergilla* 'with its own rind').

[26] 5.10.16 *suo sibi argumento* 'with his own argument'; 12.1 (heading) *suo sibi lacte* 'with her own milk'; 16.19.12 *sua sibi omnia indumenta* 'all his costume'; 19.12.9 *vites suas sibi omnes* 'all his vines'.

used the collocation because for him it had an archaic ring, but he probably did not fully understand its meaning.²⁷

4 *SUUS* INSTEAD OF *EIUS*

The remaining question concerns other uses of *suus* instead of *eius*. In general, Latin uses the possessive pronoun *suus* whenever possessor and grammatical subject are identical. Elsewhere, it is mainly *eius* which is used. However, there are three more contexts in which both early and classical Latin use *suus* rather than *eius*. The first context consists of cases in which there is no subject, as with impersonal verbs. Here it is naturally the constituent whose semantic function comes closest to that of a subject which can govern a reflexive possessive pronoun:

(33)   eosque qui secus quam decuit vixerunt peccatorum suorum tum maxime
         paenitet.   (Cic. *Div.* 1.63)

         And those people who have lived differently from how one ought to then
         regret their mistakes most.

The impersonal *paenitet* requires the person who feels regret to be in the accusative. In the absence of a grammatical subject, this experiencer constituent comes closest to subjecthood and thus governs a reflexive possessive.²⁸

The second context is subordinate clauses which are highly dependent on their main clauses:

(34)   [*sc.* Amphitruo] eos legat, Telobois iubet sententiam ut dicant suam.
                                                                     (Pl. *Am.* 205)

         He [*sc.* Amphitruo] sends them as envoys and orders them to tell the
         Teloboians his terms.

The *ut* clause here is an object clause. Its close connection with the main clause can be seen from the fact that it follows the sequence of tenses. In

²⁷ The other tokens are: *Apol.* 6 *sua sibi urina* 'with his own urine'; *Apol.* 69 *sua sibi voce* 'with his own voice'; *Fl.* 9.17 *suis sibi manibus* 'with his own hands'; *Fl.* 16.14 *suo sibi lectulo* 'in his bed' (unemphatic); *Fl.* 18.20 *suo sibi discipulo* 'with his pupil' (unemphatic); *Fl.* 23.5 *in sua sibi copiosa domo* 'in his own wealthy house'; *Met.* 1.6 *a suis sibi parentibus* 'by her own parents'; *Met.* 1.10 *in suis sibi domibus* 'in their own houses'; *Met.* 4.32 *cum sua sibi perspicua pulchritudine* 'despite all her manifest beauty' (unemphatic); *Met.* 6.30 *cum suo sibi funiculo* 'with her own rope'; *Met.* 7.28 *suam sibi fasciam* 'her breast-band' (unemphatic); *Met.* 8.14 *in suo sibi pervolutata sanguine* 'having rolled around in her own blood'; *Met.* 9.40 *in suum sibi cubiculum* 'into his own room'.
²⁸ Traditional grammars speak of a 'logical subject'. For subject properties of experiencers see Palmer 1994: 40–4.

such cases *suus* can refer either to the subject of the clause it is in or, as here, to the subject of the main clause. It is only the context and common sense which show that the terms the Teloboians are to be told are the terms of the main clause subject, Amphitruo, and not the terms of the envoys themselves. The contrast between *suus* and *eius* comes out clearly in the following example:

(35)   videtque ipse ad paupertatem protractum esse se
            suamque filiam esse adultam virginem,
            simul eius matrem suamque uxorem mortuam.   (Pl. *Trin.* 109–11)

He sees that he himself has been reduced to poverty, that his daughter is a grown-up girl, and that at the same time her mother, his wife, has died.

Here the two instances of *suam* show the connection with the main clause subject: the first modifies the girl, who is the daughter of the subject, the second modifies the deceased woman, who was the wife of the subject. The wife was of course also the daughter's mother, but since the daughter is neither subject of the main clause nor subject of the accusative and infinitive, the connection between her and her mother is established with *eius*.

The third context in which *suus* rather than *eius* is used has to do with the original meaning of *suus*, which seems to have been 'his own' rather than just 'his'. Thus if speakers want to emphasise the close connection between two elements, they can use *suus* non-reflexively. We saw this above in example (20); the construction is best known in collocations of the type *suum cuique* 'to each his own'.[29]

The situation in the Romance languages is somewhat different. *Meus* 'my', *tuus* 'your', *noster* 'our' and *voster* 'your' survive in Italian as *mio*, *tuo*, *nostro* and *vostro*, without any real change in meaning. In the third person, however, there has been a remarkable change. Latin used to distinguish between reflexive *suus* and non-reflexive *eius*. Morphologically, *suus* is like the other possessive adjectives, but it is unmarked for number, that is, it can mean 'his/her' as well as 'their'. *Eius* is the genitive of *is* and as such it does not agree with its head noun in case, number and gender; it means

---

[29] Because of the close proximity between *suus* and *quisque* the two sometimes came to be regarded as a single element, leading to case attraction. E. Löfstedt (1956: II.114) mentions case attraction of *suus* in *suae cuique parti* (Liv. 3.22.6) for *suos cuique parti* 'to each part its own people', and attraction of *quisque* in *omnia . . . suo quoque loco* (Var. *R.* 1.22.6) for *omnia . . . suo quidque loco* 'all . . . each in its place'. In Plautus the latter type of attraction occurs twice: *suo quique* [= abl.] *loco* 'each in its place' (*Mos.* 254, *Poen.* 1178), in a phrase almost identical to the one in Varro. Some instances without attraction have interesting patterns of verb agreement: *suos quisque visunt* 'each goes to see his own' with plural verb agreement (*Epid.* 212, cf. also *Rud.* 980). With *uterque* the same occurs: *cum amica sua uterque . . . eatis* 'each of you should go with his girlfriend', with the verb in the second person plural and the noun modified by a third-person possessive.

'his/her', but not 'their', for which the genitive plural *eorum/earum* has to be used. The Romance languages have given up the distinction between reflexive and non-reflexive possessives, but have introduced a consistent differentiation between singular and plural possessors. Thus Italian uses *suo* for 'his/her', regardless of reflexivity, and *loro* for 'their', again regardless of reflexivity. In other words, in the singular the reflexive possessives have ousted the non-reflexive forms, and in the plural both reflexives and non-reflexives have been ousted by the genitive plural *illorum* 'of those' > *loro* 'their' (the latter is a very late development). *Loro* still betrays its origin in that it does not inflect like other adjectives.[30]

The usage of *suus* where the classical rules demand *eius* is claimed to be colloquial (H–S 175). If the reason is that this usage foreshadows later developments, it has to be said that linguistic innovations need not start as colloquialisms. If, on the other hand, the reason is that this usage is the result of a certain confusion of construction types, the register may well be colloquial; but then we also expect the confusion to go both ways: we should not only find *suus* instead of *eius*, but also *eius* instead of *suus* (on this type see below). What is more, such confusion ought not to be restricted to possessive *suus* and *eius*, but ought to affect forms like *se* and *eum* as well. A certain amount of confusion between *se/sibi* and *eum/ei* does indeed occur in the context of indirect speech in Plautus:

(36)   dicit capram quam dederam servandam sibi
         suai uxoris dotem ambedisse oppido.   (Pl. *Mer.* 238–9)

         He says that the she-goat I had given him to watch over had completely
         eaten up his wife's dowry.

(37)   eum fecisse aiunt sibi quod faciundum fuit.   (Pl. *Poen.* 956)

         They say he did what he had to do.

(38)   omniaque ut quidque actum est memoravit, eam sibi hunc annum con-
             ductam,
         relicuum id auri factum quod ego ei stultissimus homo promisissem.
                                                             (Pl. *Bac.* 1097–8)

         He has told me how each and everything was done; that the woman was
         hired by him for this year and that the money which I had promised
         him, complete fool that I am, was the amount still outstanding.

---

[30] The French equivalent has become more similar to adjectives because it inflects for number: *leur* (singular) versus *leurs* (plural). Wackernagel (1928: 81) points out how unusual in a Latin/Romance context the development from a noun to an adjective is; nominalisation of adjectives is much more common.

In the first sentence, the speaker uses the indicative in the relative clause to show that this is not part of the indirect speech; but the reflexive *sibi*, which refers back to the main clause subject, would only have been appropriate in indirect speech. The second sentence is similar. The old man who is the subject of the accusative and infinitive is said to have done what everybody has to do sooner or later: he died. The relative clause is in the indicative to mark that it is not part of what people say. Since the relative clause is therefore not closely connected with the accusative and infinitive, we would expect non-reflexive *ei*; but Plautus uses the reflexive *sibi* as if the relative clause were still part of what people are talking about. The third sentence shows the opposite kind of confusion. The subject of *memoravit* is a soldier who hired a prostitute; part of the money for her was paid by the speaker of the sentence, who thought he was giving it for a different purpose. The first accusative and infinitive contains *sibi*, as one might expect, because *sibi* refers back to the subject of the main clause. This is followed by a second accusative and infinitive, on an element of which the subsequent relative clause depends. The subjunctive in the relative clause makes it clear that it is still part of the indirect speech. The dative pronoun in it refers back to the main clause subject, which is why we would expect *sibi*; but Plautus uses *ei* as if the relative clause were no longer part of the indirect speech.

Does Plautus confuse possessive *suus* and *eius* in the same way? Let us begin with the latter.[31] Plautus has 131 tokens of possessive *eius*.[32] Of these, 129 follow the classical rules. Only two tokens are exceptional:

(39)   . . . si vidulum
hunc redegissem in potestatem eius, iuratust dare
mihi talentum magnum argenti.   (Pl. *Rud.* 1378–80)

He swore that if I had returned this trunk into his power, he would give me an Attic silver talent.

(40)   itan tandem hanc maiiores famam tradiderunt tibi tui,
ut virtute eorum anteperta per flagitium perderes?   (Pl. *Trin.* 642–3)

Did your ancestors really hand down this good reputation to you so you could squander in a shameful way all they had won through their excellence?

---

[31] I leave out cases where *eius* is a genitive in object function because possessive pronouns and adjectives are rare in object function (but they do exist: *meo . . . prae metu* in *Am.* 1066 means 'out of fear of me', and *erilis . . . metus* in *Am.* 1069 means 'fear of the mistress'). The decision between object function and other functions is not always straightforward: *potestatem eius* in *Per.* 602 has an objective genitive ('power over her'), but in *Rud.* 1379 the same phrase has a possessive genitive ('his power').

[32] I exclude *earum* in *Truc.* 532, which is merely a conjecture.

The first sentence contains indirect speech again. The conditional clause is part of it, as indicated by the subjunctive. However, *eius* is used as if the clause were not part of the indirect speech. The second sentence is more problematic. Final clauses are highly dependent on their main clauses and hence typically follow the sequence of tenses and have reflexive pronouns if there is reference to the main clause subject. Consecutive clauses are less dependent, need not follow the sequence rules (although they often do), and typically do not contain reflexive pronouns if there is reference to the main clause subject. The subordinator *ut* can introduce either clause type. Since in this example the *ut* clause is preceded by cataphoric *ita*, one might tend towards a consecutive interpretation, in which case *eorum* would be the appropriate pronoun. However, one can also detect final overtones in the *ut* clause: the speaker indignantly asks if the ancestors did all their work in order that the addressee could throw his inheritance away.[33]

If *eius* hardly ever encroaches on the territory of *suus*, is the opposite true? Does Plautine usage foreshadow later developments? There are 448 tokens of the possessive pronoun *suus*. Most of these conform to the classical norms outlined above, that is, they indicate a connection with the subject of the clause they are in or with the subject of the main clause if they are in a subordinate clause closely connected with it. Also in accordance with the classical norms are the cases in which *suus* marks a connection with an accusative dependent on *aequum est* 'it is fair', *decet* 'it is fitting' and *oportet* 'it is appropriate' or with a dative dependent on *honos est* 'it is honourable' and *lubido est* 'it pleases'.

But there are also several cases in which *suus* is not used reflexively. I have already mentioned that *suus sibi* need not be reflexive; Plautus uses the collocation non-reflexively in four cases. In general *suus* can be used non-reflexively if it is emphatic and means 'one's own'. This usage, which is also typical of classical Latin, always occurs when *suum* is nominalised:

(41) ne penetrarem me usquam ubi esset damni conciliabulum
      neu noctu irem obambulatum neu suum adimerem alteri
      neu tibi aegritudinem, pater, parerem, parsi sedulo. (Pl. *Trin.* 314–16)

      I have carefully avoided entering any place where one has a tête-à-tête with loss, and I have avoided roving about at night, taking away from someone else what is his, and giving you grief, my father.

Here *suum* signifies what belongs to someone else as opposed to the speaker's own possessions. The emphasis based on an implicit contrast

---

[33] For this kind of final clause see Nisbet 1923.

should be obvious. There are six more tokens of non-reflexive, nominalised, emphatic *suum* in Plautus.[34]

Just as classical and even more common are occurrences where emphatic *suus* is non-reflexive and adjectival:

(42)   nunc eam vult suae matri et patri, quibus nata est, reddere ultro.
                                                                   (Pl. *Cist.* 718)

         Now, of her own accord, she wants to return her to her own mother and father, the ones she was born to.

(43)   ... ei sunt nati filii gemini duo,
         ita forma simili pueri uti mater sua
         non internosse posset quae mammam dabat.   (Pl. *Men.* 18–20)

         Two twin sons were born to him, boys so much alike that their own wet-nurse, who was giving them her breast, could not distinguish between them.

The subject of example (42) is the foster-mother of the girl referred to with the pronoun *eam*. Now that the real parents are available, the foster-mother has lost her role and refers to the natural parents as the girl's own parents. In example (43) the emphasis on *sua* should also be self-evident: not even their own wet-nurse can tell the twins apart, so other people will find it entirely impossible. This type is rather frequent in Plautus, who has ten more tokens of it.[35] The following is similar:

(44)   DO. salvus sis, adulescens. SAG. siquidem hanc vendidero pretio suo.
                                                                   (Pl. *Per.* 579)

         DO. Good afternoon, young man. SAG. I'll have one if I sell this woman for the price she deserves.

Here *suus* is also emphatic and indicates an inherent characteristic of the woman, who is the object in the conditional clause: the price she deserves.

But whereas in all the cases above the reflexive possessive is fully expected, there are also instances where its presence is against the classical rules. Two of these involve interference from an intervening construction:

(45)   iam de istoc rogare omitte – non vides nolle eloqui? –
         ne suarum se miseriarum in memoriam inducas.   (Pl. *Per.* 642–3)

         Stop asking her about this now – can't you see that she doesn't want to tell? – so you don't remind her of her misery.

[34] *Capt.* 400, *Cur.* 180, 488, 495, *St.* 693, *Trin.* 156.
[35] *Bac.* 931, *Capt.* 91, *Mer.* 454, 973, *Poen.* 848, 1083, *Ps.* 185, *St.* 133, 200, *Trin.* 214.

(46)   illine audeant
id facere quibus ut serviant
suus amor cogit?   (Pl. *Ps.* 205b–6)

Would they dare do this to people into whose service their love presses them?

In both examples the possessive pronoun can hardly be said to be emphatic or contrastive. In the first sentence the most natural explanation for the reflexive possessive (and the reflexive object pronoun) is that the parenthetic construction led to a certain amount of confusion. The parenthesis consists of an 'accusative and infinitive' construction, albeit without an overtly expressed accusative, dependent on *non vides*. If an object were dependent on *eloqui*, this could be modified by a reflexive possessive pronoun referring back to the subject of the accusative and infinitive; for instance, Plautus could have written *non vides nolle eloqui patriam suam* 'can't you see that she doesn't want to tell you what her country is'. The following subordinate clause does of course not depend on the parenthetic expression, but it is not surprising that the choice of pronouns is influenced by it. The second sentence involves what Kühner and Stegmann (K–S II.315–19) call 'relative Verschränkung', that is, the relative pronoun is made a part of a subordinate *ut* clause, which in turn depends on *cogit* in the subordinate clause one syntactic level above it. Such a complex construction can easily lead to some inconsistencies. Here the *ut* clause has not just usurped the relative pronoun of the following, higher clause, but has also caused *suus* rather than *eius* in this second clause.

However, non-emphatic *suus* can also occur in subordinate clauses in the indicative when no confusion can explain its presence:

(47)   mater quod suasit sua | adulescens mulier fecit.   (Ter. *Hec.* 660–1)

The young woman did what her mother advised her.

(48)   quin divum atque hominum clamat continuo fidem,
de suo tigillo fumus si qua exit foras.   (Pl. *Aul.* 300–1)

What's more, he immediately implores gods and men if smoke somehow manages to escape from his roof to the outside.

The first example comes from Terence and shows the spread of *suus* to relative clauses in the indicative. We seem to be dealing with an extension of the use of *suus* from highly dependent subordinate clauses to less dependent ones. The second example is from Plautus and shows the same phenomenon in a conditional clause. This usage foreshadows Romance developments,

but it is rare; the example from Plautus is the only one of its kind. We find
the same development in Cato:

(49)   tum erit tempestiva [*sc.* materies], cum suum semen maturum erit.

(Cato *Agr.* 31. 2)

It [*sc.* the wood] will be ready when its seed is ripe.

Again the *cum* clause ought to contain *eius* according to the classical rules.
The fact that this construction also occurs in Cato, a writer whose style is
relatively neutral in his book on agriculture, should make us guard against
speaking of a colloquialism too easily.

But *suus* also occurs in main clauses when one might expect *eius*. Some
cases are easy to explain:

(50)   ei nunc alia ducendast domum, | sua cognata Lemniensis.

(Pl. *Cist.* 99–100)

Now he has to marry another girl, his relative from Lemnos.

The man referred to with the dative pronoun *ei* is not the grammatical
subject, a role which is given to his relative from Lemnos. However, the
grammatical subject has the semantic role of patient, while the dative
pronoun here expresses the agent and hence selects a reflexive possessive
pronoun. The following example is slightly different:

(51)   deinde illi actutum sufferet suus servus poenas Sosia.   (Pl. *Am.* 1002)

Then his slave Sosia will immediately pay the price to him.

The slave Sosia is the grammatical subject. This noun phrase is modified
by *suus*, which is connected with *illi* in the same clause. The semantic role
of this dative pronoun is somewhat vague. Amphitruo, whom it refers to,
is certainly the beneficiary of this punishment, but he is also the one who
administers it. Perhaps it is this agentive function which explains the direct
reflexive possessive modifying the subject.

However, we also find cases where there is an agentive subject and a
direct object in the same clause, but non-contrastive *suus* is selected by the
latter:[36]

(52)   quin voco ut me audiat nomine illam suo?   (Pl. *Rud.* 236)

Why don't I call her by her name so she can hear me?

Suus is clearly not emphatic and could be left out. Its reference is unambiguous here because the subject is a first person. We find the same constellation

---

[36] For the few occurrences of similar constellations in Cicero see K–S 1.604.

four more times; by the same constellation I mean a first- or second-person
subject in agent function followed by a direct object in the same clause
with *suus* referring to the latter.[37] Note also that the construction is not
excluded if the subject is a third person as well:

(53)   nam is illius filiam | conicit in navem miles clam matrem suam.

(Pl. *Mil.* III–12)

For this soldier puts that woman's daughter onto the ship behind her
mother's back.

This construction is ambiguous only in theory; only in theory could *matrem
suam* refer to the soldier's mother rather than the girl's, while within the
context of the narrative it is perfectly clear whose mother is being referred
to.[38]

The following case looks deceptively similar to previous ones, but here
the rationale for choosing a reflexive possessive modifying the subject may
be different:

(54)   iubet salvere suus vir uxorem suam.   (Pl. *Mer.* 713)

Her husband is greeting his wife.

The reflexive *suam* modifying *uxorem* is natural and expected, as it indicates
a connection with the grammatical subject. However, *suus* modifying this
subject and indicating a connection with the direct object is rather odd.
Perhaps the context can help to explain this oddity. The speaker is a
husband hiding away his neighbour's mistress. Now the speaker's wife is
returning unexpectedly early. He is embarrassed and tries to gloss over the
awkward situation he is in by addressing his wife in this facetious manner.
It is not inconceivable that he uses the same possessive type twice in order
to underline the close bond between himself and his wife.

Finally, there are also cases in which there is a grammatical subject and
a dative, and the reflexive possessive is governed by this dative:

(55)   mittam hodie huic suo die natali malam rem magnam et maturam.

(Pl. *Ps.* 234)

Today, on his birthday, I'll send him a big and full-grown hard time.

Again the reference of *suus* is unambiguous. It can only refer to the person
in the dative, as the subject is a first person. Equally unambiguous is the
similar constellation in *Men.* 973. In *Am.* 194 nominative and dative are
both third persons, but the context disambiguates the passage.

---

[37] The tokens are in *Aul.* 639, *Bac.* 849, *Men.* 903, *Mos.* 1171.
[38] A similar constellation, disambiguated by the context, occurs in *Rud.* 1225.

It is only now, after establishing to what extent Plautus follows the classical rules for *suus* and *eius*, that I can look at the register of those cases in which Plautus does not follow what became the norm later. It has to be said from the outset that on the whole Plautus follows the classical rules closely. *Eius* encroaches on the territory of *suus* only twice, once in the context of indirect speech and once in an *ut* clause that is neither clearly final nor clearly consecutive. *Suus* instead of *eius* occurs more frequently. In four cases we find non-reflexive *suus sibi*, which I explained in an earlier section; I doubt whether this type is colloquial. Twice *suus* occurs in indirect speech where one might expect *eius*. These two cases of confusion could be argued to be an imitation of colloquial language, just like the two cases in which *eius* is used instead of *suus*. Finally, *suus* occurs in one subordinate clause in the indicative where *eius* is expected, and nine times in main clauses referring to the object rather than the (grammatical or 'logical') subject. It is only these last ten cases which could be argued to foreshadow Romance developments, but given that there are 448 tokens of *suus* in total one would go too far if one were to say that Plautus already reflects a situation which we find in later Latin.

Let us now turn to these ten cases in more detail. The one instance of *suus* instead of *eius* in a subordinate clause occurs in a dialogue between a slave and cooks in senarii (*Aul.* 300 = example (48)). Colloquialisms are not unusual in such passages, but the fact that the same construction occurs in Cato (*Agr.* 31.2) makes me wonder whether we are not dealing with unmarked language; after all, even in dialogue colloquial elements only form one part of the whole, while most elements are simply unmarked for register. What about the remaining nine passages with *suus* in main clauses? It has been argued that high-register forms are more frequent in sung passages (Haffter 1934; Happ 1967); colloquialisms should be more frequent in senarii. While checking distribution patterns of this kind is worthwhile for certain figures of speech and morphological archaisms, it normally leads to no results for grammatical words. In our case we do not have enough tokens for statistical analyses anyway, but it should be noted that the tokens we have are distributed in a completely unremarkable way over the various verse types: two are in senarii, four in 'long verses', and three in *mutatis modis cantica*.[39] It is more interesting to see who the speakers of the nine passages are and what genres they belong to. One passage (*Bac.* 849) is a highly stylised threat uttered by a pompous soldier; another is found in the mouth of Menaechmus, a free-born man, and

---

[39] For the term cf. Don. *De com.* 8.9.

again we are dealing with a threat (*Men.* 903); yet another threat is issued
by an old man (*Mos.* 1171). Such passages are typically not informal. But
it is remarkable that the remaining six passages all belong to slaves. While
slaves are often characterised by racy colloquialisms and other low features
such as the use of Greek phrases, they also use highly elevated language
on occasion. Some of the six tokens are found in contexts where higher
register is not unusual: one is in Sosia's famous battle report (*Am.* 194),
another is in a 'good servant's speech'[40] (*Men.* 973), a third is in a delayed
prologue spoken by a slave (*Mil.* 112), and a fourth is in a threat uttered
by the clever Pseudolus (*Ps.* 234). *Rud.* 236 is in an elaborate *canticum* sung
by a slave girl who will turn out to be a free-born Athenian. Only *Aul.* 639
is in a dialogue with certain colloquial features. The conclusion must be
that *suus* instead of *eius* is probably not colloquial, despite statements to
the contrary in several grammars.

5 CONCLUSIONS

In this chapter I have examined possessive pronouns from a number of
different perspectives. As far as their position vis-à-vis their head nouns is
concerned, hyperbaton is so frequent in Plautus that it should be considered unmarked within the context of early drama; but its rarity in early
prose shows that we are dealing with Plautine *Kunstsprache*, not with a
phenomenon that is unmarked in all contexts. Pre-modifier hyperbaton
is emphatic in about half of the cases, while post-modifier hyperbaton
is rarely emphatic. Metre does have some influence on such word order
patterns, but it is limited.

The type *suus sibi* seems to be unmarked, not colloquial as earlier studies
suggest. It is remarkable that we find *suus sibi*, but not *meus mihi* or *tuus
tibi*. I have tried to explain the absence of the latter two types by proposing
a diachronic derivation of *suus sibi* different from previous ones: *suus sibi*
began with emphatic *suus* and a dative pronoun that underwent what I call
'reflexivity attraction' for want of a better term.

Occasionally Plautus uses *suus* where one might expect *eius*. In a few
instances we seem to be dealing with genuine confusion, for example in
the context of indirect speech. Here we may be dealing with a true colloquialism. Elsewhere, however, the occurrence of *suus* cannot be explained
in this way. These instances foreshadow later developments. They do not
seem to be colloquial, though, and they are still very rare.

---

[40] A discussion of this genre can be found in Fraenkel 2007: 167–9.

CHAPTER 7

Greeting and farewell expressions as evidence for colloquial language: between literary and epigraphical texts

Paolo Poccetti

I GREETING AND FAREWELL EXPRESSIONS AS INDIVIDUAL ACTS AND SOCIAL PERFORMANCE

Greetings and farewells are among the most conspicuous aspects of inter-personal interaction in many different cultures and thus are a constant subject of anthropological, ethnological and sociological interest. From a linguistic perspective such expressions belong to colloquial language in its broadest sense, as they are inextricably connected to conversation and dia-logue. Greetings and farewells are founded on a system of verbal interaction between individuals that varies according to cultural conventions, context, and the status and relationship of the interlocutors. To a much greater extent than most linguistic features, they require an interlocutor – though the interlocutor may not be actually present. Greetings and farewells also tend to come in clusters: the first interlocutor to utter one expects a reply or other reaction adequate or commensurate to it. Consequently these expressions are individual acts that belong to ritual performance governed by social conventions, meaning that speakers have a relatively limited free-dom of linguistic choice (cf. Letessier 2000).

Indeed in modern western societies a speaker greeting or taking leave of a given person in a given context has a rather restricted set of options, such as 'hello', 'hi', 'good morning', and 'goodbye'. These formulae often cannot be literally translated between languages because their meaning comes not from their lexical significance but from conventions that are strictly language-specific (cf. Cardona 1976: 205).

The essential nature of this social performance is obvious in Plautus, where the omission of greetings may give rise to explicit comment and to anger:

(1)   BA. eho, an non priu' salutas? SI. nulla est mihi salus dataria.
        BA. nam pol hinc tantundem accipies.   (Pl. *Ps.* 968–70)

BA. Oh, indeed! And no 'good-day' first, eh? SI. I have no good day spareable. BA. Then you'll find me equally generous.[1]

Anyone present at an interaction, even if he is not the addressee, may feel aggrieved at the omission of a greeting, as such omission can be interpreted as a declaration of the intention to ignore him:

(2)   LY. Charmidem socerum suom
Lysiteles salutat. CH. di dent tibi, Lysiteles, quae velis.
CA. non ego sum salutis dignus? LY. Immo salve, Callicles.

(Pl. *Trin.* 1151–3)

LY. Lysiteles, sir, greets his father-in-law Charmides. CH. God grant your every wish, Lysiteles! CA. Don't *I* deserve a greeting? LY. Yes, and you have mine, Callicles.

Languages contain a range of greeting and farewell formulae of different lengths for use in different contexts. They can range from brief one-word expressions (e.g. English 'hi', 'hello', 'bye', Latin *salve, vale*) to more detailed and complex formulae (e.g. 'Good morning! How are you?') according to the circumstances and the relationship between the interlocutors. In Latin the equivalent of 'How are you?' is most often *quid agis?*, *quid agitur?*, or *quid fit?*, and these phrases tend to follow the basic greeting formula *salve*. There are a number of examples in Plautus and Terence, where such extended greetings stimulate personal interaction and open up dialogue (cf. Gaide 2001):

(3)   salve. quid agitur?   (Pl. *Ps.* 457)

       Greetings! How's it going?   (tr. E. Dickey)

(4)   bone serve, salve. quid fit?   (Pl. *Bac.* 775)

       Ah! my good servant, how goes it?

(5)   O Syre noster, salve: quid fit? quid agitur?   (Ter. *Ad.* 883)

       O dear Syrus, greetings! What's up? How are things?

(6)   Paegnium, deliciae pueri, salve. quid agis? ut vales?   (Pl. *Per.* 204)

       Good morning, Paegnium, you little darling! What's the news? How are you?

---

[1] Translations of Plautus, unless otherwise indicated, are taken from the Loeb edition by Paul Nixon. Other translations are my own or the volume editors' unless otherwise indicated.

(7)   eugae, Demipho, | salveto. quid agis? quid fit?   (Pl. *Mer.* 283–4)

         Aha! Demipho! Good day to you! How are you! How goes it?

There are significant genre differences in the use of such phrases. In comedy they are common at the start of dialogues, but in tragedy, despite the presence of a large amount of dialogue, such greeting formulae are very rare (see Roesch 2008: 210). One can assume that in this feature, as in so many others, comedy comes closer to the conversational practices of everyday life than does tragedy.

Other literary genres provide further evidence for the use of the interrogative phrase *quid agis?* in a range of types of colloquial language. They suggest some diachronic change in its use: whereas in Plautus this phrase appears only as an accompaniment to the basic greeting *salve*, in classical Latin it may replace *salve* altogether. For example:

(8)   ibam forte via Sacra, sicut meus est mos,
         nescio quid meditans nugarum, totus in illis.
         accurrit quidam notus mihi nomine tantum,
         arreptaque manu 'quid agis, dulcissime rerum?'
         'suaviter, ut nunc est,' inquam, 'et cupio omnia quae vis.'
                                                        (Hor. *Sat.* 1.9.1–5)

         By chance I was walking on the Via Sacra as is my custom, mulling over some trifle and wholly absorbed in it, when someone known to me only by name comes running up, seizes my hand, and says, 'How are you, dearest?' 'Not bad, as things are now', I say, 'and I hope you get all you want.'

Here Horace, describing a meeting with an undesirable person, has this character use *quid agis?* as a greeting, accompanied by the vocative *dulcissime rerum* (a 'term of affection for family, lovers and friends', Dickey 2002: 322). Such a greeting produces an informal and intimate tone that contrasts sharply with the speaker's minimal acquaintance with Horace, and therefore it is presented as unsuitable and irritating in this context. The functional equivalence of *quid agis?* to English 'how are you?' is shown by Horace's reply.

The phrase *quid agis?* could be used reciprocally, as a reply to a greeting using it. Cicero highlights this usage in producing a pun involving the contrast between such usage (= English 'how are you doing?') and the phrase's literal meaning 'what are you doing?':

(9)   idem tribuno plebi potentissimo homini M. Druso, sed multa in re
       publica molienti, cum ille eum salutasset <et> ut fit dixisset: 'quid agis,
       Grani?' respondit 'immo vero tu, Druse, quid agis?'   (Cic. *Planc.* 33)

       When the tribune M. Drusus, a very powerful man but much engaged in
       political intrigue, greeted him and said, 'How are you doing, Granius?'
       he responded, 'What about you, Drusus, what are you up to?'

Pliny tells us that it was frequent in letters of familiar tone:

(10)   et hercule quousque illa vulgaria 'quid agis? ecquid commode vales?'
                                                         (Plin. *Ep.* 3.20.11)

       and by Hercules, how long shall we keep up that commonplace 'How
       are you doing? I trust you're doing well?'

Plautus suggests that the use of *quid agis?* or an equivalent was part of a
proper greeting when he has Alcumena defend herself to her husband by
saying:

(11)   ecastor equidem te certo heri advenientem ilico
       et salutavi et valuissesne usque exquisivi simul,
       mi vir, et manum prehendi et osculum tetuli tibi.   (Pl. *Am.* 714–16)

       Why mercy me, when you came home yesterday I certainly did welcome
       you the moment you appeared, and asked you in the same breath if you
       had been well all the time, and seized your hand and gave you a kiss.

And he depicts the same couple using this type of two-part greeting in
direct speech:

(12)   Amphitruo uxorem salutat laetus speratam suam ...
       valuistin usque? exspectatun advenio?   (Pl. *Am.* 676–9)

       Gladly does Amphitryon greet his darling wife ... Have you been well
       all the time? Are you glad to see me?

This two-part greeting is composed of (a) a section in which Ampitruo
greets his wife and expresses pleasure at her well-being, material that can be
conveyed by means of various expressions belonging to the lexical family
of *salus* (*salutare, salvere, salus*) in the present tense, and (b) a section in
which Amphitruo asks about her health and affairs in his absence, using
valere in the past tense.

The verb *valere* is most commonly used in fixed formulae for leave-
taking; these formulae vary by genre and by register. They include the
imperative *vale*, which appears mostly in oral contexts, and phrases such
as *cura* (or *fac* or *da operam*) *ut valeas* and *opto* (or *iubeo*) *te valere*, which

are more common at the ends of letters. In fact all these formulae occur not infrequently in letters, but Plautus allows us to see that the imperative *vale* is more characteristic of oral usage and the constructions with *cura* etc. more characteristic of letters (cf. Cugusi 1983: 57).

In some cultures, such as Twareg, the beginning of an interaction may involve an extensive dialogue in which both interlocutors inform each other in detail about their health, work, family, and so forth (Cardona 1987: 97). Generally speaking, ethnolinguistic work suggests that in less advanced, more rural societies greeting expressions are longer and less formulaic than in urbanised cultures (cf. Cardona 1987: 96). Some traces of this anthropological feature can be seen in Plautus when one interlocutor reproaches another for an inadequately detailed reply to his own solicitous inquiries:

(13)   EP. quid agis? perpetuen valuisti? TH. varie. EP. qui varie valent,
        capreaginum hominum non placet mihi neque pantherinum genus.
        TH. quid tibi vis dicam nisi quod est? EP. ut illae res? TH. probe.
        EP. quid erilis noster filius? TH. valet pugilice atque athletice.
                                                              (Pl. *Epid.* 17–20)

        EP. Well? Enjoyed good health all this time, have you? TH. Oh, check-
        ered. EP. Folks of checkered health – your goatish or your panther-like
        variety – I can't abide. TH. What do you want from me but facts? EP.
        How about the campaign? Speak up. TH. First rate. EP. And our young
        master? TH. In fighting trim, fit as an athlete.

The inquiries in this passage thus should not be considered a theatrical resource used to protract a dialogue, but as depiction, perhaps realistic depiction, of the actual practice of certain individuals (see Fraenkel 1960: 111).

Greeting formulae are often intended to establish human contact or provide a basis on which further interaction can proceed. Thus in Plautus' *Mercator* the youth Charinus and his father think over how to approach each other and start the dialogue reciprocally:

(14)   DE. quid illuc est quod solus secum fabulatur filius?
        sollicitus mihi nescioqua re videtur. CH. attatae!
        meu' pater hicquidem est quem video. ibo, adloquar. quid fit, pater?
        DE. unde incedis, quid festinas, gnate mi?   (Pl. *Mer.* 364–7)

        DE. What's the boy babbling about, all to himself? He seems worried
        over something or other. CH. Oh Lord! There he is, there's my father!
        I'll up and speak to him. How goes it, father? DE. Where do you hail
        from? Why so flustered, my lad?

2 ORAL AND WRITTEN COMMUNICATION: DISTANT AND FICTITIOUS DIALOGUES IN LETTERS AND INSCRIPTIONS

One of the chief interests of greeting formulae for the student of colloquial language is the interaction between oral and written speech in their representation. One aspect of this are the different verbs used to specify an act of salutation in oral utterances (e.g. *salutem dicere, nuntiare*) and those made in writing (e.g. *salutem scribere*). Obviously the importance of greeting expressions in both oral and written communication mean that they can be found in a variety of contexts, determined both by the rules of literary genres and by the social rules that control personal interactions. In written texts that do not attempt to imitate spoken dialogue, the greeting expressions are usually significantly different from those the same interlocutors would employ in oral conversation.

Cicero calls letters *amicorum conloquia absentium* 'a conversation with absent friends' and states that *epistulas cotidianis verbis texere solemus* 'we are accustomed to weave letters out of everyday language'.[2] Nevertheless Cicero's letters, like those of other Romans, used greeting and farewell formulae very different from those probably in use in oral conversation. There was an ancient rhetorical convention that a letter should be more elaborate than oral speech (see Cugusi 1983: 28 ff.), but when it comes to greeting formulae variation in letters is minimal. Of course, for published letters such as those of Cicero our understanding of this subject is complicated by the difficulty of determining which elements belong to the original drafting of the letter and which, if any, were added at the time of publication. Letters have numerous colloquial features but are nevertheless characterised by fixed and distinctive epistolary conventions (e.g. the 'dear' used at the start of letters in English) that clearly separate them from actual dialogue (cf., for Cicero, Garcea 2002, 2005). Letters may well convey actual dialogue, but that dialogue is not expressed precisely as it would have been had it taken place face to face.

On the other hand dramatic texts do not convey actual dialogue at all, rather fictional dialogue. The difference matters, because what is said in a play may have to do with concerns that would be irrelevant in real dialogue, such as the needs of the audience. In the case of greetings in Plautus and other dramatic texts departures from the conventions of spontaneous conversation may be caused by the practical necessities of conveying

---

[2] Cic. *Phil.* 2.7.17, *Fam.* 9.21.1 (quoted by Thomas, this volume p. 255).

information about entrances and exits and identifying the characters as they arrive.

To complicate matters further, letters and other non-dramatic texts may also represent fictional dialogue, as the addressee may be a person who will never be able to answer, or even entirely imaginary. In considering letters a distinction must be made between private letters and public ones, which were considered by ancient authors to belong to different genres (cf. Cugusi 1983: 105 ff.). A private letter is conceived of as distant dialogue, in that it expects a reply and performs an interaction across space and time. Though it may be published, such availability to the wider world is secondary. On the other hand a public letter is written for publication; its purpose is the disclosure of thought. Public letters mostly concern political or philosophical material and are often addressed to distinguished personalities (such as the letters to Caesar attributed to Sallustius or, in Greek literature, Plato's letters to Sicilian tyrants). They may convey the appearance of dialogue, but in fact no reply is expected or imagined.

Another type of fictitious dialogue, much more common among ordinary people in the Hellenistic and Roman world, is that found in sepulchral inscriptions with greetings to or from the deceased. The Romans, like other populations of ancient Italy, imitated the Greek convention of addressing the dead with greetings also used to living persons, such as Greek χαῖρε and Latin salve, (h)ave, vale. In Greek this custom is attested as far back as Homer, who depicts Achilles saying to Patroclus' corpse χαῖρέ μοι, ὦ Πάτροκλε, καὶ εἰν Ἀΐδαο δόμοισιν, 'Farewell, Patroklos, I hail you even in the House of Hades' (Il. 23.19). Greek funerary inscriptions show its widespread use among common people across the Mediterranean from around the fourth century BC onwards (Guarducci 1995: III.150).

In the Roman world, an enormous quantity of Latin inscriptions from the late Republican period onwards attests this practice of imitating oral greeting. The bilingual epitaph of a Roman citizen buried in Greece demonstrates the correspondence between Greek and Latin usage:

(15)   Q. Avili C. f. Lanuvine, salve.
        Κοίντε Ἀουίλλιε Γαίου υἱὲ Ῥωμαῖε χρηστὲ χαῖρε.
                                            (CIL I² 2259 = ILLRP 961)

    Greetings, Quintus Avilius from Lanuvium, son of Gaius.
    Greetings, excellent Roman Quintus Avillius son of Gaius.

A particularly Latin feature of this practice is the combination of two different greeting expressions:

(16)   salve, salvos seis.   (*CIL* I² 2273 = *ILLRP* 981)

         Greetings, may you be well.

(17)   have et vale.   (*CIL* VI 23685 = *CLE* 64)

         Greetings and farewell.

(18)   salve, vale.   (*CIL* I² 3146 = *ILLRP* 819)

         Greetings, farewell.

(19)   bene rem geras et valeas.   (*CIL* I² 1202 = *ILLRP* 970)

         May you prosper and be well.

This Latin feature of a double greeting is occasionally used in Greek epitaphs for Romans. From the same cemetery as example (15) we have:

(20)   Γάειε Καστρίκιε χρηστὲ χαῖρε καὶ ὑγίαινε. (Couilloud 1974: no. 492)

         Excellent Gaius Castricius, greetings and be well!

The verb ὑγίαινε 'be well' is uncommon as a greeting in classical Greek, and its appearance here as part of the compound expression χαῖρε καὶ ὑγίαινε seems to be a literal translation of a Latin model such as *salve vale*.

   Literary poetry also contains examples of this compound greeting, as Catullus' lament to his brother:

(21)   atque in perpetuam, frater, ave atque vale.   (*Catul.* 101.10)

         And forever, brother, hail and farewell!

or Virgil's depiction of Aeneas' farewell to Pallas:

(22)   salve aeternum mihi, maxime Palla, | aeternumque vale. (*Aen.* 11.97–8)

         Magnificent Pallas, forever hail and forever farewell.

Such literary instances are likely to be a reflection of common greeting expressions addressed orally to the deceased and inserted in sepulchral inscriptions.

   On a literal level, this tendency of both Greeks and Romans to use to the deceased expressions commonly employed in everyday life is paradoxical. These basic greeting expressions have lexical meanings referring to health and well-being: *salve* 'be well', *vale* 'be healthy'. So Servius in his commentary on Virgil remarks, quoting Varro, that the expressions *salve* and *vale* when addressed to the dead must not be understood in their etymological

meaning but need to be seen merely as farewell formulae pronounced by
the living to the departing dead:

(23)   Varro in libris logistoricis dicit, ideo mortuis 'salve' et 'vale' dici, non quod
        aut valere aut salvi esse possunt, sed quod ab his recedimus, eos numquam
        visuri. hinc ortum est ut etiam maledicti significationem interdum 'vale'
        obtineat, ut Terentius 'valeant qui inter nos discidium volunt', hoc est
        ita a nobis discedant, ut numquam ad nostrum revertantur aspectum.
        ergo cum mortuo dicitur 'vale', non etymologia consideranda est, sed
        consuetudo, quod nullis 'vale' dicimus nisi a quibus recedimus.
                                              (Serv. *Aen.* II.97; cf. Riese 1865: 253)

        Varro in his *Libri logistorici* says that for this reason one says 'be safe' and
        'be well' to the dead, not because they are capable of being either safe or
        well, but because we are departing from them, never again to see them.
        Hence it arose that 'be well' can have even the meaning of a curse, as
        Terence [has characters say] 'be well' when they want to get away from
        each other, meaning 'may they depart from us in such a way that they
        never return to our presence'. Therefore when one says 'be well' to a dead
        person, we should look not at the etymology, but at the usage, because
        we say 'be well' only to those from whom we depart.

This contrast between the lexical and social meanings of such expressions
may give rise to puns, especially in Plautus (see Roesch 2005: 929):

(24)   AR. vale, <vale>. PH. aliquanto amplius valerem, si hic maneres.
        AR. salve. PH. salvere me iubes, quoi tu abiens offers morbum?
                                              (Pl. *As.* 592–3)

        AR. Farewell! PH. I should fare much better if you'd stay with me.
        AR. And God bless you! PH. You ask God to bless me when you curse
        me yourself by going?

When greeting formulae are used in funerary contexts a comparison of literary documentation and epigraphic materials reveals a more complicated
picture. In address to the dead the difference between Latin terms for greeting (*salve*, (*h*)*ave*) and farewell (*vale*) is neutralised: the two are used together
to emphasise that real interaction with the deceased is no longer possible.
As is well known, this Latin distinction has no parallel in Greek, which
uses the same term (χαῖρε) for both greeting and farewell (like modern Italian *ciao* in colloquial speech). Indeed Greek χαῖρε means not only 'hello'
and 'goodbye' but also a number of other things, including 'welcome' and
'cheers!', and so can be used in place of a wide range of Latin expressions.

    The Romans' awareness of this difference is revealed in ironic depictions
of those who imitated Greek manners. An instance is a well-known passage
in Lucilius, where T. Albucius, 'who aspired to be more Greek than the

Greeks' (Adams 2003a: 353) is addressed in a mock-Greek fashion with χαῖρε and his *praenomen* (address by *praenomen* was characteristic of Greeks at an early period when they had not yet grasped the complexities of the Roman name system). Significantly Lucilius makes it clear that a greeting rather than a farewell is indicated by χαῖρε when he adds *cum ad me accedis* 'when you approach me': such specification would not be necessary from a Greek perspective:

(25)   Graecum te, Albuci, quam Romanum atque Sabinum,
        municipem Ponti, Tritani, centurionum,
        praeclarorum hominum ac primorum signiferumque,
        maluisti dici. Graece ergo praetor Athenis,
        id quod maluisti, te, cum ad me accedis, saluto:
        'chaere – inquam – Tite'. lictores, turma omnis chorusque:
        'chaere, Tite'. Hinc hostis mi Albucius, hinc inimicus.
                            (Lucil. 88–94 M. = 87–93 W. = 89–95 K. = 2.19 C.)

A Greek – not a Roman or Sabine, or a native of the town that gave birth to Pontus and Tritanus, to centurions, to first-class men, front-rank soldiers and standard-bearers – that's what you preferred to be called, Albucius. A Greek 'hello' to you, then, just as you preferred, when you come to meet me, the praetor at Athens, 'Khaire, Titus,' I say. And the band of attendants and bodyguards all go in unison: 'Khaire, Titus'. This is why Albucius is my foe and enemy.

Given the Romans' widespread bilingualism χαῖρε would have been commonly understood, and since the incident being described took place in Athens the use of Greek could have been justified by the locality. But the situation (address to a Roman official in the presence of his entourage) made such a greeting disrespectful to Albucius, as is shown by the resentment Lucilius says he bore to the speaker.

As mentioned earlier, the distinction between greeting and farewell may be neutralised in Latin sepulchral inscriptions, so that there seems to be no difference between the use of *salve* and *(h)ave* and that of *vale*. For example:

(26)   Nicanor, have, mei amantissume.   (*CIL* I² 1345 = *ILLRP* 963)

        Greetings, Nicanor, my dearest.

(27)   C. Maeci. T. Pu( ) l. salve.   (*CIL* I² 2130 + 21326 = *ILLRP* 960)[3]

        Greetings, G(aius) Maeci(us) freedman of T(itus?) Pu(blius)!

However, sometimes we find *salve* at the beginning of an epitaph and *vale* at its close, in parallel to the conversational practice. In metrical inscriptions

---

[3] Text following Aurigemma 1941.

these expressions often stand outside the verse structure (Conso 1996: 300), showing that they were considered an external framework. This practice sets metrical funerary inscriptions apart from more literary poetry such as that cited in examples (21) and (22), in which the greeting and farewell formulae are necessarily integrated into the verse structure.

3 PRAGMATIC AND METALINGUISTIC FUNCTIONS

In addition to the roles we have already examined, expressions of greeting and farewell have a metalinguistic function of marking the beginning or end of an interaction; this role applies equally to oral and to written communication. As we have seen, some sepulchral inscriptions reproduce conversational patterns by using *vale* addressed to the deceased to conclude a text. Other epitaphs contain greetings and/or farewells addressed by the deceased to the reader, and in these *vale* can be replaced by *abi* 'go away!'. This farewell literally expresses an invitation to wayfarer to continue on his way but functionally points out that the text has come to an end:

(28)   have. numquid vis? vale.   (*CIL* vi 25092.5)

         Greetings. Do you want anything further? Farewell!

(29)   hospes, quod deico paullum est, asta ac pellege . . . dixi. abei.
                                                 (*CIL* i² 1211.8 = *ILLRP* 973)

         Friend, I have only a little to say, stand here and read it . . . I have spoken.
         Depart.

In these two texts the imperatives *vale* and *abi* are functionally equivalent in the sense of conveying 'I have nothing else to tell you'. This function could also be considered a colloquial one, as farewell formulae have this function in live conversation as well.

   More common in Latin funerary inscriptions is the use of greeting and farewell formulae to engage in a sort of conversational interaction between the reader and the deceased, with a reciprocal exchange of politeness. The reader by reading the inscription receives greetings from the deceased (or sometimes the tombstone) speaking in the first person, and at the same time by pronouncing the written words aloud (as usual in ancient reading practice) he or she greets the deceased in turn:

(30)   have et vale, quae optas eveniant tibi et tuis.   (*CIL* vi 23685 = *CLE* 64)

         Hail and farewell, and may what you wish befall you and yours.

(31)   Primitiva have! et tu quisquis es vale.   (*CIL* v 1939 = *CLE* 1585)

         Hail, Primitiva! And to you, whoever you are, farewell.

(32)   bene valeas, quisquis es qui me salutas.   (*CLE* 65)

         May you fare well, whoever you are who greets me.

(33)   Gemella salve! salvete mei parentes! et tu salve quisquis es.   (*CIL* vi 6457)

         Greetings, Gemella! Greetings, my parents! And greetings to you, who-
         ever you are.

Such inscriptions form an imaginary dialogue, whose purpose was to compel the wayfarer/reader to pay some regards to the deceased in the manner
of verbal interaction between living persons.[4] This type of imaginary conversation can now be glimpsed only through epigraphic materials and is
not preserved in literary texts.

Because of their range of key functions greeting expressions are among
the first topics learned by foreign-language learners. They are also easily
borrowed between languages, and indeed Latin (*h*)*ave* may have been
borrowed from Punic – a well-integrated borrowing, obviously, and one
that did not involve any knowledge of Punic on the part of its users (Adams
2003a: 205; for similar borrowings in modern languages see E–M s.v. *ave*).
Latin (*h*)*ave* also developed meanings and functions independent of those
the term had in its original language; the origin seems to have been a verb
meaning 'to live' (Sznycer 1967: 139; Adams 2003a: 231), so the development
would presumably have occurred via an acclamation such as 'long life!' Such
evolution is paralleled in modern languages, for example colloquial French
ciao, which unlike its Italian model is used only for farewells and not for
greetings; an additional twist is that this formula originated as a formal
and respectful greeting meaning 'I am your servant' (Cortelazzo and Zolli
1979–88: s.v.) and has now become a highly colloquial usage.

In Plautus (*h*)*ave* is not common as a greeting; the standard terms are
salve and *salvus sis*. But the Punic-derived term is used to characterise Punic
contexts and characters and thus occurs repeatedly in the *Poenulus*, where
avo (not (*h*)*ave*, which is presumably a morphological adaptation of the
Punic form to the Latin greeting system) is presented as the standard way of
greeting people of Punic origin. This usage indicates both that use of (*h*)*ave*
was not yet widespread in Plautus' day and that Romans of that period were
aware of the term's Punic origins. However, we have no proof that Punic
people used *avo* or anything corresponding to it as a common greeting
form; the use of *avo* may have had more to do with Roman stereotypes
of Punic greeting behaviour than with actual Punic practice (Glück and
Maurach 1972: 116).

[4] As pointed out by Campanile (1976), though as Conso (1996: 300) stresses, it is not always easy to
identify the different parts in such dialogues.

In Plautus' dialogue between the Roman Milphio and the Carthaginian Hanno, the Roman does not give the impression of knowing much Punic beyond the greeting formula. The passage is a good example of use and translation of the greeting expression in an oral context by a person who pretends to know Punic:[5]

(34)   MI. vin appellem hunc Punice?   990
         AG. an scis? MI. nullus me est hodie Poenus Poenior.
         AG. adei atque appella quid velit, quid venerit,
         qui sit, quoiatis, unde sit: ne parseris.
         MI. avo. quoiates estis aut quo ex oppido? . . .   994
         HA. avo. MI. salutat. HA. donni. MI. doni volt tibi   998
         dare hic nescioquid. audin pollicitarier?
         AG. saluta hunc rursus Punice verbis meis.   1000
         MI. avo donnim inquit tibi verbis suis.   (Pl. *Poen.* 990–1001)

MI. Want me to speak to him in Punic? AG. You know it? MI. I? There's not a Punicker Punic living. AG. Step up and speak to him, find out what he wants, what he's come for, who he is, his origin, his city: spare no questions. MI. Avo! Where are you people from, what town? . . . HA. Avo! MI. Good-day, he says. HA. Donni. MI. A donation – he wants to give you something or other. Hear him promise? AG. Return him his good-day in Punic for me. MI. Avo donni says he to you for himself.

In fact in his reply Milphio is unable to do anything other than repeating his interlocutor's greeting and providing an approximate translation with the Latin generic term *salutare*.

From the first century BC (*h*)*ave* becomes common with a greeting function equivalent to that of *salve* and *salvus sis*. In this sense it is attested in imperial Latin as an opposite of *vale*:

(35)   subit igitur alia classis et illi quidem exclamavere 'vale Gai', hi autem 'ave,
        Gai'.   (Petr. 74.7)

        So another group came up and the first ones cried 'Gaius, farewell!',
        while the new ones said 'Gaius, hail!'

This usage is also indirectly attested in a letter from Caelius to Cicero:

(36)   simul atque 'have' mihi dixit, statim quid de te audisset exposuit
                                                  (Caelius *apud* Cic. *Fam.* 8.16.4)

        and as soon as he said 'hello' to me, he at once told me what he had
        heard about you.

---

[5] On the Punic passages in the *Poenulus* see the essays in Baier 2004.

In the Republican period (*h*)*ave* is also used as an expression of welcome to visitors, and in this function it occurs on the threshold of a famous Pompeian house (*CIL* x 872; see also Zevi 1991: 71). If this inscription is to be dated before 80 BC, it is also an instance of Roman influence on Pompeian society of the Samnite period (Poccetti 1993a: 93). Once again we see cross-linguistic influence in the use of a greeting expression, and indeed (*h*)*ave* in the sense of 'welcome' seems to have been common in Pompeii, as evidenced by a number of graffiti.[6]

4 OTHER PRAGMATIC FUNCTIONS IN DIALOGUE

Greeting expressions can allow a speaker to introduce himself to his inter-locutor and to others. Such usage is particularly likely when the speaker refers to himself in the third person, as:

(37)   PA. Palaestrio Acroteleutium salutat.   (Pl. *Mil.* 900)

         PA. Palaestrio presents his compliments to Acroteleutium.

(38)   CH. servos salutat Nicobulum Chrysalus.   (Pl. *Bac.* 243)

         CH. Greetings to Nicobulus from servant Chrysalus, sir.

(39)   GN. plurima salute Parmenonem | summum suom inpertit Gnatho.
                                                           (Ter. *Eu.* 270–1)

         GN. Gnatho presents his dear Parmeno with his very best greetings.

(40)   LY. iubet salvere suo' vir uxorem suam.   (Pl. *Mer.* 713)

         LY. Greetings from your husband to his wife, my dear!

The use of the third person entails the provision of two pieces of informa-tion, the speaker's identity and that of his interlocutor(s), and thus allows definition of the context. For this reason such third-person greetings are frequent in drama: they allow the playwright to introduce new characters and make their identities clear to characters and audience alike.

The usage is also common in the headings of letters, where it occurs both in official or formal letters and in familiar or private ones, as these examples from Cicero illustrate:

(41)   Marcus Quinto fratri s(alutem).   (*Q. fr.* 1.1)

         Marcus to his brother Quintus, greetings.

---

[6] E.g. *CIL* IV 1883, 2071, 2148, 3022, 3069; further references in *TLL* s.v. *ave* 1.55–60.

(42)   Tullius Terentiae suae s(alutem) d(icit).   (*Fam.* 14.12.1)

Tullius sends greetings to his Terentia.

(43)   M. Tullius M. f. Cicero pro cos. s(alutem) d(icit) cos. pr. tr. pl. senatui.
                                                              (*Fam.* 15.1.1)

Marcus Tullius Cicero son of Marcus, proconsul, sends greetings to the
consuls, praetors, tribunes of the plebs, and senate.

In both drama and letters considerations of practicality make the third-
person address form usable without regard to register. In ordinary face-to-
face interaction, however, such considerations would rarely have applied,
and such evidence as we have suggests that in oral interaction this type
of greeting was restricted to formal registers. One preserved example is
the customary address of the combatants to the emperor before games, as
recorded by Suetonius:

(44)   sed cum proclamantibus naumachiariis, 'have imperator, morituri te
        salutant!' respondisset, 'aut non', neque post hanc vocem quasi venia
        data quisquam dimicare uellet, diu cunctatus an omnes igni ferroque
        absumeret, tandem e sede sua prosiluit ac per ambitum lacus non sine
        foeda vacillatione discurrens partim minando partim adhortando ad pug-
        nam compulit.   (Suet. *Cl.* 21)

But when the combatants in the naval battle declared 'Hail, emperor,
those who are about to die salute you!' and he responded 'Or not about
to die', and after those words no-one wanted to fight, as if they had been
excused, he hesitated for a long time whether to destroy them all with
fire and sword, but finally he leapt from his seat and running around the
perimeter of the lake with his ridiculous wobbling gait compelled them
to fight partly by threats and partly by encouragment.

This greeting, though almost exclusively an oral utterance, was clearly
formal rather than colloquial. Indeed the sentence *have imperator, morituri
te salutant* is rhetorically constructed with a chiastic structure in which
two greeting expressions enclose the identities of the emperor and the
gladiators.

Another case of formal third-person greeting may come from an interesting fragment of a *praetexta* attributed to Naevius:[7]

(45)   Vel Veiens regem salutat Vibe Albanum Amulium
        comiter senem sapientem: contra redhostitur salus.   (Naev. *com.* 5 R.)

'Vel Vibe of Veii politely greets the wise old king Amulius of Alba.' The
greeting is returned.

---

[7] The text requires restoration: see Bettini 1982: 166, whose version is followed here.

Undoubtedly the fragment depicts a formal greeting between a Latin king of Alba and an Etruscan ruler from Veii.[8] The two monarchs' social equality is emphasised both through the central position of *regem* 'king' (Havet 1905) and through the symmetricality of the designation of their origins. The name of the Etruscan king, Vel Vibe, is authentically Etruscan: Vel is one of the most common names in extant Etruscan inscriptions (Rix 1991: 98–9), and Vibe is is also well attested.[9] This equality leads one to suppose that each greeted the other in his own language, as in modern diplomatic meetings between heads of state.

It is however unclear whether the first sentence should be taken as direct speech or as the narrator's description. In the first case, reflected in the translation given above, Vel Vibe would be introducing himself as the Etruscan king of Veii and offering a formal greeting to the king of Alba; this interpretation is supported by the consideration that the fragment comes from a dramatic context in which third-person address would be practically useful for the audience. In the second, the entire text would simply be third-person narration in the historical present, which must be the case for the second half of the second line in any case.

In some passages of Plautus one can suspect that the formality of third-person greeting is retained even in the dramatic context. This may be the case in examples (38) and (39) above, where there is a status difference between speaker and addressee. When the two are related, third-person address seems to convey respect and/or solicitude, as in examples (2), (12) and (40) above and:

(46)   Mnesilochus salutem dicit suo patri.   (Pl. *Bac.* 734)

    Mnesilochus sends best wishes to his father.

(47)   Mars peregre adveniens salutat Nerienem uxorem suam.   (Pl. *Truc.* 515)

    Mars, arriving from abroad, doth greet his spouse, his Neriene.

This usage resembles the formula used in the headings of letters, and indeed the expression in example (46) is presented as reproduction of a written message.

5 FURTHER METALINGUISTIC FUNCTIONS

There are two interrogative phrases using the same root as the basic greeting *salve*: *salven?* and *satin salve?* (or *satin salvus?*). These phrases show

---

[8] On the historical context of this story see Tandoi 1974: 271.
[9] With variations such as *Vipe, Vipi, Vipiena* and *Vipina*. The collocation Vel Vipe is also attested as a personal name of non-royal individuals (Rix 1991: Ta 1.93, Vs 1.133).

a grammaticalisation process, in that they represent clauses and mean
literally 'are you well enough?' Though not very common, these expressions are well distributed in different contexts, time periods and literary
genres with claim to contain colloquial language; such a distribution suggests that the phrases were generally present throughout the Latin language. One function they have is that of encouraging someone reticent
to talk, as in the following example where Perseus is addressed by his
father:

(48)   regiam ingressus perturbato vultu in conspectu patris tacitus procul con-
         stitit. cui cum pater 'satin salve?', et quaenam ea maestitia esset interrog-
         aret eum, 'de lucro tibi' inquit 'vivere me scito.'   (Liv. 40.8.1–2)

         He entered the palace with a distressed expression and stood in silence,
         within his father's presence but at a distance. When his father said 'Are
         you okay?' and asked him why he was sad, he replied, 'Know that you
         are lucky that I am alive.'

Similarly in the next example *salven* serves to convey concern for the
addressee; here it also echoes the preceding greeting in a stylistically marked
fashion:

(49)   salva sis. salven advenio? salven accersi iubes?
         quid tu tristis es? quid ille autem aps te iratus destitit?
                                                              (Pl. *Men.* 776–7)

         And you. Do I find all well here? Is all well, that you have me summoned?
         Why are you so gloomy? Yes, and why is he standing aloof there, angry?

Here too the phrase invites the addressee to open his heart or at least engage
in a conversation, perhaps like English 'come on':

(50)   satine salve? dic mihi.   (Pl. *Trin.* 1177)

         All right, are you? Tell me.

In other contexts *satin salve* can have a somewhat different function.
Livy reports Cincinnatus using it to the envoys from the Senate:

(51)   ibi ab legatis, seu fossam fodiens palae innixus seu cum araret, operi certe,
         id quod constat, agresti intentus, salute data in vicem redditaque rogatus
         ut, quod bene verteret ipsi reique publicae, togatus mandata senatus
         audiret, admiratus rogitansque 'satin salve?' togam propere e tugurio
         proferre uxorem Raciliam iubet.   (Liv. 3.26.9)

         He was found there by the legates, whether leaning on a spade while
         digging a ditch or when he was plowing, in any case engaged in some
         agricultural work; and when greetings had been given and returned they

asked him to put on his toga to hear the instructions of the Senate, as a good omen for himself and for the state. He, astonished and asking 'Is everything all right?' ordered his wife Racilla to bring his toga quickly from the hut.

Here the speaker is clearly not encouraging immediate explanation on the part of his visitors; the question must be a general expression of concern along the lines of 'Is something wrong?'

A related expression is *sunt vestra salva?*, as in the following example where a teacher urges students to check their own affairs; here the function must be an exhortation or a weak command:

(52)   <nos aliter> didicimus, dicebat enim magister: 'sunt vestra salva? recta domum. cave circumspicias; cave maiorem maledicas.'   (Petr. 58.13)

      We had a different sort of schooling, for the teacher used to say, 'Are all your possessions safe? Go straight home; be careful not to stop and look around you, and be careful not to speak ill of your elders.'

The parallelism between *sunt vestra salva?* and *satin salve?* is based on the fact that *salvus/-a sis* is usually a mere variation of *salve*, as in the following examples of replies in comedy:

(53)   PI. salvos sis, Mnesiloche. MN. salve.   (Pl. *Bac.* 536)

      PI. Mnesilochus! bless you! MN. Same to you.

(54)   CR. O Mysis, salve! MY. Salvo' sis, Crito.   (Ter. *An.* 802)

      CR. Hello, Mysis! MY. May you be well, Crito!

The connection between *salvus* and *salve* is also emphasised by word plays:

(55)   PE. ego sum. salve. PH. salva sum quia te esse salvom sentio.
                                                          (Pl. *Epid.* 558)

      PE. I am. God save you! PH. I am saved, now that I see you are safe.

The Sabellic languages do not appear to have had any equivalent of the verb *salvere* and therefore of the imperative *salve*; in greetings they used a phrase corresponding corresponding to *salvus sis*, as is indicated by sepulchral inscriptions containing greetings to the deceased:

(56)   statie silie. salavs s ( )   (Rix 2002: Cm 18; cf. Poccetti 1983)

      Statius Silius, greetings

(57)   αλαπονις πακϝηις οπιες. πιω-αις. εκο σαλαϝς. ϝαλε.

(Rix 2002: Lu 40)

Alponius Oppius son of Paquius [. . .], greetings! Farewell!

(58)   [sacra]crix herentatia. vára sonti. salas. vali.   (Rix 2002: MV 6)

Vara daughter of Sontius, priestess of Venus, greetings! Farewell!

(59)   [s]acracrix cibat. cerria licina. saluta salaus.   (Rix 2002: MV 7)

Here lies Licina Saluta priestess of Ceres. Greetings!

The expression *salas, salaus* began as a masculine singular but became morphologically invariable, so that in examples (58) and (59) it is used for women. Examples (57) and (58) also use what appears to be the Latin *vale* (ϝαλε), showing a very close parallel with Latin sepulchral inscriptions and raising the possibility of direct influence from Roman epigraphic practice (Campanile 1976). The possibility of such influence need not, however, cause us to conclude that Sabellic languages did not have their own analogous greeting expressions. An indirect clue to their existence is provided by the worship of the divinities *Salus* and *Valetudo* in the Sabellic-speaking areas (Letta 1996: 337); such divinities points to the existence of these lexical items in a broader sense. All this points to close similarities between Latin and Sabellic greeting practices, something that would have facilitated communication between the communities.

The farewell formula *vale*, when used in curses, may have the meaning 'go to hell!' For example:

(60)   valeant | qui inter nos discidium volunt: hanc nisi mors mi adimet
        nemo.   (Ter. *An.* 696–7)

        Those who want us to be separated can go to hell! No-one except death
        shall take this woman away from me.

Ancient commentators drew attention to this usage, as Servius quoted in example (23) above.

There are also phrases that indicate a refusal of greetings. The shortest of these, *sat salutis*, appears to be fairly rude:

(61)   ARG. mater, salve. ART. sat salutis.   (Pl. *As.* 911)

        ARG. How do you do, mother? ART. Enough of your how d'ye do-ing!

(62)   AS. salve. TR. sat mihi est tuae salutis. nil moror. non salveo.

(Pl. *Truc.* 259)

AS. I hope you're in good health, sir. TR. Got enough of your good
healths. No use for 'em. Ain't I good-healthy?

Longer expressions seem to be less rude (see also example (1) above):

(63)   LA. salve. PL. salutem nil moror.   (Pl. *Rud.* 852)

LA. Good morning. PL. Don't you good-morning me!

6 GREETING EXPRESSIONS AS A SOURCE OF DELOCUTIVE VERBS

In a number of languages greeting expressions give rise to new words
describing the act of using them and having meanings like 'say hello', 'say
goodbye', and so on. Two Latin verbs, *salutare* and *salvere*, belong to this
category; indeed the term 'delocutive' was invented by Benveniste primarily
to describe these verbs.[10] Delocutives are verbs derived from a phraseology
directly linked with a speech act; thus *salutare* comes not simply from *salus*
or *salvus*, but from *dicere 'salutem'*, while *salvere* comes from *dicere 'salve'*.

Different languages form different delocutive verbs in the semantic field
of greetings. For instance English 'to welcome' is a delocutive verb derived
from 'welcome!', but in French there is no equivalent delocutive verb
*bienvenir from *bienvenu!* Similarly English has not formed the verbs '*to
hello' or '*to goodbye'. In late Greek the verb χαιρετίζω is attested with
the meaning 'to say χαῖρε', that is in delocutive function, in parallel to
εὐδαιμονίζω, μακαρίζω, σκορακίζω which mean 'to say ὦ εὔδαιμον, ὦ
μακάριε, εἰς κόρακας' (Perpillou 1996: 76 ff.).

In Latin there are three delocutive verbs connected with greetings:
salutare, *salvere* and *valedicere*. The greeting *(h)ave* did not produce a
delocutive, even though its morphological paradigm was modelled on *salve*
owing to its similar function.[11] The verb *salutare* is used both to make greetings and to describe the process of greeting; both functions are attested from
Plautus. We have seen (examples (37), (38), (44), (45), (46), (47) above) the
third-person use of *salutare* in greetings, and it is also so used in the first
person singular and plural:

---

[10] Benveniste 1958. See also J. Knobloch 1961– s.v. *délocutif.* The classification of *salutare* as delocutive
has been rejected by Mignot 1981, but without convincing arguments.

[11] See above and Mignot 1969: 140, who wrongly attributes the morphological adaptation to the
'tendence qui pousse à ranger les verbes de salutation dans la 2e conjugaison'.

(64)   mi homo et mea mulier, vos saluto.   (Pl. *Cist.* 723)

Good day to you, my dear sir, and to you, ma'am.

(65)   etiam nunc saluto te, <Lar> familiaris, priu' quam eo.   (Pl. *Mil.* 1339)

And now once more, God of this household, I salute thee before I go!

(66)   iterum te saluto.   (Pl. *Rud.* 1055)

Good morning to you again, sir!

(67)   Aetoli cives te salutamus, Lyce.   (Pl. *Poen.* 621)

We citizens of Aetolia bid you good morning, Lycus.

The descriptive use is also attested in the first person:

(68)   forte aspicio militem.
        adgredior hominem, saluto adveniens. 'salve' inquit mihi,
        prendit dexteram, seducit, rogat quid veniam Cariam;
        dico me illo advenisse animi causa.   (Pl. *Cur.* 337–40)

It so happens I see a military man. Up I step and say good day to him.
'Good day to you', says he, and seizes my hand, takes me aside, and asks
what I have come to Caria for. 'A pleasure trip', says I.

(69)   erum saluto primum, ut aequomst; postea
        siquid superfit, vicinos inpertio.   (Pl. *Ps.* 455–6)

Greetings to my master first, as is proper; then, if there are any left, I let
the neighbours have some.

The formal, respectful tone that attaches to this verb when used as part of
a greeting in the third person (see above) can also apply in the first person:

(70)   saluto te, vicine Apollo, qui aedibus
        propinquos nostris accolis, veneroque te   (Pl. *Bac.* 172–3)

Thee I greet, neighbour Apollo, who dost dwell adjacent to our house,
and I do implore thee . . .

The delocutive *salvere* has a narrower range of uses. This verb has delocutive function only in certain phrases, such as *iubeo* (*te*) *salvere*, literally 'I
order (you) to be well', which expresses a weak causativity and considerable
politeness and means something along the lines of 'I pay (you) my warmest
regards' (Fruyt and Orlandini 2008). Thus:

(71)   salvere Hegionem plurumum | iubeo.   (Ter. *Ad.* 460–1)

I pray Hegio to be very well.

The delocutive sense can also be used in requests to pass on greetings to a third party, as frequently at the ends of letters:

(72)   Dionysium iube salvere.   (Cic. *Att.* 4.14.2)

         Greetings to Dionysius.

(73)   salvebis a meo Cicerone.   (Cic. *Att.* 6.2.10)

         Greetings from my son Cicero.

The last of the three, *valedicere*, is not common and occurs only in descriptive function:

(74)   reges Parthorum non potest quisquam salutare sine munere: tibi
         valedicere non licet gratis.   (Sen. *Ep.* 17.11)

         No-one may greet the Parthian kings without a gift; I may not say farewell
         to you for free.

(75)   quo tempore tibi . . . valedixi   (Sulp. Sev. *Dial.* 1.3.1)

         when I bade you farewell.

The different uses of these three verbs explain why only *salutare* has survived into Romance (Italian *salutare*, French *saluer*).

7 INTERACTION BETWEEN SOCIAL CONVENTION AND PERSONAL CHOICE IN DIALOGUE

Greetings require replies. Just as Plautus depicts characters complaining about omitted greetings (examples (1) and (2) above), he also depicts complaints about omitted replies to greetings:

(76)   CH. quin tu salutem primum reddis quam dedi? | NI. salve.
                                                              (Pl. *Bac.* 245–6)

         CH. Why don't you return my greeting first, sir? NI. How d'ye do.

An adequate reply needs to correspond to the original greeting, as emphasised here:

(77)   PE. salva sies. PH. salutem accipio mihi et meis. PE. quid ceterum?
         PH. salvos sis: quod credidisti reddo.   (Pl. *Epid.* 548–9)

         PE. Good day to you. PH. I accept your good wishes for me and mine,
         sir. PE. What else? PH. Good day to you – I repay your loan.

This utterance insists on two terms identifying a greeting exchange: *credere* 'give, commit' and *reddere* 'give back, return'. This use of *reddere* is well paralleled elsewhere; in addition to example (51) above, note:

(78)   salute accepta redditaque   (Liv. 7.5.4)

     when greetings had been given and returned.

The verb *accipere*, which here occurs with *reddere*, may also replace it, indicating that acceptance of a greeting is shown by an adequate reply:

(79)   dicta acceptaque salute   (Ov. *Met.* 14.11, 271)

     when greetings had been given and accepted.

8 PATTERNS OF SYMMETRY AND RECIPROCITY IN REPLIES

The need for symmetry and reciprocity in Roman greetings[12] could be met in a variety of ways. One was a simple repetition of the same words in the same order, as:

(80)   PE. salva sies... | PH. salvos sis.   (Pl. *Epid.* 548–9)

     PE. Good day to you... PH. Good day to you.

Another was the return of the same greeting formula but with the order of its elements inverted, either symmetrically (ABBA) as in these examples:

(81)   CH. O Pistoclere, salve. PI. salve, Chrysale.   (Pl. *Bac.* 183)

     CH. What ho, sir! How are you? PI. And yourself, Chrysalus?

(82)   LE. O pater, pater mi, salve. CH. salve multum, gnate mi.

                                           (Pl. *Trin.* 1180)

     LE. Oh father, father dear, God bless you! CH. And you, my dear boy, and you!

or with slight variation:

(83)   mi frater, salve! – o soror, salve, mea.   (Pompon. *com.* 49 R.)

     'Greetings, my brother!' 'Greetings, my sister!'

A third possibility was the use of terms different from but still closely related to those of the original greeting, as for example *salve* versus *salveto* or *salvus sis*:

---

[12] This is not, of course, a feature specific to the Romans but is common in many cultures; see Braun 1988: 303.

(84)   AC. salve, architecte. PA. salva sis.   (Pl. *Mil.* 902)

AC. Good day, master builder. PA. And good day to you.

(85)   AM. salve, adulescens. SC. Et tu multum salveto, adulescentula.

(Pl. *Rud.* 416)

AM. Good morning, sir. SC. And a very good one to yourself, my little lady.

(86)   PL. pater salveto, amboque adeo. DA. salvo' sis.   (Pl. *Rud.* 103)

PL. Good day to you, father – to both of you, in fact. DA. And to yourself.

(87)   TR. salvere iubeo te, Misargyrides, bene. | DA. salve et tu.

(Pl. *Most.* 568–9)

TR. A very good day to you, Misargyrides. DA. Good day!

It is also possible to respond to a greeting in Latin without repeating the actual words involved. One way to do that is to use an entirely different greeting formula, as:

(88)   AG. salvos sis, leno. LY. di te ament, Agorastocles.   (Pl. *Poen.* 751)

AG. Good day, pimp. LY. God bless you, Agorastocles.

(89)   TR. di te ament plurimum, Simo.
         SI. salvos sis, Tranio. TR. ut vales? SI. non male.
         quid agis?   (Pl. *Most.* 717–19)

TR. God bless you, Simo, bless you bountifully! SI. A good day to you, Tranio! TR. How are you, sir? SI. Not bad. What about you?

Another is to produce an expression that leaves the words of the original greeting understood, as:

(90)   DI. salva sis. AS. et tu.   (Pl. *Truc.* 123)

DI. Greetings! AS. And to you.

(91)   TR. iterum te saluto. DA. et ego te.   (Pl. *Rud.* 1055)

TR. Good morning to you again, sir! DA. The same to you.

This *et tu* greeting response is also attested in funerary inscriptions, as in examples (31) and (33) above and:

(92)   ave! et tu!   (*CIL* x 2752; see also Campanile 1976)

        'Hail!' 'And to you!'

A literary documentation of this epigraphic usage is provided by Petronius, who has Trimalchio request an epitaph that concludes:

(93)   vale. – et tu.   (Petr. 71.12)

        'Farewell.' 'And to you.'

It is paralleled in Greek: χαῖρε – καὶ σύ (Guarducci 1995: III.527).

9 TWO FORMULAE IN DIACHRONIC AND
SYNCHRONIC PERSPECTIVE

The most basic greeting formulae, the imperatives of *salvere* (*salve*, *salvete*, *salveto*) clearly antedate our earliest literary texts by a considerable margin. They can be identified in archaic Latin and Faliscan inscriptions dated from the seventh to the fifth century BC. Example (94) comes from a Faliscan inscription of the seventh century BC that depicts an exchange of courtesies during a banquet:

(94)   salvete sociai ofetioskaiosvelosamanos salveto salves seite iofete menenes.[13]

Though not entirely straightforward in interpretation, this text clearly contains several different forms of *salvere*: the present imperative (imperative I) *salvete* addressed to a group of women (*sociai*), the future imperative (imperative II) *salveto*, and the collocation *salves seite* (probably corresponding to Latin *salvi sitis*). The last two seem to be addressed to the same people and thus constitute a repeated greeting; it is presumably the reply from the women who received the original greeting.

Another epigraphic documentation of the *salveto* form comes from a pot of *c.* 630–620 BC:

(95)   salvetod tita[14]

        Greetings, Tita!

[13] Vetter 1953: no. 243. A revised edition with a commentary of this complicated text is provided by Prosdocimi 1990. The text quoted here refers to the parts generally accepted, which are relevant to our matter.
[14] Published by Colonna 1980; see also Hartmann 2005: 35.

The parallel of Greek χαῖρε, which on account of its use in toasts was sometimes written on drinking vessels in collocations such as χαῖρε καὶ πίε,[15] suggests that example (95) was inscribed on the pot with similar motives.

This future imperative (imperative II) form is probably not a mere variant of the present imperative *salve*. In general such imperative forms are typical of legal texts (especially laws and wills) and other directive expressions containing 'rules of conduct' (Risselada 1993: 128). Because this type of imperative neutralises the distinction between second and third person, it may be a kind of subjectless or impersonal form (Rosén 1999: 115). Future imperatives also occur in conversational texts and there have a different use, designating orders out of the control of the speaker (Risselada 1993: 122 ff.; Rosén 1999: 114 ff.) and thus coming close to being an expression of wishing. This is clearly the use of the greeting *salveto*: the speaker has no power over the addressee's health or well-being, and thus the expression is essentially a wish rather than an order.

The use of the future imperative *salveto* in greetings is clearly not an artificial invention of Plautus: it long predated him and belongs not only to Latin but also to at least one other Italic language. Likewise the juxtaposition of present and future imperatives in greetings, seen in Plautus in examples (85) and (86) above, belongs to archaic Faliscan as well as Latin and therefore must be a feature of actual conversational language rather than Plautus' invention.

There is some evidence in Plautus for a usage of *salveto* different from that of *salve*. The future imperative is more common as the reply to a greeting than as the initial element (cf. example (85) above), but it can also be used to initiate greetings, as in example (86) above and:

(96)   adgrediar. O bone vir, | salveto, et tu, bona liberta.   (Pl. *Per.* 788–9)

        I'll up to them! Aha, my good sir, greetings! And to you, my good freedwoman!

A particularly interesting use of the form is:

(97)   tu erus es: tu servom quaere. tu salveto: tu vale.   (Pl. *Men.* 1076)

        It's you who are my master. You, seek another slave! Good day to you, sir.

As Havet (1898: 287) notes, here '*salveto* n'est pas un bonjour ordinaire'. With this greeting the slave Messenio recognises his new master, and with

---

[15] References in Colonna 1980; further documentation in Guarducci 1995: III.491 ff.

the *vale* that follows it he abandons the person he previously considered his master. It is notable that the future imperative is the form chosen for this particularly loaded greeting.

Another greeting worthy of more detailed examination is *iubeo* (*te*) *salvere* (and variants), which can replace *salve*. Normally *iubeo* designates a strong order, but in this type of expression it is clearly much weaker, and the first-person form is performative: *iubeo te salvere* is a description of the action of saying *salve*. This expression seems to indicate solicitude or a delicate tone, as it tends to be accompanied by further politeness expressions:

(98)   iubeo te salvere et salvos quom advenis, Theopropides,
        peregre gaudeo.   (Pl. *Mos.* 1128–9)

        Well, well, sir! And it's glad I am to see you well, on your return,
        Theopropides!

(99)   iubeo te salvere voce summa, quoad vires valent.   (Pl. *As.* 297)

        Good day to you – as loud a one as my lungs allow!

This sense is also found in third-person usage, as in example (40) above.

When this expression is used in the imperative (*iube… salvere*), it constitutes a request to pass on greetings, as in example (72) above. This usage may also be attested in the Faliscan inscription quoted as example (94): Rix (1993: 86) suggests that (*i*)*ofeteqe menes*(*i*) might correspond to Latin *manere iubete* and be an invitation to someone to remain.

This important Faliscan document therefore demonstrates that a number of Plautine greeting and politeness formulae date back to a very early period and were shared by other Italic languages. Such information is significant for our understanding of the communication between Latin speakers and other populations in archaic Italy.

CHAPTER 8

Colloquial and literary language in early Roman tragedy

Hilla Halla-aho and Peter Kruschwitz

I INTRODUCTION

Roman tragedy has not received the same amount of careful examination as Greek tragedy – not even the tragic œuvre of Seneca and those few other tragedies that happened to survive in full.[1] Partly the fragmentary nature of the textual corpus is to blame, but also, and this is perhaps even more important, the fact that Roman tragedy never managed to leave behind its smell of being secondary, of being derivative, and of being inferior to the Greek models. Nevertheless, some aspects of Roman tragedy, even early Roman tragedy, are reasonably well understood.

Performances of literary and subliterary tragic plays were an integral part of Roman dramatic festivals and were very much appreciated by all strata of Roman society.[2] Leading Roman intellectuals felt that Roman tragedians and tragedies were roughly equal to their Greek counterparts (or even better still).[3] And, in fact, one of the most important reasons why Romans felt so strongly about their tragedies and tragedians was the art and nature of the tragic language.[4]

From a linguist's point of view, the language of Roman tragedy (and, in more general terms, of Roman drama) is a fascinating, artistic and artificial construction – but it could nevertheless have included colloquial features;

---

[1] This is not to say that Roman tragedy has been neglected; indeed over the past fifteen years there has been a significant increase in work on the subject, most notably by Lennartz 1994, Dangel 1995, Schierl 2006, Boyle 2006, Baldarelli 2004, Scafoglio 2006, Erasmo 2004, Manuwald 2000, 2001, 2003, and Faller and Manuwald 2002.

[2] Lennartz 2003: 98–100 with references. Modern scholars have thought that tragedy in particular provided social cohesion and raised an awareness of social, political and ethical state norms, see e.g. Gruen 1992: 183 ff. as well as many articles in Manuwald 2000 and Peglau 2000.

[3] Cf. e.g. Cic. *De orat.* 3.27, *Fin.* 1.5 (*mihi quidem nulli satis eruditi videntur quibus nostra ignota sunt*), *Ac.* 1.10 (*non verba sed vim*). For Cicero and the early Latin poets see Zillinger 1911 and Shackleton Bailey 1983, esp. 243–4. See also Quint. *Inst.* 10.1.97 and Gel. 6.14.5.

[4] For recent work on Roman tragic language see Lennartz 1995–6, 2003; Peglau 2000; and Bagordo 2002.

the principal aim of this paper is to determine whether it did, but we shall also examine the nature of tragic language in a broader sense.

2 THE MATERIAL

Before this research question can be dealt with in a meaningful way, it is important to remind oneself how fragmented, heterogeneous and problematic the material of this study is, and what the material's specific peculiarities and implications are.

First of all, Roman Republican tragedies are literary plays. Over the last twenty or thirty years, scholars have taken great pains in pointing out the 'orality' of early Roman drama in general, usually overstating it. From a linguistic point of view we are in all cases dealing with written texts, not oral utterances; and this by definition means we are dealing with stylised forms of language, and in this case of literary language (as opposed to the language of non-literary texts such as inscriptions, papyri, and so on).[5] Moreover, as early Roman tragedy was written in verse, we will deal with a manifestation of stylised language which to a certain degree must be biased by formal requirements for the author, namely the need to create and to maintain a certain rhythmical flow (cf. e.g. Nowottny 1965: 99 ff.). And, furthermore, an aspect that is often forgotten: much of what Republican actors uttered on the stage, they sang, and this will certainly have had an impact on the language used in those portions of the play.[6]

The second aspect that needs to be mentioned is the transmission of the texts, both in a technical sense (in secondary tradition as quotations in other writers' works) and in the sense of completeness (they are highly fragmentary). It is far too simplistic to see Livius Andronicus as the *primus inventor* of Roman tragedy, Naevius as his successor, Ennius as the model for a relatively sober style, and then Pacuvius and Accius as those who finally paved the way for the highly elaborated dramatic manner and language of Roman (and, consequently, European) tragedy, until tragic production more or less came to a standstill in the first century BC. Even though scholars seem to be willing to attribute most of the *adespota* to the better-known

---

[5] Moreover, the texts have a pragmatic perspective completely different from that of any type of oral utterance, an aspect that only can be touched in passing here; for general reference cf. Hannappel and Melenk 1984.

[6] Jocelyn 1972: 1002 (cited below in section 3.2) and Jocelyn 1969: 40–1. The difference in stylistic level between spoken and sung parts is very pronounced in Plautus, and less so in Terence. A similar development seems to have occurred in tragedy as well, although we have less evidence; Ennius seems to make a clearer distinction than Accius.

playwrights (without any real justification),[7] there is scattered evidence for a much broader tradition already at an early stage. The *carmen Nelei*, for example, according to Charisius (*GL* 1.84 = 106 Barwick) of the same date as Livius Andronicus' *Odusia*, has often been seen as a tragic rather than an epic composition (even though there is insufficient evidence for a conclusion either way).[8]

In addition one needs to be aware of the differentiation between Latin tragedy in Greek costume (*crepidata* et al.) and in Roman costume (*praetexta*), even though these terms were mostly introduced in a post-creative period (see Beare 1964: 264–6). It has been argued that these genres showed considerable differences in language and style, even though there is no such distinction between plays with mythical and those with historical themes in Greek tragedy.[9]

Another question is: how representative is the material which has survived the highly selective process of secondary transmission? There is no straightforward answer to this question. However, certain factors causing bias in the transmission process as a whole can be pinned down, and these may indeed have had a direct influence on the linguistic quality of the material: apart from authors such as Cicero and Gellius, who have a genuine interest in the playwrights and their art, fragments are usually preserved in grammarians and lexicographers – and here it is usually the odd, rare, or intriguing phrase or word that caught the later author's interest (cf. Clackson and Horrocks 2007: 174). This issue does not affect the question of how representative the material is in terms of its quality, but it clearly affects the amount of preserved evidence for certain phenomena.

A final issue is the tragedians' position in Roman literary history; interestingly enough, modern scholars are far from being consistent in their approach to this aspect. Whereas the very category of 'early Roman tragedy' does not leave any doubt that one is looking at the outset of the genre in Roman literature, some scholars seem to believe that even as late as the time of Pacuvius or Accius there was still no proper Latin poetic language,[10] others, however, more plausibly hold that especially Pacuvius and Accius already were harvesting what earlier tragic playwrights, ever

---

[7] See e.g. Lennartz 2003: 83–4 with n. 1.   [8] Cf. Suerbaum 2002: 285–6.
[9] For a recent comprehensive study of this genre see Manuwald 2001.
[10] See e.g. Schierl 2006: 30: 'Pacuvius' Wortungetüme sind ein Extremfall, aber letztlich repräsentativ für eine Zeit, in der sich durch Übersetzungen griechischer Vorlagen die lateinische Literatursprache auszuformen und zu etablieren begann. Erst im Rahmen dieses Prozesses zeigten sich die Grenzen.'

since Livius Andronicus, had grown.[11] And by the beginning of the second century BC at the latest there seems to have been a clear distinction between tragic, comic and epic language features.[12]

3 TOWARDS A DESCRIPTION OF THE LANGUAGE OF EARLY ROMAN TRAGEDY

What was 'the' language of early Roman tragedy?[13]

3.1 Ancient views

The fragmentary state of early Roman tragedy adds to the general need to pay attention to the question of how Roman writers and intellectuals themselves felt about the language of this particular genre. There are a number of relevant sources, but it is not always easy to determine what is said about the actual language, and what is said with respect to a tragic performance. What the archaic tragic poets themselves thought about their language is virtually unknown, though one might assume that especially Accius in his didactic poems would have said something about this on a theoretical level. The satirist Lucilius has been (ab)used to prove that even at an early stage the pomposity of tragic language was criticised, but many of Lucilius' statements are either obscure or inconclusive when the actual evidence is more closely examined.

---

[11] Lennartz (2003: 85) points out that the earliest poets made choices that the later ones use as petrified elements of tragic language. Erasmo (2004: 31 ff.) sees Livius Andronicus, Naevius and Ennius as creators, and wishes to see Pacuvius and Accius 'theatricalizing tragedy'. Jocelyn (1972: 1002) shows that Ennius 'used the metrical patterns and the kind of language which Livius Andronicus fixed in broad outline and others developed. What contributions he made himself we cannot ourselves see, the remains of his own scripts and those of most of his predecessors being so scanty. A hundred years later men who affected powers of discernment found the tragic scripts of Livius hardly worth reading but those of Ennius delightful because of their relatively simple verbal style, a style which contrasted with the ornate and artificial one developed by Pacuvius.'

[12] Cf. e.g. Jocelyn 1969: 31–40. The difference between Latin tragic and comic language, even though never as sharp as that between the different genres of Attic drama, nevertheless existed from the very beginning (Jocelyn 1969: 39; also useful is Blänsdorf 2000 on the influence and contribution of Livius Andronicus). Lennartz (1995–6: 168–9) maintains that when Livius Andronicus started his work, he had, in addition to his Greek epic and tragic models, native pre-literary traditions to make use of, and that the register distinction observable already in earliest epic and tragedy is traceable to those traditions (Saturnians in epic and iambotrochaic in drama).

[13] Often in linguistic research on the textual remains of the ancient world the fact that one is dealing with a certain textual corpus of fragmentary nature leads towards the assumption that these fragments form an entity; one must however bear in mind that what we have got is a very heterogeneous collection of bits and pieces from a plethora of authors who merely have in common that they wrote texts of the same literary genre. For a similar observation on a different textual corpus see Kruschwitz and Halla-aho 2007: 32–4.

Perhaps the best-known feature of the language of early Roman tragedy[14] is a fancy for compound nouns: *sesquipedalia verba*, as Horace puts it (see p. 133 below for this passage), words of a foot and a half's length (foot refers to the measurement, not to the technical term of metre).[15] When discussing tragic language in more detail, most sources use imagery of height/position (*sublimis* 'elevated'), size (*grandis* 'grand'), capacity (*tumor*, *tumidus* 'swollen'),[16] or impact (*fortis*, *vehemens* 'powerful', 'vehement').[17] It is clear that these qualities, even if characteristic of the tragic register, are not exclusive to it:[18] other genres can show similar features (due to this sometimes turning 'tragic' in flavour), and tragedy consists by no means exclusively of passages with those qualities. There is in fact considerable variation in tragic language.

Indeed two passages from Cicero's *Orator* seem to imply that there are colloquial elements in tragic language. In the first passage Cicero discusses the general difficulty of defining 'the best' in language, as this is pre-eminently a matter of taste:

sed in omni re difficillimum est formam, qui χαρακτήρ Graece dicitur, exponere optimi, quod aliud aliis videtur optimum. Ennio delector, ait quispiam, quod non discedit a communi more verborum; Pacuvio inquit alius: omnes apud hunc ornati elaboratique sunt versus, multo apud alterum neglegentius; fac alium Accio; varia enim sunt iudicia, ut in Graecis, nec facilis explicatio quae forma maxime excellat. (Cic. *Orat.* 36)

---

[14] This is the common view. One might wonder, however, if it really is restricted to tragedy: is Plautus' obsession with endless made-up, Greek-sounding names so different?

[15] Especially Pacuvius, and in particular his infamous line *Nerei repandirostrum incurvicervicum pecus* ('Nereus' upturnsnouted and roundcrooknecked flock', i.e. dolphins!), have faced ancient criticism, see Quint. *Inst.* 1.5.67 (*dure videtur struxisse Pacuvius* 'Pacuvius however seems to have made some very awkward compounds') and 1.5.70 (*vix a risu defendimus* 'can hardly protect... from ridicule' (all trans. D. A. Russell)). Quintilian sees compound nouns of this type as a feature of the Greek language, not of Latin, and this is what his criticism is aiming at; Lucil. 211 K. (= 212 M. = 235 W. = 5.21 C.) might aim at the same thing (as many scholars have suggested, see e.g. most recently Manuwald 2003: 120–2 or Schierl 2006: 30 and 493), but is hard to evaluate, as no context whatsoever has been transmitted. (There is, however, scattered evidence that Lucilius criticised aspects of tragic diction, see Lucil. 605–6 ff. K. = 597–8 M. = 729–30 W. = 26.19 C.) For a more general treatment of such coinages of words cf. Lennartz 1995–6.

[16] Cf. e.g. Euanth. *De fab.* 3.5, Donatus on Ter. *An. praef.* 1.5, *Ad.* 638, 789.

[17] Cf. e.g. Mart. 8.18.8 *cum posset tragico fortius ore loqui*. Should Boethius *Consolatio* 2.2.12 *tragoediarum clamor* be seen in a similar context? (At any rate, Boethius' evidence, even though referring to a *praetexta* of Pacuvius, is so late and unclear that it is very hard to tell whether this is actually a judgement regarding the quality of the text, or – perhaps more likely – a remark on the way plays were produced in the time of Boethius; Manuwald 2001: 194–5 is unhelpful.)

[18] Gel. 6.14.1–6, for example, makes it very clear that *sufflatum atque tumidum* are perversions of the grand style (*ubertas*), a style that is characterised by *dignitas* and *amplitudo*. And interestingly enough, the tragedian Pacuvius is mentioned as a model of *ubertas* in the very same section (whereas Terence is mentioned as example of the middle style and Lucilius is listed as model for the plain style). Cf. also Leo 1913: 230 (with n. 2–4) and Martin 1974: 335.

It is always difficult to describe the 'form' or 'pattern' of the 'best' (for which the Greek word is χαρακτήρ), because different people have different notions of what is best. 'I like Ennius,' says one, 'because his diction does not depart from common usage.' 'I like Pacuvius,' says another, 'for all his lines are embellished and carefully elaborated; in Ennius there is much careless work.' Suppose that another likes Accius. There is a difference of opinion, as there is in the case of Greek authors, and it is not easy to explain which type is the most excellent. (trans. H. M. Hubbell)

The second passage that is of interest here deals with a similar aspect, namely the need for variation of style and tone in speeches, and Cicero once again gives a poetic parallel:

an ego Homero, Ennio, reliquis poetis et maxime tragicis concederem ut ne omnibus locis eadem contentione uterentur crebroque mutarent, non numquam etiam ad cotidianum genus sermonis accederent: ipse numquam ab illa acerrima contentione discederem? sed quid poetas divino ingenio profero? histriones eos vidimus quibus nihil posset in suo genere esse praestantius, qui non solum in dissimillimis personis satis faciebant, cum tamen in suis versarentur, sed et comoedum in tragoediis et tragoedum in comoediis admodum placere vidimus: ego non elaborem? (Cic. *Orat.* 109)

Am I to yield to Homer, Ennius and all the other poets, and more especially the tragic poets, the privilege of not employing in all passages alike the same impassioned style but of changing their tone frequently, even of passing over at times to the language of everyday life, while I myself am never to depart from that most vehement and impassioned manner? But why do I cite poets of divine genius? We have seen actors whose superiors in their own class cannot be found, who not only gained approval in utterly different parts while confining themselves to their own proper spheres of tragedy and comedy, but we have also seen a comedian highly successful in tragedy and a tragedian in comedy. Should I not take equal pains? (trans. H. M. Hubbell)

Cicero emphasises that the speaker needed to use various styles, and not use the same *contentio* ('rhetorical style', as Ferri and Probert (this volume p. 25) translate – 'rhetoric that made use of all possible rhetorical embellishments', one may add) everywhere. Cicero here says that not even epic and tragic poetry always use the same form of language, *acerrima contentio* (typical of epic or tragic register), but often turn to everyday language use. As Ferri and Probert rightfully point out, not everything in a high poetic register should be considered alien to everyday language use, at least not by default. What this means, however, is that there is considerable stylistic variation within the tragic register, from the high-flying, grand expression to the more common expression that is equally part of spoken everyday registers of language.[19] We think that *cotidianum genus sermonis* here cannot be taken to refer to colloquial language use (which would abandon the tragic register for a moment), but rather to a less embellished style of speaking within the tragic register and in the poetic context, a style with fewer poetic ornaments and thus approaching everyday language.

Another well-known passage, Hor. *Ars* 89–98, makes a similar observation, confirming the stylistic variation in tragedy:[20]

> versibus exponi tragicis res comica non vult;
> indignatur item privatis ac prope socco   90
> dignis carminibus narrari cena Thyestae.
> singula quaeque locum teneant sortita decenter.
> Interdum tamen et vocem comoedia tollit,
> iratusque Chremes tumido delitigat ore;
> et tragicus plerumque dolet sermone pedestri   95
> Telephus et Peleus, cum pauper et exsul uterque
> proicit ampullas et sesquipedalia verba,
> si curat cor spectantis tetigisse querella.

A theme for Comedy refuses to be set forth in verses of Tragedy; likewise the feast of Thyestes scorns to be told in strains of daily life that well nigh befit the comic sock. Let each style keep the becoming place allotted it. Yet at times even Comedy raises her voice, and an angry Chremes storms in swelling tones; so, too, in Tragedy Telephus and Peleus often grieve in the language of prose, when, in poverty and exile, either hero throws aside his bombast and Brobdingnagian words, should he want his lament to touch the spectator's heart. (trans. H. R. Fairclough)

In order to touch the hearts of the audience, as Horace puts it, even tragic language had to make use of *sermo pedestris*,[21] closer to the normal linguistic usage. With this sense it comes close to what Cicero means by *cotidianum genus sermonis*. And it should have become clear by now that neither Cicero nor Horace is speaking about colloquial language, but generally about variation within a particular register. What seem to be colloquial elements, if there are any, should be considered part of this variation within the given register.

---

[19] Cf. Cic. *De orat.* 3.177 (discussed by Ferri and Probert, this volume pp. 27–8), on the common element in the languages of conversation, rhetoric and drama).

[20] The entire passage is based on Aristotle, *Rhetoric* 3.7; see (in addition to the commentary itself ad loc.) Brink 1963: 97–9.

[21] This does not even necessarily imply that the language gets close to prose. *TLL* s.v. *pedestris* 971.37 ff. refers to *versus humiliores*, and has in addition to this passage also Hor. *Sat.* 2.6.17 *quid prius illustrem saturis musaque pedestri*.

3.2   Modern approaches

Modern attempts to define the tragic language of the Romans are scattered, and nothing much has ever been done in a systematic way. One of the severe disadvantages that apply to early Roman tragedy (as opposed to comedy) is the lack of coherent passages of noteworthy length. One of the more interesting and promising approaches to the language of Roman comedy, for example, has been research into how Roman playwrights differentiate between their characters (of different social standing, gender and age) by linguistic means.[22] This can be done for a corpus of texts as fragmentary as early Roman tragedy only to a very limited degree; it does seem, however, that there is some evidence for employment of linguistic characterisation, in particular by using features of technical languages (Lennartz 2003).

Tragic language is usually characterised in the following way. It was stylistically below epic but above the highly stylised passages of Plautine comedy. It made frequent use of archaisms, neologisms (e.g. abstracts, nominal suffixation), metaphorical expressions and rhetorical figures. Expressive sound effects were very important; these were produced first and foremost by (sometimes excessive) alliteration. One typical feature is the use of vocabulary and phraseology from special languages, most importantly from sacral, legal, official and military language. This mixture has received from critics evaluations such as 'pompous', 'artificial' and 'baroque'.[23]

Lennartz has made the point that in fact the typical ingredients of Roman tragic language from Livius Andronicus onwards – alliteration, assonance, chiasmus, parallelism, synonyms, etc. – are all common elements in all poetic genres of ancient times.[24] The only respect in which they are 'tragic', according to Lennartz, is the greater extent to which they are used in Roman Republican tragedy.

What is interesting, although not perhaps surprising, is that most of these components are Roman, not that much Greek. In his commentary on Ennius, rich in linguistic detail, Jocelyn writes: 'It would be foolish to assert that the Attic τραγικὴ λέξις had no influence on poets constantly adapting Attic plays but the forms of elevated speech already familiar to third- and second-century Roman audiences should be considered the dominating

---

[22] Particularly worth mentioning are studies by Maltby (1979, on the language of old men in comedy) and Adams (1984, on female speech).
[23] Cancik 1978: 338–41; also Petersmann and Petersmann 1991: 202–4. For a list of features in individual authors see also the introductions of Schierl 2006 and Dangel 1995.
[24] Lennartz 1995–6: 170–1. Goldberg (2000: 54–5) points out that emphatic alliteration and morphological parallelism are typical stylistic mannerisms even in comedy.

influences.'²⁵ The essentially Roman character of tragic language, although easily neglected in the general context of adaptations, is not difficult to understand. Even though it was otherwise adapted from Greek models, Roman tragedy needed to use elements of elevated speech that would be recognisable to the heterogeneous audience, which consisted not only of the educated upper classes of Roman society.²⁶

What then has been said about the particular aspect of tragic language and colloquialisms? Jocelyn (1972: 1002) states:

> The manner in which Ennius' tragic heroes spoke from the stage did not differ drastically from that which contemporary Romans used on formal occasions. They spoke no special language as the Attic heroes were made to do even by the realist Euripides. Nevertheless they spoke more elaborately and in a more obviously old-fashioned way than did Roman orators and the rhythms of their speech had the regularity of poetry. When they sang, as they did more often than in the Attic plays Ennius translated, their vocabulary and style elevated considerably but never beyond the imaginable limits of urban Latin.

Lennartz draws special attention to different stylistic levels inside the tragic register, pointing out how careful one should be when attributing individual words or constructions to different registers and/or sociolects. He sees elements from different spheres of spoken language as important elements in the tragic poets' repertoire (2003: 85):

> Es sind durchaus Ausdruckselemente des in den täglichen Tätigkeitsfeldern gesprochenen Lateins der alten Zeit, die wir finden, und damit der kraftvollen Sprache des Publikums der *ludi scaenici*, die es schließlich zu unterhalten galt.

Thus, both Jocelyn and Lennartz highlight the mixed nature of tragic language, consisting of both highly poetic language and elements of colloquial registers. Jocelyn stressed more the educated side of colloquial, but Lennartz is ready to allow for the presence of words even from the normal everyday life of the Roman farmer.

---

²⁵ Jocelyn 1969: 43. Cf. also 1969: 42: 'Three sources have been suggested for the origin of the types of phrasal elaboration characteristic of certain parts of early Roman drama: the modes of public speaking taught in Greek schools and practised by Roman politicians, the Attic τραγική λέξις and the formulae of Roman law and religion.' See further Jocelyn's index for Greek syntax and vocabulary.

²⁶ Even the Greek words in the tragic scripts are not necessarily derived from the Greek tragedy that was the source of the Roman version. Contemporary Latin contained many words of Greek origin that were simply part of the common language, and their appearance in tragedy should not be viewed as Greek influence from the plays the tragedians were adapting (see Lennartz 1995–6). For example, *stola* in Ennius is at times a 'Latin' word, at times Greek taken over from the source (Lennartz 1995–6: 192–4).

One aspect pertaining to this theme is the standardisation of written language. In many cases where there is a difference in use between tragic (or comic) language and the classical authors, it is a matter of formative processes in the written (and literary) language. Thus, if the tragic poets use a linguistic feature that is absent from Caesar and Cicero, they are not necessarily using a colloquial feature, as opposed to the written norm, since there was no written norm, in the classical sense, at the time they were writing. Among these features in the tragic language are, e.g., the differing use of *consecutio temporum* (Casaceli 1976: 43–5), of diathesis (see below, 5.10), and of verb government.[27]

4 ORALITY, COLLOQUIALISMS AND THE TRAGIC LANGUAGE

Given that the language of Roman tragedy is usually characterised in modern studies as 'rhetorical', 'archaic', 'pompous' and even 'artificial', consisting of archaic, sacral, legal, official, rhetoric and military elements, is there any place in it for colloquialisms at all? At least Cicero seems to have been fully aware of the artificiality of the language of tragic texts and the degree of its detachment from reality, when he concludes a passage on the absurdity of fear of death, quoting Pacuvius at length:

non intellego, quid metuat, cum tam bonos octonarios fundat ad tibiam. (Cic. *Tusc.* 1.106)

I do not understand what he is afraid of, seeing that he pours out such a stream of the fine eight-foot verses. (transl. J. E. King)[28]

Roman drama of the third and second centuries BC in all cases was meant to be played to an audience. That means: to a certain degree the tragedies must have been conceived as 'oral' texts, at least partly close to natural speech – otherwise they could not have been performed successfully to large audiences of heterogeneous intellectual capabilities.[29] Tragedy did not generally try to give an illusion of conversational language, as comedy often did, but nevertheless it was meant to evoke feelings, and for this purpose there was also a need for certain feeling of immediacy.

---

[27] See Casaceli 1976: 47–50 for examples; cf. Cic. *Tusc.* 3.20 *male Latine videtur sed praeclare Accius... poeta ius suum tenuit et dixit audacius* on Accius' use of *invidere* with the accusative.

[28] King's translation has 'seven-foot', which was changed here, as King was using an outdated edition.

[29] Cf. e.g. Castagna 1992: 84 ff. On the linguistics of the dialogue in Roman drama (Terence in particular) see Müller 1997.

Lennartz (2003: 104–5) points out that starting with the preconception that tragedy always represents high-register language will lead to misinterpretations. He discusses words that appear in tragedy, are avoided by classical authors, but turn up again later in the history of Latin (2003: 108–19). These can be claimed to be words of the common language that the tragic poets felt comfortable in using, and that supposedly stayed in use in conversational language (but cf. below, section 5).

As in the case of archaism, we are often lacking a trustworthy contemporary label for features of tragic language. A typical case is that in which a linguistic feature later was an outright archaism, but may well have been an element of the common language at the time of the play's composition (cf. Chahoud, this volume pp. 54–5); see e.g. Jocelyn (1969: 363) on *nequiquam* in Ennius: 'It therefore looks as if in Ennius' day *nequiquam* belonged fully to the common language but very soon after dropped out, to be employed henceforth only by poets and poeticising historians.' On the other hand, if a linguistic feature was colloquial in Cicero's time, it is difficult to tell whether it was so for e.g. Ennius and his contemporaries, as Jocelyn (1969: 338) remarks on *em* in Ennius: 'Here it seems to indicate an exasperated tone of voice. In a tragedy of the classical period it would be an extreme colloquialism; one cannot be sure about its exact status in early second century drama.'

All this seems to imply that there is a certain overlap between spoken, natural language and written, stylised, 'spoken' language in Roman drama.[30] Any colloquialism, as one of the most obvious features of spoken language, should therefore be an element of that overlap. Thus one could illustrate the situation as in Figure 8.1 (implying that tragedy resembles conversational language to an even lesser degree than comedy).

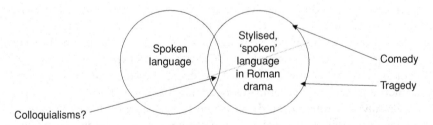

Fig. 8.1 Spoken language and written reflections of spoken language in Roman drama

[30] Generally for spoken language see e.g. Clark 1996; Schiffrin *et al.* 2001; Fiehler *et al.* 2004.

Perhaps even more so than with other genres and text-types, the definition of 'colloquial' is essential to finding out what is colloquial in tragic
language and what is not. The language of Roman tragedy has been characterised as artificial due to its excessive use of elements that were meant to
raise the tone of the register to tragic heights. On the other hand, in dramatic texts more than elsewhere the presence of a certain amount of orality
and also colloquial language has been regarded as natural. As has been
pointed out above, the search for colloquialisms in Roman tragic language
means looking for elements that bordered on the colloquial but nevertheless were not too informal to be used in the tragic register; again it is a
matter of variation inside the tragic register, not a shift of registers entirely.

Furthermore, we suggest that there is no one typical case of 'colloquialism
in tragedy' but that those cases that are found to be potential candidates
for colloquial status have to be evaluated individually, and they will form a
continuum from 'more colloquial' to 'less colloquial'. There will, however,
be no examples of such colloquialisms that were too close to actual lower-
register spoken language.

In the end, it does not matter so much that there is no one thing called
'colloquial' – we are looking for variation inside literary, or in any case
written, language. One label 'colloquial' clearly is not enough, and in each
separate case one will need to give further definitions on what colloquial
means, depending on the context, approach, etc. The difficulty, or better,
impossibility, of defining colloquial language springs from the nature of
linguistic variation itself. It does not lend itself to one simply formulated
continuum, not even two or three. Hence, in addition to practical even
if indefinable labels like colloquial, explanatory remarks will always be
required from the linguist or philologist.[31]

This is why, as Clackson (this volume p. 9) observes, the term is hardly
used by linguists. But as classical philologists we have less material to work
on, material that is highly restricted in nature. We are working on a less
detailed level of linguistic variation than linguists working on modern
languages. That is why simple labels like colloquial continue to be used
widely, as this volume among others shows. There is in ancient texts
something that often is comfortably classified as colloquial.

Usually this nomination derives from the distribution of the feature in
question in other texts: if it is found mainly in e.g. comedy and private

---

[31] Moreover, one's native language will have an effect on what one sees as colloquial, how one views the
relationship between colloquial and standard written, and so forth. Languages differ with regard to
their standards and the distinction between spoken and written language, both for historical reasons
(the circumstances under which the standard came into being) and for language-dependent reasons
(the amount of e.g. inflexional morphology). To a certain extent, one is always a prisoner of one's
own native language, and this is reflected in views on the ancient material.

letters, it will be a candidate for a colloquialism. The combined testimony of Plautus, Terence and Cicero's letters, as against that of classical prose, seems to be one traditionally and generally accepted way to identify colloquial language (cf. Adams quoted by Chahoud, this volume p. 55). As a result of this investigation one most probably will (at least in the overwhelming majority of cases involving tragic fragments, given the high, even artificial, register of the genre) find only *seemingly* conversational language (cf. Chahoud, this volume p. 44): colloquialisms that were not necessarily part of actual conversational registers, but features that were at home in informal written language and, as such, sometimes used in formal (or higher-register) written language for a special effect, as in the case of tragedy.[32] The individual evaluation of the features would greatly benefit if we had more context for the fragments and so were able to undertake a contextual analysis of what was used and why.

In literary texts, whatever their true nature with regard to conversational language, colloquialisms are intentional, a deliberate choice of the author in question. It is clear, almost a priori, that colloquial elements in Roman tragedy (or in fact in tragedy in general) cannot be meant to be perceived as a comic element. For, as Cicero pointed out,

poematis enim tragici comici epici melici etiam ac dithyrambici, quo magis est tractatum [a Latinis], suum cuiusque est, diversum a reliquis. itaque et in tragoedia comicum vitiosum est et in comoedia turpe tragicum; et in ceteris suus est cuique certus sonus et quaedam intellegentibus nota vox. (Cic. *Opt. Gen.* 1.1)

For there is something individual about tragic poetry, comedy, epic, melic, and also dithyrambic, the more it is cultivated, something distinct from the other genres. Thus it is the case both that a comic element is wrong in tragedy and that a tragic element is unseemly in comedy; also in the other genres, each has its own distinct sound and as it were a voice known to those who understand such things.

Colloquial expressions were used in tragic language as one element that contributed to the characteristic affective expression of the tragic register.

5 COLLOQUIAL ELEMENTS IN THE LANGUAGE OF ROMAN TRAGEDY

What follows is a representative, but by no means exhaustive, collection of features that have been adduced as features of colloquial language in

---

[32] The term 'fingierte Mündlichkeit' has been used for this element in literary texts (Goetsch 1985). 'Mündlichkeit in geschriebenen Texten is nie mehr sie selbst, sonderns stets fingiert und damit einen Komponente des Schreibstils und oft auch der bewussten Schreibstrategie des jeweiligen Autors' (Goetsch 1985: 202). Even drama, 'die semiorale Gattung', only occasionally tries to give an illusion of true spoken language (Goetsch 1985: 214–15).

Roman tragedy, and an evaluation of these.[33] In the analysis we reserve
the term 'colloquial' for those features that, in our view, either are, or give
an illusion of being, elements of conversational language (as opposed to a
literary *Kunstsprache*).[34] We begin with lexical items.

5.1 flaccere

(a)   sin flaccebunt condiciones repudiato et reddito

          (Enn. *scaen.* 301 R. = p. 356–7 no. 373 W. = 304 J.)

          But if our terms go lax, then cast her off and give her back.

(b)   an sceptra iam flaccent   (Acc. *trag.* 3 R. = p. 326–7 no. 1 W. = 105 D.)

          Or else droops his sceptre?

In Ennius, this verb is used in a fragment from *Thyestes*.[35] Jocelyn
notes: 'The metaphorical use of *flaccere* is odd but cf. Cicero, *Q. fr.*
2.15.4 *Messala flaccet*... Ennius may have been employing a current
colloquialism.'[36]

On passage (b) Casaceli (1976: 79) observes: 'Similmente al v. 3 abbiamo
an sceptra iam flaccent, dove il grecismo eleva il tono banale del verbo, adop-
erato, secondo la testimonianza di Varrone, per indicare un difetto fisico.'

Flaccere is attested in Afranius (*com.* 65 *disperii, perturbata sum, iam
flaccet fortitudo*) similarly of incorporate things (also later in Apul. *Apol.* 25
cur vestra oratio rebus flaccet, strepitu viget). In addition to the passage in
Cicero mentioned above, it is used of animate beings also in Lucilius 294
K. = 310 W. = 275 M. = 7.7 C. (*hic est Macedo si Gentius longius flaccet*).
This distribution of *flaccere*, not used by Plautus and Terence, is not easy to
interpret. Elsewhere Jocelyn (1969: 264) lists *flaccere* among other similar
formations of tragic language that do not appear in comedy (at least not
in Plautus and Terence), e.g. *clarere, frondere, nigrere, senere*. Given the
derivation from *flaccus*, and the contexts of the attestations, we find it

---

[33] We will not be concerned with such necessary elements of dramatic language as interjections (*heus,
eheu, eho tu*), use of vocatives, etc. as these have very little to do with colloquial language. We have
concentrated on the writings of Ennius, Pacuvius and Accius.

[34] The text of the fragments is that of Jocelyn (1969) for Ennius, Dangel (1995) for Accius and Schierl
(2006) for Pacuvius, unless otherwise stated. References are to Ribbeck 1871 (R.) and Warmington
1967 (W.) as well as to Dangel 1995 (D.) for Accius, Jocelyn 1969 (J.) for Ennius and Schierl 2006
(Sch.) for Pacuvius. Translations of the fragments are from Warmington (1967).

[35] The context, as well as the entire action of the play, have been subject to various suggestions, see
Jocelyn 1969: 412–19 (414 on this fragment).

[36] Jocelyn 1969: 425. Jocelyn takes *condiciones* as the object of *repudiare* (and *reddere*?). Warmington
(1967) translates *repudiare* according to the meaning 'to reject formally, as a prospective wife or
husband', with the object *eam* understood, see *OLD* s.v. *repudio*.

probable that *flaccere* carried derogatory connotations, but, as the absence from comedy suggests, the derivational type may not have been typical of actual conversational language.

5.2 segregare, fervere

(a)   nedum cum fervat pectus iracundiae
                        (Acc. *trag.* 2 R. = p. 326–7 no. 3 W. = 107 D.)

when seethes the breast with anger full

(b)   aere atque ferro fervere
                        (Acc. *trag.* 631 R. = p. 536–7 no. 616 W. = 79 D.)

glowing with bronze and iron

(c)   ore obscena dicta segregent
                        (Acc. *trag.* 511 R. = p. 498–9 no. 504 W. = 16 D.)

to . . . dispart words of ill-boding import from their tongues.[37]

Casaceli (1976: 79) identifies a colloquial feature in the transferred use of *fervere* and *segregare* in the verses quoted above: 'Dal *sermo cotidianus* è tratto l'uso traslato di *segregare* al v. 511 *ore obscena dicti segregent*, dove però l'espressione è impreziosita dalla rarità del costrutto *obscena dicti*, e di *fervere* al v. 2 *fervat pectus iracundiae* e al v. 631 *aere atque ferro fervere*, incalzato al verso successivo dalla metafora letteraria *insignibus florere*.'

But the *TLL* records the transferred use of *fervere* in classical poetry,[38] and there seem to be no good reasons for seeing an origin in conversational language. Also for *segregare* the transferred usage is widely attested, even in prose.[39] Thus, these verbs do not seem to be particularly colloquial, rather poetic, especially *fervere*.

5.3 nitidare

(a)   eam secum advocant, eunt ad fontem, nitidant corpora
                        (Enn. *scaen.* 125 R. = p. 264–5 no. 139 W. = 136 J.)

They call to her to come with them, they go to the spring; and they cleanse their bodies.

---

[37] Warmington (1967) prints *obscena dictu*, and Ribbeck (1871) *obscena dicti*.
[38] *TLL* s.v. *ferveo* 592.37 ff.: Hor. *Carm.* 1.13.4 *fervens . . . iecur*, Hor. *Epist.* 1.1.33 *fervet avaritia . . . pectus*, Ov. *Fast.* 2.732 *fervet multo linguaque corque mero*; also in Accius (450 R. *heu! cor ira fervit caecum, amentia rapior ferorque*). The example quoted at 5.2 (a) is the only one of *ferveo* with a genitive (*TLL* 592.43).
[39] *OLD* s.v. *segrego* has many examples of transferred use, e.g. Sen. *Ep.*, Pl., Tac., Cic. *de Orat.* and *Fin.*, Liv. With the bare ablative (as in *ore . . . segregent*) cf. *me curae somno segregant* Turp. *com.* 52 R.

(b)   quin ad Dircaeum fontem adveniunt; mundulae | nitidantur ungulae
             quadripedantum sonipedum[40]
             (Acc. *trag.* 602–3 R. = p. 548–9 no. 656–7 W. = 399–400 D.)

             But when to the fountain of Dirce they come, the hoofs o' the horses,
             whose four feet go thumping full gallop, are washed clean and neat.

Jocelyn (1969: 279) sees in *nitidare* a poetic neologism, but Lennartz
(2003: 113) reconstructs an origin in conversational language: 'ein
von *nitidus* in banal-expressivem Zusammenhang jederzeit mögliches
Faktitivum der gesprochenen Sprache'. He refers to later attestations in
Columella and Marcellus (a medical writer of the fifth century), but it is
unlikely that we are dealing with a linguistic continuum here. The other
attestations are so late, especially Marcellus, that it seems very difficult to
claim that the same verb remained in use in conversational language all
through the centuries, even if the form happens to be the same (cf. *rarenter*
below, 5.4). This of course does not rule out an origin in conversational
language in Ennius' or Accius' time.

5.4 rarenter, celeranter, famulanter

(a)   sed quasi aut ferrum aut lapis | durat rarenter gemitum †conatur trabem†
             (Enn. *scaen.* 66–7 R. = p. 246–7 no. 86–7 W. = 109–10 J.)

             But like unto stiff strength of iron or stone she strained to draw sobs
             fitfully.[41]

(b)   sed quis hic est qui matutinum cursum huc celeranter rapit?
             (Acc. *trag.* 123 R. = p. 354–5 no. 82 W. = 249 D.)

             But who is this runs hither hurryingly in early morning?

(c)   deum Cadmogena natum Semela adfare et famulanter pete!
             (Acc. *trag.* 642 R. = p. 544–5 no. 647 W. = 445 D.)

             In a menial manner address and pray the god the son of Cadmus' daughter
             Semele.

Lennartz thinks, on the basis of attestations in Cato and later in the
Mulomedicina Chironis, that *rarenter* belonged to conversational language of the farmers and veterinarians.[42] Plautus has only *raro* (as does,

---

[40] Here we have adopted Warmington's (1967) text.

[41] Warmington (1967) translates with *conatu trahens*.

[42] Lennartz 2003: 109–10. In tragedy *rarenter* occurs also at Andr. *trag.* 24, in comedy two times in
    Caecilius. Mannheimer 1975, Lennartz's source here, does not give exact references.

interestingly, Vegetius' *Mulomedicina*). Varro (*apud* Gel. 2.25.8 = *L.* fr. 11 Funaioli) observes *alii 'raro' dicunt, alii 'rarenter'* in connection with adverbs and their derivation from adjectives. Naturally the Cato example points to a prosaic use of common language, but nevertheless we think that the presence in Chiron probably does not belong to the same continuum, at least not on the spoken level of the language.[43] Jocelyn (1969: 261) labels the word a poetic coinage, and refers to the use of adverbs in -*ter* in tragedy and Plautine comedy (there especially at verse ends).[44]

Of these three, *celeranter* appears to be an Accian *hapax* (*TLL* s.v. *celero*), and *famulanter* is attested again very late.[45] Thus, as in the case of *nitidare* above, the colloquial character of these three adverbs remains to be proven on other grounds. Furthermore, the absence of *rarenter* from Plautus casts some doubts over Lennartz's view.

5.5 hoc corpus

quamquam annisque et aetate hoc corpus putret
(Pac. *trag.* 340 R. = p. 300–1 no. 376 W. = 249 Sch.)

Though this my body rots with years and age.

The use of *hic* in reference to the first person is attested in comedy and thought to be colloquial.[46] Here naturally *corpus* and not *ego* has to be the subject of *putret*, and thus *hoc corpus* can only be a substitute for *meum corpus*. We find this use of *hic* not especially colloquial. More probably it is an affective expression typical of dramatic language.[47]

5.6 inibi est

profecto aut inibi est aut iam potiuntur Phrugum
(Pac. *trag.* 205 R. = p. 248–9 no. 229 W. = 151 Sch.)

The event is either near at hand for sure, or else they're masters of the Phrygians now.

---

[43] *Rarenter* is attested also in Novius and Pomponius Bononiensis, later in Gellius and Apuleius.

[44] See Casaceli 1976: 37–40 for this type of adverb in Accius.

[45] The *TLL* records *famulanter* (s.v. *famulor*) at Dracontius, *De laudibus dei* 2.72 and Greg. Tur. *DLH* 9.41; cf. Casaceli 1976: 39–40.

[46] Schierl 2006: 507; H–S 180, e.g. Pl. *St.* 751 *fugit hoc libertas caput*. The text at Acc. *trag.* 605 R. = p. 534–5 no. 611 W. = 402 D. *hoc anima corpus liquerit* is uncertain.

[47] Hofmann and Szantyr (H–S 180) mention the movement of the hand in connection with the demonstrative.

The expression *inibi est* 'almost there, near at hand' has been considered a colloquial usage (Schierl 2006: 332). It is used in comedy by Caecilius (188 R.), Afranius (208 R.) and Pomponius (66 R.). Then it is found in Cic. *Phil.* 14.5 *quod sperare nos quidem debemus, patres conscripti, aut inibi esse aut iam esse confectum.*[48]

The Ciceronian passage (*Phil.* 14.5) does not seem to have a colloquial character. For Cicero, this use of *inibi* may have had an archaic sound. But, in the absence of parallels from Plautus and Terence, and as the fragment of Pacuvius itself does not seem to call for a colloquial expression in any way, we conclude that this was not in common colloquial use at Pacuvius' time.[49]

5.7 habere = habitare

ubi habet? urbe agrone?

(Acc. trag. 537 R. = p. 508–9 no. 541 W. = 212 D.)

Where keeps he? In the city or afield?

This use of *habere* is attested in comedy, then in an inscription (*CIL* VI 38274),[50] and a couple of times in late Latin.[51] According to Lennartz (2003: 116) this use must have been current 'in der lebendigen Sprache'. Lennartz is probably right, although we again express doubts as to whether the later evidence reflects the same phenomenon, and a spoken continuum of hundreds of years. In a context of dialogue and of an actual question, this sense of *habere* probably reflects actual conversational usage.

5.8 hoc *for* huc

eaque ivi hoc causa ut ne quis nostra auribus verba cleperet

(Acc. trag. 292 R. = p. 422–3 no. 280 W. = 594 D.)

This too is the reason for my coming hither – that no man's ears should steal our words.[52]

This form is usually thought to have been common in old Latin.[53] Casaceli has proposed a different view: 'È in realtà una forma propria del latino arcaico e della *Umgangssprache*, mentre *huc* appartiene alla lingua colta'

---

[48] *TLL* s.v. *inibi* 1611.17–27 and H–S 283.

[49] In addition, the word *inibi* is found once in Plautus, three times in Cato, once in the *Bellum Africum*, once elsewhere in Cicero (*Agr.* 1.20), later once in Vitruvius and Celsus and then frequently in Gellius.

[50] *D.M. Damas fecit coiugi Daphnidi quae abuit ad nymfas*, a Roman funerary inscription.

[51] *TLL* s.v. *habeo* 2401.6–24. Late Latin examples are in Dictys (fourth century) and Paulinus of Nola.

[52] Ribbeck (1871) and Warmington (1967) give the last three words in the order *verba cleperet auribus*.

[53] N–W II.613, with many examples from Plautus; Servius notes the use of *hoc* for *huc* in old Latin.

(Casaceli 1976: 13). However, *huc* is transmitted in tragedy (e.g. Acc. *trag.* 123 R. = p. 354–5 no. 82 = 249 D., Enn. *scaen.* 189 R. = p. 308–9 no. 247 = 201 J.), and there seem to be no good reasons to modify the traditional view.

5.9 Frequentative verbs: erogitare

qui neque cuiatis esset, umquam potuimus
multa erogitantes sciscere

(Acc. *trag.* 625–6 R. = p. 540–3 no. 634–5 W. = 81–2 D.)

Though we kept asking many a question, at no time were we able thus to learn wherefrom he came, nor . . .

Lennartz connects this and other frequentative verbs with the need of conversational language for phonetically 'stronger' words. At the same time, they provided means for the powerful expression needed in tragic language (Lennartz 2003: 116–17).

Jocelyn notes in connection with *adventant* (Enn. *scaen.* 68 J. *multii alii adventant, paupertas quorum obscurat nomina*) that tragedy often uses an intensive form with no perceptible difference in meaning from the simple form normally used in comedy. On the other hand, comedy has similar formations as well, verbs that were not used by the classical purists. Jocelyn comments: 'it is erroneous to label them all vulgarisms; many must have been poetic formations' (1969: 231).

Here probably both motivations (*volkssprachlich* and poetic) are applicable, differently for different verbs.

5.10 Active vs deponent verbs

Lennartz (2003: 108–11) has discussed *ruminari* and *adoriri*. According to him (p. 110), *Verkehrssprache* did not like deponents. Tragedy favoured active forms, similarly to comedy, and actives were thus part of common language ('allgemeine Ausdrucksweise'), not any special stylistic level.[54] Ennius has *contemplare* as active, although Terence already had it as deponent, and chooses thus the 'normal' voice in place of the 'modern' one. Then Accius has the active, according to Lennartz, as an established feature of tragic language.[55]

---

[54] Similarly Risicato 1950: 50–2. Lennartz (2003: 112–13) attributes *adoriant*, similarly to the odd word *verruca* and *itis* (indicative second person plural for imperative) to the specific sphere of military language.

[55] Lennartz 2003: 111–12, with examples of active verbs on p. 112 n. 96.

However, the preference for active forms in conversational language cannot be stated as a general rule. For example, in the case of *opino/opinor* the deponent form was more common in comedy, and the distribution (active: two times in tragedy, twelve times in comedy; deponent: once in tragedy, extremely often in comedy) thus points more to the direction that the deponent form was normally used in conversation (see Schierl 2006 on Pac. *trag.* 70 Sch., pp. 219–20 and Jocelyn 1969: 288 on *opino*).[56] Different verbs clearly had different distributions. This may have more to do with variation and the developing standard of the literary language, rather than an opposition between written/poetic and conversational.

MORPHOSYNTAX

5.11 quod superest socium

tunc quod superest socium mittis leto? An lucti paenitet?
(Acc. trag. 491 R. = p. 494–5 no. 492 W. = 134 D.)

As for the rest, do you then send what remains of your comrades to death? Are you now sorry for your grief?

The use of *quid/quod* + a partitive genitive of persons has been identified as a colloquial feature. In this function, *quid* is found in comedy (e.g. Pl. *Poen.* 856 *nescio quid viri sis*, Ter. *Hec.* 643 *quid mulieris uxorem habes*), but also in Caesar (*Civ.* 3.29.3 *quid militum transvexisset*). The variant with *quod* seems to be attested only here and in a wall inscription from Pompeii (*CIL* IV 5213 QVD TV MVLIIIRO | RVM (sic) DIFVTVISTI, QVOD TV [. . .]).[57] In view of the Pompeian example (the content of the inscription and the analogical formation of the genitive plural in *mulierorum*) there is naturally a strong temptation to see this use of *quod* + genitive as highly colloquial. However, the parallel construction with *quid* does not seem to have been strictly colloquial, if we are to judge by its presence in Caesar. Thus, even the character of *quod* + gen. cannot be exactly determined.

Nevertheless, it is interesting to have a potential colloquialism in the same verse with the poetic word *letum*. If *quod. . . socium* has a colloquial flavour to it, this passage shows how the poets strove for affective expression with different stylistic means even inside one verse.

---

[56] See further Jocelyn 1969: 175, 206, 317 for examples of varying uses of the active and deponent verbs.
[57] H–S 56. See Väänänen (1966: 118) on *CIL* IV 5213.

5.12 interea loci, quovis gentium

(a) interea loci | flucti flaccescunt, silescunt venti, mollitur mare
(Pac. *trag.* 76–7 R. = p. 194–5 no. 82–3 W. = 63 Sch.)

Meanwhile the billows drop and drop, the winds fall quiet, the sea sinks soft.

(b) iussit proficisci exilium quovis gentium
(Acc. *trag.* 599 R. = p. 530–1 no. 602 W. = 560 D.)

He has ordained you go to banishment where in the world you will.

The use of the genitive in *interea loci* and *quovis gentium* has been labelled as colloquial.[58] The phrase *interea loci* is attested in comedy (e.g. Pl. *Men.* 446, Ter. *Hau.* 256), but apparently not elsewhere before late Latin,[59] and it remains impossible to say anything definite on its colouring in the dramatic writers.

Similar constructions are found in Cicero, *res erat... eo iam loci* (*Sest.* 68), and correspondents, *aliquo terrarum* (Decimus Brutus in Cic. *Fam.* 11.1.3). It thus looks as if expressions like *quovis gentium* had a place also in the colloquial registers. Consequently, it could have been used to give strength to the thought 'ordered to go, no matter where'.

In addition, we may note that in the same verse with *quovis gentium* there is a use of the plain accusative with *proficisci*, *proficisci exilium*, that usually is regarded as a feature of archaic language (cf. *domum ire, rus ire* where *domum* and *ius* are close to adverbials) (Casaceli 1976: 53–4).

5.13 praesente his

est res aliqua quam praesente his prius maturare institit
(Acc. *trag.* 428 R. = p. 466–7 no. 418 W. = 528 D.)

There is some matter which he formerly has set himself to bring unto fulfilment with these men present.

The incongruence of number in *praesente his* appears to be a feature of official language. The construction is attested also elsewhere in early Latin (e.g. Pomponius, *com.* 47 *praesente amicis*, 168 *praesente testibus*, Novius, *com.* 57 *praesente omnibus*).[60] Warmington reconstructs as a possible context

---

[58] Schierl 2006: 213; Casaceli 1976: 54; H–S 53–4; Petersmann 1999: 292–3.
[59] *TLL* s.v. *interea* 2184.61 ff. records instances at Symmachus *Epistulae* 1.5.1 and 3.23.
[60] *TLL* s.v. *praesens* 838.55–69; Hofmann and Szantyr (H–S 445) refer to *Protokollstil.* Casaceli (1976: 56–7) sees a connection to popular language as possible as well.

a conference about Tydeus' plans to kill Agrius' sons, something that would fit in well with *praesente his* being an official formula.

Interestingly, this construction occurs in the *Rhetorica ad Herennium* in a passage (*praesente multis, Rhet. Her.* 4.16; discussed by Ferri and Probert, this volume p. 21) illustrating a *genus exile*, or *frivolus . . . et inliberalis . . . sermo*, i.e. a debased version of the simple style, that should be composed of correct and well-chosen words. Ferri and Probert refer to the substandard use of fossilised *praesente* functioning as a preposition, but note that as the construction is attested even in the school author Terence, it should not be viewed as strictly ungrammatical. But an element of official phraseology would be just as much out of place in rhetorical style.

All in all, this seems to be a feature of the phraseology of official documents and records, and not any type of colloquialism.

OTHER FEATURES

5.14 bene facis

bene facis: sed nunc quid subiti mihi febris excivit mali?[61]

(Acc. *trag.* 155 R. = p. 366–7 no. 122 W. = 169 D.)

Well done! But now what sudden malady is this that a fever has aroused in me?

Bene facis is found in Plautus, Terence and Cicero (*Fin.* 3.16 and *Att.* 7.3.3, 12.43.2). Thus, *bene facis* probably is colloquial, part of educated conversational phraseology.[62]

5.15 Locational vs directional expressions with verbs of motion

The variation in constructions signifying location and goal of motion has been noted in several places as a typical colloquial feature.[63] Examples are, e.g., Acc. *trag.* 437–8 R. *conlocat sese in locum*, and conversely Acc. *trag.* 406 R. *in stabulo inmittens*, Acc. *trag.* 670 R. *in monte Oeteo <sunt> illatae lampades* and Acc. *trag.* 231 R. *quo me ostendam*. The last example presents a conflation between *quo me vortam* and *ubi me ostendam* (Lennartz 2003: 123).

We suggest that, when it comes to early Latin and the tragic poets, this tendency should be considered more as an issue relating to the developing standard written language. There was not yet a standard concerning these

---

[61] Ribbeck (1871) and Warmington (1967) give *civit*, not *excivit*.
[62] Cf. Bagordo 2002: 46, 'eine Dankesformel der gelehrten Unterhaltung'.
[63] Casaceli 1976: 59; Lennartz 2003: 123; H–S 277. See also Kruschwitz and Halla-aho 2007: 42.

expressions according to which these examples might be seen as colloquialisms, even if they do reflect variation in spoken language.

5.16 Accusative and infinitive without the subject accusative

(a)   numquam erit tam immanis, cum non mea opera extinctum sciat,
       quin fragescat (Acc. *trag.* 337–8 R. = p. 440–1 no. 331–2 W. = 325–6 D.)

       Never will he be so savage that he'll not break when he is made aware
       that this man by my help was not destroyed.

(b)   sed civitatem video Argivum incendere
                              (Enn. *scaen.* 291 R. = p. 344–5 no. 343 W. = 288 J.)

       And I see he sets the Argives' town ablaze.

(c)   deumque de consilio hoc itiner credo conatum modo
                              (Enn. *scaen.* 292 R. = p. 346–7 no. 344 W. = 289 J.)

       I think too, 'twas by counsel of the gods that you did lately venture on
       this journey.

(d)   id ego aecum ac iustum fecisse expedibo atque eloquar
                              (Enn. *scaen.* 135 R. = p. 270–1 no. 154 W. = 148 J.)

       That he was fair and just in doing it I will unfold and tell.

In earlier research the use of such infinitives without the subject accusative was regarded as a feature of colloquial language (Casaceli 1976: 45–6; Frobenius 1910: 61–2). Accusative subjects are often omitted in Republican drama, but the context always precludes ambiguity (Jocelyn 1969: 289). Only *eum* and *eos* are missing as subject accusatives (Frobenius 1910: 62). However, as the construction is attested in many different genres (in Cicero's letters, in historiography after Caesar, and in the Augustan poets),[64] there seem to be no grounds for attributing the construction specifically to spoken language.[65] It is essentially variation within written language.

5.17 Parataxis and asyndeton

Parataxis is (and especially earlier it was) seen as a basic feature separating conversational language from the typical hypotactic organisation of written language (see Chahoud, this volume pp. 59–60). As such, it has been

---

[64] H–S 362 (with the label of colloquial language).
[65] It is not typical in non-literary Latin or in Petronius, see Adams 2005c.

considered a typical ingredient of dramatic speech, even that of tragedy (Frobenius 1910: 59–60; Casaceli 1976: 41–3). Often however it remains doubtful whether a paratactic organisation is a substitute for a hypotactic one, e.g. *certatio hic est nulla quin monstrum siet: hoc ego tibi dico et coniectura auguro*,[66] 'Here can there be no dispute that it is a monstrous brood. This I say unto you and foretell it as from a sign' (Enn. *scaen.* 245–6 R. = p. 326–7 no. 296–7 W. = 248–9 J.). In at least one respect, this conception has truth to it: parataxis for accusative and infinitive seems to have been a construction of the conversational language, often used in place of the infinitive one (see Halla-aho 2009: ch. 4 with references). But even there certain common verbs serve as sentence adverbials rather than governing verbs, e.g. *credo*, Enn. *scaen.* 151 R. = p. 288–9 no. 197 W. = 159 J. *constitit credo Scamander, arbores vento vacant* (but on the other hand, *credo* with the accusative and infinitive at Enn. *scaen.* 292 R. = p. 346–7 no. 344 W. = 289 J. *deumque de consilio hoc itiner credo conatum modo*).

Concerning asyndeton, Casaceli notes on verses Acc. *trag.* 437–8 R. = p. 470–1 no. 424–5 W. = 533–4 D. *constitit congnovit sensit, conlocat sese in locum celsum; hinc minibus rapere raudus saxeum grande et grave*: 'Qui, infatti, in una sequenza disarmonica di tempi e modi che riflette l'improvvisazione della lingua parlata, si inserisce un elemento di alta letterarietà quale l'infinito storico, spia di un'elaborazione artistica che si nasconde sotto la patina di una sintassi svincolata da esigenze di fredda letterarietà' (Casaceli 1976: 42). Another example of this type of asyndeton is Enn. *scaen.* 74–5 J. *adiuverit | statuerit steterit*.[67] Here it is a matter of literary devices. The asyndetic sequence *constitit congnovit sensit* has been used to convey an idea of quick action, like the historical infinitive *rapere* in the following sentence.[68]

5.18   Use of the accusative

(a)   atque eccos unde certiscent
                 (Pac. *trag.* 107 R. = p. 198–9 no. 99 W. = 82 Sch.)

And see them, there they are, from whom doubts may be settled.[69]

---

[66] Text according to Warmington (1967).
[67] Ribbeck (1871) assigned this to Accius (357–8 R.), similarly Warmington (1967: p. 444–7, no. 351–2 W.).
[68] See H–S 469. For further examples of asyndetic connection (on sentence level) in Ennius see Frobenius 1910: 84–6.
[69] Warmington's (1967) translation with *certiscant*.

(b)   atque eccum in ipso tempore ostentum senem
                    (Pac. *trag.* 283 R. = p. 258–9 no. 251 W. = 178 Sch.)

Why, see him! There in the very nick of time the old man is disclosed.

These passages are interesting examples of the range of usages of the accusative case. The accusative is used of persons who are possibly arriving on the stage, or the speaker otherwise wants to draw the hearer's attention to them. In dramatic language this can be done with the ellipsis of a verb (*vide* or the like), and was undoubtedly accompanied by the movement of the hand.

5.19   Incoherent syntax

(a)   mater gravida parere se ardentem facem | visa est in somnis Hecuba
                    (Enn. *scaen.* 50–1 J. = p. 234–5 no. 38–9 W. = *inc. trag.* 5–6 R.)

My mother Hecuba, heavy with a child, in a dream thought she gave birth to a burning brand.

This is a conflation between *parere se facem vidit* and *parere facem visa est*, quoted by Cicero in his discussion of dreams in the *De divinatione*. Jocelyn points out that Ovid imitates the construction in *Ep.* 17.237–8 *fax quoque me terret, quam se peperisse cruentam | ante diem partus est tua visa parens* (1969: 223).

(b)   †alter†[70] terribilem minatur vitae cruciatum et necem
           quae nemo est tam firmo ingenio et tanta confidentia
           quin refugiat timido sanguen atque exalbescat metu
                    (Enn. *scaen.* 22–4 R. = p. 230–1 no. 27–9 W. = 18–20 J.)

[?] threatens my life with butchery and torture terrible, horrors at which there is none so steadfast in spirit, none endowed with such firm trust that his blood would not flee him in his fright and himself not turn white with fear.

Cicero quotes this passage in the *De oratore* (3.218) in his discussion of how to present fear. Jocelyn suggests understanding *quin refugiat timido sanguen atque exalbescat metu* as a 'pictorial substitute' for a verb like *timeat*, and taking *quae* (i.e. *cruciatum et necem*) as its object (1969: 196).

Regarding both (a) and (b), it is possible to think that in Ennius' time, at least in dramatic language, similar strict rules concerning the logical

---

[70] Text is according to Jocelyn who does not accept Ribbeck's *mater* (see his discussion, 1969: 190–2). Warmington (1967) prints *mater* and translates 'mother threatens my life . . .' Jocelyn thinks that the *cruciatus et nex* Alcmeo is terrified by are those resulting from a trial he was to face (1969: 192–4).

syntactic sequence were not applicable. However, Lennartz assigns (a) and other conflations to the deliberate design of the author, who created the construction in order to strengthen the image in question.[71] Especially in example (b) this motivation seems very probable, in view of the apparent horror of the speaker (Alcmeo), horror that is given an expression in the incoherent syntactic structure. Ultimately, the source of these incoherences is in the conversational language, even if the author created them on purpose (cf. Chahoud, this volume p. 60, with reference to Adams 2005b), as he most probably did. Nevertheless, we would not classify them as colloquialisms.

6 CONCLUSIONS

We have presented cases that have been adduced as candidates for colloquial language use in Roman tragedy. Only a minority of them (*habet, bene facis*, partly frequentative verbs) were classifiable as certainly colloquial, if by colloquial we mean features that are part of spoken conversational registers, or ones that are seemingly conversational and as such at home in less formal written and dramatic language. Many features (*nitidare, inibi est, quod socium, interea loci*, adverbs in *-ter*) are possibly colloquial, but there is no decisive evidence concerning their status at the time the tragedies were written. One case was clearly an example of the official style (*praesente his*). Others look more like poetic usages (*flaccere, fervere, segregare, hoc corpus*, partly frequentative verbs). Certain features belong to the category 'variation within written language' (parataxis and asyndeton, accusative and infinitive without the subject accusative). Furthermore, in other cases we are dealing with cases in which there was a great amount of variation before the later processes of standardisation of written language (active and deponent verbs, locational and directional expressions). While these do reflect variation in spoken language, they should not be regarded as colloquial, since at the time of their writing the standard of written language was not yet established in the way it was later. Thus, these features do not represent choices made by the author against the written standard. Syntactic incoherence may have been used to create special effects at heated points, contributing to the affect typical of tragic language. But this strategy of

---

[71] Lennartz 2003: 120. See Lennartz 2003: 119–25 for more examples of syntactic incoherence in tragic language. For further examples of contamination in Ennius see Jocelyn (1969: 295) on *ius atque aecum se a malis spernit procul*: 'an odd phrase; *spernere* normally takes a simple object in republican drama'. He adduces examples from Plautus where *spernere* occurs with *segregare*, and the latter verb clearly must be understood here as well.

the author should not be called colloquial language use. It perhaps finds its place better under the concept of 'orality' (similarly the use of the accusative in *eccum* and *eccos*). In addition, the change in syntactic standards is one possible factor.

This collection of examples shows that there is not much in tragic language that can be considered strictly colloquial. What is clear, however, is that these examples testify to the richness of the linguistic means that the poets made use of and the amount of stylistic variation within the tragic register.[72]

[72] Hilla Halla-aho's contribution to this chapter is part of the 'Centres of Excellence in Research' programme 2006–11, Academy of Finland.

CHAPTER 9

The fragments of Cato's Origines

John Briscoe

Cato's *Origines* marked the beginning of Latin historiography, as earlier authors, beginning with Fabius Pictor, had written in Greek.[1] It was composed in the latter part of his long life (234–149 BC)[2] and consisted of seven books, of which the first three dealt with the foundation of Rome, the regal period and the origins of the cities of Italy (hence the title), while the remaining four contained an account of Roman history from the First Punic War to 149. He included in the *Origines* (something unique in ancient historiography) at least two of his speeches, one, delivered in 167, arguing in the Senate against declaring war on Rhodes (95), the other, delivered shortly before his death, supporting a bill to set up a special court to try Ser. Sulpicius Galba for his treatment of the Lusitani (108–9); the remaining fragments of his speeches (there are 254 in Malcovati)[3] are not considered here.[4]

Cato wanted to write impressively, and to that end looked for appropriate vocabulary and stylistic devices wherever he could find them. He took words from poetry and he neologised (see Briscoe 2005: 60), and, in principle, there is no reason why he should not, on occasion, have made use of features derived from the spoken language. To identify such elements, however, is very difficult: the only substantial texts earlier than Cato are the plays of Plautus, which certainly contain much that belongs to the spoken language, but also elements which are high-register. And even if one were to find a usage in Cato which occurs elsewhere only in dialogue

---

[1] It is a great pleasure to offer Jim Adams, my colleague in Manchester for twenty-three years, this token of my admiration and friendship.

[2] See, e.g., Astin 1978: 1 n. 1; Briscoe 2008: 353.

[3] Malcovati 1976: 1.12–97, though not all are verbatim citations. I cite fragments of the speeches as *orat.* with Malcovati's enumeration (*TLL* now cites that of Sblendorio Cugusi 1982).

[4] The fragments are cited by their number in Peter 1914; a new edition of the fragments of the otherwise lost Roman historians, with English translation and commentary, edited by Tim Cornell and prepared by a team of which I am a member, will have a different enumeration. Cornell himself has contributed the entry on Cato.

in Plautus, when so much else is lost, it would not follow that it is a deliberate colloquialism. With no pre-existing prose literature, it was, of course, natural that Cato's Latin would have much in common with the spoken language of his time (cf. Till 1935: 12 = 1968: 33). But Cato did not create Latin prose 'out of nothing'[5] and there would have been a discernible difference between the Latin of speeches delivered in the Senate or before a *contio,* or of generals' written reports to the senate, and ordinary conversation.[6]

In what follows, items which might appear, or have so appeared to others, to be in some way colloquial, will be examined in relation to their distribution across Latin literature, to see whether they might be instances of 'a current, and possibly "popular" ... usage normally excluded from higher literary genres except to achieve a special effect'.[7] There is, of course, always the possibility that what was a colloquialism at the time of Cato was no longer one at that of Cicero, and vice versa.

Of the 144 fragments 88 appear to be verbatim citations,[8] the equivalent of about five pages of Oxford text. They are quoted by ten different authors, the large majority by Gellius, Nonius, Charisius, Servius (Danieline version) and Priscian. Most are cited for linguistic reasons, but in no case does the citing author say that there is anything colloquial about his quotation. The only fragments of any length are 83, the account of the exploits of a military tribune in 258 BC, and 95, the fragments (seven separate passages) of the Rhodian speech. Both are cited by Gellius, but not for linguistic reasons.

Fragment 7 reads *agrum quem Volsci habuerunt campestris plerus Aboriginum fuit,* 'Most of the land in the plain which the Volscians possessed belonged [*sc.* originally] to the Aborigines.'[9] This is an instance of *attractio inversa*: we expect *ager,* but the subject is attracted into the case of the relative. The phenomenon occurs in Plautus, Terence, Lucilius, a letter of Pompey to Cicero, Varro, Columella, and in the speech of the freedmen in Petronius. With this distribution, nobody has doubted that it is indeed

[5] Adams 2005b: 73; Briscoe 2005: 58. The use of the phrase by both of us is not coincidence: as I recall, I took it from a comment by Jim Adams on an early draft of my chapter.
[6] Adams 2005b: 73; Briscoe 2005: 58. In Britain the decline of political oratory and the domination of the broadcast media mean that there is now far less difference between the way a politician speaks in the House of Commons or during an election campaign and his or her ordinary conversation.
[7] Adams *et al.* 2005: 7 n. 8, quoted by Chahoud, this volume p. 54.
[8] The prayer at the end of 12 may not be a verbatim citation. 133–43 are listed under the rubric *incertorum Catonis librorum reliquiae selectae*: 137 may not be a verbatim citation and 138 certainly comes from a speech (*orat.* 80).
[9] See K–S II.289, H–S 567, Till 1935: 14 = 1968: 35, Fraenkel 1964: II.139–41, Austin 1971 on Virgil *Aen.* 1.573.

of colloquial origin. The exception[10] is Virgil *Aen.* 1.573 *urbem quem statuo vestra est:* as Fraenkel argued (1964: II.139–41), for Virgil the construction was a solemn archaism, not a colloquialism. It is also used by Cato at *orat.* 158 *agrum quem vir habet tollitur,* cited by Servius (Danieline version) on the passage of Virgil. The effect is to emphasise *agrum* (it is probably coincidence that the word occurs in both fragments of Cato) and Cato will have employed it for that reason, not because it was a colloquialism.

Fragments 28 *igitur tertio pedato bellum nobis facere* 'to therefore make war on us at the third time of asking' and 136 (not certainly from the *Origines*; cf. n. 8) *in his duobus bellis alteras stipendio agrique parte multati, alteras oppidum vi captum, alteras primo pedatu et secundo,* 'In these two wars they were punished by a fine and the loss of part of their land, on another their town was captured by force, on another with the first and second attack', are also relevant.[11] *pedatus/-um,*[12] attested only in the ablative and with a numeral, occurs also at *orat.* 41, cited together with 28 by Nonius 89 L., and elsewhere only at Plautus *Cist.* 526 and the appendix to Optatus (late fourth century AD). According to Julius Romanus, whom Charisius is following (see Adams 2007: 208–9), the word was still used in Campania in his day. In 136, *orat.* 41 and Plautus the word appears to mean 'attack', and Heraeus (1902: 263) thought that it was originally a military term widened to apply to other kinds of attack. That, however, makes little sense in 28, where it seems to refer to an ultimatum delivered on three occasions (cf. Nonius' *repetitu*). There is no trace of three ultimata in Roman fetial procedure, but Cato is clearly talking about another people making war on Rome, who may have used such a procedure. It may be that Cato did indeed take a word from the language of soldiers, used it in its original sense in 136, in a widened one at *orat.* 41, and then, innovatively, of an ultimatum at 28. It is scarcely likely that the word was restricted to Campania in the first half of the second century BC.

Another pair is made of fragments 74 *laserpitium pro pulmentario habet* 'he regards asafoetida as a relish' and 75 *multo pulmento usi* 'using a lot of hors d'oeuvres'. *pulmentum* and *pulmentarium*[13] have similar distributions.

[10] Kühner and Stegmann (K–S II.289) also cite [Sen.] *Her. O.* 410, but there *hic* and *hunc* have equal attestation and both Zwierlein (1986) and Chaumartin (2002) print the former.
[11] See Heraeus 1902: 263, *TLL* x/1.965.16 ff.; Adams 2007: 208–10.
[12] *pedato* is attested by the MSS of Nonius in 28 and in 136, from Charisius, by the excerpts of Cauchius (J. Cuyck) from a now lost MS, *pedatu* by N, the eighth-century MS which is the principal evidence for the text of Charisius, and the MSS of Plautus.
[13] *OLD* correctly defines *pulmentum* as 'a small portion of meat or fish eaten as a starter to a meal' (cf., e.g., Hor. *Sat.* 2.2.34) and *pulmentarium* as 'anything (a vegetable, condiment, etc.) used to flavour a *pulmentum*'. L–S wrongly give 'sauce, condiment, relish' for *pulmentum* (Chassignet 1986: 33 translates both words as *ragoût*, Beck and Walter 2001: 195–6 as *Zukost*). See now *TLL* x/2.2593–5.

The former occurs in Plautus, Varro, Horace, *Satires* and Apuleius, the latter in Lucretius, Horace, *Satires*, Phaedrus, Seneca, Columella, Persius, the Elder Pliny and Juvenal. But that is of little significance: words of the culinary register will largely be used in the spoken language and one does not expect to find them often in high literature; if Cato wanted to talk about food, this was the language he had to use.[14]

Fragment 78 reads *mapalia uocantur ubi habitant, ea quasi cohortes rotundae sunt.* 'Their dwelling places are called *mapalia*; they are like round stables.' This is an example of what was the original sense of *cohors*, belonging to the agricultural register. *OLD* give the definition 'a space surrounded by farm buildings, farmyard' (cf. Nonius 117 L. *cohortes sunt villarum intra maceriam spatia* 'The *cohortes* of villas are spaces inside the wall'). But Cato must have been referring to a roofed building and 'stable' thus seems the best translation.[15] Apart from agricultural writers (it occurs also at *Agr.* 39), it is found in a fragment of Varro, in Vitruvius, Ovid and Martial. Again, the distribution is of little significance: if Cato wanted to compare the dwelling-places of the Carthaginians to farm buildings, he had to use words of the agricultural register, normally, no doubt, occurring in spoken Latin, but not colloquialisms.

Fragment 83[16] is the account of the exploits of the military tribune in 258 BC, during the First Punic War (his name appears in the sources variously as Caedicius, Laberius and Calpurnius Flamma, but Cato, in accordance with his usual practice, probably did not give the name).[17] The fragment consists of two parts, the first (Gel. 3.7.3–17) being a paraphrase by Gellius, the second (Gel. 3.7.19) a verbatim citation. The style of the former is not dissimilar to that of Cato, partly, no doubt, because of Gellius' archaising tendencies, partly because of the influence of the original.[18] The vocabulary, too, may sometimes have been taken from Cato himself, but in only one case can we be sure. Gellius says that Cato used *verruca* ('wart', 'mole') to refer to a hillock. The only other instance of this metaphor is in what has normally been taken to be a line of tragedy, *saxea erat verruca in summo montis vertice,*[19] but there the *saxea verruca* is clearly a rocky outcrop at the top of a mountain, in Cato the *verruca* is a hillock. The probability must

---

[14] For a similar phenomenon in Livy cf. Briscoe 1981: 10 n. 7.

[15] Cf. *TLL* III.1550.54 *saeptum, stabulum, area.*   [16] For bibliography see Briscoe 2005: 58 n. 38.

[17] Cf. Nepos, *Cato* 3.4, Plin. *Nat.* 8.11; there is no fragment where an individual is named.

[18] It has often been treated as if it were a verbatim citation; cf., e.g., *TLL* VII/1.663.3–4.

[19] *trag. inc.* 141, cited by Quint. *Inst.* 8.3.48 (cf. 8.6.4). Courtney (1999: 75) says that it is so taken 'without reason' and thinks it possible that these are the words which Cato attributed to the tribune: the fact that it is a trochaic septenarius catalectic is not a bad reason. Russell (2001: III.368 n. 66) thinks it may have come from a play dealing with the episode.

be that Cato himself is responsible for the invention of the metaphor. It is, however, not dissimilar to the rustic metaphors referred to by Cicero, *Orat.* 81[20] (though they are all verbs or adjectives) and one cannot exclude the possibility that Cato took it from rural speech.

The penultimate sentence of Gellius' verbal citation reads *Leonides Laco, qui simile apud Thermopylas fecit, propter eius virtutes omnis Graecia gloriam atque gratiam praecipuam claritudinis inclitissimae decoravere monumentis* 'Leonidas the Spartan, who did something similar at Thermopylae – because of his virtues the whole of Greece adorned his special glory and esteem with monuments of the most renowned distinction.'[21] We have here an instance of the 'detached nominative':[22] *Leonides Laco* has no predicate, but is picked up by *eius* (the nominative, as often, is followed by a relative clause). It is indeed likely that the idiom, which serves to emphasise the nominative, was used in conversation, but it is found elsewhere in literature (Adams 2005b: 92 cites Cic. *Fin.* 3.11, Livy 1.40.2), and is to be regarded as focalisation, not lax syntax. It also occurs in the text of laws (see *Lex Agraria* (*RS* 2) 15, *Lex Cornelia de* XX *quaestoribus* (*RS* 14) 2.41–4), as well as in a *senatus consultum* reported by Livy at 41.9.10: if this last is not authentic, Livy will have deliberately imitated a construction found in legal Latin. Much of the language of Roman legislation, *senatus consulta* etc., remained unchanged over long periods, and it is likely that the usage will have occurred in laws passed in the first half of the second century BC. But Cato adopted it to add force to what he was saying about Leonidas, not because it was a legalism or a colloquialism.

Fragment 95,[23] the Rhodian speech, contains five items which Till (1935 = 1968) and/or Calboli (1978) saw as colloquialisms.

(i) Fragment 95a (Gel. 6.3.14). *secundae res laetitia transvorsum trudere solent a recte consulendo atque intellegendo,* 'Prosperity, because of the happiness it produces, tends to push people sideways, away from making correct decisions and judgements.' Calboli (1978: 281–2) regards *transvorsum trudere* as colloquial. As he says, *tra(ns)vorsus* is a term often used in

---

[20] See Ferri and Probert, this volume p. 27. [21] On *claritudinis inclitissimae* cf. Briscoe 2005: 59.

[22] See H–S 29, Calboli 1986: 1090–3, Adams 2005b: 92–3; for resumptive *is* in the idiom cf. *TLL* VII/2.463.54 ff. Madvig (1873: 592) and Peter (1914: 80) emended it away, replacing *qui* with *quia* and *quidem* respectively.

[23] I merely mention in passing 93, where Cato calls the north-west wind *cercius*, rather than the normal *circius*. He is writing about Spain, and Adams (2007: 225–9) observes that Cato's orthography is reflected in Spanish *cierzo* (he argues that the word is of Celtic origin). Cato may have been representing the way he had heard the word pronounced in Spain, but, obviously, one cannot talk of a colloquialism.

the agricultural register (by Cato himself at *Agr.* 45.3, 48.2), but his only evidence for seeing it as colloquial[24] is that *de traverso* 'all of a sudden' occurs at *Rhet. Her.* 4.14, in a passage described by its author as being written in *sermo infimus et cotidianus* (cf. above, pp. 18–19); its occurrence at Cicero *Att.* 15.4a is consistent with that view, though *e(x) tra(ns)verso* is used in a number of passages which there is no reason to regard as colloquial. But in the sense of 'carried off course' there is no case at all for seeing *tra(ns)versus* as colloquial: it occurs first at Ennius *scaen.* 270 V. (229 J.), next in Sallust and Valerius Maximus (*OLD* s.v. 2b).

For Calboli *trudere* is colloquial as being a harshly realistic synonym for 'push' ('shove' in English; he says that the Italian equivalent is *cacciare*). The verb occurs in Plautus and Terence, but also in Cicero (speeches, philosophical works and letters), Lucretius and Virgil (it is absent from Caesar, Sallust and Livy), and the case for regarding it as colloquial is weak.

(ii) 95b (Gel. 6.3.16) *si nemo esset homo quem vereremur.* 'if there were not a single man whom we feared' *nemo ... homo* is declared to be a colloquialism by both Till (1935: 13 = 1968: 34) and Calboli (1978: 289–90). The usage is frequent in early Latin, but as both admit, is also common in Cicero (nine instances in the speeches, three in the philosophical works, five in the letters): it may have been the sort of pleonasm common in ordinary speech, but the Ciceronian evidence indicates that it was not felt to be particularly colloquial, and in any case Cato used it as a way of emphasising his point, not for any colloquial character it may have had.

(iii) 95b (Gel. ibid.) *si quis advorsus rem suam quid fieri arbitrantur* 'if anyone thinks that something is being done against his interests'. Till (1935: 14 = 1968: 36) claims that the plural with *si quis* (found also at *orat.* 51) is colloquial. This use of the plural with pronouns such as *quis, quisque* and *uterque* and nouns such as *pars* (note also *omnis Graecia ... decoravere* in 83, cited above p. 158) is particularly common in old Latin, largely avoided in Cicero and Caesar (though attempts to emend away the few instances attested are misguided), but frequent in Sallust and Livy. There is no reason to regard it as colloquial.[25]

(iv) 95c (Gel. 6.3.26). Till (1935: 15 = 1968: 37) sees *derepente* 'suddenly', together with other adverbs compounded with *de-*, as colloquial. In fact it

---

[24] Following Marouzeau 1954: 195.
[25] See K–S I.22–3, H–S 436–7; *pars* + plural occurs at Cassius Hemina 9, Licinius Macer 23.

is common in old Latin, including Ennius and Accius; it occurs in Varro *Men.* and not again before Suetonius.[26]

(v) 95e (Gel. 6.3.37) *nobis impune est* 'we are not punished'. Till (1935: 15 = 1968: 38) declares that this is very probably colloquial, but adduces no arguments. *impune esse* occurs at *Agr.* 5.2, twice in Plautus, twice in Cicero, four times in Livy and three times in Ovid.[27]

We thus see that of the eleven items discussed, four (95 *transvorsum trudere*, *si quis* + plural, *derepente*, and *impune esse*) have no claims to be colloquial, and in two (74 *pulmentum*, *pulmentarium*, 78 *cohortes*) Cato was dealing with subjects where he had no alternative to employing words which were normally used in the spoken language, but which were not colloquialisms. In two more (83 detached nominative and 95 *nemo homo*) we have usages which were, indeed, no doubt used in conversation, but are also found in high literature. In the case of 28, 136 *pedatus/-um* Cato may have taken a word from the language of soldiers, using it once in its original sense and once innovatively, while at 83 *verruca* it is possible that he employed a rural metaphor. The *attractio inversa* in 7 is a clear case of a colloquialism employed for emphasis. But in all cases Cato's aim was to write impressively, not to impart a colloquial flavour to his history. That is not, of course, to deny that if we had the whole work, one might come to a different conclusion.

[26] Cf. Calboli 1978: 300, though it is unclear whether or not he agrees with Till. Calboli's statement that it occurs at Tac. *Hist.* 1.63 (*sc.* §1) is an error, presumably deriving from *TLL* v/1.629.16–17, where it is, apparently, a conjecture based on the misapprehension that the second Medicean has *raptisae repente*. Calboli misses the passages of Suetonius (*Tib.* 23, *Ves.* 23.4).

[27] *TLL* vii/1.721.29 ff.; Calboli (1978: 316–17) is misleading.

PART III

Classical Latin

CHAPTER 10

Hyperbaton and register in Cicero

J. G. F. Powell

I INTRODUCTION

'Hyperbaton' is the name given, originally by rhetoricians, to the phenomenon in both Latin and Greek word order whereby words that are or
seem to be syntactically connected (e.g. a noun and an adjective which
agrees with it) occur some distance apart, separated by other words that
are in grammatical terms less closely connected. A convenient example is
given at *Rhetorica ad Herennium* 4.44: *instabilis in istum plurimum fortuna
valuit: omnes invidiose eripuit bene vivendi casus facultates*, 'Unstable Fortune has exercised her greatest power on this creature. All the means of
living well Chance has jealously taken from him' (trans. H. Caplan). *Rhet.
Her.* defines the feature as *quae verborum perturbat ordinem* '[the figure]
which disturbs the order of words'; its name, which the Romans translated
by *transgressio* or *traiectio*, means 'stepping over', implying that it is a dislocation of some more usual order in which one would not need to step
over anything. Standard grammars usually present it as a departure from
'normal' or 'natural' order, although (as it is unnecessary to point out in the
distinguished company of the contributors to this volume and especially
of its honorand[1]) any such definition begs a large question about what is to
count as normal or natural. Furthermore, the listing of hyperbaton among
the 'figures of speech' (which has been conventional from ancient times to
Kennedy's *Latin Primer* and beyond) tends to carry at least for a modern
reader the implication that it is an artificial rhetorical feature, belonging
perhaps to a formalised literary register at some distance from ordinary
speech.[2]

---

[1] Who himself published an important article on Latin hyperbaton nearly forty years ago (Adams
1971).

[2] It should here be noted that Quintilian *Inst.* 8.6.65 ff. sees hyperbaton largely as a means of aesthetic
enhancement of composition, without expressing a view on whether it represents a departure from
ordinary usage; Quintilian's comments at *Inst.* 9.4.23–32 are disappointingly vague and provide no
further enlightenment on the issue.

Scholars in the field of modern linguistics recognise the phenomenon of hyperbaton, terming it 'discontinuity', but there have been few attempts either among traditional philologists or among linguists to explore the matter either systematically or comprehensively in relation to Latin.[3] The fullest recent study of Latin hyperbaton is Devine and Stephens 2006: 524–610, part of a large-scale theoretical treatment of Latin word order which cannot be discussed here: it will be apparent that my approach is very different from theirs. I do not address here (interesting though it is) their principal question, which is how to account for the phenomena of Latin word order in terms of generative theory. I have a more modest purpose: to try to determine as clearly as possible what the phenomena actually are (initially keeping an open mind as to what kind of theory might best describe them).[4] Certain linguistic concepts are indispensable for any satisfactory description: in particular, the terms 'topic(alisation)' and 'focus', which derive from functional linguistics, will recur, though to many classicists they may not even now be very familiar. Topicalisation is what happens when a word or phrase is placed first in a sentence so as to indicate what the sentence is about: in 'Talent Mr Micawber has; capital Mr Micawber has not' the words *talent* and *capital* are topicalised. What is said about the topic is the 'logical predicate'. A word has 'focus' if, from a semantic or logical point of view, it is more important or prominent than other words in the surrounding context: focus may be conveyed by word position, by the addition of words e.g. particles, or by stress or intonation in speaking. Roughly it is equivalent to what is traditionally called 'emphasis', though it is a more precise term, since 'emphasis' could also refer to a manner of pronunciation or delivery applied to a whole utterance ('speaking with emphasis'). The usage of these terms among linguists varies to some extent; I differ from some others in making a distinction between, on the one hand, the logical categories 'topic' and 'predicate' which refer to (usually well-defined) divisions of a sentence, and on the other, the pragmatic category 'focus', which is a matter of

---

[3] See e.g. Madvig 1856: 418–19 (brief and clear summary); Ahlberg 1911 (useful study of earlier Latin prose usage); Marouzeau 1922: 215–19, 1938: 96–102, 1949: 150–62; K–S II.618–20; Foucault 1964: 66–7 (brief discussion of Latin); H–S 689–94 (with further bibliography at 693–4); Skard 1970; Lundström 1982: 31–8 (a study of hyperbaton involving possessive pronouns, directed towards solving one particular textual problem in Cicero); Bolkestein 2001; Pinkster 2005b.

[4] This chapter is a provisional preview of an on-going project, on which I embarked in 2003–4 with the aid of a Leverhulme Research Fellowship, and to which I am now returning after an intervening period of heavy administrative commitments. Much detailed work on the texts remains to be done, and at this stage I unavoidably concentrate on general principles and provisional hypotheses yet to be fully tested; but from the reader's point of view this may not be a disadvantage.

degree.[5] In my usage, focus may be a characteristic of either topics or predicates, although the main focus of a sentence is usually (for reasons that should be obvious) on the logical predicate or part of it.

Statistical surveys of the frequency of 'hyperbaton' are often rendered less useful than they might be, because of the tendency to lump together different types of real or apparent discontinuity which have different underlying causes and may turn out to have different distributions: in section 2 of this chapter I shall point towards a clearer (probably not at this stage exhaustive) classification of different types of hyperbaton. My other main purpose in this chapter is to reopen the question of the relationship of hyperbaton to register in Latin prose (verse is entirely outside the scope of this discussion), and I provisionally take Cicero as my main source of examples,[6] for the simple reason that he is the only author from the classical period whose corpus of genuine texts embraces a sufficient range of identifiably different prose genres and registers. With due care, it appears possible within this corpus to isolate variations due to genre or register (as opposed, say, to chronological variations or matters of authorial preference) with a reasonable degree of certainty – a task which could be difficult or impossible in connection with other areas of Latin.

It is usual to rank Cicero's works on a scale of formality, with the letters to Atticus, say, at the colloquial end,[7] and this can be adopted as a rule of thumb: if a feature occurs significantly more often in the Atticus letters than in the speeches, that may well indicate that it is a colloquial feature, bearing in mind the reservations expressed in Chapters 1–5 of this volume regarding the difficulties of defining and identifying colloquialism.[8] The speeches, on the whole more formal than the letters, show an appreciable variation in style,[9] although we should avoid thinking in terms of a simple linear

---

[5] For example, Panhuis's (1982) concept of 'rhematicity' seems to me to amalgamate these two theoretically separable categories.

[6] In this chapter, works of Cicero are referred to by abbreviated title alone.

[7] The cue for this comes doubtless from Cicero himself, who for example refers to his exchanges of letters with Atticus as 'familiar conversation' (*sermo familiaris*, *Att.* 1.9.1). In an often quoted passage written to his friend Papirius Paetus (*Fam.* 9.21.1) Cicero distinguishes the 'everyday' and 'plebeian' language of informal letters from the language of political or forensic oratory, and also the 'more subtle' language of private lawsuits from the 'more ornate' style of criminal trials: for this and other relevant passages see Hutchinson 1998: 5–9. Cf. Ferri and Probert, this volume p. 39 and Thomas, this volume, p. 255.

[8] Pinkster in this volume (p. 189) points out with justification that the epistolary style is an example of informal *writing* rather than informal speech, and does not necessarily reflect speech patterns; but the weight of this is lessened by his observation that letters in the ancient world were customarily dictated. Actually, dictation can lead to its own problems unless one is highly practised in it, since it proceeds at a speed so much slower than ordinary speech.

[9] See Laurand 1938; Albrecht 2003: esp. 11–27 and 79–85. Classifications of Cicero's speeches according to style often tend to rely on Cicero's own (*Orator* 102) tripartite division into 'plain', 'middle' and

scale: there are likely to be several variables, including register (here most of the speeches are likely to lie within a reasonably narrow range, reflecting the formal contexts for which they were written – except maybe where an isolated 'low' feature is introduced for particular effect),[10] communicative function (narration, logical argument, humour and other types of *captatio benevolentiae*, emotional appeal), and degree of rhetorical elaboration. The nature of the audience makes a difference: a senatorial speech may differ in style from a speech before the popular assembly, a speech in a private lawsuit from a defence speech in a public criminal trial.[11] Often the style varies from one section of a speech to another: for example, introductions and perorations may be more ornate, and perorations in particular more emotionally charged, than the narrative or argumentative portions of a speech.

The problem of characterising registers or styles is raised in a particularly acute form by the phenomenon of hyperbaton in Latin and Greek, because while some scholars have been willing to allow that it was a feature of ordinary language in at least some sense, others have found it hard to believe that it could ever have been a part of 'natural' or 'ordinary' language at all. Judgements about what is or is not possible in ordinary language are often subjective: one is tempted to say in principle (with some risk of exaggeration) that there is no linguistic feature so weird that it cannot be part of the ordinary rules of some language spoken somewhere on earth. Though familiar to classicists as a feature of written texts, hyperbaton is largely absent from most well-known modern languages and is quite rare among the world's languages in general: parallels have been cited from the Slavonic languages (though as a fairly rare feature on the whole),[12] from native North American languages (e.g. Fox),[13] and from Australian Aboriginal languages,[14] and that is about the sum total of it. But this shows that it can occur in at least some spoken languages and is not in principle excluded by some universal rule of grammar; the 'adjacency principle' cited by Givón (2001: 1.281) is correctly said not to be an absolute rule. Occasionally, indeed, one comes across fortuitous examples of separation of normally adjacent elements, even in English. Years ago I overheard an academic colleague say something like: 'I saw a good yesterday programme

'grand', which may be useful as a rough guide but is lacking in precision: H–S 689; Albrecht 2003: 21–2 n. 68.

[10] See Quint. *Inst.* 8.3.22, discussed above by Ferri and Probert, this volume p. 32.
[11] Senatorial and popular speeches: Mack 1937; private and public cases: Powell and Paterson 2004: 9.
[12] Serbo-Croat: D. Bennett 1987, cited by Adams (1994b: 132); Polish: Siewierska 1984.
[13] Dahlstrom 1987, cited by Givón 2001: II.13.
[14] Hale 1983; Austin and Bresnan 1996, cited by Givón (2001: 1.282).

on television.' Doubtless that would be counted as an error by the usual rules of English, yet it might prompt one to imagine that there could be spoken languages (especially those with inflections to mark adjectival agreement) in which such an order might be quite normal. Other things being equal, it is not unknown for spoken languages to display, both in word order and in other respects, a freedom which does not surface frequently in the formal written language.[15] There is, in other words, no intrinsic feature of hyperbaton that predicts, before we start, that it will turn out to be an artificial literary feature rather than a feature of natural spoken language (or even, indeed, of substandard linguistic performance).

Existing assessments of the role of hyperbaton in Latin style vary quite markedly. While some scholars have argued that hyperbaton in literary Latin prose was an artificial feature derived from imitation of Greek (e.g. Skard 1970, criticised by Adams 1971), others see it as a survival from a prehistoric state of the language (Devine and Stephens 2006: 602). Fraenkel (1968: 76) opted firmly for a colloquial origin for hyperbaton: 'Das nachweisliche uralte Mittel der emphatischen Sperrung entstammt nicht der Redekunst oder irgend einer literarischen Gattung, vielmehr ist es in der Umgangssprache zuhause, freilich nicht in der Sprache einer ruhigen Mitteilung, sondern in der Sprache, die dem Ausdruck einer inneren Bewegung dient, wenn der Sprechende gedrängt wird eine Einzelheit, bisweilen im Gegensatz zu etwas anderm, mit starkem Nachdruck hervorzuheben.'[16] In contrast, Adams (1971: 1) argued that hyperbaton in prose is 'artistic', stopping short of calling it artificial, but then qualifies this further, adding 'rather than natural to ordinary speech'; and then again (p. 10): 'Though it had a limited place in the colloquial written language of the upper classes... it was certainly not natural to the fabric of popular speech.' While I would agree that the use of various types of hyperbaton in literary prose can often be artistic, and while Adams's article has demonstrated quite clearly how one particular form of it became a literary mannerism in some kinds of later Latin prose, I think this formulation needs to be

---

[15] In English, the behaviour of quantifiers like 'only' has attracted attention: while the traditional rules of formal written English state that they should be placed immediately before the word they qualify, as in 'I saw only one magpie', colloquial language allows separation 'I only saw one magpie.' Devine and Stephens (2006: 524) draw the same parallel.

[16] Note also the remark of Albrecht (2003: 14 n. 16): 'in inflectional languages, such transpositions offer themselves quite naturally even to untrained speakers. Cicero, therefore, does not depart from common usage, but exploits its stylistic potential.' One could wish for more evidence as to the habits of untrained speakers of inflectional languages, but the claim seems prima facie sensible enough. Cicero, *Orator* 229–30, sometimes quoted in this context, implies only that hyperbaton sometimes sounded artificial, not that it always did.

refined, since it seems to me to postulate too sharp a dichotomy between 'artistic' prose on the one hand and 'ordinary speech' on the other. Artistic composition may sometimes reflect features of ordinary speech better than inartistic composition does; compare the last letter you received from your solicitor or bank manager with the dialogue in a first-class novel. The absence or rarity of some kinds of hyperbaton in some Latin texts in the 'lower' literary genres, noted by Adams, may not after all indicate that it is an artificial literary feature. Nor should we conflate two different oppositions: that between oral and written on the one hand, and that between formal and informal (or high and low) on the other. It is possible that a feature may be characteristically oral, without being necessarily 'colloquial' in the accepted sense. Certainly in English there exist features (some reducible to writing, others of course not) that are characteristic of formal oral performance, but which would not be found often in colloquial speech: a straightforward example is the up-and-down intonation used by English newsreaders and reporters, which would hardly pass muster in most informal conversational contexts. I shall suggest in due course that one kind of hyperbaton may be a candidate for inclusion in this category.

2 TYPES

Before we can venture a better answer to the question of the distribution of hyperbaton among the registers of Republican literary Latin, we need to have a secure classification of the different types of hyperbaton, or, more precisely, of the different phenomena that may be classified under that heading. There are naturally a number of criteria that can be used, the most obvious being the nature of the separated words (adjective and noun, for example), the nature of the intervening material (particle, pronoun, verb, etc.), and the distance of separation. The challenge is to find the significant differentiating features.

I take it as generally agreed that when a noun phrase[17] is split by words that do not form part of the phrase, we have an instance of hyperbaton. Viewed in traditional grammatical terms, the syntactic role of the noun phrase is not affected by the intervening word or words: there is no difference from a syntactical point of view, for example, between *bonos consules habemus* and *bonos habemus consules*, since both the continuous

---

[17] In conventional linguistic terminology a noun plus its modifiers (e.g. adjectives, demonstratives, possessive genitives) is called a 'noun phrase'. The noun is the 'head' of the noun phrase; modifiers may be further qualified by 'sub-modifiers'.

noun phrase *bonos consules* and the discontinuous *bonos. . . consules* function in the same way, as object of *habemus*. One should not at the moment insist that the constituent which splits the noun phrase should be a higher-order constituent (e.g. the verb): to presuppose this would beg too many questions, though I believe that it is a useful further distinction to make.

What then counts as a discontinuous noun phrase? There are several types of Latin word order phenomenon which might be candidates for inclusion, but which on closer inspection turn out to be something different. These may be divided, first of all, into (1) those which are noun phrases but are not genuinely discontinuous, and (2) those which are discontinuous, but are not genuine noun phrases.

2.1 Noun phrases, but not genuinely discontinuous

(i) Noun phrases involving a sub-modifier, e.g. *via multo longior* where *multo* modifies *longior* and the combined phrase *multo longior* modifies *via*. Probably few if any would seriously wish to count this as an example of hyperbaton. It is worth noting the well-known fact that normal Latin practice is to 'wrap' the noun + main modifier round any sub-modifiers.[18] This can lead to quite complex structures, especially where the main modifier is a participle or where the construction is rhetorically expanded by co-ordination; but however far away the main modifier appears to be from its noun, there is nothing that interrupts the continuity of the noun phrase as a whole; everything inside it belongs to it.

(ii) Noun phrases involving two (or more) modifiers, e.g. an adjective and a qualifying genitive. Here it is not easy to determine the grammatical and stylistic constraints on the choice of one order from the several available, but again we should note the tendency to 'wrap' the adjective–noun group round the genitive, e.g. *complures eiusdem amentiae scelerisque socios* (*Catil.* 1.8). *Complures. . . socios* might look superficially like a hyperbaton, as the adjective and noun are separated, but again, the noun phrase is not discontinuous, as everything inside it clearly belongs to it. A striking example from *Marc.* 5 (which deceived Fraenkel (1968: 96) into calling it

---

[18] The order however varies according to where the focus lies within the noun phrase. It is common, for example, to find the order modifier – head – submodifier, as in e.g. Cic. *Fin.* 5.32 *confecti homines senectute*, and this is a better candidate to be called hyperbaton as it involves the interposition of a higher-order constituent; cf. Devine and Stephens 2006: 575–8. I do not pursue here the wider question of the ordering of constituents within the noun phrase, which has attracted a relatively large amount of attention in the literature: see e.g. Marouzeau 1922; Devine and Stephens 2006: 314–523 with further bibliography.

a 'hyperbaton'): *omnes nostrorum imperatorum, omnes exterarum gentium potentissimorumque populorum, omnes regum clarissimorum res gestas* 'all the deeds of our commanders, all those of foreign nations and the most powerful peoples, all those of the most famous kings' – all one continuous noun phrase.

(iii) The phenomenon of the 'sandwiching' of certain adverbials between a main modifier (especially a demonstrative) and a noun. Often the 'sandwiched' element is a prepositional phrase, e.g. *hosce ex urbe sicarios* (*S. Rosc.* 74). Again, this is a single referring expression, 'these assassins from the city'; this example is particularly clear because there is nothing else in the sentence for *ex urbe* to depend on. As regards the phrase's inner structure, it is certainly implausible to regard *ex urbe* as a sub-modifier of *hosce*; but what is there to prevent us from regarding it as a modifier of *sicarios*? In this case it would be precisely equivalent to an adjective (as it might be *hosce urbanos sicarios*, avoided doubtless because of the alternative meaning 'witty assassins'). It might be objected that in Classical Latin a prepositional phrase is not normally treated as an adjective equivalent; but this pedagogic 'rule' is not borne out by actual usage and in fact prepositional phrases are used in Latin with adjectival force (as in *otium cum dignitate*),[19] and this is made easier when they are accompanied by another modifier (e.g. a pronoun).[20] Again this is not real discontinuity: everything in the sandwich belongs to it. More examples in Kühner–Stegmann (K–S II.620.Anm.1).[21]

Superficially, again, a phrase like *plura praeterea praedia* (*S. Rosc.* 133), embracing an adverb between the two case-marked elements, might look like a hyperbaton. We after all say 'more farms besides', not 'more besides farms'; and undoubtedly, *praeterea* could have been placed elsewhere in the sentence without breach of normal Latin conventions. But here *praeterea* belongs at least on the logical level, if not in terms of strict syntax, together with the noun phrase; in full the meaning is 'more farms other than the estate already mentioned' and that is a single referential expression; hence

---

[19] See also *senectutem sine querela* (*Sen.* 7) with Powell 1988: 117; K–S I.213–16.

[20] Compare the use of definite article + adverb or prepositional phrase + noun in classical Greek, which allows noun phrases of the type οἱ Ἀθήνῃσι φιλόσοφοι 'the philosophers at Athens' but not *Ἀθήνῃσι φιλόσοφοι 'philosophers at Athens'.

[21] Sometimes, adverbial or prepositional phrases that are less closely connected appear in 'sandwiched' position, e.g. *operam rei publicae fortem et strenuam praehibuit* (Cato, *Origines* fr. 83 Peter), where *rei publicae* is clearly to be taken more closely with the verb than with either component of the noun phrase; more than one explanation of these is possible, and only a more systematic study of these instances would show which is the most plausible.

it seems reasonable to treat it as, in practice, a single continuous noun phrase even though the precise syntactical relations of its elements may be a matter for debate.

2.2 *Discontinuous, but not genuine noun phrases*

(i) Where one constituent is a complement, e.g. *quem exspectari imperatorem in castris hostium sentis* (*Catil.* 1.27). *Quem . . . imperatorem* looks superficially like a hyperbaton, but it seems hardly open to doubt that the correct analysis is 'who, you realise, is being waited for in the enemy camp <u>as a commander</u>', with *imperatorem* as complement. A notorious example sometimes given to illustrate the separation of adjectives from 'their' nouns is *nostra semper feretur et praedicabitur, L. Lucullo dimicante cum interfectis ducibus depressa hostium classis est, incredibilis apud Tenedum <u>pugna illa navalis</u>, nostra sunt tropaea, nostra monumenta, nostri triumphi* (*Arch.* 21). But the meaning is not 'that sea battle of ours . . .' (if that were the case, *feretur* would have no meaning): *nostra* is the complement, and it means 'that sea battle (etc.) will always be spoken of <u>as ours</u>'.[22]

It is doubtless sometimes difficult to draw the line between an attributive adjective in hyperbaton and an adjectival complement, but usually the context solves it. Contrast for example *ne <u>bestiis</u> quoque quae tantum scelus attigissent <u>immanioribus</u> uteremur* (*S. Rosc.* 71), literally 'so that we should not experience as more ferocious the beasts which had been in contact with such a crime', where *immanioribus* is clearly a complement, with *vereor mehercule ne aut <u>gravioribus</u> utar <u>verbis</u> quam natura fert, aut levioribus quam causa postulat* 'I declare I am afraid that I may either use stronger language than I would naturally use, or else weaker than the case requires' (*Quinct.* 57), where *gravioribus* is clearly an attribute of *verbis* (it refers to a category of language). In the former example *immanioribus* is in the regular complement position before the verb (and does not form a noun phrase with *bestiis*). In the latter, *gravioribus . . . verbis* is a discontinuous noun phrase exemplifying a regular type of hyperbaton (see 2.5 (ii) below); two different constructions of *utor* are in question.

(ii) Where the second constituent is in apposition, e.g. *gravissimus auctor in Originibus dixit Cato* (*Tusc.* 4.3). Here the easiest interpretation is 'a very weighty authority says in his *Origines* – I mean Cato'. Nouns in apposition

---

[22] Further examples in Devine and Stephens 2006: 539; but despite the complexities of their theoretical analysis, they fail to distinguish clearly between adjectives which are complements – and therefore do not belong to the same noun phrase as the nouns they refer to – and attributive modifiers.

are often loosely connected and may be treated as an 'afterthought' or in linguistic terminology a 'post-topic' or 'tail': it is not at all surprising that they fail to appear juxtaposed with the noun phrase in apposition to which they stand.[23] Extensions of this usage, involving a phrase in apposition containing several words, appear especially frequently in the historical writers: many examples from Sallust and Tacitus are given by Adams (1971: 8–9). These may superficially be mistaken for hyperbata, but they seem to be in a quite different category.

(iii) Probably the most challenging category to analyse, but among the most common and important in a 'topic-prominent' language such as Latin, is that in which one constituent is topicalised.[24] The key point here is that it is possible in Latin for a noun alone to be the topic of a sentence, and for the attribute which agrees with it to function as the logical predicate or part of it.[25] Take as an example *verba, ut supra diximus, legenda sunt potissimum bene sonantia* (*Orat.* 163). The word *verba* is strongly topicalised, and the logically correct translation is something like 'As regards the words, as we have said above, the ones to be chosen above all are those which are pleasant-sounding' or 'The words that are to be chosen are the pleasant-sounding ones.' The relationship between *verba* and *bene sonantia* is that of logical topic and logical predicate, which is different from the relationship of noun and attribute within the same noun phrase, and more analogous to that of subject and complement (indeed, in English we have to recast it as subject and complement in order to make the sense explicit). Like subjects and complements, topics and predicates agree grammatically, but (I would argue) are not to be treated as part of the same noun phrase.[26] Hence I would not classify this as a hyperbaton in the strict sense.

---

[23] Compare Rosén (1999: 150–1), who draws attention to the frequency of 'appositional' word order in early Latin and particularly in comedy.

[24] Some progress was made in this direction by Panhuis (1982), who applied the theory of 'functional sentence perspective' developed by the Prague school of linguists on the basis of the Slavonic languages (for some of the problems of Panhuis's method see Powell 1984). Better typological parallels are to be found in Finnish and Hungarian: see Perrot 1994 and, for the concept of a 'discourse-configurational' language, K. É. Kiss 1995. Devine and Stephens (2006: 16–17, 26) recognise the importance of topicalisation in Latin, but never in practice focus on it as a primary issue.

[25] As Devine and Stephens (2006: 598) point out, a similar pattern does in fact occur in the archaic English idiom 'Answer came there none', although as they also point out it is not plausible to regard this as a straightforward dislocation of 'There was no answer.'

[26] A generativist account might well treat the topicalised noun as having been *extracted from* what is at a deeper level a single noun phrase, but that is a different issue.

2.3 Other related phenomena

One should also probably leave on one side a number of other phenomena which are sometimes classed as hyperbaton. I mention two of these:

(i) The common phenomenon sometimes called 'prepositional hyperbaton' (as in *summa cum laude, hac de re*) where, in a prepositional phrase, an adjective or other modifier is placed before the preposition. While it does seem that some minor shift of emphasis may be conveyed by placing the modifier before the preposition, this order is routine in Classical Latin and hardly seems comparable with the other phenomena we are here considering.

(ii) Conjunct 'hyperbaton', called *coniunctio* in Latin (*Rhet. Her.* 4.38), in which a phrase of the form 'A and B', involving a co-ordinating conjunction, is split by another constituent placed before the conjunction, as in English 'good men and true' or Latin *impuro homini ac nefario* (Cic. *Har.* 28). This is not so much a hyperbaton as a form of ellipsis, in which e.g. 'good men and true' is to be interpreted as short for 'good men and true men'. For this common feature see e.g. Kühner-Stegmann (K–S II.620–1).

2.4 Genuine discontinuity with intervening postpositive

Leaving on one side the above categories, we come now to those noun phrases which are genuinely discontinuous. These may be further classified according to the number and type of constituents in the intervening material, and according to the order of the enclosing constituents of the noun phrase itself – head first or modifier first.

Even here, however, we shall find that a relatively large proportion of discontinuous noun phrases are split by nothing more alarming than an emphatic particle such as *quidem* or *quoque*, a connective particle in the opening gambit of a sentence such as *enim, autem, igitur*, a weak personal pronoun attracted to immediate post-focus position (as admirably elucidated by Adams 1994b), or a part of the verb *esse* treated similarly (Adams 1994a). All of these can be classified together as 'postpositives' and it can often happen that a noun phrase is split by more than one postpositive, or by a postpositive together with another word or words (e.g. *Sen.* 84 *quid habet enim vita commodi?*). In the further categorisation of hyperbaton, particles and weak pronouns can be treated as invisible, so that e.g. *quid habet enim vita commodi* would be treated as if it were *quid habet vita commodi*.

Instances involving interposition of parts of *esse* need a separate category, since although the verb *esse* often behaves like a postpositive, grammatically it is still a fully-fledged verb, i.e. a higher-order constituent than any surrounding noun phrase. There are also further complexities to do with distinguishing the subject from its complements, distinguishing the existential from the copulative sense of *esse*, and so on, which need not be gone into here.

2.5 *Genuine discontinuity with stronger words intervening*

Where the intervening material consists of a word or words stronger than a postpositive, one may distinguish three types. I have provided these with distinguishing names: 'long-range' hyperbaton, 'short-range' hyperbaton, and 'double-focus' hyperbaton.

(i) I shall first examine 'long-range' hyperbaton, in which there appears to be no theoretical limit on the number or type of constituents that can intervene. Extreme examples of this can be found from time to time, such as the famous sentence <u>*magna*</u> *dis immortalibus habenda est atque huic ipsi Iovi Statori, antiquissimo custodi huius urbis,* <u>*gratia*</u>, *quod hanc tam taetram tam horribilem tamque infestam rei publicae pestem totiens iam effugimus*, 'Great are the <u>thanks</u> we owe to the immortal gods and to Jupiter Stator himself, the most ancient guardian of this city', etc. (*Catil.* I.11), <u>*quae*</u> *vobis potest cum hoc gladiatore condicionis aequitatis legationis esse* <u>*communitas?*</u>, 'What could you and this gladiator either in moral or legal or diplomatic standing possibly have <u>in common?</u>' (*Phil.* 6.3), or <u>*tantamne*</u> *unius hominis incredibilis ac divina virtus tam brevi tempore* <u>*lucem*</u> *adferre rei publicae potuit...?*, 'Could <u>glory</u> <u>so brilliant</u> be brought to the Republic in such a short time by the incredible and divine excellence of one man?' (*Man.* 33).[27] To this type belongs also the *Rhetorica ad Herennium*'s second example <u>*omnes*</u> *invidiose eripuit bene vivendi casus* <u>*facultates*</u> (4.44; see above, p. 163).

For 'long-range' hyperbaton, the following rules may be tentatively stated:
(a) The first element of the enclosing noun phrase always belongs to a certain restricted range of semantic categories which include determiners

---

[27] Cf. H–S 691; more examples in Pearce 1966: 168–70; Fraenkel 1968: 75–6, 106.

(e.g. demonstrative and interrogative adjectives; neuter pronouns with partitive genitive) and quantifiers (e.g. adjectives denoting quantity or size, including *magnus, multus, omnis, summus* and their opposites; also adverbials denoting degree or measure of difference[28] such as *tam, quam, multo, tanto, quanto*). A similar class of words was defined for Greek by Dover (1960: 20–4) and named 'preferential words'. Pearce (1966: 168) noted that certain categories of pronominal and adjectival modifiers tend to occur in first position in what he calls 'enclosing' word order in prose. Adams (1994b: 122–30, 1994a: 19–24) identifies certain categories of words (demonstratives, adjectives of quantity or size, etc.) as tending to bear focus and to attract postpositives towards themselves. Devine and Stephens (2006: 542–4) list further categories of pre-modifiers found in hyperbaton, but do not distinguish between long-range and short-range hyperbaton.

(b) No element of the clause precedes the first word of the enclosing noun phrase, except another preferential word or a conjunction.

(c) The second element of the enclosing noun phrase is usually the last stressed constituent in the sentence or clause (but not necessarily the last constituent of all).

(d) The verb, often an auxiliary, is unfocused, and is placed after the main focus of the sentence, which may be either the first word of the enclosing noun phrase or a later constituent.

As just seen, the types of words which may occur as the first element in a long-range hyperbaton are narrowly specified. This suggests a linguistic rule rather than a stylistic quirk: if long-range hyperbaton were merely an affectation why should it not have extended to other types of modifier (e.g. attributive adjectives)? For the fact that there seem to be no clear constraints on the length[29] of a long-range hyperbaton, there are easy typological comparisons with other languages: witness English 'stranding' with interrogatives (e.g. 'What did the man with the yellow raincoat travelling from Waterloo to King's Cross on the tube last Saturday see?', 'Who did you think of giving your copy of Aristotle with the fine leather binding to?').

The feature is relatively common in a range of genres and registers, and is found in Latin prose as far back as we can ascertain: Ahlberg (1911: 89) quotes an example from a speech of Cato the Elder, *quid illos bono genere*

---

[28] The tendency of these words to appear in hyperbaton was noticed already by Madvig 1856: 419; E. Löfstedt 1956: II.397–8.

[29] Given a constant syntactical structure. Further research needs to be done to establish the categories of grammatical constituents (subject, object, etc.) that can appear in long-range hyperbaton.

natos, magna virtute praeditos, opinamini animi habuisse? (fr. 58 Malcovati =
Gel. 10.3.17; Fraenkel 1968: 135–7). In contrast to the form shortly to be
discussed, it does not seem to be primarily a focusing device. Although
the clause-initial pronouns, adjectives, etc. do often seem to bear focus, it
seems artificial to claim that they always bear the main focus: for example
in *quam illa crudelis esset futura victoria* (*Fam.* 4.9.3) the main focus seems
to be on *crudelis*, and in *magnum tamen adfert mihi aetas ipsa solacium*
(*Amic.* 104) it appears to be on *aetas ipsa*.

(ii) 'Short-range' hyperbaton is, I would be tempted to claim, always
a focusing device.[30] This is a type in which (ignoring postpositives) only
one, always comparatively unfocused, constituent intervenes between the
separated elements: e.g. *ex tua putabam voluntate me statuere oportere* 'I
thought I ought to decide this in accordance with what *you yourself* wanted'
(*Att.* 1.5.5); *vetus opinio est iam usque ab heroicis ducta temporibus* 'It is an
ancient belief which has survived even from the *Heroic* Age' (*Div.* 1.1). We
saw above that in long-range hyperbaton there is a clear restriction on the
types of words that can come in first place, but short-range hyperbaton
shows no such constraint. It is true that the 'preferential' words do indeed
often occur as part of a short-range hyperbaton, but other types of modifier
(e.g. *heroicis*) are also found there. Nor is there a restriction on the order of
the enclosing constituents – either the head or the modifier may be found
in first place.

However, it makes a difference whether the head or the modifier comes
first. If the modifier comes first, as in the above two examples, it is usually
just the modifier that bears the focus, while if the head comes first the whole
enclosing phrase is focused.[31] As examples of the latter one may take *hunc*

---

[30] The observation that (in general terms) hyperbaton (sometimes) conveys focus or emphasis is not
by any means new. Marouzeau (1922: 217), in concluding the first volume of his study of Latin word
order (the volume devoted to nominal groups or noun phrases), already observed that hyperbaton,
which he called *disjonction*, was a method of placing the first element of the nominal group *en relief*,
i.e. in a position of prominence, observing that this could be achieved also by simple first positioning
without hyperbaton, but that hyperbaton guaranteed this effect: 'là où elle est employée, la mise
en relief en résulte nécessairement'. Adams (1971: 2) stated: 'Disjunction usually places emphasis on
one of the two words disjoined' citing Fraenkel (1928: 162–8) and Hofmann–Szantyr (H–S 690). He
quotes as an example *vereor mehercule ne aut gravioribus utar verbis quam natura fert, aut levioribus
quam causa postulat* (Cic. *Quinct.* 57; cf. p. 171 above), commenting as follows: '*gravioribus* is thrown
into relief to highlight its antithesis with *levioribus*'. Adams himself later adopted the term 'focus'
in his groundbreaking studies of the position of weak pronouns and the verb *esse* (1994a, 1994b).
Devine and Stephens (2006: 524–602) introduce many complexities into the analysis of hyperbaton,
but on the basic point that hyperbaton encodes focus they are in agreement with their predecessors.
[31] Devine and Stephens (2006: 531–48) have some insight into this issue. They classify these two categories as 'premodifier hyperbaton' and 'postmodifier hyperbaton', but since they do not distinguish

Fannium qui scripsit historiam generum esse scripseram Laeli 'this Fannius who wrote the history I had said was the son-in-law of Laelius' (*Att.* 12.5b), where the point at issue is that one of two easily confused Fannii was identified as the son-in-law of Laelius (not whose son-in-law he was, nor what relation he bore to Laelius); or *est ornamentum Academiae proprium meae* 'it is a suitable ornament for my Academy' (*Att.* 1.4.3), where Cicero is not distinguishing his Academy from some other, nor his Academy from his Lyceum, but equally stresses both components of the phrase.

(iii) A rarer type may be provisionally called 'double-focus' hyperbaton, in which not only the enclosing noun phrase but also an intervening constituent carries focus. This is to be distinguished from long-range hyperbaton, because the first element of the enclosing noun phrase is not a 'preferential' word, and from short-range hyperbaton, because in the latter the intervening word or phrase is unfocused. The precise mechanics of this type have still to be elucidated and it is uncommon enough not to be further considered in this preliminary sketch: I content myself with mentioning a few examples, beginning with the *Rhetorica ad Herennium*'s first example *instabilis in istum plurimum fortuna valuit* (4.44), where evidently *plurimum* is focused as much as *instabilis*. Further cases occur in the *Rhetorica ad Herennium*'s examples of the grand style (4.12): *qui satis idoneam possit in eum poenam excogitare, qui prodere hostibus patriam cogitarit* '. . . who could excogitate a penalty fitting enough for him who has bethought himself to betray his country to the enemy', where *in eum* is focused as the antecedent of *qui; urbs acerbissimo concidat incendio conflagrata* 'the city would collapse set in flames by a most horrific conflagration' (rhythmical considerations may be at work here); *se non putant id quod voluerint ad exitum perduxisse, nisi sanctissimae patriae miserandum scelerati viderint cinerem* 'they do not think that they can bring what they desire to its conclusion unless in their wickedness they have seen the piteous ashes of their most holy fatherland'. In view of this, it could well be that this particular kind of hyperbaton was seen as characteristic of the grand, if not over-grand, rhetorical style. Instances in Cicero himself are not easy to find, though one may cite *statim cruentum alte extollens Brutus pugionem Ciceronem nominatim exclamavit* 'at once Brutus raising high his bloody dagger shouted for Cicero by name' (*Phil.* 2.28). But this is a purported quotation from Antony, and could well therefore be untypical of Cicero's

systematically on the one hand between long-range and short-range pre-modifier hyperbaton, and on the other hand between short-range post-modifier hyperbaton and effects of topicalisation, their discussion is not as clear as it could be.

usage: we would not be surprised to find that Antony's oratory tended to the grander and more emotional end of the spectrum.

3 DISTRIBUTION

Armed with the above provisional typology of hyperbaton, we can begin to look statistically at its distribution among genres and registers. This work remains to be done; at the present stage I can offer only a few preliminary suggestions and observations with particular reference to Cicero. The type 'double-focus' hyperbaton will for the time being be ignored, as occurring insufficiently often in the samples taken.

(i) First, many of the examples of 'hyperbaton' quoted in works on word order (up to and including Devine and Stephens 2006) are in fact examples of category 2.2 (iii) above, where one of the co-referential elements is topicalised. Since topicalisation is a pragmatically defined feature, one would expect its distribution to depend primarily on communicative function: for example, one might expect letters or expository works, which change topic rather often, to show the feature more frequently than, for example, narratives. It is beyond the scope of the present study to investigate whether the frequency of topicalisation, or of this special case of it, varies for register in Ciceronian Latin or any other Latin – not least because its presence in any particular passage is not necessarily evident to inspection, but can be established only by close examination of the context in each case.

To take just one text as a sample, in the course of my search for hyperbata in *Pro Roscio Amerino* I found a number of instances which should, rather, be placed in this category. These often involve a topicalised noun combined with a pronoun modifier (determiner or quantifier) in logical predicate position: e.g. *iudicium inter sicarios hoc primum committitur* (*S. Rosc.* 11). This looks superficially like a hyperbaton, with the modifier *hoc* separated from its noun *iudicium*. But it is clear enough that *iudicium* is placed first and taken out of its expected place (with *hoc*) because it is the topic of the sentence: '[as for] a case of murder, this is the first to be sent for trial'. Similar is *cupiditates porro quae possunt esse in eo qui . . . ruri semper habitarit?* (*S. Rosc.* 39). *Cupiditates* is topicalised, as shown by the fact that it comes before the normally sentence-initial interrogative, and the topicalisation is reinforced by *porro* 'moreover': 'As for desires (for wealth, power, etc.), which of them can exist in a man who has always lived in the country?' The pattern is particularly common with the negative *nullus* postponed until the end, as in 'Answer came there none': e.g. in *ego servum habeo nullum* (*S. Rosc.* 145). To overtranslate: 'as far as my having slaves is concerned, I have – none'.

The phenomenon can occur also with other grammatical patterns such as noun + possessive genitive: *nomen refertur in tabulas Sexti Roscii, hominis studiosissimi nobilitatis* (*S. Rosc.* 21). Here the phrase *nomen refertur in tabulas* is topicalised: the main information of the sentence starts at *Sexti Roscii*. One could, again, overtranslate: 'As for someone's name being put in the list, it was that of Sextus Roscius (of all people!), a man extremely loyal to the cause of the nobility.' Note that both the topicalisation of *nomen*..., with the resultant anticipation of a possessive genitive, and the focus on *Sexti Roscii*, are so strong that they override any temptation to take *Sexti Roscii* as qualifying *tabulas*, the noun immediately preceding it: maybe there was a break in pronunciation after *tabulas*.

(ii) Long-range hyperbaton, as indicated above, is distributed fairly widely and does not (as far as I can see at this preliminary stage) seem to be particularly marked for register.[32] Certainly, it is most at home in sentences with some degree of complexity, since otherwise there would not be enough intervening constituents to distinguish it from short-range hyperbaton. Its more extreme manifestations do seem to occur in oratory and, within that, in contexts with a somewhat higher than usual rhetorical or emotional 'temperature'. But the phenomenon as a whole is certainly not confined to passages of that sort, and it is in fact relatively common in all genres of Cicero's prose, whether speeches, letters, or philosophical works. Furthermore, it is clear that Cicero cultivates this type of hyperbaton partly for rhythmical reasons; yet it is not clear that he could have done this had it not been a normal feature of the language in the first place.

(iii) Short-range hyperbaton I have identified as specifically a focusing device, which I believe also to be natural to the language as spoken in Cicero's time. It is largely absent from some styles of writing, and those are in fact the styles where one would expect focusing devices to be avoided: e.g. the objective, textbook style of Cato's *De agricultura*,[33] or the military

---

[32] See above, pp. 174–6. It is avoided by the historians in the Sallustian–Tacitean tradition, perhaps not for reasons of register but because of their ideal of brevity, and possibly also just because in formal literature it sounded too Ciceronian (compare their avoidance of the *esse videatur* clausula).

[33] Some apparent examples are quoted by Ahlberg 1911: 89–91 and Adams 1971: 2; of Adams's examples only *validam habet naturam* (*Agr.* 157.1) is a genuine example of short-range hyperbaton. Most of the others are effects of topicalisation and/or of what Hofmann and Szantyr (H–S 690) call 'volkstümliche Epexegesen': Cato has a habit of adding an adjective in loose apposition to a

dispatch as exemplified in the early books of Caesar's *Commentarii*.[34] In
formal speeches of Cicero, its use is very restrained: again I take *Pro Roscio
Amerino* as a sample. The following instances are, I think, all that occur in
this speech, and they all occur at points of relatively high rhetorical tension
(although there are also many rhetorically elaborate passages in the speech
which do not display any instances of short-range hyperbaton). Five of
them involve modifiers of the 'preferential' category (which evidently lend
themselves more easily to separation):

magnam vim, magnam necessitatem, magnam possidet religionem paternus mater-
   nusque sanguis (66)
aliqua fretus mora (110)
summum admisisse dedecus existimabant (111)
maxime videtur grave (112)
haec acta res est (149).[35]

The speech yields only two further examples:

mandati constitutum est iudicium, non minus turpe quam furti (111).

Here there is clearly a strong focus on *mandati* as shown by the antithesis
with *furti*.

quod speravit sese apud tales viros aliquid ad perniciem posse innocentis (141).

Here, if this is a genuine example,[36] the genitive *innocentis* is placed second
and this therefore is an example of 'head-first' hyperbaton in which there
is strong focus on both elements. 'The destruction of an innocent man' is
a phrase which would certainly lend itself to such focus in this context.

   Adams (1971) correlates the frequency of hyperbaton in the speeches
with the traditional distinction between 'plain' and 'ornate', but the facts
seem to be more complicated. We have seen that the *Pro Roscio Amerino*,
usually reckoned a relatively 'grand' speech and certainly one where there
is abundant, if sometimes suppressed, emotional tension,[37] shows a low
frequency of hyperbaton – hardly higher than that noted by Adams for
the 'plain' *Pro Caecina*. But the frequency also varies within speeches.

topicalised word, several words later, in order to specify more exactly the scope of the topic: thus
   e.g. *harundinem prende tibi viridem* 'take a reed – I mean a green one' (160).
[34] Adams 1971: 6, citing Fraenkel 1956.
[35] On this type of order see Adams 1994a: 40–3 comparing *his decreta verbis est* (*Catil.* 3.15) and *altera
   promulgata lex est* (*Phil.* 1.21).
[36] Note that *posse* in section 141 is a minority reading absent from the main MS tradition.
[37] Another relevant factor, which I have not so far been able to investigate fully, might be chronological
   variation across Cicero's career. It is possible to conceive that Cicero's first major venture into defence
   oratory in the public courts would show a different pattern from the efforts of his mature years –
   yet one could not predict in advance what the variation might be. Again the work is still to be done.

In the *Pro Archia*, it is striking that after one instance of short-range hyperbaton in the exordium (*memoriam recordari ultimam*, 1) there are none in the main passage of legal and factual argumentation (sections 4–11). Hyperbata of this kind only appear again in the second part of the speech, on the benefits of poetry and on the merits of Archias himself as a poet – a section of argument which Cicero himself confessed at the end of the speech to have been *a foro aliena iudicialique consuetudine* 'alien to the forum and to the normal practice of the courts', where in other words Cicero presents himself (not necessarily entirely ingenuously) as dealing from a personal point of view with self-consciously non-forensic issues. It may well be Cicero's real or purported personal involvement, rather than any increased ornateness of the rhetoric, that accounts for the increased frequency of focusing constructions. A similar explanation may hold for the *Pro Plancio*, a speech in which Cicero is concerned to defuse the prosecution by adopting an exaggerated and self-conscious pose of friendly relations towards the accuser Laterensis, and to defend Plancius partly on the basis of his political loyalty to Cicero himself: again, therefore, there is an unusual degree of personal involvement on the part of Cicero as advocate, to which the higher than usual frequency of focusing constructions gives verbal expression. Here as elsewhere, one cannot do the linguistic analysis without also taking into account the rhetoric.

The frequency of hyperbaton in the letters is apparently higher than in formal oratory. In the first book of the letters to Atticus (equivalent to a medium-length speech) I have counted twenty-six examples.[38]

Long-range

haec est adhuc informata cogitatio (1.1.2)
nullam video gravem subesse causam (1.10.2)[39]
nullae mihi abs te sunt redditae litterae (1.15.2)
tanto imposito rei publicae vulnere (1.16.7)
nihil est damni factum novi (1.16.9)
quanta sit in Quinto fratre meo comitas (1.17.2)
omnis in tua posita est humanitate mihi spes huius levandae molestiae (1.17.4)
illud inest tamen commodi (1.17.7)
nullam a me volo epistulam . . . pervenire (1.19.1).

---

[38] All cited here. There may of course be doubt about the inclusion or exclusion of particular instances or types, and their distribution within the book may also be worthy of attention: on the stylistic variety even within the individual books of the *Ad Atticum* see Albrecht 2003: 69.

[39] This example and 1.16.7 exemplify a variant of long-range hyperbaton in which a noun phrase is split into three: *nullam video gravem subesse causam* and *nihil est damni factum novi*. The pronominal always goes first, as in ordinary long-range hyperbaton; but the precise analysis of these patterns awaits further study.

Short-range

A number of these are split only by a part of *esse* (which is more or less
a postpositive: see Adams 1994a) but should be counted nevertheless:

summa hominum est opinio (1.2.2)
consul est egregius (1.14.6)
molestia sum tanta adfectus (1.17.1)
summum erat periculum (1.17.9)
si mihi tantum esset oti (1.19.1)
multo essem crebrior (1.19.1)
contentionem fore aliquem (1.19.7).

The following[40] are split by a stronger verb than *esse*, or by a participle
with or without auxiliary, and in all of these instances, it seems to me,
the focusing function is clearly to be seen:

summam adhibebimus diligentiam (1.1.2)
ex tua putabam voluntate me statuere oportere (1.5.5)
humanitatis sparsae sale (1.13.1)
summo proposito periculo (1.16.5)
in tua posita est humanitate *and* huius levandae molestiae (1.17.4)
aures nactus tuas (1.18.1)
omnes profudi vires (1.18.2)
non odio adductus alicuius (1.18.2).

It is not clear whether the following example should be counted; it may
be an example of short-range hyperbaton but *alacris* may be a complement:

non ita . . . alacris exsultat improbitas (1.16.7).

One remaining example is hard to explain; if the text is right, it involves the
postponement of a possessive, which may place it in a special category:[41]

Pompeius togulam illam pictam silentio tuetur suam (1.18.6).

As a check on this I chose at random another book of the letters to
Atticus, the eleventh. The style and tone of this book are significantly
different from those in evidence in the first. It is much more elliptical,
since by its date of composition, 48 BC, Atticus and Cicero were still more
intimate than in the years leading up to Cicero's consulate; and Cicero's
mood in *Att.* 11 is much less positive, since it covers the period of his great
falling-out with his brother. But the frequency of hyperbaton is almost
exactly the same – twenty-seven instances in a book of roughly similar

---

[40] These may be the eight examples referred to by Adams 1971: 5–6.
[41] On hyperbata involving possessives see Lundström 1982: 36; Albrecht 2003: 113 citing Menk 1925.

length. The obvious provisional indication is that hyperbaton shows a consistent presence in the letters to Atticus, and must be regarded as a feature of the language which is at home in informal styles, possibly in fact more regularly so than in the speeches.

It has been suggested in general terms (Devine and Stephens 2006: 603) that there is a higher frequency of hyperbaton in the philosophical works, where the use of focusing devices is in place both because of the need for logical exposition and because of their evocation of relaxed and expansive conversational style (on the model of Plato's dialogues). This seems borne out by an examination, again *exempli gratia*, of the first fifty sections of the *De divinatione*, where there are sixteen instances of hyperbaton and a majority of them belong to the short-range (focusing) category.[42] Yet these particular instances, at any rate, do not seem especially bound up with the making of logical distinctions in the course of a philosophical exposition (as Devine and Stephens suggested);[43] rather, the function seems more often to be to highlight a rhetorical point. They are as follows:

vetus opinio est usque ab heroicis ducta temporibus, eaque et populi Romani et omnium gentium firmata consensu (1).

This comes from the very beginning of Cicero's prologue, before the dialogue begins, and the repeated emphasis on the universality of divination in both time and space (and hence the importance of the topic to be discussed) is rhetorically entirely in place.

ut Stoicorum magis argumenta confutet quam hominum deleat religionem (8).

The focus on *hominum* makes sense: 'to destroy the religion *of humankind*' – and may convey a nuance of 'ordinary people' as opposed to Stoics.

caput exstitisse Panisci (23)
Vastitatem esse Italiae (49; the personified 'Devastation of Italy').

Focus is in place in these two instances of head-first hyperbaton, as these are striking and unusual portents, while in *aquilae admonitus volatu* (26) the eagle is implicitly contrasted with other, more ordinary, birds which Deiotarus was in the habit of watching.

Then three examples where the function does appear to be the making of a logical distinction:

---

[42] The four instances of long-range hyperbaton (sections 6, 23, 29 and 31) call for no special comment; nor does *quam habeat vim* (9).

[43] A more promising area to find the expository, distinction-making function of short-range hyperbaton is that of Roman law texts; certainly the phenomenon seems very obvious in the passages of the *Institutes* of Gaius studied by Orinsky 1923: 83–6.

auspiciis utuntur coactis (27)
et augurum et haruspicum comprobat disciplinam (33)
auctoritatem habet vetustatis (34).

In the next example Quintus stresses a rather unexpected or unpalatable
aspect of his Stoic doctrine, that we should adopt divination because it
works, even if we do not know why, for Nature does not reveal her secrets;
hence the focus on *obscuritate naturae*:

latet fortasse obscuritate involuta naturae (35).

Finally the following example calls for more complex elucidation. At
first sight this seems to be a counter-example to the thesis that short-range
hyperbaton encodes focus, since the main point of contrast is obviously
se, not *maturam* – 'that *he himself* should meet an early death, rather than
Africanus' young daughter':

aequius esse censuit se maturam oppetere mortem quam P. Africani filiam adulescentem (36).

But an extra subtlety is gained from supposing that *maturam* also is focused,
for *matura mors* does not mean precisely a 'speedy death' (as the Loeb
translator has it); it means a *timely* death, and it can then be seen that
there is a further contrast between *maturam* and *adulescentem*: 'he thought
it was fairer that *he himself* should meet death *in the fullness of his age*,
than that Africanus' daughter should meet it *while still a young girl*'. This
interpretation is not special pleading, because it not only works in context
but enriches our understanding of the passage. I would expect further
applications of the principle to bear similar fruit.

4 CONCLUSION

It appears to emerge provisionally from the above preliminary exploration –
further research may confirm or amend this picture – that, as far as the Latin
usage of Cicero goes, there is no firm reason to suppose that hyperbaton is,
in itself, either a formal rhetorical feature or a colloquial feature. Rather, it
has uses in both formally rhetorical and informally conversational genres
of writing, but its frequency in any given text varies primarily on the basis
of the detailed communicative function. I am tempted to surmise that
it is, in fact, a generalised *oral* feature which surfaces in those kinds of
written prose texts (letters, dialogues, and the less formal parts of speeches)
which approach most closely the character of a reasonably close imitation
or evocation of oral discourse.

As Adams correctly noted in 1971, throughout Cicero's corpus its use is relatively restrained. It seems that it was the narrative writers of the generation just after Cicero (especially Nepos and Livy) who discovered that the constant use of short-range hyperbaton as a focusing device[44] could create rhetorical variety and elaboration. There might be a temptation to take this as a sign of over-luxuriance and to compare it unfavourably with the restraint of Cicero, but this would be just a matter of taste. The usage of Nepos and Livy need not be seen as decadent or artificial; it is simply a more highly coloured way of writing. I would be tempted, further, to link it with the practice of public oral recitation of literature which was at that period coming into vogue, and to compare it perhaps (as a rough equivalent) with the English newsreader's intonation I mentioned earlier – which is also a focusing device natural to the language but taken to extremes.

Rhetoricians and literary critics should continue to be interested in hyperbaton just as they are interested in the use of any other feature of language, but hyperbaton needs to be lifted out of the category of 'rhetorical figures' and to take its place where it primarily belongs – in the grammar of the language. Only after it has been properly analysed as a linguistic phenomenon can we hope to make meaningful generalisations about its usage in either literary or colloquial contexts.

---

[44] Even to the extent of placing focus on words that do not at first sight look as though they ought to have it: Devine and Stephens (2006: 605–6) have trouble with a number of passages from Livy in this respect. But their readiness to assume that Livy had internalised a different syntax from Cicero is indicative of a tendency towards ad hoc explanations. Rather we should assume that the focus is where it seems to be, and appreciate the literary effect: e.g. Livy 1.7.2 *novos transiluisse muros* emphasising that the walls are brand-new.

CHAPTER 11

Notes on the language of
Marcus Caelius Rufus

Harm Pinkster

Marcus Caelius Rufus (*c.* 88–48 BC) is the author of seventeen letters to Cicero preserved in Book 8 of Cicero's *Epistulae ad familiares*, totalling thirty pages in the Oxford Classical Text.[1] We also possess nine letters of Cicero to Caelius (*Fam.* 2.8–16, eighteen pages OCT), three of which are reactions to preserved letters of Caelius. I will be concerned with those letters that were exchanged between the two when Cicero was proconsul in Cilicia (fifteen letters by Caelius – total number of words 5,275[2] – and eight by Cicero – 2,011 words), written between May 51 BC and November 50 BC. The size of the two corpora is large enough and the circumstances in which they were writing were sufficiently stable to see whether there are differences between the language of the two men.

Caelius had a good reputation as orator, as is testified by Cicero himself and by Quintilian:[3]

† quam eius actionem † multum tamen et *splendida* et *grandis* et eadem in primis *faceta* et *perurbana* commendabat *oratio*. graves eius contiones aliquot fuerunt, acres accusationes tres eaeque omnes ex rei publicae contentione susceptae; defensiones, etsi illa erant in eo meliora quae dixi, non contemnendae tamen saneque tolerabiles. (Cic. *Brut.* 273, my emphasis)

His delivery was offset by a style brilliant and impressive, conspicuous especially for its cleverness and wit. He made some important public speeches and three merciless prosecutions, all of which arose out of political ambition and rivalry. His court speeches in defence of himself and others, although inferior to those which I have mentioned, were not negligible, indeed quite tolerable. (trans. H. M. Hubbell, Loeb)

---

[1] The author would like to thank the anonymous referee and Eleanor Dickey for their very helpful comments and suggestions.
[2] The *senatus consulta* in Cael. *Fam.* 8.8.5–8 are not in this total.
[3] There is a detailed discussion of Caelius as an orator in Cavarzere 1983: 46–61.

multum ingenii in Caelio et praecipue in accusando multa *urbanitas*, dignusque vir
cui et mens melior et vita longior contigisset. (Quint. *Inst.* 10.1.115, my emphasis)

Caelius had much talent, and a notable wit, especially in prosecuting; he deserved
a wiser mind and a longer life. (trans. D. A. Russell, Loeb)

Quintilian (*Inst.* 4.2.123–4) quotes one longer passage of Caelius
(Malcovati 1976: no. 162.17: four sentences, seventy-five words) to illustrate the technique of 'combining the true facts with a plausible picture of
the scene' *qualis est illa M. Caeli in Antonium descriptio* 'such as that well
known description of M. Caelius that he used against Antonius', which
he then qualifies in the following way: 'Nothing can be more plausibly
invented, more strongly censured, or more vividly portrayed.'[4]

Aper, in Tacitus, *Dialogus* 21.4, while recognising Caelius' qualities in
general (the speeches manifest the *nitor* 'elegance' and the *altitudo* 'sub-
limity of style' that was typical of his time), mentions a few characteristics
of Caelius' speeches he considers less positive: *sordes verborum* 'unrefined
words', *hians compositio* 'disjointed arrangement of the words' and *inconditi
sensus* 'shapeless periods' (see Mayer 2001: 156–7).

The fragments from the speeches that we have, including the longer
one mentioned, do not allow a linguistic comparison with the letters. We
have no ancient comments on the language of the letters of Caelius (nor
on the language of Cicero's, apart from Fronto's general remark quoted in
note 12). We can be pretty sure that the language of the letters we have
would not qualify as *splendida* or *grandis* (but satirical wit is definitely
present), whereas Aper's qualifications might be pertinent to some extent.
However, the evaluations quoted above prove beyond doubt that the quality
of the language of the letters, whatever it is, is not due to an insufficient
command of the Latin language, to an insufficient education (in fact, his
apprenticeship on the forum was supervised by Cicero and M. Licinius
Crassus), or any similar cause. Like any language user Caelius must have
been able to adapt his language to the circumstances (the reader, the topics
he was writing about, and the communicative goal(s) of his letters).[5] We
may even assume that his ability to adapt was more than average, given
his training and education. We therefore can a priori assume that allowing
for one or two slips of the pen (and imperfections in the manuscript
tradition) the wording of the letters is what Caelius considered adequate
in the circumstances.

[4] Trans. D. A. Russell (Loeb).
[5] I paraphrase Quirk *et al.* (1985: 25–7) in their section 'Varieties [of English] according to attitude'.

What were the circumstances?[6] When Cicero left for his province he asked Caelius to keep him informed of the situation in Rome (Cael. *Fam.* 8.1.1), more specifically about those developments that were relevant to Cicero himself (Cic. *Fam.* 2.8.1). The function of the letters was not so much to give an ordered account of the actual events in Rome (Caelius tells us (*Fam.* 8.1.1) that he had someone else write a detailed report in addition to his own letters; the verbatim reports in 8.8.5–8 are an exception), but to report Caelius' personal estimate of the situation and of the events to come (*Fam.* 2.8.1). The letters were certainly not meant for circulation. Given the intimate relationship that existed between the two men and the type of information the letters contained Caelius most likely adopted an informal variety of Latin, a type of letter that Cicero elsewhere called *familiare et iocosum* 'informal and gossiping' (*Fam.* 2.4.1). With other correspondents Caelius probably used a more formal or neutral variety of Latin, in the same way as Cicero's letters vary depending on which correspondents they were addressed to.[7] However, Caelius was writing to Cicero, the orator of his time, then still an important statesman, a generation older than Caelius himself, and Caelius was an ambitious young man. There is no reason to assume that by choosing an informal variety he could afford to be negligent or go as far as using slang.

The topics include political events (notably the delicate relationship between Caesar and Pompey), social events (accusations and prosecutions, divorces and adultery), family affairs, Caelius' anxiousness to obtain panthers for his Games, his worries about the Parthian situation, etc. Some are more serious than others, some require more detail and precision of description, and some are more 'technical' and require the use of less common words and expressions. Some topics lend themselves more readily to a narrative mode of discourse than others. Caelius' language varies with the topics he addresses, as a comparison of his carefully worded advice in *Fam.* 8.6.1 and his gossip in 8.7.2 will easily demonstrate.

Cicero's letters are mostly reactions to Caelius' reports and they vary with the topics as well. A good example is Cicero's reaction (*Fam.* 2.13.3) to Caelius' last-minute modification of the first part of his letter (*Fam.* 8.6.5). Now and then he writes in detail about his daily activities. An example is the passage about his actions as a commander against an expected Parthian attack (*Fam.* 2.10.2–3), which can be read as a first draft of the official report he plans to send to Rome later, when the campaign will be finished

---

[6] See Hutchinson 1998: 141–8 on the context of Cael. *Fam.* 8.6.
[7] See Albrecht's section 'Types of letters' (2003: 67–71) and Hutchinson 1998: 7–8.

successfully. It contains the only ablative absolute, a typical feature of the narrative mode,[8] in these letters: *Parthico bello nuntiato* 'after news had arrived about the Parthian war'.

A few words about the medium, (letter) writing. If any form of writing is really written and not spoken language it is letter writing. Whereas written plays, orations and dialogues try to convey a sufficient number of linguistic features to suggest oral communication, this is not the case in letter writing (unless it contains a report of a conversation). Informal writing does not per se imply the use of features that are typical of spoken language. There is informal and formal writing alongside informal and formal speaking. Letters written by or for uneducated people or people with an insufficient knowledge of Latin are also written language (see Halla-aho 2009). One should therefore be careful with the use of terms like 'colloquial'.[9]

Caelius' letters were dictated, with an occasional addition in Caelius' own handwriting (8.6.5 is such an addition, as we know from Cic. *Fam.* 2.13.3). This might have left 'oral' traces in the language of the letters. Speculative candidates are the few harsh asyndeta mentioned by Burg (1888: 72) and Cavarzere (1983: 67). Burg says that with his 'frequent' use of asyndeton Caelius follows the 'sermonis antiqui et vulgaris simplicitatem', but he adds 'simulque eo consilio ut graviorem concitatioremque orationem faciat'. One of his examples is:

[Laterensis] in tabulas absolutum non rettulit, ordinum iudicia perscripsit. (Cael. *Fam.* 8.8.3)

Laterensis made his entry in the record – not 'acquitted', but the verdicts of the several categories. (trans. D. R. Shackleton Bailey, Loeb)

In spoken language the contrast between the two clauses would appear from the intonation contour. However, dictated written language is not equivalent to recorded spoken language. Unlike recorded language, dictated language is intended to be read by another person. Instead of taking the asyndeton quoted above as the mechanical notation of an unintended asyndeton I assume that Caelius had the choice between dictating a syndetic and an asyndetic version and that he preferred the latter, perhaps to achieve

---

[8] On this letter and other 'military narrative' passages in Cicero's letters see Hutchinson 1998: 80–100. For the use of the ablative abs. in narrative (letters and orations) in Cicero see Van Gils 2003: 54–7.

[9] Of course 'literary' letters also existed in antiquity. On Cicero's plans to introduce this genre in Rome and make a selection (and adaptation) of his own letters see Cavarzere 2007: 35–40. Letters that were not meant for publication as literary may nevertheless have aesthetic or artistic aspirations and qualities; see Hutchinson 1998 on Cicero's letters. For common characteristics of Cicero's letters and the 'documentary' letters found in Vindolanda and elsewhere see Cugusi 1998: 174–85.

the effect mentioned by Burg. Instead of being simple, it may just as well be refined.

Modern scholars vary in their appreciation of the language of Caelius' letters. Badian (*OCD* s.v. *Caelius*) calls it 'a delightful, informal style'. Hutchinson (1998: 142) mentions Caelius' 'obvious literary talent'. Shackleton Bailey, in his commentary on the *Epistulae ad familiares*, is less charmed by Caelius' language. He blames Caelius' 'careless writing' (*ad* 8.14.4), talks of a 'happy-go-lucky style' (*ad* 8.4.2), and observes that 'limits can hardly be set to the vagaries of such a writer as Caelius' (*ad* 8.4.3). Other scholars refrain from terms like the ones mentioned while describing the language as the product of, on the one hand, the intimate relationship between Caelius and Cicero and the content of the letters, and on the other hand Caelius' age and character (e.g. Leeman 1963: 137–8). The result of these factors is a variety of language with many elements that are regarded as reflections of spontaneous, spoken language, in other words: 'colloquialisms'. A survey of 'colloquialisms', more or less along the lines of Hofmann (1951), can be found in Cavarzere (1983: 62–78). More details can be found in Becher (1888) and Burg (1888). However, as Cavarzere (1983: 71) rightly observes, many of the elements mentioned are not typical of Caelius. They are also common in Cicero's letters and in those of his other correspondents. Has Caelius more or less, or a different mix, of these elements? Or are there levels of colloquialism and has Caelius (more) expressions belonging to a lower level (see above: *sordes verborum*)?

The lexicon is perhaps the area that has attracted most attention, and at first sight it is a relatively unproblematic topic that yields clear results. Lebek (1970: 134) mentions fourteen words used by Caelius that are entirely absent from the works of Cicero, his correspondents, and Caesar. He concludes: 'Jedoch scheinen die Lizenzen des Briefschreibers [i.e. Caelius] . . . über das sonst im familiären sermo der guten Gesellschaft Übliche bisweilen hinauszugehen.' Plausible as this may seem (one word in every two pages), how does one reconcile it with the fact that in his first letter to Caelius (*Fam.* 2.8.1) Cicero, while joking about the extensiveness of the report that Caelius attaches to his letters (see above), uses the hapax *compilatio* 'burglary' and the unique combination *gladiatorum compositiones* 'pairings of gladiators'? Observations on the distribution of a word as such are not sufficient. In the first place, there is nothing to prevent Caelius (or anybody) inventing a new word and it need not be (very) informal on that account. Secondly, there is also nothing to prevent Caelius using a word that is (mainly) attested outside classical prose. It may have been the most appropriate word in the context, because there was no synonym available, because it was the right expression in the semantic field at hand, or because it evoked the connotation that suited best. Two words may serve as an illustration.

In *Fam.* 8.1.4 Caelius tells Cicero that *subrostrani* 'people who lounge near the Rostra (*sub rostris*), city loafers' (*OLD*'s translation) had spread the news that Cicero was dead. As to its formation and its meaning the word is fully transparent: it resembles *suburbanus* 'situated close to the city', which is common enough in all sorts of texts from Cato onwards.[10] The word was certainly not meant as a compliment by Caelius. We will probably never know whether it was Caelius' invention nor whether it was used in informal speech. In the same paragraph Caelius uses the unique expression *embaeneticam* [*sc. artem*] *facere* for Q. Pompeius. The precise meaning of *embaenetica* is unclear,[11] though the adjective must be derived from the Greek verb ἐμβαίνειν meaning 'to embark' or, possibly, 'to make embark'. Shackleton Bailey (1977: 384) translates 'operating boats', Constans (1936: 220) 'promener des touristes en barques'. Whatever it meant, the job that Pompeius was said to be performing in Bauli was certainly not one that befitted a man of his position. Here again Caelius may have invented the expression for the occasion or taken it from a semantic field that is not well represented in our corpus of texts. The expression may have been intended as denigratory. This does not make it informal or, even worse, vulgar. It may have been clever instead. Cicero jokingly asked Verres whether people were to assume *naviculariam, cum Romam venisses, esse facturum* 'that you were going into the shipping business when you reached Rome' (*Ver.* 5.46) (trans. L. H. G. Greenwood, Loeb), another unique expression and not, for that reason, informal. It is also not easy to think of synonyms for the two words discussed. Caelius did not choose an informal wording from a set of alternatives, at least as far as we know.

Reading through a very detailed commentary like the one by Cavarzere, one sometimes gets the impression that, if we acted in the same way with Cicero, we would find a lot of 'unclassical' expressions.[12] Just one example: in his first letter to Caelius, already referred to, Cicero uses the expression

---

[10] For derivatives in *-anus* see Kircher-Durand 2002: 133–6.

[11] The *OLD* calls it 'probably corrupt'; for the history of scholarship see Cavarzere 1983: 209–10, adding W. Schneider 2000: 516–18.

[12] That may have been the reason why Fronto was of the opinion that one should read 'all letters of Cicero', even more so than 'all his orations', because 'there is nothing more perfect than Cicero's letters' (Fro. *Ant.* 3.10, pp. 107–8 van den Hout). For other statements on or imitiations of Cicero in antiquity see Cugusi 1998: 167–70.

decem ipsos dies 'exactly ten days' (*Fam.* 2.8.3).[13] This use of *ipse* is uncommon outside Cicero (see *TLL* s.v. *ipse* 332.13 ff.). Is the fact that it is Cicero who uses *ipse* in this way more often, and also outside his letters, sufficient for us not to regard it as 'colloquial'? The questions raised so far resemble the ones discussed by Adams (Adams *et al.* 2005).

It is easier to assess the level of formality of a lexical feature in a text if it also occurs elsewhere. I will turn to the word *validissime*, first attested in Caelius:

quin ego, cum pro amicitia validissime faverem ei..., postquam factum est, obstipui et mihi visus sum captus esse. (Cael. *Fam.* 8.2.1)

Even I, who as a friend was wholeheartedly on his side ... was dumbfounded when this happened, and felt as though I had been cheated. (trans. D. R. Shackleton Bailey, Loeb)

Cavarzere (1983: 218) seems to regard *validissime* as the superlative of *valde*. *Valde* is often used with verbs as an intensifier, to express a high degree of emotional (*placet* 'to please') or intellectual (*probo* 'to approve') appreciation. It is used in this way a few times in Plautus, in combination with *placet* and *deamo* 'to love utterly'; Plautus also has *valide* in the same meaning, for example in combination with *amo* 'to love'. Plautus has also a few instances of *valide* and *valde* in combination with other verbs where it functions as a manner adverb ('vigorously', 'powerfully'), in correspondence with the adjective *validus*. With the exception of a few instances in Varro it is in Cicero's works, especially his correspondence, that *valde* is found in large numbers (*c.* 350 instances: 25 in the orations, 75 in the dialogues, 140 in the letters to Atticus, 110 in the other letters), of which about one quarter occur in combination with gradable adjectives and adverbs. The total number exceeds that of all the other texts on the *Bibliotheca Teubneriana Latina* CD-ROM together.

Caelius has eight instances of *valde* in its intensifier meaning, a large number given the size of his corpus.[14] From Caesar we have only one instance, in a letter preserved with Cicero's letters (*Att.* 9.7C.1); the same is true of other correspondents. The form is absent from many other authors, but it occurs in Petronius – once in Encolpius' narrative, five times spoken by a freedman, one has the impression with less restrictions than in Cicero –

[13] Shackleton Bailey translates 'ten clear days' and elsewhere uses the translation 'whole'. This may suggest that *ipse* is used with a different meaning from usual. *Ipse* in these contexts indicates that it is 'ten days and nothing else'.

[14] In *Fam.* 8.17.2 *valde depugnare* 'to fight desperately' (paraphrasing Shackleton Bailey's translation), *valde* is an adverb of manner.

and also in the Vindolanda Tablets (*valde desidero* 'I miss you strongly', 347b1). The 'informal' status of *valde* therefore looks settled, although it 'should not be overrated, for the word not only occurs in Cicero's letters and dialogues but in the speeches'.[15]

As for *validissime*, Celsus has *validissime excitat . . . aqua* 'a most powerful excitant is water' (3.20.3), where it may be taken in its manner meaning 'forcefully'.[16] The form *valdissime* is found in a letter on papyrus dated 5–2 BC *te valdissime decriminatum* [sc. *esse*] 'that you have been utterly defamed' (*Stud. Pal.* 14.17.4–5) and in Seneca *valdissime diligunt* 'they love most devotedly' (*Dial.* 10.8.4). In Pliny the Younger editors read *valdissime*, where some of the manuscripts have *validissime* (five instances in combination with the usual verbs). It looks therefore as if Caelius' use of the non-syncopated form *validissime* in the sense 'extremely' is unique. Cavarzere (1983: 218), who assumes that Pliny also has the non-syncopated forms, suggests that non-syncopated forms continued to exist after Plautus, but were during the classical period banished to the 'lingua dell'uso, in genere più conservativa'. Our Caelius instance would then be the only manifestation of this continuous stream in the classical period.

But there may be another explanation. On closer examination, the verbs with which Caelius uses *valde* are very similar to those used by Cicero. The combination *valde + faveo* does not occur in the classical period, so *validissime faverem* is also exceptional from this point of view. Although the verb presupposes a certain emotional attitude, it means 'offering (active) support'. *Validissime* may well be the superlative of *valide*, the adverb of *validus*. Caelius was thus a 'fervent supporter'. Of course, this makes the expression no less unique, but there is no need to assume the type of conservative undercurrent that was popular in earlier accounts of the history of Latin. There is a close parallel for this use of *valide* in Pliny the Elder:

nemo umquam ulli artium validius favit. (Plin. *Nat.* 30.14)

No other of the arts ever had a more enthusiastic patron. (trans. W. H. S. Jones, Loeb)

The last lexical item to discuss is *suus* as found in the manuscript M in *Fam.* 8.14.4 and accepted by Shackleton Bailey:

---

[15] Brink 1971 on *valdius oblectat* in Hor. *Ars* 321. For Cicero's use of *valde* see Orlandini 2003. Wölfflin 1879 is still useful.

[16] It is used in its meaning 'forcefully' by Ammianus (24.2.10) and in the *Historia Augusta* (23.4.5). There are a number of instances in Christian authors. Augustine combines it once with *amo* (*Conf.* 1.15).

si sine suo periculo fieri posset, magnum et iucundum tibi Fortuna spectaculum parabat. (Cael. *Fam.* 8.14.4)

If it were not for the personal risk involved, Fate is preparing a mighty and fascinating show for your benefit. (trans. D. R. Shackleton Bailey, Loeb)

'Despite the following *tibi* I retain this reading in the sense of *proprio* (K.–S. 1.606), though if right it is an extreme example of Caelius' careless writing; but cf. Sen. *Dial.* 9.15.6 . . . ' (Shackleton Bailey 1977: 433). Most editors, instead of granting Caelius an extreme example of carelessness, have preferred to emend to *summo* 'extreme' or *tuo* 'your'. Böhm (1979) has tried to show that *summo* is in fact how we should interpret the reading of M. I do not believe that Shackleton Bailey's translation 'personal' for *suo* is possible. The parallels he adduces do not support it, nor does the reference to Kühner–Stegmann. But there may be another way to defend the transmitted reading. *Periculum* may indicate both the risk that threatens something or somebody or the threat that comes from something or somebody (for the latter meaning see *TLL* s.v. 1469.47 ff.). In both cases the entity involved may be in the genitive, as in the first (*omnium*) and third (*praedonum*) example below. For the first ('objective') case it is not difficult to find parallels with a possessive pronoun instead of a genitive, as in the second example below (*meo*). The *TLL* has no pronominal parallel for the third ('subjective') example.[17] The emendation *tuo* in the Caelius text is evidently an attempt to supply a threatened person ('objective').

. . . quis hoc statuit umquam aut cui concedi sine summo <u>omnium</u> periculo potest, ut eum <iure potuerit occidere, a quo metuisse se dicat ne ipse posterius occideretur?> (Cic. *Tul.* 51)

. . . who ever laid down such a principle as this, or who could have this granted him without extreme danger to the whole body of citizens, that he might lawfully kill a man, if he only said that he was afraid of being hereafter killed by him? (trans. C. D. Yonge)

at enim non sine <u>meo</u> periculo, Crassus inquit, possum, Sulpici, te reprehendere, quoniam Antonius mihi te simillimum dixit sibi videri. (Cic. *De orat.* 3.47)

'All the same,' said Crassus, 'I can't find fault with you without running some risk on my own account, because Antonius said that in his view you and I are extremely like one another.' (trans. H. Rackham, Loeb)

---

[17] For the use of possessive pronouns for 'objective' relations see also K–S 1.599. *TLL* s.v. *meus* 921.12 ff. refers to the frequent use of *meus* 'mine' for a 'subjective' relation. There is no precise parallel.

nam aestate summa, quo tempore ceteri praetores obire provinciam et concursare consuerunt aut etiam in tanto praedonum metu et periculo ipsi navigare . . . (Cic. *Ver.* 5.80)

During the height of summer, the season when it has been the practice of all other governors to move actively about and inspect their province, or even, when the risk of attacks by pirates was as formidable as it then was, to put to sea themselves . . . (trans. L. H. G. Greenwood, Loeb)

Turning now to *suo*, we may first ask whether *sine periculo tout court* would do as well (it would, as in the example that follows) and, then, what *suo* adds.

cum ei dicerem tibi videri sponsionem illam nos sine periculo facere posse . . . (Cic. *Fam.* 7.21.1)

When I told him that in your opinion we could safely make the stipulation . . . (trans. D. R. Shackleton Bailey, Loeb)

The referent of the reflexive possessive pronoun, unlike *meus* and *tuus*, has to be found in its immediate context. It is often the subject of the clause in which it occurs, but it may be another constituent of that clause, and it may also be the subject of the immediately governing clause. There are in fact even more possibilities (see Bertocchi 1989; K–S 1.600–17). In our case *suo* cannot be related to a constituent of its own clause. The first candidate to relate it to is *Fortuna* in the main clause. Evidently *suo periculo* cannot be interpreted as 'the risk that threatens *Fortuna* itself' (an 'objective' interpretation), but maybe it means 'the risk that emanates from *Fortuna* itself'. At this point we return to Kühner–Stegmann, not to the page Shackleton Bailey refers to, but to page 1.599, Anm. 6, where they draw attention to the fact that the Latin possessive pronoun has a wider range of meanings than the German one. The *OLD* s.v. *suus* 11 has examples under the heading 'his distinctive or characteristic'. *Sine suo periculo* means 'without the risk that is typically involved when Fate does its work'.

The result of the preceding discussion is still a unique expression. But if the reader agrees that it is entirely in accordance with the semantic and syntactic rules of Latin there is nothing wrong with it being a unique expression. That does not make it 'colloquial', and it is certainly better to look for an explanation along the rules of Latin than to defend it as an extreme example of carelessness.

I now turn to a few syntactic items. First a few remarks about sentence structure. It is difficult to make a comparison between the sentences of Caelius and Cicero in their mutual correspondence. The first difficulty consists in the fact that we have to decide what counts as a sentence. If we define a sentence as a string of words between two periods and include strings that are separated by one or more semicolons, the results are affected by the fact that Shackleton Bailey has relatively more semicolons in Caelius' text than in Cicero's. If we use a syntactic definition, as I do for this purpose, and consider a sentence a string of words that has no syntactic interdependence with a preceding or following string, then the strings separated by semicolons will count as sentences. This is not as easy as it seems at first sight, because in the case of asyndetic co-ordination one might opt for independent sentences instead of clauses. It is also difficult to make a distinction between (explicitly) co-ordinated clauses (belonging to one sentence) and co-ordinated sentences; in spoken language it is usually not difficult to hear the difference. Essentially I follow Shackleton Bailey's decisions (also his deletions and additions) and equate his semicolons with full stops.[18] The second difficulty consists in establishing the number of clauses that make up a sentence. I count as clauses the main and finite subordinate clauses as well as participial clauses (predicative participles and ablative absolutes), gerundi(v)al clauses, and accusative and infinitive clauses, including those lacking a verb.

Working in this way I found that on average Caelius' sentences are longer in terms of the number of words they contain (Caelius 14.3 words per sentence, Cicero 12.8), and are more complex in terms of the number of clauses per sentence (Caelius 2.8, Cicero 2.4). Conversely, Cicero has more words per clause (5.4) than Caelius (5.0). If one examines sentence length in more detail, it turns out that Cicero has more (very) short sentences (25 per cent are between one and five words, 35 per cent between six and ten), Caelius more sentences of 11–15 words and also more very long sentences. This can be seen in the radar diagram below (Figure 11.1). In this diagram 7 types of sentence length are distinguished (from 1–5 words to 31–60 words) and for each type the percentage is indicated (running from 0 per cent in the middle to 35 per cent at the outside).

The number of predicative participles in Caelius is almost twice as great as in Cicero (20.2 per cent of all clauses, versus 4.1 per cent of all clauses), and Caelius has many more ablative absolutes (13 versus 1). Why? My estimate is that this has to do with the fact that there is more narrative in Caelius, which is not strange in the light of the communicative goal of his

---

[18] The result of this approach is the following. Number of sentences: Caelius 369, Cicero 158. Number of clauses: Caelius 1,048, Cicero 376.

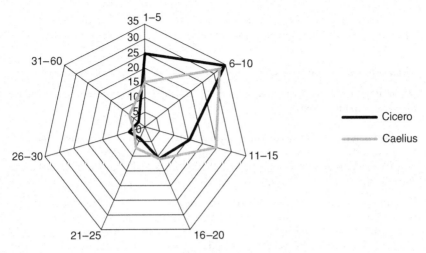

Fig. 11.1 Sentence length in Cicero and Caelius

letters in comparison with Cicero's.[19] At the same time the frequency of these clause types contributes to the fact that on average Caelius' clauses are shorter.

Caelius and Cicero have practically the same amount of clauses that are 'encapsulated' in their governing clause (Caelius 87 clauses, 7 per cent of all clauses; Cicero 26 clauses, also 7 per cent). I give one example below with two encapsulated clauses. I find this form of sentence building more difficult to read than a form in which clauses follow each other, and it may be more sophisticated. This has no obvious connection with the degree of formality of the structure:

atque hoc e[g]o diligentius facio quod, cum otiosus sum, plane ubi delectem otium meum non habeo. (Cael. *Fam.* 8.3.1)

I am all the more punctilious about it, because when I have no work at hand there is simply nowhere for me to amuse my leisure. (trans. D. R. Shackleton Bailey, Loeb)

More remarkable is the relative frequency of complement clauses that precede their main clause in Caelius (29, 2.7 per cent of all clauses, versus Cicero 6, 1.5 per cent). Two examples are given below. The relative order of main and subordinate clauses is (partly) determined by discourse factors: the clause with topical information, that is information related to the

---

[19] For the ablative absolute as a typical feature of narrative discourse see Paschoud and Wirz 2007.

preceding discourse or otherwise accessible to the reader, has the best chance of coming first. The material is insufficient to arrive at firm conclusions.

mea porro comitia quem eventum sint habitura nescio. (Cael. *Fam.* 8.4.3)

What is going to happen in my own [elections] I don't know. (trans. D. R. Shackleton Bailey, Loeb)

tu si Pompeium, ut volebas, offendisti, qui tibi visus sit et quam orationem habuerit tecum quamque ostenderit voluntatem (solet enim aliud sentire et loqui neque tantum valere ingenio ut non appareat quid cupiat), fac mihi perscribas. (Cael. *Fam.* 8.1.3)

If you found Pompey, as you wanted to do, be sure to write and tell me what you thought of him, how he talked to you, and what disposition he showed. He is apt to say one thing and think another, but is usually not clever enough to keep his real aims out of view. (trans. D. R. Shackleton Bailey, Loeb)

In the example given below a constituent of the subordinate clause (*tu*) is placed at the beginning of the sentence in a clause to which it does not belong. This phenomenon is called 'fronting' or 'topicalisation'. In a way it resembles the sentence structure of the preceding examples in that topical information is placed early in the sentence. This structure is often considered 'colloquial'. There are seven instances in Cicero and only eleven in Caelius.

tametsi tu scio quam sis curiosus et quam omnibus peregrinantibus gratum sit minimarum quoque rerum quae domi gerantur fieri certiores. (Cael. *Fam.* 8.1.1)

However, I know how curious you are and how much everybody abroad likes to be told of even the most trifling happenings at home. (trans. D. R. Shackleton Bailey, Loeb)

Another 'colloquial' feature, recently discussed by Adams (1995b: 117–18, 2003c: 19), is the use of the second person subjunctive without *ut* with verbs like *rogo* 'to ask' to express a request or instruction. Caelius has it in combination with *fac* (an example is given above) and with *velim* 'I'd like' (twice), which Cicero uses three times, more or less set directive expressions.

Caelius uses *rogo* without *ut* once (see below), whereas Cicero has one instance of the 'formal' (Adams) *rogo ut* (*Fam.* 2.10.4), or rather *ut . . . rogo*, as almost always in his letters. Caelius has *peto* 'to request' once. Cicero uses it often, seventy times in his letters (not in our corpus). He uses it with *ut* sixty-four times, without *ut* – probably – in order to avoid repetition of *ut* four times, and only two times without such a reason.[20] Caelius also has *moneo* 'to warn' (once),[21] possibly *admoneo* (Cael. *Fam.* 8.4.5), and *suadeo* 'to advise' (twice), which Cicero has in a letter to Caelius of a later date (*Fam.* 2.16.7).[22]

The bare subjunctive is also found outside the class of verbs discussed so far. Cicero has *oportet* 'it is proper' only once in these letters (*Fam.* 2.14), but that is nevertheless the regular expression. Caelius uses *impetro* 'to obtain' once without *ut* (see below), a very uncommon usage throughout latinity.[23] Lambinus proposed to read *ut reprehenderem*. Remarkable is not only the absence of *ut* but also the length and the complexity of the subordinate clause and the fact that it precedes its governing verb:

sed quoniam suspicaris minus certa fide eos <esse quos> tibi misi, tamquam procurator sic agas rogo. (Cael. *Fam.* 8.11.4)

But since you suspect that the persons I sent are not altogether trustworthy, please act as though you were my agent. (trans. D. R. Shackleton Bailey, Loeb)

postea quam vero comperi eum collegam temptasse . . . ipsum reprehenderem et ab eo deprecarer iniuriam quem vitam mihi debere putaram impetrare a me non potui. (Cael. *Fam.* 8.12.1)

But when I found that he had been sounding his colleague . . . I could not bring myself to tax him personally and ask a man who I thought owed me his life not to do me harm. (trans. D. R. Shackleton Bailey, Loeb)

Apart from *fac*, *velim* and *oportet*, where there was no real choice, Caelius had the choice between the *ut* expression and the bare subjunctive. In the letters we have and which I discuss he opted for the bare subjunctive, even in the last example in which some form of formal demarcation of the subordinate clause would seem easier for the reader. This means on the one hand that the recipient of the letter (Cicero) was capable of processing the text, and on the other hand that the degree of transparency of the sentence structure created by the use of *ut* was not felt necessary by every educated writer. Was Caelius 'informal' or was Cicero 'overformal'? The

---

[20] Avoidance of repetition can be suggested for Cic. *Att.* 3.25 *illud abs te peto des operam ut* . . . (by contrast, . . . *a te peto ut des operam* . . . *ne* . . . – *Fam.* 15. 12. 2); *Fam.* 13.34.1, 13.39.1, 13.55.2. The two other bare subjunctives are in *Fam.* 15.8 and 16.14.2.

[21] *Moneo* + subjunctive is found elsewhere in Cicero (see also *TLL* s.v. *moneo* 1411.9 ff.).

[22] Cicero advises Caelius with respect to his attitude towards Dolabella, the same context in which Caelius had used *suadeo* + bare subjunctive before. Cicero has *suadeo* without *ut* also in *Fam* 7.7.1. Caelius uses *censeo* 'to recommend' once with a bare subjunctive in a later letter (8.16.5). This use of *censeo* is common from Plautus onwards and is best regarded as a set phrase (material in *TLL* s.v. *censeo* 794.23).

[23] *TLL* s.v. 601.50 has Pl. *Trin.* 591 and a few other, non-literary or late, instances.

last example is especially interesting in this context. Are we to assume that in spontaneous spoken language such a sentence would have been interpretable and was it even typically colloquial? Or is it written language dictated by a very good public orator who uses an option that Cicero did not use that often?

The next item I want to discuss is the extent to which both authors separate modifiers from the nouns to which they belong (i.e. hyperbaton or discontinuity of a noun phrase). I make a distinction between three types of hyperbaton: (i) hyperbaton caused by an intervening particle like *enim* 'you know' or *quidem* (see below), (ii) hyperbaton caused by a constituent that is neither a particle nor part of the noun phrase, (iii) hyperbaton by multiple constituents that are not part of the noun phrase. Discontinuity is a characteristic feature of the Latin noun phrase (see C. Lehmann 1991). Type (i) is more or less unavoidable. The other two are optional and more interesting when the language of different authors is examined. Examples of the three types are given below:

Plancus quidem tuus Ravennae est... (Cael. *Fam.* 8.1.4)

Your friend Plancus is at Ravenna... (trans. D. R. Shackleton Bailey, Loeb)

si quid in re publica maius actum erit... et quem ad modum actum sit et quae existimatio secuta quaeque de eo spes sit diligenter tibi perscribemus. (Cael. *Fam.* 8.1.2)

If there is any major political event... I shall be careful to write you a full account of the manner of it and of consequent views and expectations. (trans. D. R. Shackleton Bailey, Loeb)

illud nunc a te peto, si eris, ut spero, otiosus, aliquod ad nos, ut intellegamus nos tibi curae esse, σύνταγμα conscribas. (Cael. *Fam.* 8.3.3)

Now I have a favour to ask. If you are going to have time on your hands, as I expect you will, won't you write a tract on something or other and dedicate it to me, as a token of your regard? (trans. D. R. Shackleton Bailey, Loeb)

The relative frequency of the three types can be seen in the graph below (Figure 11.2), in which the absolute numbers have been adjusted on the basis of the number of words of the two corpora (and not the number of noun phrases). Caelius has more instances of type (iii), but they are not rare in Cicero, who, elsewhere, has instances with a very long distance between the separated constituents (Adams 1971: 13). The attributes involved and the pragmatic reasons to separate them from their heads are the same

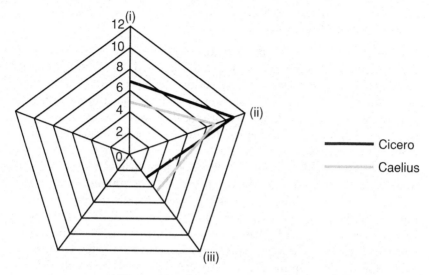

Fig. 11.2 Hyperbaton in Cicero and Caelius

in both authors.[24] Caelius seems to have found more reason to use this option.

A common feature of letters are expressions that indicate transition to another subject. Prepositional phrases with *de* 'about' serve that purpose and so do subordinate clauses introduced by *quod*. An explicit form of attracting the attention for a new topic with *quod attinet ad* 'as for' is shown in the first example below (six instances in Caelius, only three in Cicero's letters). In the other example *quod* alone signals 'Now for something new/different', remarkably enough at the beginning of the first letter of the exchange of letters during Cicero's stay abroad:

quod ad tuum decessum attinet, illud tibi non possum polliceri, me curaturum ut tibi succedatur. (Cael. *Fam.* 8.10.5)

As regards your departure from Cilicia, I cannot promise to procure the appointment of a successor. (trans. D. R. Shackleton Bailey, Loeb)

quod tibi decedens pollicitus sum me omnis res urbanas diligentissime tibi perscripturum, data opera paravi qui sic omnia persequeretur ut verear ne tibi nimium arguta haec sedulitas videatur. (Cael. *Fam.* 8.1.1)

Redeeming the promise I made as I took my leave of you to write you all the news of Rome in the fullest detail, I have been at pains to find a person to cover the

---

[24] Absolute numbers for type (i) Caelius 13, Cicero 7; (ii) 24:11; (iii) 12:3.

whole ground so meticulously that I am afraid you may find the result too wordy.
(trans. D. R. Shackleton Bailey, Loeb)

Caelius uses *quod* expressions seven times, while there is no instance of
this construction in the letters of Cicero discussed here (though Cicero
uses it elsewhere, especially in contexts like *quod scribis*... 'as for your
observation...').[25] The use of such expressions is sometimes considered
'colloquial'. Although I do not doubt that they were also used in spoken
language, they are not a 'colloquial' feature, nor are they especially 'informal'. Transitional signals are a necessary feature in any form of longer
discourse. The fact that Caelius has more of them than Cicero probably is
to do with the different roles the two had in their communication.

To conclude: it is difficult and often wrong to apply the notion 'colloquial' to the language of letters in general and to Caelius' letters in particular. We may assume that his letters show an informal way of writing. Most
of the features involved are not unique to Caelius, although he uses some
expressions more often than Cicero. Lexical items are particularly risky to
establish the level of formality of a text, since they are closely connected to
subject matter. Caelius' language sometimes seems to be evaluated more
on the basis of what we know about his personality and the few remarks in
Tacitus than on the basis of the data.

---

[25] For the use of this type of *quod* clause in Cicero's correspondence see Garcea 2003b.

CHAPTER 12

Syntactic colloquialism in Lucretius

Tobias Reinhardt

Although (or because?) it is a truism that Lucretius admits colloquial features in his *De rerum natura*, there are surprisingly few studies explicitly devoted to the language and style of this author, and certainly no book-length treatment exists as we have for a number of Latin poets. Commentators tend to note what they regard as colloquial usages, but are usually not free to pause and justify their assessment. The most substantial single publication on colloquialism in Lucretius to date remains that of Diels (1922), which is concerned primarily with morphological and lexical colloquialism and promises another study on syntactic colloquialism (Diels 1922: 59). Diels did not live to complete it.

Diels's general view was that the instances of colloquialism in Lucretius reflect the language of the farmers around whom the poet supposedly grew up and lived. At the time, scholars disagreed about the extent of the colloquial element in Lucretius' language (see Heinze 1924: 47; Ernout 1923: 155), whereas modern scholars are also likely to question the general explanatory rationale which underlies it. Moreover, it is fair to say that a certain disconnect has become the norm between scholars who are interested in details of Lucretius' language, at least when considered within the context of Latin usage in general and poetic usage in particular, and those who work on Lucretius as a literary or philosophical text and on what one might call his ideological position, whether it is within the didactic tradition, within the intellectual landscape of the Hellenistic period, or narrowly within the Epicurean tradition. One of my aims in this paper is to facilitate dialogue between these camps of scholars.

It is quite common to regard Lucretius as what one might call 'permissive' in his language and style. Leumann (1947: 122) writes: 'Alles in allem steht Lukrez mehr sprachlich als zeitlich mitten inne zwischen Ennius und Vergil.' As an objective statement of the facts, that remains uncontentious, but the assessment is meant to be more than that: the implied suggestion is that Lucretius exercised less stylistic control than Virgil did, simply because

Latin poetic language was less standardised when the *De rerum natura* was composed (see also Bailey 1947: 1.72). Nowadays our understanding of Lucretius' wide array of persuasion techniques is much improved, and we are thus more ready to reckon with Lucretius' didactic intentions where Leumann saw the literary environment impinging on the poet. Lucretius frequently appropriates his opponents' narratives with all the features which characterise them, and questions and undermines them in a second step (see below, pp. 226–7). The invocation of Venus in the proem of Book 1 is a famous example, in which traditional hymnical patterns of praising a deity and crediting her with wondrous works are then called into question by atomistic explanations of the same phenomena which are submitted later (Mansfeld 1995). This technique of appropriation followed by rejection seems to require a conscious selection and previous analysis of linguistic and stylistic features. I propose to keep an eye on the question whether we can locate with more precision and with reference to specific usages the claims of the two competing modes of explanation.

The variety of styles and of modes of writing in Lucretius is astonishing, and to try to draw up a classification is probably as difficult as it is in the case of Plato; cf. Thesleff (1967). Any such classification would include highly poeticised passages, expository passages, and so-called diatribes as general categories (see also Kenney 1971: 26–9). Once one started to classify passages, it would become apparent that the categories are problematic at least when the presence or absence of colloquial features is of interest: e.g. a passage explaining an aspect of atomistic doctrine may differ from one describing the early history of man in that the latter may at times be focalised through the eyes of early man, whose naive perception of the world may be conveyed through colloquial usages (see below, pp. 213–14). By 'diatribes' the passages at the end of the two central books are meant (3.830–1094, 4.1030–1287), which show many of the features of that elusive genre and try to rid the reader of fear of death and mistaken attitudes regarding emotional attachment and sensual pleasure respectively.[1] In some cases the presence of colloquial features might run against the generic expectation created by the passage, e.g. in highly poetical contexts or in cases where philosophical doctrine is expounded in comparatively matter-of-fact terms (cf. below, p. 220). Clearly the fact that didactic poetry is epic according to the divisions of ancient literary criticism partly accounts for this expectation on the part of many scholars. Apart from types of passage, we may also want to distinguish modes in which the narrator speaks. An

[1] See Kindstrand 1976: 25–49; Wallach 1976; R. Brown 1987: 137–9.

important one is a direct address to or engagement with the reader (a distinctive feature of the didactic mode in general), which can occur in any of the types of passage mentioned above; a second one is what one might call a critical comment, when the narrator drops out of an opponent's persona that he has temporarily adopted and glosses what precedes with a caustic remark, often phrased in forceful, colloquial terms (2.1040–3, esp. *desine... exspuere ex animo rationem* 'do not spew out reason from your mind', with Hofmann–Ricottilli 318–19).

As far as methodology is concerned, I will be relying on a range of criteria, but will carefully avoid the kind of cross-over between different criteria which the editors (p. 66) rightly regard as methodologically unsound. On occasion, I will be arguing from the distribution of a certain feature; however, since my focus is syntax, I am less likely to draw on parallels from subliterary sources, simply because these texts tend to exhibit very basic syntax only. I will also touch on matters of the lexicon or of style where they can serve to contextualise syntactic features, or where a rigid distinction between style and syntax would be artificial (see e.g. H–S 686); and trivially, colloquial features have whatever function they have in conjunction with other features, which may be archaisms, poeticisms, Hellenisms, or instances of Lucretian idiosyncrasy or boldness. Apart from introducing instances of colloquialism and describing them, my concern is to show what function they serve in Lucretius' didactic project: whether they are adopted for pragmatic reasons, whether they play a role in the engagement of the reader or in connection with the numerous argumentative strategies Lucretius adopts, or whether they are functional in generating or exhibiting a certain view of the world.[2] Given the constraints of space, I am interested in the larger picture and in general plausibility, not in a watertight proof of the colloquial status of every single feature. Thus I am more ready than I might otherwise be to use a soft – in terms of the burden of proof – psychological criterion, along the lines of Hofmann's classification (this volume pp. 45–51), rather than a harder criterion like distribution.

I begin with a usage which is not in an obvious way functional with a view to Lucretius' didactic enterprise and might be taken to be an instance of Lucretius' 'permissiveness', although, or so I shall argue, it should not so be viewed. Einar Löfstedt (1956: 1.348 n. 1) has observed that on a number of occasions Lucretius attaches *-ve* to the interrogative pronoun *quis, qui* and the relative pronoun *qui* where sense would seem to require *-que*. Thus:

---

[2] Built into the narrative of the *De rerum natura* are distinctive views on political issues (Cabisius 1985; Fowler 1989) or on perceptual experience (Catrein 2003: 165–99).

nam tibi de summa caeli ratione deumque
disserere incipiam et rerum primordia pandam,
unde omnis natura creet res, auctet alatque,
<u>quove</u> eadem rursum natura perempta resolvat . . .

                                        (1.54–7)

For about the highest principle of heaven and of the gods I shall begin to converse,
and I will lay out the first beginnings of things, from which nature creates all
things, augments them and nourishes them, <u>or</u> to what nature dissolves them once
they have perished . . .

When Seneca quotes these lines in *Ep.* 95.11 (and when Nonius 670 L.
cites 5.71 *quove modo*), they change the text to *-que*, but ample parallels
from Roman comedy through to late Latin show that *-ve* should stand. As
Löfstedt points out, on occasion this use of *-ve* may have recommended
itself because it avoided confusion with *quisque*, but the fact that *aut* can
be used alternatively (as in Verg. *Aen.* 1.369 *sed vos qui tandem, quibus
aut venistis ab oris* 'but you, who are you, or from which shores have
you come?') and that Lucretius elsewhere uses *quareve* (e.g. 3.730) shows
that this cannot be the whole story; Löfstedt thus suggests that there is a
psychological and syntactic dimension to the feature. Many of the early
appearances of the feature in Plautus and Terence are in emotive or at least
lively questions which include two elements of close semantic similarity or
even equivalence (e.g. Ter. *Hec.* 643 *sed quid mulieris | uxorem habes aut
quibus moratam moribus?*, 'But what sort of woman do you have for a wife,
or how does she behave?'); alternatively, the two parts of the question can
stand in asyndeton (Pl. *Trin.* 118 *quin eum restituis, quin ad frugem conrigis?*,
'Why don't you set him straight, why don't you reform him to honesty?').
Haffter (1934: 53–60) is right when he discusses this feature in the context of
other 'exhaustive constructions' ('erschöpfende Ausdrucksweisen') which
likewise mimic the speech of someone who is excited or exasperated. While
in late Latin the construction seems no longer to have been perceived as
emotive,[3] it is striking that in Virgil's *Aeneid* it continues to occur in emotive
speech (1.369, quoted above; 9.376 *state, viri. quae causa viae? quive estis in
armis?*, 'Stop there, you men. Why are you on the road? Or why are you
armed?')[4] or in reported speech reflecting the speech patterns of an emotive
speaker (10.149–50 *memorat nomenque genusque | quidve petat quidve ipse
ferat* '[he had gone to the king] and told him his name and nation, or

---

[3] On problems of definition of terms like vulgarism or colloquialism as applied to late Latin see R.
Coleman 1999b.
[4] See Hardie 1994: 140–1 ad loc. for further references on the usage in Virgil.

what he wanted or what he himself offered'). My point is now that the occurrence of this feature in what looks on the face of it like expository passages in Lucretius does not suggest that the poet had a tin ear for its usual application and availed himself of it simply because it was there, i.e. that its presence in the text is evidence for Lucretius' 'permissiveness'. Rather, it suggests that even in expository passages Lucretius' voice is meant to sound more urgent and involved than the average epic narrator.

Another feature related to the issue of permissiveness vs conscious selection of features is the picking up of a noun with a pronoun which does not agree with the noun but rather with a synonym of it. A psychological explanation for this kind of thing is easily found of course, and to associate the phenomenon with spoken discourse or its artful imitation in written texts has obvious plausibility.[5] Thus in

> fulgit item, cum rarescunt quoque nubila caeli;
> nam cum ventus eas leviter diducit euntis
> dissolvitque ...   (6.214–6)

There is lightning also, when the clouds in the sky grow thinner; for when the wind gently stretches them as they move and dissolves them ...

it is *nubes* which is picked up, not *nubila*.[6] There is an interesting, though less striking, use of the same device in Ovid:

> hoc pecus omne meum est; multae quoque vallibus errant,
> multas silva tegit, multae stabulantur in antris.
>   (*Met.* 13.821–2)

All these animals are mine; many besides are wandering in the valleys, many are hidden by the forest, many are kept in cave-rooms serving as barns.

These words are spoken by Polyphemus, attempting to woo Galatea. They must be seen alongside a range of other features of his speech which subtly undermine his claims to sophistication (see Hopkinson 2000 ad loc.). Thus I would be inclined to see it as intentional colouring in Lucretius rather than an inadvertent feature. There is, I would argue, a cumulative effect of

---

[5] Cf. e.g. Petr. 115.18 *quicquid feceris, omnia haec eodem ventura sunt*, with Petersmann 1977: 51. See Collinge 1953 for a collection of similar passages.

[6] Lucretius is prone to this kind of confusion especially with regard to the notion 'cloud': cf., in addition to 6.215–16; 6.187–8 *ne tibi sit frudi quod nos inferne videmus | quam sint lata magis quam sursum extructa quid extent*, where *lata* and *extructa* fail to agree with *nubibus* in 185; 1.351–3 *crescunt arbusta et fetus in tempore fundunt, | quod cibus in totas usque ab radicibus imis | per truncos ac per ramos diffunditur omnis*, where *totas* agrees with *arbores* and Lucretius in fact wrote *arbusta*.

such features regarding the tone the narrative has in the perception of the reader.

Sometimes Lucretius uses constructions which, if they occurred in spoken conversation or in literary texts reflecting it on occasion, would be explained as momentary instances of imperfect performance, due to the lack of organisation which they reveal. In 2.716–17 he speaks of atoms which entered the (human?) body but which were then expelled, *quae neque conecti quoquam potuere neque intus | vitalis motus consentire atque imitari* 'which were not able to link up with any part nor find agreement with the life-giving motions inside the body and imitate them'. While *imitari* is of course regularly construed with an accusative, *consentire* takes the dative or a prepositional phrase with *cum*. To say ad hoc that *consentire* is 'transitive' here (so Bailey 1947 ad loc.) smoothes over the oddity of the expression. One can well imagine someone stringing together a sentence like that in conversation, but would imagine that in a literary work the word order would have been normalised. A comparable, though less striking, case is 6.1239 *vitai nimium cupidos mortisque timentis* '[lack of concern for their relatives would punish them], too desiring of life and fearful of death as they are'; some present participles of transitive verbs can of course regularly take the genitive, but *timens* with the genitive is otherwise unexampled. I would assume that the construction of *cupidus* has been allowed to carry over; alternatively, the fact that *metuens* can take the genitive may account for the construction of *timens*.

One of the psychological motivations underlying colloquial language which Hofmann plausibly identified is an aversion to abstractions, including abstract nouns (this volume p. 49). It is against this background that the question can be raised whether some striking uses of the substantivated infinitive in Lucretius should count as syntactic colloquialisms.[7] That texts recognised to contain colloquial usages offer unusual instances of this syntactic phenomenon is beyond dispute, but it is hard to differentiate between cases which ought to be termed colloquial, archaic, or merely bold. In general, infinitives in Lucretius are frequent: Kollmann (1975: 282) counts 2,450 instances of the infinitive in the 7,415 verses of the *De rerum natura*, compared to 1,259 in the 9,896 verses of Virgil's *Aeneid*, 1,737 in the 12,095 verses of Ovid's *Metamorphoses*, and 300 in the 2,188 verses of Virgil's *Georgics* (which is notable because the latter is a didactic poem too, showing that the fact that Lucretius' poem is a didactic one does not by itself account for the frequency of the infinitive). In standardised prose

---

[7] See Wölfflin 1886; H–S 343–4; Metzger 1974.

the use of the substantivated infinitive is fairly tightly restricted (see K–S 1.664–6), and it is apparent that Lucretius' uses of the feature often deviate from this standard. Some notable passages are:

> praeterea meminisse iacet languetque sopore
> (4.765)

besides, during sleep memory lies inactive and is relaxed

> nec fuit ante videre oculorum lumina nata,
> nec dictis orare prius quam lingua creatast
> (4.836–7)

nor was there sight before the light of the eyes arose, nor speaking with words before the tongue

> non erat ut fieri posset mirarier umquam,
> nec diffidere, ne terras aeterna teneret
> nox   (5.979–81)

it could not happen that they should ever experience wonder or fear that eternal night might hold the earth

> et prius est armatum in equi conscendere costas
> et moderarier hunc frenis dextraque vigere
> quam biiugo curru belli temptare pericla.
> et biiugos prius est quam bis coniungere binos
> et quam falciferos armatum escendere currus
> (5.1297–1301)

and it is an earlier practice to mount a horse in arms and direct it with the bit and exercise force with the right hand than to brave the dangers of war on a two-horse chariot. And to use a two-horse chariot was earlier than combining two and two, and armed men climbing a scythed chariot (cf. 5.1250–1, 5.1379–81)

> nil adeo magnum neque tam mirabile quicquam,
> quod non paulatim minuant mirarier omnes
> (2.1028–9)

nothing is so great and so admirable that all men will not reduce their wonder about it by degrees.

Some trends may be illustrated with reference to this necessarily selective sample of evidence. Especially in Book 4, which is broadly concerned with epistemological matters, verbs denoting psychological activities are preferred candidates for substantivated infinitives,[8] as they are in texts which are recognised to exhibit colloquial usages. One can compare Pl. *Bac.* 158 *hic vereri perdidit* 'he has lost his sense of shame', Persius 1.27 *scire tuum* 'your knowledge' (see also Kißel 1990: 124 on Persius 1.9–10), and Petr. 52.3 *meum enim intellegere nulla pecunia vendo* 'I won't sell my expertise for any money', where the construction of the infinitive with a possessive pronoun is notable.[9] With regard to the last two passages, Stefenelli (1962: 106) points to corresponding expressions in Romance (cf. *il sapere* in Italian, *le savoir* in French, *el saber* in Spanish), which suggests their presence in spoken late Latin. One may wonder, though, whether in 4.836–7 the infinitive is not adopted because it is functional: the Epicureans are opposed to the notion that the abilities humans or other living beings have are hard-wired into them, one reason being that a divine power is most likely to be credited with this; instead, they assume that creatures find themselves with, e.g., the faculty of sight and then discover through trial and error how it can be used. This idea may be brought out by saying that the activity or the concept of seeing (rather than the faculty of sight) did not precede the eyes in existence. Another pattern is the occurrence of the substantivated infinitive in complex sentences involving *priusquam* or *antequam* (4.836–7, 5.1297–1301); this is not a frequent phenomenon in other texts, and it is plausible to regard it as due to the subject matter about which Lucretius talks (the chronology of the achievements of human civilisation) and the way he lays out his material on the one hand, and a preference for the construction on the other. On 2.1029, where *mirarier* is used as an object of *minuant*, Bailey (1947: II.962) cites the Pompeian graffito, *CIL* IV 6768 *et gelidae cursu minuerunt quaerere silvam*, as the closest parallel for the construction, and rightly points out that it is also analogous to another colloquial construction, *mittere* + infinitive (cf. below, p. 211).

Another colloquial construction is *habeo* with the infinitive, as in 6.711 *item in multis hoc rebus dicere habemus* 'even so in many cases we have this to say' (see R. Coleman 1971, 1976; Adams 1991a). From this construction the Romance future evolved, although in its earliest occurrences – in Cicero's *S. Rosc.* 100 and Lucretius – it is not itself future in sense, but rather expresses possibility. The distribution in Cicero's works is interesting: it soon drops out of the speeches along with a number of other colloquialisms, while it continues to be used in the philosophical works.

---

[8] While Lucretius in the whole poem uses no noun meaning 'memory', *visus* in the sense of 'sight' is used elsewhere (e.g. 4.217).

[9] It occurs in Plautus and Cicero's letters, but not in Sallust, Caesar or Livy (K–S 1.666; H–S 343).

The latter are as *Übersetzungsliteratur* amenable to syntactic Hellenisms, and the occurrences might thus be explained as reflections of Greek ἔχω + infinitive; Robert Coleman (1971: 215) is right, however, that neither Cicero in the speeches nor Lucretius are prone to syntactic Hellenisms. 6.711 is an authorial comment addressed to the reader, where a slightly informal tone would not be surprising.

In 3.100–1 Lucretius writes *harmoniam Grai quam dicunt, quod faciat nos | vivere cum sensu, nulla cum in parte siet mens* '[other philosophers assume that the mind is not located at a particular place in the body, but is a kind of vital state of it while we are alive] which the Greeks call a "harmony" which makes us live and feel, although the intelligence is not situated in any particular part'. The accusative with infinitive after *faciat* is very rare in archaic Latin, then occurs here and elsewhere in Lucretius (e.g. 3.301), is then used occasionally in poetry, and is frequent in late Latin (against the trend that outside formal contexts the accusative with infinitive tends to be replaced with clauses; see H–S 353–4). In Verg. *Aen.* 2.538–9 it occurs in Priam's speech just before he is murdered by Pyrrhus (*nati coram me cernere letum fecisti | et patrios foedasti funere vultus* 'you made me see my own son's death before my eyes and defiled the face of a father through the killing').

Another colloquial construction which plays a role in the text's attempt to engage the reader is *mitte* + infinitive in negative commands, as in 6.1056–7 *illud in his rebus mirari mitte, quod aestus | non valet e lapide hoc alias impellere item res* 'in this matter don't be amazed that the current emanating from the stone cannot move other things too'.[10] We can compare Pl. *Per.* 207 *mitte male loqui* 'stop being abusive' and Ter. *An.* 904 *mitte orare* 'don't beg me', as well as the similar usages Pl. *Per.* 312 *pressare parce* 'do not exercise pressure on it' and 642 *rogare omitte* 'ask her no more'. Related is the use of the indicative *mitto* + infinitive, as in Ter. *Hau.* 900 *mitto . . . osculari* 'I say nothing of kisses' and Lucretius 4.471 *hunc igitur contra mittam contendere causam* 'I will therefore forego to plead against a man who . . .', where the tone is very hard to gauge: *contendere*, when used of litigation, is unparalleled with *causa* as an accusative object (cf. *TLL* s.v. 669.7–70 and 73–5; Munro 1928: 250). One wonders if this reflects a usage of legal procedure which has left no further trace in the written record.[11]

An interesting sentence is 1.455–8 *servitium contra paupertas divitiaeque, | libertas bellum concordia cetera quorum | adventu manet incolumis natura*

---

[10] See Landgraf (1878: 40–1), who points out that it is another feature which Cicero, after using it as a young man, eventually omitted from the speeches; and L. Löfstedt 1966: 74–82.
[11] On this sort of thing cf. Bailey 1947: II.664 on 1.411.

abituque, | *haec soliti sumus, ut par est, eventa vocare* 'by contrast, slavery, poverty, wealth, freedom, war, unity, as well as other things through whose appearance and disappearance the nature (of things) remains stable, these things we are accustomed to call, as is appropriate, accidents'. The basic construction of this sentence has been described as an 'absolute nominative' by Holtze (1868: 3–4), and as an anacoluthon by Bailey (1947: II.675 ad loc.). The string of nouns in asyndeton in lines 455–6 can be paralleled from elsewhere in Lucretius (1.633–4, 1.685, 1.744, 1.808, 1.820–1, and 1.680, which shows two infinitives in asyndeton). What makes it appropriate to see a syntactic colloquialism here is the resemblance to patterns of spoken discourse which are in evidence in modern languages as well, i.e. the way in which a number of items are listed, then resumed by a pronoun (cf. the accusative *haec* here) or some equivalent expression ('all those things'), with which a predicate then forms a syntactic unit. Of course literary texts show constructions which are explainable in terms of broadly comparable psychological mechanisms without being colloquialisms,[12] but given evidence introduced earlier that the voice of the narrator in Lucretius is generally less restrained than is customary in epic, the assumption of a conversational feel to the construction is plausible.

In 5.170–4 Lucretius writes: *nam gaudere novis rebus debere videtur* | *cui veteres obsunt; sed cui nihil accidit aegri* | *tempore in ante acto, cum pulchre degeret aevom,* | *quid potuit novitatis amorem accendere tali?* | *quidve mali fuerat nobis non esse creatis?*, 'For it is apparent that he must rejoice in new things who is offended by the old; but he who has not experienced something troubling in time past, when he has lead a beautiful life, what could ignite the love for novelty in such a man? Or what evil had there been if we had not been made?' Here W. A. Merrill (1907) wanted to normalise to *creatos,* but other editors retain the dative. The assimilation in 5.174 of the predicative noun in the infinitive with the dative of the person affected is sometimes explained as an analogy to sentences like Cic. *Att.* 9.2a.1 *impetrabis... a Caesare ut tibi abesse liceat et esse otioso* 'you will obtain permission from Caesar to be absent and out of public life', sometimes as a syntactic Hellenism (so H–S 350, tentatively); the latter seems a less attractive explanation in Lucretius. The few other occurrences of the construction, in speeches in Ovid (*Met.* 8.555, 690–1) and Horace (*Epist.* 1.16.61), suggest that it was felt to be colloquial, which would also

---

[12] Like *attractio inversa,* on which see Fraenkel 1954, which is used in colloquial texts as well as in Republican legislation.

fit the general tone of the passage (a challenging question posed to the reader). In 5.174 we also have *-ve* for *-que* as discussed above (pp. 205–7).

Lucretius frequently uses impersonal verbs in personal constructions and vice versa; one can observe the same variability compared to classical usage in archaic Latin and in late Latin, which suggests that it remained a feature of the living language throughout antiquity. Once more each case needs to be considered individually if one is to form a view whether a given instance is archaic or colloquial.[13] In 4.984 *magni refert studium atque voluntas,* | *et quibus in rebus consuerint esse operati* | *non homines solum* 'application and inclination are important, and what those things are which not only men ... tend to undertake', the normally impersonal *refert* is used in a personal construction, but with a thing rather than a person as a subject. One can compare Plin. *Nat.* 7.42 *incessus atque omne quicquid dici potest in gravida refert* 'the way she walks and everything that can be mentioned are important during pregnancy', and earlier the plural construction in Pl. *Per.* 593 *te ex puella prius percontari volo quae ad rem referunt* 'I want you to address some questions which bear on the matter to the girl first', of which our passage is a natural development. The personal use of *refert* is too rare to establish its stylistic level with reference to distribution, but the existing parallels are at least consistent with colloquial status. In Lucretius 4.984 it seems to be adopted for convenience. *Opus est* in personal construction (*OLD* s.v. *opus* 13) is better attested and also has a distribution which suggests a colloquial ring, although it is to be found in Horace's odes once (*Carm.* 1.15.25) and once in Caesar (*Gal.* 5.40.6); in Lucretius there is e.g. 3.967 *materies opus est ut crescant postera saecla* 'matter is necessary for later generations to grow' and 2.20–1 *corpoream ad naturam pauca videmus* | *esse opus omnino* 'we see that for the bodily nature few things are necessary'. A more interesting case is 5.1262–3 *tum penetrabat eos posse haec liquefacta calore* | *quamlibet in formam et faciem decurrere rerum* 'then it became clear to them that this material, once liquefied through heat, could run into any shape or form', which contains an unparalleled impersonal construction of *penetrare* (*TLL* s.v. 1069.40–2), later developed by Tacitus in *Ann.* 3.4.2 *nihil tamen Tiberius magis penetravit quam studia hominum accensa in Agrippinam* 'nevertheless, nothing made a stronger impression on Tiberius than men's burning interest in Agrippina' (see Woodman and Martin 1996: 96–7 ad loc.). The passage in Lucretius raises inter alia the question whether new constructions and word formations (of which there are many

---

[13] See Holtze 1868: 3–4 and Bailey 1947: 1.88–9 for collections of instances in Lucretius; E. Löfstedt 1911: 44–7 for a historical survey; Bauer 2000: 93–150.

in Lucretius) can have colloquial register. This is arguable in the present case, because the construction of *penetrare*, concrete and almost pictorial as it is, is likely to be modelled on *in mentem venit* (which also inspired the less colourful *occurit*, cf. H–S 359), itself a colloquial expression, and because a colloquial tone would suit the context of the passage, which is concerned with how the early, primitive humans discovered the technique of processing ore so as to produce weapons and tools. The infinitive which depends on *penetrabat* and in particular the phrase *formam et faciem rerum* seems to reflect their point of view rather than the narrator's, and it would be in keeping with this perspective to say that the insight was 'sinking in' (to use a comparable, but not equivalent, English rendering). While *facies* can have the plain technical meaning 'form' (*OLD* s.v. 7; *TLL* s.v. 49.60 ff.), many of the instances for this use play on or show awareness of the more elementary meanings 'physical and outward experience (of men and animals)' and 'face'. Thus Var. *L.* 6.78 *'facere' a facie qui rei quam facit imponit faciem* 'the word "to make" is from *facies* because it imposes a *facies* onto a thing', or Sen. *Ep.* 24.13 *non hominibus tantum, sed rebus persona demenda est et reddenda facies sua* 'we should strip the mask, not only from men, but from things, and restore to each object its own aspect'. I thus suggest that here *facies* is not just a synonym of *forma* but has the sense of 'aspect', 'features', which reflects the early humans' naive view of the world around them. A related issue is the use of transitive verbs as intransitive ones and vice versa, which I will not pursue here.

Latin poetic language tends to avoid prepositional phrases in many cases where these would have been used in prose. Instead, simple cases are more frequently used; explanations for this phenomenon which have been offered include syntactic archaism (R. Coleman 1991, 1999a: 79–81) and a wider tendency to avoid function words in poetic narrative (Adams and Mayer 1999b: 11). One effect of having simple cases instead of prepositional phrases is an increased scope for ambiguity, which helps account for the perceived richness of poetic narrative. It is remarkable that against this trend Lucretius is a preposition-heavy author (see also Bailey 1947: 1.106–7). Apparently he does not aim for this kind of ambiguity, and is happy to include function words otherwise not used in poetry outside comedy (see below, p. 222). Some prepositional phrases in Lucretius arguably reflect colloquial usages.

The replacement of the dative through a prepositional phrase formed with *ad* is a usage which is to be regarded as a colloquialism on grounds of its distribution and afterlife; see Hofmann and Szantyr (H–S 86, 220), who observe that the origin of the usage may be situations where a prepositional phrase with *ad* expressing a direction is interchangeable with the dative of the person affected (cf. Pl. *Capt.* 360 *praecipe quae ad patrem vis nuntiari* 'instruct (him) what message he is to bring to your father' with 400 *numquid aliud vis patri nuntiari?* 'Do you want no further message to be brought to the father?'). A common feature in late Latin and one which lives on in the Romance languages, it is found from very early on. In Lucretius there is e.g. 1.750 *quod ad sensus nostros minimum esse videtur* 'what appears to be smallest to our senses', with which we may compare Cic. *Att.* 8.3.6 *invidiosum ad bonos* 'arousing hatred with the honest men' and Prop. 1.18.29–30 *quodcumque meae possunt narrare querellae* | *cogor ad argutas dicere solus aves* 'whatever tale my laments can relate, I am forced to tell, alone, the singing birds'.[14] Its occurrence in Cicero's letters and in elegy, a genre which admits of elevated conversational features but is less amenable to archaism, tells against explaining it as the latter in Lucretius.

The use of *de* as a genitive equivalent is sometimes sweepingly called a colloquialism, but already in 1956 Väänänen showed that it is often pragmatically motivated and that we can distinguish several types of use under this general heading, not all of which show the required distribution. In technical language, for instance, there are many such uses which are clearly due to the enhanced precision of expression (see Adams 1995a: 430–8). *de* phrases replacing partitive genitives, however, have a colloquial distribution: in classical Latin, this replacement involving *de* is restricted to a few standing phrases (e.g. *homo de plebe*), but it is frequent in Roman comedy, and is also to be found in subliterary Latin (*Tab. Vindol.* II, no. 310, recto, col. 2 *mittas per aliquem de nostris* 'he may send it through one of us') and the non-urbane parts of Petronius' *Satyrica* (see Petersmann 1977: 72–3). The same can be said, if to a lesser degree, about prepositional phrases with *ex.* In Lucretius we find e.g. 2.104 *et cetera de genere horum*[15] 'and the other things of their kind' and 2.183 *nunc id quod superest de motibus expediemus* 'and now we will explain what remains of the topic of motions'.[16] Possibly showing the 'partitive' use of *ab*, but usually explained differently, is 2.50–2 *audacterque inter reges rerumque potentis* | *versantur neque fulgorem reverentur ab auro* | *nec clarum vestis splendorem purpureai* '[and if] they boldly

---

[14] See also *TLL* s.v. *ad* 557. 78–558.39.

[15] *de* is in the *recentiores* but usually printed by the editors.

[16] *expedire de aliqua re* is late and rare (*TLL* s.v. 1612.83–1613.2), which makes me hesitant to take *de motibus* with *expediemus*.

mingle with kings and potentates, if they revere neither the shine of gold nor the bright light of crimson garment', where *vestis . . . purpureai* shows that *ab auro* can be seen as the replacement of a genitive, although what kind of genitive is not obvious – the Epicurean, materialist way of looking at the world would make it natural to see the shine of the gold as a part of it which physically emanates from it.[17] There is a wider issue here: to what extent do grammatical categories like the types of the genitive which we habitually distinguish embody a view of the world which an author like Lucretius may not share?

The causal use of *prae* and, to a lesser degree, *ab* in cases where a simple *ablativus causae* might be used also has a distribution typical for colloquial usages (see H–S 134). Instances in Lucretius are 4.1166–7 *cum vivere non quit | prae macie* 'when she cannot live because she is so thin', which comes from a diatribe-like passage where euphemistic nicknames which lovers give to girlfriends with obvious blemishes are ridiculed, and 3.74–5 *ab eodem saepe timore | macerat invidia* 'envy consumes (them) through the same fear'; however, the causal use of *ab* has a wider distribution,[18] and its colloquial status is less clear-cut.

Prepositional phrases can also replace parts of *ipse*. *Per se* is the best known instance of this usage, frequent in late Latin and discussed in detail by Einar Löfstedt (1911: 335–7). In Lucretius we find *per se* used in this way in 2.646–7 *omnis enim per se divom natura necessest | inmortali aevo summa cum pace fruatur* 'for the nature of divinity herself must enjoy an immortal life in deepest peace'; cf. also *per te* in juxtaposition with *ipse* in 1.407 *alid ex alio per te tute ipse videre* 'you (will be able to) see for yourself one thing after another', an address to the reader. Harder to parallel, but similar in type, is the use of *ab se* in 4.467–8 *res secernere apertas | ab dubiis, animus quas ab se protinus addit* '[for nothing is more difficult than] to separate apparent things from doubtful ones, which the mind adds by itself', with which we can compare Pl. *Mil.* 939 *datne ab se mulier operam?*, 'Is the girl herself lending us help?' In 4.468 I would suggest that *ab se* has been adopted because it is functional: it is a key tenet of Epicurean epistemology that all perceptions are true and that episodes of misapprehending something are to be explained by assuming that accurate perceptual data have been

---

[17] If that is correct, then many of the parallels cited by Munro 1928: 122–3 ad loc. are not pertinent, since they represent varieties of the causal use of *ab* (on which see below). Fowler (2002: 130 ad loc.) suggests a syntactic Hellenism, which cannot be ruled out given that kings and other single rulers are to be found in 2.50. On such replacements in Greek see Tzamali 2000.

[18] Especially Livy uses it on a number of occasions, cf. 8.29.13 *ingenti ardore militum a vulnerum ira*, 42.62.3 *ferocia ab re bene gesta*.

badly processed and distorted by the mind. This idea is emphasised by the expression *ab se*.

Another expression involving a preposition which can be called colloquial because it exhibits the lack of logical rigour which Hofmann associated with many colloquialisms is 6.393 *nulla sibi turpi conscius in re* 'not aware of any evil deed'. The adjective *conscius* is normally construed with simple cases or accusative with infinitive when used in the sense of 'aware of', or with *in* + ablative in the sense of 'being privy'. Here we have the former sense, but the construction with *in*; I have found no other instance of this usage (cf. *TLL* s.v. 372.61). There are many other cases where Lucretius uses prepositional phrases instead of simple cases or other constructions, but these do not have a sufficiently strong claim to being colloquial to feature here.

Many noteworthy uses of the dative can be found in Lucretius, some of which are deviant and some of which are likely to be colloquial in some sense. The matter would merit (and require) a separate study, beginning with a full list and classification of all relevant instances.[19] Bailey (1947: 1.92–3) notes the tendency to use a dative in cases where a 'possessive or objective' genitive would have been equally possible, and observes that in a substantial number of cases metrical convenience cannot be the reason for adopting the dative. I list some examples:

<u>seminibus</u> si tanta est copia
(2.1070)

if there is such a quantity of seeds
[possessive dative, replacing a subjective genitive]

ramique virescunt | <u>arboribus</u>
(1.252–3)

the branches of the trees grow green
[possessive dative, replacing a partitive genitive]

quae <u>partibus</u> eius | discidium parere . . . posset
(1.219–20)

which can bring about the break-up of the parts
[adnominal dative with *discidium*, replacing a subjective genitive; dative of disadvantage, if taken as part of the verb phrase *discidium parere*]

---

[19] For an extensive if largely unanalysed collection of passages featuring noteworthy datives in Lucretius, compiled after Lachmann's edition but before much of the later work on the text had been carried out, see Holtze 1868: 39–45.

quae . . . creant incendia <u>silvis</u>
(1.903)

which cause fires of the woods
[adnominal dative, replacing a subjective genitive]

fit quoque uti pluviae forsan magis ad caput <u>ei</u> | tempore eo fiant
(6.729–30)

it is also possible that there is perhaps more rain at its source at that time
[possessive dative, replacing a partitive genitive *eius*]

multaque praetera tibi possum commemorando
argumenta fidem <u>dictis</u> conradere nostris
(1.400–1)

I could mention many further proofs, thereby scraping together credit for my sayings
[dative of advantage with the verb phrase *fidem corradere*, replacing a subjective genitive (*fides* = 'plausibility', cf. *TLL* s.v. 683.67 ff. for the construction) or objective genitive ('faith, belief in')].

Havers (1911: 3 ff.) used the term 'sympathetic dative' as a generic label for six different uses of the dative, of which the possessive dative used of persons (e.g. Pl. *Mil.* 26 *quo pacto <u>ei</u> pugno praefregisti bracchium* 'how your fist did smash his forearm') is more frequent than the other types. [20] Indeed, it is this dative most scholars have in mind when they talk about the sympathetic dative. However, Pinkster (2005a: 242–3) cites examples from Pliny's *Naturalis historia* in which non-human and non-animate entities are 'affected' and placed in the dative, e.g. 1.69 [*herbae*] *quibus flos antequam caules exeant* 'plants which produce flower before stalk', thus showing that the restriction to persons is artifical and due to too narrow a selection of evidence. It will be clear that several of the examples from Lucretius given above are comparable. Pinkster (2005a: 242–3) observes that the *Naturalis historia*, although it looks at nature from the perspective of its usefulness for human beings, is 'the largest work in Latin that is not chiefly anthropocentric in its subject matter', which helps account for the deviant uses of the sympathetic dative. In a related way the datives in question in Lucretius, as used of inanimate objects, convey a sense of empathy with the world and as a consequence a move away from human concerns. This might sound impressionistic were it not for the fact that the narrative itself invites its readership on a number of occasions to let go of their egotistic

---

[20] A critique of the notion of the 'sympathetic dative' is to be found in Adams 1995a: 449–60.

way of looking at the world and view their own fate instead in the context of abstract cosmic events (2.1168–74, 3.964–9). How colloquial, then, are such datives? An informed answer to the question would have to start from the full survey of data in Lucretius which I mentioned above, and Adams (1995a: 450) rightly cautions against generalisations – already Einar Löfstedt (1956: II.213) pointed out that the usage is frequent in what he called *Volkssprache*, in technical prose, in poetry, and in stylised prose of the Imperial period. Yet even with this caveat, it is noteworthy that the dative of the person affected is markedly more frequent in the conversations of the freedmen in Petronius' *Satyrica* than in the urbane passages (Petersmann 1977: 84). What is thus safe to say is that the instances for this usage will *include* cases which had a colloquial ring for contemporary readers or which, while colloquial in type, were recognisably adopted for pragmatic reasons. 1.400–1 above may serve as an illustration of the first possibility: it is a forceful address to the reader, in which the narrator pointedly craves acceptance for the arguments he offers. In a sentence where there is also a 'sympathetic' dative of the person involved (*tibi*), the dative *dictis* is juxtaposed with *corradere*, a colloquial word used in comedy to describe the scraping together of money.[21]

A well-recognised colloquialism, showing a typical distribution, is the use of adverbs with *esse* in place of *se habere, fieri, vivere* or similar verbs,[22] e.g. Ter. *Ph.* 527 *sic sum; si placeo, utere* 'that's what I am like; if you like it, do business with me' or Cic. *Q. Rosc.* 29 *sic est vulgus* 'that is the way of the crowd'. In Lucretius there is 3.307 *sic hominum genus est* 'so is the race of men', on which Heinze (1897: 93) intriguingly comments: 'durchaus nicht zu vergleichen mit bequem-lässigen Ausdrücken, wie Cicero pro Rosc. Am. 30, 84 *sic vita hominum est*'. But why not? In 3.288–306 Lucretius explains in terms of atomistic theory why certain species have temperaments of a certain kind, and then moves on to human beings, describing in rather concrete terms that education provides merely superficial polish (3.307–8 *quamvis doctrina politos | constituat pariter quosdam* 'although training makes some equally polished') and that innate bad qualities cannot (literally) be eradicated (3.310 *nec radicitus evelli mala posse putandumst* 'and one must not think that flaws can be torn out with the roots'). To introduce these points with a phrase which is colloquial and thus mildly forceful would not be jarring.

---

[21] Cf. Pl. *Poen.* 1363 *credo conradi potest* and *TLL* s.v. *corradere* 1026.80–1027.7; see more generally Hofmann–Ricottilli 319 n. 3.

[22] See Landgraf 1878: 38, 1914: 174; Housman 1919: 71; H–S 171; Hofmann–Ricottilli 337.

The replacement of pronouns with or without preposition with pronominal adverbs (e.g. *hinc, unde, inde*) is a feature which in classical Latin on the evidence of its distribution is situated at the border between colloquialism and usages acceptable in standardised prose.[23] It also has a number of specialised usages e.g. in legal language (*unde petitur* = 'the accused', Ter. *Eu.* 11), and some have argued that its origin actually is in what has been dubbed *Kanzleisprache* (see Bagordo 2001: 90), but Löfstedt (1911: 181) rightly observes that this would be hard to square with the frequency and wide distribution of this feature and its afterlife in the Romance languages. Instances in Lucretius are outside strongly colloquial contexts like the 'diatribes' (see this volume, p. 204). They include, however, 1.54–6 *nam tibi de summa caeli ratione deumque | disserere incipiam et rerum primordia pandam, unde* [= *a quibus*] *omnis natura creet res, auctet alatque* (see this volume, p. 206), which is a matter-of-fact address to the reader about Lucretius' plans, where a slightly conversational tone would not be out of place (note 1.57 *quove* for *quoque*), but there are also passages which are simply expository, like 5.200–3 *principio quantum caeli tegit impetus ingens, | inde* [= *cuius*] *avidam partem montes silvaeque ferarum | possedere, tenent rupes vastaeque paludes | et mare* 'first, of all that the vast expanse of the sky covers, a greedy part is taken up by mountains and forests full of wild animals, and parts are held by rocks, huge swamps and the sea'.

Pleonastic accumulation of particles which are similar or identical in meaning is another feature of colloquial language; it can be explained in terms of the lack of intellectual discipline and stylistic control which oral communication often exhibits. In poetry where otiose words are normally avoided, such usages are striking.[24] *Etiam* and *quoque* in combination are frequent already in Plautus and Terence, in the sequence *quoque etiam*, *etiam* followed by and separated from *quoque*, and *quoque* followed by and separated from *etiam*. Lucretius uses *etiam quoque*, and *etiam* followed by and separated from *quoque* (3.292, 5.153, 5.517, 5.604, 6.503). All these passages are of an expository nature. Interestingly, Lucretius once (5.751) also uses *item quoque*, a collocation not found elsewhere but which may or may not have been felt to have a colloquial register as well. By the same token, Lucretius uses *quippe etenim* twenty times, though it occurs only once elsewhere (in Apul. *Apol.* 72, where it is best explained as a mannerism consciously lifted from Lucretius). The mechanism underlying such duplications is plausibly explained by Einar Löfstedt (1911: 59): the

[23] See H–S 208–10; E. Löfstedt 1911: 180–1; Palmén 1958.
[24] Informative discussion in E. Löfstedt 1911: 59–64, 1956: II.219–32; see also Wölfflin 1880: 427.

semantic value of particles can weaken, but at the same time sense requires their continued presence, which results in duplication. We should probably suspect a similar mechanism at work at 3.440, where *quippe etenim* occurs, but not in a justification of what preceded; rather, a new argument is offered, coming to the same conclusion as the previous one, so that sense would require something like *praeterea* (see Heinze 1897 ad loc.). If Löfstedt's psychological explanation is along the right lines (and the text is sound), then it is tempting to speculate why this kind of semantic weakening can occur in the *De rerum natura*. Part of the explanation may be that Lucretius, unlike any other Latin poet, relies on a rudimentary formulaic technique comparable to that used in Homeric epic. A study describing if not explaining this technique is that of Minyard (1978).[25]

One of the psychological mechanisms which according to Hofmann account for colloquial usages is a lack of mental or intellectual application (*Denkträgheit*). A feature which arguably stems from such lack of application but which can also readily harden into a mannerism without a recognisable stylistic register is the combination of a noun with a semantically faint verb (esp. *facere, capere, dare, reddere, sumere*) used to replace a simple verb. In Lucretius instances include 1.740 *principiis tamen in rerum fecere ruinas* '[these men] have come to a crash as far as the first beginnings are concerned', from a polemical passage which dismisses the findings of natural philosophers other than Empedocles and is the only instance in Lucretius where persons rather than things are the subject; cf. 6.572–3 *ruinas... facit*, 1.747 *facient... pausam*, 2.934 *huic satis illud erit planum facere atque probare* 'this will be enough to make clear to him and to prove',[26] 4.41 *in sua discessum dederint primordia* '[body and soul] have each dissolved into their first-beginnings', with Munro (1928: 232) on further instances of such phrases. In this case distribution likewise suggests that the usage is colloquial (see Landgraf 1878: 20–1; Hofmann–Ricottilli 385). We may also compare, for similarity in type, the semantic paleness of the underlined expression in 3.1071–2 *quam bene si videat, iam rebus quisque relictis* | *naturam primum studeat cognoscere rerum* 'for if he could see this well, he would drop everything else and first make an effort to learn the nature of things', which talks in counterfactual terms about someone (representing man in general) who opts out of his normal rat-race-like existence.

---

[25] See also H–S 674 on *quasi si*, which occurs once in Lucretius (4.1014).
[26] A faded proverbial expression, cf. Pl. *Rud.* 1132 *faciam ego hanc rem ex procliva planam tibi* and *As.* 663 *nam istuc proclivest quod iubes me planum conlocare*.

We proceed to some devices which help in articulating the didactic narrative, in that they clarify, reinforce, lend structure or bring out logical connections. Many of these usages are rare in poetry, because poetry normally has less need for such devices; some of them can plausibly be called colloquial. Still, these need to be seen in the context of other, related usages, which is why I shall cast my net a bit wider.

Clarification devices include *propterea... quia* (e.g. 3.1070) and *propterea... quod* (e.g. 2.735), where the causal relationship could be expressed by the conjunction alone. *Propterea* is not used in poetry outside Plautus, Terence[27] and Lucretius, but is of course widespread in prose. *Hoc... quod/quoniam* has the same function. Lucretius uses *hoc* in the sense of 'therefore' on a number of occasions (e.g. 4.553, 622), and sometimes in correlation with the causal *quod* (2.125–7) and with *quoniam* (4.1093, on which see R. Brown 1987: 233 ad loc.).[28] The distribution of *hoc* in this sense (comedy, Horace's *Satires*, late Latin; not Verg. *G.* 2.425, see Mynors 1990: 157 ad loc.) suggests colloquial status.[29]

A stylistic feature which likewise has clarifying function is the seemingly pleonastic use of *sic* and *ita* (*sc.* unrelated to *sic(ut)... ita*), e.g. in 1.1114–17 *haec sic pernosces parva perductus opella; | namque alid ex alio clarescet nec tibi caeca | nox iter eripiet, quin ultima naturai | pervideas: ita res accendent lumina rebus*, 'So you will acquire understanding of these matters with little effort; for one thing will be illuminated by another, and dark night will not conceal the path from you, so that you cannot see the utmost recesses of nature; so will real things create light for real things' (see E. Löfstedt 1950: 7–9), which is the end of the book, a forceful address to the reader,[30] but at the same time there is also an argument being made about the self-perpetuating illumination which a grasp on truth affords. The feature as such occurs in a variety of texts, but striking instances like 1.1114–17 are not normally found in stylised prose or poetry. With *haec sic pernosces* here cf. Cic. *Att.* 5.21.5 *hoc tu ita reperies* 'you will find it is so'.

It is common in a number of languages, including Latin and English, to repeat for the sake of clarity a conjunction or pronoun in spoken discourse, especially when attempting to build longer, complex sentences. For obvious reasons the device is frequent in technical treatises too, where it is more

---

[27] Both Plautus and Terence use *propterea... quod* as well as *propterea... quia* (or reverse order).

[28] On the usage see Wölfflin and Meader 1900: 376; E. Löfstedt 1956: 1.262–5; *TLL* s.v. *hic*, 2745.57–78.

[29] On the question whether *hoc* is a causal ablative, as one might suspect on the evidence of Lucretius, or an accusative, see E. Löfstedt 1956: 1.262–5 (accusative); H–S 575.

[30] Note the three compounds formed with *per-*, a type which is rare in poetry apart from the genres which are more amenable to colloquialism; see Axelson 1945: 37–8; H–S 164; Müller 1997: 236.

likely to be functional rather than meant to bestow conversational flair (which is not to say that in colloquial contexts there is no clarifying effect). The feature is inconspicuous when there is a certain distance between the two occurrences of the word in question, but becomes mannered when that is not the case. In Lucretius we find

> fiet <u>ut</u>, ante oculus fuerit qui dexter, <u>ut</u> idem
> nunc sit laevus et e laevo sit mutua dexter.
>
> (4.324–5)

it will happen that the eye which was previously the right eye,
that the same one is now the left one and in turn the left one becomes the right,

where some editors change the first *ut* to *ita*, but Löfstedt (1956: II.227) rightly compares Pl. *Am.* 495 *suamque ut culpam expetere in mortalem ut sinat* '[it would not befit a god] if he allowed a mortal to face the consequences for his guilt' and Cic. *Att.* 3.5 *tantum te oro ut, quoniam me ipsum semper amasti, ut eodem amore sis*, 'Only that I ask of you, since you have always loved me for my own sake, that you maintain the very same love.' (Many colloquial features are interdependent with others, as opposites relative to a notional baseline; see Hofmann–Ricottilli 349 and Chahoud, this volume pp. 60–1). Just as Lucretius can aim for hyperclarity by repeating conjunctions, he can omit conjunctions or pronouns elsewhere. In 4.1174 *nempe eadem facit – et scimus facere – omnia turpi* 'indeed, she does all the things which the ugly woman does, and we know she does them', talking about the disgusting cosmetic routines of a beautiful woman, a pronoun with *facere* is omitted (see H–S 362).

Expressions which mark out steps of an argument include *principio*, signalling a first step, and *praeterea*, *porro* and *item*, which signal a move to a new point. That spoken conversation, in which paratactic construction is preferred to hypotactic construction, has a need for such structuring devices too is obvious, and the uses of *porro* in lively exchanges in comedy is significant, as well as the fact that it is rare in poetry and, when used, occurs in texts like Horace's *Satires*.[31] Notable are also *tum porro* (e.g. 1.298, 1.426, 1.520) and *hinc porro* (e.g. 4.1244, twice in Plautus), with which we may compare *perge porro*, which is used in lively conversation in Roman comedy as well as in animated dialogue in Cicero (cf. above, pp. 220–1 on semantic fading).

Like some other didactic poems, the *De rerum natura* has a developed internal addressee, Memmius, as well as being directed at a wider secondary

---

[31] On *porro* in Lucretius see Calboli Montefusco 1972; R. Brown 1987: 350.

readership.[32] We have already encountered various devices which engage
the audience in a way that is unusual for epic poetry, and the impact of some
of these devices is enhanced by the fact that they are colloquialisms in some
sense. To these we add now a number of first-person verbs of saying and
thinking in parenthesis;[33] these are common in comedy, but are otherwise
mostly absent from poetry, except for specific contexts (speeches in epic,
e.g. Verg. *Aen.* 1.387, 6.368; addresses to the girl in love elegy; dialogical
bucolic poems, e.g. Verg. *Ecl.* 3.10). They are also used in oratory, which is
not surprising given their function (see below):

- *ut opinor* seventeen times, e.g. 2.184, 3.626, 3.676, 3.876, 3.963; cf. Pl.
  Am. 574, *Aul.* 77, Ter. *Hec.* 598 (*ut ego opinor*), *Eu.* 563, *An.* 179.
- *opinor* without *ut*, 1.396, 2.201; cf. Pl. *Aul.* 782, *Bac.* 774, Ter. *Ph.* 615–16,
  693, 678–9.
- *credo*, 5.175 (following after 5.174 *quidve mali fuerat nobis non esse creatis*,
  on which see above, p. 212); cf. Pl. *Aul.* 110, *Capt.* 889, Ter. *Ph.* 140.
- *inquam*, 2.257, 3.341, 5.620; cf. Pl. *Am.* 94, *Cist.* 606, Ter. *Hau.* 694, *An.*
  715.
- *ut dico*, 4.1207; cf. Ter. *Ph.* 479.

All of these are 'expressions of contact' (*sc.* with the addressee), cf. Anna
Chahoud's remarks above (pp. 58–9). They are, however, not equivalent
in function: on a superficial level, (*ut*) *opinor* and *credo* convey caution,
modesty, and hesitation; *inquam* is more forceful and assertive. Müller
(1997: 177–86) has pointed out with reference to Terence that (*ut*) *opinor* is
used by sociologically inferior speakers when addressing someone of higher
status, among equals, and in self-address. It would not normally be used by
a superior speaker addressing an inferior one, as there is usually no need for
qualification of the speaker's remarks. *Credo* is similar but more forceful,
and expresses a stronger longing for approval or consideration of what is
being said. *Inquam* is used by sociologically superior speakers, who can
afford highmindedness or aloofness.

In Lucretius these parentheses can (i) be devices of realism which add
to the characterisation of the narrator persona by making him sound
conversational (in 5.620 the narrator refers back in a self-conscious way to
the beginning of the paragraph in 5.614), modest, clever, or sardonic (5.175),
as well as modulate his status relative to the addressee by making him sound
by turns humble and authoritative, (ii) play a role in the presentation of an
argument, in that they can assert or draw attention to the plausibility of an
assumption (3.341, 3.676; in 3.963 *iure, ut opinor, agat* '[Nature] would be

---

[32] See Mitsis 1994 and the entire collection of which it forms part; Fowler 2000.
[33] Hofmann and Szantyr discuss parenthesis under syntax (H–S 472–3) and style (H–S 728–9).

right, I think, to argue in this way' is a comment on Nature who has just spoken in a prosopopoeia; in 2.201 *ut opinor* is used to signal the narrator's presumptions about the audience's views).

Occasionally Lucretius directly addresses the reader, e.g. in 3.206–7 *quae tibi cognita res in multis, o bone, rebus | utilis invenietur et opportuna cluebit* 'if this matter is known to you, my good man, it will be found advantageous, and you will call it useful'. In his disturbingly effective book on possible interpolations in Lucretius, Deufert (1996: 242–4) has argued that these two lines are spurious. Apart from arguments about the train of thought of the passage, Deufert suggests, referring to *TLL* (s.v. *bonus* 2085.56 ff.) and Kenney (1971: 103 ad loc.), that the address *o bone* is otherwise only found in comedy and satire and thus at too low a stylistic level given that Memmius, to whom the *De rerum natura* is dedicated, is an aristocrat. Interpreters since Merrill, when they have not suspected the text, have assumed an address to someone other than Memmius, e.g. the 'general reader' (see Townend 1978: 276). The question whether Lucretius might be distinguishing two audiences through addresses of different stylistic level is an intriguing one which we cannot pursue further here, and while the distribution of the address *o bone* warrants calling it colloquial, the general type of address and the parallels do not seem to warrant calling it a rough (and hence offensive) colloquialism (see also Dickey 2002: 129–62, esp. 145).

Another 'expression of contact' is direct addresses to the reader on which urgency is bestowed through the pleonastic use of personal pronouns. Instances include 1.407–8 *sic alid ex alio per te tute ipse videre | talibus in rebus poteris* (see above, p. 216) and 4.1149–52 *et tamen implicitus quoque possis inque peditus | effugere infestum, nisi tute tibi obvius obstes | et praetermittas animi vitia omnia primum | aut quae corpori' sunt eius, quam praepetis ac vis* 'and yet you could escape the danger despite being entangled and held back, if you do not stand in your own way and overlook all flaws of the soul and of the body which the person whom you prefer and desire has'. Hofmann and Szantyr (H–S 174) go as far as to associate the use of reinforcements like *tute* with spoken language (rather than colloquial language in a weaker sense),[34] but then draw attention to the frequency of the usage in Cic. *Att.* 4.5.5, the famous consolatory letter Servius Sulpicius Rufus sent to Cicero on the occasion of the death of his daughter Tullia, whose tone is conversational but also composed, dignified and at places oldfashioned.

---

[34] On *tute* see the note in R. Brown 1987: 275 on 4.1150.

Lucretius occasionally uses sentence questions without an interrogative particle, addressed to the reader. These are forceful and can convey a range of emotions, including indignation and incredulity, or can be equivalent to an exhortation.[35] Their distribution does justify calling them colloquial, with the qualification that they are regularly used in emotive passages in oratory too. An instance of how Lucretius employs them is 2.206–9 *nocturnasque faces caeli sublime volantis | nonne vides longos flammarum ducere tractus | in quascumque dedit partis natura meatum? | non cadere in terras stellas et sidera?*, 'The nightly torches of the sky, flying along high up, do you not see how they draw long traces of flames in whatever direction nature has given them a course? [Do you not see how] stars and celestial bodies fall to earth?' The extract comes from a difficult passage, whose general line of thought has been clarified by West (1964). Lucretius argues that the natural movement for bodies, those in the perceptible world and in that of the atoms, is downwards, and that they move in other directions only if there are additional forces at work (examples given include blood splurting out of a pierced artery, and pieces of wood pushed under water and rebounding). 2.206–9 is another instance of this pattern: the question beginning *nonne vides* relates to celestial bodies whose movement is determined by additional forces,[36] while 209 is then concerned with the behaviour of these bodies when these forces are withdrawn (see West 1964: 98–9). Line 209 thus stands in a contrast with what precedes, and demands added emphasis.[37] Arguably a sleight of hand depends on this added emphasis too: the forces governing celestial phenomena are much less transparent to the observer than those in the examples cited earlier, and Lucretius' forceful question suggests that it is obvious that the stars fall down once they are no longer subject to additional forces.

In 3.894–9 Lucretius speaks in the character of mourners who are grieving for a young father:

'iam iam non domus accipiet te laeta neque uxor
optima, nec dulces occurrent oscula nati   895
praeripere et tacita pectus dulcedine tangent.
non poteris factis florentibus esse tuisque
praesidium. misero misere' aiunt 'omnia ademit
una dies infesta tibi tot praemia vitae.'

---

[35] See H–S 460–2; Petersmann 1977: 261.
[36] On *nonne vides* as a typical didactic structuring device see Schiesaro 1984.
[37] That 209 contrasts with what precedes shows that the question mark at the end of 208 is the right punctuation, and that we are not dealing with an instance of the pattern *nonne... non... (non)*, where *non* introduces additional question(s) which are logically at the same level as what precedes (H–S 462). Lucretius uses *nonne vides* fifteen times, but never follows it up with *non*.

'No longer will your flourishing home welcome you, nor your best of wives, nor will sweet children run towards you in order to steal a kiss and will deeply touch your heart in silent sweetness. You will not be able to thrive and be a bulwark for your family. The poor man', they say, 'one fatal day, miserably, took all these prizes of life away from him.'

He then goes on to show that the views expressed by these mourners are misguided, on the grounds that the deceased will no longer be able to desire any of the things he lost.

As a whole, the extract is representative of a strategy that Lucretius frequently adopts: an attitude which is from his point of view undesirable or misguided is first appropriated, in this case by introducing it in direct speech, and then rejected, undermined or otherwise discredited (see above, p. 204). Lucretius evidently took the view that many such attitudes are embodied in literary texts or in ordinary ways of thinking; these attitudes thus 'enter' his poem as literary allusions to certain texts, as episodes of focalisation, or even as direct 'quotes' (as here). My primary interest is the underlined infinitive of purpose. Hofmann and Szantyr (H–S 344) regard it, especially when used alongside verbs of motion like *occurrere*, as an archaism, but note its frequency in late Latin and Romance. The construction has some currency in Augustan poetry, but there it is frequently explained as a syntactic Hellenism; its use with verbs of motion in comedy and satire (from Lucilius) suggests that there was also an indigenous Italic use.

The mourners' sentiments might be termed old-fashioned, but more relevantly they are clichéd, and there are notable correspondences with funerary inscriptions: the *domus laeta*, the *uxor optima*, the notion of a father as *praesidium* of his family, the idea that one day can take away all of life's goods (see Bailey 1947 ad loc.). If these were just atavisms rather than the kind of things people thought and said on such occasions, Lucretius would fail in his didactic endeavour. Readers must be able to recognise and – briefly – empathise with these sentiments in order to be cleansed of them in a second step. Penney (1999: 255) raises the question why in Latin poetry the infinitive is preferred to the supine to express purpose after verbs of motion. One possibility he considers is that poetry follows everyday language in this respect, which would mean that the infinitive of purpose persisted in Lucretius' time as a feature of everyday spoken language rather than re-emerging in late Latin. He says rightly that this is 'beyond demonstration', but we can add to his discussion that it would be more in keeping with Lucretius' didactic purpose if the infinitive of purpose was a feature of contemporary spoken language rather than an archaism. This is not to say that the two are mutually exclusive categories:

retention of archaic usages is not unusual in colloquial language (Adams and Mayer 1999b: 10).

Some recurrent themes of this chapter were syntactic colloquialism and its role in reader engagement, the issue of 'permissiveness', and colloquialism that is functional with reference to Lucretius' didactic purpose. I end with a few observations. This study would have profited from closer attention to other first-century poets whose work shows a colloquial element, notably Catullus and Horace's *Satires* and *Epistles*. But apart from constraints of space, there are few monographs or substantial articles on which one could draw in order to put Lucretius into perspective, e.g. in cases where a usage is earlier attested in comedy and the question is whether it ought to be seen as colloquial or rather archaic (see, however, Richard Thomas's and Stephen Harrison's contributions in this volume). Moreover, it does seem that we need finer distinctions within the sphere of colloquialism. For instance, I have commented on occasion on usages that feature in comedy and in Cicero's speeches (not just the early ones) when he is seeking to make a connection with the audience, but are usually absent from poetry or historiography; it would be artificial to exclude such usages on grounds of distribution.

CHAPTER 13

Campaigning for utilitas: style, grammar and philosophy in C. Iulius Caesar

Andreas Willi

I INTRODUCTION

C. Iulius Caesar is not a name that readily springs to mind in the context of an inquiry into the relationship between 'colloquial' and literary Latin; for 'Caesar is incomparably the most "correct" of classical authors, if by "correct" we mean that he observes the "rules" of Latin orthography, grammar and word-order that would later become standardised by Palaemon and others' (Hall 1998: 18). Caesar's linguistic self-discipline, which famously restricts the vocabulary of the *Bellum Gallicum* to less than 1,300 lexemes, is so thorough that it even affects and excludes forms, words and constructions which can hardly be called 'colloquial' if this term is taken as the opposite of 'literary'.[1] However, if we admit that colloquial Latin can also be taken to refer to 'the Latin used conversationally by the upper . . . classes during the Republic' (Dickey, this volume p. 66), in other words be equated roughly with what ancient theoreticians referred to by terms such as *cottidianus sermo* (*Rhet. Her.* 4.14; cf. Ferri and Probert, this volume pp. 14, 39), then Caesar might even be called the most colloquial of Latin authors: there is little in his writings which could not also have been said, without much stylistic effect, in a standard upper-class conversation of his time. All the more, though, the inclusion of a chapter on Caesar in this collection might seem pointless: for whether we call nothing or everything 'colloquial', the lack of substantial diastratic differentiation in the primary material provides little scope for illuminating comments.[2]

---

[1] Cf. e.g. the avoidance of the third person plural in *-ere*, shared with Cicero (E. Löfstedt 1911: 36–9; Leumann 1977: 607–8 with literature), of the genitive plural *deum* (Pascucci 1973: 490) or of the genitive of quality with third-declension adjectives (E. Löfstedt 1956: 1.155–62); on the selection and number of lexemes (excluding names and technical terms) see Eden 1962: 94–8, Pascucci 1973: 493–5 and Hall 1998: 17.

[2] This statement does not imply that there is no stylistic variation in the *Bellum Gallicum* and the *Bellum civile* (cf. E. Löfstedt 1956: II.307–8; Eden 1962: 113–15), only that nothing which we do

Our present focus will therefore be different. Instead of searching for marked (non-)colloquialisms in Caesar's writings, we will ask why he adopts such a smooth style and what this tells us about his (and some of his contemporaries') ideas on the relationship between colloquial and literary Latin. If we had only the *Bellum Gallicum* and the *Bellum civile*, such an endeavour might yield little but empty speculation. Fortunately, however, we possess, in a fragmentary state, a primary source that has rarely been fully explored or, I will suggest, understood. Mainly this is because Caesar the general and politician tends to eclipse Caesar the man of culture and learning who, according to Cicero (*Brut.* 252, 261), was not only one of Rome's foremost orators – second to none but Cicero himself (Quint. *Inst.* 10.1.114) – but who had also reached this perfection *multis litteris et eis quidem reconditis et exquisitis summoque studio et diligentia* 'through extensive reading even of inaccessible and little known texts, through extraordinary and most careful learning'. The neglected source I am referring to is Caesar's treatise *De analogia*, the remains of which consist of less than three dozen short fragments mainly culled from ancient scholars and grammarians such as Gellius, Probus, Charisius, Pompeius and Priscian and nowadays accessible in the collections of Funaioli (1907: 145–57) and Klotz (1927a: 177–85, the text and numbering adopted here).

2 DATE AND CONTEXT OF CAESAR'S *DE ANALOGIA*

According to Suetonius (*Jul.* 56.5), Caesar wrote the two books of *De analogia*: *in transitu Alpium cum ex citeriore Gallia conventibus peractis ad exercitum rediret* 'while crossing the Alps when he returned from Cisalpine Gaul to the army after he had held courts of law'. This information, together with the fact that the treatise was dedicated to Cicero (Gel. 19.8.3) and should therefore postdate the reconciliation of Caesar and Cicero in 56 BC, points to a composition in the spring of 55 or 54; in the winter of 54–53 Caesar stayed with the army, and in the spring of 52 the revolt of Vercingetorix hardly left any time to spare during a hurried journey (Dahlmann 1935: 259). Moreover, Hendrickson (1906) has made a good case for the year 54 from reading some of the introductory words, which are quoted by the proud dedicatee (Cic. *Brut.* 253 = fr. 1), as a reply to Cicero's *De oratore* of 55 BC:

read there was normally excluded from either (a) 'higher' prose (i.e. 'colloquial' ∼ 'non-literary') or (b) an educated conversation (i.e. 'colloquial' ∼ 'belonging to the *sermo cottidianus*'); it is risky to assert (b) even for a 'slip' like the third person plural perfect *sustinuere* and *accessere* in *Civ.* 1.51.5 and 3.63.6 (cf. Rosén 1999: 187–9).

ac si <ut> cogitata praeclare eloqui possent, nonnulli studio et usu elaboraverunt, cuius te paene principem copiae atque inventorem bene de nomine ac dignitate populi Romani meritum esse existumare debemus: hunc facilem et cotidianum novisse sermonem nunc pro relicto est habendum.

And even if not a few people have worked hard in theory and practice to ensure that brilliant ideas can also be brilliantly expressed – and we must admit that you, who are more or less the leading force and the inventor of this richness, have done a great service to the name and dignity of the Roman people – to master this straightforward everyday style must nowadays be regarded as a relic.

These words seem to react to *De orat.* 3.38 and 3.48, where Crassus refuses to dwell on the ability of speaking *Latine* and *plane*:

neque enim conamur docere eum dicere, qui loqui nesciat; nec sperare, qui Latine non possit, nunc ornate esse dicturum . . . praetereamus igitur praecepta Latine loquendi, quae puerilis doctrina tradit et subtilior cognitio ac ratio litterarum alit aut consuetudo sermonis cotidiani ac domestici, libri confirmant et lectio veterum oratorum et poetarum.

For we do not try to make an orator out of someone who cannot speak; nor to hope that someone who cannot speak good Latin, will now be able to make elegant speeches . . . Let us therefore pass over the precepts of how to speak good Latin, which are taught at elementary school, strengthened by the more advanced systematic study of grammar or by regular exposure to everyday language at home, and finally corroborated by books and the reading of old orators and poets.

What is here referred to as *Latine dicere* and taken for granted recalls the unornamented 'simple style' characterised as *sermo purus et Latinus* in the *Orator* (79) and already described with the same term as in the above passages by the *Rhetorica ad Herennium* (4.14: *id quod ad . . . cottidianum sermonem demissum est*). It thus appears that Caesar wants to complement the *De oratore*, where Cicero failed to give adequate guidance because of his elitist attitude: in *De analogia* we are supposed to learn more precisely what *Latine dicere* means. Given this background, its dedication to Cicero makes perfect sense, and since we know from a slightly later letter by Cicero how keen he was at that time to learn about Caesar's opinion on his literary output (Cic. *Q. fr.* 2.16.5), we may also hypothesise, with Hendrickson (1906: 110), that 'Cicero himself would have forwarded a copy [of the *De oratore*] to Caesar at his winter headquarters in Cisalpine Gaul'.

3 CONTENTS AND BACKGROUND

If Caesar felt that knowledge of an unadorned *facilis et cotidianus sermo* – the kind of *sermo* we do find in the *commentarii* – was something that could not simply be taken for granted but had to be taught, just as much as Cicero's *ornatus*, the question arises how he went about doing so in *De analogia*. How did he determine what was, or was not, admissible in the target style?

Most of the fragments are tantalisingly uninformative. Apart from the one already quoted (which is preceded by the statement that Caesar also held 'that the selection of words is the basic principle of eloquence', *verborum delectum originem esse eloquentiae*), only one is of a general nature. Unsurprisingly it is this one which was most often cited in antiquity. In Gellius' rendering it reads (fr. 2 = Gel. 1.10.4): *tamquam scopulum sic fugias inauditum atque insolens verbum* 'you should avoid like a rock in the sea any word that is unheard of or unusual'. Nearly all the other fragments concern specific minutiae of Latin usage and grammar, such as the correct formation of various case forms[3] (e.g. fr. 6: accusative plural *fagos*, not *fagus*; 8: accusative singular *turbonem*, not *turbinem*;[4] 9: genitive plural *panium*, not *panum*; 10: genitive singular *die*, not *diei*; 11: nominative plural *isdem*, not *idem*; 16: nominative-accusative singular *lac*, not *lact*; 22: nominative singular *pubis*, not *pubes/puber*; 23: dative singular *ornatu*, not *ornatui*; 26b: ablative singular *iubare*, not *iubari*, despite 25a, 25b and 26a on the ablative in *-i* of neuters in *-ar, -e, -al*; 27: genitive plural *partum*, not *partium*), the assignment of grammatical number (fr. 3: *harena*, not *harenae*) and gender (fr. 18: masc. *crinis*; 19: ntr. *pollen*), word formation (fr. 28: *mortus*, not *mortuus*; 29: *ens* as participle of *esse*), syntax (fr. 12: *se* vs *sese*)[5] and orthography (fr. 17: genitive singular *Pompeiii*, not *Pompei*).[6] Thus, despite the randomness of what is transmitted, it is clear that *De analogia* did not just establish, or argue for, abstract rules, but entered into a discussion of a wide range of concrete topics.

What is more difficult to say on the basis of these fragments alone is whether Caesar's main aim was to provide stylistic guidance in every major

---

[3] Fr. 31 (= Gel. 6.9.13, on *e*-reduplicated perfects like *memordi, pepugi, spepondi*) may not belong to *De analogia* (despite Klotz 1927a: 185); no other fragment deals with verbal conjugation, and Fronto (p. 224.15–16 van den Hout) summarises the contents of *De analogia* as *de nominibus declinandis, de verborum aspirationibus et rationibus* 'about the declension of nouns, about the aspiration and regularities of words'.

[4] The fragment (Char. p. 183.19–24 Barwick) must be corrupt when it compares *caro, caronis* (*sic*), but the usual correction to *Cato, Catonis* is doubtful in the light of phonemic restrictions on analogical pairings (cf. fr. 13, Siebenborn 1976: 72–5); a better reading would be *carbo, carbonis*.

[5] Doubting the authenticity of the fragment (Char. p. 142.4–7 Barwick: *sese* in indirect reflexive usages), Klotz (1910: 223–39) observes that Caesar uses *sese* for emphasis; however, the theory in *De analogia* does not always fully agree with Caesar's practice (cf. §8, Oldfather and Bloom 1927: 596–7).

[6] Klotz (1927a: 185) further suggests that Caesar may have codified in *De analogia* the superlative spelling *-imus* instead of *-umus* (cf. Quint. *Inst.* 1.7.21, Isid. *Orig.* 1.27.15). Similarly, the question of initial /h-/ (cf. n. 3) was partly (though not exclusively: Catul. 84, Gel. 13.6.3 with Nigidius fr. 21 Funaioli) an orthographical one.

area of uncertainty or whether the grammatical suggestions he made were introduced as (probably selective) illustrations of some overarching principles. A number of considerations suggest the latter. Firstly, the *scopulum* rule (fr. 2) would be unhelpful to anyone wanting to know, say, what the 'pure' dative singular of a *u*-stem noun like *ornatus* was: the problem was precisely that neither *ornatu* nor *ornatui* were *inaudita atque insolentia verba* (cf. Lomanto 1993: 667–70). Secondly, most but perhaps not all of the issues mentioned in the fragments appear to have been real cases of doubt – although we have to concede that we may never know for sure whether a genitive plural *partum* or a participle *ens* sounded as outlandish in Caesar's time as our lack of relevant attestations suggests; after all, the similarly awkward-looking nominative-accusative *lact* was used by Varro (*Men.* 26, *L.* 5.104) and Pliny (*Nat.* 11.232, 22.116), and *partum* could be found in Ennius (*Ann.* 593 V. = 600 Sk.). Thirdly, and most importantly, the title *De analogia* itself points to something theoretically more advanced than a 'Primer of Good Latin'. It positions the treatise in the midst of a fierce debate among Hellenistic and Roman grammarians, orators and philosophers (cf. Dahlmann 1935: 265–71).

This is not the place to discuss in detail the controversies between the so-called 'analogists' and their opponents, the 'anomalists' (cf. e.g. Siebenborn 1976: 97–109). In a nutshell, it may be said that the analogists stressed the regularities in grammar, by pointing out paradigmatically predictable patterns, whereas the anomalists highlighted any breech of such regularity principles and thereby questioned whether language was governed by anything other than mere convention; hence, some of their strongest evidence came from word derivation (e.g. Var. *L.* 8.56: *Parmensis* ← *Parma*, but *Romanus* ← *Roma*), synonymy (e.g. Var. *L.* 8.71: *aedes Deum Consentium*, but regular genitive plural *deorum*) and homonymy (e.g. Var. *L.* 8.63: dative = ablative in some nouns, but not in others). Moreover, given the largely negative, empiricist and anti-theoretical thrust of their arguments, the anomalists' position had the advantage of simplicity and they could weaken that of the analogists further by stressing the latter's internal disagreements. Thus, whereas the Alexandrian grammarian 'Aristarchus, Varro says, thought that analogical word forms should be used, to the extent that common usage permits', his Pergamene counterpart Crates of Mallus may have been more fundamentalist, thinking 'that analogical forms ought to be substituted for forms in common use'.[7] Such a divergence between two analogical positions shows that we must clarify not only whether a

---

[7] Blank (2005: 238), who shows that the older view, according to which Crates was an anomalist, is based on a misreading of Varro's *De lingua Latina*.

particular figure was an analogist or an anomalist but also whether he adopted one or the other viewpoint in a prescriptive or a descriptive manner. For instance, from Varro's text it appears that the Stoic Chrysippus, who wrote three books περὶ ἀνωμαλίας in which he demonstrated *similes res dissimilibus verbis et dissimiles similibus esse vocabulis notatas* 'that similar things were denoted by dissimilar words and dissimilar things by similar words' (Var. *L.* 9.1), was nevertheless in favour of analogically correcting oblique forms on the basis of the nominative and vice versa (cf. Var. *L.* 10.59); in other words, he was descriptively an anomalist (accepting that irregularities are real), but prescriptively an analogist (trying to do something about them).[8] People like Aristarchus and Crates, meanwhile, were analogists both descriptively (playing down irregularities) and prescriptively (with Aristarchus apparently being more ready to make concessions when analogy crassly contradicted common usage), whereas empiricists like Sextus had to be descriptive as well as prescriptive anomalists (cf. Sextus Empiricus, *Adversus mathematicos* 1.191–3).

Returning to Caesar, his title *De analogia* clearly suggests an analogist attitude of some sort, and many of the fragments point to a form of prescriptive analogism grounded in the descriptive recognition of anomalism (e.g. fr. 3 = Gel. 19.8.3 *Gaius enim Caesar... in libris quos ad M. Ciceronem de analogia conscripsit 'harenas' vitiose dici existimat, quod 'harena' numquam multitudinis numero appellanda sit* 'for Gaius Caesar finds in the books about analogy, which he dedicated to Cicero, that *harenae* is wrong, since *harena* "sand" should never be used in the plural').[9] However, the case of Aristarchus vs Crates (vs Chrysippus) shows that even within the world of prescriptive analogism there were various positions, and we must therefore still ask which one Caesar was taking.

4 CAESAR THE POPULIST OR CAESAR THE NATIONALIST?

Whereas the grammatical fragments of *De analogia* have largely been neglected in historical and literary scholarship, two articles published in recent years have attempted to integrate this material into a larger picture of Caesar as a statesman. Although they come to widely divergent conclusions, both of them assume that Caesar's prescriptivism is of the 'fundamentalist' type.

---

[8] On Chrysippus see further e.g. Steinthal 1890: 359–73 and M. Frede 1978: 71–3.
[9] The plural *harenae* was widely used, not just in poetry (e.g. Verg. *Aen.* 1.107), but also in cultivated spoken and written language (cf. the context in Gellius, Liv. 22.16.4, Suet. *Aug.* 80, etc.).

According to Sinclair (1994), Caesar had observed in his court-hearings how the provincials in Gaul struggled to master a 'Ciceronian' elite language based on Roman upper-class *consuetudo*. In order to win the support of these groups, he decided to remove the barrier to their social advancement by propagating a 'democratic grammatical agenda', in which *ratio* was paramount and *consuetudo* at best played a role of arbitration when *ratio* did not provide a satisfactory solution. Caesar's 'impulse' to subject the Latin language to systemisation would thus introduce the anti-libertarian principles of political thought informing the later Principate.

In contrast to this, Hall (1998: 28) concludes that 'imposing linguistic order on the world against the intrusion of barbarisms, and imposing political order on it against rebarbative tribesmen, are two sides of the same intellectual coin'. Here Caesar is not making 'democratic' advances to provincials, but promoting a 'Latin ringfenced against contamination by obvious rhetorical baggage or alien artistic ornament . . . , a deliberately calculated expression of uncompromising *Romanitas*'. The creation of a pure, analogist Latin, the Latin of the *Bellum Gallicum*, is primarily to be seen as directed against foreign, especially Greek, influences: it is nationalist rather than populist.

There are obvious weaknesses in both of these readings. For instance, one might object to Hall that, while every attempt to set up linguistic norms has something potentially 'national' about it, to construct an anti-Greek Caesar is hardly more promising than to construct an anti-Greek Cicero. Having spent several years in the East and having studied with Apollonius Molon in Rhodes, Caesar himself used Greek freely in speech and writing,[10] and he greatly admired Greek culture (cf. e.g. Suet. *Vit. Ter.* 7 on Terence as a *dimidiatus Menander*). The fact that *De analogia* (fr. 22) promoted the Latin declension pattern for Greek words and names (e.g. accusative *Calypsonem*, not *Calypso*) is just the unavoidable result of an analogist's mindset and need not have anything to do with nationalism.[11] And as for Sinclair's views, we may wonder whether Caesar in 54 BC really needed the support of some poorly educated provincials as much as that of the Roman aristocracy and, more generally, if the publication of a style guide is the most promising way to amass a political following.

In our context, however, the main shortcoming of these readings is their unquestioned belief in Caesar's linguistic fundamentalism and, in

---

[10] Cf. Caes. *Gall.* 5.48.4, Cic. *Q. fr.* 2.16.5, Plutarch, *Caesar* 2 and 46, *Pompey* 60, Suet. *Jul.* 82.2; see further Kaimio (1979: 130–1, 255–6), who even concludes from Plin. *Nat.* 1 Ind. xviii that Caesar wrote his *De astris* in Greek.

[11] For the discussions about this issue see further Var. *L.* 10.69–71, Quint. *Inst.* 1.5.58–64.

connection with this, their disregard for the intellectual debate in which *De analogia* takes part. To start with, Cicero himself states that Caesar *rationem adhibens consuetudinem vitiosam et corruptam pura et incorrupta consuetudine emendat* 'by applying analogy corrects mistaken and corrupt usage by pure and incorrupt usage' (*Brut.* 261). In other words, Caesar's analogy does not operate freely, overruling usage in the name of a greater good. According to Cicero, the result of a Caesarian correction is still in line with one form of *consuetudo*, which would not (or not necessarily) be the case if only *ratio* counted. Moreover, only such a mitigated form of analogy is in line with the *scopulum* rule, and Poccetti (1993b: 621) is therefore certainly right when he states that a closer inspection of the fragments of *De analogia* reveals how Caesar did not blindly espouse the analogists' cause, but rather positioned himself in the midst of the 'complex cultural kaleidoscope' of a period which was strongly imbued with eclecticism. In Poccetti's view, the *consuetudo*-based *scopulum* rule acts as a final check against an exaggerated application of analogical principles: first, 'abstract' analogy establishes that Y would be better than X, but if Y is an *inauditum atque insolens verbum*, whereas X is not, Y must not be used out of respect for *consuetudo*.[12]

However, this is not exactly what Cicero is saying (cf. Dihle 1957: 193–4; Siebenborn 1976: 111–12). Cicero speaks of *two* forms of *consuetudo*, one *vitiosa*, the other *pura*. Hence, both 'good' Y and 'bad' X are anchored in *consuetudo*. What Caesar's analogy does is merely help to decide which one is 'good'; whereas what is outside *consuetudo* to begin with need not be considered at all since the *scopulum* rule is applied at the start, not at the end, of the selection process.[13] Caesar's analogism is thus as non-fundamentalist as analogism could possibly be, and with its restriction to cases of *variatio* within *consuetudo*, which foreshadows Varro's reconciliatory position,[14] it would have been equally unsuited for a populist and for a nationalist agenda. The uneducated provincial still had to know what options were

---

[12] Cf. similarly Leeman 1963: 157; Dahlmann 1935: 262–4 remains somewhat contradictory.

[13] In practice, *De analogia* may have overstepped these limits occasionally, for why should for instance a participle *ens* be 'correct' when *consuetudo* apparently knew neither this nor any competing form (fr. 29; cf. Collart 1954: 148 n. 3)? Note, however, that the matter certainly called for debate on a theoretical level: contrast *potest* : *potens* = *est* : $X \rightarrow X$ = *ens* with *abest* : *absens* = *est* : X.

[14] Cf. Var. *L.* 10.74 on the *analogia quae derigitur ad usum loquendi* (i.e. the individual's analogy); Siebenborn 1976: 96–7 and Müller 2001: 200 and 195, after Collart 1954: 149–57, on the primacy of *consuetudo* in Varro (e.g. *L.* 9.2–3, 9.35, 9.114) and his differentiation of a *consuetudo recta* and a *consuetudo depravata/mala* (*L.* 9.11, 9.18). Contrast the stricter attitude depicted in Var. *L.* 9.20 (*verbum quod novum et ratione introductum quominus recipiamus vitare non debemus* 'we must not shrink back from accepting a word which is new and established through analogy') and enacted by people like Sisenna (Cic. *Brut.* 259, Gel. 2.25.9; Rawson 1979: 343–5).

available through *consuetudo*, and even the staunchest defender of *Romanitas* was given no means to prevent *consuetudo* from adopting 'un-Roman' elements.

5 *RATIO, NATURA, AUCTORITAS*

Now, if for Caesar analogy should operate only where different forms of *consuetudo* compete, it might be asked whether that does not make his analogism meaningless. After all, even an anomalist had to decide in cases of doubt and might therefore have conceded that *ratio* could usefully be applied here.[15] However, *ratio* was not the only possible criterion available. According to a Varronian fragment (fr. 268 Funaioli), [*Latinitas*] *constat... his quattuor: natura analogia consuetudine auctoritate* 'good Latin rests on these four criteria: nature, analogy, usage, and authority'.[16] The relative weight given to each of these could vary, so that assigning the first rank to *consuetudo* still left open the possibility of deciding between competing forms of *consuetudo* with the help of either *natura* or *auctoritas* rather than *analogia (ratio)*. In order fully to understand the implications of Caesar's position, we must briefly look at these alternatives in turn.

Varro's *natura* is a somewhat elusive concept (cf. Siebenborn 1976: 151–4). In the fragment cited, he exemplifies it by arguing that the use of a form *scrimbo* instead of *scribo* would simply be 'unnatural' (presumably because no-one ever uses or used *scrimbo*, nor would anyone postulate *scrimbo* for the sake of analogy), but the term also evokes the old discussion between those who believed in a natural (φύσει) connection between *signifiants* and *signifiés* and those who held that *signifiants* were assigned to *signifiés* through an act of – potentially[17] arbitrary and conventional – nomenclature (θέσει). Thus, a proponent of the φύσει view could have argued that a *consuetudo* variant *Y* is better than its competitor *X* because *Y* is closer to the 'inherent nature' of the concept denoted, as shown for instance through etymology.

There is one fragment of *De analogia* which leaves no doubt about what Caesar thinks of such naturalist theories of language (fr. 4 = Gel. 19.8.7). Having established that *caelum* 'heaven', *triticum* 'wheat' and *harena* 'sand' should not be used in the plural, he asks his addressee: *num tu harum rerum natura accidere arbitraris quod 'unam terram' et 'plures terras' et*

[15] Cf. the anti-analogist voice in Var. *L.* 8.26, where the acceptance of variation is then preferred.
[16] Cf. Quint. *Inst.* 1.6.1 with a slightly different list; from Cic. *Orat.* 157 one might also add *suavitas*, i.e. 'euphony' (Siebenborn 1976: 154–5).
[17] Not all θέσει proponents believed in a purely arbitrary relationship of *signifiants* and *signifiés*: cf. n. 19.

'*urbem*' et '*urbes*' et '*imperium*' et '*imperia*' *dicamus, neque* '*quadrigas*' *in unam nominis figuram redigere neque* '*harenam*' *multitudinis appellatione convertere possimus?*, 'Do you think it is due to the nature of these things that we can speak of one *terra* "earth" and several *terrae*, of one *urbs* "City" and several *urbes*, of one *imperium* "supreme power" and several *imperia*, but cannot turn the word *quadrigae* "horse-team" into the singular or the word *harena* "sand" into the plural?' The expected answer is 'No', and the viewpoint we are invited to share is unmistakably conventionalist.[18]

Turning to *auctoritas*, Caesar could hardly have put a similarly dismissive rhetorical question to his dedicatee. We remember Cicero's words in *De orat.* 3.48: *praetereamus igitur praecepta Latine loquendi, quae... libri confirmant et lectio veterum oratorum et poetarum* (cf. above, §2). For someone like Cicero, who was even prepared to accept the occasional archaism merely for the sake of *ornatus* (*De orat.* 3.39), *auctoritas* would have been a more obvious choice than *ratio* in deciding between competing variants (cf. Fögen 2000: 136–8).

6 INVENTING EPICUREAN GRAMMAR AND STYLE

To sum up the results reached so far, we have seen that (a) despite its title the *De analogia* assigned first rank to *consuetudo*, not *ratio*, in the relative weighting of possible criteria of *Latinitas*, and (b) the fact that *ratio*, not *auctoritas* (or *natura*), was placed second is itself worth noting, especially given the well-known traditionalist attitudes of large parts of the Roman establishment. We are now in a position better to define the place of Caesar's treatise – and with it, of Caesar's stylistic choices more generally – on the intellectual map of the Roman first century BC.

What is most remarkable about (a) is its pragmatic, undogmatic, approach to language: it implies an empirical analysis of current *consuetudo* whilst recognising that *consuetudo* is not always uniform. Together with the unconventional stance adopted in (b), this yields a combination that is neither in line with Alexandrian grammar à la Aristarchus (where the basic procedures are theoretical rather than empirical) nor particularly close to the linguistic thinking in the philosophical schools most interested in such matters: Stoicism and (Neo-)Pythagoreanism. It is true that the descriptively anomalist position of someone like Chrysippus (above, §3) has an

---

[18] Cf. in this context also Morgan (1997) on Caes. *apud* Suet. *Jul.* 77 *nihil esse rem publicam, appellationem modo sine corpore ac specie* 'the *res publica* is nothing, just a name without substance and form'.

intrinsic affinity with a *consuetudo*-focused empiricism, but a true Stoic would not have dismissed as absurd the idea that something in language 'happens by nature' (*natura accidere*); and similarly, a Pythagorean would have firmly believed in a φύσει-governed relationship between *signifiants* and *signifiés*,[19] while being less ready to compromise on the imposition of analogy through respect for *consuetudo*.

Yet, there is one philosophical school with whose principles Caesar's unique combination of (a) and (b), and also his dismissal of *natura* as a factor in the shaping of language, tallies well: Epicureanism. Admittedly, Lucretius' Epicurean 'Bible' *De rerum natura*, also published in 54 BC, has little to say about language, except for a digression on its origin from animal sounds (Lucr. 5.1028–90). In a sense, language has thus come about φύσει even for an Epicurean, but Lucretius makes it clear that his is not a φύσις origin which informs the actual relationship of *signifiants* and *signifiés*: instead, this relationship is governed purely by human *utilitas*, as demonstrated by a passage from Epicurus' *Letter to Herodotus* (75–6), where the author underlines the function of language as a tool for unambiguous, concise communication among groups of people who have come to an agreement about its use.[20]

Unsurprisingly this teaching fits in well with wider Epicurean theories about the world. According to these, the cosmos is governed by natural laws as a consequence of orderly atomic motion. However, because of the existence of the *clinamen* or 'swerve', which can make atoms collide unpredictably, there is no absolute determinism and mankind is able and invited rationally to apply its free will within the framework defined by the natural laws. Crucially, the fact that chance may sometimes shatter a rational plan must never discourage such rational action, for the ideal Epicurean will remain 'reactively creative' even in the face of adversity, his highest aim always being *utilitas* for the community.

Now, what has been described under (a) and (b) above constitutes a sort of parallel microcosmos. *Consuetudo* is the communal linguistic framework over which the individual has as little say as over the laws of nature, and it is subject to influences which make it unpredictable. However, within the framework set by *consuetudo* there is room for individual choices, and these must be governed by *ratio* because only *ratio* has the potential of optimising the usefulness (*utilitas*) of language as a communicative tool. If

---

[19] Technically, the Pythagoreans promoted the θέσει view, but since they believed in a name-giver with a superior insight into the nature of things, their position was ultimately similar to that of the Stoics (cf. Collart 1954: 259–60, 262).

[20] On these passages see now Atherton 2005; Verlinsky 2005; Reinhardt 2008.

one disregards other functions of language, it is not useful, for instance, to retain a dative *ornatu* next to another dative *ornatui*.

It is this strictly utilitarian view of language which explains why Epicureanism traditionally had an uneasy relationship with the arts of rhetoric and literature. This was particularly obvious in the case of the (deliberately?) unpolished earliest philosophical treatises in Latin by Amafinius and Rabirius,[21] but even the Greek Philodemus, a friend of Caesar's family, who was interested in questions of literary style and perhaps more flexible in such things than many Epicureans, maintained that form and content should not be separated because style was primarily a means to an end. Thus, for a person with Epicurean leanings it would have been difficult to appreciate Cicero's *De oratore* with its emphasis on *ornatus*. A text like Caesar's *Bellum Gallicum*, on the other hand, which claimed to be nothing but an artless military report, would have been something of an ideal, even when in reality there was much art behind the artlessness.

7 CAESAR AND EPICUREAN ROMANNESS

We are now beginning to see an intrinsic connection between Caesar's linguistic theories and his literary style. Any Roman Epicurean should not only have aimed for a Caesarian style, devoid of *ornatus* while efficiently communicating facts, but also adopted a Caesarian view on what constitutes good Latin. For such an Epicurean, Latin, like any language, was essentially a means of communication, and therefore the community of its speakers – not their ancestors (*auctoritas*) or some abstract principle (*natura*) – had to define what was, or was not, admissible (*consuetudo*); but since any community may have its disagreements, a fair method of solving these was also required, and for this purpose nothing could serve better than *ratio*, the distinctive capacity of humankind.

So everything would fall into place if we could assume that Caesar's thinking about, and making use of, language was informed by Epicureanism. Fortunately, there are good reasons to do so, since Caesar's Epicureanism has been firmly established by other scholars looking at literary and historical rather than linguistic and stylistic evidence.[22] The Epicurean's pragmatic approach to adversity and his 'reactive creativity' aiming at *utilitas* for the community provides the structural backbone of *Bellum*

---

[21] Cf. Cic. *Ac.* 1.5, *Tusc.* 1.6, 2.7, 4.6–7.
[22] See especially Rambaud 1969 and Pizzani 1993, e.g. on *fortuna* in the commentaries, Caesar's speech in Sallust's *Catilina* or the *clementia Caesaris*.

Gallicum and *Bellum civile* alike. Whatever the political realities and pro-pagandistic aims behind these texts (Rambaud 1966), their presentation is informed by philosophical principles – and we now realise, undoubtedly as Cicero did (*Brut.* 262),[23] that they are also written in the utilitarian style that naturally suited those principles.

To Cicero, however, a philosophy whose highest good was *utilitas* must have seemed exceedingly primitive (cf. *Pis.* 70). Caesar, in turn, must have been aware of this disdain, for *De analogia*, in an elegantly oblique manner, set the issue straight. Its dedicatory sentence (quoted in §2 above) presents Cicero as the *inventor* of a new Latin style, whereas Caesar himself acts as the advocate of an almost forgotten one. In Rome, where the *mos maiorum* was commonly acknowledged to be the most important social guideline, the latter, 'Caesarian', role was inevitably to be valued more highly. Moreover, the same sentence associates 'tradition' with the use of a *facilis sermo* – a *facere*-related, pragmatic, *sermo* – whereas the innovation focuses on thoughts (*cogitata eloqui*). Given the opposition *facere* vs *cogitare*, an attentive reader could not fail to remember that Rome's greatness was the result of acting, not thinking. Hence, the Epicurean linguistic pragmatism advocated by *De analogia* turns out to be the perfect embodiment of traditional Roman values, and any dissenting school of thought, however more sophisticated it may look, will only be the less 'Roman' for it.

8 CONCLUSION

It is time to conclude. At the outset, we observed that Caesar may be called both the most and the least colloquial of all Latin writers, since his 'Style without Qualities' excludes both what would have been heard *only* in ordinary conversation (e.g. vulgarisms) and what would *never* have been heard there (e.g. poeticisms). Among stylists, the latter restriction required a more explicit formulation than the former – hence the *scopulum* rule. In a wider sense, however, the *scopulum* rule could also be interpreted as an injunction against vulgarisms and the like; after all, in the context of, say, a general's report to the Senate a vulgarism too would have been an *inauditum atque insolens verbum*. If we believe Cicero when he suggests that *De analogia* was principally giving guidance in cases of doubt, we will probably best explain the occasional disregard for its precepts in Caesar's

---

[23] Leeman (1963: 175–7), Brugnoli (1993) and Lomanto (1994–5: 53–5) stress the half-heartedness of Cicero's praise.

other writings along these lines.[24] As long as no educated person wrote *mortus* or *partum* in a formal text – however advisable their adoption might seem to an analogist – Caesar himself could not admit them in such a register because his readers would otherwise have 'stumbled' and the communicative flow would have been disturbed.[25] In a speech to his army, however, things might have been different *if* the 'unusual' variants were widespread enough in oral Latin to be unmarked.[26] Thus, Caesar apparently used the analogically regular, but otherwise less 'grammatical', active form *frustrabo* instead of *frustrabor* in addressing his soldiers (Caes. *orat.* fr. 9 Klotz).[27]

In a more speculative vein, we may finally ask what would have happened if Caesar's *De analogia* had made a more lasting impact. As it is, Cicero's *De oratore* won out, Cicero himself became *the* model of *Latinitas*, and *auctoritas* – including, ironically, Caesar's own *auctoritas* – got precedence over Epicurean *consuetudo cum ratione*. However, at least in theory the latter could have prevailed over standardisation, so that the gap between spoken/colloquial and written/literary Latin would not have become as wide as it did. Presumably, the Romance languages would still be what they are now, but we might not think of them as something distinctly different from Latin, for no 'classical' Latin would have come into being. And given all this, it might even be that in hindsight Caesar would have disapproved more of the 'archaisms' or 'poeticisms' allowed for *ornandi causa* by his highly respected dedicatee, Cicero (*De orat.* 3.39), than of the 'colloquialisms' and 'vulgarisms' used consciously or unconsciously by his less respected imitators, including the author of the *Bellum Africum* whose un-Caesarian style has been described so well by the dedicatee of the present volume.[28]

---

[24] For examples see Oldfather and Bloom 1927; Dahlmann (1935: 264) argues that Caesar's 'analogistische Theorie bezieht sich lediglich auf die Beredsamkeit', but the style of the *commentarii* is clearly informed by similar ideas.

[25] On Caesar's respect for generic conventions see Adams 2005b: 74–7, after Eden 1962: 78–94 and Leeman 1963: 175–7.

[26] *Mortus* is attested in Pompeii (*CIL* iv 3129; cf. also N–W iii.529); on *partum* see §3.

[27] Already found in Pl. *Bac.* 548 and Pompon. *com.* 79, and frequent in later Latin (Flobert 1975: 294), active *frustro* is likely to have been common in first-century spoken language. Similarly, *u*-stem datives in -*u* were used by Caesar in speeches and in the *Anticato* (Gel. 4.16.8, with Caes. *orat.* fr. 2 and *Anticato* fr. 5 Klotz), though perhaps not in the *commentarii* (Oldfather and Bloom 1927: 594–5).

[28] Adams 2005b.

CHAPTER 14

The style of the Bellum Hispaniense and the evolution of Roman historiography

Jan Felix Gaertner

I INTRODUCTION

The *Bellum Alexandrinum*, *Bellum Africum* and *Bellum Hispaniense*, which have been transmitted to us as a sort of continuation of Caesar's *Bellum civile*, are not only important sources for our knowledge of the historical events of the 40s BC. They also have long been recognised as precious pieces of evidence for the stylistic diversity of Latin in the first century BC. At least since the end of the nineteenth century the three pseudo-Caesarian *Bella* have been interpreted as a reflection of colloquial/substandard[1] Latin and stylistically classed as second-rate literature. This is particularly true of the *Bellum Hispaniense*. Already humanists such as Lipsius, J. J. Scaliger or G. J. Vossius qualified its style as 'horrid' (*horridus*) or 'somewhat harsh' (*duriusculus*);[2] the early editor Goduinus thought that the author's mother tongue was not Latin;[3] Clarke (1753: 457) and Oudendorp (1737: II.940) speculated that the work was a soldier's diary, and Madvig, Norden, Klotz, Pascucci, Diouron and others have sketched the image of an author who tries to write in an elevated style but constantly fails and reveals his lack of education.[4]

When looked at more closely, this traditional characterisation must seem rather implausible. First of all, there are several features that contradict the hypothesis of a hastily written soldier's diary. It is commonly

---

[1] Previous scholars have used the terms 'colloquial', 'non-classical' and 'vulgar' indiscriminately (cf. Chahoud, this volume pp. 42–4, 53–4). I employ 'colloquial' in its strict sense ('typical of the spoken language', 'non-literary') but have to be similarly imprecise when paraphrasing earlier scholarship.

[2] Cf. Lipsius 1611: 513; Scaliger 1655: 3; Vossius 1677: 67; see also Davisius 1727: 685; Cellarius 1755: 679.

[3] Cf. Goduinus 1678: 430; Wölfflin 1893: 597, 1902: 163.

[4] Cf. Madvig 1873: 289; Koehler 1877; Degenhart 1877; Mommsen 1893: 614; Norden 1899: 211; Ahlberg 1906: 31; Sihler 1912: 248–50; Holmes 1923: III.298; Klotz 1927b: 7; Kalinka 1929: 116; Drexler 1935: 208–27; E. Löfstedt 1956: I.190–1; Way 1955: 305–7; Adcock 1956: 107; Canali 1966: 123–4; Pascucci 1965: 47; Richter 1977: 213; Diouron 1999: lxx–lxxxiii.

agreed that the speeches in 17.1–3 and 42.4–7 and Gnaeus Pompeius' letter in Chapter 26 are written in polished Latin and show no signs of
negligence or incompetence.[5] Furthermore, the quotations of Ennius at
23.3 and 31.7[6] presuppose some acquaintance with Roman poetry, as does
the comparison with the fight of Memnon and Achilles at 25.4, which is
likely to reflect a similar comparison in Furius Bibaculus' epic on Caesar's
Gallic war.[7] Moreover, the summarising ablatives absolute at 1.1, 4.1, 18.1,
al. and the careful use of the historical infinitive (1.2, 29.5, 33.4, 41.1) and
sentence-initial *esse* to introduce background information (3.1, 30.1, 34.2,
35.2) indicate that the author is aware of the stylistic conventions of military
reports and of some of the techniques of historical narratives.[8] This observation is corroborated by the author's description of the duel between Q.
Pomponius Niger and Antistius Turpio (25.3–7), which sounds very much
like Quadrigarius' famous account of the duel between Manlius Torquatus
and a *Gallus quidam* (*hist.* 10b; see Diouron 1999: 103). Thus, the *Bellum
Hispaniense* is obviously not the work of an uneducated soldier.

    A second point that should make us question the traditional character-
isation of the *Bellum Hispaniense* is its transmission. Already Petrarch and
later Davisius, Morus and others have stressed that many of the obscuri-
ties and syntactic problems must be attributed not to the author but to
the transmission.[9] Like the *Bellum civile* and the other pseudo-Caesarian
Bella, the *Bellum Hispaniense* ultimately depends on a single Carolingian
manuscript.[10] Towards the end of his task, the scribe of the archetype seems
to have grown weary, and the *Bellum Hispaniense*, being the last work of the
collection, has been badly mutilated: the end of the work is missing, several
episodes survive only in fragmentary form, and often the train of thought
is distorted by *lacunae*, errant repetitions or transpositions (see Diouron
1999: lxxxix–xc for details). Hence, unparalleled phenomena such as the
genitives absolute transmitted at 14.1, 23.5[11] or the fragmentary sentences

[5] Cf. Richter 1977: 220–3; Diouron 1999: lxxx. Sihler (1912: 250), Pötter (1932: 60–2) and Richter (1977:
   223) thought that these passages were written by a different author. However, the speeches contain
   many features that are typical of the remaining work (e.g. *intensiva*, accumulation of synonyms;
   cf. also the similarities in phrasing between 17.3 and 19.4 and see Seel 1935: 64).
[6] Cf. also Wölfflin 1902: 166–7 on 5.6.
[7] Cf. Furius Bibaculus fr. 15 Courtney; Hor. *Sat.* 1.10.36–7; Courtney 1993: 197; P. Brown 1993: 187–8;
   Diouron 1999: 103. Cf. also the Patroclean motifs at 23.3–8.
[8] On these features see Adams 2005b: 74–5; K–S II.601; Diouron 1999: lxxii.
[9] Cf. Petrarch, *Historia Iulii Caesaris* ch. 26 (Razzolini 1879: 650): 'multa hoc historiae in loco
   scriptorum vitio confusa praetereo'; Davisius 1727: 685; Morus 1780: 734 (quoted by Oberlinus
   1805: 736 = 1819: 736; Möbius 1830: 416–17); Mommsen 1893: 607; Holmes 1923: III.298.
[10] Cf. V. Brown 1972: 39, Diouron 1999: lxxxix against Hering 1963: 94–6.
[11] Cf. H–S 142, where these passages are compared with Liv. 30.26.7, Luc. 8.158. However, the former
   of these putative parallels can be interpreted as a genitive of quality (thus Weissenborn and Müller

at 1.1, 12.6, 27.2 are likely to result not from the author's incompetence but from the *fata libelli*.[12]

Finally, there is also a methodological point, which concerns the development of Latin prose style and the opposition of 'classical/standard' vs 'non-classical/substandard/colloquial/vulgar' Latin. The traditional verdict on the author's style presupposes that already in the 40s BC there was a commonly accepted notion of what constituted 'good' or 'exemplary' Latin. However, this is far from certain. In fact, it is even fairly improbable given the non-classical styles of well-educated first-century writers such as Varro, Nepos or Sallust and given the contemporary debates on proper Latin usage.[13] Hence, the traditional characterisation of the *Bellum Hispaniense* is based on a retrojection of the classical norm.

The preceding remarks show that a careful reexamination of the linguistic evidence is needed. On the following pages, I shall first discuss those features which have been used to prove the colloquial/substandard style of the work;[14] in so doing, I shall demonstrate that most of the alleged substandard usages are attested also in Cicero and Caesar or in Latin historiography or poetry and can thus hardly be classified as colloquial or non-literary phenomena.[15] In a second step I shall develop a more plausible

---

1965 ad loc.), and in the latter passage the genitive depends on the implied subject *Cornelia*: see Mayer 1981: 106–7 for discussion and parallels. A closer parallel could be *Lex XII* 3.1, but see H–S 142 against Marx 1909: 447, Klotz 1927b: 68.

[12] The poor transmission may also be responsible for 1.3 *contra cludebant* (SURT, *claudebant* NMV, cf. 27.6 *contra clausisset*), 42.4 *gentium et civiumque* (cf. *TLL* s.v. *et* 906.38–42; *contra*: H–S 523), and the use of *licet* + pluperfect subjunctive attested at 16.3 (MURTV transmit not *licet* (SN) but *et*, which could suggest *etsi*; on *licet* + pluperfect subjunctive see *TLL* s.v. *liceo* 1364.83–1365.17). At 22.7 the train of thought is bumpy, and the transmitted text (including the construction of *quod* with accusative and infinitive) is probably corrupt (but see Pascucci 1965: 271 with Sal. *Jug.* 100.5 (*quod* del. Eussner), Liv. 26.27.12). The same holds for *dum... distenti essent* (23.2): Wölfflin (1898: 369) compares *cum... distenti essent* at 12.5, 27.1 and rightly suspects that the text is corrupt (however, *dum* + imperfect subjunctive is attested at Nep. *Timol.* 1.4 and in Livy (1.40.7, *al.*), cf. *TLL* s.v. *dum* 2219.34–2220.28). Cf. also Heubner 1916: 39 and Pascucci 1965: 183 on 6.3.

[13] Cf. Adams 2005b: 95; Willi, this volume pp. 231–4; and Suet. *Aug.* 86–7 with Ferri and Probert, this volume pp. 29–30. On the relation of colloquial and standard languages see Clackson, this volume pp. 10–11.

[14] Cf. imprimis Heubner 1916: 34–9; Faller 1949: 138–59; Pascucci 1965: 46–60; Richter 1977: 218–19; Diouron 1999: lxx–lxxxiii.

[15] I shall not discuss features which are not securely attested (see n. 12). Also, there is no need to dwell on passages that have been misinterpreted by previous scholars: contrary to what Pascucci (1965: 220) and Diouron (1999: lxxiii–iv) claim, *propter quod* (13.6, cf. Cic. *Ver.* 4.135, *Tusc.* 3.74) and *nocte tota* (16.2, cf. Caes. *Gal.* 1.26.5, *Civ.* 1.81.3) conform with classical Latin. Pascucci's (1965: 178) and Diouron's (1999: lxxiii) view that at 6.1 *quoniam* means 'just as' seems improbable, because this usage is attested only in a few late texts (cf. H–S 628) and the common use of *quoniam* for 'given that', 'since' perfectly suits the context. *castra contra ad oppidum posuit* (34.1) is interpreted by Pascucci (1965: 349–50) and Diouron (1999: lxxii) as an anticipation of the colloquial tendency to accumulate prepositions, but see *TLL* s.v. *contra* 741.54–5 where this passage is rightly cited next

interpretation of the author's stylistic aims and define the place of the *Bellum Hispaniense* in the evolution of Roman historiography.

2 SUBSTANDARD OR NON-CLASSICAL PHENOMENA?

Many typical features of the *Bellum Hispaniense* which have been interpreted as colloquial/substandard are attested in the classical prose of Caesar and Cicero, but occur more frequently in Nepos, Sallust or Livy. This applies to the plu-pluperfect forms *fuit captum* (20.3), *fuisset conspectus* (38.3),[16] the use of the pluperfect indicative of *esse* (13.7, 16.2, 40.6) and *habere* (14.2) in place of the perfect or imperfect indicative,[17] the use of *habere* with a perfect participle[18] and of the ablative of the gerund instead of a present participle (12.4, 36.3, 40.6),[19] to the ablative of duration (3.1, 5.7, 16.2),[20] the ablatives of location *planitie* (25.2) and *lateribus* (30.1),[21] *quod cum* (20.1, 29.3)[22] and the use of *civitas* for *oppidum* (1.1, 8.5, 26.4),[23] *qua re* for *cur* (16.4)[24] and *utrorumque oppidorum* for *utriusque oppidi* (7.3).[25] All these phenomena were perfectly acceptable in the prose of the first century BC, but feature rarely in Caesar and

---

to *B. Hisp.* 1.1 *quo facilius praesidia contra compararet* under the adverbial use of *contra* 'de infestino animo . . . de bello' (cf. also Verg. *Aen.* 10.308: [*sc. aciem*] *contra in litore sistit*). According to Corbett (1962: 77–9) and Pascucci (1965: 257) *se deiecit* (19.3) is used in a diluted sense and reflects the fondness of colloquial Latin for compounds of *iacere*; given the exact parallels for *se de muro deicere* (Gracch. *orat.* 48 p. 192 M., Caes. *Civ.* 1.18.3) and the other attestations of *se deicere* (see *TLL* s.v. 394.45–395.2) this seems implausible.

[16] Cf. K–S 1.165–7; Lebreton 1901: 203–7 and e.g. Caes. *Civ.* 3.101.4, Cic. *Cael.* 64, Nep. *Ep.* 8.3, Sal. *Jug.* 52.3, 109.3.

[17] Cf. Caes. *Gal.* 2.6.4, 3.16.2, 4.4.3. This usage is particularly frequent in the *Bellum Africum* (see Wölfflin and Miodonski 1889: 72), Nepos, Sallust (e.g. *Jug.* 39.3, cf. Kroll 1927: 290), Livy (e.g. 4.51.5, 22.56.4) and Augustan poetry: cf. K–S 1.140–1, H–S 321.

[18] In the *Bellum Hispaniense* the phenomenon is confined to three classical iuncturae, viz. *constitutum habere* (8.6, 19.3, 28.3, cf. Caes. *Civ.* 3.89.2), *positum habere* (7.3, cf. Caes. *Civ.* 3.62.4) and *spem propositam habere* (22.7, cf. Cic. *Div. Caec.* 72, *Rab. perd.* 15). See also *TLL* s.v. *habeo* 2453.61–5.

[19] See Bennett 1.450–2, K–S 1.751–3, H–S 380 for parallels.

[20] Cf. Ahlberg (1906) 25–7, 28–9 with parallels from Cicero (e.g. *Tusc.* 1.38, *Off.* 2.81) and Caesar (*Gal.* 1.26.5, *Civ.* 1.7.7, *al.*); cf. also Sal. *Jug.* 54.1, Liv. 25.16.5 and E. Löfstedt 1911: 52–3, Pascucci 1965: 174–6, H–S 148.

[21] Cf. K–S 1.353–4; the closest parallels can be found in Sallust (*Hist.* 2.98.5), Livy (e.g. 22.4.6) and Augustan poetry (cf. F. Bömer 1969–86 on Ov. *Met.* 2.33, 3.111, 5.289).

[22] Cf. Klotz 1927b: 78; K–S II.322; H–S 571. A different matter is *qui etsi* (12.6), which is not classical but can be compared to Var. *R.* 2.4.8 *quae enim* (cf. Klotz 1927b: 65).

[23] Cf. *TLL* s.v. *civitas* 1232.84–1233.10 with e.g. Cic. *Ver.* 3.85, 3.121, Nep. *Han.* 3.2, Liv. 34.17.12. Pascucci (1965: 124) compares Caes. *Gal.* 3.20.2.

[24] Cf. Pascucci 1965: 239: 'popolare', but see E. Löfstedt 1911: 324–5 and e.g. Caes. *Gal.* 1.14.2, 1.19.1, Cic. *Mur.* 36.

[25] Cf. K–S 1.649, Krebs and Schmalz 1905–7: II.705 for parallels.

Cicero because these two authors were theorising about, and striving for, a much stricter and more systematic use of Latin than was common in their day.[26]

The last point can be corroborated further, for many of the alleged substandard phenomena previously identified in the *Bellum Hispaniense* are not so much violations of an existing norm as reflections of the fact that a standard did not yet exist.[27] In particular, this is true of the morphological peculiarities adduced by Pascucci and Diouron. The rare form *nullo* (dative, 25.1) is attested in Caesar (*Gal.* 6.13.1, *Civ.* 2.7.1) and Sallust (*Jug.* 97.3),[28] the ablative singular ending *-i* of the comparatives *superiori* (23.2), *inferiori* (23.5) and *aequiori* (25.2) has parallels in Cicero, Caesar and other prose authors;[29] the form *cornum* (accusative singular; 30.7, 31.4, 31.5) is rare in prose,[30] but remained common in (mostly epic) poetry;[31] the verbs *coagulare/-i*, *conviciare/-i* and *depopulare/-i* were not confined to the use as *deponentia*;[32] and as regards *carrus/carrum*, Caesar certainly employs the masculine, but the neuter is reported to be more common by Nonius 287 L. (p. 195.24–8 M.) and in the case of many other authors we cannot decide which declension is used, since *carrorum*, *carris* and *carrum* (accusative) are ambiguous; hence, the claim that *carrum* is a substandard usage is unfounded.[33]

Similarly, the syntax was still fairly flexible. The table at *TLL* s.v. *potior* 334.16–34 shows that the construction of *potiri* with a genitive (1.1, 2.1) or accusative (16.3) was certainly not substandard in the 40s BC and that the

---

[26] Cf. Adams 2005b: 86, 95 and Willi, this volume pp. 231–4.

[27] Cf. Willi, this volume pp. 231–4 with nn. 3–9.

[28] Cf. also *nullae* (dative) at Coel. *hist.* 26 and see N–W II.528.

[29] Cf. Caes. *Civ.* 3.40.1 *ex superiori … loco* (= *B. Hisp.* 23.2) and see N–W II.266–9 for further attestations, including several Ciceronian passages, where modern editors changed transmitted *-i* to *-e*. Moreover, at least two of the three attestations in the *Bellum Hispaniense* are doubtful: at 23.2 (*superiori* TV, *superiore* SNMUR) the transmission is split (cf. also *superiore*); at 25.2 *in aequiori* is Klotz's conjecture for the corrupt readings *in aequore* S, *in aequo* N, *iniquiori* URT and *iniquiore* V.

[30] But cf. e.g. Var. *R.* 3.9.14, Col. 6.2.7, 7.10.3, Gel. 1.8.2, 14.6.2.

[31] Cf. Lucr. 2.388, Ov. *Met.* 2.874, *al.*, V. Fl. 3.156, Sil. 2.124, *al.* and N–W I.529–30, *TLL* s.v. *cornu* 962.74–82.

[32] For *depopulare/-i* see *TLL* s.v. 585.80 'frequentat solus Liv. (82ies) qui utramque formam promiscue habet' and cf. the active forms transmitted at Enn. *scaen.* 369 V., V. Fl. 4.429 and the passive forms at Caes. *Gal.* 1.11.4, 7.77.14, Liv. 5.24.2, 8.11.12 *al.* The other two verbs are so rare in this period that we cannot be certain which usage was perceived as more acceptable: cf. *TLL* s.vv. *coagulo* 1378.41–3 (the only contemporary parallel is Varro *apud* Gel. 3.10.7) and *convicior* 872.53–6 (with Var. *R.* 2.5.1, Liv. 42.41.3 (both use deponent forms)); see Klotz 1927b: 291–2, Zimmerer 1937: 91 for similar changes in *genus verbi* in late annalistic prose and Sallust.

[33] Cf. also the neuter forms at Hist. Aug. *trig. tyr.* 8.5, Porphyrio on Hor. *Sat.* 1.6.104 and see *TLL* s.v. 499.36–47.

use with the ablative only gradually became the standard construction in Augustan times.[34] Likewise, the use of *plenus* with an ablative (cf. *B. Hisp.* 5.1) has never been fully replaced by the use of the genitive (cf. Cic. *Ver.* 4.126, Caes. *Civ.* 1.74.7) and features several times in Augustan poetry and post-classical writers;[35] and finally even the occasional[36] use of prepositions with city names (*ad*: 6.2, 40.7, 42.1; *ab*: 12.3, 37.3, 41.6) has many parallels in early Roman poetry and historiography and is later also attested for the emperor Augustus (cf. Suet. *Aug.* 86.1).[37] None of these usages is likely to have been perceived as a substandard phenomenon in the 40s BC, and it would be wrong to use the rare attestations in the *Bellum Hispaniense* as evidence for the author's incompetence.

Once we subtract the material discussed so far, there still remain many features that have been interpreted as colloquial. In most cases, the classification is, however, anything but well grounded.[38] Many usages are archaisms rather than colloquialisms. Thus the undeclined future infinitive (13.3 *se* (plur.) *scutum esse positurum*),[39] *clam* with accusative (3.2, 16.1, 35.2),[40] the preference for the ablative of quality over the corresponding genitive (15.2, 20.4),[41] and the use of impersonal *potest* with infinitive (3.5),[42] *cum* with indicative for *postquam* or *ubi* (3.6),[43] *simul* for *simulac*

[34] In the *Bellum Hispaniense* the ablative already prevails (13.4, 19.6, 34.5, 40.6). Not only Sallust (5x) and Nepos (5x), but even Cicero (*Rep.* 3.35, *Fin.* 1.60, *Off.* 3.113, *Fam.* 1.7.5) and Livy (4x) occasionally employ *potiri* with a genitive (other than *rerum*); *potiri* with accusative features e.g. at Sal. *Hist.* fr. inc. 32, Nep. *Eum.* 3.4, Liv. 3.7.2.

[35] See *TLL* s.v. *plenus* 2408.60–2409.17 with Verg. *Aen.* 5.311, Ov. *Fast.* 4.432, 5.124, Col. 10.310 and Sen. *Nat.* 2.26.2.

[36] Cf. the locative *Cordubae* (32.4), the ablatives of location *Hispali* (36.1) and *Gadibus* (39.3), the ablative of origin *Gadibus* (42.1) and the accusatives of direction *Cordubam* (32.4) and *Hispalim* (39.3). The prepositions at 4.1, 4.4, 6.1 and 27.5 conform with classical usage because the author refers not to the city, but its surroundings.

[37] For *ad* see Bennett II.237–8, *TLL* s.v. 490.48–79, H–S 219 and e.g. *trag. inc.* 86, Cato *orat.* 29 p. 21 M., Sis. *hist.* 56, Cic. *Phil.* 12.8, Caes. *Civ.* 3.101.1; for *ab* see Kühnast 1872: 359, *TLL* s.v. 14.42–52 and e.g. Pac. *trag.* 318, Cic. *Phil.* 5.23, Caes. *Civ.* 3.108.2, Sal. *Cat.* 40.5, *Jug.* 104.1 (cf. Kroll 1927: 297), Liv. 1.27.4, *al.*

[38] On the fluid boundaries of the category 'colloquial' see also Chahoud, this volume pp. 58–63 and Adams 2005b: 86, 91.

[39] Cf. Gel. 1.7.6–10, where C. Gracchus (*orat.* 34 p. 185 M.), Quadrigarius (*hist.* 43, 79) and Valerius Antias (*hist.* 59) are quoted; cf. also Cato *hist.* 104, Sulla *hist.* 20, Sal. *Jug.* 100.4, Liv. 26.45.5 (v. l. *datura*), and K–S 1.59, Zimmerer 1937: 94, H–S 343, E. Löfstedt 1956: II.11.

[40] Cf. *TLL* s.v. *clam* 1247.33–51. The use of the ablative seems to be younger, cf. *TLL* ibid. 51–60, H–S 282. *clam a praesidiis* (18.4) is corrupt, cf. Wölfflin 1892b: 278–9.

[41] Cf. H–S 67, 117–18, Pascucci 1965: 229.

[42] Cf. *TLL* s.v. 145.5–146.18 (first at Cato *Agr.* 90 and later attested mostly in legal writers and Livy, cf. Ogilvie 1965: 435).

[43] The phenomenon is common in early Latin (see Bennett 1.82) and rare in classical prose (but cf. Caes. *Gal.* 6.12.1, 6.18.3, Eden 1962: 91–2); it survives in historiographical prose, cf. Liv. 4.44.10, *al.*; Kühnast 1872: 241; K–S II.336–7; H–S 621.

(4.2, 31.5),[44] *uti* for *ut* (3.2, 4.2, 9.2, 22.1, 31.5),[45] *propter* for *prope* (5.5)[46] and *hoc* for *huc* (5.2, 8.1, 29.4, 38.2, 41.4)[47] are all common in early Latin but rare in late Republican and later prose.[48] Given the author's quotations from Ennius and the archaising tendencies in other historians, it seems unlikely that we are dealing with archaic features that survived in colloquial Latin; instead, it is more probable that the author consciously employed these archaic usages to give his account a grander or more elevated tone. The same applies also to other non-classical usages which have close parallels in poetry – e.g. the non-prepositional accusative of direction of country names (35.3, cf. 22.7),[49] the use of *esse* with a present participle (29.2),[50] or the dative of direction (16.3, 38.6)[51] – and to a few artificial mannerisms such as the extensive use of litotes[52] and of the subjunctive in relative clauses.[53]

The author's archaising and poeticising tendencies should also make us question the traditional classification of pleonasm, which is one of the most characteristic features of the *Bellum Hispaniense* (cf. Heubner 1916: 27–9). Diouron and Pascucci have interpreted the author's fondness for pleonastic expressions and *ubertas* as a reflection of colloquial Latin.[54] However, the use of *nocturno tempore* (2.1, 22.6; cf. Cic. *Catil.* 3.18, Nep. *Milt.* 7.3), *nullo tempore* (36.1, 42.5), *omni tempore* (3.3), *matutino tempore* (6.3) and *insequenti tempore* (15.6, 18.6, 23.1, 27.1, 27.5) instead of *noctu, numquam,*

---

[44] Cf. K–S II.360; Pascucci 1965: 161; Jones 1906: 92; Bennett I.106 and Cato *Agr.* 48.2, Enn. *Ann.* 87 (see Skutsch 1985 ad loc.).

[45] Cf. H–S 632.

[46] Cf. K–S I.529; H–S 246 and *TLL* s.v. *propter* 2118.24–2119.9 with many parallels from early Latin poetry (e.g. Enn. *Ann.* 19) and prose (e.g. Cato *Agr.* 9) and late annalistic works (e.g. Sis. *hist.* 22, 53).

[47] Cf. Serv. *Aen.* 8.423; *TLL* s.v. *huc* 3072.73–6 contra Klotz 1927b: 51; Kalinka 1929: 118. Possibly, the use of *acsi* without preceding *secus, aeque* vel sim. at 13.5 also belongs into this category; it is attested primarily in Festus and legal authors (starting with Alfenus (cos. 39 BC), *Dig.* 33.8.14; cf. *TLL* s.v. *atque* 1083.77–1084.36).

[48] Cf. also Pascucci 1965: 199 on *grumus* (8.6, 24.2), Serv. in *GL* IV.442.25 and *TLL* s.v. 1124.69–77 on *circumcirca* (41.4), and see Faller 1949: 133–4 for further archaic expressions.

[49] Cf. K–S I.481; Bennett II.235–6 and e.g. Andr. *poet.* II Blänsdorf, Verg. *Aen.* 3.254. See *TLL* s.v. *proficiscor* 1712.15–16, K–S I.481, H–S 50 for (rare) parallels in contemporary prose.

[50] Cf. K–S I.159; E. Löfstedt 1911: 245–9; H–S 388 and Pascucci 1965: 314: 'arcaismo-volgarismo, accetto anche alla lingua poetica' (and in classical prose, e.g. Caes. *Gal.* 3.19.6).

[51] Cf. K–S I.320, H–S 100–1.

[52] Cf. e.g. 8.2, 8.5, 25.7, 39.2 and see Klotz 1927b: 46; Kalinka 1929: 117 on *non parum* (3.4, 24.4).

[53] Cf. *B. Hisp.* 13.6, 16.4, 22.4, 27.6, 32.7, 35.2, 35.3, 36.4, 37.1, 38.1. The parallel use of indicative and subjunctive at 37.1 shows that the author is striving for *variatio*; cf. Klotz 1927b: 36: 'beabsichtigte Feinheit', Diouron 1999: lxxviii. Another artificial and poetic feature is the *traiectio* of subjunctions, cf. 2.1, 3.2, 3.7, 4.2 al. (*cum*), 7.3 (*ut*), 14.3 (*quod*), 14.2, 23.6, 25.8, 27.1, 36.3, 40.5 (*dum*), and see Schünke 1906, K–S II.615. For further poetic usages (e.g. *iter ante* (2.1, cf. Wölfflin 1902: 163–4), *pelagus* (40.6, but cf. Adams 2007: 404), *pyra* (33.4), *insequenti luce* (10.1, 19.3, 19.5)) see Kalinka 1929: 119, Faller 1949: 136–7; cf. Adams 2005b: 83–5 for poetic elements in *B. Afr.*

[54] Cf. Pascucci 1965: 51, Diouron 1999: lxxv; see also E. Löfstedt 1956: II.173–98, esp. 173.

semper, mane and *post(ea)* is probably not a colloquialism but an artificial mannerism.[55] Moreover, expressions such as *maiores augebantur copiae* (1.4) or *cum celeri festinatione* (2.1) closely resemble the poetic techniques of prolepsis (cf. H–S 414) and 'amplificatory pleonasm',[56] and other iuncturae (e.g. 29.2 *planities aequabatur*,[57] 40.7 *rursus . . . recurrit*[58]) are paralleled even in classical prose. Thus, the fact that an expression is a pleonasm cannot prove that it has a colloquial ring.[59] Likewise, other emphatic devices such as the use of intensive verbs (*adflictare, intentare, occultare, agitare*), *simplicia pro compositis* (*prehendere, sequi*) or *composita pro simplicibus* (*convallis, deurere, deposcere, depugnare*) only reveal the author's striving for expressiveness.[60]

In the end, few usages can be justly called colloquial or substandard.[61] The adverb *intro* (41.5),[62] *belle habere* ('to be well', 32.7),[63] the use of *suus* for *eius* and vice versa (8.6, 31.4),[64] *hoc* for *ideo/ita* ('consequently', 1.5),[65] *homo* for *is* (18.1),[66] *cum . . . ut* (8.6),[67] *renuntiare quod* (36.1)[68] and the phraseological contaminations at 3.7 *respondit ut sileat verbum*

---

[55] Klotz (1927b: 42) rightly emphasises that the author also employs the adverbs, e.g. *noctu* (6.1, *al.*).

[56] Cf. Diggle 2005: 643 and F. Bömer 1969–86 on Ov. *Met.* 6.66 for parallels and literature.

[57] Cf. Cic. *Ver.* 4.107.

[58] Cf. e.g. the use of *rursus* with *revertere, se recipere* and *reducere* at Caes. *Gal.* 4.4.5, 5.34.4, 6.3.3. In view of these parallels, 4.1 *ante praemisit*, too, must seem perfectly acceptable (but cf. the different construction at Caes. *Gal.* 7.9.4 *multis ante diebus . . . praemiserat*).

[59] Cf. also 29.8 *propius appropinquassent* (Pascucci suspects contamination of *propius accedere* and *magis appropinquare*, but *propius* may indicate a relative degree ('fairly closely')) and 35.4 *rursus . . . denuo* (paralleled only at Pl. *Poen.* 79, but not necessarily colloquial in the 40s BC, cf. Adams *et al.* 2005: 7 n. 8).

[60] Apart from *depostulabant* (1.5, cf. *TLL* s.v. 593.1–9), all the verbs adduced by Diouron (1999: lxxv) are common in classical prose. Moreover, the use of *simplicia pro compositis* and *composita pro simplicibus* is also typical of Roman poetry, and *intensiva* are characteristic of old Latin and Sallust (cf. Kroll 1927: 293). This squares well with the author's poeticising and archaising tendencies.

[61] The military expressions gathered by Diouron (1999: lxxvi–lxxvii) are unparalleled in classical prose, but not colloquial/substandard features; the same holds for Canali's (1966: 135) list of words which are unparalleled in the remaining *Corpus Caesarianum*.

[62] Cf. *TLL* s.v. 54.33–9: 'sermonis humilioris'; the closest parallels in prose are Cato *Agr.* 157.14 and Col. 9.12.1.

[63] Cf. Pascucci 1965: 342; *TLL* s.v. *habeo* 2452.14–36.

[64] Klotz (1927b: 60) compares Cic. *Quinct.* 85; see Meusel 1887–93: 11.321–2 and Kroll 1927: 296 for parallels in Caesar and Sallust.

[65] Cf. 41.5 *hoc* Fleischer, *hac* SRTV. Most parallels come from comedy and Horace's satires, see *TLL* s.v. *hic* 2745.57–2746.19.

[66] Cf. H–S 198, Pascucci 1965: 249, *TLL* s.v. 2882.13–53, and Quad. *hist.* 10b: *dum se Gallus . . . constituere studet, Manlius . . . de loco hominem iterum deiecit.*

[67] Cf. H–S 620. E. Löfstedt (1936: 66) criticises Wölfflin and Miodonski (1889), R. Schneider (1905) and others for eliminating similar accumulations of subjunctions at *B. Afr.* 4.3, 40.5, 50.3.

[68] This construction is exceptional within the *Bellum Hispaniense* (cf. *nuntiare* + accusative and infinitive at 18.6) and can be compared to *dicere quod* at Pl. *As.* 52, Cato *Fil.* 1 p. 77.1–2 Jordan and in Silver Latin and later authors (cf. *TLL* s.v. *dico* 985.80–986.24, Marx 1909: 444). *praeterire quod* at 10.2 conforms with Ciceronian usage (cf. e.g. *Clu.* 188).

facere and 25.5 *ut prope videretur finem bellandi duorum dirimere pugna*[69] are
fairly isolated phenomena.[70] More striking is the author's use of *bene* with
magnus (1.2, 4.2, 12.4, 13.4, 15.6, 16.2, 22.6, 35.2, 35.3, 40.2, 41.1), *multus* (12.6, 34.6, 36.4) and *longe* (25.2).[71] The parallels at *TLL* s.v. *bonus*
2125.53–2126.80 indicate that this usage has an informal or casual ring (cf.
Klotz 1927b: 38; Kalinka 1929: 117), but the phenomenon is also attested in
Ennius (*Ann.* 32 *al.*, cf. Porphyrio on Hor. *Carm.* 3.24.50). Given that the
author is fully capable of using the superlative (6.1, 6.3, 13.7, *al.*), his use
of *bene* is probably functional: as elsewhere he may consciously strive for
ubertas,[72] imitate the style of his favourite Latin poet Ennius (thus Wölfflin
1902: 161–2), or, like some of the late annalists,[73] affect casualness.

The reassessment of the linguistic evidence shows that the *Bellum Hispaniense* is not a substandard, but rather a 'pre-standard' work in the sense
that there was not yet a commonly accepted norm of 'correct' literary Latin
in the 40s BC. Moreover, most of the non-classical features attested in this
work have parallels in contemporary historiography and earlier Latin prose
or poetry. This suggests that the author of the *Bellum Hispaniense* never
wanted to compose a *commentarius* in the Caesarian style but consciously
placed himself in the tradition of (mildly) archaising and poeticising historiography. This interpretation not only squares well with the author's use of
historiographical themes (see p. 244 above) but also calls for a more precise
definition of the work's place in the evolution of Latin historiographical
prose and especially of its relation to late annalistic historiography.

[69] The latter expression is unparalleled; the former has its closest parallel at Cassiodorus, *Historia
Ecclesiastica* 9.34.1 (see E. Löfstedt 1956: II.154–72; Corbett 1962: 74–7; Pascucci 1950: 193; 1965:
154–6 (also on the similar use of *tacere* in late Latin); cf. also Pl. *Per.* 493 *res . . . quam occultabam
tibi dicere*). Less striking is the combination of *nihil merere* (cf. *TLL* s.v. *mereo* 810.24–35) and
merere cur/quare (cf. *TLL* s.v. 808.32–4) at 16.4 (see K–S 1.818 on adverbial *nihil* for *non*). The other
examples of contamination collected by E. Löfstedt (1956: II.157) and Diouron (1999: lxxiii) are not
convincing. At 19.4 *tali virtute et constantia futurum me in te esse praestabo*, the verb *praestare* is
employed in the sense of 'to vouch for', cf. *OLD* s.v. 14b, Cic. *Tusc.* 5.29; at 22.4 *qui cum certum
comperissent legatorum responsa ita esse gesta quemadmodum illi rettulissent* the words *ita esse gesta
quemadmodum . . .* are an accusative and infinitive dependent on *responsum*: cf. *OLD* s.v. *responsum*
1b with Cic. *Ver.* 1.50, Curt. 5.3.11 *triste responsum . . . redditur non esse veniae locum* and K–S 1.696
with Caes. *Gal.* 7.48.1 *crebris nuntiis incitati oppidum ab Romanis teneri*. The construction at 22.7
neque sibi ullam spem . . . propositam habere can be compared to Cic. *Div. Caec.* 72 *habet spem, quam
propositam nobis habemus*; at 28.4 the text is insecure (*dividi* V, *dividit* SURT, *dividitur* N) and
probably corrupt (cf. Pascucci 1965: 309); 39.1 *saluti suae praesidium parare* is not a conflation of
sibi praesidium parare and *suae saluti consulere*, but simply a case of *praesidium parare* used with an
abstract object: cf. *OLD* s.v. *salus* 1, *TLL* s.v. *praesidium* 886.38–41, Cic. *Phil.* 10.9 *praesidia vestrae
libertati paravit*.

[70] *Se reportant* (40.2), too, could be colloquial (cf. Pascucci 1965: 375); *clanculum* (32.8) might be an
archaic feature: cf. *TLL* s.v. 1260.29–57.

[71] Cf. also *vehementer* at 30.2, 38.2.

[72] Cf. Norden 1899: 211; Canali 1966: 125 against Klotz 1927b: 38.

[73] See Zimmerer 1937: 98–9 on Quadrigarius' similar use of *cumprime* and *adprime* (*hist.* 7, 15) and cf.
the casual tone of *ut dico* and *ut ante dixi* at Quad. *hist.* 10b (see also Albrecht 1983: 118).

3 THE *BELLUM HISPANIENSE* AND THE LATE ANNALISTS

In an important article Eden (1962) has shown that several of the hall-marks of the style of the late annalists also feature in Caesar's *commentarii*, but that Caesar has made a great effort to reduce or refine the manner-isms of annalistic historiography. The author of the *Bellum Hispaniense* had less reservation against the late annalists, but in many respects fol-lows their example rather closely. His seemingly simple account not only formally resembles the traditional, diary-like, presentation of annalistic historiography,[74] but also exhibits most of the linguistic peculiarities of late annalistic prose. Many of the morphological and syntactic character-istics of the *Bellum Hispaniense* have close parallels in the fragments of the late annalists.[75] Furthermore, the author's fondness for poetic expressions can be compared to similar tendencies in Coelius and Quadrigarius.[76] Also, neither the late annalists nor the author of the *Bellum Hispaniense* strive for the periodic style of Cicero or Caesar; instead, both prefer paratactic constructions and link their sentences by means of demonstrative and re-lative pronouns and adverbs such as *ita*.[77] Moreover, both make extensive use of compound verbs instead of *simplicia*,[78] of *coepisse* with infinitive instead of a simple perfect[79] and of expressions of the type *facere* + noun (e.g. *iugulationem facere* at 16.4, 22.6).[80] Like Sisenna (*hist.* 51, 127) and Quadrigarius (*hist.* 37), the author of the *Bellum Hispaniense* occasion-ally employs the ablative of the gerund instead of the present participle (cf. p. 246 above); like Calpurnius Piso, he does not refrain from abrupt changes of subject;[81] like Quadrigarius, he does not avoid close repetitions,[82]

---

[74] Cf. Asellio's polemic (*hist.* 1–2) and Klotz 1927b: 6–7.

[75] See nn. 28, 32, 37, 39, 46 above on the dative of *nullus*, changes in *genus verbi*, the use of prepositions with city names, undeclined future infinitives, and *propter* for *prope*.

[76] Cf. Fro. p. 56.23 van den Hout, Gel. 17.2.3 and see Wölfflin 1908: 16–17, 21–2; Zimmerer 1937: 97, 99, 113–14.

[77] Cf. *ita* at 1.2, 1.4, 3.6, *al.*, Quad. *hist.* 48, 81, Sis. *hist.* 7 and see Kroll 1927: 284–5.

[78] Cf. *ita* at 1.2 with n. 60 above and Coel. *hist.* 44 *congenuclat*, Quad. *hist.* 57 *conlaudavit*, 93 *conger-manescere*, Sis. *hist.* 104 *persubhorrescere*; see Zimmerer 1937: 110.

[79] Cf. *B. Hisp.* 1.1, 3.2, 4.4, 5.3, 6.3, 9.1, *al.*, Asel. *hist.* 7 *orare coepit*, Quad. *hist.* 10b, 72, 92 (see Zimmerer 1937: 114–15), Sis. *hist.* 52, 131. The phenomenon also features in Caesar (cf. Eden 1962: 81 and *Gal.* 3.23.2, 4.27.7, *al.*). Nevertheless, E. Löfstedt (1911: 209–10), Devoto (1940: 257) and H–S 319 classify the phenomenon as 'colloquial'.

[80] Diouron (1999: lxxiv) gives further examples; cf. Coel. *hist.* 38 (*finem*), Asel. *hist.* 14 (*iter*), Quad. *hist.* 5 (*consilia*), 54 (*castra*), Val. Ant. *hist.* 16 (*senatus consultum*), 58 (*foedus*), 59 (*res divinas*), Sis. *hist.* 10 (*bellum*).

[81] Cf. Diouron 1999: lxxii, *B. Hisp.* 2.1, 14.4, *al.* and Calp. *hist.* 27 with Eden 1962: 90; see also Kroll 1927: 285–6 on Sallust.

[82] Cf. e.g. *B. Hisp.* 1.1–2 *compararet... comparata*, 2.1 *confectis... conficiendum* and Quad. *hist.* 10b *constitit... constiterunt... percussit... percutit*; Schibel 1971: 18. See also Calp. *hist.* 27. Eden (1962: 83–4) gives Caesarian examples (e.g. *Gal.* 1.49.1–3, *Civ.* 3.97.2).

occasionally chooses an informal tone,[83] exploits the devices of assonance and alliteration,[84] uses collective singulars,[85] and frequently employs
the *praesens historicum*,[86] pleonastic expressions,[87] iterative or intensive
verbs,[88] and immediate polyptota.[89]

The similarities show that the heterogeneous style of the *Bellum Hispaniense* has a close precedent and probably its model in the similarly
uneven and pre-classical style of the late annalists. However, the work is
not a mere continuation of the annalistic tradition, but also moves towards
a more mature and classical historiographical style. Like Caesar in the later
books and like Livy, the author of the *Bellum Hispaniense* does not share
the late annalists' preference for *oratio obliqua* but uses speeches and letters
to structure and dramatise his account.[90] Whereas the word order in the
late annalists was rather inflexible (cf. Eden 1962: 80), the word order in
the *Bellum Hispaniense* can occasionally be quite artful,[91] and the author
varies between the normal word order *factus est* and the emphatic form *est
factus*.[92] Furthermore, he is more selective (or 'classical') than the annalists in his use of adverbs in *-tim*[93] and avoids rare compounds such as
persubhorrescere (cf. nn. 60 and 78). Finally, also his archaising is more
moderate than that of Quadrigarius or Sallust.[94]

4 CONCLUSION

The analysis of the *Bellum Hispaniense* illustrates how problematic the concept of colloquial Latin is. As we have seen, the boundaries between literary

---

[83] See pp. 250–1 and nn. 66, 73 above.   [84] Cf. Pascucci 1965: 57; Zimmerer 1937: 116–17.

[85] Cf. *B. Hisp.* 23.7 *eques*, 30.2 *hostis*, Quad. *hist.* 11 *militem*, 46 *hostem* and see Zimmerer 1937: 100.
Wölfflin (1908: 18–20) suspects Ennian or Naevian influence.

[86] Cf. Pascucci 1965: 141–2 and Wölfflin 1908: 11; Zimmerer 1937: 122; Kroll 1927: 289 for references.

[87] Cf. pp. 249–50 above and Wölfflin 1908: 11.   [88] Cf. p. 250 above and Zimmerer 1937: 110.

[89] Cf. *B. Hisp.* 5.6 *morti mortem . . . tumulos tumulis*, 20.1 *castra castris* (∼ 23.1), 31.7 *pes pede premitur*,
armis teruntur arma, Quad. *hist.* 10b *scuto scutum* and see Wölfflin 1902: 166. Further points of
contact are the phrases *in ea caede* (in this form only at Cato *hist.* 83 p. 79.7 Peter, *B. Hisp.* 6.4) and
procul dubio (first at Cato *hist.* 83 p. 79.6 Peter, Lucr. 3.634, *B. Hisp.* 25.3, Liv. 39.40.10), the use of
partim in place of a noun (*B. Hisp.* 3.8, Quad. *hist.* 89, cf. Wölfflin 1908: 15), and the interest in
colourful, military and other, details (cf. e.g. *B. Hisp.* 16.2, 32.2, Quad. *hist.* 10b, Sis. *hist.* 82).

[90] Cf. Klotz 1927b: 7; Zimmerer 1937: 123; Eden 1962: 79–80.

[91] E.g. 2.1 *multis iter ante rebus confectis*; cf. Heubner 1916: 26–7.

[92] Cf. Pascucci 1965: 48; Diouron 1999: lxxv–lxxvi.

[93] He only employs *partim* (13x), *confestim* (3x) and *interim* (28.4), thus avoiding adverbs like *pilatim*
(Asel. *hist.* 14), *pedetemptim* (Quad. *hist.* 92), or *iuxtim, certatim, manipulatim, vicatim, festinatim,
dubitatim, praefestinatim, celatim, vellicatim, saltuatim, properatim* (Sis. *hist.* 3, 7, 28, 31, 47, 65, 75,
117, 126, 127, 137). Generally, such adverbs are characteristic of archaic Latin, cf. Funck 1893: 103,
contra: Schaffner-Rimann 1958: 9–10.

[94] E.g. the author avoids forms like *transvorsum, facies* (genitive), or *ponti* (ablative); cf. Zimmerer 1937:
90–104; Albrecht 1983: 118 on Quadrigarius, and e.g. Kroll 1927, McGushin 1977: 17–21, Schmal
2001: 129–31 on Sallust.

and colloquial/non-literary usages are often fluid. Many features previously classified as colloquial are so common in Latin historiography and even in Cicero and Caesar that they can hardly be said to reflect spoken as opposed to written Latin. Moreover, a standard of exemplary, literary Latin seems to have evolved only towards the end of the Republic and in the early Principate. In this period, Roman historiography gradually moved away from the uneven and highly idiosyncratic style(s) of the late annalists to the more balanced style of Livy, Curtius and Tacitus. The *Bellum Hispaniense* is part of this development. Its mix of ostentatious diary-like simplicity, occasional laxness and a fondness for poetic expressions reflects the influence of the late annalists, but its more selective vocabulary and moderate archaising point ahead to the more classical style of Livy. Refined readers of the first century BC such as Cicero would have certainly deplored its immature and mannered annalistic style and its lack of a *tractus orationis lenis et aequabilis* ('gentle and even flow of sentences'),[95] but few contemporaries would have thought that the *Bellum Hispaniense* was a reflection of colloquial, substandard or non-literary Latin.

[95] Cf. Cicero's comments on the style of Sisenna (*Leg.* 1.7) and Coelius (*De orat.* 2.54).

CHAPTER 15

Grist to the mill: the literary uses of the quotidian in Horace, Satire 1.5

Richard F. Thomas

The engagement of the *Satires* of Horace with everyday Latin has generally been a given.[1] After all, the poet himself programmatically referred to them as *sermo merus*, straight conversation (*Sat.* 1.4.48), not to be compared to the high-register language of an Ennius, for example (1.4.60–1). But it does not take much to see that this position is disingenuous, as studiedly disingenuous as Catullus' praise of Cornelius Nepos and diminution of his own work as 'trifling', or as selectively true as Cicero's distinction:

quid tibi videor in epistulis? nonne plebeio sermone agere tecum? nec enim semper eodem modo. quid enim simile habet epistula aut iudicio aut contioni? quin ipsa iudicia non solemus omnia tractare uno modo. privatas causas et eas tenuis agimus subtilius, capitis aut famae scilicet ornatius. epistulas vero cottidianis verbis texere solemus. (*Fam.* 9.21.1; cf. p. 39 above)

But tell me now, how do you find me as a letter writer? Don't I deal with you in colloquial style? The fact is that one's style has to vary. A letter is one thing, a court of law or a public meeting quite another. Even for the courts we don't have just one style. In pleading civil cases, unimportant ones, we put on no frills, whereas cases involving status or reputation naturally get something more elaborate. As for letters, we weave them out of the language of everyday. (trans. D. R. Shackleton Bailey)

That is certainly true of the letters as a whole as compared to the speeches, but within the entirety of the former, restrictions clearly apply depending on the formality of situation, ease or lack of ease with the addressee, and the purpose of any given letter. Nevertheless for Horace it is abundantly clear that the *Satires* traffic constantly in colloquialisms. The patterns are somewhat more frequent in *Satires* 1 than in the second book,[2] and the *Epistles* generally admit fewer instances than the *Satires*, but this can only be partially, and I believe minimally, attributed to raw developmental

---

[1] I am grateful to an anonymous referee for some useful suggestions.
[2] See Müller-Lancé 1992: 249 for the raw figures.

issues, or even to the influence from higher-register hexameter, Virgilian in particular. The *Epistles* generically pass themselves off as addressed and sent to elite Roman figures, whose status helps shape the genre. The *Satires* on the other hand are populated by slaves, pimps, witches, Priapic statues, boatmen, low-life women, fortune-tellers and men in the street. As with the *Odes*, genre obviously shapes the use of language.

There is a general laxity to the *Satires* that permits and admits certain words and usages that might not be permitted elsewhere. But these instances may be found indiscriminately side-by-side with so called high-register practices, simply for the sake of *variatio*. So for instance the metrically and semantically equivalent adjectives *fessus* and *lassus*. Ruckdeschel rightly notes that *lassus*, which appears five times in Petronius (*fessus*, never) can be shown to have a colloquial essence to it.[3] Yet in the poem on which this study focuses (1.5), the particular appearance is worth noting: 37 *in Mamurrarum lassi deinde urbe manemus* 'after that we were tired out and stayed in the house of the Mamurrae'. There is nothing particularly colloquial about the line itself, any more than there is at 94 where the non-colloquial alternative occurs, in a similar updating of the itinerary: *inde Rubos fessi pervenimus* 'next we arrived tired out at Rubi'. Similarly at 17–18 *tandem fessus dormire viator | incipit* 'finally the traveller got tired and fell asleep'. Fatigue napping and falling asleep are features of travel, and certainly of this journey (cf. also 48 [*imus*] *dormitum ego Vergiliusque* 'Virgil and I go off for a nap'; 83–4 *somnus tamen aufert | intentum veneri* 'I had my mind set on sex but dozed off'), and the poet may simply have wanted *variatio* when he chose to use *lassus* at 37. What matters however is that he was *able* to make use of the word, precisely because of the genre within which he was working. In the *Aeneid* on the other hand Virgil could use the adjective only in a simile, of poppies weighed down by the rain: 9.436–7 (*lassove papavera collo | demisere caput* 'or when poppies with weary head have drooped their heads'), never of human tiredness.

Ruckdeschel has gathered together most of the examples of *sermo cottidianus* from throughout the Horatian corpus, and it is not my purpose to study the overall use in Horace, but rather to take one poem, and consider it from the perspective of the colloquial coming into contact with the literary, with the tension and aesthetically potent effects that result, and to observe the transformation of register that can be part of a poet's audacious and creative manipulation of language and style. Even the use of

3 Ruckdeschel 1910: 51; also Bonfante 1937: 30–1 = 1994: 105–6. *Lassus* occurs at *Sat.* 1.5.37, 1.10.10, 2.2.10, 2.7.94, 2.8.8.

sermo cottidianus in the *Satires,* or elsewhere, needs to be approached with caution. Ultimately it is inadequate to register percentages of colloquial versus uncolloquial; rather every instance needs to be scrutinised to determine what it *means* that such elements are present, whether they might have a diachronic literary pre-history, or if not what the synchronic literary function might be.

If for instance, to generalise, diminutives may be said, where their diminutive status is not felt, to constitute one class of words generally colloquial in flavour, the examples of *Satire* 1.5 may be noted: 36 *vatillum;* 45 *villula;* 47 *clitellas;* 69 *pusillo;* 87 *oppidulo.* In raw philological terms *vatillum* (diminutive of *vannus* < **vatnos*) appears before Horace only at Varro *R.* 3.6.5 (likely 37 BC, that is, after the actual journey to Brundisium took place, but just before the publication of *Satires* 1), where it is truly diminutive and not particularly colloquial, rather almost technical in sense, designating a peacock 'poop scooper': *pastorem earum cum vatillo circumire oportet ac stercus tollere ac conservare, quod et ad agri culturam idoneum est et ad substramen pullorum* 'the peacock man should go around with a little scoop and pick up their droppings since it is a good manure as well as good for the chicks' litter'. In Horace the use is belittling and derisive, indicating the absurdity of Aufidius Luscus' petty pretensiousness, in part by the bathetic lowering of tone at the end of the tricolon, abundans by syllable-count, decrescens in meaning: *praetextam et latum clavum prunaeque vatillum* 'his toga with its broad stripe and little pan of coal' – all part of the amusement of Horace and the grandees.[4] As for 45 *villula,* the 'house by the Campanian bridge', owner unnamed, which provided firewood and salt, was clearly of a rudimentary type and was soon succeeded by a grander stop: 50 *hinc nos Coccei recipit plenissima villa* 'after this the well-stocked house of Cocceius took us in'. This diminutive therefore has a function that is literary, rhetorically meaningful and contrastive, so it can hardly be listed simply as evidence of the colloquial for the *Satires.* Similarly at 47 *clitellas* occurs in the context of a mock-elevated scene, *hinc muli Capuae clitellas tempore ponunt* 'next at Capua our mules put down their saddle-bags on the early side'. At 69 *pusillo* is appropriately in the (indirect) speech of the clown Messius Cicirrus, while at 87 *oppidulo* (metrically tractable) points to the context: they stayed in the town (little

[4] Porphyrio ad loc. explains the little pan of coals: *quem* [sc. *Aufidium Luscum*] *sibi risui fuisse ait, quod magni penderet indutum se esse latoclavo ac praetexta, et de balneis publicis prunas sibi domuma mediastinis adferri,* 'Horace says they made fun of Aufidius Luscus for making a big deal of being dressed in the broad stripe and praetexta, and of having coals from the public bath delivered to his house by slaves.'

or otherwise), whose name will not fit in the hexameter – *quod versu dicere non est* 'which you can't say in hexameter' – a name as unusable as *oppido* itself. Satire can make such play, but in doing so it is doing something different from simply using *sermo cottidianus*.

Similarly outside *Satire* 1.5, more allusive motivations may be at work, which obscure the simply quotidian nature of specific forms. Take for instance *auriculam* at 1.9.77, where Horace acknowledges the plaintiff's subpoena by offering his earlobe for the latter to touch, as a sign of willingness to serve as a witness (76–7 *ego vero | oppono auriculam*). The form has been noted by those attending to colloquialisms, but it is insufficient simply to enter the data (see Ruckdeschel 1910: 13). Precisely in the mid thirties at the latest Virgil adapted Callimachus *Aetia* 1, fr. 1.22 Pfeiffer (Ἀπόλλων εἶπεν ὅ μοι Λύκιος... 'Lycian Apollo said to me...') in verses that would stand as the fountain-head of the Callimachean *recusatio* in Rome: *Ecl.* 6.3–4 *Cynthius aurem | vellit et admonuit* 'Apollo tweaked my ear and gave me some advice'. At the end of *Satire* 1.9, then, Horace may be seen as attenuating the Virgilian *aurem* with a hypochoristic diminutive (*auriculam*), perfect in the context of modernising the Homeric intertext of his lines and in this display of allusivity: 1.9.78 *sic me servavit Apollo* 'so it was Apollo saved me' alludes to Hom. *Il.* 20.443 τὸν δ᾽ ἐξήρπαξεν Ἀπόλλων 'him did Apollo rescue'. The adversary to whom Horace offers his ear, and whose actions are seen as the workings of Apollo (*sic me servavit Apollo*) looks just like the Virgilian *Cynthius*, the Callimachean Apollo of that poet. At the same time Horace converts a culturally banal Roman gesture: a juristic ritual becomes an Apollonian ear-tweak. In this whole process Horace also 'Callimacheanises' the Lucilian intertext at the very end of a poem that is immediately followed by *Satire* 1.10, which, continuing the discussion of *Satire* 1.4, precisely theorises the Callimachean deficiencies of Lucilius for his lack of Callimachean concision and *ars*. Even outside the *Satires* Horace has ulterior motives in his use of the diminutive, for instance at *Odes* 2.7.9–10, of his days on the 'wrong side' at Philippi: *tecum Philippos et celerem fugam | sensi relicta non bene parmula* 'no hero, I left my shield behind, when I experienced with you Philippi and a speedy retreat'. It is quite natural for the poet of *c.* 23 BC to use the diminutive, which utterly suits his stance as a lyric (not epic) poet in the tradition of Callimachus, and as one not so committed to the Republican cause: back then he had a shield, but like all good lyric poets he threw it away, and it was a little one at that.[5]

---

[5] For the preceding and further study of the literary nature of the end of *Sat.* 1.9, see Thomas 2009: 332–4.

Satire 1.5, the 'Journey to Brundisium', which famously never gets to Tarentum, the *telos* of the politically charged odyssey towards which Maecenas and his retinue were directed, immediately poses an obvious problem for a topic such as this. Even if Porphyrio had not told us as much, the remains of Book 3 of Lucilius' *Satires* (thirty-seven fragments amounting to sixty lines or parts of lines) make it quite clear that the journey is a literary one, and in a tradition of literary journeys, so that any word, phrase or line of it may for the ancient reader of Horace have converted what appears colloquial into something different, depending on what Lucilius was doing with his own linguistic register, and also depending on how Horace interacted with that prior effect. The poem emphatically puts into practice the Callimachean theory laid down in *Satires* 1.4 and 1.10: good as he may have been, and he was certainly more polished than his predecessors, Lucilius simply will not do in the current poetic culture in which polish, revision and perfection in writing are what matters:

> ... fuerit Lucilius, inquam,
> comis et urbanus, fuerit limatior idem　　　　　　　　65
> quam rudis et Graecis intacti carminis auctor
> quamque poetarum seniorum turba; sed ille,
> si foret hoc nostrum fato delapsus in aevum,
> detereret sibi multa, recideret omne quod ultra
> perfectum traheretur, et in versu faciendo　　　　　　70
> saepe caput scaberet vivos et roderet unguis.
> 　　　　　　　　　　　(*Sat.* 1.10.64–71)

Granted Lucilius was cultured and urbane, granted he was more polished than one would expect from an author of a raw genre untouched by the Greeks, more polished also than the host of older poets; but if the fates had brought him down in time to this modern age of ours, there's much you'd find him trimming as he cut back everything that went beyond perfection, constantly scratching his head and biting his nails to the quick as he composed his verse.

Long before Horace tersely ends *Satire* 1.5 (the shortest of the book to this point) with the faux-weary utterance *Brundisium longae finis chartaeque viaeque est* 'Brundisium is the end of my long work and journey' (1.5.104), readers familiar with the Lucilian model will have followed the ways in which Horatian revision of the model is effected. The wording *longae... chartae*, though at odds with the actual length of 104 lines, defines the poem as an epic, and Horace has done plenty to help affirm that final *sphragis*. As I have suggested elsewhere,[6] the poem approximates

---

[6] Thomas 2006: 62. There have been good recent treatments of *Sat.* 1.5's play with epic by Gowers (1993) and Harrison (2007: 86–9).

itself to epic, and avails itself of high-register style, syntax and figures
throughout:

elegant temporal markers

(9–10) *iam nox inducere terris | umbras et caelo diffundere signa parabat;*
(20–1) (including *cum-inversum* construction) *iamque dies aderat, nil
cum procedere lintrem | sentimus;* (39) *postera lux oritur multo gratissima;*
(77–8) *incipit ex illo montis Apulia notos | ostentare mihi;* (86) *quattuor
hinc rapimur viginti et milia raedis;* (94) *inde Rubos fessi pervenimus;*
(96) *postera tempestas melior*

chiastic anaphora

(11) *tum pueri nautis, pueris convicia nautae*

personification

(1–2) *egressum magna me accepit Aricia Roma | hospitio modico;* (45–6)
proxima Campano ponti quae villula, tectum | praebuit; (50) *hinc nos
Coccei recipit plenissima villa;* (73–4) *nam vaga per veterem dilapso
flamma culinam | Volcano summum properabat lambere tectum;* (77–
8) *incipit ex illo montis Apulia notos | ostentare mihi;* (78) *quos torret
Atabulus;* (79–80) *nisi nos vicina Trivici | villa recepisset;* (81) *udos cum
foliis ramos urente camino;* (83) *somnus tamen aufert;* (84–5) *immundo
somnia visu | nocturnam vestem maculant ventremque supinum;* (97–8)
dein Gnatia Lymphis | iratis exstructa dedit risusque iocosque

apostrophe

(24) *ora manusque tua lavimus, Feronia, lympha*

epic formularity for characters

(27–8) *huc venturus erat Maecenas optimus atque | Cocceius;* (31–2)
Maecenas advenit atque | Cocceius Capitoque simul Fonteius; (40)
Plotius et Varius Sinuessae Vergiliusque; (52) *Sarmenti scurrae pugnam
Messique Cicirri*

high invocation to Muses

(51–4) *nunc mihi paucis | Sarmenti scurrae pugnam Messique Cicirri, |
Musa, velim memores et quo patre natus uterque | contulerit litis*

golden or similarly artful lines for closure

(4) *differtum nautis cauponibus atque malignis;* (26) *inpositum saxis late
candentibus Anxur;* (36) (tricolon abundans) *praetextam et latum
clavum prunaeque vatillum;* (38) *Murena praebente domum, Capi-
tone culinam;* (49) *namque pila lippis inimicum et ludere crudis;*

(61) *saetosam laevi frontem turpaverat oris*; (85) *nocturnam vestem maculant ventremque supinum*; (93) *flentibus hinc Varius discedit maestus amicis*

metonymy, alliteration and high-register language
(73–4) *nam vaga per veterem dilapso flamma culinam | Volcano summum properabat lambere tectum.*

Simply viewed from features such as the preceding, the poem is indeed a miniature masterpiece, a Callimachean epyllion demonstrating all the poet's attention to artistry and poetic elevation. Except, of course, just to take the last example, the poem shows us what high literature avoids, in that case a grease fire in a *taberna* or *caupona* in central Italy.

Horace has taken the great men of his day, politicians, poets and grammarians, and put them – and himself – into the lowly hovels and flesh pots of Italy. There could be no greater contrast between high style and the low subject matter which is the subject of the poem, much of it having to do with bodily function and other matters absolutely outside the bounds of epic decorum:[7]

7–8:	Horace gets e-coli or other stomach poisoning
14–15:	kept awake by pesky midges and marsh-frogs
16–17:	drunken boatman and traveller sing of their girlfriends, content presumably execrable
19:	boatman on his back snoring
21–3:	pissed-off traveller beats up boatman and mule
25:	eat breakfast
30–1:	Horace puts black ointment on his ?conjunctivitis-diseased eyes
35:	they laugh at the petty pretensions of a local functionary
48:	Maecenas goes to play ball (like Trimalchio)
56–70:	clowns flyting about servile status, cuckolding, deformities
71–4:	grease fire
80–1:	green firewood makes them tear up
82–4:	local girl fails to turn up for sex; Horace has wet dream
88–92:	bread at unnamed town cheap and excellent (only positive information of little use since the town is unnamed), unlike that of Canusium
95:	rain makes things unpleasant

---

[7] See Cucchiarelli 2001: 56–76 for the ironic use of epic language and for the assimilation to comedy.

97–100:   they have a good laugh at local superstitions, anti-semitic joke
                 thrown in.

    The style of the poem is utterly at odds with what it communicates, the brute realities of human existence, with the mighty and the lowly sharing the stage. This is the context in which the actual elements of the poem's *sermo cottidianus* are to be set. Ruckdeschel (1910), Bourciez (1929) and Bonfante (1936, 1937) among them record most of the words, other than those already treated, that can be put down to *sermo cottidianus*; I have chosen some the most prominent. Their function is to contribute to the differences among the players in the drama of *Satire* 1.5; as such they are grist to the mill of Horatian poetics:

4   *cauponibus* 'shopkeepers': also at 1.1.29. Forms in *-o, -onis* are generally considered to belong to the colloquial register (Ruckdeschel 1910: 9–11), but in the *Satires* this instance (compared say to *Sat.* 1.2.68 *mutto*) has no intrinsic colloquial force, rather introduces an occupation that is part of the everyday world of the poem (like *leno* at *Sat.* 2.3.231, *Epist.* 2.1.172).

12–13   *ohe,* | *iam satis est* 'hey, enough already': the exclamation *ohe*, expressing exasperation (also at *Sat.* 2.5.96–7 *donec 'ohe iam'* | . . . *dixerit*) is clearly appropriate in the mouth of the boatman, so in context is perfectly appropriate as a means of character portrayal, and Aristotle would presumably have approved. The phrase itself was clearly a durable colloquialism: Pl. *Cas.* 249 *ohe, iam satis, uxor, est*; Mart. 4.89.1 *ohe, iam satis est* (Ruckdeschel 1910: 55).

14–19   A decidedly casual and paratactic stretch of narrative, with nouns repeated resumptively and an absence of pronouns: *nauta . . . viator . . . viator . . . nauta*.

14   *culices* 'midges': Bonfante (1936: 221 = 1994: 71) notes the limited range, suggesting the realm of *sermo cottidianus*, but that is because high literature does not deal with such creatures – as opposed to insects that figure through simile or other means in literary texts (*apis, formica, asilus*, etc.).

15   *cantat* 'sings away': while it is true that frequentatives often have a colloquial force (Ruckdeschel 1910: 20–3), poetic reality also generates this form: what annoys Horace is the fact that the two go on singing about their girlfriends. At *Satire* 1.10.19 the form is derogatory in a similar way, again suggesting true tedious repetition: *nil praeter Calvum et doctus cantare Catullum*;

likewise *Sat.* 2.1.46 *tota cantabitur urbe*, *Epist.* 1.19.9 *mandabo siccis, adimam cantare severis.* Horace uses it of himself at *Odes* 1.6.17–19 *nos convivia, nos proelia virginum* | . . . *cantamus vacui,* again suggesting repetition and preoccupation.

16   *multa prolutus vappa* 'soused with too much sour wine' – appropriate to context. Ruckdeschel (1910: 86–7) points to Plautus *Cur.* 121b *propere prolue cloacam.* But even Virgil could admit the word where appropriate, namely for the striking and enthusiastic imbibing of the Carthaginian Bitias from his cup of gold and jewels: *Aen.* 1.739 *pleno se proluet auro.* This use, like that of line 16, is part of the *enargeia* of the passage. *vappa* 'flat wine' has a colloquial feel to it, and survives first here in this sense (also *Sat.* 2.3.144, and appropriately App. Verg. *Copa* 11; Persius 5.77; Plin. *Nat.* 14.64; Mart. 12.48.14). Its earliest survival is in a transferred sense ('worthless person'; cf. 'dregs': Catul. 28.5; then Hor. *Sat.* 1.1.104; 1.2.12; Sen. *Con.* 2.4.12; *Priap.* 14.6 *PLM)* and clearly colloquial. Plin. *Nat.* 14.125 explains: *nec non aliqua est musti picea natura vitiumque musto quibusdam in locis iterum sponte fervere, qua calamitate deperit sapor: vappae accipit nomen, probrosum etiam hominum, cum degeneravit animus* 'and must in fact has a somewhat pitchy nature, and in some places has the flaw of spontaneously fermenting for a second time, through which disaster its flavour is ruined. It is then called *vappa,* a pejorative term also for humans whose spirit has deteriorated.'

21   *cerebrosus. . . unus* 'a crack-brained one': also at Lucil. 514 M. (= 519 W. = 510 K. = 15.15 C.) *insanum hominem et cerebrosum* 'a crazy crack-brained fellow'. That is what he is; again, appropriate characterisation, and the combination with *unus* (references here) gives a vivid sense of the man's social order. Once Lucilius has used such a word the issue of high vs colloquial register becomes moot. Knox (1986: 91) has shown that 'there is nothing intrinsically colloquial about the suffix' -*osus* in Latin poetry, and 91 *lapidosus* and 97 *piscosi,* descriptive uses of places, have a mock epic feel to them.[8]

23   *dolat* 'beats up': *dolo* (*OLD* s.v. '*del-,* cf. Skt. *dálati,* Gk. δαιδάλλω, δέλτος') is essentially a technical term in origin 'hew or chop into shape'; cf. Cic. *Div.* 2.86, of wooden lots used

[8] Cf. Knox 1986: 92–4 on Virgil's use of such -*osus* words (including these two), often to represent Greek -οεις or πολυ- adjectives.

in divination, *quis robur illud cecidit, dolavit, inscripsit?* 'who chopped down the oak, cut the wood into shape, inscribed the lots?' Horace's transferred use ('make chop suey out of?') is the first attested, and one might have looked for it in comedy if it were an actual colloquialism, but its absence may be accidental since it is already used by Pomponius (*fl.* 89 BC) in an obscene sense: *com.* 82 *dolasti uxorem.* In the present context it is colourful as context (a brawl) and register come together; cf. Apul. *Met.* 7.17 *dedolare aliquem crebris ictibus.*[9]

30–1   *hic oculis ego nigra meis collyria lippus | illinere* 'here my eyes got enflamed so I smeared black ointment over them': *lippus* (also at *Sat.* 1.3.25; 1.7.3) is otherwise only in Plautus, and after Horace in Vitruvius and the Elder Pliny, but it is the very subject that belongs to the everyday, and there is no reason to assign *lippus* itself, in absolute terms, to a particular register. On the other hand the sentence in which it here appears is remarkable for its communication of personal, bodily functions.

32–3   *ad unguem | factus homo* 'a man formed to perfection': the figurative use of *ad unguem* is transferred from using the fingernail to test perfection, for instance of a join in marble (*OLD* s.v. 1b). First used of a person in Horace, it has a colloquial or proverbial feel to it (see Otto 1890: 357), though it also appears at *Ars* 294, and Virgil would soon use it in a different but also transferred sense in a context that seems quite formal (though with *in* for *ad*, which could make a difference): *G.* 2.277–8 *nec setius omnis in unguem | arboribus positis secto via limite quadret* 'nevertheless, when all your trees are set out, every pathway should form a perfect square with clear-cut line' (i.e. form a quincunx).

61   *turpaverat* 'had disfigured': Ruckdeschel (1910: 25) treats adjectivally formed verbs such as this, and the same verb is also found in the *Odes*, but in contexts of a lower register: 1.13.9–11 *candidos | turparunt umeros inmodicae mero | rixae*; 4.13.12 *te quia rugae turpant.* Horatian lyric is as open to such diction as Horatian satire, if that is what the context calls for.

These instances generally appear in the sections of the poem (clearly demarcated as is best shown by Shackleton Bailey's paragraph divisions in his Teubner edition) devoted to those mundane but colourful figures with

---

[9] For this instance see Ruckdeschel (1910: 80).

whom Horace and his other elite companions come into contact, but from whom they are implicitly distinct – though Horace himself crosses the line with his own bodily problems. In the end it is not possible – or desirable – to see the artful use of colloquialism as much different, in the hands of the Callimachean artist, from his use of any other register. *Sermo cottidianus* is as literary as speech of the highest epic, tragic or lyric register, as it imports into its literary context the flavour of the street and is in the process transformed into a literary phenomenon.

CHAPTER 16

Sermones deorum: *divine discourse in Virgil's* Aeneid

Stephen J. Harrison

I INTRODUCTION

This contribution looks at some of the divine scenes in the *Aeneid* and the language used by gods in speeches, considering them as a special case of the presence and transformation of colloquial language in a high literary context.[1] The language of the *Aeneid* is generally acknowledged to be a *Kunstsprache*, an artificial construction,[2] and the language of these scenes is likely to be especially stylised given that they feature the most elevated category of characters in the most elevated of poetic genres. Nevertheless, here I try to show how the artificial language of epic in these scenes of divine conversation echoes typical features of colloquial speech, characteristically combining such traces of familiar discourse with high poetic elements. I also suggest that stylistic choice in these scenes is more often determined by the dramatic and literary requirements of plot, scene or characterisation than by any consistent theory of the language of the gods in general.

2 'COLLOQUIALISM' IN THE *AENEID*

First, we face the issue of defining 'colloquial' features in literary texts. Anna Chahoud's analysis in Chapter 4 of this volume (section 3.2) provides a useful list of colloquial features of language in Latin, and I will here try the experiment of applying it as a template for analysing Virgil's text. On the purely lexical level, 'colloquial' expressions in a high poetic text such as the *Aeneid* can be picked out through lexical parallels with lower, more 'colloquial', texts which are traditionally thought to be closer to common speech usage (e.g. Roman comedy, private letters, subliterary documents),

---

[1] It is a great pleasure to dedicate this piece to Jim Adams, *viro humano utriusque doctissimo linguae.*
[2] The most useful modern studies on the language of the *Aeneid* outside commentaries are Cordier 1939, Wilkinson 1959, Görler 1982, 1985 and 1999, Lyne 1989, Horsfall 1995: 217–48, O'Hara 1997 and the relevant sections of the manuals of Lunelli 1980 and Maurach 1995. I hope I can be excused for making frequent reference to Harrison 1991, where I collected much useful material.

and some examples of this will be cited below. More prevalent, but more difficult to define, are larger stylistic features which point to traces of conversational situations in literary contexts. Here I find useful Chahoud's categories of these features, as follows (I will refer to these categories as Chahoud 1, etc.):

1. Expressions of contact, e.g. exclamations, curses, fossilised imperatives, stereotyped questions, forms of address
2. Loose syntax showing the emotion of the speaker, e.g. parataxis, parenthesis, anacoluthon, simplified constructions, emotive collocation of words
3. Brevity, e.g. brachylogy, interruptions, aposiopesis, ellipsis, euphemism, pregnant usages
4. Redundancy, e.g. anaphora, pleonasm, periphrasis, exaggeration
5. Irony, e.g. understatement, litotes
6. Imagery, e.g. metaphor, ambiguity, concretisation of abstracts
7. Diminutives.

As Chahoud herself acknowledges, it is sometimes difficult to decide whether some of the features are colloquial or not in a literary text; in a poetic context, this problem is particularly acute, as some features in the list above are established elements in poetry long before Virgil (e.g. Chahoud 4, 5 and 6). Nevertheless, this investigation will try to trace 'colloquial' features as presented and transformed within the literary *Kunstsprache* of Virgilian epic, looking not only at lexical items but also at how broader conversational features are translated into the very unconversational medium of Virgilian hexameters. I will briefly consider four sample scenes of divine conversation in the *Aeneid*, which involve the three major divine characters in all possible combinations: 1.227–97 (Venus, Jupiter), 4.90–128 (Juno, Venus), 10.5–117 (Jupiter, Venus, Juno), 12.791–842 (Jupiter, Juno).

3 VENUS AND JUPITER (*AENEID* 1.227–97)

In this famous scene Venus complains to her father Jupiter about the current tribulations of her son Aeneas, and is comforted by Jupiter's prophecy of Aeneas' future establishment of the Roman nation; Venus' speech covers lines 229–53, Jupiter's lines 257–96. Neither speech contains many obviously colloquial lexical items, though both contain many features of conversational situations, naturally adapted to an elevated literary context. Anaphora (Chahoud 4) is particularly frequent in Venus' speech, expressing high emotion and indignation, especially in lines 231–7:

> quid meus Aeneas in te committere tantum,
> quid Troes potuere, quibus, tot funera passis,
> cunctus ob Italiam terrarum clauditur orbis?
> certe hinc Romanos olim, volventibus annis,
> hinc fore ductores, revocato a sanguine Teucri,   235
> qui mare, qui terras omnis dicione tenerent,
> pollicitus, quae te, genitor, sententia vertit?

How has my Aeneas managed to commit such a crime against you, how have the Trojans managed this, to whom (after enduring such losses) the whole of the world is closed because of Italy? When you firmly promised that from them with the rolling years would come the Romans, from them would come great leaders, descended from the bloodline of Teucer called back to Italy, who would hold the sea and all lands under their sway – what opinion, father, has changed you?

This colloquial feature is however carefully arranged in the poetic context: *quid* is placed symmetrically at the beginning of the consecutive lines 231 and 232, a positioning nicely varied in the consecutive lines 234 and 235, where *hinc* occurs as second and first word respectively, while in line 236 *qui* is repeated much more rapidly and neatly juxtaposed with the polar pairing *mare... terras*. As in formal Ciceronian rhetoric, an important influence on Virgil's speeches in general, 'colloquial' features such as anaphora are given a literary colour and become artistic devices as well as reflections of ordinary speech. Other features of these lines which have a colloquial air are the initial *certe* of line 234 (the adverb usually occurs in this first sentence position in Plautus, is found relatively rarely in Cicero, and used only twice elsewhere in Virgil, both in speeches)[3] and the generally confused nature of Venus' syntax in lines 234–7 (only in line 237 does the sentence construction *pollicitus... Romanos... fore ductores qui tenerent* become clear). This confusion (Chahoud 2), like the dense anaphora, primarily reflects Venus' heightened emotional state, and characterisation is a key feature explaining the language here. Especially interesting is the phrase *quae te... sententia vertit?* in line 237: here the expected phrase is reversed with *sententia* as subject rather than object (Venus should surely say that Jupiter has changed his view rather than vice versa), perhaps another element of loose emotional syntax (Chahoud 2).

---

[3] 32 of the 45 examples of *certe* in Plautus are in initial position; only 27 of the 732 examples in Cicero are in initial position, and of those 10 occur in letters; for the other two Virgilian examples see *Ecl.* 8.107 and 9.7 (both in direct speech, the second in initial position).

Much the same can be said of the final lines of Venus' speech:

> nos, tua progenies, caeli quibus adnuis arcem,
> navibus (infandum!) amissis, unius ob iram
> prodimur atque Italis longe disiungimur oris.
> hic pietatis honos? sic nos in sceptra reponis?
>
> (1.250–3)

We, your issue, to whom you accord heaven's citadel, having lost our ships (evil unspeakable!), are betrayed through the anger of one person and kept a long distance apart from the shores of Italy. Is this the honour due to *pietas*? Is this the way you restore us to rule?

Here we find a number of colloquial features gathered together at the rhetorical climax of the speech: the emotive juxtaposition of *nos* and *tua* (Chahoud 2), the breathless style of 250–1, where appositions and subordinate clauses are presented before the main verb eventually arrives in 252 (Chahoud 2), the parenthesis of *infandum* (Chahoud 2),[4] the invidious euphemism of *unius*, clearly referring to Juno (Chahoud 3), and of course the final pair of quick-fire questions, with the first compressed by the omission of *esse* (Chahoud 1 and 3). Once again, however, this is tempered by higher stylistic features which remind us that this is an epic poem: the poetic term *progenies* (see Harrison 1991: 66) and the hyperbaton *Italis... oris*, which might even reflect in the word order the separation which the phrase expresses.

The emotional passion of Venus' speech is countered by the reassuring rhetoric of her father:

> parce metu, Cytherea: manent immota tuorum
> fata tibi; cernes urbem et promissa Lavini
> moenia, sublimemque feres ad sidera caeli
> magnanimum Aenean; neque me sententia vertit.
>
> (1.257–60)

Refrain from fear, goddess of Cythera: the destiny of your people remains unchanged for you; you will see a city and the promised walls of Lavinium, and you will carry great-hearted Aeneas aloft to the stars of heaven, and no opinion has changed me.

---

[4] Chahoud's classification of parentheses as a colloquial feature is strongly supported by the evidence of the *Aeneid*: of the sixty-five parentheses usually marked in modern editions in *Aeneid* 1–6, forty-six occur in direct discourse.

Jupiter opens with the use of the contracted form *metu* for the dative *metui*:[5] this form seems to have been a colloquial usage.[6] It was used by Lucilius, perhaps for convenience in hexameters (280 M. = 304 W. = 284 K. = 7.11 C. *anu noceo*, 1288 M. = 1234 W. = 1305 K. = H52 C. *victu praeponis honesto*); according to Gellius' discussion of the form (4.16.5–9) Julius Caesar approved it as the proper dative form in his lost work on linguistic analogy and used it in his speeches (see above, pp. 232f.). Such forms are used sparingly by Virgil in the *Aeneid*, more often than not in speeches (6.465 *aspectu* (Anchises to Aeneas), 698 *amplexu* (Aeneas to Anchises), 3.541 *curru* (Anchises to Trojans), 9.605 *venatu* (Numanus Remulus to Trojans)).[7]

This pronounced colloquialism, marking a shift to conversational mode, is followed by an instance of pleonasm (Chahoud 4), in which Jupiter uses both the possessive adjective *tuorum* and the pronoun *tibi*: this hyper-emphasis on the second person is both colloquial and indicates Jupiter's proclaimed focus on his daughter's interests which she had denied in her preceding speech. Again characterisation is important here in lexical choice. This considerable colloquial colour is balanced here by some more lofty phrasing: *sidera caeli* is likely to be an older phrase from Latin epic (cf. Lucretius 1.788 *sidera mundi*), while *magnanimus* clearly echoes the Homeric epithet μεγάθυμος (e.g. *Iliad* 1.123) and is very likely to have occurred in Ennius (Harrison 1991: 98).

In this initial example, then, we can see the complex reflection of spoken language in the discourse of the gods presented in the *Aeneid*. On the one hand, there are clear traces of colloquial features in these divine speeches: general conversational features are plainly present, though modified by their elevated epic context and poetic framework. On the other hand, elevated and poetic features are present too, reinforcing the high literary level of the epic genre and the dignity of its characters. Above all, the dramatic situation and the need to characterise the feelings of speakers take pride of place: literary function is more important than consistency of lexical level. We will see these features reinforced in our further examples.

---

[5] The form is surely a contraction of the dative rather than an ablative – there is no certain example of *parcere* with ablative before the fourth century (the *neve opera tua parcas* transmitted at Cato *Agr.* 1.1 is cited by Pliny *Nat.* 18.26 with *operae*) – see *TLL* x/1.339.70 ff.

[6] Plautus *Rud.* 294 *sunt nobis quaestu et cultu*, and the contraction *usust* (*usu est*) at *Mer.* 854, *Mil.* 1073, *Rud.* 1085, *Truc.* 721; cf. Cicero *Fam.* 10.24.3 *impetu... resistat*, 10.31.4 *senatu scribam* and especially 16.4.2 *sumptu ne parcas*; see Leumann 1977: 442–3.

[7] To these four examples add the three I have found which are not in speeches: 1.476 and 7.724 *curru*, 7.747 *venatu*.

4 JUNO AND VENUS (*AENEID* 4.90–128)

In this entertaining episode of divine double-crossing, Juno suggests to Venus (4.93–104) that Aeneas stay at Carthage and marry Dido, thus preventing his journey to Italy; Venus replies (105–14), apparently consenting, though she knows from Jupiter's speech in Book 1 (just examined above) that Aeneas is destined to leave Carthage. Juno then sets out how Aeneas and Dido will come together (4.115–27), promising a proper form of marriage (though in fact only a parody form of marriage will be forthcoming).

Juno begins with splendid irony (Chahoud 5) at 93–5:

> egregiam vero laudem et spolia ampla refertis
> tuque puerque tuus (magnum et memorabile numen),[8]
> una dolo divum si femina victa duorum est.

Splendid indeed is the glory and mighty the spoils that you and your boy are winning (such a great and memorable divine power), if a single woman is overcome by the deceit of a pair of gods.

Other colloquial features here are the pleonastic *tuque... tuus* (it is more than clear to whom the *puer* Cupid belongs) and the parenthesis (Chahoud 2); on the other hand, the lines show poetic features of alliteration (*magnum et memorabile numen, dolo divum... duorum*) and intricate word order (*una... divum... femina... duorum*, where the opposing nouns and numbers are neatly balanced against each other in an *abab* structure).

In her reply, Venus expresses an insincere uncertainty:

> sed fatis incerta feror, si Iuppiter unam
> esse velit Tyriis urbem Troiaque profectis,
> miscerive probet populos aut foedera iungi
> tu coniunx, tibi fas animum temptare precando.
> perge, sequar.   (4.110–14)

But I am carried away by fate's power, so as to be uncertain whether Jupiter wishes there to be a single city for the Tyrians and for those who set out from Troy, or whether he approves of the mixing of these peoples and the joining of such bonds. You are his wife – for you it is right to try his mind with prayers. Carry on and I shall follow.

---

[8] The Carolingian MSS **p** and **n** read *nomen*, 'reputation', worth considering (and read by Geymonat and Conte) given Ovid *Met.* 10.607–8 *habetis | Hippomene victo magnum et memorabile nomen* and Silius 4.184–5 *egregium Ausoniae decus ac memorabile nomen, | si dent fata moras aut servent foedera Poeni*. Adopting this reading would involve repunctuation, placing a colon after *tuus* and removing the parentheses, with *si* explaining *nomen* rather than *laudem*.

Here the loose construction *fatis incerta feror, si* reflects the conversational tone and Venus' deceptive hedging (Chahoud 2), while the terse *perge, sequar* (brachylogy for *si pergis, sequar*) is similarly colloquial (Chahoud 3). The metaphor of *fatis incerta feror* seems to be nautical, with Venus colourfully imagining herself as a ship without direction, though here one might debate whether this image is a poetic or colloquial feature; a similar ambiguity might be claimed for the polyptoton *tu . . . tibi*, a form of varied anaphora (Chahoud 4) which has some colloquial force (especially with the ellipsis of *esse* in both clauses, Chahoud 3) but which is strongly poetic in Latin, here perhaps with a tinge of honorific prayer-style, *Du-Stil*.[9]

Juno's final speech setting out how the union of Aeneas and Dido will be accomplished shows a similar stylistic mixture. It begins with a pair of lines of suitably imperious and didactic brevity:

> mecum erit iste labor. nunc qua ratione quod instat
> confieri possit, paucis (adverte) docebo.   (4.115–16)

That will be my task. Now, I will tell you briefly how what is now in store can be accomplished – pay attention.

Here the characterisation of Juno as a ruthless and efficient operator in her own cause is paramount, though colloquial colour is clearly important: the terse form of *mecum erit iste labor* and *paucis* [sc. *verbis*] *docebo* is clear (Chahoud 3), and the imperative parenthesis (*adverte*) is a typical feature of Virgilian speeches (see Harrison 1991: 61) which recalls colloquial patterns (Chahoud 2). But the immediately following lines again reassert the text's high poetic level:

> venatum Aeneas unaque miserrima Dido
> in nemus ire parant, ubi primos crastinus ortus
> extulerit Titan radiisque retexerit orbem.
>
> (4.117–9)

Aeneas and most wretched Dido prepare to go together into the forest, when tomorrow's Sun lifts up his first risings and reveals the world with his rays.

The careful distribution of the matching names *Aeneas* and *Dido* at the ends of the two halves of line 117,[10] the allusive *Titan* (= 'sun'; cf. Cicero *Arat.* 343 Traglia), the elaborate phrase *primos ortus . . . extulerit* with its poetic plural, and the alliteration of *extuleritque Titan radiisque retexerit orbem*, all belong to high poetic style, though as at *Aeneid* 10. 244 *lux*

---

[9] On Virgilian polyptoton see Harrison 1991: 101. *Du-Stil* in Latin poetry: see conveniently Harrison 1991: 80.

[10] On such pointed placing of names in the *Aeneid* see conveniently Harrison 1991: 288–90.

crastina we may be dealing with a poeticised version of the colloquial *dies crastinus* (Plautus *St.* 635; cf. *Men.* 175 *stellam crastinam*). In this scene as a whole, we see an interesting mixture of stylistic levels which incorporates some colloquial features as well as epic diction.

5 JUPITER, JUNO AND VENUS (*AENEID* 10.1–116)[11]

In this episode, the only divine council of the *Aeneid*, we find the only three-way exchange of speeches between the poem's main divine characters. The scene is deeply revealing about the characterisation of the gods and about domestic relations on Olympus: Venus and Juno attempt to wheedle and manipulate their (respective) father and husband/brother, while Jupiter resorts to economy with the truth to pacify his difficult wife and daughter. Jupiter opens up, demanding to know why his ban on war in Italy has been defied:

> caelicolae magni, quianam sententia vobis
> versa retro tantumque animis certatis iniquis?
> abnueram bello Italiam concurrere Teucris.
> quae contra vetitum discordia? quis metus aut hos
> aut hos arma sequi ferrumque lacessere suasit?
>
> (10.6–10)

Great dwellers in heaven, why has your resolve been reversed, and why do you vie with hearts of hate? I had forbidden Italy to clash with the Trojans in war. What is this discord contrary to my ban? What fear has urged one side or the other to follow the course of arms and provoke the sword?

Jupiter begins this scene in high Ennian style, addressing the assembled gods with the epic compound *caelicolae* (*Ann.* 445 Sk.), using the Ennian interrogative *quianam* (*Ann.* 121 Sk.) and an Ennian verb and construction (*Ann.* 262 Sk. *certare abnueo*); these archaic Ennian echoes may have a primarily intertextual purpose in echoing the divine council of the first book of Ennius' *Annales* which raised Romulus to divine status (*Ann.* 51–5 Sk.; see Harrison 1991: 57), but they also serve to characterise Jupiter as dignified and impressive. The conversational flavour is conveyed by the series of three questions with which the speech opens, and by the omission of *esse* in both line 2 (with *versa*) and line 9 (with *discordia*): but once again we find intricate poetic word order in the careful placing of the opposing *Italiam . . . Teucris* (nicely avoiding the easy exact match *Italos* by using the 'land for people' *Italiam*) at the two ends of the two halves

---

[11] In this section I make especially free use of (and occasionally correct) my commentary in Harrison 1991.

of the hexameter. On the other hand, the excited questions of lines 9–10 have colloquial elements: *hos . . . hos* is a vivid and colloquial version of *hos . . . illos* (see Hofmann–Ricottilli 340), and the unusual and colourful phrases *arma sequi* and *ferrum lacessere* reflect the speaker's lively feelings.

Venus' passionate reply urging Aeneas' case (18–62) is the longest of the scene's speeches. Lines 25–30 show its mixed style:

> Aeneas ignarus abest. numquamne levari   25
> obsidione sines? muris iterum imminet hostis
> nascentis Troiae nec non exercitus alter,
> atque iterum in Teucros Aetolis surgit ab Arpis
> Tydides. equidem credo, mea vulnera restant
> et tua progenies mortalia demoror arma.   30

Aeneas is away and unaware. Will you never allow them to be relieved from siege? Once more an enemy with another army threatens the walls of growing Troy, and once more there rises against the Trojans the man from Aetolian Arpi, Diomedes. Yes, I am sure of it, a wounding for me lies ahead, and I, your offspring, am a mere delay to mortal arms.

The compressed and terse *Aeneas ignarus abest* (Chahoud 3) is succeeded by the indignant rhetorical question and exaggeration (Chahoud 1 and 4) of *numquamne . . . sines*; on the other hand, *nascentis* seems to be poetic *simplex pro composito* for *renascentis*, a poetic feature,[12] while the artful collocation of *Teucros Aetolis*, juxtaposing the traditional hostile pair of Trojans and Greeks,[13] and the learned epithet *Aetolis* for *Arpis* (pointing to the Greek foundation of the Italian city) are both further poetic devices. Likewise, in the last two lines we find balancing lexical features: the colloquial *equidem credo* (three times in Plautus) is matched by the poetic and archaic *progenies* (see Harrison 1991: 66).

Juno's speech also shows high indignation, especially in its dramatic opening:

> quid me alta silentia cogis
> rumpere et obductum verbis vulgare dolorem?
> Aenean hominum quisquam divumque subegit   65
> bella sequi aut hostem regi se inferre Latino?
> Italiam petiit fatis auctoribus (esto)
> Cassandrae impulsus furiis: num linquere castra
> hortati sumus aut vitam committere ventis?
> (10.63–9)

[12] I missed this feature here at Harrison 1991: 65; for poetic *simplex pro composito* in general see the references collected at Harrison 1991: 68.
[13] See n. 10 above.

Why do you force me to break my deep silence, and lay open in words my hidden grief? Did any man or god compel Aeneas to take the path of war, to attack King Latinus as an enemy? Grant that he made for Italy on the authority of destiny – driven by the ravings of Cassandra: did we urge him to abandon his camp, or trust his life to the winds?

Each of these three sentences contains a lively rhetorical question, and the first of them combines a phrase already established in poetry (*silentia... rumpere*, cf. Lucr. 4.583) with a vivid metaphor (Chahoud 6) from the healing of a wound (*obductum*). The second question contains a Homeric imitation in the pairing *hominum... divumque* (cf. *Iliad* 1.544 ἀνδρῶν τε θεῶν τε), the third a colloquial parenthesis (Chahoud 2) and some poetic alliteration (*vitam... ventis*). Again in this scene we see colloquial features juxtaposed with more elevated elements to produce a complex epic *Kunstsprache* which nevertheless bears clear traces of representing speech.

6 JUPITER AND JUNO (*AENEID* 12.791–842)

In this crucial scene in the poem, Jupiter tells Juno to stop aiding Turnus and to allow the Trojans to win the war in Latium; Juno agrees, but extracts the price that Aeneas' people will no longer be called Trojans, and that the hated name of Troy will be abolished. In agreeing to this, Jupiter states further that the resulting Roman race will honour Juno more than any other people. Jupiter opens in dramatic manner:

> quae iam finis erit, coniunx? quid denique restat?
> indigetem Aenean scis ipsa et scire fateris
> deberi caelo fatisque ad sidera tolli.
> quid struis? aut qua spe gelidis in nubibus haeres?
>
> (12.793–6)

What will the end be now, my consort? What is left then? You yourself know, and admit that you know, that Aeneas is owed to heaven as a local god and that he is being raised by destiny to the stars. What are you up to? Or what do you hope for in hanging on in the cool clouds?

Four questions in four lines, indeed two quick-fire pairs in each of two lines, set the lively and conversational tone, and the lexical evidence of line 793 points the same way: *quae iam finis erit?* (with its splendid metafictional speculation about how the poem will finish, cf. Fowler 1997: 260) looks like a heightened version of the colloquial *quid iam?* 'what now?' (Pl. *Epid.* 56, *Mil.* 322, *Mos.* 460, Cael. *apud* Cic. *Fam.* 8.15.1), while the use of *denique* 'then' afforcing interrogatives in brief questions is equally familiar in tone

(Pl. *Bac.* 294 *quid denique agitis?*, *Cas.* 915 *quid fit denique?*, *Truc.* 401 *quid denique agitis?*). The situation is similar with the two questions of line 796, which echo the famously brusque questions of Mercury to the recalcitrant Aeneas in Carthage at 4.271: *quid struis? aut qua spe Libycis teris otia terris?*: *struere* in the sense of 'plot, devise' is a comic usage (Pl. *As.* 72, Ter. *Hau.* 514), as is the use of *qua spe* in questions – cf. Ter. *Eu.* 1025 *quid nunc? qua spe aut quo consilio huc imu'?* The reference to 'cool clouds' seems a mere ornamental detail, but surely here there is a poetic play on Plato's famous 'etymology' (*Cratylus* 404c) of Juno's Greek name Hera, derived from Greek *aer* 'cloudy air' (see O'Hara 1996: 239).

This colloquial tone is joined by some more formal features in the next lines, though the rapid questions continue:

> mortalin decuit violari vulnere divum?
> aut ensem (quid enim sine te Iuturna valeret?)
> ereptum reddi Turno et vim crescere victis?
> desine iam tandem precibusque inflectere nostris,   800
> ne te tantus edit tacitam dolor et mihi curae
> saepe tuo dulci tristes ex ore recursent.
> ventum ad supremum est.   (12.797–803)

Was it fitting for a god to be pierced by a mortal wound? Or that his lost sword should be returned to Turnus (for what could Juturna manage without you?) and that the strength of the defeated party should increase? Cease now at last, and be turned by my prayers, to prevent so great a pain from eating you up in silence, and to stop sad complaints repeatedly streaming back to me from your sweet mouth. We have reached the end.

Line 797 combines a terse rhetorical question with careful poetic arrangement: the opposing pair *mortalin... divum* is neatly distributed at either end of the hexameter, and the words *decuit violari vulnere divum* (referring to the future god Aeneas' wounding at 12.318–23) provide chiastic initial alliteration. In lines 798–9 we find a conversational parenthesis (Chahoud 2) juxtaposed with an alliterative poetic phrase, *vim crescere victis*. In lines 801–2 Jupiter uses vivid emotional language (Chahoud 2) in the image of being eaten up by pain and in the collocation *dulci tristes* (he expects kisses from Juno's mouth but gets only complaints), and employs *edit*, the archaic/colloquial form of the subjunctive *edat*;[14] the archaic tone lends dignity to the king of the gods, but the colloquial element reminds us that

---

[14] *Edat* appears in two of the three capital MSS here, but is rightly rejected by modern editors as a normalisation; for *edit* cf. Pl. *Aul.* 672, *Capt.* 461, *Men.* 90, Horace *Epod.* 3.3. This form seems to preserve the original optative: see Leumann 1977: 573–4.

this is a conversational context. The impersonal *ventum ad supremum est*, on the other hand, seems to introduce the telegraphic and lapidary language of Roman military discourse, what Fraenkel called the 'war-bulletin' style, which can be amply illustrated from military historians. Once again we see a mixture of stylistic registers.

Juno's reply shows a similar mixture of styles, e.g. at 808–17:

> ista quidem quia nota mihi tua, magne, voluntas,
> Iuppiter, et Turnum et terras invita reliqui;
> nec tu me aeria solam nunc sede videres   810
> digna indigna pati, sed flammis cincta sub ipsa
> starem acie traheremque inimica in proelia Teucros.
> Iuturnam misero (fateor) succurrere fratri
> suasi et pro vita maiora audere probavi,
> non ut tela tamen, non ut contenderet arcum;   815
> adiuro Stygii caput implacabile fontis,
> una superstitio superis quae reddita divis.

Because indeed that wish of yours, great Jupiter, is known to me, I have left behind both Turnus and the earth, though against my will. You would not now be seeing me alone in my cloudy seat, suffering things deserved and undeserved, but I would be standing girt with flame at the very battle-line itself and dragging the Trojans into battle against their enemies. Juturna (I admit it) I did urge to aid her poor brother, and approved her greater daring to save his life, but not that she should use weapons or draw a bow. I swear by the inexorable head of the stream of Styx, the one binding power which is given to the gods of heaven.

The confused word order of Juno's opening, including the split vocative address to Jupiter (*magne... Iuppiter*), shows her emotional state and conversational mode (Chahoud 2). *Ista quidem* with *quidem* limiting a pronoun is a colloquial Plautine usage – we find *iste quidem* similarly at Plautus *Mer.* 730, *Mos.* 235 – and it is worth noting that *quidem* itself occurs only five more times in the whole *Aeneid*, of which four instances are in direct speech.[15] Equally colloquial is the asyndetic polar expression *digna indigna*: cf. Plautus *As.* 247 *dignos indignos adire*, *Capt.* 200 *indigna digna habenda sunt*. This conversational start is then balanced by a number of elevated poetic features in 813–17: in 813 we find a parenthesis (Chahoud 2), but also an implied etymology of the name Juturna (*iuvare Turnum*) in the phrase *succurrere fratri*, a regular feature of Virgilian poetic style (O'Hara 1996: 240). Likewise, the syntax of line 815 is decidedly poetic, employing a true zeugma where supplying the verb *contendere* with *tela*

---

[15] 3.628, 10.385, 11.49, 11.378, 12.234 (only 10.385 is not in direct speech).

leads to a phrase which is strictly illogical:[16] the plural *tela* implies either arrows or weapons in general, neither of which goes well with *contendere*, which applies only to drawing a bow. Once again a divine speech combines colloquial elements with elevated poetic usage.

7 CONCLUSION

Investigation of some key scenes of divine conversation in Virgil's *Aeneid* leads to the unsurprising conclusion that such speeches of the gods characteristically combine the high register of epic poetry with traces of colloquial usages. These traces are often closely mixed with poetic elements, and it is often hard to tell whether a particular feature is poetic or conversational, but there are enough instances to show that echoing conversational usage is a key feature of Virgilian divine discourse. Occasionally, we can see that such conversational usages are archaic rather than contemporary, especially in the mouth of Jupiter, who might naturally be expected to show an archaic linguistic dignity as the father of the gods, however dubious his words and function in the poem.[17] Above all, the prime purpose of the divine scenes of the poem seems to be characterisation of the individual deities; though the mixture of colloquial and poetic elements is clear and relatively consistent, even if the two elements are often hard to untangle from each other, literary purposes are understandably supreme, and the colouring of individual divine characters remains the prime determinant of how the gods speak in the *Aeneid*.

[16] On true zeugma (two complements with one verb which strictly fits only one of them) and the contrast with syllepsis (two complements with one verb which fits both) see Kenney 1971: 160.
[17] For Jupiter's problematic character in the *Aeneid* see Lyne 1987: 75–99.

PART IV

Early Principate

CHAPTER 17

Petronius' linguistic resources

Martti Leiwo

Petronius uses many linguistic devices to characterise his narrative and the persons he describes, employing resources from the fields of vocabulary, morphology, syntax, code-switching, rhetoric and pragmatics;[1] the only major linguistic possibility that he leaves underexploited is the description of pronunciation.[2] Many studies of Petronius' language deal with the idiosyncrasies of his expressions, but the subject is still not fully understood, in part because his work is a literary creation that deliberately violates the literary conventions of classical Latin (see Adams 2005b: 77–8; Herman 2003: 139). The difference between this prescriptive or normative good literary Latin and the Latin of Petronius is notable. So, how can we define the language of Petronius?

The study of Petronius' language begins with the understanding that it varies both by genre (e.g. between dialogue and narrative) and by social context (e.g. between the speech of one character and another). Much has already been written on different aspects of this variation;[3] here my aim is to examine a few specific usages and see what light they can shed on Petronius' linguistic and literary technique.

The *Satyricon* involves many different genres (see e.g. Petersmann 1977: 26; Callebat 1998: 10–2, 25–6; Biville 2003: 50–2), and Petronius writes according to his conceptions of the respective genres (oratory, epic poetry, tragic drama, derisive poetry) and also tries to use different registers for

---

[1] I would like to express my warmest thanks to Eleanor Dickey for her exceptional criticism and help in all matters, especially with my English. I am also very grateful to my research assistant Riku Partanen for providing me with examples and excellent ideas.

[2] See Daheim and Blänsdorf 2003: 96–7. The omission is not absolute, as some variant spellings in the text of Petronius probably indicate non-standard pronunciations, e.g. Hermeros' *saplutus, dupundii, dupunduarius* (37.6, 58.4, 58.5); it is possible that additional variant spellings may have disappeared in the course of the text's transmission. Although Roman writers did not often use variant spellings to characterise individuals' speech, regional and social differences in pronunciation existed (see Adams 2007) and sometimes appear in Latin literature by means of variant spellings (e.g. Catul. 84).

[3] See e.g. Petersmann 1977, Pinkster 1987, Boyce 1991, and the various pieces in Herman and Rosén 2003.

lower-class dialogue, middle-class dialogue, first-person narrative and, perhaps, 'foreigner speak'. Much previous work has concentrated on words
or structures that are 'colloquial', 'vulgar', or in the 'wrong' place in the
middle of urban speech, or on loan words that were thought to be examples
of *Volkstümlichkeit* (see Petersmann 1977: 25 with corrections of some of
these views).[4] In such discussions 'colloquial' usually refers to the variety
spoken by the more educated characters and 'vulgar' to the speech of the
uneducated freedmen. Several scholars have observed that, in the *Cena*, the
language of (some) freedmen is different from that of other speakers.[5] For
example, the language of Dama (41.10–12), Seleucus (42.1–7), Phileros
(43.1–8), Ganymedes (44.1–18) and Echion (45.1–46.8; see also Boyce 1991:
76–83) involves more deviations from formal literary language than that
of, for example, Ascyltos, Encolpius and Eumolpus. The latter are clearly
more educated, as Encolpius informs us: *et tu* (Ascyltos) *litteras scis et ego*,
'You are a man of letters; so am I' (10.5) and *Eumolpus tanquam litterarum
studiosus utique atramentum habet*, 'Eumolpus, as a man of letters, has
always got ink with him' (102.13).[6] An additional complication is genre-
based fluctuation within the speech of a single character, most notably in
the case of Encolpius, who serves as a narrator and also appears in dialogue
(R. Beck 1975).

There are difficulties with the traditional approach of taking Petronius'
dialogue passages simply as representations of non-elite speech of the middle of the first century AD (see Clackson and Horrocks 2007: 237). I shall
show that, in analysing linguistic resources and conversational contexts, it
is possible to find elements of literary prose and elements of non-literary
prose (see also Biville 2003: 50–2; Adams 2003c: 11–12). On the most basic
level, the people who were the models for Petronius' freedmen cannot
have spoken exactly like the characters in the *Satyricon* because of the
clearly literary character of Petronius' work. Actual dialogue tends to have

---

[4] The literature on Petronius is enormous. Works between 1975 and 2005 are collected and admirably
analysed by Vannini (2007), and Boyce (1991: 14–32) provides a survey of earlier studies.
[5] The first important study of the differences of language between educated and uneducated speakers in
Petronius was that of Abbot (1907). He speaks first of 'words and phrases which belong to the people's
speech and are at variance with formal usage' (1907: 44) but then turns to use terminology such
as 'colloquial elements', 'colloquial forms' (1907: 45), 'colloquial speech' (1907: 46), 'colloquialisms'
(1907: 48) etc., see also Petersmann 1977: 23–5. For research on 'vulgarisms' and style see Vannini
2007: 319–29. The terms 'vulgar', 'colloquial', 'informal', *sermo inliberalis*, *sermo urbanus* are freely
used without much theoretical discussion about different varieties and registers. Some uncertainty
also arises from the state of the transmitted text (see Petersmann 1977: 29–36), but we shall try to
deal with material that is generally accepted.
[6] Translations of Petronius are by P. G. Walsh, Clarendon Press 1996 unless otherwise noted.

different internal organisation and different cohesion from that of a written representation,[7] and Petronius' dialogue is an artistic creation.

I WORDS AND IDIOMS

Petronius is rich in using words, in part because of the variety of his subject matter and genres; had Cicero written a work like the *Satyricon*, many more words would have been considered acceptable in good prose by the ancient grammarians. A few points are particularly striking about Petronius' lexical resources. He chose many words from military language and used different professional varieties freely (see the excellent collection of Heraeus 1937). He also used proverbs and contemporary idioms and took advantage of a rich collection of Greek-based vocabulary. His code-switches seem to mock the high classes more than the low ones, since his usage resembles that found in Cicero's letters more than that of extant documentary texts.[8] He also knew that speech may vary between individuals[9] and to some extent portrayed such variation, though he did not use this method frequently (Highet 1998; Boyce 1991). I give two examples that seem to show a more subtle way of imitating an idiolect than simply morphological idiosyncrasies or code-switches.

Petronius uses the idiom *ad summam* as a concluding particle fourteen times in the text. Six of the fourteen are used by Hermeros, who speaks only six lines in the *Cena*.[10] In comparison with the distribution of this idiom elsewhere,[11] it seems that Petronius puts it into Hermeros' mouth to highlight his idiolect. It is used repeatedly in the middle of rapid and rhetorically well-arranged speech. Petronius uses short clauses, rhetorical questions and gnomic language and, in addition, characterises the type with several Greek loans (37–8, 57). These simple loans, in reality, would not show that Hermeros was bilingual, and if Petronius was trying to

---

[7] See Halla-aho 2009 for a discussion of the complexity of defining the differences between spoken and written Latin.

[8] Swain 2002: 138; Adams 2003a: 308–23, 344–7, 348–50. For inscriptions see Leiwo 2002: 173–4. For Latin letters see Halla-aho 2009; for Greek letters see Leiwo 2009.

[9] See also the characterisation in Boyce 1991: 90–4.

[10] 37.5, 37.10, 38.2, 57.3, 57.9, 58.8. Though unnamed, the speaker identified as *is ipse qui supra me discumbebat* (57.1) must be Hermeros.

[11] Encolpius: fifty-three lines, uses *ad summam* once (2.8); Servus (*qui vestimenta dispensatoris perdiderat*): one line and once (31.2); Trimalchio: sixty-two lines and three times (71.1, 75.10, 77.5); Echion *contubernalis*: one line and once (45.12); Eumolpus thirty-one lines and once (105.3); and, finally, Proselenos three lines and once (134.9).

characterise him as bilingual by means of such language he misunderstood the essence of language contacts.[12]

The idiom *ad summam* is not particularly colloquial. It was used in all registers and genres, even in philosophy (Cic. *Fin.* 4.21.60), but its origin probably was in simple totalling (*Tab. Vindol.* 11.178.7 etc., cf. Suet. *Aug.* 71), so it fits in well with the character of Hermeros the business agent (Bodel 1984: 144–5). It does not belong to archaic discourse, as it is not used in comedy, but it is found in Cicero's letters.[13] The idiom is absent from Augustan poetry apart from one example in Horace's *Epistles* (1.1.106); Seneca uses it three times in his letters to Lucilius and twice elsewhere.[14]

This overall pattern shows that this idiom was used especially in familiar registers, but that it was not socially restricted. Hermeros uses it clumsily, however, with little summing up or closing function, and one can suspect that Petronius was trying to give the impression that Hermeros repeated it nervously without real meaning. If this is so, it is a characterisation by use of idiolect, although this kind of idiolect is hardly attested in non-literary data to prove our suggestion.

When Hermeros (58.2, 58.5, 58.7), Trimalchio (74.15, 74.17, 75.10) and Scintilla (69.1) are angry and upset, they use the structure *curabo* + subjunctive (see also Highet 1998; Adams 2003c: 19). These are the only examples of this construction in Petronius, which means that he chose them intentionally. The omission of *ut* in constructions such as this one is widespread in other texts, but so is its presence;[15] it seems that the use of *ut* with *curabo*

---

[12] See Adams 2003a, Thomason 2001, and the excellent books on the effects of language contact in Carelia and Estonia (Ingria), respectively, by Sarhimaa 1999 and Riionheimo 2007. The latter is a good reason to learn Finnish. Riionheimo analyses all previous theories of language contact, and offers an excellent study of interference between morphologically complex systems of Finnish, Ingrian Finnish and Estonian.

[13] For example, Cic. *Fam.* 8.14.4, where the writer is Caelius, and *Fam.* 14.14.2, where Cicero writes to his family.

[14] In *Ep.* 102.10 it is used in direct speech: *ad summam dicite nobis utrum laudantis an laudati bonum sit: si laudati bonum esse dicitis, tam ridiculam rem facitis quam si adfirmetis meum esse quod alius bene valeat*, 'Finally, tell us whether the good belongs to him who praises, or to him who is praised: if you say that the good belongs to him who is praised, you are on as foolish a quest as if you were to maintain that my neighbour's good health is my own' (trans. Richard M. Gummere). (The other instances are 31.2 and 119.9.) The other examples from Seneca are *Dial.* 3.6.5, and *Apoc.* 11 in direct speech: *hunc nunc deum facere vultis? videte corpus eius dis iratis natum. ad summam, tria verba cito dicat, et servum me ducat. hunc deum quis colet*, 'Now do you want to make this man a god? Look at his body, born when the gods were angry. And finally, if he can say three consecutive words together, he can have me as his slave. Who will worship this god?' (trans. Allan Perley Ball).

[15] For an excellent analysis of parataxis and asyndeton see Halla-aho 2009. She suggests that the variation between *rogo* (etc.) + subjunctive and *rogo* (etc.) *ut* + subjunctive depends not on register but on syntactic contexts: the asyndetic construction as the shorter alternative was used more in contexts where the subordinate verb was close to the governing verb, and the predication was short

is common in all registers.[16] Yet Petronius uses only the variant without *ut*;[17] the examples are as follows:

(1)   curabo domata sit Cassandra caligaria.   (74.15, Trimalchio)

I'll surely tame that Cassandra in jackboots.

(2)   recte, curabo me unguibus quaeras.   (74.17, Trimalchio)

Right, then, I'll make you go for me tooth and claw.

(3)   iam curabo fatum tuum plores.   (75.10, Trimalchio)

I'll soon see that you have something to whine for.

(4)   curabo iam tibi Iovis iratus sit   (58.2, Hermeros)

I'll see to it that Jupiter falls on you.

(5)   curabo longe tibi sit comula ista besalis et dominus dupunduarius.
                                                                (58.5, Hermeros)

I'll see to it that those cheap curls of yours and your twopenny-ha'penny master don't rescue you.

(6)   Athana tibi irata sit curabo   (58.7, Hermeros)

I'll see to it that Athena bears down heavily on you.

(7)   agaga est; at curabo stigmam habeat.   (69.1, Scintilla)

He's a pimp, and he'll be branded; I'll see to that.

The topicalisation in (6) encourages the construction without *ut* by causing the subjunctive to precede *curabo*, but no such explanation is possible in the other examples, where *curabo* either begins the verbal phrase or is in the second place after the particles *recte*, *iam* and *at*. This seems to mean

and simple. In the *Mons Claudianus* Greek ostraca letters I have found strong Latin interference in the directive expressions and a lot of variation in the syntax. There is also syntactic variation that does not seem to be context-bound, which means that in non-literary material variation depends on the linguistic facilities and feelings of the letter writers (Leiwo 2009).

[16] See, for example, Pl. *Per.* 608 *curabo ut praedati pulchre ad castra convertamini*, 'I'll look out that you return to camp well laden with loot', and 610 *taceas, curabo ut voles*, 'Keep still, I'll see to it as you wish' (trans. Paul Nixon), or Cic. *Att.* 2.4.3 *magnum opus est, sed tamen, ut iubes, curabo ut huius peregrinationis aliquod tibi opus exstet*, 'It is a big piece of work: still I will do as I am told and see to it that this little tour is not entirely unproductive for you' (trans. E. O. Winstedt).

[17] There seem to be no syntactic constraints either, though the space between the governing verb and the subordinated verb is short. However, it is short in Pl. *Per.* 610 as well (see also n. 20 on *amabo*).

that for Petronius the asyndetic structure belonged more to rapid speech than the *ut* construction (cf. Labov 2001: 18–19). If indeed he was making such a distinction, it is good evidence for the subtlety of his linguistic characterisation.

The construction *curabo* + subjunctive is used in the same way demonstrating anger and threat in Sen. *Con.* 9.2(25).20 (*iratus*) and Phaed. 5.2.6 (a soldier) so we can see that Petronius had literary models. This idiom is not attested in comedy, although in both Plautus and Terence the future *curabo* is used by members of lower social groups when they agree to take care of something.[18]

This use of the first person future must come from the use of the verb *curare* to introduce clauses that indicate the intentions of the speaker, whether positive or negative, and it is used in all situations by people who are accustomed to take care of things entrusted to them: slaves, servants and soldiers. This weakened semantic value of *curabo* is attested also at the higher levels of society: Cicero uses it in his letters merely as a greeting formula meaning more or less 'I'm thinking of you and of your interests'.[19] Clearly *curare* could be used to introduce wishes or intentions, as in the ubiquitous formula *cura ut valeas* 'take care of yourself', 'farewell' and in example (4) above: *curabo, Iovis tibi iratus sit!*, 'I'll take care/take it to my heart/I wish (i.e. 'I would have it taken care of, but in reality can't do much about it') that Jupiter's anger would fall upon you.' Jupiter's anger is something one cannot procure at one's own will, so the notion of wishing is appropriate. One can, perhaps, compare this semantically weakened use of the first person future *curabo* with the *amabo* structure common in Plautus, where the first person future has been reduced to an equivalent of 'please' with questions and orders.[20]

---

[18] Of the fourteen instances of *curabo* 'I'll take care of it' in Plautus and Terence five are uttered by persons of clearly servile origin (*servus, libertus, ancilla*), eight by persons who lack authority (*matrona, parasitus, meretrix, virgo*), and finally three by senile old men, who by definition are always swindled in Roman comedy: Pl. *Am.* 949 (*Alcumena matrona*), *As.* 827 (*parasitus*), *Bac.* 227 (*Chrysalus servus*), *Bac.* 1152 (*accurabo; Soror meretrix*), *Men.* 207 (*Erotium meretrix*), *Per.* 608 and 610 (*virgo*), *Per.* 843 (*Lemniselenis meretrix*), *Ps.* 232 (*Pseudolus servus*), *Rud.* 779 (*Daemones senex*), *St.* 682 (*Stephanium ancilla*), Ter. *An.* 171 (*Sosias libertus*), *An.* 685 (*Mysis ancilla*), *Ph.* 713 (*Demipho* (*senex?*)).

[19] Cic. *Fam.* 4.13.7 *ego, quae pertinere ad te intelligam, studiosissime omnia diligentissimeque curabo*, 'On my side, I shall give the most devoted and painstaking attention to what I see is of importance to you . . .' (trans. W. Glynn Williams); cf. *Fam.* 6.4.5, 6.22.3, 10.3.4, 13.6a.5.

[20] See Adams (1984: 61–3) and below, pp. 334f. Plautus uses *amabo* seventy-seven times, of which only three take an *ut* clause. The most common constructions used are the imperative (e.g. Pl. *As.* 894 *dic amabo, an fetet anima uxoris tuae?*) and a question (e.g. Pl. *Bac.* 1121 *quid hoc est negoti nam, amabo?*).

2 FUTURE AND PRESENT

A well-known element of Petronius' language is his use of the present tense where a non-native Latin speaker would expect a future (see Petersmann 1977: 167–9). Serbat has shown that in certain contexts and text genres the 'Latinity' or correctness of these usages should not be examined by attempting to fit them into our traditional schema of tense usage, which presupposes a rigorous distinction of time between past, present and future, and then labelling the exceptions just plain errors. Drawing heavily on examples taken from Plautus, Serbat demonstrates that the Latin present tense can also be a non-temporal, unmarked form whose time value is largely defined by context and verbal semantics (Serbat 1975: 385–90). In conversation the future is often used to tell us something about the attitude of the speaker to a future state of affairs, and about his or her present intentions as regards them.

Many examples in Plautus and in the speeches of the freedmen in Petronius show that the use of the present tense where a non-native Latin user would expect a future is largely genre-related and can mostly be found in texts that are artificial imitations of speech. This is good evidence for the nature of the present and the future tense in discourse. The future has strong intentional essence (see e.g. *Tab. Vindol.* III.645.13–16), and it is also used in directive expressions, especially in military language, whereas the present is factual (see e.g. *Tab. Vindol.* III.670.i.4–5). By using these aspectual and semantic elements the writers strive to give their texts the casual informality of real conversation and to highlight their characters' motivations by means of linguistic nuances. In other words, the usage is a descriptive element of colloquial style in any register, rather than a substandard variety of Latin.

However, it has been stated (Serbat 1975: 386; Petersmann 1977: 168–9) that in main clauses (except in conditionals) the use of *praesens pro futuro* belonged to familiar and low social registers, and that Petronius put it in the mouths of his freedmen for that reason. I think rather that as a native speaker of Latin Petronius followed normal conversational practice. In some cases the present tense is pragmatically better motivated than the future, and in other cases semantic context seems to rule out the use of the future. If the temporal relations are clear to the interlocutors, the present tense also avoids redundancy (Serbat 1975: 386) and thus makes room for other linguistic information. Hints of the widespread use of the present tense instead of the future in all social levels can be found in the *Satyricon*, for even the supposedly more cultivated persons use it at least in conditional constructions (Petersmann 1977: 167–8), as does Cicero in his letters (*Att.* 10.8.5). The scarcity of appropriate works makes it difficult to study this usage in other writers, but the grammarian Sergius tells us that it was in common use among the intelligentsia of his day:

(8)   tempora tria sunt, praesens praeteritum et futurum. sed praeteriti species sunt tres, inperfecta perfecta plusquamperfecta. praesens est, cum agitur. advertamus haec: in nulla enim re sic fit soloecismus etiam a doctis. praesens est, dum agitur: ceterum si non agatur, non est praesens: non possum dicere lego, nisi dum lego, dum in ipso actu sum. ergo si mihi dicas 'lege mihi Vergilium', et dixero lego, soloecismus est. nam cum adhuc in re non sim, quo modo praesens tempus adsumo? ergo debemus dicere legam.
                        (Sergius, *Explanationes in Donatum lib.* 1: *GL* IV.2.507.37–508.4)

        There are three tenses, present, past and future. But there are three divisions of the past, imperfect, perfect and pluperfect. The present is when something is happening. Let us emphasise this, for in no (other) matter is there so much solecism even on the part of learned men. The present is while something is happening: if it is not happening, it is not present. I cannot say 'I read' except while I read, while I'm in the act itself. Therefore if you say to me 'read me some Virgil', and I respond 'I read it', it is a solecism. For when I am not yet engaged in the act, how can I use the present tense? Therefore we ought to say 'I shall read it'.

Sergius' condemnation of this usage does not show that it was characteristic of a low register or members of low social classes, since he explicitly states that this usage, unlike others that he would label as solecisms, was commonly used by learned men (whether in conversation or in writing is not clear, but it is notable that the example he gives is conversational). His condemnation seems to be founded on the illogicality of the usage given his simplistic conception of the Latin tense system.

I comment here on some examples of *praesens pro futuro* given by Petersmann (1977: 167–70):

(9)   nec sursum nec deorsum non cresco   (58.5)

        I won't swell or shrink by an inch.

This expression occurs as part of a heated threat (see example (5)) and serves to strengthen that threat. It is not at all connected to the real chain of events contained in the threat, and the present tense is not temporal (cf. Serbat 1975: 385–6). The next example belongs to the same outburst of anger, in which, it must be confessed, Hermeros' use of tenses is somewhat muddled due to his emotional state:

(10)   exi, defero lamnam.   (58.8)

         Come on, I'm putting my money down.

Hermeros is already in the act of 'placing the bets', and wants to emphasise his superiority: the act can be repeated as many times as one wishes, and he is the winner of all those challenges. In the immediately following clause (*iam scies patrem tuum mercedes perdidisse,* 'You'll soon realise that your father wasted his funds on your fees') the future is quite in place and definitely temporal. But in (10) it would really be strange. Hermeros generalises his strong position as regards his opponent and does not limit it to some particular instance in the future.

(11)   'quid dicis', inquit, 'amice carissime? aedificas monumentum meum que-
         madmodum te iussi?'   (71.5)

         'Tell me, my dearest friend, he said, will you order my tomb according
         to my instructions?'

In this case Trimalchio is addressing Habinnas, and although the events will take place in the future, there is no need to stress this, as Trimalchio is obviously not yet dead.[21] The futurity can be inferred from extralinguistic context. Furthermore, Trimalchio probably conceives the facts pertaining to his monument as generally known, and as an omnipotent master over his household and a sovereign and sometimes even tyrannical host to his guests he has no doubts that his wishes will be fulfilled. So the present tense also expresses certainty: Trimalchio has already decided these things in the present or past and considers them almost done. One can compare his comments about his will (e.g. *omnes illos in testamento meo manu mitto* 'I'll free them all in my will' (71.1, my trans.)): they are all expressed in the present tense, considered as written down and actual. To the same sphere of certainty belongs also the next example:

(12)   permittitis tamen finiri lusum.   (33.2)

         Allow me, however, to finish the game.

There can be no doubt in Trimalchio's mind that the guests will allow him to finish his game. Moreover, the game is going on as he speaks, which

---

[21] In theory it could be that the tomb is imagined as being constructed during its owner's lifetime – some funerary inscriptions record the existence of this practice with the formula *se vivo fecit* 'erected for himself while still alive' – but that would be a very forced interpretation of this particular passage.

creates a continuum between the present and the future, and it is not necessary to project the 'allowance' linguistically into the future. This is not a polite question, but a simple statement of facts by a man who has the authority to decide what happens during his own dinner party. In the absence of interrogatives or other hedging linguistic markers the present tense makes it impossible to answer 'no' to this statement.

(13)   spero tamen iam veterem pudorem sibi imponit [*sc.* venter].   (47.3)

          I now have hopes that my stomach will be regular as before.

Despite the English translation, in this loosely arranged asyndetic wish the present tense is more natural and appropriate, even if the clause seems to be a wish for a future state of being after taking some 'pomegranate-rind and pinewood dipped in vinegar'. The present refers to a chronic state affecting Trimalchio, the problems and the growling of his stomach, and he is constantly wishing it would cease. So this is a neutral wish without reference to a specific state of being in the future.

(14)   sive occidere placet, <cum> ferro meo venio, sive verberibus contenta
          es, curro nudus ad dominam.   (130.3)

          If your verdict is to be execution, I shall come to you with my sword; if
          you are satisfied with a whipping, I shall hasten to my mistress unclothed.

In this example the present tense is pragmatically better motivated than the future. Encolpius/Polyaenus wants to win over Circe's good will, and therefore assures her of the immediacy of his desires with the inchoative present tense: 'I am starting to come . . . I am (already) running'. The use of the future would have made the statement more hypothetical.

(15)   quid porro ad rem pertinet, si dixero Licham Tarentinum esse dominum
          huiusce navigii . . .?   (100.7)

          What difference does it make if I tell you that Lichas of Tarentum is
          master of the ship?

Here the reason for the use of the present tense instead of the future is the expression *pertinere ad rem*. In questions such as the above *quid porro ad rem pertinet* the interrogative main clause acts more like a modal sentence modifier revealing the attitudes of the speaker than like a real question. The answer to Encolpius' inquiry is delivered in the hypotactic conditional clause. The clause *quid ad rem pertinet . . .* , 'What does it matter . . . ', is emphatic in order to demonstrate the speaker's attitude and guide the remaining discourse to the direction that he wants. In such circumstances the present tense is more natural than the future, for if something is important, it is important regardless of temporal relations. Being of importance is here a general state of affairs, not a process that starts in the future. Therefore, the unmarked present tense conveys the sense of general applicability in the best way possible.

(16)   habeo tamen, quod caelo imputem, si nos fata coniunxerint.   (127.6)

     But if the Fates unite the two of us, I shall be in heaven's debt.

Here, in the light of Circe's denial that she is the more famous Circe, daughter of the sun, the present tense *habeo* might refer more to an inherent quality in Circe herself ('but maybe there's something divine in me') than to the events wished for in the conditional clause, and therefore the present tense would even be the more correct tense in this context (see also Rosén 1992: 110–11).

Thus it is possible to provide pragmatic and semantic explanations for the use of the present tense in all the above examples (9–16). Such explanations render explanations by social varieties unnecessary: pragmatics and genre are the factors that seem to guide Petronius in his use of the present tense, not the imitation of social dialects.

With these two different linguistic issues, the use of fairly ordinary idioms (such as *ad summam* and *curabo* + *subjunctive*) and the use of the present tense in discourse, I have tried to highlight the multiple linguistic resources that are at a good writer's disposal. Petronius skilfully used conspicuous linguistic resources like morphosyntactic variation, lexical items and simple loan words, gnomic expressions and proverbs. But he also took advantage of other, more subtle, linguistic devices, and attention to such devices can reveal aspects of language use that have nothing to do with register.

What could be done with the language of Petronius is to make an exact description of all linguistic elements in their context, keeping in mind stylistic questions as well as purely linguistic ones. Such a description would reveal a continuum that starts with colloquial elements taken from planned spoken language and ends with highly artificial written language.

CHAPTER 18

Parenthetical remarks in the Silvae

Kathleen M. Coleman

I INTRODUCTION

Most of the poems in the *Silvae* have a personal addressee, usually a senator or an equestrian; sometimes the emperor. Depending upon the status of the recipient and the relative gravity of the topic, Statius may adopt a more – or less – jocular tone. Short parenthetical remarks that are characteristic of colloquial language usually lend an air of informality when they are employed in literary works. Hence we would expect to find them in a poem such as Statius' hendecasyllables to Plotius Grypus, complaining about the unsuitable present that Statius received from him for the Saturnalia; indeed, the climax of the long list of items that Statius would have preferred to Grypus' gift contains two colloquial parentheses within a sentence of four lines (4.9.42–5):

> ollaris, rogo, non licebat uvas,
> Cumano patinas vel orbe tortas,
> aut unam dare synthesin (quid horres?)
> alborum calicum atque caccaborum?

Couldn't you, please, have sent preserved grapes, or plates turned on a Cumaean wheel, or a table-set (why are you shuddering?) of plain white mugs and dishes?

Parenthetic formulae of request (*rogo*, 42) are characteristic of colloquial speech, which favours parataxis over hypotaxis (H–S 472; Hofmann 1951: 129–30, 199). The parenthesis anticipating the interlocutor's reaction (*quid horres?*, 43) is a feature commonly displayed in an informal context, such as Cicero's letters to Atticus (Hofmann 1951: 116): cf. Cic. *Att.* 3.25 *neque enim – sed bonam in partem accipies – si ulla spes salutis nostrae subesset, tu pro tuo amore in me hoc tempore discessisses*, 'And indeed (you won't take this amiss), if there were any lingering hope of my restoration, caring for me as you do you would not have left Rome at this time.'[1]

The ancient rhetoricians recognised parenthesis as a figure, and gave it a name (Schwyzer 1939: 4–8; Lausberg 1998: §860). Quintilian supplies a definition and an example (*Inst.* 9.3.23, quoting Cic. *Mil.* 94):

> unum [*sc.* schema] quod interpositionem vel interclusionem dicimus, Graeci παρένθεσιν sive παρέμπτωσιν vocant, cum continuationi sermonis medius aliqui sensus intervenit: 'ego cum te (mecum enim saepissime loquitur) patriae reddidissem.'

> What we call *interpositio* or *interclusio*, and the Greeks *parenthesis* or *paremptosis*, namely the insertion of a phrase in the middle of a continuous utterance: 'when I restored you (for he very often talks with me) to your country'.

The explanatory aside, sustaining the impression of viva voce communication with an audience, is characteristic of oratory (Roschatt 1884: 240–4), and is frequently flagged with a causal connective (Roschatt 1883: 22–4 = 1884: 208–10).[2] Indeed, the purpose of parenthesis is very often explanatory or justificatory, so that the connectives *nam* and *enim*, frequently found in parentheses in colloquial speech (Hofmann 1951: 117), are underlined in the examples that follow, to signal this function. In Quintilian's Ciceronian example, quoted above, the explanatory aside introduced by *enim* contributes something of an air of confidentiality, and maps the orator's train of thought in a manner that reflects the twists and turns of everyday speech. Such an effect is 'informal', hence 'colloquial'.[3]

The tonal range of parenthesis is wide, and adds considerably to the atmosphere and character of the *Silvae*. The dialogue of comedy, and the one-sided dialogue of intimate letters (such as Cicero's to Atticus),[4] are characterised by looseness of syntax and studded with colloquial parentheses; Donatus' remarks on the parenthetic exclamations, interjections and exhortations of comedy have already been mentioned (Ferri and Probert, this volume p. 37). Parenthesis may occur also in the more elevated genres

---

[1] Trans. D. R. Shackleton Bailey. Translations from the *Silvae* are adopted, where appropriate, from K. Coleman 1988, Shackleton Bailey 2003, and Gibson 2006; light adaptations include, where necessary, the insertion of punctuation to mark the parentheses. For the *Thebaid* I use the powerful verse rendering by Melville 1992, and for Quintilian, *Institutio Oratoria*, Russell 2001.

[2] Roschatt published two studies under the same title: his dissertation (Roschatt 1883) was reprinted the following year as the first half of a more comprehensive article (Roschatt 1884: 189–219).

[3] For the antithesis between formal and colloquial see Clackson, this volume pp. 7–11.

[4] Demetrius, *On Style* 223 δεῖ ... εἶναι γὰρ τὴν ἐπιστολὴν οἷον τὸ ἕτερον μέρος τοῦ διαλόγου, 'a letter may be regarded as one of the two sides in a dialogue'.

of both prose and verse.[5] The historians use it in a variety of ways. Some
of these can be illustrated from *Annals* 3, on which a pair of recent commentators have contributed illuminating remarks (Woodman and Martin
1996): Tacitus frequently uses parenthesis for subjective authorial comment to separate two narratives (*Ann.* 3.16.1), or to introduce background
material (*Ann.* 3.56.2) or additional evidence (*Ann.* 3.66.2–4) or a more
loosely related digression (*Ann.* 3.24.1). The effect is that the authorial
voice becomes more audible, since the parenthetic mode draws attention
to the intervention by the architect of the discourse. The explanatory
parenthesis that supplies background detail, common in oratory (Roschatt
1884: 238), can be employed to illustrate the omniscience of the narrator;
this is closely related to the way in which Callimachus, in the *Hymns*
and *Aetia*, uses parentheses as a vehicle for a display of arcane knowledge – what one might term the 'learned footnote' style. This mannerism,
taken over by Virgil and Ovid, is also in evidence in the *Silvae*, and
must therefore be distinguished from more obviously colloquial parentheses, which tend to be shorter and more 'chatty'; such parentheses are also
employed by Callimachus, but in the *Iambi* and the *Epigrams* (Tarrant 1998:
143).

Statius remarks of two of the poems in the *Silvae* – on the oddly shaped
tree on Atedius Melior's estate on the Caelian Hill (2.3), and on the demise
of Melior's parrot (2.4) – that they were composed *quasi epigrammatis
loco*, and he goes on to include in the same category the subsequent poem
(2.5), on the death of Domitian's favourite lion (2 *praef.* 14–18). But the
stylistic register of the *Silvae* is far different from that of epigram, being
characterised by elaborate hyperbaton, extensive mythological embroidery
and bold paradox. Both the terms 'mannered' and 'baroque' have been
applied to it. Splashes of colour from the colloquial register are all the
more striking against this background, lending a flash of intimacy to the
client-poet's habitually deferential stance – a stance that is, in any case,
adapted according to metre and genre, so that the jocular hendecasyllables
to Plotius Grypus (which demonstrate other colloquial features too),[6] or

---

[5] General treatments of parenthesis in Greek and Latin: Boldt 1884: 159–79, Schwyzer 1939, Marouzeau
1954: 242–5; in colloquial Latin: Hofmann 1951 (cf. Hofmann–Ricottilli, with Ricottilli's addition at
378 n. 1 on §106); in Cicero's letters: Bolkestein 1998; in the orators: Grünewald 1912, Roschatt 1884;
in the historians: Schmitt 1913, Comber 1976; in Callimachus: Lapp 1965: 52–3; in Catullus, Virgil,
and other Augustan poets: G. Williams 1968: 711–72, Tarrant 1998; in Ovid: Albrecht 1964, Kenney
1970.

[6] E.g. 4.9.9 (Statius' gift of his *libellus*) *praeter me mihi constitit decussis*, 'cost me (apart from my
personal contribution) ten *asses*': 'the elliptical use of the pronoun instead of noun and possessive
adjective sounds colloquial' (K. Coleman 1988: 226).

the verse letter composed to Vitorius Marcellus (4.4), are natural hosts for parenthetical remarks that might be less readily accommodated in some of the more formal tributes to other patrons, even though Statius himself in his prefaces stresses the extempore nature of the original compositions, delivered viva voce on the occasions being celebrated.

The sense of immediate verbal delivery in the *Silvae* is heightened by the use of mythological spokespersons, whom Statius introduces to enhance the discourse with an atmosphere of charm or whimsy, and who are often responsible for conveying extravagant compliments to the addressee that might sound patently false if Statius were to voice them *in propria persona* (K. Coleman 1999). Being quoted in *oratio recta*, such speeches might be expected to accommodate colloquialism, depending upon the register being adopted and the relative status of spokesperson and addressee, and to contribute thereby to the characterisation; yet, parentheses occur in slightly fewer than half the speeches in the *Silvae*.[7] This distribution suggests that they are used for artistic purposes, to characterise the speech of chosen individuals, rather than as a standard ingredient of the spoken register, thereby guaranteeing that their contribution to the characterisation will be all the more subtle and striking.

It is not, however, always obvious what constitutes a parenthesis, especially in a text as corrupt as the *Silvae*. If it is an utterance syntactically independent of its surroundings, then a parenthesis may either be a phrase or clause inserted within a sentence; or it may be an independent sentence, or series of sentences, interrupting the sequence of thought within a larger narrative.[8] Even when the text is not in dispute, it is frequently difficult to decide whether or not a particular subordinate clause or independent sentence constitutes a parenthesis; and since systems of punctuation that make the interpretation clear are a modern invention, an inventory of instances inevitably involves value-judgements. Parenthetical insertions sometimes confused scribes, so that a corruption may hide an original parenthesis;[9]

---

[7] Parentheses occur in the speeches of Eros to Venus (1.2.65–102), Venus to Eros (1.2.106–39), Venus to Violentilla (1.2.162–93), Apollo to Asclepius (1.4.61–105), Calliope to Lucan (2.7.41–104), Volturnus to Domitian (4.3.72–94), the Sibyl's prophecy (4.3.124–63), and the Scotsman to Crispinus (5.2.144–9). They are absent from the speeches of Curtius to Domitian (1.1.74–83), Diana to her nymphs (2.3.24–6), Pan to Melior's tree (2.3.43–52), Hercules to Pollius (3.1.91–116 and 166–83), Claudius Etruscus to his father (3.3.182–204), Venus to Earinus (3.4.32–45), Eros to Earinus (3.4.95–7), Earinus to Asclepius (3.4.100–5), Janus to Domitian (4.1.17–43), Priscilla to Abascantus (5.1.177–93).

[8] The flexibility of Latin word order accommodates parentheses that frequently cannot be rendered parenthetically in English translation.

[9] Goodyear 1982: 11 = K. Coleman *et al.* 1992: 221 (on Justin 17.3.6).

but such instances, being predicated on an ellipse of logical connection, make it very hard to recover the text with much optimism.[10] Conversely, an easy emendation may be preferable to forcing a parenthesis out of the paradosis.[11] The Appendix lists the parentheses that it is possible to identify with some confidence; in the discussion below, rather than treat every instance in detail, I shall first identify various sorts of expression – usually brief – that commonly occur parenthetically, and then discuss the types of effect for which longer parentheses are habitually employed in the collection.

2 COMMON TYPES OF PARENTHESIS

In addition to formulae of request and parentheses anticipating the addressee's reaction (mentioned in section 1), the *Silvae* are distinguished by exclamations, exhortations and expressions of credulity and sufficiency (and their opposites), which contribute a sense of lively dialogue and engagement, even while their diction usually reflects the ornate poetic register that typifies the collection.

2.1 Exclamations

The narrator's sympathy, horror, outrage and other reactions are often signalled by a parenthetical exclamation. As one might expect in a collection dominated by *epicedia* and commemoration of the deceased, *heu* occurs frequently, sometimes in first position in its colon, but never postponed further than second position.[12] The reiteration of the previous word after *heu* (*Silv.* 5.5.33–4 *iuvat heu, iuvat inlaudabile carmen | fundere*, 'It helps, alas, it helps to pour out a song that is not to be praised') is an epic mannerism (V. Fl. 3.272, Sil. 5.154) employed once by Martial for an exaggerated show of distress after a jaunty and colloquial opening addressed

---

[10] For a warning against forcing a parenthesis out of a corrupt passage see Goodyear 1969: 20 = K. Coleman *et al.* 1992: 89–90 (on Corippus, *Iohannis* 7.508–9).

[11] E.g. 1.4.63–4 *teneamus adorti | tendentes* (Markland: *tendatis* M) *iam fila colos*, 'Let us go and grasp the distaff as it stretches the threads', where Vollmer (1898) prints *teneamus adorti | (tendatis iam fila!) colos*. Another instance occurs at 2.7.116–19, where a four-line parenthesis addressed to Lucan in the middle of a request to him to be present, no matter where he is now, was eliminated by Heinsius' substitution of *seu* for *tu* at line 116, so that three alternative locations for Lucan's soul are described, instead of only two (107 *seu*, 111 *seu*, 116 *seu*); the parenthesis is preferred, however, by Courtney 1990.

[12] First position: 2.1.50, 3.3.176, 5.1.165, 5.3.217. Second position: 1.4.60, 2.1.26–8, 2.7.24, 4.7.35–6, 5.5.33, 5.5.62.

to his book (1.3.3):[13] *nescis, heu, nescis dominae fastidia Romae*, 'Ah, little, little do you know the haughty ways of Lady Rome.' In one instance in the *Silvae*, *heu* is combined with another distressed exclamation, *pudet*, to underline the disgrace of an (hypothetical) heir wishing for the testator's demise (4.7.35–6): *optimo poscens (pudet heu) propinquum | funus amico* 'demanding for his admirable friend – shame on him! – that death will come soon'. This combination, in either order, is attested exclusively in poetry, in its higher registers,[14] with three exceptions: Mart. 2.18.1, another instance lamenting the practice of *captatio* (although this time the parasite, who is the speaker himself, is cadging not an inheritance but a meal), Mart. 14.101.2, where the 'speaker' is a *boletar*, a serving-dish for mushrooms, and Petr. 119.19, where the effect is bombastic; clearly it is the grand style that Martial and Petronius are mocking.

Parenthetical *pudet*, without *heu*, conveys the embarrassment of the rivergod representing the Volturnus, who delivers a speech of gratitude to Domitian for having tamed the river's former torrent by bridging it with the Via Domitiana (*Silv.* 4.3.79–80):

> qui terras rapere et rotare silvas
> assueram (pudet!), amnis esse coepi.

I who (shame on me!) used to snatch up the lands and whirl away forests have begun to be a river.

The same gesture of the admission – or accusation – of guilt is conveyed by the absolute use of *pudet* in a parenthesis three times in the *Thebaid*, each in a speech delivered at a moment of high dramatic tension. Hippomedon, drowning in the river Ismenus, shouts at Mars (9.506–7): *fluvione (pudet!), Mars inclite, mergis | hanc animam?*, 'Shame, great Mars! Will you | Drown my soul in a river?'; Apollo expostulates to Diana at the death of Teiresias (9.653–5): *en ipse mei (pudet!) inritus arma | cultoris frondesque sacras ad inania vidi | Tartara et in memet versos descendere vultus*, 'I too – for shame! – saw powerless | My prophet with his arms and wreath of bay, | Turning his eyes to me, go down to Hell'; Creon rages at Eteocles' cowardice (11.283–4): *at tu (pudet!), hostia regni, | hostia, nate, iaces*, 'But you, my son, lie scapegoat – yes, for shame! – | The scapegoat of the realm.' The material in the archive of the *Thesaurus Linguae Latinae* yields only four precedents, all of them contributing a markedly subjective gloss on the narrative: Ov. *Met.* 14.278–9 (Macareus, describing Circe's transformation

[13] *TLL* vi/2.2673.37–8 (Rubenbauer); Citroni 1975: 25.
[14] *TLL* vi/2.2673. 45–8 (Rubenbauer); Hofmann 1951: 14.

of Ulysses' men into swine) *et tetigit summos virga dea dira capillos,* | – *et pudet et referam – saetis horrescere coepi,* 'and the goddess grazed the tops of our heads with her grim wand – I am ashamed to describe it, but describe it I will – and I began to grow rough with bristles', *Pont.* 1.8.45–6 (the poet reminisces about the *horti* he used to tend) *quibus ipse solebam* | *ad sata fontanas, nec pudet, addere aquas,* 'where I in person – I'm not ashamed to admit it – used to carry the spring water to the plants', Sen. *Thy.* 90–3 (the ghost of Tantalus, to Jupiter) *magne divorum parens* | *nosterque (quamvis pudeat), ingenti licet* | *taxata poena lingua crucietur loquax,* | *nec hoc tacebo,* 'Mighty parent of gods, and my parent too (however much this may shame you), even though my prattling tongue be condemned to punishment and torture, I shall not keep quiet about this', [Sen.] *Her. O.* 1266–8 (Hercules, astonished at his own tears) *invictus olim voltus et numquam malis* | *lacrimas suis praebere consuetus (pudet)* | *iam flere didicit,* 'My face, once immoveable and accustomed never to react to its own misfortune with tears, has now learnt (how shameful!) to weep.'[15]

Nefas, first employed parenthetically in a literary work by Catullus (68b.89 *Troia (nefas!) commune sepulcrum Asiae Europaeque,* 'Troy – horror! – the mutual tomb of Asia and Europe') is an indignant exclamation that signals involved reaction (Tarrant 1998: 150); as such, it is not a colloquialism but a mark of high style (Hofmann 1951: 198). It is used three times in the *Aeneid* (7.73, 8.688, 10.673), and it becomes a favoured parenthesis in Statius, occurring four times in the *Thebaid* (3.54, 4.193, 11.360, 12.83), once in the *Achilleid* (1.133) and three times in the *Silvae* (van Dam 1984: 395): cf. *Silv.* 2.6.2–3 (to Flavius Ursus, on the death of his *puer delicatus,* Philetos) *miserum est primaeva parenti* | *pignora surgentesque (nefas!) accendere natos,* 'Sad it is for parents to put fire to young children and (outrage!) growing sons', 5.3.8–9 (Statius' reaction upon his father's death) *funestamque hederis inrepere taxum* | *sustinui trepidamque (nefas!) arescere laurum,* 'and I have allowed the fatal yew to creep over the ivy and the trembling laurel to wither, an unspeakable thing!' In the mouth of Calliope, addressing the dead Lucan on the occasion of his birthday, the third instance of parenthetic *nefas* is particularly significant, illustrating her emotions getting the better of her discourse towards the end of her speech, since it is matched in the concluding line by another parenthesis, even more emphatic, combined with anaphora and a repeated exclamatory *o* (2.7.100–4):

---

[15] I am grateful to Dr Hugo Beikircher, Generalredaktor of the *Thesaurus Linguae Latinae,* for collating parenthetical instances of *pudet* in the Thesaurusarchiv for me.

sic et tu (rabidi nefas tyranni)
iussus praecipitem subire Lethen,
dum pugnas canis arduaque voce
das solacia grandibus sepulchris,
(o dirum scelus, o scelus!) tacebis.

And so even you (outrage of a crazy tyrant!), bidden plunge into Lethe as you sang of battles and with lofty utterance gave solace to grand sepulchres (O foul crime, O crime!), shall be silent.

Exclamatory parentheses involving phrases construed with a relative or interrogative pronoun convey heightened emotion: excitement or, more usually, grief. Cf. 1.6.60–1 (an exhibition of dwarves fighting as dinner-entertainment in the Colosseum) *edunt vulnera conseruntque dextras | et mortem sibi (qua manu!) minantur*, 'They deal wounds and mingle fists and threaten one another with death – by what hands!', 2.1.33–4 (among the credentials that Statius offers for the privilege of mourning Melior's *puer delicatus* with him is his experience in mourning his own father) *cum proprios gemerem defectus ad ignes | (quem, Natura!)*[16] *patrem*, 'when at fires of my own I lamented (whom, Nature?) my own father', a parenthesis famously described by Politian as 'quasi singultu impeditus', 3.5.49 (Laodamia, whose grief at Protesilaus' death drove her mad) *et quam (quam saevi!) fecerunt maenada planctus*, 'and she whom lamentation (how cruel!) made Maenad',[17] 5.5.38 (Statius, who had so often comforted bereaved parents, has now lost his own adoptive child) *ille ego qui (quotiens!) blande matrumque patrumque | vulnera, qui vivos potui mulcere dolores*, 'I am that man who (so many times!) could gently soothe the wounds of fathers and mothers, who could soothe living grief'.[18] The parentheses punctuate the train of thought to convey urgency of emotion and empathy with the addressee.

---

[16] This punctuation, proposed by Gronovius in 1653, conveys the close relationship between the deceased and the bereaved that is implied whenever Statius invokes Natura in a funerary context (Håkanson 1969: 49), and is therefore preferable to the alternative interpretation, whereby *quem* is taken as the equivalent of *qualem*, and the phrase is punctuated *quem, Natura, patrem!*, i.e. 'when at fires of my own I lamented fainting (O Nature!) what a father' (Shackleton Bailey 2003: 105). But the translation normally offered (e.g. by Håkanson, and by van Dam 1984: 90), 'whom, o Nature! my own father', is meaningless, and it is necessary to take *quem* as an exclamatory interrogative.

[17] For *quam saevi* Cruceus proposed *tam saevi*; but the ugly *cacemphaton* (Lausberg 1998: §964) that is created by the repetition of *quam* suits the horrid topic.

[18] As observed by Gibson 2006: 410, 'there is no need to emend to *totiens*; the parenthesis adds to the intensity of Statius' lament'.

2.2 Exhortations

A ritual injunction to fling open the doors, *Pande fores*, opens *Silv.* 4.8, celebrating the birth of a child to Julius Menecrates, son-in-law of Statius' wealthy Neapolitan patron, Pollius Felix. But the same phrase occurs in parenthesis in the *epithalamium* for L. Arruntius Stella and his bride, Violentilla (1.2.16–17): *nosco diem causasque sacri: te concinit iste | (pande fores), te, Stella, chorus*, 'I learn the day and the reason for the ceremony. It is you, Stella, you that choir (fling wide the gates!) is singing.' Here the parenthetic expression of the injunction conveys excitement and anticipation, rather than a casual aside.

2.3 Expressions of credulity and sufficiency

Parenthetic expressions of credulity and sufficiency, or their opposites, are a colloquial feature well attested in oratory to create suspense before a particularly extravagant claim or striking revelation (Roschatt 1884: 232) and widely exploited by Ovid as a vehicle for conveying subjective comment, especially in the miraculous context of metamorphosis (Albrecht 1964: 74). Statius expresses breathless wonder at the tranquil passage of the hitherto tempestuous river Anio, as it flows through Manilius Vopiscus' estate (1.3.20–2):

> ipse Anien (miranda fides!) infraque superque
> saxeus, hic tumidam rabiem spumosaque ponit
> murmura . . .

Anio himself (wondrous to tell!), full of rocks above and below, here rests his swollen rage and foamy din . . .

In the *epicedion* for Claudius Etruscus on the death of his father, Statius comments on the paradox that a son thinks his father's life too short (3.3.20–1):

> . . . celeres genitoris filius annos
> (mira fides!) nigrasque putat properasse Sorores.

A son thinks his father's years too swift (wonderful but true!), thinks the dark Sisters went too fast!

Such expressions of credulity (or incredulity) can take the form of a parenthetical question, 'who would believe/doubt/deny?', usually inserted before the remarkable claim is made, to create suspense: cf. Ov. *Met.* 6.193–4 (Niobe) *sum felix (quis enim neget hoc?) felixque manebo | (hoc quoque quis dubitet?): tutam me copia fecit,* 'I am lucky (who would deny it?) and I'll remain lucky (who would hesitate at this too?): plenty has made me safe', 7.690 (Cephalus) *hoc me, nate dea (quis possit credere?), telum | flere facit,* 'This weapon, son of a goddess (who could believe it?), made me weep.' Such is Statius' excited outburst to Domitian at the start of his *soteria* on the recovery of Rutilius Gallicus from illness (1.4.4–6):

> es caelo, dis es, Germanice, cordi
> (quis neget?): erubuit tanto spoliare ministro
> imperium Fortuna tuum.

Heaven and the gods love you, Germanicus (who would deny it?): Fortune blushed to strip your Empire of such a worthy servant.

Also Ovidian, although sparingly employed in his work, are parenthetic expressions of sufficiency employing the nuclear phrase *satis est*, sometimes in an expanded form: cf. *Met.* 6.502–3 (Pandion to Philomela) *tu quoque quam primum (satis est procul esse sororem), | si pietas ulla est, ad me, Philomela, redito,* 'You too (it is enough that your sister is far away), if you have any respect for me, come back to me as soon as possible', *Am.* 2.1.11–12 (concerning Ovid's successful start at epic, and noteworthy for the parenthetic *memini* in the preceding line) *ausus eram, memini, caelestia dicere bella | centimanumque Gygen (et satis oris erat),* 'I dared, I remember (and my eloquence was sufficient), to tell of the wars in heaven and Gyges of the hundred hands', 3.8.59–60 (usurped in his beloved's affection by a soldier) *tantum ne nostros avidi liceantur amores | et (satis est) aliquid pauperis esse sinant* 'only let them not, in their greed, bid on our loves and (it is enough) let them allow the poor man something'. Distinctly colloquial is Venus' aside to Eros, describing the lengths to which she has gone to supply Violentilla with appropriate jewellery (*Silv.* 1.2.127–9):

> huic Hermum fulvoque Tagum decurrere limo
> (nec satis ad cultus), huic Inda monilia Glaucum
> Proteaque atque omnem Nereida quaerere iussi.

For her I have bidden Hermus and Tagus flow with tawny mud (there's not enough for her adornment), for her Glaucus and Proteus and every Nereid must search for necklaces of Ind.

There is a similar ring to Statius' claim that there is no need to trouble Apollo for the explanation of the curious growth-habit of the tree on Melior's estate, since it is enough if the Naiads and the fauns inspire his poem (2.3.6–7):

> ... vos dicite causas,
> Naides et faciles (satis est) date carmina, Fauni.

Naiads, you tell the tale and you, obliging Fauns (no more is needed), give me my poem.

These parenthetic claims of sufficiency, or the lack of it, help with the punctuation at the end of the poem to Sleep, where Statius, desperately insomniac, asks merely that the god graze him with the tip of his wand; here the colloquial tone of the parenthesis in the final line is matched by that of the preceding lines, where Statius self-deprecatingly abjures the full embrace of the god, allowing that it be reserved to others (5.4.16–19):

> ... nec te totas infundere pennas
> luminibus compello meis (hoc turba precatur
> laetior); extremo me tange cacumine virga
> (sufficit), aut leviter suspenso poplite transi.

And I do not ask you to pour all your feathers over my eyes (a happier crowd prays for this); touch me with the extreme tip of your wand (it is enough), or pass by gently with lifted knees.

3 PARENTHETICAL EFFECTS

Longer parentheses, or clusters of shorter ones, sometimes contribute a very distinctive atmosphere. I shall discuss these effects in four categories: characterisation, subjectivity, the 'learned footnote', and picking up the threads (resumptive iteration).

3.1 Characterisation

Because parenthesis is employed sparingly in the speeches delivered by the spokespersons in the *Silvae*, when it occurs it contributes to the characterisation of the speakers and, being in direct speech, conveys a colloquial tone.[19] Eros uses parenthesis three times in a speech of thirty-eight lines to his mother, prevailing on her to persuade Violentilla to accept Stella's suit (1.2.65–102). His parentheses are tactful asides pointing out to Venus that, in making Stella and Violentilla fall in love with each other, he has been carrying out her wishes (74–5, 79–80):

---

[19] In speaking of the use of parenthesis in the Augustan poets, Tarrant (1998: 153) explicitly avoids the term 'characterisation', preferring to describe its contribution to the '*ethos* of a speaker or participants in a dialogue'. Its role as a tool of characterisation seems more overt in the *Silvae*.

hunc egomet tota quondam (tibi dulce)²⁰ pharetra
improbus et densa trepidantem cuspide fixi.
. . .

ast illam summa leviter (sic namque iubebas)
lampade parcentes et inerti strinximus arcu.

Him I once pierced with all my quiver – it was your pleasure – as he trembled in
a hail of darts, no mercy. . . As for her, I lightly grazed her with the tip of my
brand – for such was your command – and a flaccid bow.

At the climax of the speech, a third parenthesis employs exclamatory *pro!*
(untranslatable in English) to add emphasis to the further exclamation that
follows, in which Eros again flatters his mother by alluding to her power
(1.2.101–2):²¹

> . . . pro! quanta est Paphii reverentia, mater,
> numinis! hic nostrae deflevit fata columbae.

How he reveres Paphos' deity, mother! He bewailed our dove's demise.

The same parenthetic exclamation, followed by an exclamatory statement
of the power of the goddess, is addressed by Galatea to Venus in the
Metamorphoses, a passage to which Statius must surely allude (Ov. *Met.*
13.758–9): *pro! quanta potentia regni* | *est, Venus alma, tui!*, 'How mighty
is your power, dear Venus!' In Eros' speech, this exclamation, and the
two preceding parentheses, are the tactics of a wheedling child, subtly
manipulating his mother's vanity to ensure that he gets his way.

Parentheses contribute significantly to the characterisation in other
speeches too. Apollo, inviting Asclepius to join him in curing Rutilius
Gallicus' illness (1.4.61–105), employs two parentheses that support the
impression of him as a verbose and somewhat self-important deity. In
the first instance, instead of postulating a parenthesis, it is arguable that
the phrase can be construed in apposition to the indirect statement that
forms the subject of the verb; but a parenthesis would be an early signal
of Apollo's wordy and inflated style later on (1.4.62–3): *datur (aggredienda
facultas)* | *ingentem recreare virum*, 'The chance is offered, one to be seized,
to restore a man of mighty mould.' In the god's subsequent résumé of Gallicus' career, the reference to Gallicus' campaign in Galatia is so phrased as
to give the initiative to the Galatians, in order to tuck in a parenthetical

²⁰ The parenthesis *tibi dulce* has a parallel at *Theb.* 7.236 *ita dulce Iovi*, glossing the mustering of the
forces of Aonia, Euboea and Phocis by Mars.
²¹ *TLL* x/2.1440.14–26 (Ramminger).

reference to the attack on Delphi by the Gauls in 279 BC, which Apollo conceives as a personal assault (1.4.76–7): *hunc Galatea vigens ausa est incessere bello | (me quoque!)*, 'Lusty Galatia dared assail him in war (me too).' The colloquial overtones of the parenthesis nicely capture the frank atmosphere of a god-to-god conversation.

In addition to the parenthetic exclamation *pudet!*, discussed in section 2.1, the speech delivered by the river Volturnus contains a parenthesis comparing the river's former silted state with the sluggish river Bagradas in North Africa, to be capped by the claim that, in its newly enlarged bed, its sparkle and tranquillity will challenge the river Liris and the sea (4.3.88–94):

> ne me pulvereum gravemque caeno
> Tyrrheni sinus obluat profundi
> (qualis Cinyphios tacente ripa   90
> Poenus Bagrada serpit inter agros),
> sed talis ferar ut nitente cursu
> tranquillum mare proximumque possim
> puro gurgite provocare Lirim.

so that the bay of the Tyrrhenian deep does not wash against me in a dirty state and laden with mud (like the Punic Bagradas snaking with its silent stream among the Cinyphian fields), but such shall I flow that with my sparkling current I can challenge the calm sea and my neighbour the Liris with my pure flood.

This parenthesis, demonstrating geographical knowledge, verges on the 'learned footnote' variety, discussed in section 3.3, except that the purpose of the 'learned footnote' is to embellish the narrative with the learning of the author *in propria persona*, and the references are usually more allusive and amount to a definable excursus. Here, the parenthesis, too pointed to qualify as an excursus, seems above all to fit the *persona* of the boisterous young rivergod who, like all teenagers, is obsessed with comparing himself to his peers. His 'learning' is restricted to identifying his rivals: the river Bagradas flows near Carthage; the river Cinyps flows between the Syrtes, and the adjective *Cinyphius* is used as the equivalent of *Libycus*.[22] It is a nice touch that Volturnus disposes of the unfavourable comparison in an aside, whereas his claim to outdo worthy rivals occupies the main clause at the climax of his speech.

Finally, a corrupt passage has been construed so as to put parenthetical remarks into the mouth of a mortal, the Scotsman who is envisaged

---

[22] For these details, and the transposition of the case-endings in the manuscript (*Cinyphius . . . Poenos*), see K. Coleman 1988: 126.

lecturing Statius' young addressee, Crispinus, on the exploits of his father, Vettius Bolanus, in Caledonia (5.2.144–9):

> hic suetus dare iura parens, hoc caespite turmas
> adfari victor; speculas (*Davies*: vitae specula *M*) castellaque longe   145
> (aspicis?) ille dedit, cinxitque haec moenia fossa;
> belligeris haec dona deis, haec tela dicavit
> (cernis adhuc titulos); hunc ipse vocantibus armis
> induit, hunc regi rapuit thoraca Britanno.

Here your father was accustomed to give laws, on this turf he addressed the squadrons in victory; he provided lookouts and forts far and wide (do you see them?), and surrounded these walls with a ditch; these are the gifts, these are the weapons he dedicated to the gods of war (you still see the inscriptions); this breastplate he himself put on when arms were summoning him, this one he seized from the British king.

The classroom style is neatly conveyed by the parenthetical query ('are you paying attention?') and the gesture drawing attention to the evidence ('you can still see the traces').

3.2 *Subjectivity*

3.2.1 *Authorial comment*

A parenthesis is frequently used to convey an authorial comment on the narrative, contributing a subjective point of view. Virgil was the first author to use this technique to create a sense of empathy with the characters in the text (Tarrant 1998: 152). Sometimes this takes the form of reporting the reaction of the authorial persona, as when Statius, attempting to comfort Flavius Ursus, laments that he helped set fire to Philetus' pyre (2.6.14–15):

> . . . hominem gemis (ei mihi, subdo
> ipse faces), hominem, Vrse, tuum

You mourn a human being (woe is me! I myself kindle the torch), *your* human being, Ursus.

At other times, the authorial persona explains – and, by implication, sympathises with – the actions of the participants within the narrative, as in Statius' description of the embalming of Priscilla, whose widower, he says, could not stand the smoke and noise of the pyre (5.1.225–8):

> hic te Sidonio velatam molliter ostro
> eximius coniunx (nec <u>enim</u> fumantia busta
> clamoremque rogi potuit perferre) beato
> composuit, Priscilla, tholo.

Here, Priscilla, your outstanding husband, covering you softly in Sidonian purple (for he could not endure the smoking pyre and the ritual cries), set you to rest in a blessed dome.

This type of parenthesis gains extra subtlety when the authorial persona is the same as the participant in the narrative, as with the *epicedion* on Statius' father's death, where the poet imagines the onlookers observing his grief – including his mother, who sees her own example emulated in his behaviour (5.3.262–4):[23]

> quos ego tunc gemitus (comitum manus anxia vidit,
> vidit et exemplum genetrix gavisaque novit),
> quae lamenta tuli!

What groanings then (an anxious band of companions saw me, my mother saw me too and recognised her example with joy), what laments I uttered!

3.2.2 Licentia

Sometimes in the parenthesis the authorial persona employs the rhetorical motif of an appeal for *licentia* or, in Greek, παρρησία (*Rhet. Her.* 4.48, Quint. *Inst.* 9.2.27–9), apologising for an exaggeration or other audacious poetic claim (Laguna 1992: 205). This is to be distinguished from comparable liturgical language anticipating a charge of impiety (3.2.13–16):

> vos quoque, caeruleum Phorci, Nereides, agmen,
> quis honor et regni cessit fortuna secundi,
> dicere quae magni fas sit mihi sidera ponti,
> surgite de vitreis spumosae Doridos antris

You too, Nereids, cerulean host of Phorcus, to whom has fallen the honour and fortune of the second realm (give me leave to call you stars of the great ocean), arise from foamy Doris' glassy grottoes.

Statius uses the parenthetical motif of an appeal for *licentia* twice. In the climax to his description of Claudius Etruscus' baths, in words reminiscent of Cyane's apology at Ov. *Met.* 5.416–17, *si componere magnis | parva mihi fas est*, 'if I am allowed to compare the small with the great' (Albrecht 1964: 212), he apologises for introducing a comparison with Domitian's villa at Baiae (1.5.60–2):

> nec si Baianis veniat novus hospes ab oris
> talia despiciet (fas sit componere magnis
> parva)

Were a stranger to come from Baiae's shores, he would not scorn the like of this (lawful be it to compare great with small).

[23] As noted by Gibson 2006: 364, 'it is on this antithesis that the parenthesis depends'.

The same apology for comparing the inferior with the superior is likewise expressed by a parenthetical motif of *licentia* in the *epicedion* addressed to Claudius Etruscus, asking permission to compare the deceased with Hercules and Apollo (3.3.56–8):[24]

> et (modo si fas est aequare iacentia summis)
> pertulit et saevi Tirynthius horrida regis
> pacta, nec erubuit famulantis fistula Phoebi.

and (if only it be lawful to compare the lowly with the highest) the Tirynthian bore the harsh convenant of a cruel king and Phoebus' flute did not blush when he obeyed a master.

A comparable parenthesis, in the context of the (questionable) legitimacy of a request, occurs in Cicero's letter to Lucceius about the commemoration of his consulship, a letter in which Cicero adopts, at times, an insistently conversational tone (*Fam.* 5.12.8):

quod si a te non impetro, hoc est, si quae te res impedierit (neque <u>enim</u> fas esse arbitror quicquam me rogantem abs te non impetrare), cogar fortasse facere quod non nulli saepe reprehendunt

Suppose, however, I am refused; that is to say, suppose something hinders you (for I feel it would be against nature for you to *refuse* any request of mine), I shall perhaps be driven to a course often censured by some.[25]

The effect of these parenthetical claims to *licentia* is deprecating and polite, a conversational strategy for (usually) flattering the addressee.

3.2.3 Sententiae

In commenting on the narrative, the authorial persona sometimes expresses a comforting truism or proverbial belief in a parenthetical aside that smacks of the colloquial register. Ovid does this (with his tongue in his cheek) when he invites his mistress to attack him, in revenge for his having attacked her (*Am.* 1.7.63–4):

> at tu ne dubita (minuet vindicta dolorem)
> protinus in voltus unguibus ire meos

But you shouldn't hesitate (vengeance will diminish grief) to have a go at my face with your nails right away.

---

[24] For the alternative identification, whereby the comparison is between Admetus/Eurystheus and Domitian, see the discussion at Laguna 1992: 273–4.

[25] Trans. D. R. Shackleton Bailey.

Pliny likewise uses a sententious parenthesis to comment on his obligation to reciprocate the affection of the community at Tifernum in Umbria, of which he is patron (*Ep.* 4.1.5):

in hoc ego, ut referrem gratiam (nam vinci in amore turpissimum est), templum pecunia mea exstruxi

Here, to express my gratitude (for it is disgraceful to be outdone in affection), I have erected a temple at my own expense.

Similar *sententiae* are expressed parenthetically in the *Silvae*. When he addresses the deceased slave-child, Glaucias, asking him to comfort the bereaved Melior, Statius anticipates the objection that the dead cannot reach the living, and meets it by expressing the notion that Charon and Cerberus do not put up obstacles to the innocent (2.1.227–30):

> . . . ades huc emissus ab atro
> limine, cui soli cuncta impetrare facultas,
> Glaucia (insontes[26] animas nec portitor arcet
> nec durae comes ille serae): tu pectora mulce

Come hither, dispatched from the dark threshold, you that alone can win all you ask, Glaucias (for neither the ferryman nor the companion of the inexorable bar blocks guiltless souls), soothe his breast.

Similarly, in describing Flavius Ursus' grief at the death of his slave, Philetus, Statius remarks parenthetically that, when it comes to affections transcending barriers of status, Fortune is blind (2.6.8–9):

> . . . famulum (quia rerum nomina caeca
> sic miscet Fortuna manu nec pectora novit),
> sed famulum gemis, Vrse, pium

You mourn a slave – for so does Fortune blindly mingle names and knows not hearts – but a faithful slave, Ursus.

In adducing mythological *exempla* to persuade his wife to retire to Naples with him, Statius expresses the *sententia amatoria* that nothing can daunt a lover (3.5.46–7):

> isset ad Iliacas (quid <u>enim</u> deterret amantes?)
> Penelope gavisa domos, si passus Vlixes

Penelope would gladly have gone to the dwellings of Ilium (for what do lovers fear?) if Ulysses had suffered it.

---

[26] The hiatus has prompted numerous attempts at emendation, e.g. *nil sontes* (Saenger), *non sontes* (Håkanson). For a thoughtful defence of the paradosis see van Dam 1984: 184. Hiatus might also deliver an aural signal that the syntax is about to be disrupted by parenthesis.

And in his poem of thanks to the emperor for a dinner-invitation, Statius makes use of the sentiment, which has a proverbial ring to it, that the prayers of the lowly also reach the gods (4.2.57–9):

> di tibi (namque animas saepe exaudire minores
> dicuntur) patriae bis terque exire senectae
> annuerint finis!

May the gods grant you (for they are said often to listen to lesser souls) to outlast twice and three times the limits of your father's old age!

3.2.4 *Expressions of loyalty*

A particular type of empathetic reaction is conveyed by Statius' tendency to insert parenthetical expressions of loyalty to the emperor, a habit that at first sight seems almost treasonably casual. But the effect is, rather, that of a default attitude that surfaces periodically; the emperor is always present in the back of his loyal subject's mind, and will naturally be mentioned or invoked in the normal course of events. Even the gods acknowledge Domitian in such asides, as when Venus predicts that, by the emperor's grace, Stella will rise to the consulship before the statutory minimum age (1.2.174–6):

> hunc et bis senos (sic indulgentia pergat
> praesidis Ausonii) cernes attollere fasces
> ante diem

Him shall you see – so continue the favour of Ausonia's sovereign – raise the twice six rods before the time.

A few lines later, Venus remarks parenthetically on the extraordinary honour entrusted to Stella, whereby he was to administer Domitian's triumph over Dacia in AD 89 (1.2.180–1):

> . . . Dacasque (et gloria maior)
> exuvias laurosque dabit celebrare recentes.

and grant him to celebrate – a yet greater glory – Dacian spoils and recent laurels.

Addressing Domitian directly, Statius, in his authorial persona, comments on the emperor's presence at the *cena* he had laid on for the people of Rome in the Colosseum, asking parenthetically which god could issue such invitations, or accept them (1.6.46–8):

> et tu quin etiam (quis hoc vocare,
> quis promittere possit hoc deorum?)
> nobiscum socias dapes inisti.

Nay, you yourself (which of the gods could thus invite, which accept invitation?) entered the feast along with us.

The motif of *serus in caelum redeas* (Hor. *Odes* 1.2.45) is parenthetically expressed in a compliment to Domitian about his palace on the Palatine, a dwelling that is the envy of Capitoline Jupiter and the rest of the gods (4.2.20–3):

> . . . stupet hoc vicina Tonantis
> regia, teque pari laetantur sede locatum
> numina (nec magnum properes escendere caelum):
> tanta patet moles . . .

The Thunderer's palace next door gapes at it and the gods rejoice that you are lodged in a like abode (do not hurry to mount high heaven yet): so great extends the structure . . .

Commenting on Abascantus' responsibilities as *ab epistulis*, Statius remarks parenthetically that no other job in the emperor's household is so busy (5.1.83–8):

> . . . ille paratis (*Gibson*: gravatis *M*)
> · molem immensam umeris et vix tractabile pondus
> imposuit (nec <u>enim</u> numerosior altera sacra   85
> cura domo), magnum late dimittere in orem
> Romulei mandata ducis, viresque modosque
> imperii tractare manu

He placed on shoulders that were ready a massive burden, a weight that could scarcely be carried (for no other task in the sacred household is more varied), the dispatch of the orders of the Romulean lord into the great world far and wide, and the handling of the powers and means of command.

As with Venus' prediction of Stella's precocious consulship, Domitian's *indulgentia* is mentioned in a parenthesis as encouragement to Crispinus to take up his appointment abroad (5.2.125–7):

> ergo age (<u>nam</u> magni ducis indulgentia pulsat
> certaque <u>dat</u> votis hilaris vestigia frater)
> surge animo et fortes castrorum concipe curas.

Come, then – for the favour of our lord pushes you on, and your joyful brother leaves clear footsteps for your prayers – rise up with zeal and assume the brave cares of the camp.

And Statius expresses the parenthetic hope that Crispinus' friend, Optatus, will receive imperial support in accompanying him on his journey (5.2.152–5):

> felix qui viridi fidens, Optate, iuventa
> durabis quascumque vias vallumque subibis,
> forsan et ipse latus (sic numina principis adsint)
> cinctus et unanimi comes indefessus amici

Happy Optatus, confident in your burgeoning youth, you will endure whatever journeys and palisades you come to, perhaps yourself wearing a sword at your side (so may the divinity of the emperor be with you) and an untiring companion of your soul's friend.

3.3 *'Learned footnote'*

The Callimachean mannerism of the learned parenthesis, mentioned in section 1, usually contains a mini-excursus on a geographical or mythological theme. In the *epicedion* addressed to Melior on the death of Glaucias, Statius interrupts a triple sequence of protases in a conditional sentence (*sive... seu... sive*) to comment that Apollo would have preferred Glaucias to Hyacinthus, and Hercules would have preferred him to Hylas; editors do not always mark off the digression as a parenthesis,[27] but it is clearly a learned aside that interrupts the sequence of alternative conditions (2.1.110–13):

> sive catenatis curvatus membra palaestris
> staret, Amyclaea conceptum matre putares
> (Oebaliden illo praeceps mutaret Apollo,
> Alciden pensaret Hylan); seu...

If he stood fast in a wrestler's lock, you would think him born of Amyclaean mother (Apollo would have hurried to take him in exchange for Oebalus' son, Alcides would have bartered Hylas), or if...

In the poem on the dedication of the shorn locks of Domitian's eunuch, Earinus, at Pergamum, Statius compares Pergamum favorably with Mt Ida, despite Ida's fame as the site of a divine rape, and then inserts a parenthesis – a mini-excursus, if not noteworthy for allusive learning – that describes the abduction of Ganymede in terms of Juno's reaction (3.4.12–16):

> Pergame, pinifera multum felicior Ida,
> illa licet sacrae placeat sibi nube rapinae
> (nempe dedit superis illum quem turbida semper
> Iuno videt refugitque manum nectarque recusat),   15
> at tu...

---

[27] E.g. none is signalled by van Dam 1984.

Pergamus, more fortunate by far than pine-clad Ida, though Ida pride herself on the cloud of a holy rape – for surely she gave the High Ones him at whom Juno ever looks askance, recoiling from his hand and refusing the nectar: but *you* . . .

A final example of the parenthetical footnote in the *Silvae* purveys geographical learning. (It has already been argued, in section 3.1, that a parenthesis conveying geographical details in the speech by the river Volturnus in 4.3 contributes to the characterisation rather than functioning as a learned excursus in its own right.) In the *epicedion* on the death of his father, Statius claims the supremacy of his poem in the hierarchy of commemorative gifts by comparison with the costliest funerary spices (5.3.41–5):

> hic ego te (nam Sicanii non mitius halat
> aura croci, dites nec si tibi rara Sabaei
> cinnama odoratas nec Arabs decerpsit aristas)
> inferiis cum laude datis heu carmine plango
> Pierio

Here, with offerings duly given (for not more gently wafts the breeze of the Sicanian crocus, nor is the scent so fragrant for you, if the Sabaeans have plucked the rare cinnamon, and the Arabian has plucked the perfumed herbs), I lament for you, alas, in Pierian song.

These 'footnotes' are far from colloquial, although, being cast as asides, they indicate a certain self-deprecating willingness to relegate the poet's learning to the background; while 'colloquial' would be a misleading definition, the parentheses convey a certain lightness of touch that contributes to the persona of the poet as a modest and engaged observer.

3.4 Picking up the threads

One feature of colloquial speech remains to be noted in connection with the parentheses in the *Silvae*: the technique of 'resumptive iteration', a type of epanalepsis. In ordinary speech, after a digression a speaker often repeats the key phrase that preceded it, to remind members of the audience what he was talking about before the digression potentially derailed their train of thought. This is a feature noted by Quintilian (referring to parenthesis this time as *interiectio*), who illustrates it with a quotation from Cicero (Quint. *Inst.* 9.3.29, quoting Cic. *Phil.* 2.64):

similis geminationis post aliquam interiectionem repetitio est, sed paulo etiam vehementior: 'bona <Cn. Pompei – miserum me! consumptis enim lacrimis infixus tamen pectori haeret dolor – bona,> inquam, Cn. Pompei acerbissimae voci subiecta praeconis'

Related to this doubling, but somewhat stronger, is repetition following a parenthesis: 'The property <of Gnaeus Pompeius – alas, alas, my tears have been exhausted, but the grief of it lies deep in my heart – the property,> I say, of Gnaeus Pompeius, was put up for sale by the strident bawling of the public auctioneer!'

After Statius' parenthetical remark about the blindness of Fortune in cases where human affections transcend social barriers, commented on in section 3.2.3, the reiteration of the key word *famulum* is paralleled by the repetition of the key word *hominem* on either side of a further parenthesis four lines later, quoted as an example of authorial reaction under section 3.2.1. The figure is sufficiently marked to justify quotation of the passage in full (2.6.8–17):

> . . . famulum (quia rerum nomina caeca
> sic miscet Fortuna manu nec pectora novit),
> sed famulum gemis, Vrse, pium, sed amore fideque   10
> has meritum lacrimas, cui maior stemmate cuncto
> libertas ex mente fuit. ne comprime fletus,
> ne pudeat; rumpat frenos dolor iste deisque,
> si tam dura placent < . . .
> . . . > hominem gemis (ei mihi, subdo   15
> ipse faces), hominem, Vrse, tuum, cui dulce volenti
> servitium, cui triste nihil, qui sponte sibique
> imperiosus erat.

You mourn a slave – for so does Fortune blindly mingle names and knows not hearts – but a faithful slave, Ursus, who deserved those tears by love and loyalty, whose soul gave him a freedom beyond lineage. Suppress not your weeping, be not ashamed. Let your grief break the reins, and if such cruelty please the gods * * * You mourn a human being (woe is me! I myself kindle the torch), *your* human being, Ursus, one that welcomed his sweet bondage, nothing resented, did everything voluntarily, imperious to himself.

This resumptive iteration (Wills 1996: 66–8) can be traced to oratory (Roschatt 1884: 220–4), where the repetition is commonly (but by no means inevitably) accompanied by a verb such as *inquam*, as in the example from the *Philippics* quoted by Quintilian above; it is occasionally imitated in Augustan poetry before Ovid, who adopted it (without, however, the give-away *inquam*) as a regular device in the *Metamorphoses* to signal return to the main theme after a digression (Albrecht 1964: 52, 84–9), whence it entered the mainstream of post-Virgilian epic (and, one might note, passages in other genres where emotions of epic proportions are on display). Its presence in the passage quoted from the *epicedion* for Flavius Ursus has been well described as evidence that 'the syntax has truly become a figure;

its reuse is not merely a mannerism but instead the connection of ideas marked with the same figure of repetition' (Wills 1996: 68).

Similar resumption, although on a less capacious scale, introduces an echo of oral delivery elsewhere too. In the *suasoria* addressed to his wife, Statius uses the figure to add emphasis to his conviction that her reluctance to accompany him to Naples does not spring from what we would nowadays call 'alienation of affection' (3.5.3–6):

> non metuo ne laesa fides aut pectore in isto
> alter amor; nullis in te datur ire sagittis
> (audiat infesto licet hoc Rhamnusia vultu),
> non datur.

I have no fear lest faith be broken or another love be in your heart. No arrows have licence to assail you (though she of Rhamnus hear and frown), no indeed.

The Sibyl's quotation of her ecstatic prophecy of Domitian's epiphany along the Via Domitiana employs the same figure, intersected by an injunction to features of the local landscape to wait patiently (4.3.124–6):

> dicebam: 'veniet (manete campi
> atque amnis), veniet favente caelo
> qui...'

I used to say, one will come (be patient, you fields and river), one will come with heaven's favour who...

And Statius' admonition to Crispinus to learn from his father's example, interrupted by a parenthetic disclaimer of the need to heed the standard *exempla*, employs the figure too (5.2.51–4):

> disce, puer (nec enim externo monitore petendus
> virtutis tibi pulcher amor: cognata ministret
> laus animos, aliis Decii reducesque Camilli
> monstrentur), tu disce patrem...

Learn, youth – for you do not have to seek the beautiful love of valour from an outsider's guidance: let kindred glory provide your courage; to others let the Decii and the returning Camilli be shown – learn of your father...

4 CONCLUSION

The *Silvae* are one of the few works where we can examine prose and verse by the same author. The first four books each contain a prose preface (that to the first book somewhat mutilated), and the fifth is accompanied by a letter to the addressee of the first poem, Abascantus. These prose texts contain a sprinkling of parentheses, alongside other colloquial features; in addition to parenthetical expressions of opinion (e.g., 4 *praef.* 11 *uti scis*, 26 *ut audio*), a common idiom occurs at 3 *praef.* 14–16:

merebatur et Claudi Etrusci mei pietas aliquod ex studiis nostris solacium, cum lugeret veris (quod iam rarissimum est) lacrimis senem patrem.

Then the filial devotion of my friend Claudius Etruscus deserved some solace from my pen as he mourned his father with unfeigned tears – something very unusual nowadays.

The parenthetical relative clause, referring to the entire clause surrounding it, is indeed a colloquial touch, familiar from letters (e.g. Cic. *Att.* 4.16.2 *rem enim – quod te non fugit – magnam complexus sum*, 'it's a big subject – as you realise – that I am grasping', Plin. *Ep.* 6.29.1 *Avidius Quietus, qui me unice dilexit et – quo non minus gaudeo – probavit*, 'Avidius Quietus, who is extraordinarily fond of me and – which pleases me no less – approves of me')[28] and from Ovid (*Met.* 3.269–70, Juno speaking about Semele: *et mater, quod vix mihi contigit, uno | de Iove vult fieri*, 'and she wants to become a mother, which has scarcely befallen me, by Jupiter alone', Albrecht 1964: 77, H–S 573). The prefaces to the *Silvae*, being addressed to a specific person, are cast as letters, topped and tailed by a regular salutation and valediction, and it is therefore no surprise to find them expressed in a colloquial manner.

The poems, however, are a different matter. Only one is explicitly a verse epistle (4.4). Five contain no parentheses: surprisingly, these include two that Statius himself classified 'in the style of epigrams' (2.4, on Melior's parrot, and 2.5, on Domitian's favourite lion); it is less surprising to find that the hieratic pose in the poem on Domitian's seventeeth consulship admits no parenthesis; but neither do the alcaics to Septimius Severus (4.5), nor the elaborate hexameters on Novius Vindex's statuette of Hercules (4.6), whereas the sapphics to Vibius Maximus (4.7) admit one, and most of the rest of the poems in hexameters do too, covering a wide range of themes and occasions. If these statistics are of any demonstrable value, it is to remind us that parenthesis is only one of a wide range of linguistic features that may convey a colloquial tone, and that the absence of parenthesis from

---

[28] This type of parenthesis is very common in Pliny: cf. *Ep.* 2.11.9, 6.27.1, 6.33.4, 7.15.3, 7.19.7, 9.34.1, 10.61.3.

a particular poem is only significant if it can be demonstrated that no other colloquial features are present either. At the other end of the spectrum, however, the tendency of parentheses to cluster in particular sections, or in speeches delivered by particular spokespersons, suggests a cumulative effect; the Appendix shows where these clusters occur. A comprehensive treatment of colloquial features in the *Silvae* would demonstrate the relationship between the occurrences of parenthesis and of other colloquialisms; a few instances have been noted above.

The effect of the parentheses in the *Silvae* ranges from mimicry of colloquial speech, as in the examples from the poem to Plotius Grypus with which I started, to the characterisation of the spokespersons to whom Statius gives the microphone, and the subjective involvement of Statius himself and the display of his learning. Parallels for many of these effects come from the Augustan poets, especially Ovid. Statius, and his spokespersons, speak like people in poetry, which indeed is what they are; '[l]iterary texts are... artistic representations of conversational modes' (Chahoud, this volume p. 58). But, in Statius, as in his Ovidian model, the purpose of parenthesis seems to be above all to reinforce the sense of communication with an interlocutor, which is one of the identifying features of colloquial language in Hofmann's classic study (Chahoud, this volume p. 49), so that, even if the exact phrasing of the parentheses reflects that of people in poetry rather than people on the street (we cannot know how common it was to hear someone exclaim *nefas!* in real life), the occurrence of the parentheses adds a sense of liveliness and immediacy that contributes to the unique texture of the *Silvae*.

APPENDIX

Note: Although the *tituli* to the poems are probably late additions, I include them below to indicate the theme of each poem. An asterisk denotes an occurrence inside a speech by a spokesperson. Instances of parenthetic *heu* on its own are omitted here, as being so common as to skew the impression of the frequency of parenthesis overall; they are listed in n. 12 above.

I	*praef.*: 22–3	
1.1	*Ecus maximus Domitiani imp.*: 86–7	
1.2	*Epithalamion in Stellam et Violentillam*: 17, 37, 64, *74, *79, *101, *128, *174–5, *180	
1.3	*Villa Tiburtina Manili Vopisci*: 20	
1.4	*Soteria Rutili Gallici*: 5, 34–5, 53, *62, *77	

1.5   *Balneum Claudii Etrusci*: 61–2
1.6   *Kalendae Decembres*: 46–7, 61

2   *praef.*: –
2.1   *Glaucias Atedii Melioris delicatus*: 20, 34, 112–13, 229–30
2.2   *Villa Surrentina Pollii Felicis*: 113–15
2.3   *Arbor Atedii Melioris*: 7
2.4   *Psittacus eiusdem*: –
2.5   *Leo mansuetus*: –
2.6   *Consolatio ad Flavium Vrsum de amissione pueri delicati*: 3, 8–9,
        14–15, 76, 93
2.7   *Genethliacon Lucani ad Pollam*: 24, *100, *104

3   *praef.*: 16–17
3.1   *Hercules Surrentinus Pollii Felicis*: 162, *172
3.2   *Propempticon Maecii Celeri*: 15
3.3   *Consolatio ad Claudium Etruscum*: 21, 56, 68–9
3.4   *Capilli Flavi Earini*: 14–15
3.5   (*Suasoria* to Statius' wife): 5, 46, 49, 81–2

4   *praef.*: 11, 26
4.1   *Septimus decimus consulatus Imp. Aug. Germanici*: –
4.2   *Eucharisticon ad Imp. Aug. Germ. Domitianum*: 22, 57–8
4.3   *Via Domitiana*: *80, *90–1, *124–5
4.4   *Epistola ad Vitorium Marcellum*: 21–2, 57, 58–60
4.5   *Ode lyrica ad Septimium Severum*: –
4.6   *Hercules Epitrapezios Novi Vindicis*: –
4.7   *Ode lyrica ad Vibium Maximum*: 35
4.8   *Gratulatio ad Iulium Menecraten*: 27
4.9   *Hendecasyllabi iocosi ad Plotium Grypum*: 42, 44

5   *epist.*: –
5.1   *Epicedion in Priscillam <Abascanti> uxorem*: 85–6, 92–3, 200,
        226–7 ˙
5.2   *Laudes Crispini Vetti Bolani filii*: 51–4, 125–6, *146, *148, 154, 164–5
5.3   *Epicedion in patrem suum*: 9, 41–3, 174–5, 262–3
5.4   *Somnus*: 17–18, 19
5.5   *Epicedion in puerum suum*: 27–8, 38

CHAPTER 19

Colloquial Latin in Martial's epigrams

Nigel M. Kay

I INTRODUCTION

Epigram is and was regarded as well down the rankings in the literary hierarchy, and was so regarded by Martial himself: in one of the final pieces of his final book he runs down the literary scale, from epic and tragedy via lyric to satire and elegy, and asks *quid minus esse potest?*, 'What can be lower?'; the answer of course is epigram (12.94.9).[1] It is low literature and as such one might expect its linguistic register to be weighted towards the colloquial, as opposed to the literary, end of the spectrum.

Many epigrams, especially those of a satiric or scoptic nature, with which I will be chiefly concerned in this paper, do indeed have evident colloquial characteristics in that they are either framed as dialogues in direct speech, or as one-sided conversations between the author and an addressee (who can be real or fictional, named or not, or simply Martial's public addressed as reader or listener). *Hominem pagina nostra sapit* 'my pages smack of mankind', says Martial (10.4.10), and his poems often describe the situations, interactions and general paraphernalia of contemporary everyday life in vivid and immediate settings. This suggests that the language he uses will be in accord, and will be colloquial in the sense that it is what would have been generally and widely heard in Martial's first-century Latin-speaking world.

However, there are clear limitations to such an assumption. At the basic level, Martial writes verse, and people do not speak in verse, and metre must influence word order and vocabulary. But there is another fundamental issue, namely that epigram, low in the literary hierarchy though it is, is nevertheless a part of that hierarchy, and is itself a literary creation. This is well evidenced in Martial's description of the type of writer he is, and the type of reader (or audience) for whom he writes: he is an *urbanus*

---

[1] For ease of reference my numeration of the epigrams follows Lindsay 1929; text and translations are mine, though it will be apparent that I have consulted others, especially Shackleton Bailey 1993.

writing for *urbani*, and they are the cultured and highly literate elite who can appreciate the subtleties of his epigram. Take 1.41:

> urbanus tibi, Caecili, videris.   1
> non es, crede mihi. quid ergo? verna es,
> hoc quod transtiberinus ambulator...
> quod fumantia qui thumatla raucus   9
> circumfert tepidis cocus popinis,
> quod non optimus urbicus poeta,
> quod de Gadibus improbus magister,
> quod bucca est vetuli dicax cinaedi...
> non cuicumque datum est habere nasum: 18
> ludit qui stolida procacitate,
> non est Tettius ille, sed Caballus.

You think yourself urbane, Caecilius. You aren't, believe me. What are you then? You're vulgar, you're like a peddlar from over the river... a raucous cook carrying his smoking sausages round sweaty inns, a less-than-optimal towny poet, a sleazy dancing-master from Cadiz, an old queer's prattling gob... Not everyone is granted sensibilities: he whose wit is boorishly aggressive is not a Thoroughbred, but a Nag.[2]

Martial's point here is that his wit is subtle and literate, and befits the *urbanus* author; he expressly does not use the type of language which might be heard amongst the uneducated and virtually illiterate characters who aim to display their wit in their everyday banter; they employ *stolida procacitas*, he, by implication, employs *urbanitas*. Elsewhere (10.3.1–2) he castigates a poor plagiarist of his work as a scribbler of *vernaculorum dicta, sordidum dentem, | et foeda linguae probra circulatricis* 'the witticisms of vulgarians, sordid abuse, and the common insults of a hawker's tongue'. This is a clear indication that his epigrams will not generally reveal the type of colloquial speech which can be termed substandard; he is a writer, and though his genre is low, his level of culture is high, and so is that of his audience/readers. This is not to say that there is no evidence of the colloquial in Martial, but what there is is likely to reflect that of a literary elite and should be recognised as such; it may of course overlap with the ordinary speech of many other types of people, but its literary genesis needs to be borne in mind.

For the present enquiry it is also unfortunate that Martial's humour rarely focuses on, or deals with, contemporary speech. Exceptions are thin on the ground, for example:

---

[2] The references in the last line are obscure, but the general import is clear.

(i) At 2.27.3–4 he attacks one Selius, a sycophantic seeker of dinner invitations at literary recitals, listing his effusive exclamations *effecte! graviter! cito! nequiter! euge! beate!* | *hoc volui!* 'you've got it! profound! bang on! wicked! wow! bliss! that's just it!'.

(ii) At 6.54 we meet Sextilianus, who includes at every opportunity in his speech a part of the adjective *tantus*, in an epigram which well illustrates how information about colloquial language is likely to come to us obliquely, because Martial's purpose in describing Sextilianus' language is only to make a sexual innuendo based on his favourite word:

> tantos et tantas si dicere Sextilianum,
>   Aule, vetes, iunget vix tria verba miser.
> 'quid sibi vult?' inquis. dicam quid suspicer esse:
>   tantos et tantas Sextilianus amat.

Should you stop Sextilianus saying 'Huge!', Aulus, the poor chap will barely be able to string three words together. 'What's he up to?', you ask? I'll tell you my suspicion. Sextilianus fancies huge men hugely endowed.

(iii) At 1.65 Martial is accused of a grammatical barbarism by one Caecilianus in terms which suggest the accusation relates primarily to speech, though again the joke is centred on an innuendo:

> cum dixi 'ficus', rides quasi barbara verba
>   et dici 'ficos', Caeciliane, iubes.
> dicemus 'ficus', quas scimus in arbore nasci,
>   dicemus 'ficos', Caeciliane, tuos.

When I say *'ficus'*, you laugh as if it were a barbarism and tell me to say *'ficos'*, Caecilianus. Those we know come from trees we'll call *'ficus'*, and we'll call yours *'ficos'*, Caecilianus.[3]

(iv) And at 14.120 Martial draws a distinction between the everyday speech of the upper classes and that of grammarians:

> quamvis me ligulam dicant equitesque patresque,
>   dicor ab indoctis lingula grammaticis.

Although knights and senators call me *ligula*, I am called *lingula* by ignorant grammarians.[4]

---

[3] Citroni's (1975) survey of the (written) evidence finds little systematic distinction between either or both second and fourth declension, and masculine and feminine gender, *ficus* in reference to anal sores and the fruit of the fig tree, and he concludes that Martial makes the remark for humorous purposes; yet, as he hints, the piece has more bite if contemporary upholders of 'correct' Latin were arguing there was, or should be, some distinction (1975: 212–13).

[4] To the extent that MSS are reliable in such matters the usual spelling in this sense ('spoon') is indeed *ligula* and *lingula* is found very rarely (see *TLL* vii/2.1396.3ff.). But both forms survive in romance

Occasionally also it is possible to draw an inference about the tone of the direct speech Martial puts in the mouths of his characters: an example of this is 8.76, which opens *dic verum mihi, Marce, dic amabo;* | *nil est quod magis audiam libenter*, 'Tell me the truth, tell me, Marcus, I pray; there is nothing I would hear with greater pleasure.' These words are spoken by one Gallicus, useless lawyer, bad amateur poet, but also patron, and with them he annoyingly persists in soliciting Martial's opinion on his various writings. It can reasonably be argued that they are intended to characterise Gallicus in that they have at least one and probably two marked features: (i) the (over)familiar tone of the praenomen address,[5] and (ii) the use of *amabo*, a word for 'please' which was once colloquial but is almost certainly an archaism and jarring by this time in speech.[6] But it is more difficult to determine precisely how Gallicus is characterised by his short speech, other than to say that the impression he gives must be adverse: the emphasis might be on overfamiliarity, on pedantic old-fashionedness, on irritating wheedling, or on a mixture of these.

In the rest of this paper I will look at three types of colloquial speech in the epigrams and deal in some detail with each of them.[7] They are (a) the interjected asides or parentheses which are frequently introduced by Martial with the purpose of providing a context of actual, often intimate, conversation, and which are a feature of all conversation; (b) Martial's use of obscenity, to the 'frankness' and 'plain-speaking' of which he draws specific attention, itself indicative of colloquiality; and (c) a specific suffix (*-arius/-aria*) which Martial often uses for humorous effects and which I suggest has a colloquial tone.

---

reflexes (e.g. Romanian *lingura* 'spoon' and Spanish/Portuguese *legra* 'scraper') and it is likely both were current in Martial's day, even if *lingula* was viewed by some as an affectation: see *REW* 5036. E–M s.v. *lingo* list other derivatives of *lingula* which drop the 'n', as e.g. *ligurrio*.

[5] See Dickey 2002: 65 ff., though a note of caution must be added about this instance: Martial uses his praenomen in reference to himself six more times (1.5.2, 1.55.1, 3.5.10, 5.29.2, 5.63.1, 6.47.6), not least because his cognomen does not fit dactylic verse (see Howell 1980: 118 and Citroni 1975: 35); on the other hand this is not dactylic verse, and in hendecasyllables and other metres Martial uses his cognomen except for here (1.1.2, 1.117.17, 6.82.4, 7.72.16, 10.9.3, 10.92.15); so the point is probably still valid.

[6] See Hofmann–Ricottilli 281–2 (§117) for its extensive use in comic dialogue and in e.g. Cicero's letters; after Cicero there are only three instances in *TLL* apart from this one (1.1956.60 ff.), two in Gellius which are marked in that they occur in addresses where the speaker is very irritated with the addressee (4.1.4, 5.21.6, cf. p. 335 below), and one in Sidonius (*carmina* 9.4 *dic amabo*, either a quotation or an archaism). Also K–S 1.199–200; Blase 1896: 485 ff.

[7] To save space I have generally not made reference to the commentaries on the individual books of Martial's epigrams, even on the few occasions when my interpretation differs; but I have consulted them all with profit. There are two useful recent bibliographies of work on Martial, by Sven Lorenz in *Lustrum* 45 (2003) 167 ff. and 48 (2006) 109 ff. covering the years 1970–2003, and by J. A. Beltrán and others, *Marco Valerio Marcial: Actualización científica y bibliográfica. Tres décadas de estudios sobre Marcial (1971–2000)*, Zaragoza 2005.

2 INTERJECTED ASIDES OR PARENTHESES

There are many parenthetic or interjected asides which aim to stimulate or keep the attention of the interlocutor/listener/reader by drawing him into conversation or debate with the author ('believe me', 'in my opinion', 'if you please', 'if I remember rightly' etc.). They serve various functions, expressing surprise, doubt, incredulity, sarcasm and so forth. They usually occur in or at the end of a clause, where they function to qualify the clause as a whole or a word in it (e.g. 12.48.5 *lauta tamen cena est, fateor – lautissima* 'it's an excellent dinner, I grant, a most excellent dinner', and 2.3.1 *Sexte, nihil debes, nil debes, Sexte, fatemur* 'Sextus, you owe nothing, you owe nothing, Sextus, I grant you'). On rare occasions they begin their clause and their tone is, or can be, more emphatic (e.g. 3.52.3–4 *rogo, non potes ipse videri | incendisse tuam, Tongiliane, domum?*, 'Well, I ask you! Mightn't it appear that you torched your house yourself, Tongilianus?').

I append a catalogue of these words and phrases which also indicates the frequency of their use in the epigrams (* indicates opening position in the clause):

puto: 1.5.2, 27.2, 80.2, 99.6, 102.2; 2. *praef.* 11*, 9.2, 41.2, 67.4; 3.55.4, 95.4; 4.26.3, 58.2; 5.11.4, 16.14, 84.10; 6.30.5, 70.2; 7.24.8, 53.9, 88.10; 8. *praef.* 4, 4.4, 29.1, 64.3; 9. *praef. epig.* 6, 63.2, 72.6, 78.2, 82.2, 94.3; 10.36.8, 79.10, 95.2, 104.19; 11.6.4, 28.2, 101.2; 12.28.2; 14.182.1; cf. *ut puta* at 2.44.2; *ut puto* at 11.75.4.[8]

crede mihi/mihi crede: *Sp.* 17.4; 1.3.4*, 15.11, 41.2; 2.32.7; 3.5.3, 16.5; 4.49.1; 5.52.7*, 53.3; 6.23.2*, 27.10, 56.3, 61.6; 9.41.3, 99.9; 10.90.5; 12.36.6; cf. *credo* at 3.72.7.[9]

rogo: 2.14.18, 25.2, 80.2; 3.44.9, 52.3*, 73.3, 76.3, 95.3; 4.84.4; 5.25.7, 44.1, 82.3*; 6.17.2, 20.4; 7.86.3; 9.25.3; 10.15.2, 21.2, 41.3, 66.1; 12.63.6; 13.58.2;[10] cf. *oro* at 11.75.2, 76.3;[11] *precor* at 5.50.7; 12.49.7 (and note *amabo* at 8.76.1, discussed above at p. 321; cf. also p. 335 below).

---

[8] For examples from other sources see Hofmann–Ricottilli 250 (§100), 376.

[9] See further *TLL* iv.1137.20 ff., 65 ff.; Hofmann–Ricottilli 279–80 (§114).

[10] See further Hofmann–Ricottilli 284–5 (§120). I have grouped together *rogo*, *oro* and *precor* (I have omitted two instances of the formulaic *parce precor* at 7.68.2 and 10.82.7) because they serve much the same function in conversational epigram and have much the same meanings. However, *rogo* is evidently much the commonest in Martial, and its particularly colloquial tone is suggested also by its absence in this usage from e.g. contemporary epic. But were *oro* and *precor* equally colloquial? Both appear in this usage in epic, but that does not rule them out of everyday speech and their presence in Martial and elsewhere suggests they were colloquial. Their attraction may however simply lie in the metrical variety they afford; it is possible they can have a more formal tone, but I cannot detect it in Martial's usage.

[11] See further Hofmann–Ricottilli 284 (§119), 379.

fateor: 1.90.5; 2.28.5; 3.12.1; 5.13.1, 27.2; 9.99.7; 10.75.2; 12.48.5; 13.103.1,
    114.1; cf. *fatemur* at 2.3.1, and *confiteor* at 3.31.1.[12]

si memini/memini: 1.19.1*; 9.8.2; 11.65.3; 12.34.2.[13]

quis nescit?: 2.62.3; 5.38.1; *quis potest negare?*: 1.64.2; 5.78.22; *quis credat?*:
    5.44.3; 9.48.9; *quis negat?*: 11.22.3; cf. 11.70.11.

3 USE OF OBSCENITY

An obvious area in which to seek colloquial language is in Martial's use
of obscenity, since the primary obscenities did not belong to the higher
literary genres, and can always be found in colloquial speech, however
defined. But here too the stricture outlined above (pp. 318–19) should be
borne in mind: Martial is aiming to amuse and entertain an audience
from the literary elite, and they expect their obscenity to be acceptable and
enjoyable in an appropriate manner, to be cultured as well as obscene, to
be distanced from out-and-out vulgarity, and in that sense to be literary.
So on the one hand a key concept Martial employs in this connection
is that of *simplicitas* 'putting things bluntly', particularly in reference to
the basic obscenities which were the currency of the street and the low
literary genres.[14] Thus he excuses, whilst simultaneously advertising (1.
praef. 9–10), his *lascivam verborum veritatem, id est epigrammaton linguam*
'unrestrained frankness of words, i.e. the language of epigrams', which he
glosses as *latine loqui* 'speaking Latin'.[15] But on the other hand it does
not necessarily follow that every use of a basic obscenity is colloquial. To
take just one example: when Martial says (6.45.1) *lascivi nubite cunni* 'get
married, wanton *cunni*',[16] what he means is 'get married, wanton women',
his purpose is praise of Domitian's moral legislation, and his vocative use of
the obscenity is as literary a device as any other, not necessarily a reflection
of everyday speech.

---

[12] See further Hofmann–Ricottilli 251 (§100) *TLL* vi/1.337.10 ff, iv.227.32 ff.

[13] Hofmann–Ricottilli 249 (§100), 376; *TLL* viii.646.72 ff, 647.35 ff.

[14] Basic obscenities are words such as *mentula, cunnus, futuere, fellare, irrumare* etc.: they are given
magisterial coverage in Adams 1982a, and I will have little further to say of them here.

[15] See also 2.8.2, 11.20.2 and 10, 11.63.4, 14.215.1.

[16] I have not translated *cunni* as 'cunts' precisely because in English it would appear to be colloquial
invective of the type 'you cunts', whereas in the Latin it is an obscene *pars pro toto* equivalent to
mulieres and has not lost its basic anatomical reference. Such personal insults, which are weakened
uses of basic obscenities referring to the genitalia and from which the anatomical meanings have all
but disappeared, are actually notable for their absence from Martial. They do occur in contemporary
Latin, both in graffiti and literary sources, though they are hardly commonplace (see Adams 1982a:
132–3 and index s.v. 'weakening'; and 1982c: 37 ff.). Perhaps Martial avoided them as *vernaculorum
dicta*, a type of the *stolida procacitas* he eschews (1.41.19 and 10.3.1, quoted above, p. 319).

In what follows I will however concentrate on Martial's use of euphemistic obscenity. The frequency of such idioms in Martial's work and elsewhere, and their tendency to use words of basic, everyday vocabulary, strongly suggest they were a feature of everyday speech;[17] I will look at some frequently used verbs as they feature in Martial's sexual vocabulary, in the order *negare, dare, facere, posse* and *velle*.

3.1 negare

The basic reference of *negare* in this sense is a refusal to perform a sexual act with another person. It is usually a female who refuses a male, and the act refused is generally unspecified, though it can be assumed to be *fututio*.[18] This is 4.38: *Galla, nega: satiatur amor nisi gaudia torquent:* | *sed noli nimium, Galla, negare diu*, 'Galla, say no: love is satiated unless its pleasures torment: but don't say no, Galla, for too long'; and see also 1.106.7, 2.25.2, 3.54.2, 4.12.1, 4.71.2–6. The verb is used once, humorously, of a male refusing a female (10.75.14). When the refusal relates to an act other than *fututio*, the act has to be specified in some way for the sake of clarity. Thus 11.104.17 *pedicare negas*, where Martial's 'wife' denies him *pedicatio;* and 4.7.1 *cur, here quod dederas, hodie, puer Hylle, negasti . . . ?* 'why, Hyllus my boy, do you refuse today what you gave yesterday?', where a boy who offered *pedicatio* one day refuses it the next, because he has become a man.

The phrase *nil negare* 'to say no to nothing' is closely related and is usually understood to refer to agreement to perform *fellatio*, largely on the evidence of 12.79.4 *quisquis nil negat, Atticilla, fellat* 'whoever says no to nothing, Atticilla, sucks'.[19] This is evidently one meaning, but the phrase

---

[17] Note e.g. Adams 1981a: 127: 'there is a widely attested group of verbs (*do, rogo, nego, promitto*) used in the pregnant sense "grant etc. intercourse" without a complement expressed. The frequency of these elliptical usages is such that they were undoubtedly well established in the ordinary language.' This article is the starting point for this section of my chapter, in which I aim to provide a survey of the sexual meanings of some such common verbs in Martial and to demonstrate how widespread and entrenched they are in his work. I have not detailed their appearances in other relevant colloquial sources because that information can be found in Adams's article: thus *posse* (122), *velle/nolle* (122), *facere* (123 with n. 4), *dare/negare* (127–8).

[18] The ellipse in this type of phrase is likely to be of e.g. *negare futuere/fututionem* and of *dare futuere/fututionem* (rather than of e.g. *dare se alicui*); note the phrases *pedicare dare* and *pedicare negare* at 11.78.5 and 11.104.17. I sometimes use the terms *fututio* and *pedicatio* in what follows because they are more precise and concise than English equivalents.

[19] I would also interpret *non negat* at 4.71.6 as meaning *fellat*, as the following translation is intended to make clear. This epigram contains three of the verbs with which I am and will be dealing in this section (*negare, dare, facere*) and is worth quoting in full: *quaero diu totam, Safroni Rufe, per urbem,* | *si qua puella neget: nulla puella negat.* | *tamquam fas non sit, tamquam sit turpe negare,* | *tamquam*

might encompass other sexual activity as well. Thus, when at 4.12 Martial says *nulli, Thai, negas, sed si te non pudet istud,* | *hoc saltem pudeat, Thai, negare nihil*, 'You say no to no-one, Thais, but if that doesn't make you ashamed let this at least make you ashamed, to say no to nothing', *negas* relates only to *fututio*, *negare nihil* to *fellatio* and perhaps also *pedicatio*; and when at 11.49.12 Martial says to the commercially rapacious Phyllis *nil tibi, Phylli, nego; nil mihi, Phylli, nega*, 'I refuse you no gift, Phyllis; say no to nothing to me, Phyllis', there seems no reason why the acts involved in *nil nega* should not include any he might demand.[20] In the absence of further information we simply do not know enough about the phrase to be certain.

3.2 dare

In its euphemistic sexual sense *dare* can be viewed as the antonym of *negare*. Thus in its basic meaning the reference is generally to an offer to perform a sexual act with another person. The person making the offer is usually female, and the act in question is often unspecified, though it can be assumed to be *fututio*.[21] In addition *dare* often refers to the performance of the act itself, when it is essentially a euphemism for the female role in intercourse, and it can carry the overtone that the act is at least consensual, and sometimes positively desired by and initiated by the female. I give examples:

(i) For an instance where the reference is to the offer, and expressly excludes the act, note 10.75.13–14, where a prostitute has become increasingly unattractive to Martial and he is eventually driven to refusing her unsolicited advances: *inferius numquid potuit descendere? fecit.* | *dat gratis, ultro dat mihi Galla: nego*, 'Surely she could sink no lower? She did. Galla offers it me for nothing, and offers me money without being asked: I say no!'

---

non liceat: nulla puella negat, | *casta igitur nulla est? sunt castae mille. quid ergo* | *casta facit? non dat, non tamen illa negat*, 'For ages I've been asking over the whole city, Safronius Rufus, if any girl says no: no girl says no. As if it weren't right to, as if it were a sin to say no, as if it weren't allowed: no girl says no. So is none of them virginal? Lots are. What then does a virginal girl get up to? She doesn't say yes, but she doesn't say no either.'

[20] Similar comments apply to 12.71. For completeness I mention also 3.61.2 *nil tibi, Cinna, nego*, which in my view may be intended to have a humorously obscene ambiguity.

[21] On the ellipse see n. 18 above.

(ii) For instances which focus more on the act than the offer see especially 2.25 *das numquam, semper promittis, Galla, roganti.* | *si semper fallis, iam rogo, Galla, nega*, 'You never give it, you always promise it, Galla, when I ask; if you always lie – I beg you, Galla! – say no!'; 2. 31 *saepe ego Chrestinam futui. det quam bene quaeris?* | *supra quod fieri nil, Mariane, potest*, 'I've often fucked Chrestina. How well does she give it you ask? Nothing could be better, Marianus'; and 10.81.3–4.

(iii) For instances where there is a focus on the female's initiation of, or desire for, the act cf. 7.30.1 and 7–8 *das Parthis, das Germanis, das, Caelia, Dacis . . . qua ratione facis, cum sis Romana puella,* | *quod Romana tibi mentula nulla placet?*, 'You give it to Parthians, you give it to Germans, you give it, Caelia, to Dacians . . . How do you square the fact that, although you're a girl from Rome, no Roman prick interests you?'; and 7.75 *vis futui gratis, cum sis deformis anusque.* | *res perridicula est: vis dare nec dare vis,* 'You want to be fucked for free, even though you're old and ugly. It's quite ridiculous! You want to give it but don't want to pay for it.' There might also be added those cases where a female is desirable to a lover because she *dat pueris* 'gives it to boys': 2.49.2, 9.32.2.

(iv) For other instances, which suggest both the offer and the act, note 2.9.1–2, 2.56.4, 4.71.6 and 14.175.2.

As with *negare*, when the reference of *dare* is to an act other than *fututio*, the reference has to be made more explicit for the sake of clarity. Thus when the act is *pedicatio* the verb acquires a complement or an explanatory clause: e.g. of a female at 11.78.5 *pedicare semel cupido dabit illa marito* 'she will allow her desirous husband to bugger her once'; also 11.104.17, and of males at 12.96.7 *hi dant quod non vis uxor dare. 'do tamen,' inquis* 'these boys offer what you don't want to offer as his wife. "But I will offer it", you say'; also 4.7.1. At 10.81.3–4 *promisit pariter se Phyllis utrique daturam,* | *et dedit: ille pedem sustulit, hic tunicam*, where Phyllis is dealing with two men who have come *mane fututum* 'for a morning fuck' and both want first turn, the meaning is 'Phyllis promised she would give it to them both simultaneously, and she did: the one raised her legs, the other her tunic', and the reference is to a double penetration schema;[22] the wit stems from

---

[22] As seems obvious, though some peculiar, overliteral explanations have been advanced by commentators (e.g. Shackleton Bailey 1993: III.318–19); *tunicam tollere* is not encountered elsewhere and may be contemporary slang (cf. modern slang 'shirtlifting').

the imprecision of the verb *dare*, and the meaning of *dedit* is both *dedit futuere* and *dedit pedicare*.

3.3 facere

Facere is a verb of even more imprecise reference in the sexual vocabulary, and is often used to key a witticism or humour about the precise kind of sex a person practices ('what does (s)he get up to in bed?'). For example, to the question of 12.86 *triginta tibi sunt pueri totidemque puellae: | una est nec surgit mentula. quid facies?*, 'You've got loads of boys and as many girls. You've got one prick and it doesn't rise. What will you do?', the reader can readily supply the answer (oral sex); cf. also 3.71.2, and, possibly, 2.17.5, 4.71.6 (see n. 19 above) and 10.64.6.

Sometimes a subordinate clause is introduced which alludes to the type of sex practiced: thus 3.83.2 *fac mihi quod Chione* 'do to me what Chione does' (Chione was a well-known fellatrix); 7.62.5–6 *non pedicari se qui testatur, Amille, | illud saepe facit quod sine teste facit* 'he who has a witness that he is not being buggered, Amillus, regularly gets up to what he does without a witness': *sine teste* is a humorous ambiguity, referring both to the testes[23] and to a witness, and the target of the humour is accused of practising oral sex; and 11.71.6 *et fieri quod iam non facit ipse sinit* 'and he allows to take place that which he can no longer do himself': the allusion here is to *fututio*.

For other instances of *facere* simply referring to sexual activity, the specific type of which can usually be deduced from the context, see 2.47.4, 2.60.4, 2.73, 7.24.8, 7.62.2, 9.27.14, 12.40.4. Compounds of *facere* also crop up in colloquial sexual contexts: at 3.79.2 *perficere* is used in the sense 'to reach orgasm', and at 9.32.4, quoted below, *sufficere* is applied to a woman accommodating three men simultaneously.

Finally, two instances should be mentioned where *facere* is used in a different type of sexual idiom. At 1.46.1 *fac si facis*, I understand the meaning to be 'do it if you're going to', and I take the phrase to be a colloquialism which need have no sexual reference,[24] but has acquired one in this particular context (where it instructs Martial to hurry up with the act of *pedicatio* he is performing). And at 7.10.1–2 *pedicatur Eros, fellat Linus: Ole, quid ad te | de cute quid faciant ille vel ille sua* the meaning is 'Eros is buggered,

---

[23] The testes here allude to the penetrative or 'active' role in sex, which was the role Martial's readers considered acceptable in men.

[24] For similar expressions cf. Sen. *Ben.* 2.5.2 *fac si quid facis*, Pl. *Per.* 659 and *Epid.* 196 *age si quid agis* (cf. above, p. 59), Pl. *Poen.* 1237 *ite si itis*; Hofmann–Ricottilli 384.

Linus sucks: what's it to you, Olus, what either of them gets up to with his own body?'

3.4 posse *and* velle

The verbs *posse* and *velle* are both used in euphemistic sexual senses (as with *dare* and *negare* an ellipse of an obscene verb like *futuere* is usually evident), and both can be used absolutely or with a personal object. Thus *posse* is used absolutely at 11.97.1 *una nocte quater possum* 'I can do it four times a night'; *velle* is used absolutely at 11.58.1 *cum me velle vides tentumque... sentis* 'when you see I want it and can tell I'm stiff'; possibly also ambiguously at 11.58.2 (if *velle* is taken as dependent on *negare*) and, of the ideal boy, at 4.42.11 *saepe et nolentem cogat nolitque volentem* 'and he should often urge me on when I don't want it, and be contrary when I do'.

Posse is used with an accusative of the person at 3.76.4 *cum possis Hecaben, non potes Andromachen* 'although you can do it with Hecuba, you can't with Andromache', 3.32.1 and 3 (four times) and 11.97.2. *Velle* with accusative might sometimes mean nothing more than 'to fancy', as at e.g. 1.57.1 *qualem, Flacce, velim quaeris nolimve puellam* 'you ask, Flaccus, the type of girl I would or wouldn't fancy', but the context is generally such that ellipse of *futuere* should be assumed. Thus at 9.32.1–4, where the subject is the ideal prostitute, four lines beginning *hanc volo* conclude with *hanc volo quae pariter sufficit una tribus*, 'I want the one who on her own can satisfy three at the same time'; and note also 6.40.4, 11.104.22 (and cf. *malo* at 3.33.1). The prevalence of the idiom is well illustrated by 5.83.2, where the infinitives *velle* and *nolle* are treated as substantives: *velle tuum nolo, Dindyme, nolle volo*, 'I'm not turned on by your wanting me, Dindymus, but by your refusing me.'

4 THE SUFFIX -ARIUS/-ARIA

Martial has interesting and varied uses of nouns and adjectives with -*arius* and -*aria* suffixes.[25] These suffixes generally attach to nouns denoting objects of some kind (though they can also attach to adjectives or even adverbs: see below), and their basic function is to describe a person who trades in, or professionally has to do with (e.g. in the army), those objects.[26] Thus at 4.64.22 the *helciarii* are people who use ropes to

---

[25] See also Watson 2002: 241–2; Watson also has useful comments on Martial's literary language, 2002: *passim*, especially 248 ff.
[26] Note the *OLD* definition s.v. -*arius*: 'very common as masc. sb. meaning "dealer in"'.

pull barges upstream, at 5.24.9 the *locarii* are people who trade in seats at gladiatorial shows, at 14.222 lemma the *pistor dulciarius* is a cook of sweet pastries, at 11.31.15 the *bellarius*[27] is a manufacturer of sweetmeats, and at 1.41.8 *salarii* are dealers in salt (perhaps salted foods also). All these words are attested elsewhere, though none of them is common.

But Martial provides another batch of words of this type of formation, some of which occur only in his work.[28] In doing this he is playing with a common suffix in order to characterise a person as so closely associated with something that he can be likened to one who trades in it or uses it in the performance of professional duties: for example 11.100, an epigram about preferred physical attributes in girlfriends, concludes *carnarius sum, pinguiarius non sum*, and the meaning is a humorous and slangy 'I'm a flesh merchant, not a fat merchant.' Here are further examples: at 4.28.7 a woman who fancies young, hairless boys is labelled *glabraria* (*glaber* refers to a hairless boy); at 4.87.3 a woman who always has a baby with her to disguise her perpetual farting is labelled *non infantaria* or 'not a baby merchant';[29] at 4.4.7 a *sabbataria* is a woman whose stock-in-trade is Sabbaths, i.e. a Jewess; at 10.3.5 a *poeta clancularius* is a poet whose occupation is characterised by the adverb *clanculum*[30] (i.e. keeping his identity secret, because he tries to pass off his rubbish as Martial's work); and at 12.58 the doubly suffixed *lecticariola* and *ancillariolus* denote respectively a woman whose amatory interest lies in litter-bearers, and a man whose interest lies in housemaids.

There are various factors which suggest we can view these humorous coinages and usages by Martial as colloquial, in that they would have been a type of humour common in the everyday speech and idiom of the time: (i) *-arius/-a* words of this type are extremely common in Latin, especially in the inscriptional evidence: the termination is so ubiquitous that it is applied to adjectives as well as nouns, and we have seen how Martial even extends it to an adverb;[31] (ii) Martial is not the only evidence for the use of this

---

[27] Accepting Shackleton Bailey's (1989: 144) excellent emendation of MS *cellarius*.

[28] Namely *pinguiarius*, *glabraria* and *lecticariola*.

[29] Conceivably 'not a wet-nurse or baby-minder': there may have been an actual profession of *infantaria*, that is someone who looks after babies, or the word might merely suggest that the woman's stock-in-trade was babies – there is humour on either interpretation.

[30] An adjective *clanculus* is only found in glosses.

[31] See Olcott 1898: 133 ff.: out of over 400 such words which he catalogues, 143 in *-arius* and 22 in *-aria* are found only in inscriptions, and others are found with new meanings in inscriptions (p. 137 with n. 1); also Väänänen 1966: 91 ff. A few random examples: *CIL* vi 9676 records a *negotians salsamentarius et vinariarius maurarius* (a merchant in Mauretanian salted meats and wines); *CIL* xiv 2302 a *pistor candidarius*, vi 9488 a *lagunar<i>a* (a female seller or maker of flagons), and vi 5972 a *margarit<aria>* (a female pearl-seller). See also Adams 1995b: 104–5 for instances from the Vindolanda letters, in which the suffix is used of some military occupations.

formation for humorous purposes, and it also appears in a poetic graffito: under a statue of Octavian a wit wrote *pater argentarius, ego Corinthiarius,* because he had a reputation for proscribing people whose Corinthian ware he coveted for his collection (Suet. *Aug.* 70 = Courtney 1993: 474–5); and (iii) these suffixes have many Romance reflexes, such as Italian *-aio* (even the double suffix *-aiuolo,* as e.g. *borsaiuolo* (a dealer in bags, humorously denoting a pickpocket) and *fruttaiuolo* (a fruit dealer)), French *-ier,* Spanish *-ero,* Portuguese *-eiro* etc.; Olcott (1898: 138) comments that 'the suffix still forms new words whenever the need is felt, even in jest, a sure test of its popularity and usefulness' (see also Staaff 1896).

5 CONCLUSION

I have aimed in this paper to provide some general thoughts about colloquial language in Martial, and have looked in some detail at three particular types of it in the epigrams. In this, as in many other matters, he is clearly a valuable and fertile resource. It is notable, for example, that his epigrams provide a significant proportion of the material which Hofmann added in his Nachträge to the first edition of *Lateinische Umgangssprache.*[32]

---

[32] Hofmann 1951, esp. 188 ff. (=Hofmann–Ricottilli, esp. 358 ff.).

CHAPTER 20

Current and ancient colloquial in Gellius

Leofranc Holford-Strevens

Aulus Gellius' theoretical attitude to current spoken usage is clear-cut (Wolanin 1999): it is a degenerate aberration from the pure Latin spoken before Augustan times (13.6.4), corrupted by the ignorant (15.5.1) and to be rejected even when not confined to the common herd (1.22.2).[1] In this judgement there is no ambiguity; it remains only to see how far theory is supported by practice.

However unwilling Gellius may be to speak like the masses of his own day, he has no objection to speaking like the masses of long ago. In *Noctes Atticae* 17.8 the philosopher L. Calvenus Taurus,[2] having invited his students in Athens to dinner, sends for oil to pour into the pot of Egyptian lentils and diced gourd on which the feast is based; a pert slave-boy accidentally brings an empty jar and, amidst much shaking and grimacing, claims *perquam Attice* that the oil is frozen: §7 μὴ γελᾶτε, *inquit*, ἔνι τοὔλαιον· ἀλλ᾽ οὐκ ἴστε οἷα φρίκη περὶ τὸν ὄρθρον γέγονε τήμερον; κεκρυστάλλωται. Taurus laughingly bids him in Latin to run and fetch some: §8 *Verbero, inquit ridens Taurus, nonne is curriculo atque oleum petis?*

That the exchange is of Gellius' own concoction is clear enough from the confusion between φρίκη and *frigus* (Holford-Strevens 2003: 232); we need therefore not worry about the kind of Latin Taurus used, or whether on such an occasion he would have spoken Latin at all.[3] It is far more important to notice the echoes of early drama, in particular comedy.

---

[1] This chapter arises out of observations made in the course of writing on Gellius' language in the context of Antonine literary trends: I have great pleasure in offering it to Jim Adams, who has done so much to further the study of different Latinities and to refine the concept of 'standard' and 'non-standard'.

[2] Not, as Gellius calls him at 18.10.3, by confusion with a then prominent family, Calvisius: see Holford-Strevens 2003: 317.

[3] See on this chapter Beall 1999.

The noun *verbero* is common enough in comedy, mostly as a vocative,[4] but afterwards appears only once, at Cic. *Att.* 14.6.1 (in the ablative singular), until the Antonine era, being signficantly absent from Petronius: Gellius has it not only here, but in 1.26.8, where again (by coincidence or not) it is a vocative put in Taurus' mouth, albeit quoting Plutarch.

The use of the present tense after *nonne* in a disguised command recalls Pac. *trag.* 16 Ribbeck[2] = Schierl *nonne hinc vos propere a stabulis amolimini?*;[5] slightly different is the mocking challenge at Pl. *Per.* 747 *nonne antestaris?*, in effect an ironic imperative *antestare*, 'Go on, get your summons witnessed', uttered in much the same spirit as Catiline's *refer ad senatum* addressed to Cicero (*Catil.* 1.20). At 1.10.2, when Favorinus is made to say *nonne, homo inepte, ut quod vis abunde consequaris taces?*, we may recall that *non taces?* is found some dozen times in Plautus[6] and twice in Terence (so too in grandiose abuse at Petr. 8.8–9);[7] but Gellius does not share the early authors' preference for plain *non* in questions (nor indeed their reluctance to place *nonne* before a consonant: 1.18.5, 1.25.6, 7.16.12, 18.7.4, 20.1.12, 20.8.4).

The adverbial ablative *curriculo* 'at the double' is found in comedy at Pl. *Epid.* 14, *Mil.* 523, 525, *Mos.* 362, 929, *Per.* 199, *Rud.* 798, 855, fr. 120, Ter. *Hau.* 733. The most interesting passage for our purposes is *Rud.* 798–9 *i dum, Turbalio, curriculo, adfert<o domo>* | *duas clavas.* Here too we have *ire* modified by *curriculo* and followed by a verb of fetching.

Not only does Gellius' vocabulary recall the early drama, but also the rhythm: *verbero, nonne is curriculo atque oleum petis?* resembles either an interrupted septenarius or the ends of two senarii.[8] This no more means that Gellius is quoting from a comedy than that the various snatches of *versus quadrati* scholars have detected in the fable of 2.29 need (or in some cases even can) be derived from Ennius (Holford-Strevens 2003: 48 with n. 3); nevertheless, it is evident that he is blending, and means to be heard blending, Plautine passages such as those cited and *Per.* 671 *abin atque argentum petis?* If the slave can speak with fashionable affectation, so

---

[4] Nineteen times in Plautus and twice in Terence, against two instances in the nominative (Pl. *Am.* 180, *Vid.* 65) and one in the accusative (Pl. *Ps.* 1205).

[5] For *non* + present in similar questions in Plautus see Lodge (1924–33), s.v. III.C.2.c.

[6] That is, besides the fuller form at *Per.* 533 *taces an non taces?*, and *Ps.* 889 *molestus ne sis; nimium iam tinnis; non taces?*, where if we do not delete *iam* as a dittography (cf. *nimium tinnis Cas.* 250) we must alter either *nimium* to *nimis* or *non taces* to *tace*.

[7] Note too Hor. *Epist.* 1.2.33 *ut te ipsum serves, nonne expergisceris?*, advice rather than command; there is advice in Favorinus' question too, but ironic.

[8] A Taurus as well read in Aristophanes as Gellius in Plautus might have said ὦ μαστιγία, ἔλαιον οὐκ οἴσεις τρέχων;, suggesting the ends of two successive trimeters.

can the master; better than Rolfe's rendering 'You rascal . . . run' would be 'Varlet, hie thee'.

The three Plautinisms, *verbero, nonne* + present indicative for a disguised command and adverbial *curriculo*, are all absent from the Corpus Frontonianum, but recur in Apuleius. *Verbero* indeed is used five times, but never as a vocative, and only in the *Metamorphoses* (8.31.5, 10.7.10, 10.9.2, 10.10.1, 10.10.3).[9] At *Soc.* 10.153 a quotation is introduced with the words *Nonne audis, quid super tonitru Lucretius facundissime disserat?*; not 'Qui ne connaît?' (Beaujeu) but 'N'entendras-tu pas?' or simply 'Entends'. *Curriculo* is used four times: twice in the context of running and fetching, *Apol.* 63.4 *iussi curriculo iret aliquis et ex hospitio meo Mercuriolum afferret*, *Met.* 10.9.4 *quam* [sc. *pecuniam*] . . . *iussi de meis aliquem curriculo promptam adferre*,[10] and twice where the sense is more loosely 'post-haste', *Apol.* 44.6 *Thallus solus, ut dixi, quod fere ad centesimum lapidem longe exul Oea est, is Thallus solus abest, sed misimus qui eum curriculo advehat* (unless the sense be 'in a chariot', which the epileptic Thallus would need), *Fl.* 21.1 *illis, quibus curriculo confecta via opus est, adeo uti praeoptent pendere equo quam carpento sedere.*

In comedy, an interrogative may be followed by *malum* to indicate the speaker's annoyance; by the classical period the usage had become sufficiently sanitised to appear in literary representations of speech – and not to appear in Petronius. It is particularly favoured in the combinations *quae malum ratio* (Cic. *Off.* 2.53, cf. *Scaur.* fr. *g, Phil.* 10.18, Liv. 5.54.6, Apul. *Apol.* 8.4) and *quae malum amentia/dementia* (Sen. *Dial.* 6.3.4, Plin. *Nat.* 7.190, 33.137, Curt. 8.14.41, cf. Cic. *Ver.* 2.54, *Q. Rosc.* 56);[11] Gellius uses it thrice (12.1.17, 13.12.8, 15.31.4), always with *quae ratio*, and the second time in his own person.[12] Fronto, who has *qua malum volup* at *Fer. Als.* 3.2 (p. 228.12 van den Hout) and *quae malum providentia tam inique prospicit* at *Nep. Am.* 2.3 (p. 236.8 van den Hout), bizarrely inserts the interjection in a relative clause at *De eloq.* 1.4 (p. 135.1 van den Hout);[13] Apuleius puts

[9] All these instances are in the singular; for the plural see Non. p. 28.27 M. (= p. 41 L.), Hier. *Epist.* 98.21.

[10] I hesitate to count the first passage with the Gellian echoes, due to personal acquaintance, posited at Holford-Strevens 2003: 22–6, since *afferre* points directly to *Rud.* 798–9; for what it is worth, the second stands near four of the five instances of *verbero*, even though they are not in the vocative (on *Met.* as possible debtor to Gellius' work see Holford-Strevens 2003: 24 n. 62).

[11] Later examples of these phrases at *TLL* VIII.236.65–71.

[12] See Cavazza 1985–: VI.99 n. 19 and in general Hofmann 1951: 32, 188.

[13] All references to Fronto follow van den Hout's second edition (Leipzig, 1988). It would be as dangerous to suppose that Fronto's copy of the *Epistulae ad Atticum* read *malum* with M (written in 1393) at 9.18.4 as to build anything on Hauler's *uuomalum*, also read *duolladom*, in Pius' letter at *Ant.* 6 (p. 165.6 van den Hout).

it in an indirect question at *Met.* 4.25.4 *quid malum fieret* 'what the devil was going on'.[14] Neither usage is found previously.

Indeed, dipping into older styles is not an error-proof procedure. Cicero's attempt at writing old Latin in his *Laws* is not free from false archaisms (Powell 2005); in English, 'derring-do' in the sense of 'heroic courage' is a misunderstanding by Spenser, popularised by Scott, of Chaucer's 'dorring don', i.e. daring to do, mediated through Lydgate.[15] Gellius too is guilty of the occasional catachresis;[16] thus it is with his use of the requesting formulae *amabo* and *amabo te*.

Amabo for 'please' in early Latin mostly follows immediately after an imperative, and is overwhelmingly used by women (Adams 1984: 61–2). When used by men (never in Terence), it implies a loss of masculinity: most drastically at Pl. *As.* 707, 711, where young Argyrippus is being ridden by the slave Libanus ('just as when you were a boy, know what I mean?', v. 703), elsewhere when they are pleading with or in thrall to women (Panciera 2007).[17] Occasionally it takes the object *te* (once in the mouth of a pleading man, *Men.* 678), and then shows more freedom in its position.

Usage, however, was to change (Adams 1984: 62–3). We do not know the speaker or context of *mea Vatiena amabo* in Laevius fr. 28 Courtney = Blänsdorf, but when Catullus invites a woman round for sex (32.1) there is no abjection. It is still a woman, namely Olympias mother of Alexander the Great, in whose mouth Varro puts *amabo* (Gel. 13.4.2);[18] but in Cicero's correspondence men freely use *amabo* and *amabo te*, which has largely ousted it, to each other; they are familiar, even affectionate, but not in the least unmanly. Indeed, at *De orat.* 2.278 *amabo te* is employed in a jest of casual misogyny.

---

[14] Cf. by euphemism *Met.* 10.16.1 *quid bonum rideret familia* ('why to goodness' Butler and Owen 1914: 21). At Ps.-Hegesippus 5.31 (*Corpus Scriptorum Ecclesiasticorum Latinorum* LXVI.370.19–20) *quae malum ratio Iohanni suaderet ut Romanos in excidium templi lacesseret* takes the place of Josephus, *De bello Iudaico* 6.95 εἰ καί τις αὐτὸν ἔρως κακὸς ἔχοι τοῦ μάχεσθαι, where κακός no doubt inspired *malum*.

[15] See *Oxford English Dictionary* s.v.

[16] Like Fronto *Ep. M. Caes.* 5.48.1 (p. 78.21 van den Hout), at 2.26.20 he uses *absque te* without the early authors' *esset* or *foret* to mean εἰ μὴ σὺ εἴης, and at 2.2.7 he even allows it with a substantive in the sense of *sine*, with no precedent unless we believe the manuscripts at Quint. *Inst.* 7.2.44 (though later writers were to use it thus with abandon); writing in an age when *dies* was often made feminine against the Republican rule, at 1.25.15, 3.4.1 he hypercorrectly uses the masculine for an appointed day.

[17] Thus at *Per.* 765 Toxilus, having strutted about like a mighty conqueror, has turned to putty in Lemniselenis' arms.

[18] Since Varro is an author whose style Gellius admires, we may take the introductory *ad hanc sententiam* to mean 'in Varro's free translation from the Greek' rather than 'in my paraphrase of Varro'.

Thereafter both expressions disappear from current usage, being absent alike from Horace and Petronius; there is one instance of *amabo* in Martial (8.76.1), where it is spoken by a man who begs to be told the truth so long as he is not told it,[19] but none in Vindolanda. By Imperial times, when love was invoked in a request, the preferred formula was evidently *si me amas*, with variations of person, number and tense, found only twice in early comedy (Pl. *Trin.* 243–4, Ter. *Hau.* 1031), but frequent in Cicero's letters and the Corpus Frontonianum,[20] besides attestations in Horace (*Sat.* 1.9.38), Petronius (48.4, 96.7, 98.8) and the Vindolanda letters (*Tab. Vindol.* 11.233.B.ii.3; see Adams 1995b: 127). By contrast, there are no instances in Gellius or Apuleius; instead Gellius uses the older courtesies, but not in the old way.

At 4.1.4 a bore of a *grammaticus* who has been holding forth about the gender and accidence of *penus* is put in his place by Favorinus: *amabo, inquit, magister, quicquid est nomen tibi, abunde multa docuisti, quae quidem ignorabamus et scire haud sane postulabamus.* The tone of the last clause needs no comment; *quicquid est nomen tibi*, an echo of Pl. *Ps.* 639,[21] is rude enough; in this context *amabo* does not seem in the least polite, not 'please' but at best 'pray'. At 5.21.6, Gellius' anonymous and no doubt fictitious friend, rebuked by a pedantic purist (*reprehensor audaculus verborum* §4) for using *pluria* instead of *plura*, retorts laughingly: *amabo te, inquit, vir bone, quia nunc mihi a magis seriis rebus otium est, velim doceas nos . . .* Here, besides *bone* 'used ironically to show the speaker's superiority' (Dickey 2002: 313), the reference to leisure, while right and proper in a Roman man of affairs,[22] indicates the unimportance of the other's concerns; again *amabo te* has nothing friendly about it.

In previous authors *amabo* and *amabo te* have always been addressed to a person whom the speaker (or the letter-writer) already knows; they may, in comedy though not in Cicero, convey reproach, but always to someone of

---

[19] Is there a hint that Gallicus' poems imitate the style of the late Republic?

[20] *Si me amas*, Marcus *Ep. Ant. Imp.* 1.1.3 (p. 86.22 van den Hout), Fronto *Amic.* 2.6 (p. 189.4 van den Hout); *si quicquam nos amas*, Fronto *Ep. M. Caes.* 5.1 (p. 69.41 van den Hout); *si quid umquam me amasti*, Marcus *Ep. M. Caes.* 5.43.1 (p. 77.9 van den Hout); *si umquam nos amasti sive amaturus umquam es*, Fronto *Ver.* 1.6.8 (p. 111.21–2 van den Hout).

[21] Surely spoken, as Acidalius saw, by Harpagus not Pseudolus, to whom it was ascribed by a dull-minded copyist because Pseudolus had given a (false) name. Those who have accepted the reattribution include Eduard Fraenkel, in his Oxford seminar of 1966.

[22] We may wonder about a *doctrina homo seria et ad vitae officia devincta ac nihil de verbis laborante* (§2) who can nevertheless rattle off the names of half a dozen authors who have used '*pluria*' sive '*compluria*' – *nihil enim differt* (§5) and cite by title a treatise on the topic by Sinnius Capito (§§9–10), even if he has to qualify its location in the Templum Pacis with *opinor*. No doubt the dialogue was invented in order to advertise knowledge of the treatise.

whom better might have been expected, as when at Pl. *Per.* 336 a girl says *amabo, mi pater*, to the father who means to sell her into slavery. However, the grammarian is manifestly a stranger to Favorinus, the purist may well be a stranger to Gellius' friend; tiresome as their behaviour is, the speakers have no claim upon them other than as fellow human beings. The nearest approach to the Gellian tone is Pl. *Mil.* 900–1, where Acroteleutium, accosted by Palaestrio, exclaims *Quis hic amabo est,* | *qui tam pro nota nominat me?*, but her question, in the third person, is addressed to, or at least answered by, Periplectomenus; to anticipate Gellius, she would have had to ask *Quis tu's, amabo,* | *qui tam pro nota nominas me?*, which would have been perfectly metrical but completely unidiomatic. These revived *amabo* and *amabo te* are peculiar to Gellius; neither Fronto nor Apuleius has them, and when Marcus uses *amabo* it is always literal, with Fronto as object.[23]

Some colloquial uses remained current from pre- to post-classical times; one such is *bene* 'very', 'thoroughly', not entirely excluded from the higher registers, e.g. *bene saepe* ('bien souvent' Marache) Enn. *Ann.* 268 Skutsch at Gel. 12.4.4.[24] Gellius has it more than once, e.g. 9.9.12 *Valerii Probi... docti hominis et in legendis pensitandisque veteribus scriptis bene callidi*; but at 17.18, in the tale of the moralist caught in the wrong bed, the tone is unmistakable: *M. Varro... C. Sallustium... loris bene caesum dicit.* Sallust was 'given a good thrashing', or 'soundly whipped' ('fustigato di santa ragione' Bernardi Perini).[25] However, we cannot be sure whether the vivid expression is Gellius' own or Varro's; in the former case it would be interesting that he did not use the Plautine *probe.*

At the end of his investigation into everyday language in Apuleius' *Metamorphoses*, Callebat (1968: 551–2) sums up his findings thus:

> Nous avons vu qu'il existe dans le roman d'Apulée un fonds linguistique naturel où se reflètent souvent les traits du parler vivant contemporain mais nous avons également noté que l'on n'y trouve guère d'éléments qui ne soient déjà bien accueillis par la langue littéraire.... Bien des traits aussi, arbitrairement rattachés au *sermo cotidianus*, doivent être interprétés soit comme des procédés narratifs expressifs, soit comme des rappels concertés de la langue des comiques.

If this is true of a novelist whose plot and characters are not always of the most salubrious, we may much more expect it of the scholar who leaves

---

[23] *Ep. M. Caes.* 2.5.1, 5.2, *Add. ep.* 7.1 *ter* (pp. 26.3, 70.2, 249.4, 249.8, 249.9 van den Hout).

[24] See *TLL* 11.2125.53–2126.83.

[25] To be sure, there is nothing colloquial about Col. 12.15.5 *bene siccatas meridianis teporibus*, for neither is there any such incongruity in the notion of drying figs well, that is to say thoroughly, rather than leaving them partly moist, as (except to the brutal mind) there is in that of thrashing well, or in the slang of the Victorian schoolboy, laying it on with science.

his study only for the company of his fellow intellectuals and his social superiors; nevertheless, Gellius did not altogether eschew usage that an earlier age would have called substandard. He is the first literary author to use *quod* to introduce reported speech (Holford-Strevens 2003: 52–3); he also uses *paucus* in the singular, an *abusio* (*Rhet. Her.* 4.45) found at *B. Afr.* 67.2, Vitr. 1.1.6, *CIL* XII.1939.1[26] and looking forward to Spanish and Italian *poco*. It is found at 9.4.5, 20.1.31 with *aes*, 'undoubtedly a current colloquialism' (Adams 1977a: 79 on Claudius Terentianus, *P. Mich.* VIII.471.10, 13, 31), but also at 4.11.11 *pauca carne quadam* 'a few kinds of meat'.[27] Although the usage is absent from Fronto and Marcus,[28] while Apuleius admits only *pauculum tempus* at *Met.* 11.29.1, it was evidently intruding into the *consuetudo*.[29]

Far more shocking is the praise Fronto bestows on Marcus for using a word we certainly do not find in Gellius or even Apuleius: Fro. *Ep. M. Caes.* 3.17.5 (p. 50.6–7 van den Hout) *quom Persarum disciplinam memorares, bene 'battunt' aisti*. Here *battunt*, the ancestor of French *battent* and Italian *battono*, is a reduced form of *battuunt*, by far the oldest example of the reduction;[30] although this verb, in Republican Latin a coarse word for beating (Pl. *Cas.* 496 *quibus battuatur tibi os*, 'to smash your face in with') and a euphemism for *futuo* (Cic. *Fam.* 9.22.4),[31] achieved a marginal acceptance in medical and culinary contexts,[32] its use with reference to

[26] From Vienne, by an author who supposes *dolose* (l.3) to mean *dolenter*, cf. *dolum* for *dolorem* XII.2033.3, whence Old French *deul*, modern *deuil*. I omit later examples such as Hyg. *Fab.* 194.4; see in general *TLL* x/1.804.45–805.35. Quite different is Hor. *Ars* 203 *foramine pauco* 'with a few holes', singular for plural by analogy with *multus*.

[27] Why not *paucis carnibus quibusdam*? Perhaps because the plural tended to suggest either the flesh on the human body or pieces of meat; evidently Gellius preferred to treat *caro* as a substance, covering (as the sequel shows) both parts of the body (womb, heart) and source-creature (sea anemone).

[28] At *Dig.* 50.8.13 *pauco tempore* appears in Papirius Justus' report of a rescript by the Divi Fratres.

[29] No doubt the usage was encouraged by Greek ὀλίγος, not only amongst the learned, but amongst Greek-speaking freedmen. I am as reluctant to believe that Gellius misunderstood Ennius' genitives plural *verbum paucum* (*Ann.* 281–2 Skutsch) as that he wrote the unmetrical *paucorum* offered by his MSS at 12.4.4.

[30] To be sure a copying error is possible; and the reduction of -*uu*- to -*u*- is known from fourth-declension genitives plural, in particular *passum* for *passuum*.

[31] Cf. English 'bang'; so *debattuere* Petr. 69.3.

[32] Plin. *Nat.* 31.104, on the medicinal uses of salt, *crocodilorum morsibus ex aceto in linteolis ita* [sc. *inposuere*], *ut battuerentur ante his ulcera*, misinterpreting Dioscorides, *Materia medica* 5.109.5 καὶ κροκοδειλοδήκτοις δὲ βοηθοῦσιν ἐνδεθέντες εἰς ὀθόνιον λεῖοι καὶ βαφέντες ἐν ὄξει στυφομένων τῶν μερῶν τοῖς ἐνδέσμοις, as if the absolute participle were τυπτομένων (so Jan–Mayhoff); Donatus on Ter. *Eu.* 381 *cuditur, id est batuitur faba, cum siliquis exuitur tunsa fustibus*; but only once each even in the subliterary 'Apicius' 4.2.28 *soleas battues*, against four instances of *tundes* (1.18, 2.1.2, 3.18.3, 7.14.2) and Marcellus, *De medicamentis* 36.4 (p. 367, ll. 2–3 Helmreich) *mittes in pilam ligneam atque illic tam diu battues, donec sit subactissimum* (contrast *contunde in pila* §3, p. 366, l. 17 and indeed in §4 *contunde, contundas* ibid., ll. 25, 29). Although single *t* is sometimes attested, as in Donatus, *tt* is confirmed not only by Romance but by Welsh *bathu* 'to coin'.

fighting belonged to the jargon of soldiers and gladiators,[33] being exhibited in the latter context by the ostentatiously unpretentious Suetonius (*Cal.* 32.2 of a *mirmillo*, 54.1 of Caligula got up as a *Thraex*). That not even Apuleius, in whom there is no lack of physical violence, finds employment for the verb makes the more striking Fronto's commendation of its literary use, in the specialised rather than the Plautine sense at that, though his greater openness towards the rougher end of the colloquial is manifest in his approval of Laberius, whom Gellius holds in some disregard (Garcea and Lomanto 2004).[34]

These are merely a few test-bores into the Antonines' linguistic usages; nevertheless, Gellius' preference for archaic colloquial over modern, if not absolute, is detectable and not surprising. More surprising, perhaps, is that Apuleius differs from him less in this regard than Fronto and his correspondents; much indeed must be allowed for the difference in genre, but the case of *battunt* demonstrates that that is not a complete explanation.

[33] Cf. van den Hout 1999: 137, on 50. 7, and in general *TLL* 11.1789.12–51. Charisius attests the neuter plural *battualia* γυμνασία μονομάχων, whence the feminine singular *bataille*, *battaglia*, etc.

[34] To be sure, in 16.7 Gellius indulges in his sport of having things both ways, citing matter of which he voices disapproval (cf. 9.4, 9.10); but he does not use the vulgar expressions himself, as he often does expressions that he cites from early authors.

CHAPTER 21

Forerunners of Romance -mente adverbs in Latin prose and poetry

Brigitte L. M. Bauer

I INTRODUCTION

As a rule of thumb linguistic change typically starts in the colloquial registers of a given language and gradually spreads to other segments of language use. High-level literature and legal texts tend to be last to incorporate linguistic innovations. The shift from object-before-verb (OV) to verb-before-object (VO) structures, for example, was first manifest in the more colloquial Latin texts and only spread to other registers at a later stage. The honorand of this *Festschrift* has analysed this change on various occasions and already in 1977 stated that 'in spoken Latin of the informal varieties VO was already established as the unmarked order, but . . . OV was preferred in literary Latin. . . . It is well-established that formal and informal codes in any language differ radically' (Adams 1976b: 97). Similarly, other major linguistic changes first manifest themselves in our sources of colloquial Latin: case loss and the spread of prepositions, the loss of other inflected forms in favour of right-branching[1] analytic forms, the spread of subordinate clauses with conjunctions and finite verbs replacing accusative with infinitive and participial constructions, and so forth.

The same pattern is found in other languages as well and at all times. The eventual morphological loss in today's French of the *passé défini* (*passé simple*), for example, which goes back to the Latin perfective paradigm

---

[1] The notion of branching refers to the linear ordering of elements that are in a hierarchical relation. In the clause *exercitum duxit* the direct object (the complement) precedes the verb, which is the head of the clause. The complement therefore branches to the left of the head. Similarly, in *deorum munus* the nominal complement (*deorum*) branches to the left of the head noun (*munus*). In *le présent des dieux* the branching pattern is exactly the opposite: the complement follows the head. In the history of Latin/Romance we find a consistent shift whereby the original left-branching structures are being replaced by right-branching equivalents. This shift is observable not only in syntax, but also in morphology, where inflectional endings have often been replaced by prepositions, auxiliaries, subject pronouns, and adverbs that precede the lexical element, as in: *grandior* being replaced by *plus grand*, *legibus* by *avec les lois*, or *amaverit* by *il aura aimé*, and so forth. For an extensive discussion of this change and the definitions of head and complement see Bauer 1995.

(Fr. *je louai* < Lat. *laudavi*), is now almost complete and can be traced in the twentieth century in the various written registers. First it had disappeared from the informal varieties of French, a process observed in spontaneous speech in the eighteenth century (Brunot 1933: 1457–8). Following this trend, authors in the nineteenth century came to use the *passé défini* in narrative parts, but the *passé composé* in direct speech (Brunot 1933: 1784–5). This pattern is still attested by the mid twentieth century in e.g. De Gaulle's *Mémoires de guerre* (1950s) and Simenon's novels featuring Maigret (1931–72). But the *passé défini* had gradually disappeared from the colloquial written documents. And although in the 1980s it was still frequently used in newspapers, by now – depending on the newspaper – the *passé défini* has been ousted in most contexts by the *passé composé*. In 1993 Grevisse wrote that while the *passé défini* had almost completely disappeared from the spoken language, 'des gens cultivés' continued to use fixed expressions that feature the verb form – but only the third singular – as in *il fut un temps* 'there was a time when' (Grevisse 1993: 1253). Otherwise instances may be found in high-level French literature, also with a marked preference for the third person singular.

The formation of Romance adverbs in -*mente* is an exception to this common scenario of linguistic change moving from colloquial to higher registers of a given language: its earliest attestations – in actual occurrence and meaning – trace back to high-level poetry. In a (2001) article, I traced the earliest instances of adjective + *mente* in poetry and prose, examining poetic texts by Lucretius, Catullus, Virgil, Tibullus, Horace, Ovid and Lucan, and prose texts by Caesar, Cicero, Sallust, Varro, Livy, Quintus Curtius, Seneca, Quintilian, Petronius and Tacitus. Comparison of occurrence and use of the instances of adjective + *mente* revealed that in prose the combination typically has purely lexical value; in poetry we find not only many more instances of the structure, but a clear predominance of lexical/adverbial value as well. On the basis of the early occurrences of adjective + *mente* I then concluded that 'adverbial use of *mente* indeed originated in poetry and spread to prose only later. This tendency is not only reflected in the frequency of *mente* in poetry, but – more importantly – in its actual use as well: the lexical/adverbial reading clearly predominates in poetry; by contrast, in prose adjective-*mente* combinations are, with a few exceptions, purely lexical' (Bauer 2001: 40).

Yet *mente* was but one variety among several other nouns that in combination with an adjective were used to convey possible adverbial value in Latin (e.g. McCartney 1920; Karlsson 1981). There were in fact three groups of noun that occurred in adjective + noun combinations expressing the way the action conveyed by the verbs was carried out. These categories are:

(a) abstract nouns meaning 'way', 'manner' (e.g. *modo, more, opere*, etc.), as:

(1)   epistularum genera duo, quae me magno opere delectant

                                                                (Cic. *Fam.* 2.4.1)

        (there are) two types of letter that please me greatly;

(b) nouns referring to body parts (e.g. *pede, manu*, etc.), as:

(2)   nemus citato cupide pede tetigit   (Catul. 63.2)

        he reached the wood eagerly on speeding feet/he reached the wood eagerly and rapidly;

(c) nouns referring to 'mind' (*mente, animo, animis*, etc.), as:

(3)   ubi cognita aequo animo sint   (Cato *Agr.* 2.5)

        when (these things) have been discussed calmly.

In this chapter I discuss the use and value of adjective + noun combinations that include non-abstract alternatives of *mente*, focusing on nouns referring to body parts – e.g. *pede, manu, pectore, lingua, corde*, etc. – and the abstract noun *animo*. The patterns that will emerge will show whether the binary evolution we observed in the history of *mente* in prose vs poetry is more general and extends to its varieties as well. Analysis will not only inform us about the earliest stages of what was going to be a grammaticalisation process, but will also further nuance the relation between varieties of Latin and their importance for diachronic linguistic research.

2 PRESENTATION OF THE DATA

In the shift from the adjective + *mente* combination to the Romance adverbial formation featuring the suffix *-mente* one observes *grosso modo* three stages of development, each representing a different reading:

(a) The combination has purely lexical value, as in:

(4)   sed mente simplicissima et vera fide . . . comites induxisse   (Petr. 101.3)

        but he had taken (us) as his companions in all sincerity and in good faith.

This adjective + noun combination features nouns other than *mente* as well, for example *ore*:

(5)   purpureo bibet ore nectar   (Hor. *Carm.* 3.3.12)

           he will drink nectar with a red mouth.

(b) The combination has lexical / adverbial value: *timida mente*, for example, may convey the notion of 'with a timid mind' or 'timidly', as:

(6)   cave... et timida circumspice mente...   (Ov. *Tr.* 1.1.87)

           therefore be careful and look around you with a timid mind/timidly.

This combination as well is attested with nouns other than *mente*, as:

(7)   taeterrima voce... canticum extorsit   (Petr. 35.6)

           he squeezed out a song with a hideous voice/he hideously squeezed out
           a song.

(c) The combination has purely adverbial value. This value is most clear in instances in which the subject of the clause is non-animate, the verb refers to an activity that does not involve any mental activity and the adjective is free of any reference to mental activity or state as well. I here give a French example because it features *mente* as a suffix. This does not mean that in Latin we do not find instances of clear adverbial use:

(8)   le vin coule lentement, mais librement du pressoir

           the wine flows slowly, but freely, from the winepress *not:* *the wine flows
           with a slow but free mind from the winepress.

Among the adjective–noun combinations with lexical and lexical/ adverbial value, those with *mente* were relatively late and caught on slowly (already McCartney 1920: 213). Other nouns that occurred earlier in these contexts will be analysed in this chapter. For this purpose I examined texts by the popular playwrights Plautus and Terence, texts by Catullus, Ovid and Horace, representing high-level poetry, and the prose authors Cato, Livy, Caesar, Sallust and Petronius, whose texts reflect different degrees of formality. The texts analysed were the following: Plautus' and Terence's entire work, Catullus' poems, Horace's *Odes* and *Epodes*, Ovid's *Metamorphoses*, Cato's *De re rustica*, Sallust's *Bellum Catilinae* and *Bellum Iugurthinum*, Caesar's *De Bello Gallico*, Livy's *Ab urbe condita*, and Petronius' *Satyricon*. I also examined the use of *corde* in the Vulgate. The data from the Vulgate will not be included in the tables, but they will be discussed in section 3.

The selection of authors and their work is partly motivated by the nature of their writings and partly by my earlier research on adjective + *mente* combinations. The authors in question, covering prose and poetry, represent various linguistic registers. Moreover, Catullus and Ovid both had many instances of adjective + *mente*, with high scores of lexical/adverbial value. Since Horace, by contrast, had just three instances, which were lexical, I include his work here as well. The differences in chronological period and style have determined my choice of prose authors.

My analysis focuses on the non-abstract nouns *pede, manu, voce, lingua, corpore, anima, corde, pectore, ore, spiritu,* and the abstract *animo*. In the selected texts, I have identified all ablative singular forms of the nouns in question. I then determined whether the noun combined with an adjective or not. As a result, this analysis is broader than my earlier ones of *mente* (2001 and 2003), in that *all* instances of the ablative singular forms have been taken into account. The importance of evaluating the occurrence of adjectives as such will later become clear. Subsequently, I categorised the adjective + noun combinations, identifying their lexical or adverbial/lexical value. This last category here includes not only instances that feature both values ('happily' vs 'with a happy heart'), but also those that are decidedly adverbial. They are included in one category because this subcategorisation may tend to be subjective. The qualification 'lexical' (as opposed to 'non-lexical') is rather straightforward and may be motivated by the presence of a preposition or a noun used in a similar way, as in:

(9)   lubentissimo corde atque animo   (Pl. *Ps.* 1321)

        with great satisfaction of heart and soul/with a greatly satisfied heart and soul.

The distinction between lexical/adverbial and adverbial on the other hand is one of degree. Moreover, with a few exceptions, most non-lexical instances are of the type lexical/adverbial. Important details about purely adverbial use will be provided in the analysis (section 3) when necessary.

In the following pages, I will first present the numerical data for each individual author. There are three tables, one for playwrights, one for poets, and one for prose authors. The presentation of the data will be followed by the discussion of the data.

3 ANALYSIS OF THE DATA

As said, all instances of the ablative of the nouns in question have been examined. Among them, there are several that include an ablative noun that is part of a prepositional phrase or that functions as complement to an adjective or verb, as the following examples, which all include an adjective, illustrate:

Table 21.1 *Adjective + Noun in early playwrights*

Noun	Author	TOTAL	NO ADJ.	WITH ADJ.	LEX.	LEX./ADV.
PEDE	Plautus	1	0	1	1	0
	Terence	0				
MANU	Plautus	16	2	14	11	3
	Terence	3	2	1	1	
VOCE	Plautus	5	1	4	0	4
	Terence	1	0	1	1	0
LINGUA	Plautus	5	3	2	2	0
	Terence	0				
CORPORE	Plautus	1	0	1	1	0
	Terence	1	1			
ANIMA	Plautus	1	0	1	0	1
	Terence	0				
ANIMO	Plautus	45	9	17 (36*)	3	14
	Terence	47	4	19 (43**)	1	18
CORDE	Plautus	6	2	4	3	1
	Terence	1	1			
PECTORE	Plautus	6	1	5	1	4
	Terence	2	2			
ORE	Plautus	2	1	1	1	0
	Terence	6	3	3	1	2
SPIRITU	Plautus	1	1			
	Terence	0				
TOTALS		150	33	74 (117)	27	47

Notes

*19 instances are of the type adjective + noun + *esse* (as in: *bono animo sum*).

**24 instances are of the type adjective + noun + *esse* (as in: *bono animo sum*).

(10)   expulit ex omni pectore laetitias   (Catul. 76.22)

        it has expelled joy from my entire heart

(11)   forti pectore notus   (Catul. 64.339)

        known for his strong breast

(12)   manu sinistra | non belle uteris   (Catul. 12.1–2)

        (that) you make no good use of your left hand

(13)   tunc Fortuna levi defudit pectore voces   (Petr. 121.102)

        then Fortuna poured out words from her capricious heart.

Table 21.2 *Adjective + Noun in poets*

Noun	Author	TOTAL	NO ADJ.	WITH ADJ.	LEX.	LEX./ADV.
PEDE	Catullus	7	0	7	3	4
	Horace	10	0	10	1	9
	Ovid	7	3	4	2	2
MANU	Catullus	4	3	1	1	
	Horace	4	0	4	1	3
	Ovid	44	27	17	10	7
VOCE	Catullus	6	0	6	0	6
	Horace	5	1	4	3	1
	Ovid	22	7	15	6	9
LINGUA	Catullus	2	0	2	2	
	Horace	0				
	Ovid	5	2	3	2	1
CORPORE	Catullus	7	1	6	5	1
	Horace	4	1	3	2	1
	Ovid	28	2	26	22	4
ANIMA	Catullus	1	1			
	Horace	0				
	Ovid	2	2			
ANIMO	Catullus	6	3	3	2	1
	Horace	0				
	Ovid	1	1			
CORDE	Catullus	6	2	4		4
	Horace	3	1	2	1	1
	Ovid	3	1	2	2	0
PECTORE	Catullus	14	4	10	5	5
	Horace	2	0	2	2	0
	Ovid	24	6	18	13	5
ORE	Catullus	10	3	7	6	1
	Horace	5	1	4	2	2
	Ovid	Too frequent to make data collection practical				
SPIRITU	Catullus	0				
	Horace	1	0	1	1	0
	Ovid	0				
	Totals	233	72	161	93	66

In these instances the adjective + noun combinations typically do not convey adverbial value.

Comparison of the results reveals several tendencies, at different levels: in terms of comparison with *mente* and in terms of differences between varieties of Latin. First of all we notice that the combining of an adjective and the nouns in question varies depending on the chronological period

Table 21.3 *Adjective + Noun in prose author*

Noun	Author	TOTAL	NO ADJ.	WITH ADJ.	LEX.	LEX./ADV.
PEDE	Cato	1	1			
	Caesar, Sallust	0				
	Livy	13	11	2	1	1
	Petronius	2	1	1	1	0
MANU	Cato	2	2			
	Caesar	3	1	2	0	2
	Sallust	20	19	1	0	1
	Livy	Too frequent to make data collection practical				
	Petronius	28	13	15	6	9
VOCE	Cato, Livy	0				
	Caesar	3	1	2	0	2
	Sallust	3	1	2	0	2
	Petronius	16	3	13	1	12
LINGUA	Cato	1	0	1	1	0
	Caesar	0				
	Sallust	3	2	1	1	0
	Livy	8	7	1	1	0
	Petronius	1	0	1	1	0
CORPORE	Cato	0				
	Caesar	1	0	1	0	1
	Sallust	7	5	2	2	0
	Livy	Too frequent to make data collection practical				
	Petronius	8	1	7	5	2
ANIMA	Cato, Caesar, Petronius	0				
	Sallust	5	5			
	Livy	0				
ANIMO	Cato	2	0	2	0	2
	Caesar	29	18	7 (11*)	2	5
	Sallust	35	22	10 (13**)	3	7
	Livy	103	56	45 (47***)	18	27
	Petronius	1	1			
CORDE	Cato, Caesar, Sallust	0				
	Livy	1	1			
	Petronius	1	1			
PECTORE	Cato	0				
	Caesar	1	0	1	1	0
	Sallust	2	2			
	Livy	4	3	1	1	0
	Petronius	10	5	5	5	0

Table 21.3 (*cont.*)

Noun	Author	TOTAL	NO ADJ.	WITH ADJ.	LEX.	LEX./ADV.
ORE	Cato, Caesar	0				
	Sallust	1	0	1	0	1
	Livy	14	12	2	2	0
	Petronius	5	3	2	2	0
SPIRITU	Cato, Caesar, Sallust	0				
	Livy	Too frequent to make data collection practical				
	Petronius	2	2			
TOTALS		336	199	128 (137)	54	74

Notes
*4 instances are of the type adjective + noun + *esse* (as in: *bono animo sum*).
**3 instances are of the type adjective + noun + *esse* (as in: *bono animo sum*).
***2 instances are of the type adjective + noun + *esse* (as in: *bono animo sum*).

and the type of text. In Cato's text 3 instances are found (in a total of 6). In other authors these numbers are higher, but there is a distinct difference between prose and poetry: 46 nouns in a total of 63 occurrences in Catullus combine with an adjective; in Horace these numbers are 30/34 and in Ovid 85/136. In the early playwrights we find 69 instances in Plautus (total of 89) and 48 instances in Terence (total of 61). By comparison, prose has a limited number of these constructions: not only in Cato as mentioned earlier, but also in Sallust (19/73), Caesar (17/37) and Livy for all nouns analysed (*animo* (47/103), *lingua* (1/8), *pectore* (1/4), *ore* (2/12), *pede* (2/13)). Adjective + noun combinations therefore are significantly less frequent in prose than in poetry.

In addition, we notice a relatively high incidence in Livy (for *animo*, see below), in Petronius (48/73) and in the Vulgate (for *corde*, 12/64). From the perspective of language evolution we therefore observe a trend of increasingly combining the noun with a qualifying adjective, which marks the truly initial stage of what was going to be a process of grammaticalisation. In the literature on grammaticalisation this stage of development – which obviously precedes the one in which adjective + noun conveys adverbial/lexical value – as a rule is completely ignored.

Along the lines pointed out in the previous paragraph (prose vs poetry and early vs late) there is a distinction in terms of lexical vs non-lexical value as well, even if the numbers at face value may seem to suggest the opposite.

We find 66 adjective + noun instances with lexical/adverbial value in poetry, and 74 instances in prose (the totals are 159 and 128 respectively). In the playwrights the numbers are 47 of a total of 74 instances of adjective + noun. By comparison, of the 49 instances of adjective + *mente* occurrences in prose texts only one instance from Tacitus had lexical/adverbial value. Other instances were lexical (Bauer 2001: 38).

The predominance of non-lexical value in prose authors is based on Livy's high numbers. Without Livy, the lexical reading overwhelmingly predominates. Moreover, all instances with lexical/adverbial value in Livy – with one exception (1/28) – include *animo*. Caesar has combinations with lexical/adverbial value that include *manu, voce, corpore*, but in combinations with *animo* that value is most frequent. Finally, in the vast majority of these instances *animo* combines with *aequo*. *Aequo animo* was therefore the most frequent combination with adverbial value in prose as found in Sallust (4/6), Livy and Caesar (3/5), and examples are attested from the earliest texts onward, as:

(14)   ubi cognita aequo animo sint   (Cato *Agr.* 2.5)

         when (these matters) have been discussed calmly.

Among the prose authors analysed here only Petronius includes adverbial uses for a variety of other nouns, such as *manu, voce, corpore* and *ore*, for example:

(15)   clara Eumolpus voce exhortabatur   (Petr. 140.9)

         Eumolpus urged with a clear voice

(16)   ille gladium parricidali manu strinxit   (Petr. 80.1)

         he drew his sword murderously

(17)   ille manu pavida natos tenet   (Petr. 123.226)

         he holds his children shakingly.

It is striking that the only instance of *animo* in Petronius does not feature an adjective and there is only one instance of adjective + *mente*, with lexical value (*mente simplicissima*, see example (4)).

Plautus as well shows some variation in the choice of nouns, but to a lesser degree. Most instances of lexical/adverbial use include the noun *animo* (17 examples), but we also find examples among adjective + *voce* combinations (4/5), adjective + *manu* combinations (3/16) and adjective + *pectore* combinations (4/6). In the 14 instances of adjective +

animo, the 2 instances of adjective + *manu*, 4 instances of adjective + *voce* and 1 instance of adjective + *anima* and adjective + *pectore* the value is adverbial rather than lexical/adverbial. In Terence lexical/adverbial use of adjective + noun combinations is almost non-existent.

In poetry the nouns in question vary with the author, who despite diversity tends to show preference for a given noun. Lexical/adverbial uses primarily are found for *pede* in Catullus (4/7), as well as *corde* (4/6) and *pectore* (5/14). Horace favours lexical/adverbial uses in combinations with *manu* (3/4), *pede* (9/10) and *ore* (2/5). In Ovid lexical/adverbial value is attested in combinations including *pede* (2/7), *manu* (7/44), *voce* (9/22), *corpore* (4/28) and *pectore* (5/25). Other nouns occur as well, but less frequently. In fact, personal preference seems to prevail in the frequency with which the poets combine adjective and nouns: with the exception of *anima*, all nouns occur in adjective + noun combinations that have lexical/adverbial value. As said, *animo* is however remarkably rare in poets in adjective + noun combinations with adverbial/lexical value. Consequently, we find that the patterns we observed for Petronius trace back to poetic usage.

Similarly, specific uses of *animo* attested in later texts are also found in earlier documents. In my analysis of *animo* in the Vulgate (2003) I observed a strong tendency to combine adjective + noun + *esse*, as in:

(18)   bono animo estote   (Acts 27:25)

        be of good cheer.

Further analysis of *animo* shows that this same structure is common in other authors as well, as in Plautus, for example

(19)   scin quam bono animo sim?   (Pl. *Am.* 671)

        do you know how cheerful I am?

In Plautus and Terence alone, we found 43 instances of this type of structure (out of a total of 92 instances of *animo*), showing that the structure was common in colloquial Latin. For other nouns instances of this type are rare, but they do occur, for example:

(20)   scio te bona esse voce   (Pl. *Mos.* 576)

        I know that your voice is good.

Moreover, the most important findings in the Vulgate may not entail adjective + noun combinations as such, but rather the occurrence of prepositions in these contexts. In the Vulgate we not only find many prepositions with *corde* that have adverbial value, but especially so in combination with adjectives, and these prepositional constructions may convey adverbial value. In terms of frequency, we find 64 instances of *corde*, 49 of which include a preposition. Of these 49, 10 include an adjective, 8 of which have adverbial/lexical value. We find prepositional *corde*, for example, in the following types of example:

(21)   accedamus cum vero corde...   (Hebrews 10:22)

         let us go there with a true heart/true-heartedly

(22)   qui invocant Dominum de corde puro   (2 Timothy 2:22)

         who invoke the Lord with a pure heart/sincerely.

A similar example is found in Catullus, cf.:

(23)   illa vicem curans toto ex te pectore   (Catul. 64.69)

         she by contrast cared about you with all her soul.

This use tends to adverbial value, showing the intensity of her caring: 'she by contrast cared about you whole-heartedly'. Consequently in the Vulgate and occasionally in classical Latin, the combining of the preposition + adjective + noun may have adverbial value, where before that combination would typically have lexical value, as example (9) illustrated: Pl. *Ps.* 1321 *lubentissimo corde atque animo* 'with great satisfaction of heart and soul'.

Finally it is always difficult to point out the earliest attestations of any linguistic change. This is unfortunate because being able to do so might help to account for a given development. Yet, from this perspective several instances in Horace are of particular interest. Overall we find that in the texts analysed the choice of verbs is in accordance with that of the nouns: in Catullus all adjective + noun examples including *pede*, for example, combine with a verb that conveys movement; all adjective + *voce* combinations in Catullus include a verb of saying, singing or uttering, whereas *manu* examples typically combine with a verb referring to an activity involving the use of a hand (with possible idiomatic exceptions, such as 'to rear a child with severe hand').

By contrast, Horace on several occasions combines an animate subject, an object and a verb that conveys action without specifying its precise nature. The phenomenon is illustrated in English by the generic verb 'go' as in the sentence *he goes to London*, which is unspecified in terms of how *he* is getting there; by contrast *he walks to London* is specific. In Horace we find instances in which the verb as such is non-specific, as:

(24)   iniurioso ne pede proruas | stantem columnam   (Hor. *Carm.* 1.35.13–14)

         lest you overturn the standing pillar with criminal foot.

The verb *proruo* conveys the generic notion of reversing, but as such does not specify the way it is done. It is the ablative construction that provides this specification. Similarly:

(25)   ferebar incerto pede   (Hor. *Epod.* 11.20)

         I was moving with uncertain foot/uncertainly

(26)   pallida Mors aequo pulsat pede pauperum tabernas | regumque turris
                                                         (Hor. *Carm.* 1.4.13)

         pale Death knocks with impartial foot at the doors of poor huts and at the gates of royal palaces.

In some of these instances the lexical interpretation is clear, as in:

(27)   puerum minaci | voce dum terret   (Hor. *Carm.* 1.10.10–11)

         he terrified you as a boy with a threatening voice.

In other instances adverbial value is stronger, as in:

(28)   et sacrilega manu | produxit   (Hor. *Carm.* 2.13.2–3)

         and he reared you with a sacrilegious hand

(29)   si quis impia manu | senile guttur fregerit...   (Hor. *Epod.* 3.1–2)

         if anyone will strangle an old man's throat with impious hand...

These examples are interesting not only because the type of activity is specified by the occurrence of the noun, but also because the adjective that is added reveals the manner in which the specified action is carried out. As a result adjective + noun in this instance has at the same time instrumental and adverbial value. In instances of this type may reside the origins of the adverbial innovation.

4 CONCLUSIONS

Reflecting a tendency observed for the development of *mente*, examples of ablative uses of *animo* and of nouns conveying body parts reveal an uncommon dichotomy between prose and poetry: in contrast to general tendencies in diachronic linguistics this time it is in poetry, where normally we find archaisms, that we observe the first instances of linguistic innovation.

Already at the earliest stage of what was going to be a process of grammaticalisation, we notice a discrepancy between prose and poetry. In poetry combining the noun and an adjective – whatever their context – is much more common than in prose. Moreover, it is in poetry that we find a stronger variety of adjective–noun combinations in lexical/adverbial (or adverbial) use. Instances of this use in prose authors are limited in number and in type: the structure primarily includes *animo* and shows a strong preference for *aequo*. It is important to note that the earliest prose text analysed here (Cato) includes two instances of that combination, both with adverbial value. Second, the high numbers of instances of this use in Livy almost exclusively entail *animo*. By contrast, evidence from the latest author analysed here, Petronius, shows that we are dealing with a development: as in the earlier poetic texts, his lexical/adverbial combinations involve a variety of nouns. The spread of adjective + noun constructions therefore follows the patterns found for the development of adjective + *mente* (Bauer 2001).

There are more parallels. In my earlier articles on adverbs I noticed that from a diachronic perspective the main difference between *animo* and *mente* resides in the formal stability – in time and genre – of *mente* combinations, which may account for the survival of *mente* as a suffix (Bauer 2003). Conversely *animo* + noun combinations displayed important formal variety, including prepositions, genitives and so forth. Analysis in this chapter has revealed a similar formal variety, culminating e.g. in the Vulgate's importance of preposition + adjective + *corde* combinations reflecting adverbial value.

In conclusion we can therefore say that the patterns we observed earlier for *mente* in the early instances (prose vs poetry), and for *animo* in the Vulgate (variability) are similar to those involving other nouns. In view of the topic of this *Festschrift* we therefore underscore the important observation that in the development of adverbial constructions the relation between poetry and prose is the reverse of what we traditionally find.

The first question that comes to mind is: 'Why in this specific development is it prose that "catches up" with poetry and not the other way around?' Influence from Greek poetry may have been a factor. A century ago already Shorey (1910) pointed out that adjective + noun combinations in the dative featuring adverbial value are found in ancient

Greek, in Homer, and even more so in tragedies and lyric poetry. It is important to note the similarities between these constructions and their Latin counterparts: the nouns in question are of three types: (1) nouns expressing 'way', 'direction', (2) nouns referring to heart and mind, and (3) nouns referring to body parts. As in Latin, these combinations may have lexical, lexical/adverbial or adverbial value. These parallels indeed suggest that Greek influence may have been a factor, but the predominating role of poetry in the development still remains to be explained.

In my view it is the experimental character of poetry that accounts for these uses. The tendency observed in Horace may reflect this experimental innovation: combining a generic verb with a noun specifying its precise nature ('going' as opposed to 'going on foot') and then combining with an adjective that inherently specifies the manner in which the action is carried out. It may be the freedom of the creative poet that accounts for one of the major changes in the shift from Latin to Romance. Examining the instances of adjective + noun combinations in time and register therefore shows that what was to become an important colloquialism in the history of Latin/Romance can be traced back to literary creativity.

PART V

Late Latin

CHAPTER 22

Late sparsa collegimus: *the influence of sources on the language of Jordanes*

Giovanbattista Galdi

I INTRODUCTION

Unlike some other authors of the sixth century AD, such as Cassiodorus, the historian Jordanes has received very little attention in modern scholarship.[1] Besides, the evaluation of his language and style has been since Mommsen an unfavourable one, for two reasons. The first is that, since both his works are epitomes, Jordanes often employs large sections of previous authors – from the second to the sixth century AD – sometimes copying them word for word (Bergmüller 1903: 3 defines him a 'Kompilator ersten Ranges'); the other reason is that his texts contain, at least in Mommsen's (1882) edition, several late and substandard features as compared to the 'good' classical Latin, that is 'the standard language in the late Republic and early Empire'.[2] The aim of this paper is to connect, in some way, these two aspects: on the one hand, I shall show how crucial an exact knowledge of the sources is to a precise understanding of Jordanes' language; on the other, I shall discuss some morphological and syntactic peculiarities of his works. Special attention will be given here to a few substandard usages that can be considered 'colloquialisms', that is to those features which are normally excluded from literary sources of the (post-) classical period and, on the ground of several parallels in authors of the same period and, especially, in non-literary and extra-literary sources,[3] are likely to have been widespread in the spoken varieties of late Latin. I shall thus not regard as colloquial all substandard (that is not-classical) features in Jordanes, but only those which at the time when he composed his works

---

[1] The author wishes to express his deep gratitude to Anna Chahoud for her corrections and very useful suggestions.

[2] Adams 2007: 17. As is well known, linguistic anomalies occurring in late Latin sources are often seen, especially in nineteenth-century/early twentieth-century scholarship, as a mark of 'wrong' and bad Latin, with an implied judgement of value. See Chahoud, this volume p. 54.

[3] On the difference between non-literary and extra-literary evidence see Chahoud, this volume pp. 56–7.

(and often also before) were probably common in everyday language. After
a short introduction on the life and work of the author, I shall focus on his
'minor' work *Romana* in which (as it will be shown) nearly each paragraph
can be traced back to a precise model.[4]

2 THE AUTHOR AND HIS WRITINGS

All that we know about Jordanes' life comes from two paragraphs of his
Getica:

(1)   Scyri vero et Sadagarii et certi Alanorum cum duce suo nomine Candac
        Scythiam minorem inferioremque Moesiam acceperunt. cuius Candacis
        Alanoviiamuthis patris mei genitor Paria, id est meus avus, notarius,
        quousque Candac ipse viveret, fuit, eiusque germanae filio Gunthicis,
        qui et Baza dicebatur, mag. mil., filio Andages fili Andele de prosapia
        Amalorum descendente, ego item quamvis agramatus Iordannis ante
        conversionem meam[5] notarius fui.   (*Get.* 265–6)

        The Sciri moreover, as well as the Sadagarii and certain of the Alani with
        their leader, Candac by name, received Scythia Minor and Lower Moesia.
        Paria, the father of my father Alanoviiamuth, that is my grandfather,
        was secretary to this Candac as long as he lived. To his sister's son
        Gunthigis, also named Baza, the Master of the Soldiery, who was the
        son of Andela's son Andag and descended from the family of the Amali,
        I also, Jordanes, although an unlearned man, was secretary before my
        conversion.   (trans. Mierow 1915: 127, slightly adapted)

(2)   nec me quis in favorem gentis praedictae [*sc. Geticae*], quasi ex ipsa
        trahenti originem, aliqua addidisse credat, quam quae legi et comperi.
                                                                  (*Get.* 316)[6]

        Let no one believe that to the advantage of the race of which I have
        spoken – though indeed I trace my own descent from it – I have added
        aught besides what I have read or learned by inquiry.
                                                        (trans. Mierow 1915: 142)

---

[4] Quotations of Jordanes in the following pages reflect a number of late antique phonological features
(e.g. change of *u* to *o*, loss of final *-m*, confusion of *b* and *v*) which have been sufficiently treated by
earlier commentators and will not be discussed further here.
[5] It is not known exactly what this phrase refers to: it could have been a conversion from Arianism
to Catholicism, entry into a monastery, or both. See Buonomo 1997: 115–69 and Christensen 2002:
94–101, with further literature.
[6] The standard edition of Jordanes, to which I refer, is Mommsen's (1882). The *Getica* has been
more recently edited by Giunta and Grillone (1991), who introduce numerous normalisations to
the text of Mommsen. In the two passages above they make the following changes: *Alanoviamuthis*
(for *Alanoviiamuthis*), *filii Gunthigis* (for *filio*), *filii Andagis* (for *filio*), *descendentis* (for *descendente*),
agrammatus (for *agramatus*) and *Iordanes* (for *Iordannis*); *trahentem* (for *trahenti*).

Passage (1) indicates that our author, as *notarius* to a Roman *magister mili-tum* (Gunthigis) and nephew of a *notarius*, descended from a distinguished family ('non infima condicione', remarks Mommsen 1882: vi). Further-more, the passage puts him directly in connection with the area of Scythia and Moesia,[7] so most scholars assume that he was either a Goth or an Alan, both populations being well represented in that territory. The precise value of *quasi* in text (2) (*quasi ex ipsa trahenti originem*) is fundamental in this respect, since this conjunction can carry in late Latin both a comparative-hypothetic force ('as if') and a causal one ('because', 'though indeed', as in Mierow's translation). The meaning of *agrammatus* is also problematic: in reference to a *notarius* and historian who knows and employs several literary sources, it cannot simply mean 'unlearned'. Besides, the fact that – as Jordanes himself states in the prefaces – the addressees Vigilius (in the *Romana*) and Castalius (in the *Getica*) chose him to write the two works presupposes a satisfactory historical and linguistic knowledge; Giunta and Grillone (1991: xviii) diminish the strength of the adjective by explaining it as 'consuetudine tantum "humilis" qui dicitur sermonis'; this interpreta-tion appears unsatisfactory on several grounds.[8] It is instead probable that Jordanes, at the least at the time of his *notariatus*, 'had bypassed', as Croke (1987: 17) assumes, 'the conventional training in *grammatice*'.

This aspect emerges clearly in some studies of Jordanes' language, par-ticularly in those of Roxana Iordache.[9] In this connection it is crucial to recall that Latin was not Jordanes' mother tongue and may well have been even his third language after Gothic (spoken by many in Gunthigis' army) and Greek (the language of most cities in the region; see Croke 1987: 119). He may well have learned Latin at the time of his *notariatus* and deepened his knowledge of it after his conversion. Besides, the harsh judgements on Jordanes' language are obviously conditioned by the edition of Mommsen

---

[7] Besides, some sections of the *Getica* show that Jordanes was well acquainted with the east-ern regions. See on this point the discussions of Mommsen (1882: x–xiii) and Kappelmacher (1916).

[8] Jordanes occasionally employs some *formulae modestiae*, but they are confined to the prefaces of his works. They concern either the ability of the author to fulfil the task he has been given by the addressee (as in *Rom.* 3 *licet nec conversationi meae, quod ammones, convenire potest nec peritiae*) or the quality of his books (cf. *Rom.* 4 *parvissimo libello*, *Get.* 1 *hoc parvo libello*). References to his linguistic skill do not occur. Furthermore, it must be observed that Jordanes' works reveal some knowledge of classical authors, such as Virgil or Ovid. See particularly Wölfflin 1900: 361–8, Bergmüller 1903: 20–6 and Mierow 1922–3.

[9] See for example Iordache (1992: 33): 'Dans nombre de ses phrases [i.e. of Jordanes] presque chaque mot comporte une faute, voire plusieurs, de nature différente, que ce soit au point de vue de la graphie, ou bien de la morphologie, de la syntaxe, du lexique, de l'ordre des mots dans la proposition et dans la phrase.'

who sometimes chooses, among different *lectiones* of the manuscripts, the most ungrammatical ones. This point has been particularly stressed by Giunta and Grillone in their more recent edition of the *Getica*.[10] It must be noted, however, that these two scholars often make the opposite mistake by going too far in their 'normalisation' process: in several instances they arbitrarily refuse the form transmitted by the first manuscript family, particularly by the *Palatinus*, and 'correct' it through grammatically 'better' variants in the second or third one.[11] Moreover, most of their changes concern phonetic aspects, such as *u* for *o*, *e* for *i*, and vice versa: the morphology and syntax of the text (which constitute the bulk of the present contribution) are much more rarely involved.

Jordanes left us two historical works, *De origine actibusque Getarum* (or *Getica*) and *De summa temporum vel origine actibusque Romanorum* (or *Romana*), which, as the author himself states, were completed during the twenty-fourth year of the reign of Justinian, that is in AD 551–2.[12] Both works are epitomes: the *Getica* summarises the twelve volumes of Cassiodorus' *Historia Gothorum*, occasionally supplemented *ex nonnullis historiis Grecis ac Latinis* (*Get.* 3). The *Romana*, considered by Jordanes as his minor work (cf. *Get.* 1), is a world chronicle, from Adam to Justinian. The sources of the *Getica* (apart from the lost books of Cassiodorus) are mainly unknown, whereas most of those used in the *Romana* have been identified and discussed by Mommsen (1882).[13] The most frequently employed are the *Epitome* of Florus (second century) and the *Chronicon* of Jerome (fourth century), the only author besides Ablabius whom Jordanes expressly mentions by name (*Rom.* 11 *sicut Eusevius vel Hieronimus*). Less common is the use of other works such as the *Chronicon* of Marcellinus Comes (sixth century), the *Historiae* of Orosius (fifth century), the *Breviaria* of Eutropius and Rufius Festus and the *Epitome* of Ps.-Aurelius Victor (fourth century).[14]

---

[10] See Giunta and Grillone 1991: xviii–xix: 'Difficile non est statuere permulta illa errata, et syntactica et graphica, quae traduntur ex prima familia tantum [i.e. the first manuscript family], non ad auctorem nostrum esse tribuenda, sed potius ad amanuenses Germanicos.' According to Mommsen (1882: lxxii) the *Romana* is transmitted by two manuscript families, the *Getica* by three. The most important and reliable *codices* of both books (*Heidelbergensis, Valenciennensis, Palatinus* and *Laurentianus*) belong to the first one.

[11] See on this point my discussion in Galdi, forthcoming.

[12] Cf. *Rom.* 4 *in vicensimo quarto anno Iustiniani imperatoris quamvis breviter uno tamen in tuo nomine et hoc parvissimo libello confeci*; 363 *Iustinianus imperator regnat iam iubante* [sic] *domino annos* XXIII.

[13] Modern scholarship generally rejects the old theory of Enßlin (1949) according to which the text of the *Romana* is mainly based on the lost *Historia Romana* of Symmachus. See on this point the remarks of Luiselli (1976).

[14] For a full list of the sources used by Jordanes see Mommsen (1882: xxiii–xxix).

3 THE LANGUAGE OF THE AUTHOR AND
ITS RELATION TO THE SOURCES

Jordanes' language and style have mostly been neglected by modern linguists and literary critics alike. Only four monographs exist on the topic: a lexical analysis of preverbs (Lorenzo 1976) and three doctoral dissertations of the last century (Bergmüller 1903; Werner 1908 and Kalén 1939). These and other studies[15] have undoubtedly enlarged our knowledge of the author and his works (especially the *Getica*). A serious drawback, however, is that they give little or non-existent consideration to the sources. Now, the *Romana* and *Getica* being as we have seen compendia of previous works, it is evident that an accurate comparison with these texts should constitute a precondition for any linguistic analysis of the author, in order to distinguish his style from that of the source text. This applies particularly to the *Romana* whose sources, apart from a few paragraphs, are all well known and preserved. In this chapter, by means of selected examples, I shall point out the different techniques by which the author takes up and revises the text of his models in the *Romana* and their influence on his language.

3.1 Transcription of the source

In numerous paragraphs of the *Romana* Jordanes copies his source text verbatim. Specifically, this technique characterises the large section based on the *Epitome* of Florus that sums up the most relevant historical facts from the beginning of Rome until the end of the *res publica* (*Rom.* 87–110, 115–209, 224, 236, 241–7, 251–4, henceforth referred to as the Florus fragment). As Jordanes transcribes the text of Florus verbatim in about 80 per cent of these lines,[16] this section is of great interest to the textual critic. For, leaving aside those passages (for which see below) in which Jordanes deliberately changes Florus' text in terms of single words or longer sections, the

---

[15] These include several articles of Roxana Iordache (1973, 1983, 1986, 1992), who mainly focused her attention on the syntax of Jordanes. The monograph of Helttula (1987), which deals in a long chapter with the usage of absolute constructions in Jordanes and Gregory of Tours, is also very instructive.

[16] See also Mommsen 1882: xxiii: '[Flori] epitomam...Iordanes in Romanis...ita secutus est, ut excepto uno loco...aliena nulla interponeret, complura omitteret, multa in compendium redigeret, pleraque autem ipsis verbis retentis redderet.' The reasons why Jordanes follows the *Epitome* of Florus so blindly are unknown. Perhaps the antiquity of the text, which is some 150 years older than the *Breviaria* of Eutropius and Rufius Festus, generated a sort of deep deference in the author and induced him to a literal transcription. Another possibility is that, whereas several authors dealt with the Imperial period (Eutropius, Jerome, Orosius, etc.), Florus was Jordanes' main and (apart from a few passages in Rufius Festus) only source for the Republican age.

manuscripts often exhibit other kinds of deviation, which mostly involve either the orthography of the text (exchange of letters, haplography, dittography, etc.) or phonetic and morphological aspects (such as the loss of final -*m* and -*s*, omission of *h*, *u/o* confusion, etc.). Now, since our author probably had, as seen above, a satisfactory knowledge of Latin orthography and certainly would have acquired a good practice in transcribing texts during his *notariatus*, it is unlikely that he accidentally miscopied his model (an assumption which, of course, cannot be completely excluded a priori). This type of error is more likely to be the work of medieval scribes. Hence, an accurate study of these mistakes enables us to evaluate the tendency of the *Romana*'s manuscripts to alter the text and eventually to check their trustworthiness. Conversely and more to our point, the Florus fragment is of little importance to the linguist and should be used very cautiously because of the constant risk of 'slipping' into Florus' language. A few examples will illustrate the importance of this aspect.

A revealing case is the use of words meaning 'therefore'. The *Romana* (like most late Latin texts) shows a clear preference for *ergo* (eight times, excluding the section depending on Florus): *itaque* and *igitur* occur solely in the Florus fragment (sixteen and nine times respectively). It would be wrong or at least misleading to assert based on usage in that fragment that, in contrast with other writers of his age, Jordanes' style is characterised by heavy use of *itaque* and *igitur*. An analogous case is that of *quin* and *donec*, which are both attested only in the Florus section.

Apart from the long Florus fragment, Jordanes seldom copies the text of his models verbatim. When he does, however, we should act with similar caution: if some linguistic features are mainly (or solely) attested in passages taken more or less literally from a model, we should not draw general (or generalising) conclusions on the style of the author. The case of *apud* exemplifies this situation. This preposition is usually avoided in late Latin texts and, except in Gaul, it is mostly replaced by *ad* in the Romance area. The *Romana* exhibits nineteen occurrences of *apud* and sixty-seven of *ad*: looking closer, however, we notice that in eighteen cases *apud* was already present in the model, whereas this is the case with *ad* only eight times. Furthermore, the latter occasionally displays the function of other prepositions, as in *Rom.* 86 *ea* . . . , *que ad tempora Augusti imperatoris dicuntur* ('the things which are told about [*ad* = *de*] the time of the emperor Augustus').

These and similar examples show that Jordanes' own language is often 'later' than his sources in terms of vocabulary selection. This means that when he has a free choice – that is, not conditioned by the models – among different, nearly synonymous, words, he mostly picks up those which were common in late Latin authors, sometimes using them with a meaning unattested in the classical period (such as *ad* in *Rom.* 86). Late, of course, does not necessarily imply 'colloquial' in the meaning given above, since only some of the features occurring in literary texts of the late antique period appear to be widespread in the spoken usage as well. One of these is certainly *ad*, which is also largely employed in non-literary sources such as inscriptions, and survived in all Romance languages.

3.2 Adaptation of the source

More interesting for the linguist are the numerous passages in which Jordanes modifies his source text. In the following section I shall analyse these changes, which appear to depend on several parameters (the context, the source, the linguistic trends of the author, etc.).

3.2.1 Addition of single words in the text
The simplest form of adaptation of the source is the insertion of one or more words into it. This kind of change is obviously rather infrequent in the *Romana*, which, as previously noted, is essentially a short summary of previous works. Most of the examples can be found in the long Florus fragment, where Jordanes occasionally supplements his source text either for pure stylistic reasons or perhaps for facilitating its comprehension (in terms of contents and language) to a sixth-century reader. For example:[17]

(3)   lupa . . . uber ammovit infantibus matrisque gessit officium   (*Rom.* 87)

        the she-wolf moved her teats towards the children and played the role of mother,

cf. Flor. *Epit.* 1.1.3 *lupa . . . uber ammovit infantibus matremque se gessit*;

(4)   Mucius Scevola Romanorum fortissimus   (*Rom.* 121)

        Mucius Scaevola, the strongest among the Romans,

cf. Flor. *Epit.* 1.10.5 *Mucius Scaevola*;

(5)   Illyres autem, id est Veneti, seu Liburnes   (*Rom.* 180)

        the Illyrians, that is the Venetians or Liburni,

---

[17] Some further passages are collected by Erhardt in his long review of Mommsen's edition (1886: 681–8).

cf. Flor. *Epit.* 2.5.1 *Illyrii seu Liburni;*

(6)   Pyrrum clarissimum Epyrotarum Greciae regem   (*Rom.* 150)

           Pyrrus, the king of Greece and most illustrious among the Epirotes,

cf. Flor. *Epit.* 1.18.1 *Pyrrum Greciae regem.*

   Moreover, our author almost unfailingly adds the third person plural or
the cluster *populus Romanus* in all passages in which Florus speaks in first
person plural of the victories and defeats of the Romans. These changes
are essentially motivated by the ethnic and linguistic origins of the author,
who could hardly identify himself with the Romans. For example:

(7)   de Verulis et Bobillis . . . triumphavere Romani   (*Rom.* 124)

           the Romans triumphed over the Veroli and Bovilli,

cf. Flor. *Epit.* 1.16.6 *de Verulis et Bovillis . . . triumphavimus;*

(8)   populus Romanus . . . penetravit   (*Rom.* 209)

           the Roman people penetrated,

cf. Flor. *Epit.* 2.7.10 *penetravimus.*[18]

   A much more frequent phenomenon, both in the *Romana* and the
Getica, is the insertion of copulative conjunctions such as *nam, si quidem*
and (*et*)*enim* between two phrases (cf. Mommsen 1882: 194; Werner 1908:
106–10). This phenomenon, which is also attested in other late Latin texts
(see S. Kiss 2005: 571–6, esp. 576), probably arises from the author's desire
to give stronger cohesion and uniformity to his narration, based as it was
on several different source texts.[19] Interestingly enough, the usage of these
particles appears directly related to the model: in about 40 per cent of
the total number of occurrences *nam* (thirteen times), (*et*)*enim* (six times)
and *si quidem* (five times) mark either the transition from one source to
the other or a skipping of paragraphs within the same source. Conversely,
the semantic value of these connectors is practically non-existent, as the
following examples illustrate:

(9)   Gaius Caesar cognomento Caligula regnavit ann. III menses x. hic
           namque Memmium Regulum coegit, ut uxorem suam sibi loco filiae
           coniugem daret strumentaque matrimonii ut pater conscriberet.

                                                                          (*Rom.* 259)

---

[18] Note that this kind of adaptation of Florus, although very frequent, is not universal. In a few cases
Jordanes keeps (perhaps by mistake) the first person plural. Cf. Erhardt 1886: 681.

[19] The same tendency can be observed in the frequent use of the connecting relative as well as
cross-reference expressions such as *ut diximus*.

Gaius Cesar, named Caligula, reigned for three years and ten months; he forced Memmius Regulus to give him in marriage his wife in place of his daughter and to sign the marriage documents as her father,

cf. Eutr. 7.12.1 *successit... Gaius Caesar cognomento Caligula* and Hier. *Chron.* a.Abr. 2055 *Gaius Memmii Reguli uxorem duxit impellens eum, ut uxoris suae patrem esse se scriberet;*

(10) Artaxerses, qui et Ochus, ann. xxvi. hic <u>etenim</u> Sidonem subvertit
      Aegyptumque suo subegit imperio   (*Rom.* 69)

      Artaxerses, also known as Ochus, [reigned] for twenty-six years. He
      overthrew Sidon and submitted Egypt to his power,

cf. Hier. *Chron.* a.Abr. 1652 *Artaxerses, qui et Ochus, ann.* xxv, and 1670 *Ochus Sidonem subvertit et Aegyptum suo iunxit imperio.*

The repeated usage of copulative conjunctions in these and similar passages does not seem accidental: probably the author felt that in such contexts the narrative cohesion of his text was particularly compromised and thus needed to be reinforced through the addition of textual connectors.

3.2.2 *Change of one or more words*

In most instances of adaptation of the model Jordanes makes substitutions and changes in the text. This can happen on different levels: it can involve single words (as in the change mentioned above from the first to the third person plural) or concern word order in the phrase or even deeply modify the syntactic structure of the source.[20] This last type of change is probably the most interesting for the linguist as it allows us to penetrate the deeper structures of Jordanes' style and to evaluate, to a certain extent, his linguistic skills as well as his preferences and distinctive features.

In a diachronic perspective it is worth mentioning those passages where the modification of the model reveals some colloquial features that also occur in authors of the same period or in non-literary sources, for example:

(11) Romani... [Domitianum] interficere statuerunt <u>omniaque, quod</u>
      constituerat, inritum fore   (*Rom.* 265)

      the Romans decreed to kill Domitian and annul all his decisions,

---

[20] This last, more radical, technique is characteristic of those paragraphs in the *Romana* that depend on Rufius Festus. Here Jordanes modifies his model so extensively that Luiselli (1976: 95) supposed that these passages had previously been adapted by Symmachus in his lost *Historia Romana* and then copied by Jordanes. Unfortunately, we have no evidence to prove this hypothesis.

cf. Hier. *Chron.* a.Abr. 2113 *senatus decrevit, ut <u>omnia, quae</u> Domitianus statuerat, in irritum deducerentur.*

The syntactic agreement between a singular and plural neuter constitutes a well-known feature of substandard Latin, which appears to be widespread in the spoken usage. It is first attested in an official inscription (containing a *lex repetundarum*) of the second century BC (*CIL* I² 583 *utei ea omnia, quod ex hace lege factum non erit, faciant*), but most of the occurrences (not only with *omnia* but also with other neuters such as *illa, ista, pauca, multa*) are to be found in late and medieval sources.²¹ Our example is also fostered by the gradual syntactic extension of *quod*, which tends, especially in the late period, to become a universal conjunction.²² Probably Jordanes considered both constructions *omnia, quae* and *omnia, quod* syntactically correct and thus interchangeable for stylistic purposes.

The syntagma above constitutes an isolated example in the *Romana*. More significant are those cases in which the anomalous form or construction resulting from the adaptation of the model confirms some 'anomalous' (that is non-classical) linguistic tendencies of the author that also figure in other passages of his works. Noteworthy is the usage of place names, especially city names. In both books of Jordanes, the distinction between the notions 'where' and 'whither' clearly tends to disappear in favour of 'where', a phenomenon revealing of the development of the language (in the Romance idioms this distinction is mostly unknown).²³ In particular, our author tends to generalise a precise (although not universal) scheme for the indication both of state and movement: the locative with *Roma*, the accusative with the names ending in *-polis* and the ablative with all other names,²⁴ for example *Rom.* 315 *[Theodosius] veniens... Thessalonica ab Acolio... baptizatus est* 'Theodosius came to Thessaloniki and was baptised by Acolius', 380 *postquam [Belisarius] Ravenna ingressus est... Epiro revertitur* 'after entering Ravenna Belisarius returned to Epirus', 227 *[Antiochus] filios... Romae deductos... regnare genitali loco concessit* 'Antiochus brought the children to Rome and allowed them to reign in place of the father'. This tendency is so marked that it causes a change of the (usually correct) construction of the source in a few cases, for example:

²¹ Cf. Bonnet 1890: 499–502; E. Löfstedt 1911: 307–10; Norberg 1944: 55–6; H–S 431–2; Adams 1976a: 88; Petersmann 1977: 51.
²² Väänänen (1982: 218–19) observes that in Gregory of Tours *quod* refers some forty times to a masculine or feminine term (both in singular and plural).
²³ The confusion or non-distinction between the indication of state and movement is already attested in the first century AD, both in literary and non-literary documents.
²⁴ The three above-mentioned phenomena also occur in other documents of the late period; cf. Adams 1976a: 57. Specifically on Jordanes see Galdi, forthcoming.

(12)   caputque   eius   [*i.e.*   Rufini]   et   dextera   manus
         <u>Constantinopolim</u> ... circumductum uxoremque eius exulatam
                                                                 (*Rom.* 319)

and Rufinus' head and right hand were brought round Constantinople
and his wife was banished,

cf. Marcell. *Chron.* II p. 64.395.5 *caput eius manusque dextra* <u>*per totam*</u>
<u>*Constantinopolim*</u> *demonstrata*;[25]

(13)   Misahelu et Ardaburem <u>Serdica</u> in exilio misit   (*Rom.* 360)

         he banished Misahelus and Ardaburis to Sofia,

cf. Marcell. *Chron.* II p. 101.519.2 *Misahel et Ardabur* <u>*Serdicam*</u> *in exilium
missi*;

(14)   *Archelaus* <u>*Romae*</u> *adveniens*   (*Rom.* 225)

         as Archelaus came to Rome,

cf. Ruf. Fest. 11.4 *cum Archelaus . . .* <u>*Romam*</u> *venisset.*
     An analogous case is the usage of the moods in relative clauses. Mommsen
(1882: 183) first noticed that the *Romana* and *Getica* often display an apparently unmotivated subjunctive in subordinate clauses, particularly in the
relative ones ('coniunctivus locum indicativi usurpavit praesertim post
pronomen relativum'). This observation, which was partly confirmed by
Werner (1908: 95), must be revised: a closer examination of all individual
occurrences reveals on the one hand that the allegedly incorrect uses of the
subjunctive are limited to the pluperfect (in the other cases one can assume
an *attractio*) and, on the other hand, that this mood (unlike the indicative)
is mainly found in clauses having a direct logical connection with the main
sentence, which they usually explain. This mood operates as an additional
signal to highlight the temporal–logical relationship between relative and
main clause (see Galdi 2008: 321–7). Therefore, we cannot regard these
instances as 'wrong' or inappropriate, but rather as conforming to the classical practice of inserting the subjunctive in those relative clauses with an
additional (causal, concessive, etc.) value (see K–S II.292–3). For example:

(15)   [Nepus] Glycerium, qui sibi tyrannico more regnum inposuisset, ab
         imperio expellens   (*Rom.* 338)

         Nepus excluded from the command Glycerius, who had usurped power
         as a tyrant

---

[25] Jordanes' use of the neuter singular instead of the plural with the participle (*circumductum* vs
demonstrata in Marcellinus) is probably to be explained *variationis causa*.

(Glycerius' exclusion from the command is the direct consequence of his usurpation of the power.)

The preference for the subjunctive in such contexts induces Jordanes in four cases to change the indicative of the source, for example:

(16)   [Gordianus] Puppienum et Albinum, qui Maximino²⁶ occidentes
         tyrannidem arripuissent, occidit   (*Rom.* 282)

         Gordian killed Puppienus and Albinus, who had killed Maximinus and
         usurped the power,

cf. Hier. *Chron.* a.Abr. 2256 *Pupienus et <B>albinus, qui imperium arripuerant, in palatio occisi;*

(17)   [Valentinianus] contra Saxones Burgutionesque, qui plus LXXX milia
         armatorum primum Reni in limbo castra metassent, movit procinctum
                                                                (*Rom.* 309)

         Valentinianus moved his attack against Saxons and Burgundians, who
         firstly encamped with over eighty thousand soldiers in the border of the
         Rhine,

cf. Oros. *Hist.* 7.32.11 *Burgundionum... hostium novum nomen, qui plus quam octoginta milia, ut ferunt, armatorum ripae Rheni fluminis insederunt.*

Given the well-known unpopularity of the subjunctive in spoken language,²⁷ such examples show us that Jordanes' change and adaptation of the model do not necessarily imply the use of a more colloquial feature; in fact, he often goes in the opposite direction when he chooses a solution more in conformity with the classical rules. The following two passages are also instructive:

(18)   cuius [*i.e.* Crassi] conspectu... filius hostilibus telis effossus (*Rom.* 236)

         the son of Crassus was killed by enemy spears in front of his father,

cf. Flor. *Epit.* 3.11.10 *filium ducis paene in conspectu patris idem telis operuerunt;*

(19)   [Antoninus Pius] defunctus est duodecimo urbis miliario, in villa sua
         Lorio nuncupata   (*Rom.* 271)

         Antoninus Pius died twelve miles away from the city in his villa named
         Lorio,

²⁶ For the 'deviating' accusative singular *Maximino* see n. 4 above (on the change *u > o* and the loss of final *m*).
²⁷ In everyday speech the indicative tends to spread at the expense of the subjunctive, a phenomenon already attested in the Republican period. See Ferri and Probert, this volume p. 31.

cf. Hier. *Chron.* a.Abr. 2176 *Antoninus Pius aput Lorium villam Suam* XII <u>*ab urbe*</u> *miliario moritur.*

In these texts Jordanes substitutes a simple case (*conspectu, urbis*) for the prepositional syntagma of the model (*in conspectu, ab urbe*). Both instances are explicable as hypercorrect constructions[28] in reaction to the well-known spreading of prepositional clusters in the spoken language, which survived in all Romance languages.[29]

Finally, the cases in which Jordanes seems to make a 'mistake' under the influence of his source are also worthy of attention. I do not refer here to the very few passages where the author copies an ungrammatical construction from his model,[30] but rather to those in which, although the source is revised and modified, parts of it still persist in Jordanes' text, thus generating syntactic incongruence. The evaluation of these passages is often uncertain because we cannot exactly establish to what extent the model contributed to the error. For example:

(20)   <u>Spanias</u> quamvis... Saguntina cladis ab amicitiis Romanorum
        segre<g>asset, Scipio tamen <u>eos</u>... rursus Romanis coniuncxit
        rursusque resistentibus Sylla consul sedavit   (*Rom.* 212)

        even though the defeat of Saguntum estranged Spain from the Roman
        friendship, nevertheless Scipio associated them again with the Romans;
        but as they offered resistance, the consul Sulla subjugated them a second
        time,

cf. Ruf. Fest. 5.1 <u>*Hispanis*</u> *primum auxilium adversum Afros per Scipionem tulimus . . . postea ad Hispanos tumultuantes Sylla missus* <u>*eos*</u> *vicit.*

This text is taken from the large section dealing with the Republican period and refers to the subjection of Spain by Sulla. The source (here freely reworked) is the *Breviarium* of Rufius Festus (fourth century). Jordanes' use of *eos* with reference to the feminine *Spanias* is striking. This anomaly, certainly facilitated by the long distance in the text between the two words,

---

[28] An analogous example can be found in Eutropius (1.15), where the prepositional cluster *ab urbe* of the model (Liv. 2.39.5) is replaced by the simple *urbis* (*usque ad quintum miliarium urbis*).

[29] On the common usage of prepositional combinations in spoken language see also Ferri and Probert, this volume p. 30. Comparable cases are two paragraphs of the *Romana* (143 and 319) in which the pronominal adjectives *omnium* and *omnes* of the model are replaced by the stylistically higher forms *cunctorum* and *cunctas*. Cf. *Rom.* 143 *montes Caurus Falernus Massicus et pulcherrimus cunctorum Vesubius* (cf. Flor. *Epit.* 1.16.5 *pulcherrimus omnium Vesubius*) and 319 *opes cunctas Eutropius spado promeruit* (cf. Marcell. *Chron.* II p. 64.396.2 *Eutropius... omnes opes abripuit*).

[30] See for instance *Rom.* 314 *imperator sagitta saucius* <u>*in casa deportatur vilissima*</u>, where the 'deviating' construction *in* + ablative is derived from Ps.-Aurelius Victor, *Epitome de Caesaribus* 46.2.

can be due to a *concordantia ad sententiam* so that the gender of the pronoun actually concords with a masculine word similar to *Spaniae* such as *Hispani* or *populi*. This explanation finds support in two similar passages in which a feminine word (in one case even singular) is picked up by the accusative *eos*: *Rom.* 225 *[Deiotarum] senatus praefecit Galatiae. sed post haec Caesar eos redegit fecitque in provincias* 'the Senate put Deiotarus in charge of Galatia, but afterwards Caesar suppressed them and reduced them to provinces'; 310 *ideo populosas fore gentes, quia hoc apud eos solemne est* 'the population would therefore become numerous, because this usage is common among them'. Another possibility – which does not exclude the first one – is that the anomaly in *Rom.* 212 is caused (or strongly influenced) by the text of Festus, where the reference noun is masculine (*Hispanis*) and *eos* occurs in the same context as in Jordanes (*eos vicit*).

The influence of the model is more evident in the following passages:

(21)   Illyricus . . . habet intra se provincias XVIII et sunt Norici duo, Pannonias duas, Valeria, Suavia, Dalmatia, Moesia superior, Dardania, Dacias duas, Macedonia, Thessalia, Achaia, Epyros duos, Praevales, Creta

(*Rom.* 218)

Illyria contains eighteen provinces; these are the two Norici, the two Pannonias, Valeria, Suavia, Dalmatia, upper Moesia, Dardania, the two Dacias, Macedonia, Thessaly, Achaia, the two Epiruses,

cf. Ruf. Fest. 8.3 *provincias habet Illyricus* XVIII: *Noricorum duas, Pannoniarum duas, Valeriam, Saviam, Dalmatiam, Moesiam, Daciarum duas, <Dardaniam>; et in dioecesi Macedonica provinciae sunt septem: Macedonia, Thessalia, Achaia, Epiri duae, Praevalis, Creta*;

(22)   nisi [Romanus populus] . . . vicina loca cepisset, id est Lydia Caria Ellispontu utrasque Frigias   (*Rom.* 222)

if the Roman people had not conquered the places nearby, that is Lydia, Caria, the Hellespont, and both Phrygias,

cf. Ruf. Fest. 10.2 *Lydia . . . Caria, Hellespontus ac Phrygiae in potestatem populi Romani iuncta dicione venerunt*;

(23)   L<i>gures hi imis Alpium iugis adhaerentes inter Varum Magramque amnem implicitos dumis silvestribus victitabant, quos pene maius fuit invenire quam vincere   (*Rom.* 177)

these Ligurians, whom it was almost a greater task to find than to conquer, used to live in the brambles of the forests, clinging to the lofty summits of the Alps, enclosed between the rivers Var and Magra, cf. Flor. *Epit.* 2.3.4 *Liguras imis Alpium iugis adhaerentis inter Varum et Magram flumen inplicitosque dumis silvestribus maior aliquanto labor erat invenire quam vincere*;

(24)   propter necem Aterbalae et Empsalae Mecipsae <u>liberos</u>   (*Rom.* 210)

because of the death of Micipsa's sons Adherbal and Hiempsal,

cf. Ruf. Fest. 4.4 *Iugurthae, ob necatos Adherbalem et Hiempsalem, filios Micipsae regis, bellum indictum est.*

The four examples above are definitely influenced by the well-known syntactic spread of the accusative in spoken Latin, which eventually led to its diffusion at the expense of other cases in nearly all Romance languages.[31] Particularly, its use within a list (so called *Rezeptakkusativ*), as in (21), or in apposition, as in (23) and (24), instead of other cases has parallels in late Latin documents and inscriptions.[32] Furthermore, in (21) the double initial construction *habet provincias . . . et sunt* may have fostered the syntactic ambiguity between the nominative and the accusative. There is, however, another important circumstance to consider both for this and the following passage (22). The loss of final *-m* in the accusative of the first declension (as well of the other declensions) represents a well-known colloquial feature, already widespread in the Pompeian inscriptions and very often attested in the Imperial age, particularly in late (both literary and non-literary) sources.[33] Besides, certain epigraphical texts of the late period show a nominative ending *-as* (instead of *-ae*), which occurs all over the Empire, particularly in East European inscriptions (twenty-nine times, seven of which come from Moesia).[34] It has thus been assumed that in the late spoken usage of some regions people tended to generalise in the nominative and accusative of the first declension a unique ending *-a* for the singular and *-as* for the plural.[35] Since in (21) and (22) the alternation nominative/accusative mostly involves terms of the first declension, which display this structure of nominative–accusative *-a* in the singular and *-as* in the plural, it is possible that in both passages Jordanes was influenced by a late colloquial trend.

---

[31] See Norberg 1943: 87–131; Väänänen 1982: 1978; Galdi 2004: 443.

[32] Cf. Svennung 1935: 175–8, 186–95; Norberg 1943: 65–9, 94–5, 100–1; E. Löfstedt 1956: 1.81–6; H–S 28s; Adams 1995a: 446–9; Galdi 2004: 458–61, 495.

[33] See for instance Väänänen 1966: 71: 'Il n'y a pas de phénomène vulgaire qui soit plus répandu dans les inscriptions latines que la chute de *m* final.'

[34] This ending has been long debated in linguistic scholarship, which has offered both morphological and syntactic explanations. For a discussion on the topic see Galdi 2004: 59–67, with further literature.

[35] For references see Galdi 2004: 59–67.

Additionally, the source text may also have played an important role in these examples, because it displays that very construction which interferes with Jordanes' syntactic choice, so it might have caused the anomaly. So in (21) the alternation nominative/accusative is certainly influenced by the double syntactical choice in Festus, who also uses both cases and introduces them, like Jordanes, through the clusters *provincias habet* and *et . . . sunt.* In passage (22) the forms *Lydia* and *Caria* may have been prompted by the corresponding nominatives in Festus. In (23) the weight of the source is even clearer, as it contains the form *implicitos*, whereas in (24) the author appears to conflate the expression *propter necem liberorum* with that of Festus *ob necatos filios.*

In all these passages, including (20), the syntactic choice of Jordanes while reworking his models seems to remain, so to speak, halfway: although he opts for a new construction he does not completely abandon the original one and (probably unintentionally) mixes the two. Such examples show us, once again, the influence of the models on the language of the *Romana* and at the same time confirm the presence in it of some typical features of everyday speech.

Finally, in the same category belong those anomalies (usually of syntactic nature) which seem to arise from a conflation of two models. Jordanes' tendency to mix different constructions and produce various types of interference was already highlighted by Mommsen.[36] For instance, the expression in *Rom.* 277 *ideo [Caracalla] hoc nomine nanctus est, eo quod eiusdem vestium genere . . . erogans sibi nomen Caragalla et vesti Antoniana dederit* 'Caracalla obtained this name because he distributed this kind of tunics, so that he named himself Caracalla [i.e. tunic] and the tunic Antoniana' probably originates from the commingling of the two types *eiusdem generis vestes erogans* and *eiusdem vestium genere erogato.* In a similar way *Rom.* 265 *[Domitianus] Iohannem apostolum et euangelistam, postquam in fervente oleo missum non potuisset extingui, Pathmo eum insulam exulem relegavit* 'since Domitian could not kill the apostle John by putting him in boiling oil, he banished him to the island of Patmos' seems to be due to a mixture between the active construction (a) *postquam [Domitianus] in oleo missum [Iohannem] non potuisset extinguere* and the passive one (b) *postquam [Iohannes] in oleo missus non potuisset extingui.* To this general category belongs a smaller group of cases in which the author uses more sources at the same time, conflating their text, as in the following passages:

---

[36] Cf. Mommsen (1882: 182–3): 'Confusio locutionum duarum similesque sermonis perturbationes.'

(25)   cuius [*i.e.* Archelai] et <u>regnum</u>, postquam defunctus est, in provinciam <u>verso</u>, [Tiberius] Mazacam civitatem eius de nomine suo Caesaream vocitavit   (*Rom.* 258)

after whose [*i.e.* Archelaus'] death his realm was turned into a province and Tiberius renamed its city Mazaca after his own name, Caesarea,

cf. Hier. *Chron.* a.Abr. 2036 *cuius regno in provinciam verso, Mazacam nobilissimam civitatem Caesariam appellari iussit*, and Eutr. 7.11.2 *Archelaum Cappadocem, cuius etiam regnum in provinciae formam redegit*;

(26)   qui [*i.e.* Aurelianus] mox Tetricum apud Catalaunos <u>prodente</u> exercitum suum Gallias recepit   (*Rom.* 290)

Aurelianus soon obtained the Gauls while Tetricus was bringing forth his army among the Catalans,

cf. Hier. *Chron.* a.Abr. 2289 *Tetrico aput Catalaunos prodente exercitum suum Gallias recepit*, and Eutr. 9.13 *superavit in Gallia Tetricum apud Catalaunos ipso Tetrico prodente exercitum suum*;

(27)   [Claudius] occisusque Sirmium est   (*Rom.* 288)

and Claudius was killed in Sirmium,

cf. Oros. *Hist.* 7.23.1 *continuo apud Sirmium . . . interiit*, and Hier. *Chron.* a.Abr. 2287 *Claudius Sirmii moritur*.

The text of the *Romana* seems the result, in all these examples, of the syntactic combination of the two sources. So in passage (25) the 'broken' ablative absolute *regnum verso* can be ascribed to the mixture of the expressions *regno verso* of Jerome and *regnum redegit* of Eutropius. Similarly, the accusative *Tetricum* in text (26) probably arises from Eutropius, whereas the following segment (*apud . . . recepit*) is taken verbatim from Jerome. Finally, in (27) the anomalous accusative *Sirmium* indicating place originates from the conflation of the texts of Orosius (where the cluster *apud Sirmium* displays the accusative) and Jerome (where the locative *Sirmii* lacks a preposition).

4 CONCLUSIONS

The passages discussed above suggest that, at odds with the conclusions reached by Mommsen, Werner and other scholars, the language of Jordanes cannot be simply marked as unlearned or 'vulgar'. It is evident, on the one side, that our author often deviates, especially at the morphological and syntactical level, from the classical usage. This aspect is partly due to the late period in which Jordanes was working (contemporary authors often display the same or similar features) and partly to the fact that he probably learned Latin as a second or third language only for professional purposes. But besides some substandard and particularly colloquial elements, we also find several 'classical' (or hypercorrect) ones.[37] One of the most significant elements which contributed to this unusual stylistic mixture, but paradoxically has been paid little attention, is the influence of the sources: both the *Romana* and the *Getica* are compendia of previous historical works, which naturally constituted a continuous reference point for the author and conditioned his style at various levels. This process can be easily observed in the *Romana*, whose source texts are almost entirely preserved. I have shown that the exact knowledge of the models and their systematic comparison with the text of the *Romana* constitute an indispensable prerequisite for discovering the most peculiar features of Jordanes' language, in particular of his syntax.

The text of the model can be revised by different techniques. The simplest one is verbatim transcription, a procedure which is nearly generalised in all paragraphs depending on Florus. This section is very useful to textual critics, in that it helps to evaluate the reliability of the manuscripts, but tells very little about Jordanes' own style. Among the cases of adaptation of the source the most interesting ones for the linguist are those in which the author modifies longer sections of text. Interestingly enough, these changes often simplify the model through the insertion of some post-classical elements. Since these features are frequently attested both in late literary and non-literary sources (particularly in inscriptions), they are likely to have been common in the late spoken usage and can thus be regarded as colloquialisms. Some of these features have been indicated and discussed above. These are: (a) the use of *quod* with reference to a neuter plural (*omnia quod*, example (11)), (b) the loss of the syntactic distinction between 'where' and 'whither' with geographical names through the gradual generalisation of a standard scheme (examples (12)–(14)) and (c) the extension of the accusative to the detriment of other cases (examples (21)–(4)). Syntactically related to this last point is the usage of the nominative ending *-as* in the plural of first-declension names: this late colloquial feature seems to occur in two passages ((21) and (22)). On the other hand, Jordanes sometimes shows the opposite tendency, by choosing

---

[37] This aspect has partly been stressed in some studies of Iordache, for instance 1986: 332: 'Au point de vue linguistique, *Romana* et *Getica* présentent une intéressante combinaison de latin vulgaire du vɪe siècle et de latin de chancellerie (des juristes et ecclésiastiques) de l'époque tardive, sans qu'il y manquent pour autant des éléments de pur latin classique.'

some classical or hypercorrect features (as the usage of the subjunctive in causal relative clauses) which were certainly uncommon in everyday speech (see examples (15)–(19)). The cases in which Jordanes, although adopting a different construction from the source, was probably influenced by part of its text are particularly instructive: the result is a new, syntactically incongruent structure which seems to bear marks of the model, as in examples (21)–(24): however, some of these errors can also be explained by the usage of colloquial features. Finally, we have seen passages in which the anomaly arises from the syntactic conflation of two different sources, as in (25)–(27). Both types of interference (between Jordanes and the source or between different sources) confirm that the text of the models represented a constant reference point also in terms of language: but, above all and more to our point, they show that when Jordanes tried to deviate from the sources and revise their text he often was automatically influenced by late colloquial trends.

CHAPTER 23

The tale of Frodebert's tail

Danuta Shanzer

Das ist das wahrste Denkmal der ganzen Merowingerzeit.
B. Krusch (Winterfeld 1905: 60)

ne respondeas stulto iuxta stultitiam suam ne efficiaris ei similis
responde stulto iuxta stultitiam suam ne sibi sapiens esse videatur
(Proverbs 26:4–5)

What is known about how a text is transmitted affects the evaluation of its content.[1] And evaluation and classification of content in turn affect the interpretation of words and language. Literary historians must decide what it is they have in front of them using internal and, where available, external evidence too. Lexicon, syntax, metrics, *topoi*, generic markers, and more, all go into the taxonomic decision. And once a work has a place in some sort of scholarly taxonomy it may then be used (or abused). A text's nature and classification may also be interpreted in widely divergent ways by scholars who never engage each others' views. Near the end of the long period this volume covers (third century BC – eighth century AD) the *Letters of Frodebert and Importunus*, texts that some regard as serious documents and others as obvious parodies, provide a case study of such a problem. Commentary on them can easily expand to book-length.[2] My concern here will be to pinpoint the nature of a late text of controversial content, genre and characteristics (learned/vulgar, literary/colloquial, ecclesiastical/secular, written/oral, Latin/Romance). My discussion will begin with the *mise en scène* and continue with series of limited textual and interpretative problems showing how arguments even about small

[1] My thanks to Karen Dudas and Bruce Swann, our incomparable Classics librarians, who found me what I needed – fast. Ian Wood, trusty friend in the seventh century, read a draft and made helpful comments. Julia Barrow, learned and acute, both helped me think this through in conversation and contributed her expertise in ecclesiastical history when she read a draft. And Ralph Mathisen, favourite partner in early medieval epistolography, as always helped me hammer out my thoughts. This piece is for Jim, Latinist extraordinary, in gratitude for almost thirty years of wonderful guidance.
[2] P. Meyer 1867: 344; Walstra 1962 is a case in point.

philological points affect much broader assumptions about what these texts are. In Appendix 2, a working edition and translation are provided.

I GENRE TROUBLE

This volume takes as its purview colloquial and literary Latin over almost a millennium. Problems of generic classification are particularly common in late antiquity and the early Middle Ages. The former is a period of considerable generic change and recombination. The latter is a 'dark' age, when less is known about authors, audiences and literacy than in the classical period, because less literature survived. The interpretation (or misinterpretation) of works that are difficult to classify can have a disproportionate impact on literary history or even the history of external events. They are points of light, *scintillae*, in those centuries of darkness, but just what do they illuminate? If works are thin on the ground, so much greater the significance of a given item, and so much more desperately the straw is grasped. Consider the *Hisperica famina*, read in so many mutually contradictory ways: lexicographical–glossological showings-off, sapiential wisdom, rhetorical exercises or parody (Shanzer 2009). Sometimes such problems are compounded by ones of origin. Just which or whose regional literary history do Vergilius Maro Grammaticus or Aethicus Ister illuminate (e.g. Herren 1995: 51–71, 2004: 79–102)? But unlike the correspondence of Frodebert and Importunus, neither of those texts impinges on any external historical narrative.

2 THE TEXTS

The correspondence consists of five short Latin texts transmitted at the end of a collection of *formulae* (form-letters) from Sens preserved in Paris, B.N. lat. 4627.[3] They have been edited several times, the most important editions being Zeumer's (1886: 220–6) and, over forty years ago, Walstra's (1962).[4] For the purposes of this paper I will use Walstra's helpful section numbers, but for convenience will call the five items respectively *Frod.* 1, *Imp.* 2, *Imp.* 3, *Frod.* 4 and *Imp.* 5.[5] The corpus is approximately 1,250 words long. I have collated it from the photographs in Walstra 1962: 59–64.

---

[3] On the manuscript see Zeumer 1886: 34, 184 and Walstra 1962: 1–6.

[4] For previous editions, most not done from the original, see Walstra (1962: 6–7). Baluze (working in 1667) and de Rozière (in 1859) used the manuscript.

[5] The abbreviations used as titles are the names of the two putative authors, and the first number designates the position of the item in the dossier. See Appendix 1 for the new designation *Imp.* 5.

3 HISTORICAL CO-ORDINATES

Of the two principals Frodebert was located in Tours and Importunus in Paris (*Imp.* 2.14 *de Parisiaga terra*). Both were bishops (Duchesne 1910: 309, 472). The correspondence, if it is what it purports to be, can be dated fairly precisely: Importunus' episcopacy lasted only from 664 to 666.[6] Frodebert is certainly to be identified with the Chrodebert who became Bishop of Tours and was only succeeded in 682.[7] This leaves a window between 664 and 666 for the correspondence, if it is treated as documentary material.[8] If on the other hand it is a forgery (of whatever sort), Pirson has reasonably argued that the material in these letters cannot have been of interest except to contemporaries (1910: 489). A *terminus ante quem* of the first quarter of the ninth century is provided by the manuscript.[9] The text thus plausibly belongs to the third quarter of the seventh century. A gap of about a century and a half between putative date of composition and the date of the manuscript allows time for corruption in transmission (P. Meyer 1867: 346).

4 SUMMARY OF CONTENT

The tenor of the dossier is as follows.

In *Frod.* 1 Frodebert writes to Importunus to complain about the quality of a shipment of grain that the latter sent to Tours. Bread made from it proved disgusting with a vile crust on the outside and very dark crumb inside. It made far from attractive Eucharistic wafers (*Frod.* 1.8 *faciunt inde oblata non bella*). Importunus is invited to try the bread himself. The nuns have refused it. The tone of this letter is ironic at best.

War is declared in the second letter (*Imp.* 2). Importunus has heard that his grain was not acceptable. He wishes to tell some of Frodebert's

---

[6] Dubois (1969: 61 and 1995: xxv.963) notes that he signed a privilege for Soissons that is most probably dated to 664.

[7] See Walstra 1962: 16–18 for the prosopography, onomastics ('Chrodebert' > 'Frodebert') and bibliography. Chrodebert may be the same as the Chrodebert who was bishop of Paris from 656 to 663, when he was succeeded by Sigebrand, who was soon murdered to be succeeded by Importunus. An earlier connection and possibly patronage would thus be established between the two letter-writers. Sato (1990: 179), however, identifies Chrodebert with various lay Chrodeberts, including a mayor of the palace. But to do so runs in the face of *Imp.* 3.1 *nec seculari clerico*, which implies that Chrodebert was a monk (Walstra 1962: 140). The force is probably 'not a secular cleric (although you behave like one)'. I hope to treat the historical problems raised by the letters elsewhere.

[8] Walstra (1962: 22) tries to narrow it down more, to 665–6, using the alleged famine in Tours, dated by local historians to 665.

[9] Zeumer (1881: 78) dates it *c.* 817. W. Brown (2002: 354, n. 62, 2007: n. 26) confirms northern France *c.* 800–25.

deeds so that the latter never dare to relay a similar joke in the future. He accuses him of abducting or seducing the wife of Grimoald, Mayor of the Palace, and of sending her to a convent in the Touraine. There they did not read scripture, but had – <words that have been lost in a lacuna>. Their *conlocutio* was not appropriate for God. Frodebert was born in a monastery and ruined his master or lady. He is asked to forgive these 'few words.'

The third letter (*Imp.* 3) is likewise Importunus'. Frodebert is neither holy, nor a bishop, nor a secular cleric. Anyone who does not believe Importunus should look at what Frodebert did. He does the Devil's work. His parents did not love Christ when they made Frodebert in a monastery. A *domnus* apparently manumitted Frodebert in his own lifetime (i.e. not in a will), educated and raised him, but subsequently regretted it. He received no good in return for his kindness. Frodebert 'had' his wife. Furthermore he takes advantages of ladies (presumably the nuns in the convent) by stripping them of their gold, silver and virtue. He loves a pretty girl from any land. He will never be good as long as he persists on this road. He is urged to castrate himself, for the Lord judges fornicators. Importunus could say more, if Frodebert likes. Let other copies go out to many lands, he leaves this one for the master. Frodebert should either take the letter to heart or put it in <erased word>.

The fourth text (*Frod.* 4) lacks a salutation.[10] Solomon (Proverbs 26:4) said that one should not become like the fool by responding to him. Frodebert has chosen to respond thus by answering about the *falsator*, the *susurro*, the *muro*, the ungrateful man (Importunus) who forgot the man who helped and raised him (Frodebert) and trod on law and respectability. He tells lies, and destroys friendships, etc. Someone (or some people) is/are urged not to believe him. Frodebert swears by God, baptism, Sion and Sinai that Importunus is a liar. There is no greater *falsator*. But he does not frighten anyone. Such a dog doesn't discomfit a *baro*, a dog does not bark against an innocent man. Importunus is a dog in the manger. He resembles neither his father nor his mother. Such a crown befits his falsehood.

The fifth text (*Imp.* 5) addresses *domnae sanctae*.[11] They are urged not to believe these false tales. There are many liars, who resemble thieves and fools and whisperers. They will not protect them (the *domnae*). The fox barks, but not like the dog. He shows his tail, but hides his face. He cannot face a dog. But he snatches the hoopoe, not the swallow. He eats excrement. He lies like an Irishman, he always walks crooked, and says what he never

---

[10] *Frod.* 4.1 seems to be a compiler's heading (*incipiunt verba per similitudinem iuncta de fide vacua dolo plena falsatore*): Zeumer 1881: 76.

[11] See Appendix 1 on the voice of this letter.

saw. The *domnae* are again urged not to believe Frodebert. Importunus did what was right for them, but has been thrown out of their good favour.

The first three texts are clearly epistolary in form. *Frod.* 4 and *Imp.* 5 have no salutations or valedictions. *Frod.* 1 and 2 are marked *indiculum* ('letter'), but *Imp.* 3 is marked *parabola*, likewise *Frod.* 4 (even though it clearly speaks in Frodebert's voice), while *Imp.* 5 reverts to *indiculum* and recapitulates (or, as I see it, responds to) material from *Frod.* 4. The headings are unlikely to be authorial. *Frod.* 4 has the most in common with the *parabolae* of Solomon and even adverts to them in its first line. Its header, *verba per similitudinem*, invokes biblical uses of *parabola*.

5 PROBLEMS OF CLASSIFICATION

The letters certainly are 'formal text' in that they are 'planned, cohesive, and structured' (Clackson, this volume p. 9). If one is to assign them to a register, context of writing, use and audience come into play. But these are all unknowns in this equation. Assessment of their language would depend on whether they are genuine abusive letters (i.e. the documents they might seem to be)[12] or fictions written to defame both parties by some third party (Zeumer 1881: 76) or parodies written for fun by a third party.[13] These are the three options raised by previous scholars. No-one has seriously examined others' opinions:[14] all either assume that the letters are 'real' or that they are 'fictions'.[15]

6 TRANSMISSION

Study of the text's transmission cannot solve the problem. Zeumer (1881: 76; cf. Pirson 1910: 488) suggested that the presence of both sides of the correspondence in one manuscript was an argument that the dossier was the work of one person. But in light of knowledge about the preservation of outgoing and incoming letters as well as file-copies of late antique and early medieval correspondence, this argument does not stand up.

---

[12] Read as real letters of insult by Boucherie (1867); P. Meyer (1867: 344–50); Pirson (1910: 487–9); Sneyders de Vogel (1927: 425); Walstra (1962). Szövérffy (1970: 297) seems confused.

[13] Parodies (by a third party) intended to be funny: P. Lehmann 1922: 24; Brunhölzl 1990: 145.

[14] Walstra (1962: 8) counters the views of the fiction party by pointing out that the principals are historical persons.

[15] E.g. Zeumer 1881: 76: 'Dass diese wunderliche Correspondez nicht wirklich von den genannten Bischöfen herrührt, scheint mir keinen Augenblick zweifelhaft.'

Many letter collections regularly preserve dossiers with incoming as well as outgoing letters.[16] Despite the company it keeps, the correspondence cannot by any stretch of the imagination be considered form-letters.[17] It was copied by whoever assembled the *formulae* from Sens, who also started to number them as if they were part of the formulary (51, 52, 53). The suggestion (Walstra 1962: 31) that a judicial process united both sides of the correspondence at St Denis is unlikely. Someone may have tried to remove names from the text and to censor it. For example, on f. 27ᵛ the second occurrence of *Importune* has been erased, on f. 28bisʳ *in butte* (if that is what it read) has been deleted, on f. 28ʳ a large tear removed the name of the nunnery where Grimoald's wife was sent. The tear has created large *lacunae* at the ends of lines in *Imp.* 2.7–13 and at the beginnings of lines in *Imp.* 3.9–17. It is possible to guess (only approximately) how many characters may be missing by comparing the numbers of characters in complete lines at the beginning of the pages, which about average 48.5 on 28ʳ and 53 on f. 28ᵛ. F. 28bisʳ⁻ᵛ has a slight tear at the bottom that has affected *Frod.* 4.4 and 21–3.

7 CONTENT

Many have found the content of these letters somehow improbable or inconsistent with their being 'real' letters.[18] Readers are split between the more historically minded who want them to be documents and who presumably find their content authentic (if crude),[19] and the literary scholars who cannot believe that Merovingian bishops engaged in such correspondence, and prefer to see here calumny or parody (some signs of urbanity). Each side has assumed that the burden of proof lies with the other. The decision-tree can be set out thus:

1. Could the authors be the bishops Frodebert and Importunus?
   If so, are they writing to each other? To others too?
   What is their purpose? Polemic?
2. Were the letters written by a third party?
   If so, who was the audience?
   What was the purpose? Humour? Or calumny?

---

[16] E.g. Shanzer and Wood 2002: 28–57 on Avitus of Vienne's collection.

[17] *Pace* Walstra (1962: 34), who thinks that contemporaries used them as models. Also Banniard (1992: 292).

[18] E.g. Duchesne (1910: 472) 'une correspondance extraordinaire, peut-être fictive'.

[19] They could always point to the antics of Bishops Salonius and Sagittarius in Greg. Tur. *DLH* 5.20.

8 HISTORICAL REALIA

Any decision about authorship, audience and purpose will depend on internal criteria, including factual realia. There was nothing inherently improbable in a bishop being accused of impropriety with women, be they nuns or *extraneae mulieres* (Szövérffy 1970: 296; Shanzer 2002; Jong 1998: 52–7). Indeed clerical misbehaviour with nuns is the most common theme in late Latin letters about sex scandals (Shanzer 2008). The accusation of episcopal property-acquisition, practiced on *religiosae*, is likewise attested (e.g. Greg. Tur. *DLH* 9.26).

Nothing is known of the wife of Grimoald, though the mayor himself is an important historical figure.[20] So, if authentic, the correspondence could help fill a lacuna in the historical record. The affair is not the usual 'he said-she said' story. The writer(s) does/do not exhibit overt hostility to the woman.[21] She was probably a Merovingian princess, for her son Childebert was given a Merovingian name.[22] After Grimoald's fall and execution members of his family suffered persecution, including his daughter Wulfetrudis.[23] Thus, taking refuge in a monastery made sense for his wife (Walstra 1962: 20). In this narrative Frodebert emerges as a slandered or misunderstood protector. The text is likewise not hostile to Grimoald. Those who read these letters as genuine see here sympathy – at least from Importunus – for one who had recently been betrayed and had fallen.[24] Even other, pettier, aspects of the social history, complaints and foodways, have analogies. Nuns (who might be entitled princesses in this period) were known to complain about their food.[25] But even abbesses worked in the kitchen.[26]

9 COMPARANDA AND REGISTER

None of Importunus' writing survives, but examples of Chrodebert of Tours' correspondence are preserved: first a letter to Dado in *Vita Eligii*

---

[20] See J. R. Martindale 1992: 556, s.v. 'Grimoaldus 2'.

[21] Unless the accusation of impropriety with Frodebert is a slur intended to impugn the paternity of any offspring. Such a difficulty arose in connection with Fredegund and Bishop Bertramnus, see Greg. Tur. *DLH* 5.47 with Shanzer 2002: 404.

[22] Wood 1994: 222. He was 'nommé probablement ainsi par précaution'. Walstra 1962: 14; also 19 for the family of his mother.

[23] *Vita Geretrudis* 6, *MGH SRM* 11.460; Walstra 1962: 16; Wood 1994: 223.

[24] For his usurpation see Krusch 1910: 417–38; on his torture and execution see *Liber historiae Francorum* 43.

[25] Greg. Tur. *DLH* 9.39 and 10.16, for example. Also Walstra 1962: 20–1 on the increasing financial resources of powerful abbeys.

[26] Fortunatus, *Vita Radegundis* 23.

2.81 in full formal epistolary style. The second item is transmitted in two places: in a collection from St Denis (Zeumer 1886: 494–6) and, with its salutation formula intact, as a letter to Boba in *MGH Epistolae* III.[27] From these it is clear that Fr/Chrodebert could write a formal and elaborate grammatical letter of ecclesiastical content. So those who prefer to see two authors must assume that the bishops could use various styles and had something quite different in mind here. Fr/Chrodebert thus commanded two different written registers.

The letters exhibit numerous vulgar orthographical, morphological and syntactic features,[28] so many that they have been characterised as 'textes vulgaires latinisés' whose authors were not yet conscious of two language systems (Banniard 1992: 291). But one of the central difficulties in editing Merovingian Latin in Lachmannian fashion (as opposed to simply printing an authoritative manuscript) lies in distinguishing between the author and the scribe, between authentic forms and scribal corruptions.[29] A constant process of reasoning goes on: could an author who read x or said y or was z have written whatever is transmitted?

10 LITERARY SHAPING

But while the orthography and much of the syntax looks vulgar, whoever (singular or plural) wrote these letters was familiar with literary registers. One notes the salutation *domne dulcissime et frater carissime* ('sweetest lord and dearest brother') and the valedictory subscription formula with its reverse honorific: *Frod.* 1.15 *nostra privata stultitia ad te in summa amicitia* 'Our Private Foolishness to you in loftiest friendship'. Two other phrases are ironic, if read a certain way: *Frod.* 1.1 *sanctorum meritis beatificando* 'to be blessed by the merits of the saints' (as opposed perhaps to his own); likewise *Frod.* 1.16 *obto te semper valere et caritatis tuae iuro tenere* 'I wish you always to be healthy and to have the same charity you give me' (Walstra 1962: 86). The parody of epistolary salutations is a giveaway; the same goes for the epistolary initial *quod* clause ('as to the fact that . . . '), the apology for not writing at length, and the authorial subscription (Norberg 1964:

---

[27] Pp. 461–4: *oppinione religionis dulciter nominandae et caritatis vinculo ambiendae Bobae matrifamilias Chrodobertus peccator salutem in domino perhennem.*

[28] See Pirson 1910: passim and Walstra 1962: passim.

[29] Gregory of Tours' serious attempts at writing better Latin have been foiled by his editor, Krusch, who consistently aimed to print the most vulgar seeming text (Shanzer 2005: 303–6). More sophisticated syntax often shines through the readings of the Corbie manuscript. Here, we lack the higher form imitated for comparison.

296–8). The author also knew the Bible and was familiar with 'scholastic material' (Walstra 1962: 33), above all with proverbs.

These are no uneducated scrawls on walls. Content alone cannot determine whether they are what they seem to be or parodies. Nor can their transmission. But literary, philological and linguistic arguments may offer some help. One must try, but problems of interpretation have a dismaying way of turning circular,[30] and ultimately the critical reader may have to accept an argument from converging probabilities.

II FRODEBERT'S TAIL

This volume honours the author of (among many other things)[31] *The Latin Sexual Vocabulary* (1982a). Adams also wrote on the regional diversification of Latin, ending at the year 600 (Adams 2007), so it is perhaps not inappropriate to begin at the tail:

per tua cauta longa – satis est vel non est? – per omnia iube te castrare, ut non pereas per talis, quia fornicatoris Deus iudicabit. (*Imp.* 3.22)

So Importunus to Frodebert. Those familiar with the typical literary output of the Merovingian period will be surprised by the word *cauta* in a letter, particularly an episcopal one. The word occurs elsewhere in the correspondence in *Imp.* 5.5 *cauta proferit, iam non fronte*, 'He displays his tail, but never his face', but there it could refer simply to the tail of the fox. The form of Importunus' words suggests oath or entreaty, in this case by Frodebert's *cauta* (*cauda*) or penis (Adams 1982a: 37).

Archaic Romans used *testes* to refer to their testicles, because solemn oaths in the ancient Mediterranean were taken with the oath-receiver's or sacrificial animal's testicles in hand (Katz 1998). Here perhaps is a distant descendant of that idea with the penis humorously substituted for the ancestral *testes*. The latter may themselves be euphemistically present in *per omnia* and *per talis*. So far antiquarianism and anthropology. But equally important is an interpretation suggested by the Christian coda of the sentence. Importunus invokes Matthew 19:12 *et sunt eunuchi qui se ipsos castraverunt propter regnum caelorum. qui potest capere capiat.* The operation was known in Merovingian Gaul (Greg. Tur. *DLH* 10.15).

---

[30] For one example consider the historical problem of the famine: *Frod.* 1.4 *iam vicina morte de fame perire* and 10 *quod de fame nobiscum morimur*. Walstra (1962: 22) notes that it is mentioned by historians of the Touraine, but without citing any sources. A difficulty of interpretation affects external history. Is 'dying of hunger' literally true? Or was it a colloquialism (Fr. 'mourir de faim') just as it is in modern English? Or just a rhetorical position?

[31] Including the epistolographic Adams 1977a, which discusses a wonderful and undoubtedly real set of letters.

Even though the metaphor seems an obvious one, *cauda* = penis is surprisingly rarely attested in Latin. Adams (1982a: 37) notes Hor. *Sat.* 1.2.45 *caudam salacem* and 2.7.49 *turgentis verbera caudae* alone in classical Latin and no examples from late Latin, and rightly notes that Cic. *Fam.* 9.22.2 *caudam antiqui penem vocabant* does not mean that *cauda* was used for 'penis', but that *penis* was used for 'tail'. He concludes that *cauda* was an ad hoc metaphor or a coinage (Adams 1982a: 37, 221). The word's Old French derivative, *queue*, however, was used for 'penis'.[32] So there is the possibility that the word had become a vulgar Latin term for the penis.

But how to classify Importunus' use of *cauta*? Obscenity? Colloquialism? Euphemism? My epigraph contains an implicit literary and social judgement on the Merovingians, subscribed to not only by Krusch, editor of much of the *MGH*'s *Scriptores Rerum Merovingicarum*, but also by others. Pirson found nothing improbable about bishops writing such letters – after all they lived in the seventh century, in the middle of the Merovingian era (Pirson 1910: 487). Walstra clearly read the letters straight. Assumptions about what is permissible or not in the external society affect the range of possibilities considered.

Such a topic and such a lexical choice may not be as odd as they seem. In Germanic society unmentionables featured in contexts where they were absent in the classical world. The Burgundian law code (*Liber constitutionum* 98) specified that a man who stole a hawk should be punished by having the bird eat six ounces of meat on his *testones* (VI *uncias carnium acceptor ipse super testones ipsius comedat*),[33] and whoever stole a hound should be compelled to kiss its hindquarters in public (*Liber constitutionum* 97–8 *in conventu coram omni populo posteriorem ipsius canis osculetur*). The *Pariser Gespräche*'s helpful phrase for foreigners 'Undes ars in tine naso!', 'A dog's arse up your nose!', continued this tradition.[34] But the *Pactus Legis Salicae* 29.17 and 18 referred to the penis (as opposed to what was removed in *castratio*) as *virilia* or *viricula*.

12 FRANKISH INSULTS

Insults however were taken sufficiently seriously to merit a chapter *de convitiis* in the *Lex Salica* (Eckhardt 1969: 88), where penalties were assigned to various opprobrious terms: *cinitus* (*PLS* 49.1 fifteen *solidi*), *concagatus*

---

[32] *FEW* s.v. *cauda* 2a penis.

[33] *Testones* is often taken as 'breast', where the falcon would be dangerously near the thief's eye (Duby and Ariès 1987: 488), but the plural of a man's breast (*tétons?*) is odd. B8 provides a variant, *testiculos suos*, which may have originated as a gloss.

[34] The phrase was rendered in Latin as *canis culum in tuo naso* (Braune *et al.* 1969: 9–10).

(*PLS* 49.2 three *solidi*), *meretrix* (*PLS* 49.4 forty-five *solidi*), *vulpicula* (*PLS* 49.5 three *solidi*), *lepus* (*PLS* 49.6 three *solidi*) and *falsator* (*PLS* 49.2 fifteen *solidi*). The one bad name listed for a woman merits the highest penalty; insults involving specific acts against others, such as *falsator*, receive a higher penalty. A slur involving homosexuality (*cinitus* = *cinaedus*) was also serious. The fact that *concagatus* receives a far lower penalty than *cinitus* suggests that it does not mean 'buttsucker',[35] but 'coward' – 'shit-beshotten' in the sense of 'shit scared'.[36] The precise connotations of *vulpes* (thieving? devious?) and *lepus* (cowardly? homosexual? (as in *Epistle of Barnabas* 10.6)) are unclear. Two of the insults cited in the *PLS*, *vulpes* (connotative and colloquial) and *falsator* (cognitive), feature in *Frod.* 4 and *Imp.* 5 and so are probably genuine contemporary terms of insult.

There has also been embarrassment about this episcopal exchange, witness some of the translations of Importunus' *satis est vel non est?*, 'Is it completely true?' (Boucherie 1867: 26). The more moral 'Est-ce assez ou non?' = 'Is a word to the wise enough, or not?' was advocated by Walstra (1962: 162), who refers to Ter. *Ph.* 541 *dictum sapienti sat est.*[37] No-one has yet raised an obvious alternative, namely 'Is it [sc. *cauda*] long enough or not?'

And likewise for the final admonition in this letter: *se vidis amico, qui te hoc nuntiat et donet consilium verum, sed te placit, lege et pliga, in pectore repone. sin autem non vis, in butte include.* Walstra (1962: 169) reads *in butte* where there is now a *rasura*. He interprets the word as meaning 'strongbox', since Frodebert is depicted as money-grasping. The word was erased, so originally something worse perhaps stood there, or *buttis* 'barrel' had an impolite meaning.

13 AUDIENCE TO LEXICON TO FUNCTION

It may be possible to work from audience to function. Frodebert (*Frod.* 4.13) addresses the following plea to someone: *nolite domne, nolite fortes, nolite credere tales sortes.* Walstra (1962: 77) took *domne* as masculine vocative singular and the plural imperative as a polite form (193), as opposed to feminine vocative plural. This decision was linked to his interpreting *ipso domno hoc reliquo* 'I leave this to the master himself' in *Imp.* 3.24 as an allusion to copying the letter to the king (Chlothar III). But to do so violates

---

[35] So Duby and Ariès 1987: 502. Did Rouche mean 'butt-fucker' perhaps?

[36] Halsall 2003: 11. But *cinitus* is not 'covered in shit'.

[37] Also episcopal as in August. *Epist.* 40.3 *cui sapienti providenti dictum sat est.*

the clear parallelism in *Imp.* 5.1 and 14 where *nolite domnae* must refer to the nuns. Politesse thus competes with literary responsion, and a periphrastic mode of referring to the addressee in the third person (*ipso domno* instead of *tibi* or *vobis*) leads to the creation of a questionable historical narrative in which the king himself is imported into this disreputable exchange (Norberg 1964: 302). Epistolary etiquette in addressing kings likewise rules out the possibility of *ipso domno* being the king.[38] No historical Merovingian bishop thus adjured another one by his *cauta* in a letter copied to a king. *Imp.* 3 represents bishop-to-bishop communication, and *Frod.* 4 and *Imp.* 5 address the nuns.

14 LEXICON TO AUDIENCE TO FUNCTION

Imp. 5.1 *nolite domnae* etc. ostensibly addresses the religious women of Tours and contains a turn of phrase that, like the *cauta,* disturbed earlier commentators:[39]

> 3. Latrat vulpis, sed non ut canis.
> 4. Saltus init semper inanis.
> 5. Cauta proferit, iam non fronte.
> 6. Cito decadet ante cano forte.
> 7. Volat upupa et non arundine.
> 8. Isterco commedit in sofrundo.
> 9. Humile facit captia dura.

> The fox barks, but not like the dog.
> He initiates leaps that are always vain.
> He shows his tail, never his forehead.
> He will fall swiftly before a strong dog.
> He snatches the hoopoe, but not the swallow.
> He eats dung in †*so frundo.*†
> A hard hunt makes him humble.

Would a bishop have spoken of someone 'eating dung' (*isterco commedit*) to nuns? Pirson (1910: 509) took the subject of *commedit* to be the hoopoe and *in soffrundo* to mean *in suo fronde*: 'It eats dung amongst its foliage.'[40] But the subject is more probably the bishop-fox, subject of all the previous cola

---

[38] Cf. Desiderius of Cahors, *Epistulae* 1.2.6, 1.2.17, 1.3.5, 1.4.7, 1.6.15, 1.9.19: when one writes to anyone but the king's son *domnus rex* is required.

[39] E.g. P. Meyer (1867: 349) 'une grossière injure'; Norberg (1964: 295–6); Brunhölzl (1990: 145) 'la grossièreté du contenu ne cède en rien à la rudesse de la langue'; Dubois (1995: 963) 'une correspondance étonnante et cocasse'.

[40] Reasonable given Enn. *Ann.* 261 V. = 245 Sk. *russescunt frundes*. But Walstra (1962: 218–19) took the hoopoe as the subject and *in soffrundo* as 'en se résignant'.

of this tirade.[41] Addressee, grammatical subject and audience all matter. And critics have overreacted to the content at the expense of the language.

The hoopoe was associated with dung from an early period,[42] and if Importunus is merely retailing ornithological lore, then there is no problem with his mentioning the subject to nuns. But if the subject is the fox-bishop, then the eating of dung (wherever it occurs) becomes more problematic. Walstra thought the animal analogies were adapted to the nuns, who had an inferior knowledge of scripture (Walstra 1962: 23). Hardly – for a study of where these words occur reveals that the *upupa* is unlikely to be a genuine folk-element. An exegetical discussion by Jerome is relevant. The problem started with the name of the bird in Zechariah 5:9 καὶ ἦρα τοὺς ὀφθαλμούς μου καὶ εἶδον καὶ ἰδοὺ δύο γυναῖκες ἐκπορευόμεναι, καὶ πνεῦμα ἐν ταῖς πτέρυξιν αὐτῶν, καὶ αὖται εἶχον πτέρυγας ὡς πτέρυγας ἔποπος·, 'And I raised my eyes and I saw. Lo! Two women were emerging and the wind was in their wings, and they had wings like the wings of the hoopoe.' The Hebrew has *chasidah* (perhaps 'stork'). The Septuagint translated 'hoopoe', Aquila, Symmachus and Theodotion ἐρῳδιός 'heron', while the Vulgate has *milvus* 'kite'. Jerome gave the text in Latin translation twice, first using *quasi alas milvi*, and then rendering the Septuagint into Latin with *quasi alas upupae*. He then commented:

upupam autem, quam nos de Graeci nominis similitudine traximus (nam et ipsi popam appellant ab eo, quod stercora humana consideret), avem dicunt esse spurcissimam, semper in sepulcris, semper in humano stercore commorantem: denique et nidum ex eo facere dicitur, et pullos suos de vermiculis stercoris alere putrescentis. (Hier. *In Zach.* 5.9: *PL* xxv.1451A)

They say that the hoopoe, which I translated <*upupa*> from its resemblance to the Greek word (for they themselves call it the *popa*,[43] because it settles on human dung) is the filthiest of birds, always dwelling in tombs and on human dung; furthermore it is said to make a nest of dung and to feed its chicks from worms that inhabit the rotting dung.

[41] Boucherie (1867: 41) saw the fox eating *stercus in suo fundo* (i.e. comparing *frundellus = ager recens cultus* (Ducange)). For multiple types of barnyard *stercus* in Latin satire see Lucilius 1018 M. (= 1081 W. = 1107 K. = 30.15 C.) *hic in stercore humi, fabulisque fimo atque sucerdis*, 'He on the ground in the dung, the goat-beans, manure, and even pig-shit.'
[42] D. A. W. Thompson 1936: 96 citing Aristotle, *Historia animalium* 9.616a35, where it makes its nest from human dung. It sought insects in dung: Plin. *Nat.* 10.86 *obscena...pastu avis.*
[43] There is no Greek word *popa*. The Latin *popa* was a sacrificial attendant who struck the victim with a hammer. The only odd and possibly relevant usage of the word is in Persius 6.75 *ast illi tremat omento popa venter.* Kißel (1990: 856) treats *popa* as a substantive modifying *venter* 'priest stomach', presumably full of sacrificial meats. Jerome, although he read Persius carefully, seems to imply something different.

Even more relevant is a polemical use of the hoopoe, again from Jerome, in this case the peroration of the *Adversus Iovinianum*. The licentious Jovinian has an aviary not of (chaste) turtledoves, but of hoopoes, who fly around all the haunts of fetid lust.[44] Only in this context are hoopoes identified as women, specifically Jovinian's depraved women followers. It is from here that *Imp.* 5.7's use of *upupa* to refer to the low-flying (i.e. fallen) nun was derived: 'He snatches the hoopoe, but not the swallow.'[45] Jerome was expert at addressing women, particularly in exegetic contexts: *stercus* could be used before his learned ladies. But it was his satire against Jovinian that licensed the hoopoe-nuns. And there, interestingly, Jerome used the expression *stercus comedat* in a context where he drew a comparison between different choices of food (best (wheat), better (barley), worst (cow-dung)) and different levels of chastity (virginity, marriage, fornication).[46] The author of *Imp.* 5 knew some of Jerome's polemic (the *Adversus Iovinianum*) and exegesis (*In Zach.*). He used them to attack Frodebert for his suspect friendships. So the hoopoe and also the *stercus* are learned.[47]

The same applies to other features of both *Frod.* 4 and *Imp.* 5. These last two texts contain strings of insults mostly in the form of bad names:[48] *stultus* 'fool', *falsator* 'forger',[49] *susurro* 'whisperer', *muro* 'retard', 'idiot', 'blackguard',[50] *latro fraudolentus* 'dishonest thief', *adulter* 'adulterer', *raptor* 'rapist', 'abductor', *linguaris dilator* 'informer paying a verbal forfeit', *vulpes* 'fox', *bracco* 'hound', 'hunting-dog'.

Stultus is biblical and nicely contextualised as the discourse of Proverbs by *Frod.* 4.2 'Hagios Solomon'. *Susurro*, likewise (Proverbs 26:20 and 22), but it was also a favourite of the paranoid Jerome. In *Epist.* 11, an apologia to the nuns of Aemona reads: *aliter, sorores carissimae, hominum livor, aliter Christus iudicat. non eadem sententia est tribunalis eius, et anguli susurronum,*[51] 'Dearest sisters, the envy of men judges one way; Christ another. The verdict of his tribunal is not the same as that of those who

---

44 Hier. *Adv. Iovin.* 2.37 (*PL* 23.336C) *macte virtute, immo vitiis, habes in castris tuis et Amazones exerta mamma, et nudo brachio et genu, venientes contra se viros ad pugnam libidinum provocantes. et quia opulentus paterfamilias es, in aviariis tuis non turtures, sed upupae nutriuntur, quae tota foetidae voluptatis lustra circumvolent.*
45 Walstra (1962: 218–19) has the implications, if not the details, right.
46 *Adv. Iovin.* 1.7 *tamen ne quis compulsus fame comedat stercus bubulum, concedo ei, ut vescatur et hordeo.* The expression occurred in the Old Testament: see 4 Kings 18:27 and Isaiah 36:12.
47 For *stercus* see Adams 1982a: 235.
48 Contrast Importunus' detailing of what Frodebert did as opposed to what he was.
49 *TLL* s.v. *falsator* 200.71–7. Often 'forger', but when paired with *delator* in *PLS* 30.7, probably a liar or perjurer, as also in *Imp.* 5.1.
50 *TLL* s.v. *morio* 1491.73 ff., incl. Greg. Tur. *DLH* 9.41 used of *scelesti.*
51 Also *Epist.* 108.19 *susurronem quendam* and *Epist.* 125.19 *veritas angulos non amat, nec quaerit susurrones,* the latter with a similar monastic sexual context.

whisper in corners.' This cannot be coincidence. Frodebert, the Monk-Bishop,[52] recycled Jerome in his own defence.

Frod. 4.18 *psallat de trapa ut linguaris dilator* has caused puzzlement. Walstra (1962: 79) translates 'de son piège il psalmodie comme un diable loquace', perhaps because *psallere* fits the ecclesiastic Importunus. But again Jerome is the probable intermediary for this unusual *in malum* use of *psallere* as well as its retorsion in *Imp.* 5.11 *tamquam latro ad aura psallit.* In *Epist.* 117.1, again alluding to his own suspect friendships with women, Jerome cited Psalm 68:13 *postquam ergo arguendo crimina factus sum criminosus et iuxta tritum vulgi sermone proverbium, iurantibus et negantibus cunctis, 'me aures nec credo habere nec tango' ipsique parietes in me maledicta resonarunt et 'psallebant contra me, qui bibebant vinum...',* 'Therefore, after I had been turned into a criminal while making charges about crimes myself, and according to the old popular saw, while all are swearing and denying, "I do not believe I have ears, nor do I touch them", and the very walls sounded curses against me and "they sang against me, who drank wine..."' Frodebert challenges Importunus to 'sing'[53] against him like an informer put to the question, who must come up with the goods. *Linguaris* seems to be a hapax, but the coinage *linguarium* means 'verbal forfeit' (Sen. *Ben.* 4.36.2 *quod dicere solemus, linguarium dabo*). The author could have used the more biblical *laqueus* for a snare, but the Germanic *trapa*, appropriately, evokes the language of *PLS* 7.10, a bird in a trap. But possibly also colourful code-switching.

Ferri (this volume, p. 32) discusses Quintilian on the rhetorical force of *humilitas verborum* (*Inst.* 8.3.22). And here there are humble words that are not required by the context, since this is not any real sort of *Gebrauchsschrift*. But is this use part of a deliberate characterisation, comparable to literary characterisations of *rustici*?[54] Or do the words belong to the author's/authors' real speech? Or do some of the words that are normally absent from episcopal correspondence evoke other genres? In this category might belong *grunnire* (associated with pigs) or *bracco*. *Vulpis* and *canis* obviously co-feature in fable and proverb, so are at home in the parabolic discourse of *Frod.* 4 and *Imp.* 5.

But sneaky fox and barking dog had already jumped genre to feature in a fifth-century sermon by Maximus of Turin (*Sermones* 41.27). The Saviour recognised those who indicate one thing with their voices and another in their behaviour: *vulpis enim latratu canis resonat, dolo rapinam*

---

[52] Sato (1990: 176–7) dates 'l'évêque abbatial' (bishop-abbot) at Tours to the early eighth century at least.

[53] Much like English slang, 'sing', of the confession of an informer.

[54] See (for example) Adams 2007: 52–3.

fraudis exercet, 'The fox sounds with the barking of a dog, but carries out theft with tricky fraud.'[55] They too form part of the diatribic repertoire of the homiliarist. *Grunnitus* appeared only once in Augustine's works, used neutrally of a penetrating sound along with that of a saw (*De natura et gratia* 47). It is rife, however, in the satirical Jerome, who cites the *Testamentum Porcelli* in *In Isaiam* 12 *praef.* (*PL* XXIV.409D). Church fathers differed. Jerome's usage, as we saw, matters and was imitated by these authors.

But not all animals are equal. *Frod.* 4.25 rudely says *non vales uno coco*, 'You are not worth one — .' What? One cook? *Cocus* for *coquus*? Or one 'coco!' (i.e. one crowing of a rooster)? Or one rooster? Walstra (1962: 208–9) had not found a precise parallel for the worthlessness of the rooster. But there was always *gallum in suo sterquilinio plurimum posse* (Sen. *Apoc.* 7.3). This animal, unlike the fox and dog, probably comes unmediated from the world of the proverb, so the expression is spoken and colloquial.

These texts have mixed origins and a rather mixed message. Some of their vocabulary might seem popular or colloquial, but even lowly beasts are mediated by recondite exegesis. Phrases from Jerome are used in a very literary way where their original and all-too-relevant context can sound for the *cognoscente*. Colloquial turns of phrase are used for satiric point: *Frod.* 1.8 *oblata non bella* 'far from attractive Eucharistic wafers' is an ironic and colloquial litotes, like Modern English 'not pretty'.[56] Likewise *Imp.* 3.20 *amas puella bella*, an expression that goes back to Catul. 69.8 and 78.4. Both parties use an adjective conspicuous by its absence from the ecclesiastical world. A word from the spoken register emerges in writing, possibly for deliberate slumming, with scare quotes around it. In contrast, Frodebert uses *pulchras* of his refined friendships with women (*Frod.* 4.6).

While unacceptable matters are discussed (Frodebert's *cauta* and the bishop-fox eating *stercus*), in the first case *cauta* could be a euphemism and in the second the figure of the fox obscures some of the unpleasantness. But this still leaves the *cauta* in *Imp.* 5 (ostensibly addressed to the nuns). Is the allusion a simple case of distinction between front and back, where the honest end is hidden? Or is this an exegetic *cauda*? Ambrose had identified Samson's foxes (Judges 15:4) with *inprobi et fraudulenti homines* who have the tongue free to bark (Ambrose, *Expositio psalmi* CXVIII 11.29 p. 251). Or is it an allusion to *Imp.* 3.22? Frodebert never sticks out his *frons* in effrontery, but brings out his *cauda*. But that might be worse: *vulpis cauda fallit* (Maximus of Turin, *Sermones* 86.57). If that double entendre is in

[55] Others, e.g. Isidorus, *Differentiae* par. 607.70.4 distinguish between the barking of the dog (*baubo, latro*) and the yelp or snarl (*gannio*) of the fox.
[56] Cf. Hor. *Sat.* 1.4.113 *non bella est fama Treboni*, Pl. *Cas.* 851 *non belle facit*, Catul. 12.2 *non belle uteris*; frequent examples in Cicero's letters, four examples in Martial.

play, a female monastic audience seems improbable. But it is not the case (*pace* Norberg 1964: 295) that these angry men used words they would never have seen in writing.

15 RHYME

I have postponed discussing the most striking formal feature of these letters, their use of rhyme. They have sometimes been classified as verse,[57] but more commonly as prose.[58] They are sometimes treated as borderline (Szövérffy 1970: 297). Their visual impact on the reader can be powerfully manipulated by their layout on the page. For this one has only to compare Zeumer's edition (1886: 220–6) with Walstra's (1962). In the end, however, prose wins out, because it is impossible to discern any metrical schema in these texts, and, as Walstra has shown, analysis of the sentence and phrase-endings shows evidence of *cursus* (Walstra 1962: 50–6; Norberg 1968: 122).

The author or authors use(s) rhyme intentionally. Some have sought to trace the practice back to Columbanus' verse epistles (Walstra 1962: 30, 33; Banniard 1992: 293). Norberg suggested that Frodebert adopted the style as a parody of Importunus, since he accused him of lying like an Irishman.[59] But I would like to make the case that this rhyme came from prose. Solemn rhymed sermons are a known late antique phenomenon.[60] But there was another sort of oral and memorisable style of text on the border between prose and verse that employed rhyme: polemical psalms or hymns such as Augustine's *Psalmus contra partem Donati* and Fulgentius of Ruspe's *Hymn against the Arians*. Daniel Nodes has shown how one can analyse Augustine's *Psalmus* convincingly as a versified sermon, whose words facilitated propagation (Nodes 2009). Such rhymes were intended for easy memorisation and for catchiness.[61] Occasionally such moments of rhyming defiance peek through a prose text as in Victor of Vita, *Historia persecutionis Vandalicae* 3.46 (Shanzer 2004: 285–6). The use of rhyme in this instance may be homiletic–polemical: it is possible to read *Frod.* 4 and *Imp.* 5 as having a homiletic tone.[62] If the letters are a

---

[57] Schuchardt 1866: 32; Boucherie 1867: 52 citing Littré and Paris; P. Meyer 1867: 350; P. G. J. Lehmann 1922: 24.

[58] Pirson 1910: 490; Polheim 1925: 320–1; Brunhölzl 1990: 145.

[59] Norberg 1968: 111, but see Appendix 1 for a different analysis.

[60] Lietzmann 1905: *passim*; Mohrmann 1958: 61.

[61] Augustine, *Retractationes* 1.20: *volens etiam causam Donatistarum ad ipsius humillimi vulgi et omnino imperitorum atque idiotarum notitiam pervenire, et eorum quantum fieri posset per nos inhaerere memoriae, Psalmum qui eis cantaretur, per Latinas litteras feci ... ideo autem non aliquo carminis genere id fieri volui, ne me necessitas metrica ad aliqua verba quae vulgo minus sunt usitata compelleret.*

[62] *Imp.* 5.1 has some of the flavour of Matthew 7:15; *Frod.* 4 also begins in expository mode.

third party's version of an insult exchange, easy-to-remember rhymed cola make sense.

If the correspondence is genuine, however, Importunus must be seen as a willing participant knowing exactly how to engage in stylised ritual competitive abuse, not different from the 'dirty dozens' that are played on some American streets – though he may do so less skilfully than Frodebert (Boucherie 1867: 9). The correspondence becomes a consensual co-performance. In either case, however, the rhyme is a popular feature used with a sense of condescension (and disrespect), not a learned one. Banniard (1992: 294) suggested that it was used for vertical communication to an illiterate local audience, a point that cannot be proven, for there is no evidence that bishops would have taken any dispute of this sort, had it been real, to the streets. The use of exegetic sources militates against anything genuinely vernacular.[63] Banniard analysed the language of 'cette satire' as a Latinity reduced to its absolute simplicity, a point of no return, beyond which the word that it transcribes would be outside the purview of Latin. He maintains that it is built around a series of morphemes that all passed into Romance (Banniard 1992: 294). One would need to trace all the vocabulary to test this point fully, but it seems clearly untrue of words such as *stercus* and *anonna*, if true of the five lines cited by Banniard from *Frod.* 4.23–6. Meyer saw instead 'pas purement le parler vulgaire, mais un jargon mixte où . . . ce parler se fait jour à tout instant à travers l'idiome littéraire' (P. Meyer 1867: 346). This seems closer to the mark. The authors know not just templates of epistolographic idiom, but also serious exegetical sources.

Realia in the correspondence are quite circumstantial, and in contrast to other episcopal correspondence about scandals name some names.[64] There are obscure (possibly) historical details such as Frodebert's *tutor*, possibly the fearless *baro* (if the *tutor* is not God). These could be evidence that the texts are genuine. It is curious that Fr/Chrodebert had gone on record to Boba about penitence for nuns who committed adultery and had thanked her for clothes made to his manly measure.[65] These external links could likewise help anchor the man and his interests (a canonical and pastoral expert on errant nuns) and the accusations levelled at him. Jerome (who is liberally used by the correspondence) was an historical parallel for a proponent of chastity tarred with scandal involving religious women.

[63] There is however the question of flyting and Germanic practice, but that can be no more than speculation.
[64] Similarly Krusch 1910: 434, noting that the accusations make no sense if completely fictional.
[65] Gundlach 1892: 464 *gratias multas ago de linea inconsutili, bene texta, longa et larga et mihi multum amabiliter acceptam et corpori meo tamquam sciendo congrue preparata.* The cadences are suggestive. Julia Barrow has suggested to me that the item in question was a shroud. This imparts a special grim sense to *corpori meo.*

But on the other hand there is the warning whiff of generic sensitivity, details such as *Imp.* 2 *iogo tale*, the 'Proverbial' flavour of the opening of *Frod.* 4, details in the insult exchange that might indicate parody of insult exchange: *Frod.* 4.26 *non simulas tuo patre* followed by the *paraprosdokian* – *vere nec tua matre*! Literary critics might also smell a rat in *Frod.* 4.2 *ut ne similis fias stulto, nunquam respondes ei in mutto*. Does *in mutto* mean 'in a word', 'at all,' or *in multo* 'at length?' (Walstra 1962: 175–6). The passage of Proverbs alluded to (see the epigraph) presents completely contradictory advice: 'Don't answer the fool according to his foolishness lest you become like him' and 'Answer the fool according to his foolishness lest he seem wise to himself.' That said, despite *Frod.* 4.2's recommendation that one not answer or not answer at length, he followed the second course and responded in kind. Perhaps we are being invited to see this as the exchange of two *stulti*. The catalogue is extravagant when laid out side by side.

Importunus accused of	Frodebert accused of
Sending rotten grain	Taking Grimoald's wife
Being a fool	Having sex with her
Being a liar, whisperer, fool	Ruining his lord/lady
Being an ingrate	Loving the devil
Trampling on laws and decency	Being the illegitimate son of a nun
Vomiting disgusting allegations	Being manumitted by his *domnus*
Telling lies	Being an ingrate
Impugning pure friendships	Annexing nuns' wealth
Being a fraudulent thief, a murderer, an adulterer, and an abductor, a false accuser	Having sex with nuns
Being errant and envious	Having a *cauta longa*
Despised by God, trapped by the Devil	And more. . . *in praeteritio*
Being not a man, but a fox	Being a *falsator*
Being an informer	Being a thief, a blackguard, a whisperer
Being a grunting, puff-cheeked, belching, bursting, running, sweating, smelly-phlegm-emitting beast!	Being a fox
Being a hound	Collapsing before a stout dog
Being a dog in the manger	Catching fallen nuns
Not being worth a rooster	Eating dung
Not looking like his father – or his mother	Being a failed hunter
Being a disgrace to his parents	Being caught lying
	Informing like a thief
	Lying like an Irishman
	Being a crooked liar

These contradictory observations lead me to raise a fourth possibility about the texts' authorship and nature, namely that they were written by Frodebert and Importunus, but as a parodic and a consensual correspondence in which each improvises on and caps the other in a series of spiralling cadenzas. They would thus be consensual literary *jeux d'esprit*. There seem to be earlier analogies for learned contrived Gallic mock-abusive correspondence in the letters of Avitus of Vienne and Ruricius of Limoges.[66] While this may seem like an attempt to have one's cake and eat it, it is a theory that takes account of the strong subjective reactions of two reputable sets of scholars and reconciles them. Yes, the realia are accurate, yes, the correspondence is funny, but it is the *context* that is unreal and the external audience that may not be as imagined. The letters thus fit in with other ludic texts from the seventh century, including Fredegar and Aethicus Ister. One might also adduce the courtly fable of the lion, the deer and the fox in the *Gesta Theoderici regis* (Krusch 1888: 213). There a treacherous fox 'sings' when put to torture: '*vae*', inquit, '*mihi miserae, quae tantas poenas patior indigne; ut quid enim a me exquiritur, quod eum minime habuisse certa ratione cognoscitur? etenim si cor habuisset, profecto huc non redisset*', 'Alas, miserable me, who wrongly suffer such punishments. Why are they seeking back from me what it is definitely known he did not have? For if he had had a heart, he certainly would not have come back here.' Far from being Romance fight songs intended to polarise the plebs at Tours, these learned and playful texts are the products of ecclesiastics who may have exchanged them for fun, or, if one dares to imagine Merovingian *urbanitas* and a courtly environment, possibly even performed them to an appreciative audience on some seventh-century Feast of Fools.

16 APPENDIX I: THE VOICE OF THE FIFTH TEXT (*IMP.* 5)

Pirson (1910: 487) concluded that there was no longer any question of Frodebert or Importunus in the fourth and fifth pieces, but general satiric attacks. But *Frod.* 4 (though lacking epistolary headers) speaks in Frodebert's voice. Walstra (1962: 81, 212–13) reads *Imp.* 5 as a 'lettre justificative' of Frodebert, addressed to the nuns of Tours. He is right about the addressees. But the content and the rhetoric of this text make far better sense as a response of Importunus to *Frod.* 4. It echoes his forms of address, *nolite*,

---

[66] See Avitus, *Epistles* 74 and 86, and also (for a genuinely angry satirical exchange) 96–7 (with Heraclius): Shanzer and Wood 2002: 277–84 and 320–3. Likewise to be considered would be Ruricius, *Epistle* 2.35 on the fat Sedatus and the horse needed to convey him. See Mathisen 1999: 201–2 with an English translation of Sedatus' humorous reply.

domne, nolite sanctae, and turns various insults back on him (*fur, muro, susurro*), and plays with others. Frodebert (their real protector) is a false protector. The fox (one of Frodebert's insults) is Frodebert, who will fall before Importunus-the-dog (Frodebert had called Importunus a *bracco,* and the term is now triumphantly redeployed by the insultee). Importunus reverts to an allusion (again!) to Frodebert's *cauta,* for it is with his *cauta* that he hunts hoopoe. If the letter is not read as Importunus', the content is dismally repetitive, and the comment on the fox snatching the hoopoe but not the swallow makes little sense, since Importunus had not been accused of improper relations with nuns. The positive use of the dog (*Imp.* 5.6 *cito decadet ante cano forte*) likewise makes no rhetorical sense in the voice of one who had insulted his enemy with *bracco. Imp.* 5 represents the voice of Importunus in response to *Frod.* 4.

17 APPENDIX 2: WORKING EDITION AND TRANSLATION

{f. 27ᵛ} **Frodebert 1.** *Indiculum.*

1. Sanctorum meritis beatificando domno et fratri Importune.
2. Domne dulcissime et frater carissime Importune.
3. Quod recepisti tam dura: 4. estimasti nos iam vicina
morte de fame perire, quando talem annonam voluisti
largire. 5. Nec ad pretium nec ad donum non cupimus tale
anonae. 6. Fecimus inde comentum, si dominus imbolat
formentum. 7. Aforis turpis est crusta; abintus miga nimis
est fusca, aspera est in palato, amara et fetius odoratus.
8. Mixta vetus apud novella; faciunt inde oblata non bella.
9. Semper habeas gratum qui tam larga manu voluisti
donatum, dum Deus servat tua potestate, in qua
cognovimus tam grande largitate. 10. Vos vidistis in domo
quod de fame nobiscum morimur, homo.
11. Satis te presumo salutare, et rogo, ut pro nobis dignetis
orare. 12. Transmisimus tibi de illo pane; probato si inde
potis manducare. 13. Quamdiu vivimus, plane liberat nos ||
{f. 28ʳ} Deus de tale pane! 14. Congregatio puellare sancta
refudat tale pasta. 15. Nostra privata stultitia ad te in

10.,2 homo] punctuation from Zeumer   **11.,1** te . . . salutare] Norberg p. 297 points out the inversion
of the usual *non presumo te salutare.*

2.,1 Importune] P *sub ras.*   **4.,2** annonam] P *sub ras.*   **9.,4** largitate] Zeumer largitatis P   **11.,1**
presumo] presummo Pᵃᶜ

summa amicitia. 16. Obto te semper valere et caritatis tuae
iuro tenere.

1. To my lord and brother Importunus, to be blessed
through the merits of the saints.
2. Sweetest lord and dearest brother, Importunus. 3. As to the
fact that you refreshed us with such hard grain – 4. you
wished us to perish, now that death is near, when you were
willing to make a largesse of such a grain-shipment. 5. Not at
a price, nor as a gift do we want such an allowance. 6. We
made something to eat of it, but the lord stole the leaven.
7. Outside the crust is vile; inside the crumb is very dark.
It is harsh on the palate, bitter, and the smell is disgusting.
8. The old grain was mixed with the new: they made far from
pretty Eucharistic wafers of it. 9. May you always hold dear
the one whom you with such a generous hand wished
gifted, as long as the Lord keep Your Power, from whom
we have known such great generosity. 10. You saw at your
house that we are dying here at home, O Man. 11. I very much
presume to greet you and to ask that you deign to pray for
us. 12. We have sent you some of that bread. Test whether
you can eat any of it! 13. As long as we live, may the Lord
free us from such bread! 14. The convent of nuns refuses such
dough. 15. Our Private Foolishness to you in loftiest
friendship <sc. writes this greeting>. 16. I wish you always to
be healthy and to have the same charity you give me.

Importunus 2. *Item alium.*
1. Beatificando domno et fratre Frodeberto pape.
2. Domne Frodeberto.
3. Audivimus quod noster fromentus vobis non fuit
acceptus. 4. De vestra gesta volumus intimare ut de
vestros pares nunquam delectet iogo tale referrere. 5. Illud
enim non fuit condignum quod egisti in Segeberto regnum
de Grimaldo maiorem domus, 6. quem ei sustulisti sua
unica ove, sua uxore; unde postea in regno nunquam

6.,1 quem . . . 2 uxore] 1 Reg. 12:3–4

15.,2 amicitia] Walstra amicitiae P   4.,2 delectet] hoc *post* delectet *add.* P*superlin* | iogo tale] hoc *ante* iogo tale *add.* P*superlin*

habuit honore. 7. Et cum gentes venientes in Toronica
regione, misisti ipsa in sancta congregatione [. . . <in>]
monasterio puellarum qui est constructus in hon[<ore> . . .].
8. Non ibidem, lectiones divinis legistis, [. . . <sed
sermones libidi>]nis inter vos habuistis. 9. Oportet satis
obs[. . . <ervetis a vestra >] conlocutione, quem nec est a
Deo apta nec [. . .] ta 10. Sic est ab hominibus vestra
sapientia [. . . <pru>]dentiae, 11. qualem faciebat*is* [. . .]
monasterio puellarum pro pane [. . .] 12. <In> monasterio
fuisti generatus, domn [. . .] perdidesti 13. Indulge ista
pauca verba. [. . .] || {f. 28ᵛ}14. Importunus de Parisiaga
terra.

1. To my Lord and brother, Frodebert, bishop to be blessed.
2. Lord Frodebert, 3. we have heard that our grain was not
acceptable to you. 4. We wish to convey some of your deeds
so that it never give you pleasure to tell such a joke about
your equals. 5. For what you did in Sigibert's kingdom about
Grimoald the mayor of the palace was unworthy, 6. that you
took from him his only ewe, his wife. Whence subsequently
in the kingdom he never had honour. 7. And when people
were coming to the region of Tours, you packed her off to
a sacred congregation . . . the monastery of women that was
constructed in honor of . . . 8. There you did not read sacred
lections, but held <converse of lust> between yourselves.
9. It is very fit that you <abstain from your> converse, which
is neither appropriate for God, < . . . >. 10. Thus your wisdom
is from men . . . prudence. 11. Such as you did . . . in the
monastery of women instead of bread . . . 12. You were
begotten in a monastery, <your> lord/lady . . . you ruined.

7.,2 . . .] lacuna of *c.* 4 characters   **3** honore . . . 4] lacuna of *c.* 10 characters. Norberg p. 300 rightly
noted that Walstra's supplement (representing *sancto Petro*) cannot rhyme with *puellarum*.   **8.,1** . . .]
lacuna of *c.* 10 characters   **9.,2** obs . . .] lacuna of *c.* 15 characters   **3** . . .] lacuna of *c.* 20 characters
10.,2 . . . prudentiae] lacuna of *c.* 16 characters   **11.,1** . . .] lacuna of *c.* 24 characters   **2** . . .]
lacuna of *c.* 23 characters   **12.,2** domn] Editors assume a missing masculine ending, but *domnam* is
also possible. | domn . . .] lacuna of *c.* 20 characters   **13.,2** . . .] lacuna of *c.* 17 characters

---

7.,2 in²] *suppl.* Zeumer   **3** honore] Honore sanctum Petrum *suppl.* Walstra   **8.,1** . . . 2 libidinis]
suppl. Walstra   **9.,2** ervetis . . . vestra] *suppl.* Walstra   **10.,2** prudentiae¹] *suppl.* Zeumer   **12.,2**
] *suppl.* Zeumer

13. Forgive these few words. 14. Importunus from the territory of Paris.

Importunus 3. *Parabola.*

1. Domno meo Frodeberto, sine Deo, nec sancto, nec episcopo, nec seculare clerico, ubi regnat antiquus hominum inimicus. 2. Qui mihi minime credit factu tuum vidit. 3. Illum tibi necesse desiderio, quare non amas Deo, nec credis Dei Filio. Semper fecisti malum. 4. Contra adversarium consilio satis te putas sapiente. Sed credimus quod mentis. 5. Vere non times Christo, nec tibi consentit. 6. Cui amas, per omnia eius facis opera. 7. Nec genetoris tui diligebant Christum, quando in monasterio fecerunt temetipsum. 8. Tuos pater cum domna non fecit sanctam opera. 9. Propter domnus digido relaxavit se vivo, docuit et nutri[. . . \<vit\>] unde se postea penetivit. 10. Non sequis scriptura nec rendis, [. . . \<nisi in\>]iqua. 11. Memores Grimaldo; qualem fecisti damnum, [. . . \<Iesu Christo \>] et Deo non oblituit. 12. De bona que tibi fecit, quid inde [. . . \<a te recepit? 13. Mu\>]liere sua habuisti conscientia nulla, nec [. . . \<an\>]norum peracta sed contra canonica [. . . \<statuta\> 14. \<muliere extran\>]ea de sancta congregatione aput [. . .] 15. non ex devotione, sed cum gran[. . . \<de cupiditate. 16. Arguo te\>,] cur nos scimus damnas nimis [. . . \<a te esse spoliatas\>]: tollis eis aurum et argentum et honoris. 17. [. . . \<li\>]berat per has regiones. 18. Cur te presumis || {28^{bisr}} tantum dampnare suum thesaurum? 19. Quod, ut alibi, ubi eum rogas, per tua

---

6. amas . . . opera] Jo. 14:12 *qui credit in me, opera quae ego facio, et ipse facit*   **8.,1** domna] Sense requires *domna*, the nun.   **9.,2** . . .] lacuna of *c.* 3 characters   **10.,2** . . . nisi] lacuna of *c.* 13 characters   **11.,2** . . . Iesu] lacuna of *c.* 15 characters   **12.,2** . . .] lacuna of *c.* 18 characters **13.,2** . . .] lacuna of *c.* 25 characters   **3** . . .] lacuna of *c.* 26 characters   **14.,2** . . .] lacuna of *c.* 32 characters   **15.,2** gran . . .] lacuna of *c.* 28 characters   **16.,2** . . .] lacuna of *c.* 22 characters **17.,1** . . .] lacuna of *c.* 23 characters

---

3.,1 desiderio] Walstra desidero P   **8.,1** domna] Pirson domno P   **9.,1** se] Norberg te P   **2** vit] *suppl.* Walstra   **10.,2** . . . iniqua] *suppl.* Zeumer   **11.,2** Iesu Christo] *suppl.* Walstra   **3** Christo²] -um *leg.* Zeumer   **13.,1** . . . Muliere] *suppl.* Walstra   **2** nulla] Norberg nua P | annorum] *supplevi* **14.,1** . . . extranea] *suppl.* Norberg   **14.,1** muliere extranea] *suppl.* Norberg   **15.,2** gran . . . te] *suppl.* Walstra   **16.,2** . . . spoliatas] *suppl.* Walstra   **17.,1** liberat] *suppl.* Zeumer

malafacta, quod non sunt apta. 20. Amas puella bella de
qualibet terra pro nulla bonitate nec sancta caritate. 21.
Bonus nunquam eris, dum tale via tenes. 22. Per tua cauta
longa – satis es*t* vel non est? – per omnia iube te castrare,
ut non pereas per talis, quia fornicatoris Deus iudicabit.
23. De culpas tuas alias te posso contristare. Sed tu iubis
mihi exinde aliquid remandare, ut in quale nobis retenis in
tua caritate. 24. Exeant istas exemplarias per multas
patrias; ipso domno hoc reliquo. 25. Se vidis amico, qui te
hoc nuntiat et donet consilium verum, sed te placit, lege et
pliga, in pectore repone. Sin autem non vis, in butte
include.

1. To my lord Frodebert, without God, neither holy, nor
bishop, nor secular cleric, where the ancient enemy of men
reigns. 2. Anyone who does not believe me, let him see what
you have done. 3. He [*sc.* the devil] must be your object
of desire, for you do not love God, nor do you believe in
the Son of God. You have always done evil. 4. You think that
you are very wise in council against the Enemy, but we
believe that you lie. 5. Indeed you do not fear Christ, nor
does he favour you. 6. The one you love, his work do you do
in all things. 7. Nor did your parents love Christ when they
made you in a monastery. 8. Your father did not do sacred
work with the lady. 9. For that reason his master manumitted
<you> in his lifetime, taught you and fostered you,
something he repented subsequently. 10. You do not follow
scripture, nor do you do in return anything except wicked
things. 11. Remember Grimoald; the harm you did did not
remain hidden from Jesus Christ and the Lord. 12. Of the
good he did you, what of it did he receive in return from
you? 13. You had his wife with no conscience, neither . . .
against the canons, a woman who was not your relative,
14. from outside the sacred congregation with . . . 15. not out
of piousness, but with great greed [*sc.* for money]. 16. I accuse
you, because we know that the ladies have been much
despoiled by you. You take from them gold, silver and

honors. 17 . . . frees through these regions. 18. Why do you take
it upon yourself to make inroads upon their treasure to
such an extent? 19. You take this upon yourself, as elsewhere,
when you ask for it, though your evil deeds, which are not
appropriate. 20. You love a pretty girl from any land, not out
of any generosity, nor for the love of God. 21. You will never
be righteous as long as you hold to such a road. 22. By your
long 'tail' – Is it long enough or not? – by *everything*,
order yourself to be castrated so that you not perish
through such things, because God will judge fornicators.
23. I could give you grief about your other faults, if you order
me to tell you more about them, to the extent that you
keep us in your charity. 24. Let those copies go out to many
lands; this one I leave to the master [i.e. you]. 25. If you see
[him, i.e. me as a] friend who announces this and gives
you true counsel, if it pleases you, read it and fold it, put it
in your bosom [i.e. take it to heart]. If on the other hand,
you do not want [*sc.* it], close it up in <a barrel>.

Frodebert 4. *Item alia.*

1. Incipiunt verba per similitudinem iuncta de fide vacua,
dolo pleno falsatore.
2. Agios Salomon per sapientia bene scripsit hanc
sententia: ut ne similis fias stulto, numquam respondes ei
in mutto. 3. Et retractavi tam in multum. Sic respondere
iussi stulto ut confundatur <et> stultum grado nunquam
praesumat gloriare. 4. Respondi, dixi, de falsatore, nec ei
parcas in sermone, qui se plantatum ex robore, qui non
pepercit su<o ore>, vaneloquio susorrone, verborum
vulnera murone, qui sui ob<litus> adiutoris, immemor et
nutritoris, calcavit <iura et pudoris>.|| {f.28^{bisv}} qui fei
date et prioris alodis sui reparatori sordidas vomit pudoris.
5. Incredulas dicit loquellas et inprobas, quoinquinat et

2.,2 ut . . . 3 mutto] cf. Prov. 26:4 *ne respondeas stulto iuxta stultitiam usam ne efficiaris ei similis*
4.,2 plantatum] i.q. *factum*, cf. Ps. 93:3 *qui plantavit aurem non audiet*   3 susorrone] cf. Prov. 26:20
susurrone subtracto; 26:22 *verba susurronis*

2.,1 Agios] Zeumer Walstra aginos P   2 fias] Walstra fiat P   3.,2 confundatur] confundantur P^{ac} |
et] *suppl.* Walstra   4.,4 oblitus] *suppl.* Zeumer | immemor et] Walstra inmemores P inmemor est
Zeumer   5 iura . . . pudoris] *suppl.* Walstra   6 reparatori] Walstra reparatoris P

conscientias. 6. Bonum merito conquesitas, mundas,
sanctas et antiquas, pulchras, firmissimas et pulitas meas
rumpit amititias. 7. Verba dicit que nunquam vidit, ea
scribit que animus fecit. 8. Parcat, qui eum credit. 9. Et si
loquestrem non stringit furorem latro fraudolentus,
homicidium est reus, certus adulter, raptor est manifestus.
10. Innumerus fecit excessus. 11. Errando vadit quasi
caecus, fuscare temptat meum decus. 12. A Deo dispectus
et desertus, ab inimico est praeventus, et per lingua et per
pectus. 13. Nolite domne, nolite fortis, nolite credere
tantas sortes. 14. Per Deum iuro et sacras fontis, per Sion
et Sinai montis, falsator est ille factus, excogitator est
defamatus. 15. Deformat vultum et deformatus qualis est
animus, talis est status. 16. Non est homo hic miser talis.
17. Latrat <vulpis>, sed <non> ut canis. 18. Psallat de
trapa, ut linguaris dilator. 19. Maior nullus talis falsator.
20. Grunnit post talone, buccas inflat in rotore, crebat et
currit in sudore, fleummas iactat in pudore. 21. nullum
vero facit pavorem, qui non habet ad[<iu>]torem super
{secundum} meum tutorem. 22. Non movet bracco tale
baronem non [<latrat>] bracco contra insontem. 23. Non
cessare, bracco, ab exaperto sacco; [<non cessare b>]racco

7.,2 que . . . fecit] cf. Aug. *In Joh. Ev. Tract.* 20.10. *Facit animus verbum apud se, iubet linguae, et profert verbum quod fecit animus: fecit animus, fecit et lingua; fecit dominus corporis, fecit et servus: sed ut faceret servus, a domino accepit quod faceret, et iubente domino fecit. Hoc idem ab utroque factum est: sed numquid similiter?* **12.,2** praeventus] Norberg p. 303 compares Caes. *Serm.* 80.2 *diabolus, si non in opere, vel in cogitatione ac sermone subrepere; psallentes et orantes, quos viderit tam corde quam voce in dei laudibus occupari, nulla poterit calliditate praevenire.* **17.,1** Latrat . . . canis] Max. Taur. *Serm.* 41.27 *Vulpis enim latratu canis resonat, dolo rapinam fraudis exercet.* | vulpis] cf. *Imp.* 5.3 *latrat vulpis* **2** linguaris] cf. Sen. *Ben.* 4.36 *Quod dicere solemus, linguarium dabo* **20.,1** Grunnit] Hier. *In Ier.* 4, p. 267.22 *miserabilis Grunnius, qui ad calumniandos sanctos viros aperuit os suum linguamque suam docuit mendacium.* | rotore] i.q. *ructatio,* cf. Hier. *in Ezech.* 11:37 *et inflatis buccis ructare scientiam scripturarum* **22.,1** tale **2** baronem] the *tutor*? or Frodebert? **2** latrat] lacuna of *c.* 6 characters **23.,2** non . . . bracco²] lacuna of *c.* 13 characters

---

7.,2 animus fecit] *transpos.* Walstra fecit animus P **9.,2** loquestrem] Walstra loquestem P **3** homicidium] Baluze homicidum P **10** excessus] Zeumer excelsus P **12.,2** praeventus] Norberg perventus P perversus Walstra **13.,2** sortes] Walstra fortes P **15.,1** Deformat vultum] deformato vultu Zeumer | deformatus] Walstra deformatas P **17.,1** vulpis] *suppl.* Zeumer *rasura in* P | non] *suppl.* Zeumer *rasura in* P **19.,1** nullus] Walstra nullis P **20.,1** crebat] P crebrat P^{pc} **21.,2** pavorem] *leg.* Walstra **3** secundum] *seclusi* | movet] movit Zeumer **22.,2** latrat] *suppl.* Walstra **23.,1** Non . . . **2** bracco¹] *leg.* Walstra *sub ras.* | Non . . . **2** exaperto] *leg.* Walstra **2** non . . . bracco²] *suppl.* Walstra

et †salte degrassante† . . . non timere falco. 24. Non perdas
{f. 29ʳ} illo loco. 25. Non vales uno coco. 26. Non simulas
tuo patre, vere – nec tua matre! 27. Non gaudeas de dentes.
28. Deformas tuos parentes. 29. Ad tua falsatura talis decet
corona.

1. Here begin words appended in a parable about the
faithless liar who is full of deceit.

2. Holy Solomon through his wisdom wrote this opinion
rightly, that lest you become like a fool, you should never
respond to him with a word. 3. And I thought it over at great
length and I ordered that the fool be answered thus, so that
he be confounded and so that the fool not presume to boast
about his course of action. 4. 'Answer', I said, 'about the
liar, do not spare him in speech the one who believes
himself grounded in strength, who has not checked in his
mouth the empty speech of the whisperer, the wounding
words of the fool, who forgetful of the one who helped
him, unmindful of the one who raised him, has trodden on
the laws and on decency, who vomits dirty filth on good
faith given and on the one who restored to him his former
private property.

5. He tells unbelievable and wicked tales, he
contaminates consciences, 6. he breaks up my friendships
that I acquired through my good merit – clean, holy,
ancient, beautiful, very strong, and elegant. 7. He says words
he never saw, he writes what his soul dictates. 8. Let him
who believes him take care. 9. And if the fraudulent thief
does not control his gabbling madness, he is guilty of
murder, he is a clear adulterer and an evident rapist. 10. He
commits innumerable excesses. 11. He goes his way
wandering like a blind man. He tries to darken my glory.
12. Despised by God and abandoned he was caught by the
enemy – both through his tongue and his heart.'

13. 'Don't believe such filthy stories, ladies, don't believe
it, strong ones. 14. I swear by God and the sacred springs, by
Mount Sion and Mount Sinai, that man has become a liar,
and a notoriously disreputable contriver [of lies]. 15. He

23.,3 degrassante] Walstra decrasciare P decrasciante Zeumer

deforms his face, and, as his soul is deformed, so too his
state [i.e. appearance]. 16. This great wretch is not a man.
17. The fox barks, but not like the dog. 18. He sings from his snare
like an informer paying a forfeit. 19. No liar is greater than he.
20. He grunts behind [one's] ankle, he puffs out his cheeks
while belching, he bursts and runs in a sweat. 21. But he
causes no fear, who does not have an helper above my
guardian. 22. A hound doesn't move such a man, a hound
doesn't bark against an innocent.'

23. 'Don't withdraw, hound, from the open sack. Don't
withdraw, hound and . . . do not fear the falcon. 24. You will
not lose on that occasion. 25. You are not worth one rooster.
26. You don't resemble your father – nor your mother! 27. Don't
rejoice in your teeth! 28. You dishonour your parents! 29. Such a
crown befits your falsehood.'

Importunus 5. *Indiculum*

1. Nolite domnae, nolite sanctae, nolite credere fabulas
falsas, quia multum habetis falsatores qui vobis proferunt
falsos sermones. 2. Furi atque muronis similis, aetiam et
susuronis; et vobis, domne, non erunt protectoris. 3. Latrat
vulpis, sed non ut canis. 4. Saltus init semper inanis.
5. Cauta proferit, iam non fronte. 6. Cito decadet ante cano
forte. 7. Volat upupa et non arundine. 8. Isterco commedit
†in so frundo.† 9. Humile facit captia dura. 10. Sicut
dilatus in falsatura falsator vadit. 11. Tamquam latro ad
aura psallit. 12. Ut Escotus mentit. 13. Semper vadit tortus
et oc dicit que numquam vidit. 14. Nolite, domne; atque
prudentis vestras non confrangat mentis, et non
derelinquere serventes. 15. Tempus quidem iam transactus
et hoc feci quod vobis fuit adaptum, iam modo per verba
fallacia sic sum deiactus de vestra gratia.

---

7. arundine] Hier. *Adv. Helvid.* 20 *illa ad hirundinis modum lustrat uniuersa penetralia*

3.,2 non] *add.* P^pc   **4.** Saltus init] Boucherie faltus mit P?   **7.** upupa] Walstra upua P | arun-
dine] arundo P^pc   **8.,2** so frundo] soffrundo Walstra   **9.** captia] Walstra capta P   **13.,1** tortus]
Walstra toritus P   **2** oc dicit] Boucherie occidit P   **15.,3** sic sum] Walstra sexum P ne sim Boucherie

1. Do not believe such false tales, ladies! Do not believe
them, holy ones! For you have many liars who retail false
words to you. 2. Thieves and blackguards are similar, also
whisperers, and they will not be protectors for you. 3. The
fox barks, but not like the dog. 4. He initiates leaps that are
always vain. 5. He shows his tail, never his forehead. 6. He will
fall swiftly before a strong dog. 7. He snatches the hoopoe,
but not the swallow. 8. He eats dung †*in so frundo.*†

9. A hard hunt makes him humble. 10. He goes his way like
a liar caught in a lie. 11. Like a thief, he sings to the ear. 12. He
lies like an Irishman. 13. He always goes crooked and says
what he never saw.

14. Ladies, don't <sc. believe him>; and don't let him destroy your
prudent minds, and do not abandon those who serve you.

15. Time, it is true, has now passed, and I have done what was
right for you, although I now have been thrown down
from your good graces through deceitful words.

CHAPTER 24

Colloquial Latin in the Insular Latin *scholastic* colloquia?

Michael Lapidge

During the early Middle Ages, ecclesiastical legislation required of all monks that they converse in Latin (during those few hours of the day when conversation was permitted). There was accordingly a strong incentive to learn to speak Latin properly; and this knowledge, once acquired, brought an additional benefit, namely that it facilitated travel for the Latin-speaking monk, enabling him (for example) to seek food and lodging from foreign monasteries as he journeyed from non-Latin-speaking countries such as Ireland, Britain or Germany, through the former Latin-speaking provinces of Gaul and Italy, on the pilgrims' route to Rome. Spoken Latin was learned by means of conversational manuals known as *colloquia* (the name was apparently coined by the great German humanist Beatus Rhenanus (1485–1547), better known to classical scholarship as the editor of Tacitus and discoverer of Velleius Paterculus). These *colloquia* consist of imagined conversations in syntactically simple sentences, framed so as to inculcate the vocabulary necessary for conducting the business of daily life. They constitute an interesting, but minor – and accordingly neglected – genre of Latin literature.

I THE HISTORY OF SCHOLASTIC *COLLOQUIA*

The history of scholastic *colloquia* has never been written, and this is not the place to attempt it; but a few general remarks may be helpful by way of introduction to the text which will form the focus of this study. Broadly speaking, there were three periods of creative activity when imagination and effort were expended in the composition of scholastic *colloquia*. The first took place in late antique Gaul, between roughly the third and fifth centuries AD. These late antique *colloquia* were bilingual, and were designed to teach both Latin and Greek conversational vocabulary to children. Thus they consist of conversation relevant to the child's day: scenes are envisaged in which the child wakes up, summons his slave to fetch his clothing and water so that he may wash; then, accompanied by the slave, sets off to school, where he converses with the *magister scholae*; following the morning's school work, the child takes lunch, then proceeds to the baths, then eventually home and to bed. Numerous examples of these Latin–Greek *colloquia* survive from late antiquity;[1] by way of illustration I quote the beginning of one known as the 'Colloquium Leidense', so called because it is preserved in a manuscript now in Leiden (Leiden, Bibliotheek der Rijksuniversiteit, Voss. graec. 7, fol. 37v):[2]

dies. ΗΜΕΡΑ. sol. ΗΛΙΟΣ. ortus est. ΑΝΕΤΕΙΛΕΝ. solis ortus. ΗΛΙΟΥ ΑΝΑ-ΤΟΛΗ. lux. ΦΩΣ. lumen. ΦΑΟΣ. iam lucet. ΗΔΗ ΦΩΤΙΖΕΙ. aurora. ΗΩΣ. ante lucem. ΠΡΟ ΦΑΟΥΣ. mane. ΠΡΩΙ. surgo. ΕΓΡΟΜΑΙ. surrexit de lecto. ΗΓΕΡΘΗ ΕΚ ΤΗΣ ΚΛΙΝΗΣ. lectum. ΚΛΙΝΗ. vigilavit. ΕΓΡΗΓΟΡΗΣΕΝ. heri. ΕΧΘΕΣ. diu. ΕΠΙ ΠΟΛΥ. vesti me. ΕΝΔΥΣΟΝ ΜΕ. da mihi calciamenta. ΔΟΣ ΕΜΟΙ ΥΠΟΔΗΜΑΤΑ. et udones. ΚΑΙ ΤΟΥΣ ΠΙΛΟΥΣ. et brachas. ΚΑΙ ΑΝΑΞ-ΥΡΙΔΑΣ. iam calciatus sum. ΗΔΗ ΥΠΕΔΕΘΗΝ.[3]

It seems clear that the Latin was composed first, then supplied with a literal gloss in Greek, perhaps interlinear (Dionisotti 1982: 95); in the words of Carlotta Dionisotti, the *colloquia* were 'designed to teach language, the living language, that is, the vocabulary of everyday life, not literary language' (1982: 91). The corpus of these late antique Latin–Greek *colloquia* deserves attention from students of colloquial Latin.

The second high point in the career of scholastic *colloquia* was reached in the British Isles, first perhaps in Ireland or Wales, perhaps from the seventh century onwards, but with its apogee in late tenth- and early eleventh-century England, in the *colloquia* of Ælfric of Winchester (Garmonsway 1939) and his pupil Ælfric Bata of Canterbury (Stevenson 1929: 27–101; Gwara and Porter 1997). The Insular Latin *colloquia* are evidently modelled on those of late antiquity, in so far as they adopt the narrative framework of their predecessors; by now, however, the accompanying Greek gloss has been omitted (conversational Greek was not taught in Insular schools), leaving only conversational Latin. To choose one example by way of illustration, here is the opening of the *colloquia* of Ælfric Bata (*c.* AD 1000):

[1] A number are printed in Goetz 1892; the most useful discussion of this minor literary genre is Dionisotti 1982, but see also Goetz 1923: 12–23.

[2] The manuscript was written in the second quarter of the ninth century, somewhere in the middle or lower Rhine; see Bischoff 2004: 48 (no. 2182).

[3] Goetz 1892: 637. Translation: Day the sun has risen (the rising of the sun, light, light). It is already light (dawn, before daylight). In the morning I get up. He got up from the bed (bed). Yesterday he was up late. Dress me: give me [my] shoes and socks and trousers. Now I have my shoes on.

surge, frater mi, de tuo lectulo, quia tempus est nunc nobis surgendi et manus nostras lavandi, et post lavationem manuum nostrarum pergere ad ecclesiam et orationes nostras facere secundum nostram consuetudinem. da mihi prius vestimenta mea, et ficones meos huc porrige et pedules et ocreas meas, ut induam circa me, et postea surgam, et tunc pergamus sic ad latrinam propter necessitatem corporis nostri, et sic eamus ad lavandum nos.[4]

The ancestry of this conversation is clear: whereas in the late antique *colloquia* the young master summoned his slave to bring him his clothes, here a monk summons another (*frater*) to bring his clothes: English Benedictine monks did not have slaves to fetch and carry for them. The most important difference is that, by c. AD 1000, Latin was no longer a living, spoken language; the Insular Latin *colloquia* of this period are representative of what Adams helpfully calls 'Neo-Latin', that is, 'Latin used as a learned written language' (2007: 616). They are, in short, literary exercises designed to teach unusual vocabulary.

The third high point in the career of the scholastic *colloquia* resulted from the activities of a number of Dutch and German humanists in the late fifteenth and early sixteenth centuries. Once again the impetus was the (re)discovery of the Latin–Greek *colloquia* of late antiquity. Thus, for example, Johann von Reuchlin (1455–1522) discovered one such *colloquium* in 1489, and a few years later, Conrad Celtis (1459–1508) discovered another at Sponheim in 1495. Reuchlin's *colloquium* was not printed until 1729; that discovered and transcribed by Conrad Celtis was first published as recently as 1982 (Dionisotti 1982: 97–120). The interest aroused by these discoveries encouraged other humanists to attempt the composition of scholastic *colloquia*. Erasmus, for example, composed his *Familiarium colloquiorum formulae* during a stay in Paris (1495–9), although they were not published until 1518 by Beatus Rhenanus (A. Bömer 1897–9: 71–94). Other *colloquia* published at roughly this time by German humanists include the *Latinum idioma* of Laurentius Corvinus (1503) (A. Bömer 1897–9: 61–6), the *Paedologia* of Petrus Mosellanus (1518) (A. Bömer 1897–9: 95–107), the *Dialogi pueriles of* Christophorus Hegendorffinus (1520) (A. Bömer 1897–9: 108–12), and, notably, the *Manuale scolarium* and *Latinum ydeoma* by Paulus Niavis (Schneevogel).[5] Needless to say, these humanist *colloquia* are

---

[4] Stevenson 1929: 27. Translation (Gwara and Porter 1997: 81): 'Get out of your bed, my brother, because it's time now for us to rise and wash our hands, and after washing our hands to go to church and make our prayers following our custom. – First give me my clothes. Hand my shoes, stockings, and leggings here so I can put them on. After that I'll get up, and then let's go to the toilet for our need and afterwards to wash.'

[5] For Paulus Niavis see A. Bömer 1897–9: 19–55, and esp. Streckenbach 1970 (introduction and bibliography), 1972 (text), with further discussion in Streckenbach 1975.

composed in Latin that is far removed from the spoken Latin of antiquity; the humanists' intention was to provide for their students a model of elegant (written) Latin style, as may be seen a brief morning conversation in a colloquy entitled *Diluculum* (here the speakers are *Nephalius*, 'non-drinker', hence 'bore', and *Philypnus*, 'lover of sleep'):

NEPHALIUS: hodie te conventum volebam, Philypne, sed negabaris esse domi.

PHILYPNUS: non omnino mentiti sunt: tibi quidem non eram, sed mihi tum eram maxime.

NEPHALIUS: quid istuc aenigmatis est?

PHILYPNUS: nosti illud vetus proverbium, 'non omnibus dormio.' nec te fugit ille Nasicae iocus, cui quum, Ennium familiarem invisere volenti, ancilla iussu heri negasset esse domi; sensit Nasica, et discessit. ceterum ubi vicissim Ennius Nasicae domum ingressus rogaret puerum, num esset intus, Nasica de conclavi clamavit, 'non', inquiens, 'sum domi.' quumque Ennius agnita voce dixisset 'impudens, non te loquentem agnosco?' 'immo tu', inquit Nasica, 'impudentior, qui mihi ipsi fidem non habeas, quum ego crediderim ancillae tuae.'[6]

It needs hardly to be said that no Roman citizen, not even Sidonius Apollinaris, ever spoke Latin like this on the street.

2 *DE ALIQUIBUS RARIS FABULIS*

Our concern is with spoken Latin in the Insular Latin *colloquia*. As we have seen, the majority of the Insular *colloquia* were composed in England in the late tenth century, when Latin as a living language had been dead for centuries. But there is one Insular Latin colloquy which has some claim to have been composed in sub-Roman Britain, where Latin was still spoken, at least by the upper classes, in the fifth century and possibly into the early sixth. The colloquy in question is entitled *De aliquibus raris fabulis* ('Some unusual stories') (henceforth referred to as *DRF*) and is preserved uniquely in a manuscript written somewhere in Wales at some time in the tenth century (now Oxford, Bodleian Library, Bodley 572, fols. 41–50: the

---

[6] Erasmus 1533: 136. Translation (C. R. Thompson 1965: 448): 'Nephalius: I was hoping to meet you today, Philypnus, but they swore you weren't at home. Philypnus: They didn't fib altogether: I wasn't at home to *you*, but to myself I was very much at home. Nephalius: What kind of riddle is this? Philypnus: You know the old proverb, "I don't sleep for everybody." And you're not unfamiliar with the joke about Nasica. When he wanted to see his friend Ennius, the maid, on master's orders, said Ennius wasn't at home. Nasica understood and went away. But when Ennius in turn called at Nasica's house and asked if he was in, Nasica shouted from an inner room, "I'm not at home." And when Ennius, recognizing his voice, said, "You nervy fellow, don't I recognize your voice?", Nasica replied, "You're even worse: you refuse to believe me when I believed your maid!"' The story of Nasica and Ennius is from Cicero, *De orat.* 2.276.

so-called 'Codex Oxoniensis Posterior').⁷ The text of *DRF* as preserved in
the Bodleian manuscript has evidently undergone numerous campaigns
of glossing and interpolation, with the result that there are many words
and glosses (in Latin and Welsh) embedded in the text (Lapidge 1986:
94–7). The original form of the work can only be a matter of conjecture,
but it is with the original form that we are concerned. Before turning to
the language of *DRF* it is essential to try to establish the original date of
composition. The date of the manuscript provides the *terminus ante quem*;
on the other hand, the fact that *DRF* is obviously modelled on the Latin–
Greek colloquies of late antiquity provides a rough *terminus post quem* of,
say, the fourth or fifth century, when most of the surviving Latin–Greek
colloquies appear to have been composed, and when Latin was still spoken
in the western provinces. The debt of *DRF* to late antique colloquies is clear
from the very opening, where the speaker is awakened by a friend; once
awake, the speaker asks the friend to bring him his clothing in language
derived from a Latin–Greek colloquy:

'surge, <amice, de tuo lectu>lo; temp<us> est t<ibi>, si hodie surgis.'
'surgam etiam. da mihi meum vestimentum, et postea surgam.'
'ostende mihi ubi est vestimentum tuum.'
'est <hic> super pedaneum, qu<i> est ad paedes meos, vel iuxta te posui, vel
    iuxta habetur. da mihi meum c<o>lobeum, ut induam circa me. da mihi
    ficones meos, ut sint in ambulatione circa pedes meos.'⁸

Although the ancestry of this conversation is clear enough, there is no
trace in *DRF* of the Greek equivalents which accompanied the Latin conversation in the late antique colloquies. Although Greek was taught in
schools in Gaul, there is little evidence that it was taught in Romano-
British schools.⁹ What seems to have happened is that a Romano-British
(or early medieval) schoolmaster simply deleted the accompanying Greek

⁷ *DRF* has been edited by Stevenson 1929: 1–11, and more recently by Gwara 2002: 125–37. I quote
  from Stevenson's edition rather than from Gwara's, which is deformed by some grotesque conjectural
  emendations (e.g. *secabilis* in line 129 of his text), and by his attempt to normalise case endings of
  glosses. The title of the work derives from a colophon on fol. 46v of the Oxford manuscript: FINIT
  AMEN DE ALIQUIBUS RARIS FABULIS.
⁸ Stevenson 1929: 1.1–6. Translation: 'Get up, my friend, from your bed; it's time for you, if you're
  getting up today.' – 'I'm getting up already! Give me my clothing, and then I'll get up.' – 'Show me
  where your clothing is.' – 'It's here on the footstool, which is at my feet, or else I put it near you, or
  it's in the vicinity. Give me my undershirt, so I may put it around me. Give me my shoes, so that
  they may enclose my feet.'
⁹ It may be worth noting, however, that the heresiarch Pelagius, who was originally from Britain, was
  able to defend himself eloquently in Greek when he was tried for heresy at Diospolis in 415. Where
  did he learn to speak Greek, if not in Britain, where he received his education in grammar and
  rhetoric (before *c.* 380)?

gloss, leaving him with a colloquy that could be used for the less ambitious task of instruction in Latin.

2.1 Evidence for the date of DRF

There is very little information in the text of *DRF* itself to indicate when it may have been composed. At one point reference is made to a *bellum ingens* which was fought *inter regem Britonum et regem Saxonum* (Stevenson 1929: 9.22), in which victory was granted to the British. This could – in theory at least – refer to the period of conflict between the British and the English settlers which took place during the latter part of the fifth century, as described in Gildas, *De excidio Britanniae*, when Latin was still being spoken and written in the western parts of the former diocese of Roman Britain, as the writings of Gildas themselves demonstrate unambiguously.[10] But it could equally well refer to a later period, since the Welsh border remained a zone of conflict up to the Norman Conquest and beyond. Elsewhere in *DRF* a speaker describes his place of origin as follows: *Fui antea in Ibernia, vel in Britannia, vel in Francia nutritus vel fotus fui* (Stevenson 1929: 5.25–6). One might think that in the late antique period, it would still have been customary to speak of *Gallia* (or, more accurately, *Galliae*) rather than *Francia*; but in fact the Frankish settlements in Gaul began as early as the fourth century, and the term *Francia* is attested in late fourth-century authors such as Ausonius (*Mosella* 434) and Claudian (*Carmina* 21 [*De consulatu Stilchonis* 1].237). Another feature of *DRF* which could conceivably point to composition in the late antique period is a list of the titles of government officials which follows the notice that the 'king of the Saxons', after being defeated in battle, managed to escape: *tamen evassit rex et cum illo decanus .1. princeps .x. virorum, et tribunus .1. princeps duarum villarum et commes .1. qui dominatur super unam civitatem, et dux .1. qui dominatur super .xii. civitates, et patricius qui sedit iuxta regem in sede* (Stevenson 1929: 9.29–32). The author (or redactor) of *DRF* evidently copied this material en bloc from an earlier document. Several distinct recensions of the document in question are preserved in manuscripts dating from the second half of the eighth century up to *c.* 1000.[11] The earliest recension, which carries the title *Epistula*

---

[10] See Lapidge 1984: 32–48, and Sharpe 2002: 107–17, esp. 108: 'He [Gildas] wrote *De excidio* somewhere as fully Roman in culture as we can imagine surviving in Britain at this date, somewhere in lowland Britain, already affected by the English . . . a substantial romanized area stretching from (say) Wroxeter in Shropshire down through Worcestershire, Gloucestershire, and western Wiltshire into Dorset and the south coast.'

[11] The various recensions are printed and discussed by Barnwell 1991.

Hieronimi de gradus [sic] *Romanorum*, is that whose wording most closely resembles that of *DRF* (and note that the document has nothing to do with the genuine writings of Jerome).[12] The origin of the document has been much discussed, with the consensus of scholars being in favour of either a Frankish or Ostrogothic origin.[13] In either case an origin in the fifth century, when some facsimile of Roman government was still in operation, would seem to be implied. In sum this various evidence indicates that *DRF could* have been composed in sub-Roman Britain, in either the late fifth or early sixth century; but unfortunately none of the evidence is decisive. In these circumstances it is worthwhile asking whether the language of *DRF* can throw any light on its date of composition – whether, in other words, the colloquial Latin which it attempts to inculcate is a genuine reflection of the spoken Latin of sub-Roman Britain (hence of fifth- or sixth-century date), or is a later confection, produced as a literary exercise, like the colloquies of Ælfric and Ælfric Bata, at a time when Latin had ceased to be spoken as a living language in Britain. In what follows, I describe those features of the phonology, morphology and syntax of *DRF* which are attested elsewhere in colloquial Latin; references are to page and line number of the edition of Stevenson (1929: I–II).

2.2 Phonology

2.2.1 Vowels

It is well known that, in spoken Latin of late antiquity, the original ten-vowel system of classical Latin, with long and short versions of /a/, /e/, /i/, /o/ and /u/, had become simplified, as a result of loss of concern with vowel length, to a system of seven vowels. In this process /ē/ and /i/ fell together as /e/, and /ō/ and /u/ fell together as /o/.[14] The result of these mergers was the frequent orthographical interchange of *e* and *i*, and of *o*

---

[12] Barnwell 1991: 79, from St Gallen, Stiftsbibliothek, 913, pp. 93–8 (a tiny schoolbook in duodecimo format compiled by an Anglo-Saxon scribe at some point in the second half of the eighth century, from a collection of materials assembled at the Canterbury school of Archbishop Theodore and Abbot Hadrian, during the period 670–90: see Bischoff and Lapidge 1994: 534–41): *Decanus sub quo .x. homines fiunt... Tribunus qui exigit tributa et cui centuriones ministrant unius civitatis, quanti fuerunt et super unum pagum vel duos sit... Comes, sub quo una civitas sit... Dux, sub quo .xii. civitates, hoc est .xii. comitates. Patricius, qui sedet ad latus regis.*

[13] See Conrat 1908: 239–60, and Beyerle 1952: 1–23. Barnwell (1991: 82–5) inclined to favour an English origin for the document. Given the script of St Gallen 913, an English (and probably Canterbury) provenance is not in doubt; but there is no evidence that any of the titles listed in the document were used in the administration of Roman Britain or early Anglo-Saxon England, so an origin must be sought on the Continent.

[14] See, inter alia, Herman 2000: 30–2.

and *u* in texts reflecting the influence of spoken Latin. The following such spellings occur in *DRF*:

i for classical Latin *e* (see B. Löfstedt 1961: 21–56): *absidis* [for *obsides*] (10.2), *edis* [for *aedes*] (7.24), *bibliothicas* (2.17), *carissimi* [for *carissime*] (3.27), *perigrinus* (5.22), *satilites* (5.27), *satilitibus* (9.34)

e for classical Latin *i* (see B. Löfstedt 1961: 56–69): *dediceris* (3.25), *dedicit* (10.30), *itenere* (7.4), *iteneris* (7.4)

u for classical Latin *o* (see B. Löfstedt 1961: 68–88; Stotz 1996: 48–55): *accepturium* (11.19), *sapuna* (7.20)

o for classical Latin *u* (see B. Löfstedt 1961: 89–95; Stotz 1996: 61–8): *colina* (4.14), *insola* (5.23).

2.2.2 Consonants

Colloquial Latin is characterised by the interchange of voiced and voiceless consonants in intervocalic positions (see B. Löfstedt 1961: 136–49; Adams 1977a: 30–1). The following examples of such interchange are found in *DRF*:

b ~ *p*: *cipus* [for *cibus*] (3.7), *cubis* [for *cupis*] (3.3), and numerous examples of *prespiter* [for *presbyter*] (2.27, 5.7, 6.10, 6.13, 6.19, 6.22, 6.31, 8.10, 11.8, 11.11)

c ~ *g*: *fracmenta* [for *fragmenta*] (8.20); cf. *gremium* [for *cremium*] (7.28)

d ~ *t*: *cantela* [for *candela*] (7.23), *placida* [for *placita*] (3.4).

Another consonantal interchange, widely attested in spoken Latin of all periods, that of *b* and *v* (B. Löfstedt 1961: 149–59; Adams 1977a: 31–2), is represented by one example in *DRF*: *habita* [for *avita*] (5.28).[15] And it may be useful, for the sake of completeness, to list the few other consonantal interchanges which are attested in *DRF*, even though these are more characteristic of medieval Latin than of the colloquial Latin of late antiquity: *c* for *qu*: *cocus* [for *coquus*] (4.14) (Adams 1977a: 32–3; Stotz 1996: 144–5); *s* for *c* before *e*: *conseserit* [for *concesserit*] (6.28) (Stotz 1996: 185–6); and *t* for *s* before *i*: *ecletiam* [for *ecclesiam*] (5.10) and *mantionem* [for *mansionem*] (11.4) (Stotz 1996: 311).[16]

The phonology represented by *DRF* may be summarised briefly as follows. Some (but not all) of the sound changes reflected in *DRF* were widely

[15] The addition of *h-* before an initial vowel is a widespread phenomenon in medieval Latin of all periods (Stotz 1996: 158–61).

[16] B. Löfstedt (1965: 104–5) describes this phenomenon as a feature of the Latin of early medieval Ireland, rather than of the vulgar Latin of late antiquity.

attested in the spoken Latin of all parts of the Roman empire. For example, the mergers of /e:/ and /i/ and of /o:/ and /u/, represented graphically by the interchange of *i* and *e* and of *o* and *u* (Grandgent 1907: 83–7; Adams 1977a: 11; Herman 2000: 30–3), are well represented in British Latin (Mann 1971: 220–1; C. Smith 1983: 901–3; Adams 1992a: 7), not least in the Latin writings of St Patrick (Mras 1953: 102). The same mergers are also represented in *DRF* in forms such as *imbicillitas* and *absidis*, or in *accepturium* and *sapuna*.[17] So, too, the voicing of intervocalic stops (Adams 1977a: 30–1), represented in *DRF* by a form such as *cubis* for *cupis*. On the other hand, some of the sound changes which are most characteristic of spoken Latin are rarely found in *DRF*. The loss of final *-m*, for example, is well attested in British Latin (Mann 1971: 222; C. Smith 1983: 925; Adams 1992a: 7), but is represented by a sole example in *DRF* (7.27: *super foco* [for *focum*] *vel super ignem*).[18] And some of the sound changes represented in *DRF*, such as *t* for *s* before *i*, as in a spelling such as *mantionem*, are apparently first attested in Hiberno-Latin texts from the sixth century onwards. In short, the phonology of *DRF* is at best a doubtful witness to spoken Latin in late Roman (or sub-Roman) Britain.[19]

2.3 *Morphology*

2.3.1 *Nouns*

On the whole, nouns in *DRF* are declined according to their correct classical declensions and genders, with only rare exceptions.[20] The neuter noun *balneum*, which by the time of Petronius (41.11) had become masculine in colloquial Latin (Grandgent 1907: 145–6; Herman 2000: 65), is treated as neuter by the author of *DRF* – correctly, by classical standards – although he fails consistently to master its orthography: *ballenum* (7.1) and *ballneum* (7.12). But there is one development which affected the declension of nouns in colloquial Latin that is represented in *DRF*, namely that nominative and accusative plural forms of neuter nouns ending in *-a* were misunderstood as feminine terminations, and the noun correspondingly treated as feminine

---

[17] The interchange of *i* and *e* in Greek loan words such as *biblioteca* is probably not relevant to the question of colloquial Latin pronunciation. In medieval Latin, η in Greek loan words was characteristically represented as *i* (Stotz 1996: 20–1).

[18] A second example is perhaps the form *ballenio* (7.21), if it is to be understood as a spelling of *balleneum* [correctly *balneum*].

[19] Cf. Adams (2007: 594), commenting on the form *soltum* [for *solidum*] (6.17), to the effect that *DRF* (which he refers to as 'Oxon. post') 'cannot be used as evidence for a form of British Latin in the Roman period'.

[20] The noun *compes* (f.), for example, is construed as neuter: *compes de ferro factum* (5.6).

(E. Löfstedt 1911: 134–6; Herman 2000: 65). On one occasion the author of *DRF*, perhaps absentmindedly, treats *pocula* as feminine: *et poculas . . . nunc cupio accipere* (5.16–17); elsewhere, however, he declines *poculum* correctly as neuter: *et ego dabo tibi propter hoc pocula* [neuter accusative plural] (6.20), and *pocula nobis ministrat. poculum .1. potum* (8.4). Once again it is a question of whether the single form *poculas* can be interpreted as a reflex of the spoken Latin of sub-Roman Britain.

2.3.2 *Verbs*
Whereas nominal morphology underwent fairly drastic change in spoken Latin, as is reflected in the Romance languages, verbal conjugation remained more stable, the principal changes being the replacement of passive forms of the verb with synthetic (or compound) forms, and the related use of periphrastic constructions, very often involving *habere* (Herman 2000: 68–80). These developments are not, however, represented in *DRF*; what we find instead is great uncertainty about the correct conjugation of verbs. Thus, for example, on a number of occasions the indicative is used where in classical Latin the subjunctive would be required: *equitamus* [for *equitemus*]: *ut equitamus in proximam villam* (2.8); *facit* [for *faciat*]: *Exeat et custodiat oves. Similiter et subulcus facit suibus suis* (2.2); *gratulamur* [for *gratulemur*]: *et nunc gratulamur propter nostrum cibum* (8.8); *interrogat* [for *interroget*]: *Interrogat aliquis vestrum, per quam viam ingrediamur* (8.28); and *ministrat* [for *ministret*]: *surgat pincerna et pocula nobis ministrat* (8.4). It is doubtful if this usage is to be explained in terms of colloquial Latin. In other respects *DRF* provides little evidence that its author was in full command of verb conjugation. Note the following forms: *deripient* intended as third plural present subjunctive [for *deripiant*]: *ne lupi ven<i>erint et deripient eos* (2.2; see also below); *lavam* intended as first singular present subjunctive [for *lavem*]: *deportate . . . aquam limpidam, ut <de> ea lavam manus meas* (1.9); *secabis* intended as second singular present subjunctive [for *seces*]: *et accipe securim, ut ligna secabis vel abscidas de illa* (7.2); *venient* intended as third plural present subjunctive [for *veniant*]: *ne fures <v>enient <et> deripiant . . . eos diligenter* (1.9); and *venierint*, apparently intended as third plural present subjunctive [for *veniant*]: *ne lupi ven<i>erint et deripient eos* (2.2; see also above). Finally, the author of *DRF* uses several verb forms which can only be described as solecisms: *aierunt*, apparently intended as third plural perfect indicative of *aio*, which is a defective verb, and for which no perfect forms are attested (11.7);[21] *confiderunt*, intended as third

---

[21] *TLL* (s.v.) quotes Priscian: '[*verbo 'aio'*] deest praeteritum perfectum et omnia, quae ex eo nascuntur'.

plural perfect indicative [for *confisi sunt?*] (9.24);[22] *lavavi*, first singular perfect indicative [for *lavi*] (1.10); and *nostis*, apparently intended as second plural present indicative [for *noscitis*] (9.17).

2.4 Syntax

During late antiquity, the syntax of spoken Latin underwent a number of fundamental changes which are reflected in the syntax of the Romance languages. The most striking of these changes is seen in the sequence of the verb and its object in the simple sentence. Latin underwent a development from object–verb (OV) in classical Latin to verb–object (VO) in the spoken Latin of late antiquity, and hence in the Romance languages (Adams 1977a: 67–9; Herman 2000: 85–7; Clackson and Horrocks 2007: 280–1). In *DRF* the order VO outnumbers OV by 32:22 – roughly 60 per cent to 40 per cent – a marked preponderance, but by no means an overwhelming one.[23] In the letters of Claudius Terentianus (early second century), the earliest text to exhibit VO features, the preponderance of VO to OV is already 40:14 (Adams 1977a: 68). József Herman has observed that 'in most texts which we might wish to characterize as "vulgar" the proportion of verb final [*sc.* OV] sentences is 50 per cent at most' (Herman 2000: 86). In short, the preponderance of VO over OV *might* be taken as a reflex of spoken Latin; but the significant proportion of OV (40 per cent) probably implies that the author of *DRF* was familiar with the norms of written Latin of an earlier period.

A similar conclusion can be drawn from the occurrence of constructions involving the accusative and infinitive following *verba dicendi vel sentiendi*, which were preferred in written classical Latin. In late antiquity, and following the collapse of Imperial government (late fifth century), accusative and infinitive constructions came to be replaced by subordinate clauses containing a finite verb and introduced by *quod*, *quia* or *quoniam*, and it was this latter type of construction which came to characterise the Romance languages. Although *DRF* was undoubtedly composed after the collapse of Roman Imperial government, it nevertheless exhibits a marked preference for constructions with the accusative and infinitive (six examples: 4.12, 5.14–15, 5.17–18, 9.21–2, 10.3–4, 10.7–8) over those with *quod* or *quia* (two: 3.27–8, 7.9–10). This preference is presumably to be explained, once again, by the author's familiarity with the written Latin of earlier centuries.

---

[22] Cf. *TLL* iv.206.48–9: '*forma perf.* confiderunt *traditur* Liv. 44, 13, 7, *sed* -rent *edd.*'

[23] By the same token, when the verb is in the imperative, the ratio of VO to OV is 54:3; but as Adams says, 'there had always been a marked tendency for imperatives to precede their object' (1977a: 68).

Similarly, in spoken Latin of late antiquity, and hence in the Romance languages, the functions of connectives such as *an*, *ne* and *utrum* were assumed by *si* (Grandgent 1907: 10). In *DRF* we find three examples of clauses introduced by *ne* (1.13, 3.21, 7.25) and one by *utrum* (11.6), as against only one with *si* (8.31 *interrogate si . . . invenietis viam*). Again, this preference suggests the influence of written rather than spoken Latin.

2.5 *Vocabulary*

Spoken Latin in the late empire was also characterised by the emergence of certain distinctive vocabulary which subsequently became normal in the Romance languages. For example, the verb *eo* was replaced in spoken Latin with *vado*, from which derived Italian and Spanish *vado* and French *je vais* (Clackson and Horrocks 2007: 283). In *DRF* we find sixteen examples of *eo* and its derivatives, against just two of *vado* and its derivatives.[24] By the same token, a large number of words, particularly adverbs and conjunctions, which are characteristic of literary Latin, had evidently disappeared from spoken Latin by the time Roman Imperial government had collapsed, inasmuch as they do not have reflexes in the Romance languages: words such as *at*, *autem*, *donec*, *etiam* etc. (Grandgent 1907: 8). It is striking that many of these words are used by the author of *DRF*: *autem* (2.12, 6.4), *donec* (2.14, 7.24), *etiam* (8.1, 10.9, 10.19, 11.7), *postquam* (6.4), *saltem* (7.28), *sive* (2.22), *ut* (6.7, 7.28, 7.29), *utrum* (11.6) and *vel* (*passim*: 23×). In this respect, too, the language of *DRF* is more easily understood as a literary exercise modelled on earlier written Latin, than as a reflex of Latin spoken in sub-Roman Britain.

3 CONCLUSIONS

DRF was composed to teach students how to speak Latin. As we have seen, the Latin of *DRF* has many features characteristic of the colloquial Latin of late antiquity. The orthographic interchange of *e* and *i* and *o* and *u*, of *b* and *p*, *c* and *g* and *d* and *t*; nominal forms such as *poculas* (accusative plural); the significant proportion of VO constructions. In the absence of decisive internal evidence which could be used to date *DRF*, these features could arguably point to composition in Britain during the sub-Roman period.

---

[24] Examples of *eo*: 1.8 (*ite*), 2.1 (*exeat*), 2.7 (*exeas*), 4.22 (*ibo*), 5.10 (*eamus*), 7.10 (*ire*), 7.13 (*ibo*), 7.13 (*eam*), 7.17 (*eo vel ibo*), 9.3 (*ire*), 9.6 (*ite*), 11.1 (*ire*), 11.3 (*eamus*), 11.8 (*exivistis*) and 11.12 (*ite*); of *vado*: 1.12 (*vade*), 5.1 (*vade*).

And alongside these features, one might point to the author's occasional use of (what J. B. Hofmann called) 'affective' colloquial language, such as the use of *sis* (6.16), 'if you wish' (Hofmann–Ricottilli 100). On the other hand, *DRF* displays many features – the relatively high proportion (40 per cent) of OV sentences, use of accusative and infinitive constructions, use of conjunctions such as *autem* and *donec* – which were characteristic of literary Latin but which had long disappeared from the spoken language. Perhaps the awkward combination of colloquial and literary forms is best to be understood by the hypothesis that the author of *DRF* began his composition by using a late antique, arguably Latin–Greek *colloquium* (now lost) which preserved a number of features of spoken Latin; but that, during the process of redaction, introduced forms which were characteristic of literary Latin of earlier centuries. This hypothesis would imply that the redactor of *DRF* was working in an area which had formerly belonged to the diocese of Roman Britain, but at a time when spoken Latin as a living language was very much a thing of the past, and when competence in literary Latin was insecure at best, as may be seen in the frequent solecisms in the conjugation of verbs in *DRF*.

CHAPTER 25

Conversations in Bede's Historia Ecclesiastica

Michael Winterbottom

I INTRODUCTION

Bede died in 735, at the twin monastery of Monkwearmouth-Jarrow near the modern Newcastle-upon-Tyne, where he had been a monk since his childhood. He was an Anglo-Saxon, living in an Anglo-Saxon kingdom, and will have spoken the local dialect of Old English. Shortly before his death, he completed his best-known work, the *Historia ecclesiastica gentis Anglorum*, by far the most important source for the early history of Christian Britain. Like the rest of his extensive oeuvre, it was in Latin. Bede's mastery of the language owed everything to the use he made of the astonishing library built up by the founder of his monastery, Benedict Biscop, during repeated visits to the Continent. What most influenced him were not classical texts, with the exception of Virgil, but the Latin Fathers and, it need hardly be said, the Bible.[1]

Bede's narrative manner in the *Ecclesiastical History* is consistently grave and measured.[2] But he follows his models, hagiographic as well as historiographic, in allowing direct speech to play a significant part. I propose in this contribution to make some observations on the style of passages where two of his characters are represented as conversing,[3] usually in private but occasionally in public.

---

[1] For Bede's reading see Lapidge 2006: 191–228.

[2] This manner is perfectly compatible with the use of 'low' or technical words where necessary. For an example of technical vocabulary in conversation see 5.3.2 (285), where John of Beverley reports advice of Archbishop Theodore that 'periculosa sit satis illius temporis *flebotomia*, quando et lumen lunae et *reuma* oceani in cremento est' (for *reuma* cf. e.g. 3.3.2 (132), *Vita Cuthberti* 17; perhaps culled from Vegetius). I am very grateful to Michael Lapidge for placing a machine-readable text of *HE* at my disposal, and for his help and encouragement during my revision of the present contribution.

[3] I include passages where Bede gives one side of the conversation in *oratio obliqua* (cf. esp. 2.1.11 (80)). For a piquant oddity, see below, p. 425. Words in *oratio recta* are often represented as being only part of what was said (so in passage (1) below); this highlights them as especially memorable. I do *not* normally treat public utterances on formal occasions, like the dealings of Augustine archbishop of Canterbury with the British bishops in 2.2.1–5 (81–3).

Such a topic seemed appropriate in a volume devoted to colloquial Latin. But in an author like Bede, the question of colloquialism is more than usually fraught. What could Bede know of conversational Latin? He had not (perhaps) read Terence, let alone Plautus or the letters of Cicero or Petronius. Presumably Latin was spoken, at least at times, by the monks of his monastery, as by those of other houses he had visited. But we cannot know if it was spoken at any level of sophistication, or with the ease that would allow informality and experimentation. It was for the English a learnt and learned language. They may have talked, in Latin, to visitors from the Continent whose Latin was related to the developing vernacular. Bede himself might have learnt something from conversing in his youth with the well-travelled Benedict Biscop. But we have no way of knowing, and no reason to think, that the conversations in the *HE* are in any way modelled on such reality.

But matters are more complex still. We shall meet a passage (below, p. 424 n. 18) where a bishop says to a dumb youth *dicito 'gae'* ('Say *yes*': *gae* represents *gea*, the Old English form of Modern English *yea(h)*). Naturally (if the episode took place at all) he did not say *dicito*, but the equivalent in the vernacular. That will be true of almost all of the conversations 'recorded' by Bede (one exception might be that between Abbot Ceolfrith and the Irish visitor Adamnan: see below, p. 422). Bede is not telling us what his speakers actually said in Latin. At the most, he is portraying what they might appropriately have said had they been speaking in that language. In general, then, Bede's conversations are literary constructs, with no definable relation to anything that was or might have been spoken in Latin at this period.

We shall find that Bede is much concerned to vary his direct speech, taking the speakers and the circumstances into account. At times he employs a formal style, deploying features like periodisation, complex word order, elaborate figures, and rhythm. At other times the style is simpler. But if, especially in such simpler passages, we meet words, phrases or constructions that strike a modern reader as colloquial,[4] we must be very cautious in supposing that Bede intended them as such. Such items may (for example) be part of ordinary late Latin, or reflect biblical usage. Each case has to be examined on its own merits.

---

[4] We may be encouraged if such features appear *only* in Bede's direct speech, *never* in his narrative. Thus the admirable Druhan (1938: 184) remarked *en passant* that the indicative is used in indirect questions in only six places, 'all of which are found in the recital of dialogues'. He gives two examples, 2.12.3 (108) *scio... qui es* and 3.16.2 (159) *vide, Domine, quanta mala facit Penda* (neither of which would look out of place in the Bible).

2 FORMALITY AND SIMPLICITY

I begin with two passages, not at all untypical, in which a private conversation between high persons is phrased in formal language.

(1)   ... insuper adiecit: 'si ergo vis, hac ipsa hora educam te de hac provincia, et ea in loca introducam ubi numquam te vel Reduald vel Aedilfrid invenire valeant.' qui ait: 'gratias quidem ago benivolentiae tuae; non tamen hoc facere possum quod suggeris, ut pactum quod cum tanto rege inii ipse primus irritum faciam, cum ille mihi nil mali fecerit, nil adhuc inimicitiarum intulerit. quin potius, si moriturus sum, ille me magis quam ignobilior quisque morti tradat. quo enim nunc fugiam, qui per omnes Brittaniae provincias tot annorum temporumque curriculis vagabundus hostium vitabam insidias?'   (2.12.2 (108))[5]

Rædwald king of the East Anglians, who has been protecting Edwin (an exiled heir to the Northumbrian throne), agrees, under pressure from King Æthelfrith of Northumbria, to kill him or give him up to his enemies. A friend of Edwin's offers to smuggle him away; Edwin refuses. The friend's words start vigorously[6] in a relaxed word order,[7] but *ea in loca... ubi... valeant* is far more periodic. Edwin replies formally from the start (*benivolentiae tuae*), and the careful structures, marked by anaphora (*nil... nil*), rhyme (*fecerit... intulerit*) and grandiose wording (*tot annorum temporumque curriculis*), are suitable to the heroic values,[8] as well as the pathetic situation, of the speaker.

---

[5] I cite throughout by book and chapter of the *Historia Ecclesiastica* (*HE*), together with the section on the system established by M. Lapidge in the Sources chrétiennes edition (Paris 2005: 3 vols.), and (in brackets) the page of Plummer (1896: vol. 1); references to Plummer's pages appear in the margin of Colgrave and Mynors (1969). The authoritative text will in future be Michael Lapidge's Mondadori edition, the first volume of which was published in 2008. There are several easily accessible English translations.

[6] He begins another speech with equal force at 2.12.4 (110): *surge, intra...* Such imperatives show the value of direct speech in varying the tone of a long narrative work; cf. also 3.12.1 (151) (monk to sick boy) *surge, ingredere ecclesiam...*

[7] Cf. also the passage starting at 3.12.1 (151) *surge* (see previous n.); 4.3.4 (209) *obsecro dicas quod erat canticum illud laetantium quod audivi, venientium de caelis super oratorium hoc et post tempus redeuntium ad caelos* (the monk Owine; Chad answers with two periodic sentences). The 'modern' word order is very noticeable in the (later) *Colloquia Retractata* (Gwara 1996: 29–38).

[8] Not only is Edwin determined to keep to his compact, but he wishes to die, if he must, at the hands of a king (cf. Verg. *Aen*. 10.829–30 *hoc tamen infelix miseram solabere mortem:* | *Aeneae magni dextra cadis*). As the friend will report to Edwin (§4 (110)), Rædwald was persuaded by his queen not to sell for gold *amicum suum optimum in necessitate positum*, and *fidem... pollicitam servare disponit*. Edwin had earlier kept faith too, and Paulinus in §5 (111) will echo the words: *suscipiendo fidem eius* [sc. *Domini*] *et praecepta servando*. Loyalty of men towards each other and towards God is the keynote of the whole chapter. Cf. the punchline of another story at 4.20.2 (251), involving a nobleman who had disguised himself as a slave in order to escape execution following defeat in battle; when the disguise is uncovered, the victor in battle nevertheless keeps his word not to kill the man: *nec te tamen occidam, ne fidem mei promissi praevaricer.*

In the letter of Ceolfrith, abbot of Bede's monastery of Monkwearmouth-Jarrow, to Nechtan king of the Picts in southern Scotland, which is quoted *in extenso* by Bede in 5.21.2–15 (333–45), the abbot describes a conversation with Adamnan of Iona. Bede is often thought to have drafted the letter, and he may have been present on this occasion. Contrasts in the quotation are pointed up by italics.

(2)   dixi illi inter alia conloquens: 'obsecro, sancte frater, qui ad coronam te vitae, quae terminum nesciat, tendere credis, quid contrario tuae fidei habitu terminatam in capite coronae imaginem portas? et si beati *Petri* consortium quaeris, cur *eius quem ille anathematizavit* tonsurae imaginem imitaris, et non potius eius, cum quo *in aeternum* beatus vivere cupis, etiam *nunc* habitum te quantum potes diligere monstras?' respondit ille: 'scias pro certo, frater mi dilecte, quia etsi *Simonis* tonsuram ex consuetudine patria habeam, *simoniacam* tamen perfidiam tota mente detestor ac respuo; beatissimi autem *apostolorum principis*,[9] quantum mea parvitas sufficit, vestigia sequi desidero.' at ego 'credo' inquam 'vere quod ita sit; sed tamen indicio fit,[10] quod ea quae apostoli Petri sunt *in abdito cordis* amplectimini, si quae eius esse nostis, etiam *in facie* tenetis. namque prudentiam tuam facillime diiudicare reor, quod aptius multo sit eius quem corde toto abominaris, cuiusque horrendam faciem videre refugis,[11] habitum *vultus* a tuo *vultu* Deo iam dicato separare; et econtra eius quem apud Deum habere patronum quaeris, sicut facta vel monita cupis sequi, sic etiam morem habitus te imitari condeceat.'

                                                                    (5.21.14 (344–5))

The epistolary context influences the wording: Ceolfrith talks of his friend as *prudentiam tuam*, as formally as he will soon say to the king: ... *tuam nunc prudentiam, rex, admoneo* (§15); and Adamnan speaks of himself as *mea parvitas*. The rhythm, too, is very insistent, at least in the first two 'speeches'. But the topic is in any case highly important, and highly charged, for both men (*obsecro, scias pro certo*), and of course for Bede himself.

The rhetoric serves the purposes of religious argument. The whole sequence is pervaded by contrasts. Ceolfrith argues that Adamnan is misrepresenting his presumed inner convictions by wearing the tonsure he does. The emotion behind Adamnan's defence, that there is in fact no contradiction, comes out in the vehement phrase *tota mente detestor ac respuo*; and Ceolfrith tactfully acknowledges in his friend a strong antipathy

---

[9] Peter, contrasting with Simon.
[10] Colgrave translates 'it would be a sign'. But Ceolfrith means: if you wear the Petrine tonsure, it is a sign that you embrace his doctrine.
[11] 'Would shun to look upon' (Colgrave). That is not what the Latin says. Ceolfrith strains for effect, for Adamnan can hardly expect to see Simon (nor is Adamnan's *countenance* dedicated to God).

for Simon: *quem corde toto abominaris, cuiusque horrendam faciem videre refugis.*

Moving to the bottom of the social scale, we come to the famous conversation between the cowherd Cædmon and a dream apparition. Through embarrassment at his inability to sing at a feast, Cædmon had left the room as the harp, being passed around the room, was approaching him; later that evening the famous dream took place.

(3)   ... adstitit ei quidam per somnium, eumque salutans ac suo appellans nomine 'Caedmon,' inquit 'canta mihi aliquid', at ille respondens, 'nescio' inquit 'cantare; nam et ideo[12] de convivio egressus huc secessi, quia cantare non poteram.' rursum ille qui cum eo loquebatur 'at tamen' ait 'mihi[13] cantare habes.' 'quid' inquit 'debeo cantare?' et ille 'canta' inquit 'principium creaturarum'. quo accepto responso, statim ipse coepit cantare in laudem Dei Conditoris versus quos numquam audierat, quorum iste est sensus: 'nunc laudare debemus auctorem regni caelestis ... '

                                               (4.22.2 (259–60))

Both speakers speak simply. *ideo ... quia* is not markedly high in tone (at least to judge from Pl. *Mer.* 31–3 *hoc ideo fit quia | quae nihil attingunt ad rem ... | tam [ea* Ritschl] *amator profert*). Equally *cantare habes* ('you must sing', as the reply shows)[14] is not markedly low.[15] The plain and unaffected words contrast with the grand topic of the dreamt song.[16]

An equally simple exchange involves much more exalted persons. Herebald, later to be abbot of Tynemouth, relates the outcome of a riding accident,[17] brought upon himself in his youth through neglect of the advice of his bishop, John of Beverley.

---

[12] 'For it is precisely for this reason that ... ' Compare in *Homilies* 2.7, 211–13 Hurst *nam et ideo ... ut ...*

[13] *mihi* is emphatic: Cædmon cannot sing for the feasters, but he must for his divine interlocutor.

[14] Contrast (king to Colman at Whitby) *habetis vos proferre aliquid ... Columbae datum?* (3.25.11 (188)), 'can you'; 3.22.3 (174) *tu in ipsa domo mori habes* (solemn words of bishop to king: see below, p. 427), 'you will'; 4.22.5 (261) *neque enim mori adhuc habes* (those in the infirmary to Cædmon), 'you are not going to die yet'. See also 1.7.3 (19) (judge to Alban), cited below, p. 428. For the different senses see e.g. Rönsch 1875: 449 n. 13, commenting on abundant biblical and patristic material.

[15] Note in a different genre *Homilies* 2.17, 103 Hurst *dolere prout decebat habebant*.

[16] Nothing could be simpler, too, than the words uttered during the ensuing death scene of Cædmon (§§5–6 (261–2)). In the last exchange ('*non longe est.*' '*bene; ergo exspectemus horam illam*') *longe est* is not common in this sense (cf. however Cic. *Sen.* 66 *mortis, quae certe a senectute non potest esse* [v. l. abesse] *longe*; Ambrose, *Expositio psalmi* CXVIII 8.48 (*Corpus scriptorum ecclesiasticorum Latinorum* 62, p. 180, 7–8) *differ aliquantulum, non longe est finis diei*); the reply *bene* is naturally conversational (e.g. Apul. *Met.* 1.22 '*en*' inquit '*hospitium.*' '*bene*' ego), though not in any way 'low'. The usage at 2.1.11 (80) (twice) is different ('it is well that they are called ... ').

[17] John at the time commented: *o quam magnum vae facis mihi sic equitando!* (§2 (290)), relaxed and conceivably colloquial in tone. *vae* is not paralleled in *HE*, though cf. *Homilies* 2.4, 135 Hurst, where it is an exclamation, repeated in anaphora; CETEDOC gives a much later example with *magnum*. As for *o*, the only parallels in *HE* are the striking repetition in the agonised words of Æthelhun to Egbert at 3.27.4 (193): *o frater Ecgbercte, o quid fecisti? ...* (note the reaction of the OE translator:

(4)   et mane primo ingressus ad me, ac dicta super me oratione, vocavit me
           nomine meo, et quasi de somno gravi excitatum interrogavit si nossem
           quis esset qui loqueretur ad me. at ego aperiens oculos aio: 'etiam:[18] tu
           es antistes meus amatus.' 'potes' inquit 'vivere?' et ego 'possum,' inquam
           'per orationes vestras,[19] si voluerit Dominus.'   (5.6.2 (290–1))

The conversation is affecting; neither Herebald nor the bishop harks
back to their difference of opinion before the accident, and *amatus* is
strong. There is some resonance of *tu es filius meus dilectus* (Mark 1:11 =
Luke 3:22). The simplicity contrasts with a firm speech of the bishop a little
later, where in formal language he expresses his disapproval of the priest
who had baptised Herebald.[20]

To generalise from these passages: Bede can attribute formal language
to high persons even in private conversation; but they may speak as simply
as the low. What is decisive is not so much status as situation and content.
Assertion of heroic values or argument on important matters of church
custom is phrased elaborately. Solemn words between night vision and
dreamer, bishop and loving disciple, are simply phrased. But whether the
style is elevated or plain, colloquialism seems to be absent. Naturally there
are elements characteristic of conversation: addresses (2, 3), *etiam* = 'yes'
(4). That is a different matter: is 'yes' a *colloquial* word in modern English?

3 CUES

Bede's ability to match words with occasion may be tested in a number of
places where the narrator prompts us as to the tone of the direct speech.

The emotion of the speaker may be commented on. An Irish scholar
dying of a plague *inter egra tremens suspiria flebili voce talia mecum quere-
batur* (3.13.2 (152–3)). He insists in elaborate style on his past shortcomings and future fate,[21] but his words are not particularly emotional; *nisi*

'Eala, broðer Ecgbyrht, *eala, cwaeð he*, hwæt . . . '), and the remarkable exclamation at 5.14.2 (314)
o quam grandi distantia . . . Bede is there commenting in his own person on a vision of hell; the
paragraph is notably emotional, and ends with a wish introduced by *utinam*, a word only once
found elsewhere in the book, and at the beginning of this same chapter.

[18] So in a public exchange at 3.25.11 (188)). Cf. 5.2.3 (284); when the same John says to a dumb youth:
dicito aliquod verbum; dicito 'gae', Bede comments: *quod est lingua Anglorum verbum adfirmandi
et consentiendi, id est 'etiam'* (see above, p. 420). For the negative, see 5.12.4 (307) *non, non hoc est
regnum caelorum* (contrast §2 (305) *non hoc suspiceris; non enim . . .*).

[19] *tu* has preceded. So the prayers of the monks are included (so at 4.14.3 (234)).

[20] 'I know him', he says ominously (§3). *novi* governs first *eum*, then a *quia* clause, with some sense
of asyndeton. The *quia* clause is phrased in decree-like language, with rhythm. See further below,
p. 425 n. 27.

[21] One wonders if his words *audivimus autem, et fama creberrima, quia . . .* , with their echo of Verg.
Ecl. 9.11 *audieras, et fama fuit*, are meant to reflect the learning of the speaker (*doctus . . . vir studio*

forte misero mihi et indigno . . . venia propitiari dignatus fuerit [sc. *Deus*] is phrased in language whose impact has been lessened by centuries of Christian humility. We may contrast the words of a monk whose name Bede will not vouchsafe (5.14.1 (313–4)). He begins, *multum merens ac damnato similis*, to narrate a vision of hell. We are given a short extract in *oratio recta*: *in quorum vicinia (heu misero mihi)[22] locum despicio* [sic] *aeternae perditionis esse praeparatum.*[23] Again, a thegn of King Cenred of Mercia *clamabat statim miserabili voce*, when the king came to visit him and begged him to repent. He begins pathetically *quid vis modo? quid huc venisti?*, though on these simplicities something more elaborate follows: *non enim mihi aliquid utilitatis aut salutis potes ultra conferre* (5.13.2 (312)).[24]

The narrator draws attention to (mild) anger in a remarkable scene where we are given only one side of a conversation.[25] The companions of a dying nun of Barking listen to her addressing a vision, whose replies they cannot hear (4.9.4 (223)). It is only afterwards that she tells them that she has been talking to the late abbess, Æthelburh, and requesting a swift death for herself. She starts with a welcome that nicely combines formal with informal:[26] *gratus mihi est multum adventus tuus, et bene venisti.* But her next words she speaks *quasi leviter indignata* at the abbess's reply: *nequaquam hoc laeta ferre queo.* The forcible *nequaquam* marks her firmness in dealing with her visitant. So do *nullatenus* and *omnimodis* in her following remarks.[27] And when she twice prays (*obsecro*), it is for the shortest possible delay before dying.

Prayer may be accompanied by described gesture. When the monk Owine beseeches Chad, his bishop, then living in retirement at Lastingham,

---

[22] *litterarum*; it is true that he himself draws attention to his *studia divinae lectionis*). But they probably rather reflect Bede's own reading (cf. also *Epistola ad Ecgbertum* 7 (Plummer 1896: I 410) *audivimus enim, et fama est*).

[22] The parenthesis, in this context, sounds melodramatic rather than colloquial, though (for what it is worth) cf. Pl. *Mer.* 661, 701, 770.

[23] Cf. 2.1.11 (80), where Gregory the Great, *intimo ex corde longa trahens suspiria*, begins: *heu, pro dolor!* Bede only once uses *heu* in his own voice in *HE*: significantly, in a parenthesis lamenting the disloyalty of a thegn (3.14.3 (155)) *heu pro dolor, longe aliter erat*).

[24] For more on this episode see below, p. 430.

[25] Note also two points in an after-death narrative where the guide replies to a *thought* of the dead man (5.12.2 (305) and 4 (307)).

[26] Plummer (1896: II.219) remarked on *bene venisti*, comparing French *bien-venir*. One might wonder if English parallels are more relevant than Romance. The Old English version here has 'ðu eart leof wilcuma'; Latham 1975 s.v. *benevenire* cites, from a late text, 'Anglice dixit *wellecome to wike!*, quod sonat in patria illa *bene veneris ad balliviam tuam*'. The Old English verb (*ge*)*wilcumian* is transitive (= *salutare*). For Latin parallels see *TLL* s.v. *bene* 2110, 69–70, Blaise 1954 s.v. *bene* I, supplemented a little by CETEDOC.

[27] Cf. the decisive tone of John of Beverley at 5.6.3 (291) (following *si ab hoc sacerdote baptizatus es, non es perfecte baptizatus*): *nullatenus, omnimodis*. See also above, p. 424 n. 20.

he asks for permission to speak (*obsecro, pater, licet aliquid interrogare?*) *prosternens se in terram*. He then begs Chad to explain a song he had heard, using a second *obsecro* (4.3.4 (209)). Again, in his interview with Cuthbert at Carlisle (4.27.2 (274–5)), the hermit Hereberht *provolutus est eius vestigiis. Fusis cum gemitu*[28] *lacrimis*, he begins with the words *obsecro per Dominum*, and uses emotive language: *ne me deseras, sed tui memor sis fidissimi sodalis* (note the mannered word order).

Authorial comment displays itself sharply (and unusually) at 2.5.4 (91), when the three sons of Sæberht, king of the East Saxons, speak (in apparent unison) to Bishop Mellitus of London *barbara inflati stultitia*, demanding the white communion bread[29] which their father had been given in his lifetime and the people were still being given. In three utterances they make clear that for them the bread is just bread; they want to be nourished by it, but do not recognise it as the *panis sanctus*, the *panis vitae*. Their crassness shows up in their attitudes rather than in details of their language, though there is some contrast with Mellitus' Christian rhetoric (*ablui/ablutus est; participabat/participes; lavacrum vitae/panem vitae*). But their final thrust, *si non vis adsentire nobis in tam facili causa*[30] *quam petimus, non poteris iam in nostra provincia demorari*, might display in its initially relaxed word order the vigour of ordinary speech; but a velox rhythm rounds off their remarks.

St Peter (2.6.1 (92)), appearing in a vision to Archbishop Laurence when he was thinking of abandoning his mission, *sciscitabatur apostolica districtione quare gregem . . . relinqueret*. His severity[31] is expressed in a long question that draws attention to the details of Peter's own sufferings *pro parvulis Christi* (Christ is named seven times in the section). Peter, as is proper, employs language from the New Testament.[32] The editors identify

---

[28] John of Beverley's words cited above (p. 423 n. 17), were uttered *cum gemitu*.

[29] How picturesque is the phrase *panem nitidum* meant to be? One might think that *nitidus* is no more the expected epithet here than *niveus* in Juv. 5.70, where Courtney comments: 'The technical term would be *candidus*.' CETEDOC gives two parallels, one from the often colloquial Anthimus (fifth century), but the other from the respectable (but much later) Ailred of Rievaulx (twelfth century). The sons are in any case expressing their displeasure that better than ordinary bread is given to the commons. The familiar form *Saba* adds vigour to their words.

[30] The word approaches its Romance sense of 'matter, thing'. Cf. 2.1.3 (75) *cum incessabili causarum saecularium inpulsu fluctuaret*; but Bede is there citing Gregory, and will not have felt any colloquialism.

[31] Contrast the tone of the words at 4.14.3 (234) which Saints Peter and Paul tell a sick boy to pass on to a priest called Eappa: *neque aliquis de hoc monasterio sive adiacentibus ei possessiunculis hac clade moriturus est* sounds almost like the language of a charter. Similarly the royal position and circumstances of death of Oswald are elaborately stated, and there is appeal to documentation, *codicibus in quibus defunctorum est adnotata depositio*. The apostles speak as formally, and as rhythmically, as any secular magnate.

[32] Cf. the biblical language used by St Cuthbert when talking to the hermit Hereberht (4.27.2 (274)): not only 2 Peter 1:14 (cited by the editors), but also 2 Timothy 4:6 *ego enim iam delibor, et tempus resolutionis meae instat*. Note too the biblical tone of *gaudio gaude* (275); cf. e.g. John 3:29.

the passages alluded to, but unaccountably miss Hebrews 11:36 *alii vero ludibria et verbera experti, insuper et vincula et carceres.* And we should perhaps also take into account 4 Esdras 5:18 *non derelinquas nos sicut pastor gregem suum in manibus luporum malignorum.* Similarly, when Bishop Cedd has to tell off King Sigeberht, *iratus . . . et pontificali auctoritate protestatus* (3.22.3 (174)), he starts his admonition with a formula familiar from the New Testament (e.g. Luke 12:59): *dico tibi,*[33] *quia noluisti* [cf. 3 Kings 20:36] *te continere a domo perditi et damnati illius, tu in ipsa domo mori habes.*[34]

Different from all these cases is the remark that the ascetic Dryhthelm was *homo simplicis ingenii ac moderatae naturae* (5.12.8 (310)). This holy innocence is evinced by his dry responses when his friends commented on his immersion in a freezing river:

(5)   cumque . . . dicerent qui videbant: 'mirum, frater Drycthelme' (hoc enim erat viro nomen), 'quod tantam frigoris asperitatem ulla ratione tolerare praevales', respondebat ille *simpliciter . . .* : 'frigidiora ego vidi.' et cum dicerent: 'mirum quod tam austeram tenere continentiam velis', respondebat: 'austeriora ego vidi.'

The rather flowery language of the onlookers points up the stoical replies.[35]

Finally, I draw attention to a phrase used on two occasions to introduce direct speech. At 4.23.4 (264), Abbess Æbbe questions a monk named Adamnan (an Irishman, to judge from his name, but different from the interlocutor of Abbot Ceolfrith mentioned above) about a prophecy that all the buildings of Coldingham would soon be burnt to a cinder. Adamnan recounts in reply how he had during the night vigil been startled to see someone he did not know; the stranger *quasi familiari me voce alloquens* '*bene facis*' inquit '*qui tempore isto nocturnae quietis non somno indulgere sed vigiliis et orationibus insistere maluisti*'. The French translators of the Sources chrétiennes edition (2005) plump for 'avec une voix amicale'.[36] Now earlier, at 2.12.5 (110), towards the end of the story of Edwin, by this time king, Bishop Paulinus comes to him, gives him a sign, and asks him if he

---

[33] St Michael uses the phrase in a more friendly context at 5.19.12 (329). Bede there alters the wording of his source, Stephen of Ripon's *Vita Wilfridi* 56 (p. 122 Colgrave).

[34] Chad, by contrast, when it is made clear to him that he has been irregularly ordained, replies *voce humillima: . . . libenter ab officio discedo, quippe qui neque me umquam hoc esse dignum arbitrabar, sed obedientiae causa iussus subire hoc quamvis indignus consensi* (4.2.3 (205)). The narrator then remarks on the *humilitas* of the words.

[35] For *video* thus cf. *OLD* s.v. 12 ('esp. in pf. tenses'); no very close parallel is cited there, but note Pl. *Mer.* 703–4 *em quoi decem talenta dotis detuli, | haec ut viderem, ut ferrem has contumelias!*

[36] Cf. Liv. 25.18.5 *conloquium amicum ac familiare.* Note that, though this meaning is appropriate enough here, it would not be so in the passage discussed below, where Paulinus speaks in a tone of stern admonition. And what of *quasi*?

recognises it. He does; for it is the sign once given him in a dream by an unknown stranger (*vultus habitusque incogniti*), whom Bede asserts to have been not man but spirit (§3 (109)). Edwin is about to throw himself at the bishop's feet, but Paulinus *levavit eum, et quasi familiari voce adfatus 'ecce' inquit 'hostium manus, quos timuisti, Domino donante evasisti'* (a carefully crafted speech follows).[37] Here Colgrave translates 'in a voice that seemed familiar'. This is doubtless right: Paulinus' voice sounded familiar to Edwin because he had heard it in his dream at a time when he did not know Paulinus. In that case Paulinus is being identified with the night visitant, as (according to the Whitby Life of St Gregory, p. 100 Colgrave) 'people say' he was. But if so Bede gives no other hint that this is the case. If we turn back to the other passage, we should interpret similarly: the implication there is that the night visitor was the same as the priest who had lectured Adamnan in his youth (4.23.3 (263)). Adamnan told Æbbe that the stranger was *incogniti vultus*; the voice, perhaps, rang a bell that the face did not. If I am right, the phrase common to both passages has nothing to tell us about the tone of the words that succeed it in either place.

4 ADAPTING A SOURCE[38]

In his narrative of the martyrdom of Saint Alban, Bede adapts a previous account, which he found in a manuscript related to the extant Paris B.N. lat. 11748.[39] We are therefore in a position to see how he dealt with the wording of the conversation between Alban and the judge who interrogated him (1.7.3 (19)). The comparison is complicated by the fact that here as elsewhere Bede was striving not only to improve on (or at least vary) his source but also to make sense of a faulty text. It seems likely, however, e.g. that Bede replaces (a) *tu nunc perlues* with *tu solvere habes* [either 'will' or 'must': cf. p. 423 n. 14]; (b) *cuius genere familiae es?* (doubtless corrupt) with *cuius familiae vel generis es?*; (c) *ad te nihil pertinet quam* [sic] *fuerim generositatis* with the vigorous question *quid ad te pertinet qua stirpe sim genitus?*; (d) *haec . . . nec auxiliare subiectis possunt nec votorum desideria valent effectui*

---

[37] Note (beside the rhetoric of *temporalibus/temporalis*) how *ecce . . . ecce . . . tertium . . .* picks up in turn the three (very formally phrased) questions asked by the stranger in §3 (108–9). The style is entirely suited to the occasion: Bede has twice called the vision an *oraculum* (§§1, 2 (107)) sent by God.

[38] At 2.1.2 (74) Bede gives words of Pope Gregory in private conversation with his deacon Peter; they in fact come verbatim from the preface to the *Dialogues*, as Plummer knew. The famous conversation of Gregory on the topic of the Angli (2.1.11 (80)) is not necessarily written in reaction to the simpler version found in the Whitby Life (p. 90 Colgrave). Gregory speaks formally with rhetorical point. The word *frontispicium* in the sense 'face' seems to be first found in Bede (who also uses it in his commentaries), but it will certainly not be a vulgarism; Bede employs it here for variation after *vultus*, used twice earlier in the section.

[39] Printed by W. Meyer (1904: 3–81): our conversation at pp. 39 (transcript), 50 and 52 (corrected text).

mancipare (rather bureaucratic in tone) with *haec . . . nec auxiliari subiectis possunt nec supplicantium sibi desideria vel vota conplere*; and (e) *si quis ea his imaginibus reddere procuraverit* with *quicumque his sacrificia simulacris* [order!] *obtulerit.* These changes do not point in any one stylistic direction, and the itch to alter for alteration's sake (apparent elsewhere in Bede) is noticeable. But it should be observed that what we might have guessed to be traces of Bede himself, like the allusion to Verg. *Aen.* 7.648 *contemptor divum* and the rhetoric of *Christianum . . . esse Christianisque officiis vacare*, in fact take over wording of the source. In general, we should bear in mind that at least some of Bede's other miracle tales may go back to lost written sources, whose influence on his phraseology it is impossible to gauge.

5 MISCELLANEA

In the course of my discussion, I have mentioned a number of places where Bede might be thought to be employing colloquial language. I now list a number of other expressions that might be regarded as colloquial.

(6)   at ego respondi: 'habeo quidem de ligno in quo caput eius occisi a paganis
         infixum est . . . '   (3.13.2 (153))

Acca here recounts his reply to a request for a relic of St Oswald. The sentence, as it proceeds, is elaborately expressed, and *habeo . . . de ligno* may not be felt as colloquial in tone. In a narrative passage at 3.15.2 (158) Bede can write *presbyter . . . adsumta ampulla misit de oleo in pontum.* Here too the phrasing may merely reflect ordinary late usage (though note the relaxed word order).[40]

(7)   et quid ego possum puellae, si moritura est, facere?   (5.3.2 (285))

         What can *I* do for the girl . . . ?

For the dative cf. K–S 1.321 (often colloquial in classical Latin).

(8)   et dum adsiderem illi, dixit: 'vis petamus bibere?' at ego: 'volo,' inquam
         'et multum delector si potes.'   (5.3.2 (286))

         Shall we ask for something to drink? (Colgrave)

This is perhaps conversational, yet cf. Liv. 40.47.5 *nihil prius petierunt a praetore quam ut bibere sibi iuberet dari* (cf. Gwara 1996: 32 *ut des mihi bibere*; Väänänen 1981: 139). One might however take *bibere* as depending directly on *petamus*, 'seek to drink'.

---

[40] See e.g. E. Löfstedt (1956: 1.145–7). Druhan (1938: 104 'distinctly Late Latin') compares *HE* 3.10 (147) *tulit . . . de pulvere terrae*, 5.4.2 (287) *miserat . . . de aqua* (both narrative).

(9)   protulitque unus libellum perpulchrum, sed vehementer modicum
                                                              (5.13.2 (312))

The diminutive adjective *perpulcher* is found once in Terence; for a few
later examples see *TLL* s.v. 1657.18–21. For *vehementer* thus, cf. 1.12.1 (25)
gentibus transmarinis vehementer saevis (narrative), from Gildas (c. 14). The
usage goes back a long way; see the (less striking) instances given in *OLD*
s.v. 4b. The adverb looks odd qualifying *modicus*; more natural e.g. Genesis
26:13 *donec magnus vehementer effectus est*. The speech of the thegn to King
Cenred (above, p. 425), from which this sentence is taken, shows much
'modern' word order; further on we find *maior esse videbatur eorum*, and the
remarkable *moxque ut ad se invicem perveniunt* [sic], *moriar*. Some written
source may lie behind this episode.

6 SOME CONCLUSIONS

Bede will have taken hints on how to write conversations, and how to vary
their tone, by studying the practice of the texts from which he learned so
much about Latin style in general. I think especially of the Bible, and of
saints' lives: Jerome's of Hilarion and the rest, Sulpicius Severus' of Martin,
Gregory's of Benedict and other saints. Jerome could make Antony greet
a Centaur with words combining (as was only correct) a certain formality
with a touch of the colloquial: *heus tu, quanam in parte Dei servus hic
habitat?*[41] (*Vita Pauli* 7.4). Equally, he could make a married woman talk
to Malchus like a declaimer.[42] It was from such sources, not from his
companions on Tyneside, that Bede learned to write direct speech for his
characters. But just as (for example) Jerome's default style in such utterances
is redolent of the author himself, so with Bede; his speakers rarely fall below
the level of his own manner. Naturally they are at times made to say things
that would only be appropriate in conversation (e.g. *etiam* = 'yes'). They
can rarely if ever be *caught out* in colloquialism. That is, at least in part, the
result of the methodological problems raised earlier in this contribution.
A more important finding is that, within limits, they are given utterances
designed to suit their various characters and circumstances.

---

[41] Note the rhythmic clausula alongside *heus tu*.
[42] *Vita Malchi* 6.7 *cur moreris ne mihi iungaris? ego morerer si iungi velles*.

Abbreviations

Acc.	L. Accius
trag.	*tragoediarum fragmenta* (D. = Dangel 1995; R. = Ribbeck 1871; W. = Warmington 1967)
Andr.	L. Livius Andronicus
poet.	*Fragmenta poetarum Latinorum* (Blänsdorf 1995) (*Odusia*)
trag.	*Tragicorum Romanorum fragmenta* (R. = Ribbeck 1871)
App. Verg.	Appendix Vergiliana
Apul.	Apuleius
Apol.	*Apologia*
Fl.	*Florida*
Met.	*Metamorphoses*
Soc.	*de Deo Socratis*
Asel.	Sempronius Asellio
hist.	*Historicorum Romanorum reliquiae* (Peter 1914)
August.	Aurelius Augustinus (St Augustine)
Conf.	*Confessiones*
Epist.	*Epistulae*
In Joh. Ev. Tract.	*In Johannis evangelium tractatus*
B. Afr.	*De bello Africo*
B. Hisp.	*De bello Hispaniense*
Beda	Beda Venerabilis (Venerable Bede)
HE	*Historia ecclesiastica gentis Anglorum*
Caecil.	Caecilius Statius
Cael.	M. Caelius Rufus
Fam.	[Cicero] *Epistulae ad Familiares*
Caes.	C. Julius Caesar
Civ.	*De bello Civili*

Gal.	*De bello Gallico*
orat.	*oratorum fragmenta* (Klotz 1927a)
Calp.	L. Calpurnius Piso Frugi
hist.	*Historicorum Romanorum reliquiae* (Peter 1914)
Cato	M. Porcius Cato (Cato the Elder)
Agr.	*De agri cultura*
Fil.	*libri ad filium*
hist.	*Historicorum Romanorum reliquiae* (Peter 1914) (*Origines*)
orat.	*Oratorum Romanorum fragmenta* (M. = Malcovati 1976)
Catul.	C. Valerius Catullus
Char.	Flavius Sosipater Charisius
Cic.	M. Tullius Cicero
Ac.	*Academica*
Agr.	*De lege agraria*
Amic.	*De amicitia*
Arat.	*Arati Phaenomena*
Arch.	*Pro Archia*
Att.	*Epistulae ad Atticum*
Brut.	*Brutus*
Caec.	*Pro Caecina*
Cael.	*Pro Caelio*
Catil.	*In Catilinam*
Clu.	*Pro Cluentio*
De orat.	*De oratore*
Div.	*De divinatione*
Div. Caec.	*Divinatio in Q. Caecilium*
Fam.	*Epistulae ad familiares*
Fat.	*De fato*
Fin.	*De finibus bonorum et malorum*
Har.	*De haruspicum responso*
Inv.	*De inventione*
Leg.	*De legibus*
Man.	*Pro lege Manilia*
Marc.	*Pro Marcello*
Mil.	*Pro Milone*
Mur.	*Pro Murena*
Off.	*De officiis*
Opt. gen.	*De optimo genere oratorum*

Orat.	*Orator*
Phil.	*Philippicae*
Pis.	*In Pisonem*
Planc.	*Pro Plancio*
Q. fr.	*Epistulae ad Quintum fratrem*
Q. Rosc.	*Pro Q. Roscio comoedo*
Quinct.	*Pro Quinctio*
Rab. perd.	*Pro Rabirio perduellionis reo*
Rep.	*De republica*
Scaur.	*Pro Scauro*
Sen.	*De senectute*
Sest.	*Pro Sestio*
S. Rosc.	*Pro S. Roscio Amerino*
Tul.	*Pro Tullio*
Tusc.	*Tusculanae disputationes*
Ver.	*In Verrem*
Coel.	L. Coelius Antipater
hist.	*Historicorum Romanorum reliquiae* (Peter 1914)
Col.	L. Iunius Moderatus Columella (*De re rustica*)
Arb.	*De arboribus*
Curt.	Q. Curtius Rufus
Dig.	*Digesta Iustiniani*
Don.	Aelius Donatus
De com.	*Excerpta de comoedia*
Ter.	*Commentum Terenti*
Vita Verg.	*Vita Vergilii*
DRF	*De aliquibus raris fabulis*
Enn.	Ennius
Ann.	*Annales* (Sk. = Skutsch 1985; V. = Vahlen 1903)
scaen.	*scaenica* (J. = Jocelyn 1969; R. = Ribbeck 1871; V. = Vahlen 1903; W. = Warmington 1967)
Eutr.	Eutropius
Evanth.	Evanthius
De fab.	*De fabula*
Flor.	L. Annius Florus
Epit.	*Epitome bellorum omnium annorum DCC*
Fro.	M. Cornelius Fronto
Add. ep.	*Additamentum epistularum variarum acephalum*
Amic.	*Epistulae ad amicos*
Ant.	*Epistulae ad Antoninum Pium*

De eloq.	*Epistulae ad M. Antoninum de eloquentia*
Ep. Ant. Imp.	*Epistulae ad M. Antoninum Imp. et invicem*
Ep. M. Caes.	*Epistulae ad M. Caes. et invicem*
Fer. Als.	*De feriis Alsiensibus*
Nep. am.	*De nepote amisso*
Ver.	*Epistulae ad Verum Imp.*
Frod.	*Letters of Frodebert*
Gel.	Aulus Gellius
Gracch.	C. Sempronius Gracchus
orat.	*Oratorum Romanorum fragmenta* (M. = Malcovati 1976)
Greg. Tur.	Georgius Florentius Gregorius (Gregory of Tours)
DLH	*Decem libri historiarum* (*Historia Francorum*)
Hier.	Hieronymus Stridonensis (St Jerome)
Adv. Helvid.	*Adversus Helvidium de Mariae virginitate perpetua*
Adv. Iovin.	*Adversus Iovinianum*
Chron.	*Chronicon*
a.Abr.	ad annum post natum Abraham
Epist.	*Epistulae*
in Ezech.	*Commentarii in Ezechielem prophetam*
in Ier.	*Commentarii in Ieremiam prophetam*
in Zach.	*Commentarii in Zachariam prophetam*
Hist. Aug.	*Historia Augusta*
trig. tyr.	*triginta tyranni*
Hom.	Homer
Il.	*Iliad*
Hor.	Q. Horatius Flaccus
Ars	*Ars poetica*
Carm.	*Carmina* (*Odes*)
Epist.	*Epistulae*
Epod.	*Epodi*
Sat.	*Sermones* (*Satires*)
Hyg.	Hyginus
Fab.	*Fabulae* (*Genealogiae*)
Imp.	*Letters of Importunus*
Isid.	Isidorus Hispalensis
Orig.	*Origines sive Etymologiae*

Jord.	Jordanes Gothus
Get.	*Getica*
Rom.	*Romana*
Juv.	D. Iunius Iuvenalis
Liv.	T. Livius
Lucil.	C. Lucilius (C. = Charpin 1978–91; K. = Krenkel 1970; M. = Marx 1904–5; W. = Warmington 1967)
Lucr.	T. Lucretius Carus
Macr.	Ambrosius Theodosius Macrobius
Sat.	*Saturnalia*
Marcell.	Marcellinus Comes
Chron.	*Chronicon*
Mart.	M. Valerius Martialis
Sp.	*Spectacula*
Naev.	Cn. Naevius
com.	*Comicorum Romanorum fragmenta* (R. = Ribbeck 1873)
trag.	*Tragicorum Romanorum fragmenta* (R. = Ribbeck 1871)
Nep.	Cornelius Nepos
Ep.	*Epaminondas*
Eum.	*Eumenes*
Han.	*Hannibal*
Milt.	*Miltiades*
Timol.	*Timoleon*
Non.	Nonius Marcellus (L. = Lindsay 1903; M. = Mercier 1614 (page) and Mueller 1888 (line))
Oros.	Paulus Orosius
Hist.	*Historiae adversus paganos*
Ov.	P. Ovidius Naso
Am.	*Amores*
Ep.	*Epistulae (Heroides)*
Fast.	*Fasti*
Met.	*Metamorphoses*
Pont.	*Epistulae ex Ponto*
Tr.	*Tristia*
Pac.	M. Pacuvius
trag.	*tragicorum Romanorum fragmenta* (R. = Ribbeck 1871; Sch. = Schierl 2006; W. = Warmington 1967)

Pers.	Persius
Petr.	Petronius Arbiter
Phaed.	Phaedrus
Pl.	T. Maccius Plautus
Am.	*Amphitruo*
As.	*Asinaria*
Aul.	*Aulularia*
Bac.	*Bacchides*
Capt.	*Captivi*
Cas.	*Casina*
Cist.	*Cistellaria*
Cur.	*Curculio*
Epid.	*Epidicus*
inc. fab.	*incertarum fabularum fragmenta*
Men.	*Menaechmi*
Mer.	*Mercator*
Mil.	*Miles Gloriosus*
Mos.	*Mostellaria*
Per.	*Persa*
Poen.	*Poenulus*
Ps.	*Pseudolus*
Rud.	*Rudens*
St.	*Stichus*
Trin.	*Trinummus*
Truc.	*Truculentus*
Vid.	*Vidularia*
Plin.	C. Plinius Secundus (Pliny the Elder)
Nat.	*Naturalis Historia*
Plin.	C. Plinius Caecilius Secundus (Pliny the Younger)
Ep.	*Epistulae*
PLS	*Pactus Legis Salicae* (*Lex Salica*)
Pompon.	L. Pomponius Bononiensis
com.	*Comicorum Romanorum fragmenta* (R. = Ribbeck 1873)
Priap.	*Priapea*
Prop.	Sex. Propertius
Quad.	Q. Claudius Quadrigarius
hist.	*Historicorum Romanorum reliquiae* (Peter 1914)

Quint.	M. Fabius Quintilianus
Inst.	*Institutio oratoria*
Rhet. Her.	*Rhetorica ad Herennium*
Ruf. Fest.	Rufius Festus
Sal.	C. Sallustius Crispus
Cat.	*Catilina*
Hist.	*Historiae*
Jug.	*Iugurtha*
Sen.	L. Annaeus Seneca (Seneca the Elder)
Con.	*Controversiae*
Suas.	*Suasoriae*
Sen.	L. Annaeus Seneca (Seneca the Younger)
Apoc.	*Apocolocyntosis*
Ben.	*De beneficiis*
Dial.	*Dialogi*
Ep.	*Epistulae*
Nat.	*Naturales quaestiones*
Oed.	*Oedipus*
Thy.	*Thyestes*
[Sen.]	[L. Annaeus Seneca]
Her. O.	*Hercules Oetaeus*
Serv.	Maurus Servius Honoratus
Aen.	*In Vergilium commentarius: in Aeneidos libros*
Sil.	Silius Italicus
Sis.	L. Cornelius Sisenna
hist.	*Historicorum Romanorum reliquiae* (Peter 1914)
Stat.	P. Papinius Statius
Ach.	*Achilleis*
Silv.	*Silvae*
Theb.	*Thebais*
Suet.	C. Suetonius Tranquillus
Aug.	*Augustus*
Cal.	*Caligula*
Cl.	*Claudius*
Jul.	*Iulius*
Tib.	*Tiberius*
Ves.	*Vespasianus*
Vit. Ter.	*Vita Terenti*
Sulp. Sev.	Sulpicius Severus
Dial.	*Dialogi*

Tac.	Cornelius Tacitus
Ann.	*Annales*
Dial.	*Dialogus de Oratoribus*
Hist.	*Historiae*
Ter.	P. Terentius Afer
Ad.	*Adelphi*
An.	*Andria*
Eu.	*Eunuchus*
Hau.	*Heauton Timorumenos*
Hec.	*Hecyra*
Ph.	*Phormio*
Turp.	Sex. Turpilius
com.	*Comicorum Romanorum fragmenta* (R. = Ribbeck 1873)
V. Fl.	Valerius Flaccus
Val. Ant.	Valerius Antias
hist.	*Historicorum Romanorum reliquiae* (Peter 1914)
Var.	M. Terentius Varro
gram.	*Grammaticae Romanae fragmenta* (Funaioli 1907)
L.	*De lingua Latina*
Men.	*Menippeae*
R.	*Res rusticae*
Verg.	P. Vergilius Maro
Aen.	*Aeneis*
Ecl.	*Eclogae*
G.	*Georgica*
Vitr.	Vitruvius Pollio

ABBREVIATIONS FOR COLLECTIONS AND REFERENCE WORKS

ALL	*Archiv für lateinische Lexikographie und Grammatik.* Leipzig: Teubner.
Bennett	C. E. Bennett, *Syntax of Early Latin*: 2 vols. Boston: Allyn and Bacon, 1910–14.
CIL	*Corpus Inscriptionum Latinarum.* Berlin: G. Reimer, 1862–.
CLE	*Carmina Latina Epigraphica*, ed. F. Buecheler and E. Lommatzsch (Part II of F. Buecheler and

	A. Riese, *Anthologia Latina*). Leipzig: Teubner, 1895–1930.
E–M	A. Ernout and A. Meillet, *Dictionnaire étymologique de la langue latine*. Revised by J. André, 4th edn, Paris: Klincksieck, 1959.
FEW	W. von Wartburg, *Französisches etymologisches Wörterbuch*, Bonn, 1928–.
GL	*Grammatici Latini*, ed. H. Keil *et al.* Leipzig: Teubner, 1855–80.
Hofmann–Ricottilli	J. B. Hofmann, *La lingua d'uso latina*. Augmented translation by L. Ricottilli of *Lateinische Umgangssprache* (3rd edn Heidelberg 1951), 3rd edn 2003 (2nd edn 1985, 1st edn 1980), Bologna: Pàtron.
H–S	J. B. Hofmann and A. Szantyr, *Lateinische Syntax und Stilistik*. Munich: C. Beck, 1965.
ILLRP	*Inscriptiones Latinae liberae rei publicae*, ed. A. Degrassi. 2nd edn, Florence: Nuova Italia, 1963–5.
K–S	R. Kühner and C. Stegmann, *Ausführliche Grammatik der lateinischen Sprache* II. *Satzlehre*. Revised by A. Thierfelder, 3rd edn 1955 = 4th edn 1971 = 5th edn 1976, Hanover: Hahn.
L–S	C. T. Lewis and C. Short, *A Latin Dictionary*. New York: Harper, 1879.
MGH	*Monumenta Germaniae Historica*, Hanover. Subseries of this series include *Epistolae* and *SRM = Scriptores Rerum Merovingicarum*.
N–W	F. Neue and C. Wagener, *Formenlehre der lateinischen Sprache*. 3rd edn, Berlin: Calvary, 1892–1905.
OLD	*Oxford Latin Dictionary*, ed. P. W. Glare. Oxford University Press, 1968–82.
P. Köln VI	*Kölner Papyri* VI, ed. M. Gronewald *et al.* Opladen: Westdeutscher Verlag, 1987.
P. Mich. VIII	*Papyri and Ostraca from Karanis*, 2nd ser., ed. H. C. Youtie and J. G. Winter. Ann Arbor: University of Michigan, 1951.

PL	*Patrologia Latina* (*Patrologiae cursus completus, series Latina*), ed. J.-P. Migne. Paris: Garnier, 1844–.
PLM	*Poetae Latini Minores*, post Aem. Baehrens iterum recensuit F. Vollmer. Leipzig: Teubner 1923.
RE	*Paulys Real-Encyclopädie der classischen Altertumswissenschaft*, ed. G. Wissowa, W. Kroll *et al.*, Stuttgart: J. B. Metzler, 1894–1972.
REW	W. Meyer-Lübke, *Romanisches Etymologisches Wörterbuch*. 3rd edn, Heidelberg: C. Winter, 1935.
RS	*Roman Statutes*, ed. M. H. Crawford *et al.* (Bulletin of the Institute of Classical Studies, Supplement 64). University of London 1996.
Stud. Pal.	*Studien zur Palaeographie und Papyrusurkunde.*
Tab. Vindol.	*Tabulae Vindolandenses* ii and iii, ed. A. Bowman and J. D. Thomas. London: British Museum Press, 1994 and 2003.
TLL	*Thesaurus Linguae Latinae*. Leipzig: Teubner, 1900–.
W–H	A. Walde and J. B. Hofmann, *Lateinisches etymologisches Wörterbuch*. 3rd edn, Heidelberg: Winter, 1954.

References

Abbot, F. F. 1907. 'The use of language as a means of characterization in Petronius', *CPh* 2: 43–50.

Achard, G. (ed.) 1989. *Rhétorique à Herennius*. Paris: Les Belles Lettres.

Adams, J. N. 1971. 'A type of hyperbaton in Latin prose', *PCPhS* n.s. 17: 1–16.

1972a. 'On the authorship of the *Historia Augusta*', *CQ* n.s. 22: 186–94.

1972b. 'The language of the later books of Tacitus' *Annals*', *CQ* n.s. 22: 350–73.

1972c. 'Latin words for "woman" and "wife"', *Glotta* 50: 234–55.

1973a. 'The substantival present participle in Latin', *Glotta* 51: 116–36.

1973b. 'Two Latin words for "kill"', *Glotta* 51: 280–92.

1973c. 'The vocabulary of the speeches in Tacitus' historical works', *BICS* 20: 124–44.

1974a. 'On the semantic field "put – throw" in Latin', *CQ* n.s. 24: 142–60.

1974b. 'The vocabulary of the later decades of Livy', *Antichthon* 8: 54–62.

1974c. 'Were the later books of Tacitus' *Annals* revised?', *RhM* 117: 323–33.

1975. 'The Latin of the Vindolanda writing tablets', *BICS* 22: 20–4.

1976a. *The Text and Language of a Vulgar Latin Chronicle (Anonymus Valesianus II)*. London: Institute of Classical Studies.

1976b. 'A typological approach to Latin word order', *IF* 81: 70–99.

1977a. *The Vulgar Latin of the Letters of Claudius Terentianus (P. Mich. VIII, 467–72)* (Publications of the Faculty of Arts of the University of Manchester 23). Manchester University Press.

1977b. 'The linguistic unity of the *Historia Augusta*', *Antichthon* 11: 93–102.

1977c. 'The vocabulary of the *Annales regni Francorum*', *Glotta* 55: 257–82.

1978a. 'Conventions of naming in Cicero', *CQ* n.s. 28: 145–66.

1978b. 'Two unexplained misspellings in Claudius Terentianus: Greek interference in Egyptian Latin?', *ZPE* 31: 135–7.

1980. 'Anatomical terminology in Latin epic', *BICS* 27: 50–62.

1981a. 'A Type of Sexual Euphemism in Latin', *Phoenix* 35: 120–8.

1981b. 'Ausonius, *Cento nuptialis* 101–131', *SIFC* 53: 199–215.

1982a. *The Latin Sexual Vocabulary*. London: Duckworth.

1982b. 'Anatomical terms transferred from animals to humans in Latin', *IF* 87: 90–109.

1982c. 'Anatomical terms used *pars pro toto* in Latin', *Proceedings of the African Classical Association* 16: 37–45.

1983a. 'An epigram of Ausonius (87, p. 344 Peiper)', *Latomus* 42: 95–109.

1983b. 'Martial 2.83', *CPh* 78: 311–15.

1983c. 'Words for "prostitute" in Latin', *RhM* 126: 321–58.

1983d. 'Language', in A. K. Bowman & J. D. Thomas, *Vindolanda: The Latin Writing Tablets* (Britannia Monograph Series 4), London: Society for the Promotion of Roman Studies, pp. 72–4.

1984. 'Female speech in Latin comedy', *Antichthon* 18: 43–77.

1989. 'Medieval Latin and the Carolingian reforms' (review article on R. Wright, *Late Latin and Early Romance*, Liverpool 1982), *LCM* 14: 14–16 and 34–48.

1990a. 'The Latinity of C. Novius Eunus', *ZPE* 82: 227–47.

1990b. 'The uses of *neco* I', *Glotta* 68: 230–55.

1991a. 'Some neglected evidence for Latin *habeo* with infinitive: the order of the constituents', *TPhS* 89: 131–96.

1991b. 'The uses of *neco* II', *Glotta* 69: 94–123.

1992a. 'British Latin: the text, interpretation and language of the Bath curse tablets', *Britannia* 23: 1–26.

1992b. 'The origin and meaning of Lat. *veterinus, veterinarius*', *IF* 97: 70–95.

1993. 'The generic use of *mula* and the status and employment of female mules in the Roman world', *RhM* 136: 35–61.

1994a. *Wackernagel's Law and the Placement of the Copula* esse *in Classical Latin*. Cambridge: Cambridge Philological Society (Suppl. Vol. 18).

1994b. 'Wackernagel's Law and the position of unstressed personal pronouns in Classical Latin', *TPhS* 92: 103–78.

1994c. 'Latin and Punic in contact? The case of the Bu Njem ostraca', *JRS* 84: 87–112.

1995a. *Pelagonius and Latin Veterinary Terminology in the Roman Empire*. Leiden: Brill.

1995b. 'The language of the Vindolanda writing tablets: an interim report', *JRS* 85: 86–134.

1996. 'Interpuncts as evidence for the enclitic character of personal pronouns in Latin', *ZPE* III: 208–10.

1999a. 'Nominative personal pronouns and some patterns of speech in Republican and Augustan poetry', in Adams and Mayer (1999a), pp. 97–133.

1999b. 'The poets of Bu Njem: language, culture and the centurionate', *JRS* 89: 109–34.

2003a. *Bilingualism and the Latin Language*. Cambridge University Press.

2003b. 'The new Vindolanda writing-tablets', *CQ* n.s. 53: 530–75.

2003c. 'Petronius and new non-literary Latin', in Herman and Rosén (2003), pp. 11–23.

2003d. '"*Romanitas*" and the Latin language', *CQ* n.s. 53: 184–205.

2005a. 'Neglected evidence for female speech in Latin', *CQ* n.s. 55: 582–96.

2005b. 'The *Bellum Africum*', in Reinhardt, Lapidge and Adams (2005), pp. 73–96.

2005c. 'The accusative + infinitive and dependent *quod-/quia*-clauses: the evidence of non-literary Latin and Petronius', in S. Kiss, L. Mondin and G. Salvi (edd.), *Latin et langues romanes: études de linguistique offertes à József Herman à l'occasion de son 80ème anniversaire*. Tübingen: Max Niemeyer Verlag, pp. 195–206.

2007. *The Regional Diversification of Latin, 200 BC–AD 600*. Cambridge University Press.

forthcoming. *Non-Standard Latin*. Cambridge University Press.

Adams, J. N. and Brennan, P. M. 1990. 'The text at Lactantius, *De mortibus persecutorum* 44. 2 and some epigraphic evidence for Italian recruits', *ZPE* 84: 183–6.

Adams, J. N. and Deegan, M. 1992. 'Bald's *Leechbook* and the *Physica Plinii*', *Anglo-Saxon England* 21: 87–114.

Adams, J. N., Janse, M., and Swain, S. (edd.) 2002. *Bilingualism in Ancient Society: Language Contact and the Written Word*. Oxford University Press.

Adams, J. N., Lapidge, M., and Reinhardt, T. 2005. 'Introduction', in Reinhardt, Lapidge and Adams (2005), pp. 1–36.

Adams, J. N. and Mayer, R. G. (edd.) 1999a. *Aspects of the Language of Latin Poetry* (Proceedings of the British Academy 93). Oxford University Press.

1999b. 'Introduction', in Adams and Mayer (1999a), pp. 1–18.

Adcock, F. E. 1956. *Caesar as Man of Letters*. Cambridge University Press.

Ahlberg, A. W. 1906. *Durative Zeitbestimmungen im Lateinischen*. Lund: Ohlsson.

1911. 'De traiectionis figura ab antiquissimis prosae scriptoribus Latinis adhibita', *Eranos* 11: 88–106.

Albrecht, M. von 1964. *Die Parenthese in Ovids Metamorphosen und ihre dichterische Funktion*. Hildesheim: Olms.

1983. *Meister römischer Prosa von Cato bis Apuleius*. 2nd edn, Heidelberg: Lambert and Schneider.

2003. *Cicero's Style: A Synopsis Followed by Selected Analytic Studies* (Mnemosyne Suppl. 245). Leiden: Brill.

Anderson, W. B. 1927. Review of Hofmann (1926), *CR* 41: 90.

Astin, A. E. 1978. *Cato the Censor*. Oxford University Press.

Atherton, C. 2005. 'Lucretius on what language is not', in Frede and Inwood (2005), pp. 101–38.

Aurigemma, S. 1941. 'Due epigrafi riminesi', *Epigraphica* 3: 13–22.

Austin, P. and Bresnan, J. 1996. 'Non-configurationality in Australian aboriginal languages', *Natural Language and Linguistic Theory* 14: 215–68.

Austin, R. G. 1960. *P. Vergili Maronis Aeneidos liber quartus*. Oxford: Clarendon Press.

1971. *Aeneidos liber primus*. Oxford: Clarendon Press.

Axelson, B. 1945. *Unpoetische Wörter: Ein Beitrag zur Kenntnis der lateinischen Dichtersprache*. Lund: H. Ohlssons Boktryckeri.

Bagordo, A. 2001. *Beobachtungen zur Sprache des Terenz: Mit besonderer Berücksichtigung der umgangssprachlichen Elemente*. Göttingen: Vandenhoeck & Ruprecht.

2002. 'Dichtung und Philologie bei Accius am Beispiel seiner Gräzismen und Calquen', in Faller and Manuwald (2002), pp. 39–49.

Baier, Th. (ed.) 2004. *Studien zu Plautus' Poenulus*. Tübingen: Narr.

Bailey, C. 1947. *Lucretius: De rerum natura libri sex*. Oxford: Clarendon Press.

Bain, D. 1976. Review of Fantham (1972), *CPh* 71: 367–8.

2007. 'Low words in high places: sex, bodily functions, and body parts in Homeric epic and other higher genres', in P. J. Finglass, C. Collard and N. J. Richardson (edd.), *Hesperos: Studies in Ancient Greek Poetry Presented to M. L. West on his Seventieth Birthday*. Oxford University Press, pp. 40–57.

Baldarelli, B. 2004. *Accius und die vortrojanische Pelopidensage*. Paderborn: Schöningh.

Banniard, M. 1992. *Viva voce: communication écrite et communication orale du iv e au ix e siècle en occident latin*. Paris: Institut des Études Augustiniennes.

Barnwell, P. S. 1991. '*Epistula Hieronimi de gradus Romanorum*: an English school book', *Historical Research* 64: 77–86.

Barwick, K. 1964. *Charisius: Ars grammatica*. Stuttgart and Leipzig: Teubner.

Bauer, B. L. M. 1995. *The Emergence and Development of SVO Patterning in Latin and French: Diachronic and Psycholinguistic Perspectives*. Oxford University Press.

2000. *Archaic Syntax in Indo-European: The Spread of Transitivity in Latin and French*. Berlin and New York: de Gruyter.

2001. 'Syntactic innovation in Latin poetry? The origin of the Romance adverbial formation in *-ment(e)*', in A. P. Orbán and M. G. M. van der Poel (edd.), *Ad litteras: Latin Studies in Honour of J. H. Brouwers*. Nijmegen University Press, pp. 29–43.

2003. 'The adverbial formation in *mente* in Vulgar and Late Latin: a problem in grammaticalization', in Solin *et al.* (2003), pp. 439–457.

Beall, S. M. 1999. 'Aulus Gellius 17.8: composition and the gentleman scholar', *CPh* 94: 55–64.

Beare, W. 1964. *The Roman Stage*. London: Methuen.

Becher, F. 1888. 'Über den Sprachgebrauch des Caelius', *Jahresbericht über die Königliche Klosterschule zu Ilfeld von Ostern 1887 bis Ostern 1888* (Nordhausen: Kirchners Buchdruckerei): 1–41.

Beck, H. and Walter, U. 2001. *Die frühen römischen Historiker* i. Darmstadt: Wissenschaftliche Buchgesellschaft.

Beck, R. 1975. 'Encolpius at the *cena*', *Phoenix* 29: 270–83.

Bennett, D. C. 1987. 'Word-order change in progress: the case of Slovene and Serbo-Croat and its relevance for Germanic', *Journal of Linguistics* 23: 269–87.

Benveniste, E. 1958. 'Les verbes délocutifs', in G. Hatcher and K. L. Selig (edd.), *Studia philologica et litteraria in honorem L. Spitzer*, Bern: Francke, pp. 57–63 (reprinted as Chapter 23 of *Problèmes de linguistique générale*, Paris 1966).

Bergmüller, L. 1903. *Einige Bemerkungen zur Latinität des Iordanes*. Augsburg: Pfeiffer.

Bertocchi, A. 1989. 'The role of antecedents of Latin anaphors', in G. Calboli (ed.), *Subordination and Other Topics in Latin*. Amsterdam: Benjamins, pp. 441–61.

Bettini, M. 1982. 'Vel Vibe di Veio e il re Amulio', *MD* 6: 163–8.

Beyerle, F. 1952. 'Das frühmittelalterliche Schulheft von Ämterwesen', *Zeitschrift der Savigny-Stiftung für Rechtsgeschichte, germanische Abteilung* 69: 1–23.

Biber, D. 1988. *Variation across Speech and Writing*. Cambridge University Press.

Bischoff, B. 2004. *Katalog der festländischen Handschriften des neunten Jahrhunderts* II. *Laon – Paderborn*. Wiesbaden: Harrasowitz.

Bischoff, B. and Lapidge, M. (edd.) 1994. *Biblical Commentaries from the Canterbury School of Theodore and Hadrian*. Cambridge University Press.

Biville, F. 1999. 'Niveaux et états de langue chez les grammairiens latins', in Petersmann and Kettemann (1999), pp. 541–51.

    2003. '*Familia vero – babae babae!*. . . (*Satyricon* 37,9): exclamations et interjections chez Pétrone', in Herman and Rosén (2003), pp. 37–57.

Blaise, A. 1954. *Dictionnaire latin-français des auteurs chrétiens*. Turnhout: Brepols.

Blank, D. 2005. 'Varro's anti-analogist', in Frede and Inwood (2005), pp. 210–38.

Blänsdorf, J. 1995. *Fragmenta poetarum Latinorum*. Stuttgart and Leipzig: Teubner.

    2000. 'Livius Andronicus und die Anverwandlung des hellenistischen Dramas in Rom', in Manuwald (2000), pp. 145–56.

Blase, H. 1896. 'Amabo', *ALL* 9: 485–7, with *ALL* 10 (1898): 137.

Bodel, J. P. 1984. 'Freedmen in the *Satyricon* of Petronius'. Diss. Univ. of Michigan.

Böhm, R. G. 1979. 'Caelius bei Cicero, *ad Fam.* VIII.14.2.4', *Quaderni di Storia* 10: 273–83.

Boldt, H. 1884. *De liberiore linguae Graecae et Latinae collocatione verborum capita selecta*. Göttingen: Stephan Geibel & Co.

Bolkestein, A. M. 1998. 'Between brackets: (some properties of) parenthetical clauses in Latin. An investigation of the language of Cicero's letters', in R. Risselada (ed.), *Latin in Use: Amsterdam Studies in the Pragmatics of Latin* (Amsterdam Studies in Classical Philology 8). Amsterdam: J. C. Gieben, pp. 1–17.

    2001. 'Random scrambling? Constraints on discontinuity in Latin noun phrases,' in Moussy (2001), pp. 245–58.

Bömer, A. 1897–9. *Die lateinischen Schülergespräche der Humanisten*. Berlin: J. Harrwitz Nachfolger.

Bömer, F. 1969–86. *P. Ovidius Naso: Metamorphosen*. Heidelberg: C. Winter.

Bonfante, G. 1936. 'Los elementos populares en la lengua de Horacio', *Emerita* 4: 209–47 (= Bonfante 1994, pp. 60–95).

    1937. 'Los elementos populares en la lengua de Horacio', *Emerita* 5: 17–88 (= Bonfante 1994, pp. 95–159).

    1994. *La lingua parlata in Orazio*. Venosa: Oanna.

Bonnet, M. 1890. *Le latin de Grégoire de Tours*. Paris: Hachette.

Boucherie, A. 1867. *Cinq formules rhythmées et assonancées du* VIIe *siècle*. Montpellier and Paris: F. Seguin & Franck.

Bourciez, J. 1929. *Le 'sermo cotidianus' dans les satires d'Horace*. Bordeaux: Feret.

Bowman, A. K., Thomas, J. D. and Adams, J. N. 1990. 'Two letters from Vindolanda', *Britannia* 21: 33–52.

Boyce, B. 1991. *The Language of the Freedmen in Petronius' Cena Trimalchionis* (Mnemosyne Suppl. 117). Leiden: Brill.

Boyle, A. J. 2006. *An Introduction to Roman Tragedy*. London and New York: Routledge.

Braun, F. 1988. *Terms of Address*. Berlin: Mouton de Gruyter.

Braune, W., Helm, K. and Ebbinghaus, E. A. 1969. *Althochdeutsches Lesebuch*. Tübingen: Niemeyer.

Brink, C. O. 1963. *Horace on Poetry* i. *Prolegomena to the Literary Epistles*. Cambridge University Press.

1971. *Horace on Poetry* ii. *The 'Ars poetica'*. Cambridge University Press.

Briscoe, J. 1981. *A Commentary on Livy: Books* xxxiv–xxxvii. Oxford University Press.

2005. 'The language and style of the fragmentary Republican historians', in Reinhardt, Lapidge and Adams (2005), pp. 53–72.

2008. *A Commentary on Livy: Books* 38–40. Oxford University Press.

Brown, P. M. 1993. *Horace: Satires* i. Warminster: Aris & Phillips.

Brown, R. D. 1987. *Lucretius on Love and Sex: A Commentary on De rerum natura* iv, *1030–1287 with Prolegomena, Text, and Translation*. Leiden: Brill.

Brown, V. 1972. *The Textual Transmission of Caesar's Civil War*. Leiden: Brill.

Brown, W. 2002. 'When documents are destroyed or lost: lay people and archives in the early Middle Ages', *Early Medieval Europe* 11: 337–66.

2007. 'Conflict, letters, and personal relationships in the Carolingian formulae collections', *Law and History Review* 25: 323–44.

Brugnoli, G. 1993. 'Caesar grammaticus', in Poli (1993) ii, pp. 585–97.

Brunhölzl, F. 1990. *Histoire de la littérature latine du Moyen Âge*. Louvain-La-Neuve: Brepols.

Brunot, F. 1933. *Histoire de la langue française: des origines à 1900* vi. Paris: Colin.

Buonomo, L. M. 1997. 'Introduzione alla lettura delle opere di Giordane', in M. L. Silvestre and M. Squillante (edd.), *Mutatio rerum: letteratura, filosofia, scienza tra tardo antico e altomedioevo: Atti del Convegno di studi, Napoli 25–26 novembre 1996*. Naples: La Città del Sole, pp. 115–69.

Burg, F. 1888. *De M. Caelii Rufi genere dicendi*. Leipzig: Teubner.

Butler, H. E. and Owen, A. S. (edd.) 1914. *Apuleius: Apologia sive pro se de magia liber*. Oxford: Clarendon Press.

Cabisius, G. 1985. 'Social metaphor and the atomic cycle in Lucretius', *CJ* 80: 109–20.

Calboli, G. 1978. *Marci Porci Catonis oratio pro Rhodiensibus*. Bologna: Pàtron.

1986. 'Nota di aggiornamento', in E. Norden (ed.), *La prosa d'arte antica dal vi secolo a. C. all'età della rinascenza*, trans. B. Heinemann Campana. Rome: Salerno Editrice, pp. 971–1185.

(ed.) 1993. *Rhetorica ad Herennium*. 2nd edn, Bologna: Pàtron.

1996. 'The accusative as a default case', in H. Rosén (ed.), *Aspects of Latin: Papers from the Seventh International Colloquium on Latin Linguistics*. Innsbruck: Institut für Sprachwissenschaft, pp. 423–36.

Calboli Montefusco, L. 1972. 'Sviluppo del valore funzionale e semantico di *porro* dalla fase arcaica a Lucrezio', *Maia* 24: 247–60.

Callebat, L. 1968. *Sermo cotidianus dans les Métamorphoses d'Apulée.* Université de Caen.

1998. *Langages du roman latin* (Spudasmata 71). Hildesheim: Olms.

Campanile, E. 1976. 'La latinizzazione dell'osco', in *Scritti in onore di G. Bonfante.* Brescia: Paideia, pp. 109–20.

Canali, L. 1966. 'Osservazioni sul *corpus* cesariano', *Maia* 18: 115–37.

Cancik, H. 1978. 'Die republikanische Tragödie', in E. Lefèvre (ed.), *Das römische Drama.* Darmstadt: Wissenschaftliche Buchgesellschaft, pp. 308–47.

Caplan, H. (ed.) 1954. *[Cicero]: Ad C. Herennium de ratione dicendi (Rhetorica ad Herennium).* London: Heinemann and Cambridge, Mass.: Harvard University Press.

Cardona, G. R. 1976. *Introduzione all'etnolinguistica.* Bologna: Il Mulino.

1987. *Introduzione alla sociolinguistica.* Turin: Loescher.

Casaceli, F. 1976. *Lingua e stile in Accio.* Palermo: Palumbo.

Castagna, L. 1992. 'Lessico "dotto" in Pacuvio: alcuni possibili esempi', in G. Aricò (ed.), *Atti del IV seminario di studi sulla tragedia romana (Palermo 23–26 marzo 1992)* (Quaderni di cultura e di tradizione classica 10). Università di Palermo, pp. 73–88.

Catrein, C. 2003. *Vertauschte Sinne – Untersuchungen zur Synästhesie in der römischen Dichtung.* Munich: Saur.

Cavarzere, A. 1983. *Marcus Caelius Rufus: Lettere (Cic. Fam. l. VIII).* Brescia: Paideia.

(ed.) 2007. *Cicerone: Lettere ai familiari.* Milano: Rizzoli.

Cavazza, F. 1985–. *Aulo Gellio: Le notti attiche* (Prosatori di Roma). Bologna: Zanichelli.

Cèbe, J.-P. 1972–99. *Varron: Satires Ménippées. Édition, traduction et commentaire.* 13 vols. Rome: École Française de Rome.

Cellarius, C. 1755. *C. Iulii Caesaris Commentarii de bello Gallico et civili cum utriusque supplementis ab A. Hirtio vel Oppio adiectis.* Leipzig: Weidmann.

Chafe, W. L. and Tannen, D. 1987. 'The relation between written and spoken language', *Annual Review of Anthropology* 16: 383–407.

Charpin, F. 1978–91. *Lucilius: Satires.* 3 vols. Paris: Les Belles Lettres.

Chassignet, M. 1986. *Caton: Les Origines (fragments).* Paris: Les Belles Lettres.

Chaumartin, F.-R. 2002. *Sénèque: tragédies III.* Paris: Les Belles Lettres.

Christensen, A. S. 2002. *Cassiodorus, Jordanes and the History of the Goths.* Copenhagen: Museum Tusculanum Press.

Citroni, M. 1975. *M. Valerii Martialis Epigrammaton liber primus: Introduzione, testo, apparato critico e commento.* Firenze: La Nuova Italia.

Clackson, J. and Horrocks, G. 2007. *The Blackwell History of the Latin Language.* Oxford: Blackwell.

Clark, H. H. 1996. *Using Language.* Cambridge University Press.

Clarke, S. 1753. *C. Julii Caesaris quae extant accuratissime cum libris editis et MSS optimis collata, recognita et correcta.* London: Tonson and Watts.

Clausen, W. V. 1994. *A Commentary on Virgil: Eclogues.* Oxford: Clarendon Press.

Coleman, K. M. 1988. *Statius: Siluae* IV. Oxford University Press.

1999. 'Mythological figures as spokespersons in Statius' *Siluae*', in F. de Angelis and S. Muth (edd.), *Im Spiegel des Mythos: Bilderwelt und Lebenswelt – Lo specchio del mito: immaginario e realtà* (Palilia 6). Wiesbaden: Dr. Ludwig Reichert Verlag, pp. 67–80.

Coleman, K. M., Diggle, J., Hall, J. B. and Jocelyn, H. D. (edd.) 1992. *F. R. D. Goodyear: Papers on Latin Literature*. London: Gerald Duckworth & Co.

Coleman, R. 1971. 'The origin and development of Latin *habeo* + infinitive', *CQ* n.s. 21: 215–32.

1976. 'Further observations on *habeo* + infinitive as an exponent of futurity', *CQ* n.s. 26: 151–9.

1977. *Vergil: Eclogues*. Cambridge University Press.

1991. 'Latin prepositional syntax in Indo-European perspective', in R. Coleman (ed.), *New Studies in Latin Linguistics*. Amsterdam: Benjamins, pp. 323–38.

1999a. 'Poetic diction, poetic discourse and the poetic register', in Adams and Mayer (1999a), 21–93.

1999b. 'Vulgarism and normalization in the *Regula Sancti Benedicti*', in Petersmann and Kettemann (1999), pp. 345–56.

Colgrave, B. and Mynors, R. A. B. 1969. *Bede's Ecclesiastical History of the English People*. Oxford: Clarendon Press.

Collard, C. 1978. 'Colloquial expressions in Euripides' (review of Stevens 1976), *CR* n.s. 28: 224–6.

2005. 'Colloquial language in tragedy: a supplement to the work of P. T. Stevens', *CQ* n.s. 55: 350–86 (with unpublished addendum kindly provided by author).

Collart, J. 1954. *Varron grammairien latin*. Paris: Les Belles Lettres.

Collinge, N. E. 1953. 'The mental equation factor in "aberrant" syntax in Greek and Latin', *G&R* 66: 130–9.

Colonna, G. 1980, '*Graeco more bibere*: l'iscrizione della Tomba 115 dell'Osteria dell'Osa', in *Archeologia Laziale* 3: 51–55 (reprinted in *Italia ante Romanum imperium: Scritti di antichità etrusche, italiche e romane (1958–1998)*, Pisa and Rome 2005, pp. 1827–33).

Comber, M. R. 1976. 'Parenthesis in Tacitus', *RhM* 119: 181–4.

Conington, J. and Nettleship, H. 1893. *The Satires of A. Persius Flaccus*. Oxford: Clarendon Press.

Conrat, M. 1908. 'Ein Traktat über romanisch-fränkisches Ämterwesen aus einer Vatikanischen Handschrift mitgeteilt', *Zeitschrift der Savigny-Stiftung für Rechtsgeschichte, germanische Abteilung* 29: 239–60.

Conso, D. 1996. 'L'oralité fictive des inscriptions funéraires latines', in *Les structures de l'oralité en latin* (Colloque du Centre Alfred Ernout, Université de Paris IV, 2, 3, 4 juin 1994). Paris: Presses de l'Université de Paris-Sorbonne, pp. 291–304.

Constans, L.-A. 1936. *Cicéron: correspondance* III. Paris: Les Belles Lettres.

Corbett, P. B. 1962. 'On two items of colloquial usage in the *Bellum Hispaniense*', *Eranos* 60: 74–9.

Cordier, A. 1939. *Études sur le vocabulaire épique dans L'Enéide*. Paris: Les Belles Lettres.

Cortelazzo, M. and Zolli, P. 1979–88. *Dizionario etimologico della lingua italiana*. Bologna: Zanichelli.

Coseriu, E. 1980. '"Historische Sprache" und "Dialekt"', in J. Göschel, P. Ivić and K. Kehr (edd.), *Dialekt und Dialektologie: Ergebnisse des internationalen Symposions 'Zur Theorie des Dialekts' Marburg/Lahn, 5.–10. September 1977*. Wiesbaden: Franz Steiner, pp. 106–22.

Couilloud, M.-T. 1974. *Les monuments funéraires de Rhénée* (Exploration archélogique de Délos faite par l'École Française d'Athènes 30). Paris: Boccard.

Courtney, E. 1990. *P. Papini Stati Silvae*. Oxford University Press.

  1993. *The Fragmentary Latin Poets*. Oxford University Press.

  1999. *Archaic Latin Prose*. Atlanta: Scholars Press.

  2001. *A Companion to Petronius*. Oxford University Press.

Croke, B. 1987. 'Cassiodorus and the *Getica* of Jordanes', *CPh* 82: 117–34.

Cucchiarelli, A. 2001. *La satira e il poeta: Orazio tra Epodi e Sermones*. Pisa: Giardini.

Cugusi, P. 1983. *Evoluzione e forme dell'epistolografia latina*. Rome: Herder.

  1998. 'L'epistola ciceroniana: strumento di comunicazione quotidiana e modello letterario', *Ciceroniana* 10: 163–89.

Daheim, J. and Blänsdorf, J. 2003. 'Petron und die Inschriften', in Herman and Rosén (2003), pp. 95–107.

Dahlén, E. 1964. *Études syntaxiques sur les pronoms réfléchis pléonastiques en latin*. Gothenburg: Almqvist & Wiksells.

Dahlmann, H. 1935. 'Caesars Schrift über die Analogie', *RhM* 84: 258–75.

Dahlstrom, A. 1987. 'Discontinuous constituents in Fox', in Kroeber and Moore (1987), pp. 53–73.

Dammer, R. 2001. *Diomedes grammaticus*. Trier: Wissenschaftlicher Verlag Trier.

Damon, C. 1997. *The Mask of the Parasite: A Pathology of Roman Patronage*. Ann Arbor: University of Michigan Press.

Dangel, J. 1995. *Accius: œuvres (fragments)*. Paris: Les Belles Lettres.

Davisius, J. 1727. *C. Julii Caesaris et Auli Hirtii quae extant omnia*. Cambridge University Press.

Degenhart, H. 1877. *De auctoris Belli Hispaniensis elocutione et fide historica*. Würzburg: Stuber.

de Melo, W. D. C. 2007a. Review of Devine and Stephens (2006), *Lingua* 117: 1483–9.

  2007b. *The Early Latin Verb System: Archaic Forms in Plautus, Terence, and Beyond*. Oxford University Press.

De Sutter, M. 1986. 'A theory of word order within the Latin noun phrase, based on Cato's *De agri cultura*', in C. Deroux (ed.), *Studies in Latin Literature and Roman History* IV. Brussels: Latomus, pp. 151–83.

Deufert, M. 1996. *Pseudo-Lukrezisches im Lukrez: Die unechten Verse in Lukrezens De rerum natura*. Berlin and New York: de Gruyter.

Devine, A. M. and Stephens, L. D. 2006. *Latin Word Order: Structured Meaning and Information*. Oxford University Press.

Devoto, G. 1940. *Storia della lingua di Roma*. Bologna: Cappelli.

Dickey, E. 2002. *Latin Forms of Address*. Oxford University Press.

Diels, H. 1922. 'Lukrezstudien v', *Sitzungsberichte der Preussischen Akademie der Wissenschaften, philosophisch-historische Klasse*: 46–59.

Diggle, J. 2005. 'Tibullus 2.1.45–6 and "amplificatory pleonasm"', *CQ* n.s. 55: 642–3.

Dihle, A. 1957. 'Analogie und Attizismus', *Hermes* 85: 170–205.

Dionisotti, A. C. 1982. 'From Ausonius' schooldays? A schoolbook and its relatives', *JRS* 72: 83–125.

Diouron, N. 1999. *Pseudo-César: Guerre d'Espagne*. Paris: Les Belles Lettres.

Dover, K. J. 1960. *Greek Word Order*. Cambridge University Press.

Drexler, H. 1935. 'Parerga Caesariana', *Hermes* 70: 203–34.

Druhan, D. R. 1938. *The Syntax of Bede's Historia Ecclesiastica*. Washington, DC: Catholic University of America.

Dubois, J. 1969. 'Les évêques de Paris des origines à l'avènement de Hugues Capet', *Bulletin de la Société de l'Histoire de Paris et de l'Île-de-France* 96: 33–97.

1995. 'Importunus (2)', in A. Baudrillart, A. d. Meyer and R. Aubert (edd.), *Dictionnaire d'histoire et de géographie ecclésiastiques* xxv. Paris: Letouzey et Ané, p. 963.

Duby, G. and Ariès, P. 1987. *A History of Private Life*. Cambridge, Mass.: Belknap Press of Harvard University Press.

Duchesne, L. 1910. *Fastes épiscopaux de l'ancienne Gaule* ii. *L'Aquitaine et les Lyonnaises*. Paris: Fontemoing.

Eckhardt, K. A. 1969. *Pactus Legis Salicae*. Hanover: Hahn.

Eden, P. T. 1962. 'Caesar's style: inheritance versus intelligence', *Glotta* 40: 74–117.

1984. *Seneca: Apocolocyntosis*. Cambridge University Press.

Enßlin, W. 1949. *Des Symmachus Historia Romana als Quelle für Jordanes* (Sitzungsberichte der Bayerischen Akademie der Wissenschaften, philosophisch-historische Klasse, Jahrgang 1948, Heft 3). Munich: Verlag der Bayerischen Akademie der Wissenschaften.

Erasmo, M. 2004. *Roman Tragedy: Theatre to Theatricality*. Austin: University of Texas Press.

Erasmus, D. 1533. *Familiarium colloquiorum opus, ab autore postremum diligenter recognitum, emendatum et locupletatum, adiectis novis aliquot colloquijs*. Basle: J. Froben.

Erhardt, L. 1886. 'Rezension zu *Jordanis et Getica* [Mommsen, 1882] und *Jordanis de origine actibusque Getarum* [Holder, 1882]', *GGA* 17: 669–708.

Ernout, A. 1923. 'Tempore puncto', *RPh* 47: 152–63.

1954. *Aspects du vocabulaire latin*. Paris: Klincksieck.

1957. 'Le vocabulaire poétique', in A. Ernout, *Philologica* ii. Paris: Klincksieck, pp. 66–86.

Faller, A. 1949. 'Sprachliche Interpretation zum Bellum Hispaniense'. Diss. Freiburg.

Faller, S. and Manuwald, G. (edd.) 2002. *Accius und seine Zeit* (Identitäten und Alteritäten 13), Würzburg: Ergon-Verlag.

Fantham, E. 1972. *Comparative Studies in Republican Imagery*. Toronto: University of Toronto Press.

Ferri, R. 2008. 'Il latino dei *Colloquia scholica*', in F. Bellandi and R. Ferri (edd.), *Aspetti della scuola nel mondo romano*. Amsterdam: Hakkert, pp. 111–78.

Fiehler, R., Barden, B., Elstermann, M. and Kraft, B. 2004. *Eigenschaften gesprochener Sprache*. Tübingen: Narr.

Flobert, P. 1975. *Les verbes déponents latins des origines à Charlemagne*. Paris: Les Belles Lettres.

Fögen, T. 2000. *Patrii sermonis egestas: Einstellungen lateinischer Autoren zu ihrer Muttersprache. Ein Beitrag zum Sprachbewusstsein in der römischen Antike*. Munich and Leipzig: Saur.

Foucault, J. A. de 1964. 'L'hyperbate du verbe', *RPh* 38: 59–69.

Fowler, D. 1989. 'Lucretius and Politics', in J. Barnes and M. Griffin (edd.), *Philosophia togata*. Oxford: Clarendon Press, pp. 120–50.

    1997. 'Virgilian narrative: (a) story-telling', in C. Martindale (ed.), pp. 259–70.

    2000. 'The didactic plot', in M. Depew and D. Obbink (edd.), *Matrices of Genre*. Cambridge, Mass.: Harvard University Press, pp. 205–19.

    2002. *Lucretius on atomic motion: A Commentary on De rerum natura, Book Two, Lines 1–332*. Oxford University Press.

Fowler, H. W. and Fowler, F. G. 1995. *Concise Oxford Dictionary of Current English*. 9th edn rev. D. Thompson, Oxford University Press.

Fraenkel, E. 1928. *Iktus und Akzent im lateinischen Sprechvers*. Berlin: Weidmann.

    1954. '*Urbem quam statuo vestra est*', *Glotta* 33: 157–9.

    1956. 'Eine Form römischer Kriegsbulletins', *Eranos* 54: 189–94.

    1960. *Elementi plautini in Plauto* (augmented translation of *Plautinisches in Plautus* (Berlin 1922) by F. Munari). Florence: La Nuova Italia.

    1964. *Kleine Beiträge zur klassischen Philologie*. Rome: Storia e Letteratura.

    1968. *Leseproben aus Reden Ciceros und Catos*. Rome: Storia e Letteratura.

    2007. *Plautine Elements in Plautus* (translation of *Plautinisches im Plautus* (Berlin 1922) by T. Drevikovsky and F. Muecke). Oxford University Press.

Frede, D. and Inwood, B. (edd.) 2005. *Language and Learning: Philosophy of Language in the Hellenistic Age*. Cambridge University Press.

Frede, M. 1978. 'Principles of Stoic grammar', in J. M. Rist (ed.), *The Stoics*. Berkeley, Los Angeles and London: University of California Press, pp. 27–75.

Freudenburg, K. 1993. *The Walking Muse: Horace on the Theory of Satire*. Oxford University Press.

Frobenius, R. 1910. *Die Syntax des Ennius*. Nördlingen: C. H. Beck.

Fruyt, M. and Orlandini, A. 2008. 'Some cases of linguistic evolution and grammaticalisation in the Latin verb', in Wright (2008), pp. 230–7.

Funaioli, H. 1907. *Grammaticae Romanae fragmenta*. Leipzig: Teubner.

Funck, A. 1893. 'Die lateinischen Adverbia auf -*im*, ihre Bildung und ihre Geschichte', *ALL* 8: 77–114.

Gaide, F. 2001. 'A propos des intéractions verbales dans les théatre de Plaute', in Moussy (2001), pp. 959–68.

Galdi, G. 2004. *Grammatica delle iscrizioni latine dell'impero (province orientali): morfosintassi nominale.* Rome: Herder.

2008. 'Evidence for late usage of the moods in the works of Jordanes', in Wright (2008), pp. 321–7.

forthcoming. 'Les indications locales chez Jordanes à la lumière d'une nouvelle approche méthodologique', in M. Lenoble, D. Longrée and C. Bodelot (edd.), forthcoming. *De linguae Latinae usu: Actes du 13e Colloque international de linguistique latine, Bruxelles et Liège, 4–9 avril 2005.* Leuven and Paris: Peeters.

Garcea, A. 2002. 'L'interaction épistolaire entre dialogue *in absentia* et *in praesentia* chez Cicéron', in A. M. Bolkestein, C. Kroon, H. Pinkster, W. Remmelink and R. Risselada (edd.), *Theory and Description in Latin Linguistics: Selected Papers from the Eleventh International Colloquium on Latin Linguistics, Amsterdam June 24–29, 2001.* Amsterdam: Gieben, pp. 123–38.

(ed.) 2003a. *Colloquia absentium: studi sulla comunicazione epistolare in Cicerone.* Turin: Rosenberg & Sellier.

2003b. 'Rispondere con ordine alle lettere: una funzione di *quod* nell'epistolario di Cicerone', in Garcea (2003a), pp. 73–99.

2005. *Cicerone in esilio: l'epistolario e le passioni* (Spudasmata 103). Hildesheim: Olms.

Garcea, A. and Lomanto, V. 2004. 'Gellius and Fronto on loanwords and literary models: their evaluation of Laberius', in L. Holford-Strevens and A. Vardi (edd.), *The Worlds of Aulus Gellius.* Oxford University Press, pp. 41–64.

Garmonsway, G. N. (ed.) 1939. *Ælfric's Colloquy* (2nd edn 1947). London: Methuen.

Geigenmüller, P. 1908. *Quaestiones Dionysianae de vocabulis artis criticae.* (Dissertatio inauguralis.) Leipzig: Typis Roberti Noske Bornensis.

Gibson, B. 2006. *Statius: Silvae 5.* Oxford University Press.

Gils, L. van 2003. 'Narrative techniques compared in discourse and correspondence', in Garcea (2003a), pp. 47–72.

Giunta, F. and Grillone, A. 1991. *Iordanis De origine actibusque Getarum* (Fonti per la storia d'Italia 117). Rome: Istituto Palazzo Borromini.

Givón, T. 2001. *Syntax.* 2 vols. Amsterdam and Philadelphia: Benjamins.

Glück, J. J. and Maurach, G. 1972. 'Punisch in Plautinischer Metrik,' *Semitics* 2: 93–126.

Goduinus, J. 1678. *C. Julii Caesaris quae extant.* Paris: Petri le Petit.

Goetsch, P. 1985. 'Fingierte Mündlichkeit in der Erzählkunst entwickelter Schriftkulturen', *Poetica* 17: 202–18.

Goetz, G. (ed.). 1892. *Corpus glossariorum Latinorum* III. *Hermeneumata Pseudodositheana, accedunt hermeneumata medicobotanica vetustiora.* Leipzig: Teubner.

(ed.) 1923. *Corpus glossariorum Latinorum* I. *De glossariorum Latinorum origine et fatis.* Leipzig: Teubner.

Goldberg, S. M. 2000. 'Cicero and the work of tragedy', in Manuwald (2000), pp. 49–59.

Goodyear, F. R. D. 1969. 'More notes on the *Iohannis* of Corippus', *BICS* 16: 16–21, 27–8 (= K. M. Coleman *et al.* 1992, pp. 85–91).

1982. 'On the character and text of Justin's compilation of Trogus', *Proceedings of the African Classical Association* 16: 1–24 (= K. Coleman *et al.* 1992, pp. 210–33).

Görler, W. 1982. 'Beobachtungen zu Vergils Syntax', *Würzburger Jahrbücher für die Altertumswissenschaft* 8: 69–81.

1985. 'Eneide: la lingua', *Enciclopedia Virgiliana* 2: 262–78.

1999. 'Rowing strokes: tentative considerations on "shifting" objects in Virgil and elsewhere', in Adams and Mayer (1999a), pp. 269–86.

Gow, A. S. F. 1932. 'Diminutives in Augustan poetry', *CQ* 26: 150–7.

Gowers, E. 1993. 'Horace, *Satires* 1. 5: an inconsequential journey', *PCPhS* 39: 48–66.

Grandgent, C. H. 1907. *An Introduction to Vulgar Latin.* Boston: D. C. Heath & Co.

Grevisse, M. 1993. *Le bon usage: grammaire française.* 13th edn recast by A. Goosse. Paris: Duculot.

Grube, G. M. A. 1952. 'Thrasymachus, Theophrastus, and Dionysius of Halicarnassus', *AJPh* 73: 251–67.

Gruen, E. S. 1992. *Culture and National Identity in Republican Rome.* Ithaca, NY: Cornell University Press.

Grünewald, C. 1912. *Die Satzparenthese bei den zehn attischen Rednern* (Beiträge zur historischen Syntax der griechischen Sprache 19). Würzburg: C. Kabitzsch.

Guarducci, M. 1995. *Epigrafia greca.* 4 vols. 2nd edn, Rome: Istituto Poligrafico dello Stato.

Gundlach, W. 1892. *Epistolae aevi Merowingici* (Monumenta Germaniae Historica Epistolae III). Berlin: Weidmann.

Gwara, S. (ed.) 1996. *Latin Colloquies from Pre-Conquest Britain.* Toronto: Pontifical Institute of Mediaeval Studies.

(ed.) 2002. 'The *Hermeneumata pseudodositheana*, Latin oral fluency, and the social function of the Cambro-Latin dialogues called *De raris fabulis*', in C. D. Lanham (ed.), *Latin Grammar and Rhetoric: From Classical Theory to Medieval Practice.* London and New York: Continuum, pp. 109–38.

Gwara, S. and Porter, D. W. (edd. and trans.) 1997. *Anglo-Saxon Conversations: The Colloquies of Ælfric Bata.* Woodbridge: The Boydell Press.

Haffter, H. 1934. *Untersuchungen zur altlateinischen Dichtersprache.* Berlin: Weidmann.

Hakamies, R. 1951. *Étude sur l'origine et l'evolution du diminutif latin et sa survie dans les langues romanes* (Annales Academiae Scientiarum Fennicae 71.1). Helsinki: Suomalainen Tiedeakatemia.

Håkanson, L. 1969. *Statius' Silvae: Critical and Exegetical Remarks with Some Notes on the Thebaid.* Lund: C. W. K. Gleerup.

Hale, K. 1983. 'Walpiri and the grammar of non-configurational languages', *Natural Language and Linguistic Theory* 1: 5–47.

Hall, L. G. H. 1998. '*Ratio* and *Romanitas* in the *Bellum Gallicum*', in K. Welch and A. Powell (edd.), *Julius Caesar as Artful Reporter: The War Commentaries as Political Instruments*. London: Duckworth, pp. 11–43.

Halla-aho, H. 2009. *The Non-literary Latin Letters: A Study of their Syntax and Pragmatics* (Commentationes Humanarum Litterarum 124). Helsinki: Societas Scientiarum Fennica.

Halsall, G. 2003. *Warfare and Society in the Barbarian West, 450–900*. London and New York: Routledge.

Hannappel, H. and Melenk, H. 1984. *Alltagssprache: Semantische Grundbegriffe und Analysebeispiele*. Munich: Wilhelm Fink.

Hanssen, J. S. Th. 1951. *Latin Diminutives: A Semantic Study*. Bergen: John Grieg.

Happ, H. 1967. 'Die lateinische Umgangssprache und die Kunstsprache des Plautus', *Glotta* 45: 60–104.

Hardie, P. 1994. *Virgil: Aeneid Book* IX. Cambridge University Press.

Harrison, S. J. (ed.) 1990. *Oxford Readings in Vergil's Aeneid*. Oxford University Press.

    1991. *A Commentary on Vergil: Aeneid 10*. Oxford University Press.

    2007. *Generic Enrichment in Virgil and Horace*. Oxford University Press.

Hartmann, M. 2005. *Die frühlateinischen Inschriften und ihre Datierung*. Bremen: Hempen.

Harvey, R. A. 1981. *A Commentary on Persius*. Leiden: Brill.

Haugen, E. 1966. 'Dialect, language, nation', *American Anthropologist* 68: 922–35.

Havers, W. 1911. *Untersuchungen zur Kasussyntax der indogermanischen Sprachen*. Straßburg: Karl J. Trubner.

Havet, L. 1898. 'Salveto', *ALL* 10: 287–89.

    1905. 'La mise en relief par disjonction', in *Mélanges Nicole*. Geneva: Kündig & fils, pp. 225–32.

Heinze, R. 1897. *T. Lucretius Carus: De rerum natura Buch* III. Leipzig: Teubner.

    1924. Review of Diels (1923), *Deutsche Literaturzeitung für Kritik der internationalen Wissenschaft* 45: 38–49.

Helttula, A. 1987. *Studies on the Latin Accusative Absolute* (Commentationes Humanarum Litterarum 81). Helsinki: Societas Scientiarum Fennica.

Hendrickson, G. L. 1906. 'The *De analogia* of Julius Caesar: its occasion, nature, and date, with additional fragments', *CPh* 1: 97–120.

Heraeus, W. 1902. 'Die römische Soldatensprache', *ALL* 12: 255–80.

    1937. 'Die Sprache des Petronius und die Glossen', in J. B. Hofmann (ed.), *Kleine Schriften von Wilhelm Heraeus zum 75. Geburtstag am 4. Dezember 1937*. Heidelberg: C. Winter, pp. 52–150.

Hering, W. 1963. *Die Recensio der Caesarhandschriften*. Berlin: Akademie-Verlag.

Herman, J. 2000. *Vulgar Latin*, trans. R. Wright. University Park, Pennsylvania: Pennsylvania State University Press.

    2003. 'Notes syntaxiques sur la langue de Trimalcion et de ses invités', in Herman and Rosén (edd.), pp. 139–46.

Herman, J. and Rosén, H. (edd.) 2003. *Petroniana: Gedenkschrift für Hubert Petersmann*. Heidelberg: C. Winter.

Herren, M. W. 1995. 'Vergil the Grammarian: a Spanish Jew in Ireland?', *Peritia* 9: 51–71.

2004. 'The "Cosmography" of Aethicus Ister: speculations about its date, provenance, and audience', in A. Bihrer and E. Stein (edd.), *Nova de veteribus: Mittel- und neulateinische Studien für Paul Gerhard Schmidt.* Munich: Saur.

Heubner, C. 1916. *De Belli Hispaniensis commentario quaestiones grammaticae.* Berlin: Ebering.

Highet, G. 1998. 'Petronius's dinner speakers', in R. J. Ball. (ed.), *The Unpublished Lectures of Gilbert Highet.* New York: Lang, pp. 119–34.

Hine, H. M. 2005. 'Poetic influence on prose: the case of the younger Seneca', in Reinhardt, Lapidge and Adams (2005), pp. 211–37.

Hofmann, J. B. 1926. *Lateinische Umgangssprache.* 1st edn, Heidelberg: C. Winter.

1936. *Lateinische Umgangssprache.* 2nd edn, Heidelberg: C. Winter.

1951. *Lateinische Umgangssprache.* 3rd edn, Heidelberg: C. Winter.

Holford-Strevens, L. 2003. *Aulus Gellius: An Antonine Scholar and his Achievement.* Oxford University Press.

Holmes, T. R. 1923. *The Roman Republic.* 3 vols. Oxford: Clarendon Press.

Holtze, W. 1868. *Syntaxis Lucretianae Lineamenta.* Leipzig: O. Holtze.

Hopkinson, N. 2000. *Ovid: Metamorphoses, Book XIII.* Cambridge University Press.

Horsfall, N. M. 1995. *A Companion to the Study of Virgil.* Leiden: Brill.

Housman, A. E. 1919. 'Notes on Martial', *CQ* 13: 68–80.

Howell, P. 1980. *A Commentary on Book One of the Epigrams of Martial.* London: Athlone Press.

Hutchinson, G. O. 1998. *Cicero's Correspondence: A Literary Study.* Oxford: Clarendon Press.

2006. *Propertius: Elegies Book IV.* Cambridge University Press.

Innes, D. C. 1988. 'Cicero on tropes', *Rhetorica* 6: 307–25.

Iordache, R. 1973. 'Elementos vulgares en la obra de Iordanes', *Helmantica* 24: 117–34.

1983. 'L'interrogative indirecte dans les œuvres de Jordanès', *Živa Antika* 33: 149–64.

1986. 'L'emploi des adverbes "quatenus", "hactenus", "protinus" et "tenus" dans les œuvres de Jordanes', *Atti dell'Accademia di Scienze, Lettere e Belle Arti di Palermo* 5: 331–52.

1992. 'Remarques sur la subordonnée temporelle à l'époque classique et à l'époque tardive, chez Jordanes', *Linguistica* 33: 31–60.

Jakobi, R. 1996. *Die Kunst der Exegese im Terenzkommentar des Donat.* Berlin: de Gruyter.

Jocelyn, H. D. 1969. *The Tragedies of Ennius: The Fragments Edited with an Introduction and Commentary* (Cambridge Classical Texts and Commentaries 10). 2nd edn, Cambridge University Press.

1972. 'The poems of Quintus Ennius', in *Aufstieg und Niedergang der römischen Welt* I.2: 987–1026.

1979. 'Vergilius Cacozelus (Donatus *Vita Vergilii* 44)', in F. Cairns (ed.), *Papers of the Liverpool Latin Seminar* II (ARCA 3). Liverpool: F. Cairns, pp. 67–142.

Jones, J. C. 1906. '*Simul, simulac* und Synonyma', *ALL* 14: 89–104.

Jong, M. de 1998. '*Imitatio morum*: the cloister and clerical purity in the Carolingian world', in M. Frassetto (ed.), *Medieval Purity and Piety: Essays on Medieval Clerical Celibacy and Religious Reform.* New York: Garland, pp. 49–80.

Jonge, C. C. de 2008. *Between Grammar and Rhetoric: Dionysius of Halicarnassus on Language, Linguistics and Literature* (Mnemosyne Suppl. 301). Leiden: Brill.

Joos, M. 1967. *The Five Clocks* (with an introduction by Albert H. Marckwardt). New York: Harcourt, Brace and World (original publication 1962 (Bloomington, Indiana): Publication 22 of the Indiana University Research Center in Anthropology, Folklore, and Linguistics).

Kaimio, J. 1979. *The Romans and the Greek Language* (Commentationes Humanarum Litterarum 64). Helsinki: Societas Scientiarum Fennica.

Kalén, H. 1939. *Studia in Iordanem Philologica.* Uppsala: Lundequist.

Kalinka, E. 1929. *Berichte über Cäsars und seiner Fortsetzer Schriften (1898–1928)* (Bursians Jahresberichte Suppl. 224). Leipzig: Reisland.

Kappelmacher, A. 1916. 'Iordanis', in *RE* IX: 1908–29.

Karlsson, K. 1981. *Syntax and Affixation: The Evolution of MENTE in Latin and Romance.* Tübingen: Niemeyer.

Karsten, H. T. 1912–13. *Commenti Donatiani ad Terenti fabulas scholia genuina et spuria.* Leiden: Sijthoff.

Katz, J. T. 1998. '*Testimonia ritus Italici*: male genitalia, solemn declarations, and a new Latin sound law', *Harvard Studies in Classical Philology* 118: 183–217.

Kenney, E. J. 1970. 'In parenthesis', *CR* n.s. 20: 291.

1971. *Lucretius: De rerum natura Book III.* Cambridge University Press.

Kenyon, J. S. 1948. 'Cultural levels and functional varieties of English', *College English* 10.1: 31–6.

Kindstrand, J. F. 1976. *Bion of Borysthenes: A Collection of the Fragments with Introduction and Commentary.* Uppsala: Almqvist & Wiksell.

Kircher-Durand, C. 2002. 'Les dérivés en *-nus, -na, -num*', in C. Kircher-Durand (ed.), *Création lexicale: la formation des noms par dérivation suffixale* (= *Grammaire fondamentale du latin* IX). Leuven and Paris: Peeters, pp. 125–84.

Kiss, K. É. (ed.) 1995. *Discourse Configurational Languages.* Oxford University Press.

Kiss, S. 2005. 'Anaphore et coordination dans les textes latins tardifs', in G. Calboli (ed.), *Papers on Grammar* IX. *Nemo te lacrimis decoret neque funera fletu faxit. Cur? Volitas viva per ora virum: Proceedings of the Twelfth International Colloquium on Latin Linguistics (Bologna 9–14 June 2003).* Rome: Herder, pp. 571–6.

Kißel, W. 1990. *Aulus Persius Flaccus: Satiren.* Heidelberg: C. Winter.

Klotz, A. 1910. *Cäsarstudien nebst einer Analyse der strabonischen Beschreibung von Gallien und Britannien.* Leipzig and Berlin: Teubner.

1927a. *C. Iuli Caesaris commentarii* III: *Commentarii Belli Alexandrini, Belli Africi, Belli Hispaniensis. Accedunt C. Iuli Caesaris et A. Hirti fragmenta.* Leipzig: Teubner.

1927b. *Kommentar zum Bellum Hispaniense.* Leipzig: Teubner.

Knobloch, J. (ed.) 1961–. *Sprachwissenschaftliches Wörterbuch.* Heidelberg: C. Winter.

Knox, P. E. 1986. 'Adjectives in *-osus* in Latin poetic diction', *Glotta* 64: 90–101.

Koehler, A. 1877. 'De auctorum Belli Africani et Belli Hispaniensis Latinitate', *Acta Seminarii Philologici Erlangensis* 1: 367–476.

Koenen, L. 1970. 'Die "laudatio funebris" des Augustus für Agrippa auf einem neuen Papyrus (P.Colon. inv. nr. 4701; H. Volkmann gewidmet)', *ZPE* 5: 217–83.

Kollmann, E. D. 1975. 'The infinitive in Latin hexameter poetry', *Glotta* 53: 281–91.

Konjetzny, W. 1907. 'De idiotismis syntacticis in titulis latinis urbanis (C.I.L. Vol. VI.) conspicuis', *ALL* 15: 297–351.

Krebs, J. P. and Schmalz, J. H. 1905–7. *Antibarbarus der lateinischen Sprache: nebst einem kurzen Abriss der Geschichte der lateinischen Sprache und Vorbemerkungen über reine Latinität.* 2 vols. 7th edn, Basle: Schwabe.

Krenkel, W. 1970. *Lucilius: Satiren.* 2 vols. Berlin: Akademie Verlag and Leiden: Brill.

Kroeber, P. D., and Moore, R. E. (edd.) 1987. *Native American Languages and Grammatical Typology.* Bloomington, Indiana: Indiana University Linguistics Club.

Kroll, W. (ed.) 1913. *M. Tullii Ciceronis Orator.* Berlin: Weidmann.

1927. 'Die Sprache des Sallust', *Glotta* 15: 280–305.

Krusch, B. 1888. *Fredegarii et aliorum chronica. Vitae Sanctorum.* Hanover: Hahn.

1910. 'Der Staatsstreich des fränkischen Hausmeiers Grimoald I', in *Historische Aufsätze Karl Zeumer zum 60. Geburtstag als Festgabe dargebracht von Freunden und Schülern.* Weimar: Böhlau, pp. 411–38.

Kruschwitz, P. and Halla-aho, H. 2007. 'The Pompeian wall inscriptions and the Latin language: a critical reappraisal', *Arctos* 41: 31–49.

Kühnast, L. 1872. *Die Hauptpunkte der livianischen Syntax.* Berlin: Weber.

Labov, W. 1966. *The Social Stratification of English in New York City.* Washington, DC: Center for Applied Linguistics.

2001. *Principles of Linguistic Change* II. *Social Factors* (Language in Society 29). Oxford: Blackwell.

Laguna, G. 1992. *Estacio: Silvas* III. *Introducción, edición crítica, traducción y comentario.* Madrid: Fundación Pastor de Estudios Clásicos.

Landfester, M. 1997. *Einführung in die Stilistik der griechischen und lateinischen Literatursprachen.* Darmstadt: Wissenschaftliche Buchgesellschaft.

Landgraf, G. 1878. *De Ciceronis elocutione in orationibus Pro P. Quinctio et Pro Sex. Roscio Amerino conspicua.* Diss. Würzburg: Stuber.

1893. 'Der Dativus commodi und der Dativus finalis mit ihren Abarten', *ALL* 8: 39–76.

458   *References*

1914. *Kommentar zu Ciceros Rede Pro Sex. Roscio Amerino.* 2nd edn, Leipzig and
    Berlin: Teubner.
Lapidge, M. 1984. 'Gildas's education', in D. Dumville and M. Lapidge (edd.),
    Gildas: New Approaches. Woodbridge: The Boydell Press, pp. 27–50.
  1986. 'Latin learning in Dark Age Wales: some prolegomena', in D. E. Evans,
    J. G. Griffith and E. M. Jope (edd.), *Proceedings of the Seventh International
    Congress of Celtic Studies.* Oxford: Cranham Press, pp. 91–107.
  2006. *The Anglo-Saxon Library.* Oxford University Press.
Lapp, F. 1965. *De Callimachi Cyrenaei tropis et figuris* (Dissertatio inauguralis).
    Bonn: Rheinische Friedrich-Wilhelms-Universität.
Latham, R. E. (ed.) 1975. *Dictionary of Medieval Latin from British Sources, Fascicle
    1.* London: Oxford University Press for the British Academy.
Laurand, L. 1938. *Études sur le style des discours de Cicéron.* Paris: Les Belles Lettres.
Lausberg, H. 1998. *Handbook of Literary Rhetoric.* Leiden: Brill.
Lebek, W. D. 1970. *Verba prisca: Die Anfänge des Archaisierens in der lateini-
    schen Beredsamkeit und Geschichtsschreibung* (Hypomnemata 25). Göttingen:
    Vandenhoeck & Ruprecht.
Lebreton, J. 1901. *Études sur la langue et la grammaire de Cicéron.* Paris: Hachette.
Leeman, A. D. 1963. *Orationis ratio: The Stylistic Theories and Practice of the Roman
    Orators, Historians and Philosophers.* Amsterdam: Hakkert.
Lehmann, C. 1991. 'The Latin nominal group in a typological perspective', in
    R. Coleman (ed.), *New Studies in Latin Linguistics.* Amsterdam: Benjamins,
    pp. 203–32.
Lehmann, P. G. J. 1922. *Die Parodie im Mittelalter.* Munich: Drei Masken.
Leiwo, M. 2002. 'From contact to mixture: bilingual inscriptions from Italy', in
    J. N. Adams *et al.* (2002), pp. 168–94.
  2009. 'Imperatives and other directives in the letters from Mons Claudia-
    nus', in T. Evans and D. Obbink (edd.), *The Language of the Papyri.* Oxford
    University Press, pp. 97–119.
Lennartz, K. 1994. *Non verba sed vim: Kritisch-exegetische Untersuchungen zu den
    Fragmenten archaischer römischer Tragiker.* Stuttgart and Leipzig: Teubner.
  1995–6. 'Zur 'Wortabbildung' in der archaischen römischen Tragödie', *Glotta*
    73: 168–207.
  2003. 'Zu Sprachniveau und Stilbildung in der republikanischen Tragödie:
    unter besonderer Berücksichtigung sondersprachlicher und volkssprach-
    licher Elemente. Mit einem Anhang zu den Hiatstellen', *Glotta* 79:
    83–136.
Leo, F. 1913. *Geschichte der römischen Literatur* I. *Die archaische Literatur.* Berlin:
    Weidmann.
Letessier, P. 2000. 'La *salutatio* chez Plaute: adaptation ludique d'un rituel social',
    Lalies 20: 151–64.
Letta, C. 1996. 'I culti di Vesuna e di Valetudo tra Umbria e Marsica', in G.
    Bonamente and F. Coarelli (edd.), *Assisi e gli Umbri nell'antichità: Atti
    del Convegno internazionale, Assisi 18–21 dicembre 1991.* Assisi: Minerva,
    pp. 318–39.

Leumann, M. 1947. 'Die lateinische Dichtersprache', *Museum Helveticum* 4: 116–39 (reprinted in *Kleine Schriften*, Zürich and Stuttgart: Artemis Verlag 1959, pp. 131–56; Italian translation, with additional notes, in Lunelli (1980), pp. 131–78).

    1977. *Lateinische Laut- und Formenlehre.* Munich: Beck.

Lietzmann, H. 1905. *Fünf Festpredigten Augustins in gereimter Prosa.* Bonn: Marcus and Weber.

Lindsay, W. M. 1903. *Nonii Marcelli De conpendiosa doctrina.* Leipzig: Teubner.

    1907. *Syntax of Plautus.* Oxford University Press.

    1929. *M. Val. Martialis Epigrammata.* 2nd edn, Oxford University Press.

Lipsius, J. 1611. *Opera omnia quae ad criticam proprie spectant.* Antwerp: Officina Plantiniana.

Lodge, G. 1924–33. *Lexicon Plautinum.* 2 vols. Leipzig: Teubner.

Löfstedt, B. 1961. *Studien über die Sprache der langobardischen Gesetze: Beiträge zur frühmittelalterlichen Latinität.* Stockholm: Almqvist & Wiksell.

    1965. *Der hibernolateinische Grammatiker Malsachanus.* Lund: Håkan Ohlsson.

Löfstedt, E. 1911. *Philologischer Kommentar zur Peregrinatio Aetheriae: Untersuchungen zur Geschichte der lateinischen Sprache.* Uppsala: Almqvist & Wiksell.

    1936. *Vermischte Studien zur lateinischen Sprachkunde und Syntax.* Lund: Gleerup.

    1950. *Coniectanea: Untersuchungen auf dem Gebiet der antiken und mittelalterlichen Latinität.* Uppsala: Almqvist & Wiksells.

    1956. *Syntactica: Studien und Beiträge zur historischen Syntax des Lateins.* 2 vols. 2nd edn, Lund: Gleerup.

Löfstedt, L. 1966. *Les expressions du commandement et de la défense en latin et leur survie dans les langues romanes.* Helsinki: Société Néophilologique.

Lomanto, V. 1993. 'Due divergenti interpretazioni dell'analogia: la flessione dei temi in -*u*- secondo Varrone e secondo Cesare', in Poli (1993) II, pp. 643–85.

    1994–5. 'Cesare e la teoria dell'eloquenza', *Memorie della Accademia delle Scienze di Torino, Classe di Scienze Morali, Storiche e Filologiche* 5th ser. 18–19: 3–127.

Lorenzo, J. L. 1976. *El valor de los preverbios en Jordanes.* Salamanca: Universidad de Salamanca.

Luiselli, B. 1976. 'Sul *De summa temporum* di Iordanes', *Romanobarbarica* 1: 83–134.

Lundström, S. 1982. *Ein textkritisches Problem in den Tusculanen.* Uppsala: Almqvist & Wiksell.

Lunelli, A. (ed.) 1980. *La lingua poetica latina.* Bologna: Pàtron.

Lyne, R. O. A. M. 1987. *Further Voices in Vergil's Aeneid.* Oxford University Press.

    1989. *Words and the Poet.* Oxford University Press.

McCartney, E. S. 1920. 'Fore-runners of the Romance adverbial suffix', *CPh* 15: 213–29.

McGushin, C. 1977. *C. Sallustius Crispus: Bellum Catilinae. A Commentary.* Leiden: Brill.

Mack, D. 1937. *Senatsreden und Volksreden bei Cicero.* Würzburg: Triltsch.

Madvig, J. N. 1856. *A Latin Grammar for the Use of Schools*, trans. G. Woods. 3rd edn, Oxford University Press.

1873. *Adversaria critica* II. Copenhagen: Gyldendal.

Malcovati, H. (ed.) 1967. *Imperatoris Caesaris Augusti operum fragmenta*. Turin: Paravia.

1976. *Oratorum Romanorum fragmenta liberae rei publicae*. 2 vols. 4th edn, Turin: Paravia.

Maltby, R. 1979. 'Linguistic characterisation of old men in Terence', *CPh* 74: 136–47.

2007. 'The distribution of imagery by plays and characters in Terence', in P. Kruschwitz, W.-W. Ehlers and F. Felgentreu (edd.), *Terentius poeta*. Munich: Beck, pp. 143–65.

Mann, J. C. 1971. 'Spoken Latin in Britain as evidenced in the inscriptions', *Britannia* 2: 218–24.

Mannheimer, I. 1975. *Sprachliche Beziehungen zwischen Alt- and Spätlatein*. Diss. Zürich: Juris Druck.

Mansfeld, J. 1995. 'Insight by hindsight: intentional unclarity in presocratic proems', *BICS* 42: 225–32.

Manuwald, G. (ed.) 2000. *Identität und Alterität in der frührömischen Tragödie* (Identitäten und Alteritäten 3). Würzburg: Ergon-Verlag.

2001. *Fabulae Praetextae: Spuren einer literarischen Gattung der Römer* (Zetemata 108). Munich: Beck.

2003. *Pacuvius summus tragicus poeta: Zum dramatischen Profil seiner Tragödien*. Munich and Leipzig: Saur.

Mariotti, I. 1960. *Studi luciliani*. Florence: La Nuova Italia.

Marouzeau, J. 1921. 'Pour mieux comprendre les textes latins (Essai sur la distinction des styles)', *RPh* 2nd ser. 45: 149–93.

1922. *L'ordre des mots dans la phrase latine* I. *Les groupes nominaux*. Paris: Les Belles Lettres.

1938. *L'ordre des mots dans la phrase latine* II. *Le verbe*. Paris: Les Belles Lettres.

1949. *L'ordre des mots dans la phrase latine* III. *Les articulations de l'énoncé*. Paris: Les Belles Lettres.

1954. *Traité de stylistique latine*. 3rd edn, Paris: Les Belles Lettres.

Martin, J. 1974. *Antike Rhetorik: Technik und Methode* (Handbuch der Altertumswissenschaft 2, 3). Munich: Beck.

Martindale, C. A. (ed.) 1997. *The Cambridge Companion to Virgil*. Cambridge University Press.

Martindale, J. R. 1992. *The Prosopography of the Later Roman Empire* III. *AD 527–641*. Cambridge University Press.

Marx, F. (ed.) 1894. *Incerti auctoris De ratione dicendi ad C. Herennium libri* IV *[M. Tulli Ciceronis Ad Herennium libri* VI*]*. Leipzig: Teubner.

1904–5. *C. Lucilii carminum reliquiae*. 2 vols. Leipzig: Teubner.

1909. 'Die Beziehungen des Altlateins zum Spätlatein', *Neue Jahrbücher für das klassische Altertum* 12: 434–48.

(ed.) 1923. *Incerti auctoris De ratione dicendi ad C. Herennium libri* IV (M. Tulli Ciceronis scripta quae manserunt omnia I). Leipzig: Teubner.

Mathisen, R. W. 1999. *Ruricius of Limoges and Friends: A Collection of Letters from Visigothic Gaul.* Liverpool University Press.

Matthews, P. 2007. *Oxford Concise Dictionary of Linguistics.* Oxford University Press.

Maurach, G. 1995. *Lateinische Dichtersprache.* Darmstadt: Wissenschaftliche Buchgesellschaft.

Mayer, R. 1981. *Lucan: Civil War* VIII. Warminster: Aris & Phillips.

2001. *Tacitus: Dialogus de oratoribus.* Cambridge University Press.

Meisterfeld, R. 2000. 'Die unbestimmte Bestimmung: zur Entstehung des unbestimmten Artikels in den romanischen Sprachen', in B. Staib (ed.), *Linguistica Romanica et Indiana: Festschrift für Wolf Dietrich.* Tübingen: Narr, pp. 303–33.

Melville, A. D. 1992. *Statius: Thebaid.* Oxford University Press.

Menge, H., Burkard, T. and Schauer, M. 2000. *Lehrbuch der lateinischen Syntax und Semantik.* Darmstadt: Wissenschaftliche Buchgesellschaft.

Menk, E. A. 1925. *The Position of the Possessive Pronoun in Cicero's Orations.* Diss. Univ. of Iowa, Grand Forks, ND: Normanden Publishing Company.

Mercier, J. 1614. *Nonii Marcelli nova editio. Additus est libellus Fulgentii de prisco sermone et notae in Nonium et Fulgentium.* Paris: Perier, and Sedan: Iannon (reprinted Leipzig: Teubner 1826).

Merrill, F. R. 1972. *Plautus: Mostellaria.* London: Macmillan.

Merrill, W. A. 1907. *T. Lucreti Cari De rerum natura libri sex.* New York: American Book Company.

Metzger, M.D. 1974. 'Marius Victorinus and the substantive infinitive', *Eranos* 72: 65–70.

Meusel, H. 1887–93. *Lexicon Caesarianum.* Berlin: Weber.

Meyer, P. 1867. Review of Boucherie (1867), *Revue Critique d'Histoire et de Littérature* 2: 344–50.

Meyer, W. 1904. 'Die Legende des h. Albanus des Protomartyr Angliae in Texten vor Beda', *Abhandlungen der königlichen Gesellschaft der Wissenschaften zu Göttingen, philosophisch-historische Klasse,* n.s. 8: 3–81.

Mierow, C. C. 1915. *Jordanes: The Origin and Deeds of the Goths.* 2nd edn, Princeton University Press.

1922–3. 'Some remarks on the literary technique of the Gothic historian Jordanes', *Classical Weekly* 16: 140–2.

Mignot, X. 1969. *Les verbes dénominatifs latins.* Paris: Klincksieck.

1981. '*Salutare* en latin, "saluer" en français sont-ils bien des verbes délocutifs?', *BSL* 76: 327–44.

Minyard, J. D. 1978. *Mode and Value in De Rerum natura: A Study in Lucretius' Metrical Language* (Hermes Einzelschriften 39). Stuttgart: Steiner.

Mitsis, P. 1994. 'Committing philosophy to the reader: didactic coercion and reader autonomy in *De rerum natura*', in A. Schiesaro, P. Mitsis and J. Strauss Clay (edd.), *Mega nepios: il destinatario nell'epos didascalico* (MD 31), pp. 111–28.

Möbius, A. 1830. *C. Julii Caesaris Commentarii de bello civili. Accedunt libri de bello Alexandrino Africano et Hispaniensi.* Hanover: Hahn.

Mohrmann, C. 1958. 'Saint Augustin écrivain', *Recherches Augustiniennes* 1: 43–66.

Mommsen, T. 1882. *Iordanis Romana et Getica* (Monumenta Germaniae Historica v.1). Berlin: Weidmann.

1893. 'Zur Geschichte der Caesarischen Zeit', *Hermes* 28: 599–618.

Morgan, L. 1997. '"Levi quidem de re…" Julius Caesar as tyrant and pedant', *JRS* 87: 23–40.

Morus, S. F. N. 1780. *C. Iulii Caesaris Commentarii de bello Gallico et civili. Accedunt libri De bello Alexandrino, Africano et Hispaniensi e recensione Francisci Oudendorpii.* Leipzig: Weidmann.

Moussy, C. (ed.) 2001. *De lingua Latina novae quaestiones: Actes du xe Colloque international de linguistique latine, Paris-Sèvres, 19–23 avril 1999.* Leuven: Peeters.

Mras, K. 1953. 'St Patricius als Lateiner', *Anzeiger der Österreichischen Akademie der Wissenschaften, philosophisch-historische Klasse* 90: 99–113.

Mueller, L. 1888. *Noni Marcelli Compendiosa doctrina.* Leipzig: Teubner.

Müller, R. 1997. *Sprechen und Sprache: Dialoglinguistische Studien zu Terenz.* Heidelberg: C. Winter.

2001. *Sprachbewußtsein und Sprachvariation im lateinischen Schrifttum der Antike* (Zetemata 111). Munich: Beck.

Müller-Lancé, J. 1992. 'Die Funktion vulgärlateinischer Elemente in den Satiren des Horaz am Beispiel von sat. 2,5', in M. Iliescu and W. Marxgut (edd.), *Latin vulgaire – latin tardif* iii: *Actes du iiième Colloque internationale sur le latin vulgaire et tardif. Innsbruck, 2–5 septembre 1991.* Tübingen: M. Niemeyer, pp. 243–54.

Munro, H. A. J. 1928. *T. Lucreti Cari De rerum natura libri sex* ii. *Explanatory notes.* 4th edn, London: George Bell & Sons.

Murray, J. A. H. 1888. *A New English Dictionary on Historical Principles* i. Oxford: Clarendon Press.

Myers-Scotton, C. 2006. *Multiple Voices: An Introduction to Bilingualism.* Malden, Mass.: Blackwell.

Mynors, R. A. B. 1990. *Virgil: Georgics.* Oxford: Clarendon Press.

Neilson, W. A. and Knott, T. A. (edd.) 1934. *Webster's New International Dictionary of the English Language.* 2nd edn, Springfield, Mass.: Merriam-Webster.

Nisbet, R. G. 1923. '*Voluntas fati* in Latin syntax', *AJPh* 44: 27–43.

Nisbet, R. G. M. and Rudd, N. 2004. *A Commentary on Horace: Odes Book* iii. Oxford University Press.

Nodes, D. J. 2009. 'The organization of Augustine's *Psalmus contra partem Donati*', in *Vigiliae Christianae* 63: 390–408.

Norberg, D. 1943. *Syntaktische Forschungen auf dem Gebiete des Spätlateins und des frühen Mittellateins.* Uppsala: A.-B. Lundequistska Bokhandeln.

1944. *Beiträge zur spätlateinischen Syntax.* Uppsala: Almqvist & Wiksells.

1964. 'Quelques remarques sur les lettres de Frodebert et d'Importun', *RFIC* 92: 295–303.

1968. *Manuel pratique de latin médiéval.* Paris: Picard.

Norden, E. 1899. *Die antike Kunstprosa*. Leipzig: Teubner.

Nowottny, W. 1965. *The Language Poets Use*. London and Atlantic Highlands, NJ: Athlone.

Oberlinus, I. I. 1805. *C. I. Caesaris De bello Gallico et civili. Accedunt libri De bello Alexandrino, Africano et Hispaniensi e recensione Francisci Oudendorpii*. Leipzig: Weidmann.

1819. *C. Iulii Caesaris Commentarii De bello Gallico et civili. Accedunt libri De bello Alexandrino, Africano et Hispaniensi e recensione Francisci Oudendorpii*. Leipzig: Weidmann.

Ogilvie, R. M. 1965. *A Commentary on Livy: Books 1–5*. Oxford: Clarendon Press.

O'Hara, J. J. 1996. *True Names: Vergil and the Alexandrian Tradition of Etymological Wordplay*. Ann Arbor: University of Michigan Press.

1997. 'Virgil's style', in C. Martindale (1997), pp. 241–58.

Olcott, G. N. 1898. *Studies in the Word Formation of the Latin Inscriptions*. Rome: Sallustian Typography.

Oldfather, W. A. and Bloom, G. 1927. 'Caesar's grammatical theories and his own practice', *CJ* 22: 584–602.

Orinsky, K. 1923. 'Die Wortstellung bei Gaius', *Glotta* 12: 83–100.

Orlandini, A. 2003. '*Valde bella est* (Cic. *Att.* 4. 6. 4): étude sur un adverbe polysémique dans la correspondance de Cicéron', in Garcea (2003a), pp. 140–56.

Otto, A. 1890. *Die Sprichwörter und sprichwörtlichen Redensarten der Römer*. Leipzig: Teubner.

Oudendorp, F. 1737. *C. Julii Caesaris De bellis Gallico et civili Pompejano nec non A. Hirtii, aliorumque De bellis Alexandrino, Africano, et Hispaniensi commentarii*. 2 vols. Leiden: Luchtmans and Rotterdam: Beman.

Palmén, E. 1958. 'Die lateinischen pronominalen Ortsadverbien in Kasusbedeutung', *Arctos* n.s. 2: 104–42.

Palmer, F. R. 1994. *Grammatical Roles and Relations*. Cambridge University Press.

Panciera, M. D. 2007. 'Plautonic *amabo*: when men say "please" in Plautus', http://www.apaclassics.org/AnnualMeeting/07mtg/abstracts/panciera.pdf (accessed 3 February 2008).

Panhuis, D. G. J. 1982. *The Communicative Perspective in the Sentence: A Study of Latin Word Order*. Amsterdam and Philadelphia: Benjamins.

Paschoud, F. and Wirz, C. 2007. 'Emplois de l'ablatif absolu dans l'*Histoire Auguste* et Suétone', in G. Bonamente and H. Brandt (edd.), *Historiae Augustae Colloquium Bambergense* (Historiae Augustae Colloquia 10). Bari: Edipuglia, pp. 295–303.

Pascucci, G. 1950. 'Lingua e stile dell'*Hispaniense*', *Studi Urbinati di Storia, Filosofia e Letteratura* 24: 191–217.

1965. *Bellum Hispaniense: introduzione, testo critico e commento*. Florence: Le Monnier.

1973. 'Interpretazione linguistica e stilistica del Cesare autentico', in *Aufstieg und Niedergang der römischen Welt* 1.3: 488–522.

Pasquali, G. 1927. 'Lingua latina dell'uso', *RFIC* 5: 244–50 (reprinted in *Pagine stravaganti*, Florence: Sansoni 1968 II, pp. 329–35).

Pearce, T. E. V. 1966. 'The enclosing word order in the Latin hexameter', *CQ* n.s. 16: 140–71, 298–320.

Peglau, M. 2000. 'Virtutes und vitia in der älteren römischen Tragödie', in M. Braun, A. Haltenhoff and F.-H. Mutschler (edd.), *Moribus antiquis res stat Romana: Römische Werte und römische Literatur im 3. und 2. Jh. v. Chr.* Munich and Leipzig: Saur, pp. 141–67.

Penney, J. H. W. 1999. 'Archaism and innovation in Latin poetic syntax', in Adams and Mayer (1999a), pp. 249–68.

Perpillou, L. 1996. *Recherches lexicales en grec ancien.* Leuven: Peeters.

Perrot, J. 1994. 'Liberté et contrainte dans l'ordre des mots: la régulation syntaxique des variations en latin et en hongrois', *Techniques et Méthodologies Modernes Appliquées à l'Antiquité* 1: 11–32.

Peter, H. 1914. *Historicorum Romanorum reliquiae* I. 2nd edn, Leipzig: Teubner.

Petersmann, H. 1977. *Petrons urbane Prosa: Untersuchungen zu Sprache und Text.* Vienna: Österreichische Akademie der Wissenschaften.

1999. 'The language of early Roman satire: its function and characteristics', in Adams and Mayer (1999a), pp. 289–310.

Petersmann, H. and Petersmann, A. 1991. *Die römische Literatur in Text und Darstellung* I: *Republikanische Zeit* I: *Poesie.* Stuttgart: Reclam.

Petersmann, H. and Kettemann, R. (edd.) 1999. *Latin vulgaire – latin tardif v: Actes du ve Colloque international sur le latin vulgaire et tardif, Heidelberg 5–8 septembre 1997.* Heidelberg: C. Winter.

Pinkster, H. 1987. 'The pragmatic motivation for the use of subject pronouns in Latin: the case of Petronius', in *Études de linguistique générale et de linguistique latine offertes en hommage à Guy Serbat par ses collègues et ses élèves* (Bibliothèque de l'information grammaticale). Paris: Société pour l'Information Grammaticale, pp. 369–79.

2005a. 'The language of Pliny the Elder', in Reinhardt, Lapidge and Adams (2005), pp. 239–56.

2005b. 'Changing patterns of discontinuity in Latin' (handout from conference paper presented at 13th International Colloquium on Latin Linguistics, Brussels, 2005) http://www.harmpinkster.nl/index.php?section=22 (accessed September 2007).

Pirson, J. 1910. 'Pamphlets bas latins du VII siècle', in *Mélanges de philologie romane et d'histoire littéraire offerts à M. Maurice Wilmotte, Prof. à l'univ. de Liège, à l'occasion de son 25e anniversaire d'enseignement.* Paris: H. Champion, pp. 485–522.

Pizzani, U. 1993. 'La cultura filosofica di Cesare', in Poli (1993) I, pp. 163–89.

Plessis, F. and Lejay, P. 1911. *Œuvres d'Horace.* Paris: Hachette.

Plummer, C. (ed.) 1896. *Venerabilis Baedae Historiam ecclesiasticam gentis Anglorum Historiam abbatum, Epistolam ad Ecgberctum una cum Historia abbatum auctore anonymo . . . recognovit Carolus Plummer.* 2 vols. Oxford: Clarendon Press.

Poccetti, P. 1983. 'In margine all'iscrizione osca Ve 110', *Incontri Linguistici* 7: 45–51.

1993a. 'Aspetti e problemi della diffusione del latino in area italica', in E. Campanile (ed.), *Caratteri e diffusione del latino in area italica*. Pisa: Giardini, pp. 73–96.

1993b. 'Teorie grammaticali e prassi della *latinitas* in Cesare', in Poli (1993) II, pp. 599–641.

Polheim, K. 1925. *Die lateinische Reimprosa*. Berlin: Weidmann.

Poli, D. (ed.) 1993. *La cultura in Cesare*. 2 vols. Rome: Il Calamo.

Pötter, H. 1932. *Untersuchungen zum Bellum Alexandrinum und Bellum Africanum*. Leipzig: Noske.

Powell, J. G. F. 1984. Review of Panhuis (1982), *CR* n.s. 34: 75–7.

1988. *Cicero: Cato Maior de senectute. Edited with an introduction and commentary* (Cambridge Classical Texts and Commentaries 28). Cambridge University Press.

2005. 'Cicero's adaptation of legal Latin in the *De legibus*', in Reinhardt, Lapidge and Adams (2005), pp. 117–50.

Powell, J. G. F. and Paterson, J. (edd.) 2004. *Cicero the Advocate*. Oxford University Press.

Prosdocimi, A. 1990. 'Vetter 243 e l'imperativo latino tra (con)testo e paradigma', in G. Maetzke (ed.), *La civiltà dei Falisci: Atti del xv Convegno di Studi Etruschi e Italici, Civita Castellana-Forte Sangallo 28–31 maggio 1987*. Florence: Olschki, pp. 291–326.

Questa, C. 1995. *Titi Macci Plauti cantica*. Urbino: QuattroVenti.

2007. *La metrica di Plauto e di Terenzio*. Urbino: QuattroVenti.

Quirk, R., Greenbaum, S., Leech G. and Svartvik, J. 1985. *A Comprehensive Grammar of the English Language*. London: Longman.

Rambaud, M. 1966. *L'art de la déformation historique dans les commentaires de César*. 2nd edn, Paris: Les Belles Lettres.

1969. 'César et l'Épicurisme d'après les "Commentaires"', in *Actes du viiie congrès de l'Association Guillaume Budé*. Paris: Les Belles Lettres, pp. 411–35.

Razzolini, L. 1879. *Petrarca: De viris illustribus vitae* II. Bologna: Gaetano Romagnoli.

Rawson, E. 1979. 'L. Cornelius Sisenna and the early first century BC', *CQ* n.s. 29: 327–46.

Reinhardt, T. 2008. 'Epicurus and Lucretius on the origins of language', *CQ* n.s. 58: 127–40.

Reinhardt, T., Lapidge, M. and Adams, J. N. (edd.) 2005. *Aspects of the Language of Latin Prose* (Proceedings of the British Academy 129). Oxford University Press.

Ribbeck, O. 1871. *Scaenicae Romanorum poesis fragmenta* I. *Tragicorum Romanorum Fragmenta*. 2nd edn, Leipzig (reprinted Hildesheim 1962).

1873. *Scaenicae Romanorum poesis fragmenta* II. *Comicorum Romanorum Fragmenta*. 2nd edn, Leipzig 1873 (reprinted Hildesheim 1962).

Richter, W. 1977. *Caesar als Darsteller seiner Taten*. Heidelberg: C. Winter.

Ricottilli, L. 2003. 'Hofmann e il concetto della lingua d'uso', Introduction to Hofmann–Ricottilli (3rd edn), 9–69.

Riese, A. 1865. *Varro: Saturarum Menippearum reliquiae.* Leipzig: Teubner.

Riionheimo, H. 2007. *Muutoksen monet juuret – Oman ja vieraan risteytyminen Viron inkerinsuomalaisten imperfektinmuodostuksessa* (*The Multiple Roots of Change: Mixing Native and Borrowed Influence in the Past Tense Formation by Ingrian Finns*) (Suomalaisen Kirjallisuuden Seuran Toimituksia 1107). Helsinki: SKS.

Risicato, A. 1950. *Lingua parlata e lingua d'arte in Ennio.* Messina: Editrice Universitaria.

Risselada, R. 1993. *Imperative and Other Directive Expressions in Latin.* Amsterdam: Gieben.

Rix, H. 1991. *Etruskische Texte.* Tübingen: Narr.

 1993. Review of *La civiltà dei Falisci: Atti del xv Convegno di Studi etruschi ed italici, Firenze 1990, Kratylos* 38: 83–87.

 2002. *Sabellische Texte.* Heidelberg: C. Winter.

Roesch, S. 2005. 'L'échec des clôtures du dialogue dans les comédies de Plaute', in G. Calboli. (ed.), *Papers on Grammar* ix. *Nemo te lacrimis decoret neque funera fletu faxit. Cur? Volitas viva per ora virum: Proceedings of the Twelfth International Colloquium on Latin Linguistics (Bologna 9–14 June 2003).* Rome: Herder, pp. 921–32.

 2008. 'Les débuts de dialogues dans la comédie et la tragédie latines', in *Commencer et finir: débuts et fins dans les littératures grecque, latine et néolatine. Actes du colloque organisé le 29 et 30 septembre 2006 par l'Université Jean Moulin-Lyon 3 et l'ENS-LHS.* Lyons: CERGR, pp. 207–22.

Roncali, R. 1989. *Seneca: l'apoteosi negata.* Venice: Marsilio.

Rönsch, H. 1875. *Itala und Vulgata: Das Sprachidiom der urchristlichen Itala und der katholischen Vulgata unter Berücksichtigung der römischen Volkssprache.* 2nd edn, Marburg: N. G. Elwert.

Roschatt, A. 1883. *Über den Gebrauch der Parenthesen in Ciceros Reden und rhetorischen Schriften.* Erlangen: Universitäts-Buchdruckerei von Junge.

 1884. 'Über den Gebrauch der Parenthesen in Ciceros Reden und rhetorischen Schriften', *Acta Seminarii Erlangensis* 3: 189–244.

Rosén, H. B. 1992. '"Having" in Petronius', in G. Tournoy and T. Sacré (edd.), *Pegasus devocatus: studia in honorem C. Arri Nuri sive Harry C. Schnur* (Supplementa humanistica Lovanensia vii). Leuven University Press, pp. 101–17.

 1999. *Latine loqui: Trends and Directions in the Crystallization of Classical Latin.* Munich: Fink.

Ross, D. O. 1969. *Style and Tradition in Catullus.* Cambridge, Mass.: Harvard University Press.

Ruckdeschel, F. 1910. *Archaismen und Vulgarismen in der Sprache des Horaz.* Diss. Munich: Straub.

Russell, D. A. (ed.) 1964. *'Longinus': On the Sublime.* Oxford: Clarendon Press.

 2001. *Quintilian: The Orator's Education.* Cambridge, Mass.: Harvard University Press.

Sarhimaa, A. 1999. *Syntactic Transfer, Contact-Induced Change, and the Evolution of Bilingual Mixed Codes: Focus on Karelian-Russian Language Alternation* (Studia Fennica Linguistica 9). Helsinki: Finnish Literature Society.

Sato, S. 1990. 'Chrodebert concéda-t-il le premier privilège épiscopal pour Saint-Martin de Tours? Une problématique méconnue', in C. Lepelley and M. Sot (edd.), *Haut Moyen-Age: culture, éducation et sociétaé. Études offertes à Pierre Riché*. Nanterre: Publidix and LaGarenne-Colombes: Erasme.

Sblendorio Cugusi, M. T. 1982. *M. Porci Catonis orationum reliquiae*. Turin: Paravia.

Scafoglio, G. 2006. *L'Astyanax di Accio: saggio sul background mitografico, testo critico e commento dei frammenti* (Collection Latomus 295). Brussels: Latomus.

Scaliger, J. J. 1655. *Marci Manilii Astronomicon a Josepho Scaligero ex vetusto codice Gemblacensi infinitis mendis repurgatum*. Strasbourg: Bockenhoffer.

Schaffner-Rimann, J. 1958. *Die lateinischen Adverbien auf -tim*. Winterthur: Keller.

Schibel, W. 1971. *Sprachbehandlung und Darstellungsweise in römischer Prosa: Claudius Quadrigarius, Livius, Aulus Gellius*. Amsterdam: Grüner.

Schierl, P. 2006. *Die Tragödien des Pacuvius: Ein Kommentar zu den Fragmenten mit Einleitung, Text und Übersetzung* (Texte und Kommentare 28). Berlin: de Gruyter.

Schiesaro, A. 1984. '*"Nonne vides"* in Lucrezio', *MD* 13: 143–57.

Schiffrin, D., Tannen, D. and Hamilton, H. E. (edd.) 2001. *The Handbook of Discourse Analysis*. Malden, Mass. and Oxford: Blackwell.

Schmal, S. 2001. *Sallust*. Hildesheim: Olms.

Schmitt, J. 1913. *De parenthesis usu Hippocratico, Herodoteo, Thucydideo, Xenophonteo*. Greifswald: A. Hartmann.

Schneider, R. 1905. *Bellum Africanum*. Berlin: Weidmann.

Schneider, W. C. 2000. 'Vom Salz Ciceros', *Gymnasium* 107: 497–518.

Schuchardt, H. E. M. 1866. *Der Vokalismus des Vulgärlateins*. Leipzig: Teubner.

Schünke, E. 1906. *De traiectione coniunctionum et pronominis relativi apud poetas Latinos*. Kiel: Lüdtke and Martens.

Schwyzer, E. 1939. *Die Parenthese im engern und im weitern Sinne* (Abhandlungen der Preussischen Akademie der Wissenschaften, philosophisch-historische Klasse 6). Berlin: de Gruyter.

Seel, O. 1935. *Hirtius: Untersuchungen über die pseudocaesarischen Bella und den Balbusbrief*. Leipzig: Dieterich.

Serbat, G. 1975. 'Les temps du verbe en latin', *REL* 53: 367–405.

Shackleton Bailey, D. R. 1965. *Cicero's Letters to Atticus* ii. Cambridge University Press.

  1977. *Cicero: Epistulae ad familiares* i. Cambridge University Press.

  1983. 'Cicero and early Latin poetry', *ICS* 8: 239–49.

  1989. 'More corrections and explanations of Martial', *AJPh* 110: 131–50.

  1993. *Martial: Epigrams*. 3 vols. Cambridge, Mass.: Harvard University Press.

  2003. *Statius: Silvae*. Cambridge, Mass.: Harvard University Press.

Shanzer, D. R. 2002. 'History, romance, love, and sex in Gregory of Tours' *Decem libri historiarum*', in K. Mitchell and I. N. Wood (edd.), *The World of Gregory of Tours*. Leiden: Brill, pp. 395–418.

  2004. 'Intentions and audiences: history, hagiography, martyrdom, and confession in Victor of Vita's *Historia persecutionis*', in A. Merrills (ed.), *Vandals,*

Romans and Berbers: New Perspectives on Late Antique Africa. Aldershot: Ashgate, pp. 271–90.

2005. 'Gregory of Tours and poetry: prose into verse and verse into prose', in Reinhardt, Lapidge, and Adams (2005), pp. 303–19.

2008. 'Some treatments of sexual scandal in (primarily) later Latin epistolography', in S. Heilen and R. Kirstein (edd.), *In Pursuit of Wissenschaft: Festschrift für William M. Calder III zum 75. Geburtstag*. Hildesheim: Olms, pp. 393–414.

2009. 'Hisperic faminations', in A. S. Galloway and R. F. Yeager (edd.), *Through a Classical Eye: Transcultural and Transhistorical Visions in Medieval English, Italian, and Latin Literature in Honour of Winthrop Wetherbee*. University of Toronto Press, pp. 44–68.

Shanzer, D. R. and Wood, I. N. 2002. *Letters and Selected Prose of Avitus of Vienne*. Liverpool: Liverpool University Press.

Sharpe, R. 2002. 'Martyrs and local Saints in Late Antique Britain', in A. Thacker and R. Sharpe (edd.), *Local Saints and Local Churches in the Early Medieval West*. Oxford University Press, pp. 75–154.

Shorey, P. 1910. 'A Greek analogue of the Romance adverb', *CPh* 5: 83–96.

Siebenborn, E. 1976. *Die Lehre von der Sprachrichtigkeit und ihren Kriterien: Studien zur antiken normativen Grammatik*. Amsterdam: Grüner.

Siewierska, A. 1984. 'Phrasal discontinuity in Polish', *Australian Journal of Linguistics* 4: 57–71.

Sihler, E. G. 1912. *C. Julius Caesar*. Leipzig: Teubner.

Simpson, J. A. and Weiner, E. S. C. 1989. *The Oxford English Dictionary*. 2nd edn, Oxford: Clarendon Press.

Sinclair, P. 1994. 'Political declensions in Latin grammar and oratory, 55 BCE–CE 39', *Ramus* 23: 92–109.

Skard, E. 1970. 'Hyperbaton bei Cornelius Nepos', *Symbolae Osloenses* 45: 67–73.

Skutsch, O. 1985. *The Annals of Q. Ennius*. Oxford: Clarendon Press.

Smith, C. C. 1983. 'Vulgar Latin in Roman Britain: epigraphic and other evidence', *Aufstieg und Niedergang der römischen Welt* II.29.2: 893–948.

Smith, M. S. 1975. *Petronius: Cena Trimalchionis*. Oxford: Clarendon Press.

Sneyders de Vogel, K. 1927. 'Quelques remarques sur les lettres échangées entre Frodebert et Importun', in *Mélanges de philologie et d'histoire offert a M. Antoine Thomas par ses élèves et ses amis*. Geneva: Slatkine, pp. 417–25.

Solin, H., Leiwo, M. and Halla-aho, H. (edd.) 2003. *Latin vulgaire – latin tardif* VI: *Actes du VIe Colloque international sur le latin vulgaire et tardif, Helsinki 29.8.–2.9.2000*. Hildesheim: Olms.

Staaff, E. 1896. *Le suffixe -arius dans les langues romanes*. Uppsala: Almqvist & Wiksell.

Stefenelli, A. 1962. *Die Volkssprache im Werk des Petron, im Hinblick auf die romanischen Sprachen*. Vienna and Stuttgart: Wilhelm Braumüller.

Steinthal, H. 1890. *Geschichte der Sprachwissenschaft bei den Griechen und Römern mit besonderer Rücksicht auf die Logik. Erster Teil*. 2nd edn, Berlin: Dümmler.

Stevens, P. T. 1937. 'Colloquial expressions in Euripides', *CQ* 31: 182–91.

1945. 'Colloquial expressions in Aeschylus and Sophocles', *CQ* 39: 95–105.

1976. *Colloquial Expressions in Euripides* (Hermes Einzelschriften 38). Wiesbaden: Steiner.

Stevenson, W. H. (ed.). 1929. *Early Scholastic Colloquies*. Oxford: Clarendon Press.

Stotz, P. 1996. *Handbuch zur lateinischen Sprache des Mittelalters* III. *Lautlehre*. Munich: Beck.

Streckenbach, G. 1970. 'Paulus Niavis, "Latinum ydeoma pro novellis studentibus" – ein Gesprächsbüchlein aus dem letzten Viertel des 15. Jahrhunderts [I]', *Mittellateinisches Jahrbuch* 6: 152–91.

1972. 'Paulus Niavis, "Latinum ydeoma pro novellis studentibus" – ein Gesprächsbüchlein aus dem letzten Viertel des 15. Jahrhunderts [II]', *Mittellateinisches Jahrbuch* 7: 187–242.

1975. 'Das "Manuale scolarium" und das "Latinum ydeoma pro novellis studentibus" des Paulus Niavis', *Mittellateinisches Jahrbuch* 10: 232–69.

Suerbaum, W. (ed.) 2002. *Handbuch der lateinischen Literatur der Antike* I. *Die archaische Literatur von den Anfängen bis Sullas Tod: Die vorliterarische Periode und die Zeit von 240 bis 78 v. Chr.* Munich: Beck.

Svennung, J. 1935. *Untersuchungen zu Palladius und zur lateinischen Fach- und Volkssprache*. Uppsala: Harrassowitz.

Swain, S. 2002. 'Bilingualism in Cicero? The evidence of code-switching', in Adams *et al.* (2002), pp. 128–67.

Sznycer, M. 1967. *Les passages puniques en transcription latine dans le 'Poenulus' de Plaute*. Paris: Klincksieck.

Szövérffy, J. 1970. *Weltliche Dichtungen des lateinischen Mittelalters: Ein Handbuch* I. *Von den Anfangen bis zum Ende der Karolingerzeit*. Berlin: Erich Schmidt.

Tandoi, V. 1974. 'Donato e la *Lupus* di Nevio', in G. Puccioni (ed.), *Poesia latina in frammenti: miscellanea filologica*. Genoa: Università di Genova, Istituto di Filologia Classica e Medievale, pp. 263–73.

Tarrant, R. J. 1998. 'Parenthetically speaking (in Virgil and other poets)', in P. Knox and C. Foss (edd.), *Style and Tradition: Studies in Honor of Wendell Clausen*. Stuttgart and Leipzig: Teubner, pp. 141–57.

Thesleff, H. 1967. *Studies in the Styles of Plato* (Acta philosophica Fennica 20). Helsinki: Societas Philosophica Fennica.

Thomas, R. F. 1988. *Virgil: Georgics, Books 3–4*. Cambridge University Press.

2000. 'A trope by any other name: "Polysemy," ambiguity and *significatio* in Virgil', *Harvard Studies in Classical Philology* 100: 381–407.

2006. 'Horace and Hellenistic poetry', in S. J. Harrison (ed.), *Cambridge Companion to Horace*. Cambridge University Press, pp. 50–62.

2009. 'Homeric masquerade: politics and poetics in Horace's Apollo', in L. Athanassaki, R. P. Martin, and J. F. Miller (edd.), *Apolline Politics and Poetics*. Athens: Hellenic Ministry of Culture, pp. 329–52.

Thomason, S. G. 2001. *Language Contact: An Introduction*. Edinburgh: Edinburgh University Press.

Thompson, C. R. (trans.) 1965. *The Colloquies of Erasmus*. University of Chicago Press.

Thompson, D. A. W. 1936. *A Glossary of Greek Birds*. London: Oxford University Press.

Till, R. 1935. *Die Sprache Catos* (Philologus Suppl. 28.2). Leipzig: Dieterich (= 1968, *La lingua di Catone*, trans. C. De Meo, Rome: Ateneo).

Townend, G. B. 1978. 'The fading of Memmius', *CQ* n.s. 28: 267–83.

Traina, A. 1999. *Forma e suono*. 2nd edn, Bologna: Pàtron.

Traina, A., Neri, C., Oniga, R. and Pieri, B. 2002. *Stilistica latina* (augmented translation of H–S, 'Stilistik'). Bologna: Pàtron.

Tzamali, E. 2000. 'Zum Gebrauch der präpositionalen Umschreibungen bei Herondas', *C&M* 51: 119–28.

Väänänen, V. 1956. 'La préposition latine *DE* et le génitif: une mise au point', *Revue de Linguistique Romane* 20: 1–20 = *Recherches et récréations latino-romanes*. Naples 1981: 89–119.

  1966. *Le latin vulgaire des inscriptions pompéiennes*. Berlin: Akademie-Verlag.

  1981. *Introduction au latin vulgaire*. 3rd edn, Paris: Klincksieck.

  1982. *Introduzione al latino volgare*. Bologna: Pàtron.

Vahlen, J. 1903. *Ennianae poesis reliquiae*. 2nd edn, Leipzig: Teubner.

van Dam, H.-J. 1984. *P. Papinius Statius: Silvae Book II. A Commentary*. Leiden: Brill.

van den Hout, M. J. P. 1999. *A Commentary on the Letters of M. Cornelius Fronto*. Leiden: Brill.

Vannini, G. 2007. *Petronius 1975–2005: bilancio critico e nuove proposte* (Lustrum 49). Göttingen: Vandenhoeck & Ruprecht.

Verlinsky, A. 2005. 'Epicurus and his predecessors on the origin of language', in Frede and Inwood (2005), pp. 56–100.

Vetter, E. 1953, *Handbuch der italischen Dialekte*. Heidelberg: C. Winter.

Vollmer, F. 1898. *P. Papinii Statii Silvarum libri*. Leipzig: Teubner.

Vossius, G. J. 1677. *Duo tractatus aurei, unus de historicis Latinis, alter de historicis Graecis, nunc denuo subtractis prioribus exemplaribus eruditorum desiderio restituti*. Frankfurt: Moewald.

Wackernagel, J. 1928. *Vorlesungen über Syntax mit besonderer Berücksichtigung von Griechisch, Lateinisch und Deutsch* II. 2nd edn, Basle: Birkhäuser.

Wallach, B. P. 1976. *Lucretius and the Diatribe against the Fear of Death: De rerum natura III 830–1094*. Leiden: Brill.

Walstra, G. J. J. 1962. *Les cinq épitres rimées dans l'appendice des formules de Sens: Codex Parisinus Latinus 4627, fol. 27v-29r*. Leiden: Brill.

Warmington, E. H. 1967. *Remains of Old Latin*. 4 vols. Cambridge, Mass.: Harvard University Press.

Watson, L. and Watson, P. 2003. *Martial: Select Epigrams*. Cambridge University Press.

Watson, P. 1985. 'Axelson revisited: The selection of vocabulary in Latin poetry', *CQ* n.s. 35: 430–48.

  2002. 'The originality of Martial's language', *Glotta* 78: 222–57.

Way, A. G. 1955. *Caesar: Alexandrian, African and Spanish Wars*. London: Heinemann.

Weissenborn, W. and Müller, H. J. 1965. *Titi Livi Ab urbe condita libri.* Vol. vi.i. 6th edn, Berlin: Weidmann.

Werner, F. 1908. *Die Latinität der Getica des Jordanis.* Leipzig and Halle: Selle.

Wessner, P. (ed.) 1902–8. *Aeli Donati quod fertur Commentum Terenti. Accedunt Eugraphi Commentum et Scholia Bembina.* 3 vols. Leipzig: Teubner.

West, D. A. 1964. 'Two notes on Lucretius', *CQ* n.s. 14: 94–102.

Whatmough, J. 1938. Review of Hofmann (1936), *CPh* 33: 320–2.

Wilkinson, L. P. 1959. 'The language of Virgil and Horace', *CQ* n.s. 9: 181–92 (reprinted in Harrison 1990, pp. 413–28).

Williams, G. 1968. *Tradition and Originality in Roman Poetry.* Oxford: Clarendon Press.

Williams, R. D. 1960. *Aeneidos liber quintus.* Oxford: Clarendon Press.

Wills, J. 1996. *Repetition in Latin Poetry.* Oxford University Press.

Winterfeld, P. K. R. von 1905. 'Hrotsvits literarische Stellung', *Archiv für das Studium der neueren Sprachen und Literaturen* 114: 25–75 at 58–62.

Wisse, J., Winterbottom, M. and Fantham, E. 2008. *M. Tullius Cicero De oratore libri* iii v. *A Commentary on Book* iii, *96–230.* Heidelberg: C. Winter.

Wolanin, H. (1999), 'Aulus Gellius and Vulgar Latin', in Petersmann and Kettemann (1999), pp. 497–503.

Wölfflin, E. 1879. *Lateinische und romanische Komparation.* Erlangen: A. Deichert (= Wölfflin 1933, pp. 126–92).

1880. 'Über die Latinität des Afrikaners Cassius Felix', *Sitzungsberichte der königlichen Bayerischen Akademie der Wissenschaften, philosophisch-philologische und historische Classe*, pp. 381–432 (= Wölfflin 1933, pp. 193–224).

1886. 'Der substantivierte Infinitiv', *ALL* 3: 70–91.

1892a. 'Minucius Felix: Ein Beitrag zur Kenntnis des afrikanischen Lateins', *ALL* 7: 467–84.

1892b. 'Zur Konstruktion von *clam*', *ALL* 7: 278–9.

1893. 'Ennius und das *Bellum Hispaniense*', *ALL* 8: 596–7.

1898. 'Zur Differenzierung der lat. Partikeln', *ALL* 10: 367–76.

1900. 'Zur Latinität des Jordanes', *ALL* 11: 361–8.

1902. 'Sprachliches zum *Bellum Hispaniense*', *ALL* 12: 159–71.

1908. 'Die Sprache des Claudius Quadrigarius', *ALL* 15: 10–22.

1933. *Ausgewählte Schriften*, ed. G. Meyer. Leipzig: Dieterich.

Wölfflin, E. and Meader, C. L. 1900. 'Zur Geschichte der Pronomina demonstrativa', *ALL* 11: 369–93.

Wölfflin, E. and Miodonski, A. 1889. *C. Asini Polionis De bello Africo commentarius.* Leipzig: Teubner.

Wood, I. N. 1994. *The Merovingian Kingdoms 450–571.* London and New York: Longman.

Woodman, A. J. and Martin, R. H. 1996. *The Annals of Tacitus: Book 3* (Cambridge Classical Texts and Commentaries 32). Cambridge University Press.

Wooten, C. W. 1987. *Hermogenes' On Types of Style: Translated by Cecil W. Wooten.* Chapel Hill: University of North Carolina Press.

Wright, R. (ed.) 2008. *Latin vulgaire – latin tardif* VIII: *Actes du* VIII *colloque internationale sur le latin vulgaire et tardif (Oxford 6–9 sept. 2006).* Hildesheim: Olms.

Wyld, H. C. 1920. *A History of Modern Colloquial English.* London: Fisher Unwin.

   1934. *The Best English: A Claim for the Superiority of Received Standard English* (Society for Pure English Tract XXXIX). Oxford: Clarendon Press.

Zetzel, J. E. G. 1980. 'Horace's *Liber sermonum*: the structure of ambiguity', *Arethusa* 13: 59–77.

   2005. *Marginal Scholarship and Textual Deviation.* London: Institute of Classical Studies.

Zeumer, K. 1881. 'Über die älteren fränkischen Formelsammlungen', *Neues Archiv der Gesellschaft für ältere deutsche Geschichtskunde* 6: 11–115.

   1886. *Formulae Merowingici et Karolini aevi* (Monumenta Germaniae Historica Legum Sectio V). Hanover: Hahn.

Zevi, F. 1991. 'L'edilizia privata e la casa del Fauno', in F. Zevi (ed.), *Pompei.* Naples: Guida, pp. 64–89.

Zillinger, W. 1911. *Cicero und die altrömischen Dichter.* Diss. Würzburg: Straudenraus.

Zimmerer, M. 1937. *Der Annalist Qu. Claudius Quadrigarius.* Diss. Munich.

Zwierlein, O. 1986. *L. Annaei Senecae tragoediae.* Oxford: Clarendon Press.

Subject index

473

Index verborum

Index locorum

CIL I² (*cont.*)
818.3.6: 56 n. 38
1202: 107
1211.8: 110
1345: 109
2130: 109
2259: 106
2273: 107
3146: 107
21326: 109

IV
1883: 113
2071: 113
2148: 113
3022: 113
3069: 113
3129: 242 n. 26
5213: 146
6768: 210

V
1939: 110

VI
5972: 329 n. 31
6457: 111
9488: 329 n. 31
9676: 329 n. 31
23685: 107, 110
25092: 110
38274: 144 with n. 50

X
872: 113
2752: 124

XII
1939.1: 337
2033.3: 337 n. 26

XIV
2302: 329 n. 31

CLE
64: 107, 110
65: 111
1585: 110

Claudian *Carmina* 21.237: 411

Claudius Terentianus
P. Mich. VIII.471.10: 337
P. Mich. VIII.471.13: 337
P. Mich. VIII.471.31: 337

Coelius Antipater
26 Peter: 247 n. 28
38: 252 n. 80
44: 252 n. 78

Colloquia of Ælfric Bata: 407–8

Colloquium Leidense: 407

Columella
Arb. 11: 88 n. 24
R. 6.2.7: 247 n. 30
7.10.3: 247 n. 30
9.12.1: 250 n. 62
10.310: 248 n. 35
12.7.2: 88
12.15.5: 336 n. 25
12.42.2: 88
12.56.2: 88

Couilloud (1974) 492: 107

Curtius Rufus
5.3.11: 251 n. 69
8.14.41: 333

De aliquibus raris fabulis
1.1–2 Stevenson: 410
1.8: 417 n. 24
1.9: 415
1.10: 416
1.12: 417 n. 24
1.13: 417
2.1: 417 n. 24
2.2: 415
2.7: 417 n. 24
2.8: 415
2.12: 417
2.14: 417
2.17: 413
2.22: 417
2.27: 413
3.3: 413
3.4: 413
3.7: 413
3.21: 417
3.25: 413
3.27: 413, 416
3.28: 416
4.12: 416
4.14: 413
4.22: 417 n. 24
5.1: 417 n. 24
5.6: 414 n. 20
5.7: 413

Terence *Eu. (cont.)*
  563: 224
  649: 22
  1025: 276
Hau. 10: 43 n. 3
  256: 147
  514: 276
  694: 224
  733: 332
  900: 211
  1031: 335
*Hec.*522: 33
  598: 224
  643: 146, 206
  660–1: 95
Ph. 140: 224
  479: 224
  527: 219
  541: 386
  615–16: 224
  678–9: 224
  693: 224
  713: 286 n. 18
  725: 87

Theocritus
1.105: 60
5.78: 59 n. 43
11.79: 60 n. 49

Tragoediarum fragmenta
inc. 86 Ribbeck: 248 n. 37
  141: 157 n. 19

Turpilius
38 Ribbeck: 85 n. 21
52: 141 n. 38

Valerius Antias
16 Peter: 252 n. 80
58: 252 n. 80
59: 248 n. 39, 252 n. 80

Valerius Flaccus
2.55: 59 n. 44
3.156: 247 n. 31
3.272: 296
4.429: 247 n. 32
4.469: 59 n. 44
5.217–18: 43
7.93: 59 n. 44

Varro
gram. fr. 268 Funaioli: 237
Hebdomades fr. ap. Gell. 3.10.7: 247 n. 32

L. 5.97: 20
  5.104: 233
  6.78: 214
  8.26: 237 n. 15
  8.56: 233
  8.63: 233
  8.66: 40
  8.71: 233
  9.1: 234
  9.2–3: 236 n. 14
  9.5: 17
  9.11: 236 n. 14
  9.18: 236 n. 14
  9.20: 236 n. 14
  9.35: 236 n. 14
  9.114–15: 17, 236 n. 14
  10.59: 234
  10.69–71: 235 n. 11
  10.74: 236 n. 14
  fr. 11 Funaioli: 143
Men. 26: 233
R. 1.22.6: 90 n. 29
  2.4.8: 246 n. 22
  2.5.1: 247 n. 32
  3.6.5: 257
  3.9.14: 247 n. 30

Vetter (1953) 243: 124

Victor of Vita *Historia persecutionis Vandalicae*
  3.46: 392

Vindolanda: see *Tabulae Vindolandenses*

Virgil
Aen. 1.107: 234 n. 9
  1.227–97: 267
  1.231–7: 267–8
  1.250–3: 269
  1.257–60: 269–70
  1.369: 206
  1.387: 224
  1.476: 270 n. 7
  1.573: 156
  1.739: 263
  2.670: 61
  3.254: 249 n. 49
  3.541: 270
  3.628: 277 n. 15
  4.90–128: 271–3
  4.93–5: 271
  4.99: 59
  4.110–14: 271
  4.115–16: 272

CPSIA information can be obtained
at www.ICGtesting.com
Printed in the USA
FSOW04n1706060916
24660FS

9 781107 684416